WASSERSTROM

D0609598

The Open Heaven

CHRISTOPHER ROWLAND

The Open Heaven

*A Study of Apocalyptic in Judaism
and Early Christianity*

———

CROSSROAD · NEW YORK

1982

The Crossroad Publishing Company
575 Lexington Avenue, New York, N.Y. 10022

Printed in the United States of America

Library of Congress Cataloging in Publication Data

Rowland, Christopher, 1947–
The open heaven.

Bibliography: p.
Includes indexes.
1. Apocalyptic literature. 2. Rabbinical literature—
History and criticism. I. Title.
BS646.R58   220   82-7409
ISBN 0-8245-0455-0   AACR2

ACKNOWLEDGEMENTS

Biblical quotations are from the Revised Standard Version of the Bible, copyrighted
1946, 1952, © 1971, 1973, and are reproduced by permission of the National Council
of the Churches of Christ in the U.S.A.

Extracts from *The Dead Sea Scrolls in English* by G. Vermes are reprinted by permission
of Penguin Books Ltd.

Thanks are due to Soncino Press for extracts from *The Babylonian Talmud and Midrash
Rabbah*, edited by I. Epstein *et al.*

To Catherine,
Christopher, Rebekah and Benedict

Contents

Preface   ix

Abbreviations   xi

Introduction   1

Part One **What is Apocalyptic?**   7

1. Knowledge of the Divine Mysteries through Revela-
   tion   9
   Daniel and Revelation   11
   Apocalyptic Material in Judaism and Christianity   14

2. Apocalyptic and Eschatology   23
   Apocalyptic and Rabbinic Eschatologies   29
   Transcendent Eschatology   37
   The Qumran War Scroll and the Synoptic Apocalypse   38

3. Apocalypse and Apocalyptic   49
   The Apocalypse   49
   Types of Visions   52
   Apocalyptic Imagery   58
   Pseudepigraphy   61
   Summary   70

Part Two **The Content of the Heavenly Mysteries**   73

4. What is Above: the Mysteries of God, the Angels,
   and Astronomy   78
   The Heavenly World   78
   The Development of an Exalted Angel in Apocalyptic Literature   94
   Man and the World Above: the Community and the Glory of
      Heaven in the Qumran Scrolls   113
   Astronomy   120

5. What is Below: Man and his World   124
   Enoch's Journeys through the Universe   124
   The Lot of Man   126

6. What Had Happened Previously: the Interest in Past
   History in Apocalyptic   136
   The History of Israel   136
   The Creation of the World   146

7. What is to Come   156
    The Last Stages of the Present Age   156
    The Climax of History   160
    Messianic Belief   176
    The Son of Man   178

    Part Three **Towards an Understanding of the Origins
    of Apocalyptic and the Dates of the Apocalypses**   191

8. A Survey of Recent Study on the Origins of
    Apocalyptic   193

9. An Attempt to Elucidate the Origins of Apocalyptic
    Visions   214
    Excursus: Visionary Experience and Pseudonymity   240

10. Dating the Apocalypses   248

    Part Four **The Esoteric Tradition in Early Rabbinic
    Judaism**   269

11. The Meditation of Rabban Johanan Ben Zakkai and
    his Circle on the Chariot-Chapter   282

12. The Problems posed by the Esoteric Tradition in the
    Time of Rabbi Akiba   306
    The Later Mystical Tradition   340

    Part Five **Apocalyptic in Early Christianity**   349

13. Reports of Visions in Early Christian Literature to
    AD 200   358
    The Gospels   358
    The Acts of the Apostles   368
    The Pauline Letters   374
    Extra-Canonical Writings   386
    The Evidence of Montanist Visions and the *Passio Perpetuae* 392

14. Revelation   403
    Date and Setting   403
    The Composition of the Book of Revelation   413
    The Message of Revelation   423

    Conclusion   443

    Notes   449

    Bibliography   521

    Index of Ancient Sources   546

    Index of Subjects   555

    Index of Authors   558

Preface

AS THIS BOOK is the culmination of eight years study, it almost goes without saying that many have given me advice and help during that time. While it would not be possible to mention all who have contributed to my understanding of Jewish and early Christian literature, it is a pleasure to have the opportunity of acknowledging a debt of gratitude to several friends and colleagues.

The book has its origin in my doctoral dissertation. While I was doing my research, Dr Ernst Bammel, my supervisor, and Professor Charlie Moule gave me freely of their time and wisdom. Whatever value this study may have owes much to them both. From a very early stage Professor C. K. Barrett has taken an interest in my work, and I have learnt much from his perceptive comments. After I completed the first draft of the book, several friends commented on my manuscript. To Dr William Horbury and Dr John Sawyer, both of whom read the whole of the manuscript, I would like to offer my sincere thanks. Dr M. A. Knibb, Dr P. S. Alexander, the Rev. John Sweet, the Rev. Brian Beck, the Rev. Nicholas Sagovsky, Dr J. O'Neill and Mr and Mrs G. Parsons read parts of my manuscript. Their comments have been invaluable and prevented some gross errors. None of them should be held responsible for the flaws which still remain.

This book was completed in January 1979, and only one or two additions have been made to it since then. I consider that the Temple Scroll will contribute to our understanding of apocalyptic and regret not being able to include a discussion of it. I am aware that areas of New Testament thought and language, particularly the study of Ephesians and the Fourth Gospel, have been omitted from this study. I hope to examine these texts in the near future.

I much regret not having had an opportunity to take full

account of Dr Ithamar Gruenwald's important book *Apocalyptic and Merkavah Mysticism*, but I am encouraged to find much in it which coincides with my own approach to apocalyptic. The renewed interest in apocalyptic has meant an increase in the amount written on the subject. I am afraid that there are many books and articles which I have missed, and I offer my apologies in advance for any omission.

A period away from the demands of teaching allowed me to do further study. I am grateful for financial assistance from the University of Newcastle Research Fund and the British Academy, which enabled me to spend several weeks in Cambridge in the spring of 1978. I also gratefully acknowledge the generous financial support given from the Bethune-Baker Fund and the Research Fund of my College which has made the publication of this book possible.

Members of the staff of the Society for Promoting Christian Knowledge have given much support to this project over the past three or four years, and I gladly express my thanks to them.

My thanks are due to Professors Chadwick, Caird and van der Woude for permission to use material published in *The Journal of Theological Studies* and *The Journal for the Study of Judaism*.

Finally, my thanks go to my wife, Catherine. Without her help and encouragement my research would never have been completed, and this book could never have seen the light of day. My three children have borne with me with great patience during the writing of this book. The book is dedicated to them all with affection and gratitude.

C.C.R.

Abbreviations

The following is a list of abbreviations frequently used in this book.

AR	Archiv für Religionswissenschaft
ARN	Aboth de-Rabbi Nathan
Asc. Is.	Ascension of Isaiah
Apocrypha and Pseudepigrapha	R. H. Charles *The Apocrypha and Pseudepigrapha of the Old Testament*
ASTI	Annual of the Swedish Institute
b (B)	Babylonian Talmud
BJ	Josephus *Bellum Judaicum*
Ber.	Bereshith
BJRL	Bulletin of the John Rylands Library
BhM	A. Jellinek *Bet ha-Midrasch*
BR	Bereshith Rabbah
BZ	Biblische Zeitschrift
BZAW	Beihefte zur Zeitschrift für die alttestamentliche Wissenschaft
BDB	Brown, Driver and Briggs *Hebrew Lexicon of the Old Testament*
CBQ	Catholic Biblical Quarterly
Enoch	R. H. Charles *The Book of Enoch*
DB	Dictionnaire de la Bible
DJD	*Discoveries in the Judaean Desert*
EH	Eusebius *Ecclesiastical History*
EJ	Encyclopaedia Judaica
EvT	Evangelische Theologie
GT	Gospel of Truth
HTR	Harvard Theological Review
Hek.	Hekaloth
HUCA	Hebrew Union College Annual
HA	Hypostasis of the Archons
IDB	The Interpreter's Dictionary of the Bible
IEJ	Israel Exploration Journal

IOSCS	International Organisation for Septuagint and Cognate Studies
IQH	Hodayoth from Qumran
IQM	War Scroll from Qumran
IQp Hab	Habakkuk Commentary from Qumran
IQS	Manual of Discipline from Qumran
JAOS	Journal of the American Oriental Society
JB	Jerusalem Bible
JBL	Journal of Biblical Literature
JNES	Journal of Near Eastern Studies
JTS	Journal of Theological Studies
j(J)	Jerusalem Talmud
JJS	Journal of Jewish Studies
JSJ	Journal for the Study of Judaism
JSOT	Journal for the Study of the Old Testament
JSS	Journal of Semitic Studies
JTC	Journal for Theology and Church
JQR	Jewish Quarterly Review
Kautzsch	E. Kautzsch *Die Apokryphen und Pseudepigraphen des Alten Testaments*
LAB	Pseudo-Philo *Liber Antiquitatum Biblicarum*
M(ek)	Mekilta
MT	Masoretic Text
NHL	Nag Hammadi Library (ed. J. M. Robinson)
NKZ	Neue kirchliche Zeitschrift
NT	Novum Testamentum
NTS	New Testament Studies
NT Apocrypha	Hennecke, Schneemelcher, Wilson *New Testament Apocrypha*
PAAJR	The Proceedings of the American Academy of Jewish Research
PRE	Pirke de-Rabbi Eliezer
4QSl	The Angelic Liturgy from Qumran
R	Rabbah/Rabbati
Rec.	Recension
REJ	Revue des études juives
RHR	Revue de l'histoire des religions
RB	Revue Biblique
RQ	Revue de Qumran
RSR	Recherches de science religieuse
RSV	Revised Standard Version
Strack–Billerbeck	H. L. Strack and P. Billerbeck *Kommentar zum Neuen Testament aus Talmud und Midrasch*
ShS	Shir ha-Shirim

Sim.	Similitudes of Enoch
SJT	Scottish Journal of Theology
ST	Studia Theologica
TDNT	R. Kittel, G. Friedrich and G. W. Bromiley *Theological Dictionary of the New Testament*
T(os)	Tosefta
TA	Testament of Abraham
Test. Levi	Testament of Levi
TLZ	Theologische Literaturzeitung
TR	Theologische Rundschau
TSK	Theologische Studien und Kritiken
VC	Vigiliae Christianae
VT	Vetus Testamentum
ZNW	Zeitschrift für neutestamentliche Wissenschaft
ZAW	Zeitschrift für alttestamentliche Wissenschaft
ZK	Zeitschrift für Kirchengeschichte
ZKT	Zeitschrift für katholische Theologie
ZRGG	Zeitschrift für Religions und Geistesgeschichte
ZTK	Zeitschrift für Theologie und Kirche

Introduction

THE HISTORY OF research on the apocalyptic texts of Judaism and early Christianity has had a chequered history over the past hundred years or so. The discovery of new apocalypses, particularly Ethiopic Enoch, stimulated interest in this aspect of Jewish religion during the nineteenth century as a potentially important exegetical key to unlock the door which led into the thought-world of the New Testament writers. Although there has been an abiding interest in apocalyptic over the years, the character of the literature still causes perplexity to commentators.[1] Nevertheless in recent years there has been a resurgence of interest in the subject, not least among German theologians. This has been in part due to the renewed recognition of the significant role which eschatology plays in early Christian thought, but also arises from the importance given to apocalyptic in the theology of the so-called Pannenberg group.[2] The contribution of apocalyptic literature to the debate about the Christian hope has been immense, precisely because it appears to be the repository of those ideas in late Judaism which gave meaning and purpose to history as a whole.

Throughout much of the discussion of apocalyptic there has been a widespread acceptance of the close link which exists between apocalyptic and eschatology. Indeed, to many, the two words are virtually synonymous. The result of this has been to allow the study of apocalyptic to be dominated by its eschatological elements. Attempts at definition of the phenomenon of apocalyptic tend to dwell on the future hope which is manifested in the apocalyptic literature. Although, as we shall see, the word apocalyptic is still used to describe the literary form of the apocalypse, it is also more usual to find it being used to speak of a particular attitude to the world and history current in late antiquity, whose characteristic emphases are the imminent destruction of the world and utter despair about the conditions

1

of the present world order. Although, in common with modern usage, the word apocalyptic will be used to describe not only the literary genre of the apocalypse but also a distinctive religious outlook in late antiquity, there is no assumption made that apocalyptic and eschatology are alternative ways of speaking about the hope for the future. In referring to the Jewish and Christian hopes for the future, the word eschatology and its cognates will be used. It must be said, however, that this word is not the most appropriate description of many Jewish beliefs. Eschatology has connotations of the end of history, and, while it is certainly true that many Jews looked forward to the end of the present world-order, it would not be correct to suppose that the end of the world was the essential element of the Jewish hope for the future. But, for the sake of convenience, whereas apocalyptic is reserved for the description of the literary genre and a particular religious outlook evident from the apocalypses themselves, eschatology is used as a shorthand way of referring to the future hope of Judaism and Christianity.

It will probably be evident from the previous paragraph that my intention in this book has been to move away from an approach to apocalyptic which is dominated by a study of eschatological material. The consideration of Jewish eschatology has been included in this study only in so far as it is relevant to the study of Jewish apocalyptic literature. That is not to say that eschatological material does not have a significant, indeed· important, part to play within the apocalypses as they seek to expound the meaning of the universe. Nevertheless concentration on the future orientation of the apocalypses has at times given a rather distorted view of the essence of apocalyptic. Apocalyptic is as much involved in the attempt to understand things as they are now as to predict future events.[3] The mysteries of heaven and earth and the real significance of contemporary persons and events in history are also the dominant interests of the apocalypticists. There is thus a concern with the world above and its mysteries as a means of explaining human existence in the present. Apocalyptic has a vertical dimension which is just as important as any predictions made about the future. The point has been made very well by Kingsley Barrett in his discussion of New Testament eschatology:

The secrets in which apocalyptic deals are not simply secrets of the future – of the Age to Come; they include secrets of the present state of the heavenly world. Indeed, these two mysteries, of heaven and the future, are very closely allied, since in apocalyptic the significant future is the breaking into this world of the heavenly world, and to know what is now in heaven is in consequence almost the same as knowing what will be on earth. It is worth noting here that apocalyptic in its own nature involves two kinds of (limited) dualism. The contrast between this world and the other heavenly world of supra-sensual reality is often loosely described as Platonic and to be quite foreign to Judaism; but this is not so. It is difficult to draw a sharp line between apocalyptic and gnosticism – a fact with large consequences.[4]

My concern in this book will be to give due emphasis to this concern with the divine mysteries, which is so apparent in the Jewish and Christian apocalypses, and to investigate how far this type of religious outlook made an impact on Jewish and Christian religion round about the beginning of the Christian era. For this reason the approach to the literature has not been merely on the basis of matters of eschatological interest. Accordingly, certain passages which are frequently regarded as typical of apocalyptic in Judaism and early Christianity have been given only a cursory glance, for example, the so-called Synoptic Apocalypse (Mark 13 and par.) and the War Scroll from Qumran. In their place passages have been considered which seem to evince the same kind of concern as the apocalypses, namely an interest in the divine mysteries. For this reason the evidence about the speculation on the chariot-chapter of Ezekiel and the creation-story of Genesis 1 among late first century rabbis is included. There does not appear to have been a very great interest in apocalyptic matters among the rabbis, but some kind of link does appear to have existed between this speculation and the visions of the apocalypticists, which demands our attention. In early Christian literature concern with the divine world and its secrets is not confined to the book of Revelation. Various hints in other documents suggest that the contribution of an apocalyptic outlook has been extensive in early Christian theology. Some attempt will be made to assess this contribution by examining the various reports of visions in the early Christian literature.

One major omission from the Jewish literature of the period is an investigation of the way in which Philo relates to the apocalyptic outlook. This is not because I believe that such a study would be unfruitful, indeed the evidence suggests that the opposite would be the case.[5] Nevertheless it is true that Philo's writings do not exhibit the same formal characteristics as the apocalypses and the related texts studied here, though the movement of his thought and the relationship of man with the realm above is closely related to the spirituality of the apocalypses. Though, as I hope to show, the apocalypses themselves are more often than not rooted in the study of scripture, Philo's study is essentially the result of exegesis, whereas the apocalypticists claim that their insights are the result of revelation. For this reason, not to mention the question of space, a study of Philo has been deferred to a later time.

In a study of this kind, where so many difficult passages have been considered, it has been impossible to do justice to the extensive debates which have taken place on various issues. One is very conscious of the conflicting claims of a concise exposition of a particular theme and the need for sufficient exegetical detail to justify some of the positions adopted. There may appear to be some inconsistency in the way in which the different themes are treated. One of the difficulties in approaching a subject from a slightly different direction is that new material is introduced which demands some justification for its inclusion as part of the study. As a result detailed examination of certain texts has been necessary in order to demonstrate the relationship between this material and the theme of Jewish apocalyptic. What is more, the paucity of information at our disposal has, in these instances in particular, made a detailed study essential. By contrast, other sections, particularly those dealing with the content of the apocalypses and the message of the New Testament apocalypse, contain little or no exegetical discussion but are basically summaries of the material to be found in these works.

In the hope that the book may offer a starting-place for further study of the apocalypses for those who have had little or no knowledge of the subject, generally translations have been used which are readily available to most students. The main source for the translation of the Jewish apocalypses has been the collection of material edited by R. H. Charles, *The Apocrypha and Pseudepigrapha of the Old Testament* and the various translations of early Jewish works published in the series *Translations of Early Documents*. Although the latter are now out of print, many are still available in libraries, and some are being reissued. In certain instances, where English translations are not available, as is the case with some rabbinic material, I have made my own translations. In general, however, I have used the Soncino translation of the Babylonian Talmud and the Midrash Rabbah. All Greek, Hebrew and Aramaic words have been transliterated. I have used anglicized forms for the names of rabbis (e.g. Johanan for Yoḥanan) and other common terms (e.g. *merkabah* for *merkavah*). As a result there may at times appear to be some inconsistency in the way in which Hebrew words appear in English form. All biblical translations are from the Revised Standard Version.

Part One

What is Apocalyptic?

CHAPTER 1

Knowledge of the Divine Mysteries through Revelation

IN EVERY AGE man is faced by historical circumstances which present him with unfathomable problems. Innocent suffering and the triumph of the wicked are two which are the perennial concerns of mankind. Such problems were particularly pressing for a nation like Israel which had a firm belief in God's lordship over creation and history. Consequently any contrast between theological affirmations and historical realities meant that some kind of solution to the apparent contradiction between the two was most pressing. This was especially true in those circumstances where the Jewish people was subject to foreign powers. Throughout the centuries around the beginning of the Christian era the Jewish nation in Palestine had to acclimatize itself to interference and control by the powerful nations which surrounded it, the Ptolemaic dynasty in Egypt, the Seleucids in Syria, and, of course, Rome in the west. The attempt to understand the divine will in the midst of the power-politics of the ancient world had a long pedigree in Judaism. The eighth century prophets had devoted oracles to the nations surrounding Israel. Thus it is hardly surprising that at a later stage of her history the distinctive beliefs about God and history should have demanded an understanding of the Jewish nation's role in history, the relationship of the divine promises to the circumstances of the present, and the conviction that there was a divine dimension to human existence, however obscure it may seem in the present.[1] Jewish apocalyptic sought to provide such an understanding of history and this theological conviction.

According to Günther Bornkamm 'the disclosure of divine secrets is the true theme of later Jewish apocalyptic'.[2] It is concerned with knowledge of God and the secrets of the world above, revealed in a direct way by dreams, visions or angelic

9

pronouncements. As such it differs markedly from other ways of ascertaining the divine will which tend to rely on more indirect modes of discernment, like the interpretation of scripture. The character of the divine secrets which were revealed is not easily defined and includes almost anything which the human mind cannot comprehend. The subjects are varied and include descriptions of the heavenly world as well as the plans for the future of the universe.

Usually the apocalyptic movement refers to a religious current found in Jewish and Christian texts written round about the beginning of the Christian era, but this type of religion is not confined to the Judaeo-Christian tradition[3] nor to one particular period of Judaism or Christianity.[4] Nevertheless our main concern in this study will be with that religious outlook which manifests itself in certain Jewish and Christian texts written during the period extending from *c.*300 BC to AD 300. In them we have evidence of a religious perspective sufficiently coherent to be studied as an isolated phenomenon within late antiquity.

The means whereby the divine will was ascertained had a long history in Israel from the lottery of Urim and Thummim to the sophisticated exegetical techniques which were developed by the sages to gain as much advice as possible from the sacred texts.[5] While it is true that there was a variety of means of understanding the divine will, some of the questions for which answers were sought presented more problems than others. Practical matters of everyday life could usually be resolved by recourse to the scriptures. The employment of the various exegetical devices would ensure that an answer could be found for the most intractable ethical problem. There were, however, some issues which were less susceptible to answers by these means. Scripture may offer glimpses of the nature of God and his plans for the universe, but the reality of God's existence, the explanation of life's perplexities and the precise delineation of the future hope were not easily resolved on the basis of Scripture alone. What is more, the pronouncements of the sages on religious matters, however authoritative they may claim to be, were still the opinions of men which could be contradicted at a later time as circumstances changed. Therefore, it is not surprising that the answer to these problems should call forth a more radical solution. Indirect means of revelation could not provide the assurance and conviction which were necessary for those who were particularly perplexed by the circumstances which confronted them. What was required was a direct and authoritative answer to man's most pressing questions, not a variety of conflicting human opinions about the meaning of a particular passage in scripture. Many would have echoed the cry of the unknown prophet who, in Isaiah 64.1, pleads with God to rend the heavens to solve the many riddles of existence which presented themselves. The answer to this desperate plea is found in apocalyptic. The unveiling[6] of the counsels of God directly to the apocalyptic seer and thence to his readers meant that the latter were being offered an answer directly from the mouth of God himself, apparently without any risk of contradiction. Here was the authoritative pronouncement which claimed to solve the inconclusive debates of man about his world and his destiny. Thus the key to the whole movement is that God reveals his mysteries directly to man and thereby gives them knowledge of the true nature of reality so that they may organize their lives accordingly.

Daniel and Revelation

The two biblical apocalypses, Daniel and Revelation, support such a view of apocalyptic. Both are above all disclosures of the divine mysteries, Revelation explicitly so (1.1 *apokalypsis Iesou Christou*). It is this element which is the unifying factor between the two works, despite the fact that the differences between the two are quite extensive. Indeed, consideration of these differences is in itself a means of drawing attention to precisely what it is that separates these two documents from contemporary literature and sets them in a class of their own. A summary of the contents of the two books is thus called for.

Daniel can be divided into two major parts on the basis of its contents.[7] In the first part (Dan. 1—6) we have stories about a righteous Jew in Babylon called Daniel, together with the interpretation of two dreams. In the second half of the book (Dan. 7—12) we have various revelations by dream-vision or angelic pronouncement. The second half of the book contains the apocalypse proper. Revelation, on the other hand, divides quite clearly into three sections. The first three chapters are a record of John's call-vision and disclosures which are to be communicated to seven churches in Asia Minor. A new stage in the apocalypse is reached in Chapter 4 when John reports his ecstatic ascent into heaven. A series of visions then follows, most of which (though by no means all) have to do with the unfolding of the divine plan for the future of mankind. These visions extend to Chapter 22.5, after which the book concludes with a brief collection of admonitions.

A brief glimpse at the contents of the two works suggests that there are significant differences between them. The eschatology of Daniel is much less developed than that in the New Testament apocalypse. Although both refer to a belief in the resurrection (Dan. 12.2, cf. Rev. 20.12), Daniel has nothing to say about the last assize[8] and the coming of the messiah.[9] Virtually nothing is said in the latter about the character of the new age, except for the prediction of resurrection (cf. Rev. 21.1ff.). The messianic woes which were to become such an important feature of Jewish eschatology are only hinted at in Daniel 12.1f., though they form the heart of the eschatological scheme in Revelation. The *vaticinia ex eventu*,[10] on the other hand, which we find in Daniel, are completely absent in Revelation. This omission loses some of its significance, however, when the pseudonymous character of Daniel is taken into account. The detailed accounts of Israel's history, which are a feature of the apocalypses,[11] obviously depend for their impact on the pretence of being previews of future events foretold long before by holy men of the past. Nevertheless the historical determinism which is presupposed in these spurious predictions is manifest also in the carefully structured account of the prelude to the new age which is found in the sequence of seals, trumpets, and bowls (Rev. 6; 8—9; 16).

Although there is use of symbolism in Daniel (e.g. the statue in 2.31ff., the beasts in 7.1ff. and the ram and goat in 8.3ff.), this does not compare with the variety of images which are used in Revelation. In this respect Daniel, like other Jewish apocalypses, exhibits a more restrained use of the stock of images available to the apocalypticist. In addition, in every case where the imagery forms part of the dream-visions in Daniel, an interpretation is offered of the significance of that imagery. With the exception of Daniel 7, it is nowhere suggested that the imagery which forms part of the dream-visions is to be taken as anything but a pictorial presentation of events which are to take place on earth. The meaning of the dreams has to be interpreted for the seer and reader alike, e.g. Daniel 8.15ff. The distinction between vision and interpretation which is found consistently in Daniel, is not evident in Revelation. Only in one place do we find the significance of a particular vision being interpreted for John by an angel (Rev. 17). That is not to suggest that John intends us to regard his visions as consisting solely of literal predictions of the future any more than the writer of Daniel. It is probable that by John's day the stock of images used by the apocalypticists was well enough known, and the political and religious allusions so obvious, that the readers could discern the message of the visions which the various symbols were supposed to convey. Thus, in Revelation 13, when the seer sees a beast arising from the sea, the political significance of this image, already established in Daniel 7.17, would not have escaped the notice of readers who were familiar with the Jewish scriptures.[12]

The most obvious difference between the two is that Daniel, like virtually every Jewish and Christian work of a similar type, is pseudonymous. It purports to have been written by a Jew in Babylon during the Exile, whereas most commentators today would agree that it was written between 168 BC and 165 BC at the height of the crisis in Jerusalem initiated by Antiochus IV. On the other hand, it is widely accepted that the author of the whole, or at least the major part, of the New Testament apocalypse was a prophet named John who had been imprisoned on the island of Patmos (Rev. 1.9). Consequently it is hardly surprising that the legends about Jews in Babylon which form half of the book of Daniel have no parallel in Revelation. Although stories similar to these were to become an important component of the apocalyptic form, they usually had little or no revelatory content.[13]

This brief comparison of the two biblical apocalypses seems to indicate that we are not dealing here with texts whose contents fall neatly into clearly defined categories.[14] It is true that some common ideas seem to be present, e.g. resurrection, the tendency towards a panoramic view of history, urgent eschatological expectation and the vindication of the righteous. Nevertheless the unifying factor which joins both these apocalypses and separates them from other contemporary literature is the conviction that runs through both, that man is able to know about the divine mysteries by means of revelation, so that God's eternal purposes may be disclosed, and man, as a result, may see history in a totally new light. This point is also made in the opening chapters of Daniel, as 2.28 makes clear: 'There is a God in heaven who reveals mysteries'.

Such an approach to apocalyptic also does justice to the small amount of material in both apocalypses which is not in the strict sense eschatological. The 'son of man' vision in Daniel 7, for example, is, in the author's eyes, not a revelation only about the future vindication of the saints of the Most High but also a demonstration of the temporary nature of dominance of the world power now oppressing Israel. As such the revelation has the effect of unveiling the transient nature of the world-order and the rectitude of the stand of the saints. Similarly in Revelation 13 John's vision of the beast rising from the sea is not so much about a future manifestation of evil but the unmasking of the true character of the Roman state and its activities. Thus it is the significance of earthly persons and events as viewed from the divine perspective which comes across in the apocalypses. It is made clear that consideration of the world as it is would give a totally inadequate impression of reality. The dominance of pagan nations and the persecution of the righteous must be viewed in the light of the overall purposes of God. Likewise the apparent absence of the creator God from his creation has to be seen in the light of his dominion in the heavenly court and the promise of his future dominion in the world of men.

All this seems to indicate that we ought not to think of apocalyptic as being primarily a matter of either a particular literary type or distinctive subject-matter, though common literary elements and ideas may be ascertained. Rather, the common factor is the belief that God's will can be discerned by means of a mode of revelation which unfolds directly the hidden things of God. To speak of apocalyptic, therefore, is to concentrate on the theme of the direct communication of the heavenly mysteries in all their diversity. With such an understanding one can attempt to do justice to all the elements of the apocalyptic literature.

Apocalyptic Material in Judaism and Christianity

With such a definition in mind we find several documents from Judaism and early Christianity which betray an essentially similar outlook. All of them have the common emphasis that God has disclosed the mysteries of heaven and earth, past and future to the privileged seer, though the circumstances in which the revelations are said to have taken place are varied, as also is the content of the material which is revealed. Besides Daniel and Revelation an initial list of apocalyptic writings would include the following:

1 or Ethiopic Enoch[15]
2 or Slavonic Enoch[16]
Jubilees[17]
2 or Syriac Baruch[18]
3 or Greek Baruch[19]
4 Ezra or 2 Esdras[20]
Apocalypse of Abraham[21]
Testament of Abraham[22]
Testaments of Levi and Naphtali
(from the Testaments of the XII Patriarchs)[23]
Ascension of Isaiah[24]
Shepherd of Hermas[25]
3 or Hebrew Enoch[26]

The last mentioned work has been included, despite the fact that it was written well over four hundred years after the New Testament period, because it is a good example of the persistence of the apocalyptic spirit within Judaism and is typical of other works written at this period.[27] This work has been chosen because of the existence of a large-scale edition of the text together with an English translation. With the exception of the late Hebrew Enoch, none of these texts is in its original version. Nevertheless the editors of the versions we possess of these texts conjectured long ago that many of them went back to Semitic originals. The discovery of fragments of the Testament of Levi and 1 Enoch at Qumran have dramatically confirmed this suggestion, and it is probably not too conjectural to suppose that a work like the Apocalypse of Abraham goes back to a Semitic original.[28] Not all the apocalypses, however, can be shown to derive from Semitic originals, for works like Slavonic Enoch and the Testament of Abraham are probably a testimony to the existence of apocalyptic ideas in the Diaspora.[29]

One or two of the Qumran texts should be included in our consideration as examples of the same kind of religious outlook. One example is the Testament of Amram, the father of Moses, which he is said to have given to his sons before his death.[30] In form this work resembles the Testaments of the XII Patriarchs, but, like the Testament of Naphtali, incorporates an apocalypse consisting of a dream-vision. Unfortunately the text is very fragmentary, but enough is extant for us to see that it has the same perspective as other writings contained in our list.

More difficult to categorize as apocalyptic are the angelic liturgies found in Cave 4 at Qumran. Once again the texts are incomplete, and we are no longer in a position to decide whether or not these fragments ever formed part of a longer apocalyptic text. The first offers a description of the angelic liturgy and the second describes the attendants and the movement of the divine throne-chariot (the *merkabah*) (Ezek. 1).[31] Even if we cannot be sure that either text formed part of an apocalypse, both purport to offer information about the secret proceedings in the heavenly world and betray a similar ethos to apocalyptic. Also the community's understanding of its own relationship to the world above has so many similarities with the outlook of apocalyptic that it too calls for our consideration in due course.

Finally, mention must be made of the various visionary reports which are dotted all over Jewish literature. These fragments, which are now imbedded in larger works, not themselves apocalyptic, may not always have the same literary form as the full-scale apocalypse, but their character is essentially the same. Within the New Testament, for example, we have visions of the heavenly world in the manner of Old Testament visionary reports, e.g. Acts 7.56. Also there are other visionary reports like that of Peter in Acts 10.11 and the account of the baptism of Jesus (Mark 1.10f. and par). From Judaism two good examples are the vision of Cenez, which is to be found in the Biblical Antiquities of Pseudo-Philo 28, and the vision of Adam included in the Life of Adam and Eve (25ff., cf. 33.1–5). The Biblical Antiquities is a free rendering of the biblical account from creation down to the time of Saul, wrongly attributed to Philo, and written towards the end of the first century AD.[32] Cenez plays an important role in the retold story, despite the fact that he makes only a fleeting appearance in the biblical narrative (Judges 1.13; 3.9 and 11). At the end of his life he has a vision which is unique in its contents, though it has certain parallels in other apocalypses. In it he sees part of the process of creation. The passage has some links with Genesis 1, as one would expect, but there are many peculiarities which will demand our attention later in this study. The secrets which are revealed to the righteous man in this case are those concerned with cosmogony, a subject to which other apocalypticists were to turn as well (cf. Slav. Enoch 25ff.).

The Life of Adam and Eve is a work of a similar type to the Biblical Antiquities in its free rewriting of the biblical narrative, though its didactic purpose is more apparent with the inclusion of paraenetic material (e.g. 49.1ff.). The apocalypse in 25ff. obviously serves the purpose of communicating to Adam the fact that not all his descendants will suffer because of his transgression. In order to receive this message Adam is taken up to heaven, to the presence of God, and this brief description of the heavenly ascent is precisely what we find elsewhere in the apocalyptic literature (1 Enoch 14.8ff; Test. Abr. 10ff; Asc. Is. 7ff; Apoc. Abr. 15ff.).

These visionary fragments and the apocalypses listed above are distinguished from other examples of Jewish and Christian literature by the underlying conviction that they contain visions, or disclosure by heavenly envoys, which unfold various aspects of God's will and other mysteries of the world and man's life in it. Whatever the precise mode of revelation by which these mysteries are communicated, the underlying theme of all these texts is the same. Truths which are beyond man's capacity to deduce from his circumstances are revealed directly by means of the manifestation of the divine counsels.

If we stick to the approach to apocalyptic outlined above, some documents which are normally included in lists of apocalyptic literature have to be excluded. The most obvious examples are the Testament of the XII Patriarchs and the Assumption of Moses, which contains the final pronouncements of the law-giver to Joshua immediately before the former's death. There has been much discussion whether the Testaments as we have them are essentially Jewish documents which have been subject to occasional Christian additions, or, in their present form, a Jewish–Christian creation based on Jewish documents.[33] This question need not detain us at the moment, but the similarity in form and content which exists between those testaments, which we have included in our list of apocalyptic texts, and those not included permits us to examine more closely the differences between apocalyptic and other related literature at this period.

The testament has many formal similarities with the apocalypses. It usually contains stories about the life of a great figure of the past, eschatological predictions and ethical admonitions. What is more, several testaments clearly are apocalypses as well, and it therefore becomes imperative to distinguish between these different works. Thus, for example, the Testament of Abraham includes a heavenly ascent immediately before the patriarch's death. Only two of the Testaments of the XII Patriarchs can be regarded as corresponding to the apocalyptic type, and these are the two for which evidence has been found of Semitic originals, namely the Testaments of Levi and Naphtali.[34] A comparison between the Testament of Levi and the other testaments is in fact illuminating. Like the Testament of Abraham, it includes an account of a heavenly ascent and a vision of the heavenly world as well as the predictions and admonitions common to all the other testament-literature. Although other testaments contain sagacious advice from the patriarch, which was intended to be listened to and respected, this is the extent of its importance; the patriarch had learnt from his mistakes and gives the benefit of his experience to his descendants (e.g. T. Reuben 3.11ff.). There is not the same revelatory character in the majority of the testaments as we find in works like the Testament of Levi, Naphtali and Abraham.[35] The former are much closer to the biblical examples of the dying patriarch's advice and predictions about his descendants (Gen. 49 and Deut. 33). It is advice to be heeded, but it does not carry the weight of a direct revelation of God's will. The stories are closer to the edifying tales which are contained in works like Joseph and Asenath and the Genesis Apocryphon. In retelling the biblical story the writer could, and often did, take the opportunity of drawing attention to particular issues which were important to him, whether doctrinal, ethical or eschatological.

Clearly the dividing line here is a rather thin one, and it may be argued that the predictions of a dying patriarch quite quickly become an authoritative pronouncement of the divine purposes. Nevertheless it does appear that there is a distinction between works like the Assumption of Moses and the majority of the Testaments of the XII Patriarchs on the one hand and the Testaments of Levi, Naphtali and Abraham and Slavonic Enoch on the other. In the first group the character of the final pronouncements of the patriarch, as we know them from the Old

Testament, is adhered to completely. The situation in the last days of the patriarch's life is described, and his advice and predictions are recorded, but, unlike the other works mentioned, this is merely a series of verbal pronouncements. In the second group the setting in the last days of the life of the patriarch is extended by the insertion of an apocalypse as a basis for, and part of the content of, the advice which the dying man gives to his children.

The clearest demarcation, however, lies in the view which the different texts have of their own authority. Slavonic Enoch 40.1f. makes it quite clear that the basis for Enoch's advice to his children is the privilege of the previous ascent to heaven and the secrets which the seer has seen:

> And now, my children, I know all things, for this is seen from the Lord's lips and this my eyes have seen, from beginning to end. I know all things, and have written all things into books . . .

Similarly in Testament of Levi 9.3ff. the visions which Levi has received are understood to be the basis of the regulations for the offering of sacrifice. Although 10.1 suggests that the basis of Levi's authority is the information he has received from his predecessors, there does appear to be a belief in the Testament of Levi that the visions which the patriarch has received qualify him to speak with a considerable degree of authority.

However much material apocalyptic texts and related literature may have in common, the former have a much more exalted view of their authority. In its presentation of material the apocalypse offers neither pious surmise nor the result of rational speculation. The writers of the apocalypses clearly had a very high view of both the divine origin and authority of the material which they were imparting. At the end of 4 Ezra 14, for example, the apocalyptic works, which Ezra transcribes under divine inspiration are put on the same, if not higher, level as the canonical scriptures themselves and in essential continuity with them:

> And it came to pass when forty days were fulfilled, that the Most High spake unto me saying: The twenty-four books that thou hast written publish, that the worthy and unworthy may read therein: but the seventy last thou shalt keep, to deliver them to the wise among the people. For in them is the spring of understanding, the fountain of wisdom, and the stream of knowledge.

An equally self-conscious estimation of the value of such direct revelations emerges at the end of the New Testament apocalypse. Among the various admonitions with which the work concludes is a dire threat to anyone who would tamper with the contents of the book:

> I warn every one who hears the words of the prophecy of this book: if any one adds to them, God will add to him the plagues described in this book, and if any one takes away from the words of the book of this prophecy, God will take away his share in the tree of life and in the holy city, which are described in this book. (Rev. 22.18f., cf. 1 Enoch 100.6 and 104.11)

There is an allusion here to Deuteronomy 4.2, 'You shall not add to the word which I shall command you, nor take from it'. In utilizing this prohibition from Deuteronomy John appears to regard his own revelations as being of equal importance with earlier communications from God given to Moses. There is no question here of this book being regarded by its author either as a series of inspired guesses or intelligent surmise. John believes that what he has seen and heard actually conveys the divine truth to his readers. Unlike Paul, who offers his opinion to the Corinthians 'as one who by the Lord's mercy is trustworthy' (1 Cor. 7.25), John sees himself as the one who has been commissioned to write down the divine counsels for the benefit of the churches (Rev. 1.19). It is this characteristic which the apocalyptic testaments share with the other apocalypses and sets them apart from other late Jewish documents with which they otherwise have so much in common. Therefore, we should exclude from the category of apocalyptic those testaments which do not contain the essential character of apocalyptic, the disclosure of the divine secrets through direct revelation.[36]

Rather more difficult to be certain about is the work known as the Sibylline Oracles. The Sibyls were pagan oracles whose prophecies were connected with various places around the eastern Mediterranean. Reference is made to their oracles and the character of their prophecy by several Greek and Roman writers, e.g. Virgil *Aeneid* 6.77ff.[37] This well-known mode of obtaining information about the future was taken up by Jewish and Christian propagandists as a framework for predictions which have a distinctly Jewish or Christian flavour. Thus the pagan oracle is made to vindicate the beliefs of these two religions about the future and about the validity of the respective doctrines of the two religions. In form at least the Sibylline Oracles offer a similar outlook to the apocalypses. The secrets concerning the future of various towns and cities as well as the Jewish people (e.g. Sib. Or. 3.46ff. and 767–784) are disclosed through a pagan rather than a Jewish seer. It is evidence of the widespread credence which could be given to prophetic pronouncements of this kind in the ancient world.[38] Clearly Hellenistic Judaism was not slow to appreciate the value of the authority of the Sibyl as a means of justifying a Jewish approach to life and history. But while in certain respects it is a parallel phenomenon to apocalyptic, the fact that the device is used as a means of propagating a particular religious point of view should make us a little wary of seeing it in quite the same light as the other apocalypses. It is not just that we are dealing here with the peculiar phenomenon of a pagan rather than a Jewish religious authority, but also there is the difference that these oracles do not claim to be disclosures vouchsafed by the God of Israel but predictions inspired by lesser divine powers which happened to coincide with the divine mysteries. Thus, while formally the Sibylline Oracles are related to Jewish apocalyptic literature, they are to be regarded as a type of religious propaganda – literature lacking some of the key elements of the apocalyptic texts.[39]

What we are faced with in apocalyptic, therefore, is a type of religion whose distinguishing feature is a belief in direct revelation of the things of God which was mediated through dream, vision or divine intermediary. It has many parallels in contemporary pagan religion and throughout the history of religion. In the Hellenistic world there existed, what Martin Hengel has called, a quest for 'higher wisdom through revelation',[40] which has left the marks of its influence in various literary remains. The climax of this quest is to be found in the various gnostic systems of the second century where the salvation of the individual is brought about through the apprehension of hidden knowledge of the nature of reality. Knowing one's origins and destiny is just as much a concern of apocalyptic as gnosticism, though in the former this knowledge has not yet become in itself a means of salvation.[41] The point should not be missed, however, that apocalyptic is one way in which Judaism participated in the *Zeitgeist* of late antiquity. Its underlying theme is to give meaning and significance to man and his world by means of revelation. Whether the secrets be eschatological or astronomical, they are all means of satisfying man's spiritual hunger. The real meaning of events and persons, within an overall view of history, and the disclosure concerning the imminent change in the structures of society are directed to providing men and women with a way of looking at the world and God's involvement in it. This then gives coherence and significance to existence in the present when historical circumstances offered only perplexity and despair.[42]

Nor should we assume that the apocalyptic outlook is one which is to be found in Judaism and Christianity only at the beginning of the Christian era. For example, the interests of the early Jewish apocalypses reappear in the later mystical literature of Judaism.[43] The so-called *Hekaloth* literature, which tells of the journey to heaven and the various figures one encounters on the way to the heavenly palace of God, breathes the same religious spirit as the apocalypses. This outlook provided the pious Jew with an escape from a world hostile to God to the remote world of God and his angels accessible only to those selected few, whose righteousness granted them the privilege of access to the heavenly courts. These texts may be influenced by second century gnosticism, but they derive much of their distinctive imagery from the imagery of apocalyptic. The possibility of having a 'ladder in one's house' whereby one could ascend to the world above, as the Hekaloth writers put it (Hekaloth Rabbati 13.2), gave a man certainty in the present about the validity of traditional beliefs and practices. Such interests inevitably become more dominant at times of crisis, but it would be a mistake to suppose that it was only in such situations that apocalyptic flourished. The apocalyptic spirit is endemic in religion in any age, though the flight from reality became more necessary when historical circumstances lacked evidence of the fulfilment of the divine purposes, not to mention the validity of a religious view of the world. It is our intention in the following chapters to examine the nature of this religion and its influence on theology within one small period of the history of Judaism and Christianity, namely Jewish religion in the centuries immediately preceding and following the rise of Christianity and the first two hundred years of the Christian movement.

CHAPTER 2

Apocalyptic and Eschatology

APOCALYPTIC IS A word which is widely used today, not only in theological debate but also in common parlance.[1] Its secular use normally arises when social and economic events have taken such a disastrous turn that commentators look with gloomy foreboding on the future of society. Apocalyptic, when used in this context, usually denotes pessimistic prognostications about the cataclysmic demise of a hitherto ordered society and the move from the predictable to the bizarre and chaotic. In these circumstances moral norms disappear and superstition triumphs over rational explanation. The human mind is allowed free rein to indulge in wild and fanciful speculations about an imminent disaster in which abnormal and superhuman forces will be involved. Such wild speculation and gloomy prediction have their origin in the fantastic imagery and dark foreboding which figure so prominently in Revelation, and these are the features of Revelation which spring to most people's minds when they think of apocalyptic. Another feature which also stands out in Revelation, and which is regarded by many as typical of apocalyptic, is its pessimistic attitude towards the present world situation. Such an attitude can lead to utter despair about man and his world. So bad is the state of the present age and so corrupt its inhabitants, that the apocalyptic outlook cannot envisage history as the stage for the perfecting of man and society. There arises then the hope for a direct intervention of God to bring about a new order of existence. Despair about the present historical circumstances in which God's people find themselves, and the conviction that redemption can come only from and in a world beyond are usually cited as the characteristics of the contents of the apocalyptic literature.

This view is reflected in most modern studies of apocalyptic, which tend to use the term apocalyptic to describe both a particular literary genre and the eschatological material found in

23

the apocalypses.[2] Koch in his study of apocalyptic lists not only six elements which characterize the literary genre 'apocalypse' but also a group of eight motifs which distinguish the religious approach of the apocalypses.[3] A similar distinction is to be found in W. Schmithals' discussion. He gives full recognition to the aim of the apocalypses to reveal the divine mysteries, but it becomes apparent that the dominant feature of this revelation is of events in the future.[4] He considers that it is essential to extend the understanding of apocalyptic to include other writings which are not apocalyptic in form but whose religious, and particularly eschatological, ideas correspond to an apocalyptic type:

> Since this formal identifying mark (i.e. the revelatory character of the apocalypses) applies to the great bulk of apocalyptic literature, even though not exclusively to it, it is understandable that the originally literary concept 'apocalyptic' was maintained for the later emerging religio-historical description, and, by ruling out such revelational writings as give expression to a type of piety differing from the apocalyptic type, was employed to identify the religious phenomenon of apocalyptic . . . In this terminological process we find expressed the conviction that apocalyptic is a relatively closed, cohesive and independent religious phenomenon.[5]

It would appear that for Schmithals, and many other commentators, this extension of the term 'apocalyptic' to describe a particular type of religious outlook has become the dominant meaning of the word, and the general principle, though not the precise semantic development, has been followed in the previous section. Nevertheless the dominance of content in recent definitions of apocalyptic has been so great that the terminological switch becomes very important in understanding how the word is used. Not only has the original significance of the word as a description of a particular literary type become less important, but also those apocalypses which do not give evidence of a particular type of piety are excluded from the category of apocalyptic.[6]

That piety to which Schmithals refers in the quotation above is essentially the understanding of apocalyptic which has been outlined in the opening paragraphs of this section. It speaks of the imminent cataclysmic irruption of divine power into this world to bring about its destruction and then to produce another realm of goodness and light to replace the present benighted creation. Indeed, to many the word apocalyptic is really little more than a particular kind of eschatology prevalent in the early Jewish and Christian traditions.[7] What is particularly distinctive about this apocalyptic eschatology is often defined by contrasting the hope for the future as it is to be found in the apocalyptic literature with that in the Old Testament prophetic writings. The latter are said to stress the fulfilment of God's purposes within history, whereas apocalyptic emphasizes the need for intervention of a supernatural kind to destroy the old world and to create a new order of existence. H. H. Rowley summarized the attitude of the apocalypticist towards history as compared with his prophetic predecessors in the following, often quoted, words:

> The prophets foretold the future that should arise out of the present, while the apocalyptists foretold the future that should break into the present . . . The apocalyptists had little faith in the present to beget the future.[8]

The radical dichotomy between the present age and the age to come, and the despair of anything good arising out of the present, have become the basis for the construction of an apocalyptic theology, which can be set alongside other theological movements in first century Judaism. The apocalyptic movement is considered to be easily separated from other Jewish religious currents at the time by its distinctive eschatological beliefs. The contribution of the apocalypticists to the growth of Jewish religion was their peculiar development of eschatology, so that it became a cornerstone of Jewish theology. The point is made quite succinctly in the following words of J. A. T. Robinson:

> . . . with the apocalyptists eschatology developed into a subject in itself, a science of the end . . . and one could produce treatises on the last things and treatises on ethics, the one dealing with the future, the other the present. And for late Judaism the two were distinct, the apocalyptic writers giving schematic arrangements to the divine promises, the scribal tradition providing precise codification of the divine demands.[9]

> Furthermore the events with which apocalyptic deals . . . are purely supernatural occurrences . . . they are not part of the natural fabric of history . . . they have a purely supernatural origin; they come out of the blue and can be represented in the language of nature and history only in terms of the abnormal, the discontinuous and the catastrophic.[10]

These citations from modern writing on apocalyptic presuppose that it is possible to extract from the literature of Judaism a body of 'apocalyptic' material and to find in it a unified eschatological picture which varies only in relatively insignificant details. Implicit also in this view is the belief that this eschatology differs from other types which could be found in Jewish literature at this period.[11] Most attempts to define apocalyptic do in fact indicate that there are certain key elements which typify the apocalyptic eschatology: the doctrine of the two ages, a pessimistic attitude towards the present, supernatural intervention as the only basis for redemption, and an urgent expectation of a dawn of a new age. In our attempt to ascertain the essence of apocalyptic no place was found for eschatology in our definition. Perhaps this may have caused some surprise, especially in the light of the close connection which is said to exist between apocalyptic and eschatological ideas. The omission was not because it was considered that eschatology has no part to play in the apocalypses; that would be the reverse of the truth. But its presence in them is not their most distinctive feature, nor does it deserve to become the focus of attention in the study of apocalyptic to the exclusion of the other secrets which the apocalypses claim to reveal.

It may be objected that an examination of the biblical apocalypses indicates that the eschatological secrets form the backbone of both works. What really concerns the seers in these apocalypses is not the secrets of the world above but specifically the coming of the new age and the signs of its arrival. After all the God who 'reveals the mysteries' to Nebuchadnezzar reveals specifically 'what is to be' (Dan. 2.29). There is much truth in this characterization of the biblical apocalypses, though it is not the exclusive interest of the two works. The dominance of eschatology, which is apparent in them, is not typical of the rest of the apocalypses, however. Consideration of the other documents suggests that other issues loom just as large in the mind of the apocalypticist as the coming of the new age. If we compare Daniel with the early chapters of 1 Enoch, the concern with eschatology in the former is not reflected in the latter, where didactic legends and cosmology play the decisive role which eschatology and history play in Daniel.[12] The reason for the dominance of eschatology in both biblical apocalypses lies in the situations of crisis which provoked both of them. Daniel was written at the height of the troubles in Palestine caused by the activities of Antiochus Epiphanes, whereas Revelation was written with the conviction that times of real tribulation were just round the corner for the world as well as for the churches in Asia Minor.[13]

There is the belief in several apocalypses that the history of the world is at such an advanced stage that the dawn of a new age is very close (e.g. Syr. Baruch 85.10: 'For the youth of this world is past, and the strength of the creation already exhausted, and the advent of the times is very short. Yea, they have passed by; and the pitcher is near the cistern, and the ship to port, and the course of the journey to the city, and life to its consummation', cf. 4 Ezra 4. 50). The urgency is much more evident in Daniel and Revelation (Dan. 12.11 and Rev. 22.10). The note of expectation is increased in both because the historical circumstances were such that the visionaries believed that the fulfilment of the divine promises was imminent. Because of this it is only to be expected that the secrets which loom large on the mental horizon of the apocalypticist concern the future. Other matters pale into insignificance, for the simple reason that they have become less important for the seer and his readers than the mysteries surrounding the coming of the new age.

Likewise the most profound existential discussions are to be found in those apocalypses which were written during the most difficult period for Judaism, the years following the destruction of the Temple in AD 70. Syr. Baruch, 4 Ezra and the Apocalypse of Abraham offer, in their different ways, attempts to wrestle with man's lot. Nowhere else do we find such extended discussions of man's nature in the whole of apocalyptic. To that extent we are justified in supposing that a close link does at times exist between historical circumstances and the interests of apocalypticists. But such issues are always part of the concern of men who think about the human condition, though history shows that in times of crisis certain issues do tend to preoccupy the attention of individuals, precisely because they have ceased to be merely matters of abstract debate and have impinged upon the lives of the writers concerned.

The variety of emphases and interests which are to be found in the apocalypses should make us wary of raising particular elements to the level of a norm when their presence may have been dictated by the needs of the moment. Only a few of the apocalypses are dominated by urgent expectation of the coming of the new age and eschatology. The character of the material included in those apocalypses, whose origins are not so closely linked with particular historical events, is more encyclopaedic.[14] Here events have not dictated a greater emphasis on the secrets of the future to the exclusion of other mysteries. Indeed, in certain apocalypses we reach the situation where eschatology itself drops out as a matter of interest in favour of other divine secrets. A particularly good example of this is Slavonic Enoch where we have only occasional references to eschatological subjects (e.g. Slav. Enoch 39.2 and 65.6f.). Such absence is unusual, as one would expect the nature of God's plans for the future to continue to occupy the attention of the apocalypticists whatever the historical situation. Nevertheless, circumstances seem to have dictated whether eschatology dominated an apocalypse or not. An apocalypse which shows little or no interest in eschatology is no less an example of apocalyptic because of this deficiency.

We have suggested that eschatology was just one aspect of the interests of the apocalypticists. If we are reluctant to elevate the eschatological element into an essential feature of apocalyptic, even more caution is necessary when we come to define the nature of the eschatological teaching which is present in the apocalypses. It is certainly true that certain features do tend to appear in several apocalypses, particularly the messianic woes, the disasters which come upon mankind as a prelude to the new age. Frequently attested also is belief in the resurrection. We can also say that the apocalypses seem to have looked for a new age which would have formed part of the present world-order, but more often a restoration of the present universe rather than a new creation. Occasionally mention is made of the destruction of this world (e.g. 4 Ezra 7.31) but rarely is it to be found as the only and dominant view. Revelation is a good example of the way in which the establishment of a kingdom in this world precedes the coming of a new, God-given universe. There is certainly a dualism implicit in apocalyptic eschatology in its contrast between the poverty of the historical situation of the present and the glorious future which is revealed to the seer. But only occasionally is this implicit dualism turned into an explicit doctrine of two ages.[15] Messianic belief, such as it is, tends to reinforce the traditional Jewish expectation of an earthly messiah. There is some evidence to suggest that there may also have existed a belief in a heavenly redeemer in the last days, though whether that figure was thought of as the messiah is not always clear.

There is great variety not only in the contents of the apocalypses, but also in their eschatology. Consequently the contents are not easily reduced to terse summaries which encapsulate apocalyptic eschatology in a sentence or two. What is more, the emphasis on the future breaking into the present as a hallmark of apocalyptic, while not entirely absent in the apocalyptic literature, hardly summarizes the varying features of the eschatological secrets. It must, therefore, be questioned whether a particular type of eschatology can so easily be used as the characteristic feature of the hope for the future in the apocalypses.

Apocalyptic and Rabbinic Eschatologies

Another way of testing whether the eschatological material in the apocalypses offers a distinctive approach to the subject within Judaism is to compare it with other eschatological ideas of the period. As the apocalypses are our major source of information about the eschatological beliefs of Jews at the beginning of the Christian era, comparative material is not easy to come by. The Qumran scrolls contain some eschatological material, but since this material is itself so frequently linked with apocalyptic, and, in addition, can hardly have been typical of mainstream groups, it is probably advisable to exclude it from consideration at this stage. It is the other major literary monument of early Jewish religion, the rabbinic literature, which may offer some insight on the character of eschatology at this time. Obviously the material contained in the documents now extant is of varying age and value for our study. Wherever possible, therefore, consideration will be given to those elements whose pedigree seems reasonably secure.

Contrasts have often been made in the past between rabbinic and apocalyptic thought.[16] The former, with its emphasis on the Law, differs from the latter which preserved the prophetic view of history, though in a subtly altered form. Such a dichotomy can no longer be maintained,[17] for however much the interpretation of Scripture and the meaning of the Torah for the contemporary generation occupied the attention of the rabbinic schools, it is not correct to exclude an interest in eschatology or for that matter other speculative interests from the rabbinic teaching. Indeed, the essential continuity between the religion of the apocalypticists and certain early rabbinic teachers is a subject to which we shall have to return in a later chapter. By the same token it cannot be argued that apocalyptic necessarily departs to any extent from the view of God's covenant which was adhered to by the rabbis.[18] Indeed, there is plenty of material in the apocalypses to suggest that obedience to the divine commandments still had an important part to play in the religion of the apocalypticists.[19] Therefore, unless the eschatological material points in the opposite direction, there will be no good reason for supposing that apocalyptic and pharisaic/rabbinic Judaism represent two opposing streams of thought within early Judaism.

We have virtually no information about the eschatological beliefs of the teachers who flourished in the centuries before the destruction of the Temple. This should not be taken as a repudiation of eschatology on their part, for the fact is that we are generally ill-informed about the opinions of many of these teachers. In any case, such views as have come down to us have been filtered through the later rabbinic academies.[20] These rigorously processed the views of their predecessors and at the same time tended to magnify the importance of their own hero, Hillel, at the expense of other teachers. It is apparent now that many of the traditions which mention Hillel and Shammai owe their present form to the later redaction of the post-AD 70 schools. The situation is somewhat different, however, with the teachers who dominated the religious scene after the fall of Jerusalem. We have a number of pronouncements on eschatological matters from the masters of the late first and early second centuries.[21] Once again we should take care not to assume that the paucity of examples points to a lack of interest or even distaste for eschatological matters at this period. The nature of our sources (collections of, or commentaries on, legal material) makes it more likely that the ideas which would be included in the texts would be more relevant to the practice of religion than matters of merely speculative interest.

The evidence of earliest rabbinic theology is at times a little confused on the subject of eschatology. A great writer on Jewish eschatology like P. Volz rightly points to the existence of eschatological elements in early rabbinic texts, but his view of the attitude of rabbinic Judaism towards apocalyptic is dictated by other considerations. For him the enthusiasm of apocalyptic religion and its fervent expectation were features which led the rabbis to distance themselves from this type of religion.[22] The fact that only one apocalypse was included in the canon, and that in the Writings rather than the Prophets, is to him testimony enough of the rabbinic attitude towards apocalyptic in general. But the fact that only one apocalypse was included in the canon need not necessarily mean a repudiation of the teaching included in them. Doubts about the form in which the apocalyptic secrets were communicated did not prevent the rabbis sharing with the writers of the apocalypses some of the ideas which we find in these works.[23]

The years after AD 70 were obviously a time of great upheaval in Judaism. There was much reflection on the immediate past, not least the circumstances which led up to the capture of the city of Jerusalem by the Romans and the consequences of that event.[24] One factor which played a part in the disastrous events of that time was the desperate conviction that God was going to intervene on the side of his people and destroy those who were so sorely besetting them. The outlook of the people who held such views is well illustrated by. the War Scroll (1QM) from Qumran.[25] Here the elaborate preparations which were required for the proper conduct of the war of the sons of light against the sons of darkness are set out in minute detail. Dominating the beliefs of the writer is his conviction that when the chosen time arrives the heavenly host would fight on the side of the children of light in the final struggle. It goes without saying that in the light of the catastrophe of AD 70 a certain degree of circumspection was inevitable over the kind of eschatological enthusiasm found in the War Scroll. The situation of Judaism was parlous enough without further unsettling influences caused by misguided eschatological beliefs. This may help to explain the plea for caution uttered by the architect of rabbinic Judaism, R. Johanan b. Zakkai: 'If you have a seedling in your hand, and they say to you, Look, here comes the Messiah, Go out and plant the seedling first and then come out to meet him'.[26] In a similar vein R. Jose b. Halafta (c. AD 150) forbids the calculation of the date of the end (Derek, Eretz Zuta 11). Such attitudes as these are only to be expected in a period which witnessed, not only the suffering and humiliation of the war in 66–70, but also, some sixty years later, the equally bitter struggle led by Simeon b. Koseba, which led to the severe curtailment of Jewish privileges in AD 135. The amazing thing about the early rabbinic eschatological traditions is not the reserve which is sometimes encountered, but the fact that, despite the manifest failure of the eschatological hopes, they continued to linger on, to fan the flames of revolt at a later date. Indeed, it is worth pointing out in passing that Johanan's cautious statement is not in itself a repudiation of eschatological hopes but a warning not to be carried away by them.

Nowhere is the abiding influence of eschatology better exemplified than in the *Shemoneh Esreh*, which reached their final form shortly after the First Revolt and were much influenced in their content by Johanan and his school at Jamnia.[27] In these prayers which formed part of the liturgy of the synagogue there emerges the fervent hope for the rebuilding of the Temple and the establishment of the Davidic throne, which is characterized by the urgency of the plea to God:

> Benediction 14: And to Jerusalem, thy city, return in mercy, and dwell therein as thou hast spoken; rebuild it soon in our days as an everlasting building, and speedily set up therein the throne of David. Blessed art thou, O Lord, who rebuildest Jerusalem.[28]

According to b. Berakoth 28b, Johanan b. Zakkai himself lived in expectation of the coming of the messiah, whom he identified with king Hezekiah (ARN 25). But, of course, the most famous example of rabbinic eschatological zeal at this time is to be found in the support which R. Akiba gave for Simeon b. Koseba, when he pronounced that the latter fulfilled the prophecy of Numbers 24.17 as the following passage from j. Ta'anith 68d shows:

> R. Simeon b. Johai taught: My teacher, R. Akiba interpreted, A star will come forth out of Jacob. Koseba came from Jacob. When Akiba saw him, he cried, This is the king-messiah. R. Johanan said, Grass will still be growing from your cheeks and the son of David will not have come.

The small number of passages cited here indicates that eschatological ideas still had their part to play in Jewish thinking after the fall of Jerusalem and that paucity of evidence does not by any means reflect the intensity of the convictions of many of the teachers of that period. It may, however, be argued that, while it is true that the teachers of the tannaitic period did harbour eschatological hopes, these were of a purely nationalistic, this-worldly type and the elements which we find in the apocalypses did not form part of their expectation. If this were true, it would tend to support the belief that apocalyptic represents the hopes of circles which were separated from rabbinic Judaism.[29] Such a distinction between rabbinic and apocalyptic eschatology, however, seems to be difficult to maintain in the light of evidence from rabbinic literature. While it is not our intention to investigate the eschatology of the early rabbinic traditions, sufficient material will be examined to show that a dichotomy cannot be made between the apocalyptic and rabbinical eschatology. Particular attention is here given to the eschatological material which is to be found in the Babylonian Talmud, tractate Sanhedrin 94a ff.

One of the features which characterizes eschatological passages in the apocalyptic literature is the way in which a period of distress is said to precede the coming of the Messiah and the new age. Exactly this belief is to be found in b. San. 97a, in a passage which has some of the similarities with Syriac Baruch 27.1ff.[30] What also emerges in this passage is the historical determinism which makes its appearance in the overall historical perspective and is such an important feature of certain apocalypses:[31]

> Our Rabbis taught: In the seven year cycle at the end of which the son of David will come – in the first year, this verse will be fulfilled: And I will cause it to rain upon one city and cause it not to rain upon another city; in the second, the arrows of hunger will be sent forth; in the third, a great famine, in the course of which men, women and children, pious men and saints will die, and the Torah will be forgotten by its students; in the fourth partial plenty; in the fifth great plenty, when men will eat drink and rejoice, and the Torah will return to its disciples; in the sixth, (heavenly) sounds; in the seventh, wars; and at the conclusion of the septennate the son of David will come.[32]

The imagery of Gog and Magog[33] which on occasion forms part of the apocalyptic symbolism (Rev. 20.7ff.) is taken up in early rabbinic thought as the following passage from M. Eduyoth shows: 'The judgement of Gog and Magog in the age to come will endure twelve months, the judgement of the wicked in Gehenna will endure twelve months.' (2.10)[34] Here we have a feature typical of apocalypses in that the period for the judge-ment of Gog and Magog is firmly laid down. The predestined periodization of history clearly had a significant role to play within rabbinic thought as well. Indeed, there is much material in this section of b. Sanhedrin which finds parallels in the apocalyptic literature testifying to the persistence of these ideas and the abiding interest in such matters among the rabbis.

It has to be admitted, however, that some of the material in this collection comes from a period long after the major apocalypses had been written. It could, therefore, be argued that apocalyptic thought is not really typical of rabbinic Judaism in its earliest phase and its presence in the material is the result of the incorporation of apocalyptic notions into rabbinic religion. Once rabbinic Judaism became the dominant factor in Jewish religion there must have been a tendency for sectarian elements to throw in their lot with those who had hitherto been their opponents. This meant that members of fringe-groups would have imported into rabbinic religion ideas which had hitherto been alien to that movement. The lack of evidence of eschatological ideas from the pre-Destruction teachers gives this theory an air of plausibility. There are good reasons, however, for supposing that such a theory is unlikely. For one thing, it is difficult to believe that rabbinic thought was completely transformed by the inclusion of alien ideas at precisely the time when wholesale changes would have had an unsettling effect on the effort to re-establish the Jewish religion in changed circumstances.[35] Paucity of informa-tion makes certainty in such matters out of the question, but the evidence we do possess about the religion of the predecessors of the rabbis suggests that those features of eschatology which are usually regarded as the distinctive preserve of apocalyptic were already at the heart of pharisaic eschatology before AD 70.

Of prime importance among these beliefs is the notion of resurrection from the dead. The New Testament itself indicates that this notion was one of the distinguishing features of phar-isaism (Acts 23.6f. and Mark 12.18ff.). That it was one of the cornerstones of early rabbinic theology is evident from M. Sanhedrin 10.1:

> All Israelites have a share in the world to come, for it is written, Thy
> people also shall all be righteous, they shall inherit the land for ever;
> the branch of my planting, the work of my hands that I may be
> glorified. And these are they that have no share in the world to

come: he that says that there is no resurrection of the dead prescribed in the Torah . . .

Thus this belief, which is so typical of many of the eschatological
passages in the apocalypses, was of crucial importance for rabbinic theology also. Although evidence for that deterministic
view of history which we find in the eschatological section in b.
Sanhedrin is hard to come by in the pre-70 rabbinic material, the
rabbinic belief in the sovereignty of God such as we find it in,
for example, Aboth 3.16 makes it likely that such an eschatological outlook was also typical of pharisaic thought: 'All is foreseen,
but freedom of choice is given; and the world is judged by grace,
yet all is according to the excess of works.'

This contrasts with the rigid predestinarian views of the Manual of Discipline (1QS 3.15ff. and 4.15ff.).[36] But the evidence of
the apocalypses suggests that they stand closer to the dictum of
Aboth 3.16, for, while the course of history is determined and
leads up to the final inauguration of a new age, man has the
opportunity to do something in the present on the individual
level about his own relationship with God.

Another feature put forward as typical of apocalyptic is the
two ages doctrine. In the passage quoted earlier from M.
Sanhedrin we find there reference to the world or age to come.
This is a stereotyped expression in rabbinic literature and seems
to have been deeply rooted in rabbinic thought.[37] The use of this
phrase inevitably implies a distinction between the present circumstances and the glorious future which was promised. The
rabbis may have been very pragmatic in their attitudes towards
the future, a fact which is demonstrated by the saying of
Johanan b. Zakkai quoted earlier. They certainly stressed the
need for Israel to be obedient to the Torah in the present, but
that did not prevent the two ages doctrine infecting them with a
form of dualistic outlook which historical circumstances made
inevitable.

Finally we must turn to the question whether there existed in
early rabbinic Judaism a belief in the imminent arrival of a new
age. We have already noted that in the biblical apocalypses and
occasionally in the other apocalypses there is the conviction that
the writer and his generation are very near to the new age. Now
despite the cool attitude to fervent eschatological expectation
reflected in the remark of R. Johanan b. Zakkai quoted above,
there is evidence to suggest that the early tannaitic period was

marked by an intense expectation of imminent redemption. The revolt under Simeon b. Koseba is hardly explicable without the intensification of eschatological beliefs, and that is exactly what the prayers for restoration in the *Shemoneh Esreh* encouraged. The fact that three major apocalypses were written towards the end of the first century, but after the destruction of the Temple, is another indication that the failure of the First Revolt did not dampen speculation about the final resolution of Israel's difficulties but, if anything, fanned the flame of eschatological fervour. That this was the case seems to be confirmed by a short passage in the Jerusalem Talmud (j. Berakoth 5a), which suggests that there was thought to be a very close link between the destruction of the Temple and the birth of the messiah. Beliefs like this make it understandable why the early decades of the second century were times of intensified expectation:

> . . . while a Jew was working, his ox began to low. An Arab was passing by and heard the noise and said: Son of Judah, son of Judah, untether your cow, untether your plough, for the Temple has been destroyed. Then the cow lowed again, and the Arab said: Son of Judah, son of Judah, tie your ox and tie your plough, for King Messiah has been born.

In the light of this saying Johanan b. Zakkai's advice to carry on with everyday tasks instead of going out to meet every messianic claimant looks like an attempt to restrain the tendencies within Judaism of this period of those who, despite the horrors of the First Revolt, still clung to an imminent expectation of Israel's redemption.[38]

This brief review of certain aspects of early rabbinic eschatology has attempted to show that eschatological elements of a particular type cannot easily be categorized on sectarian grounds. Not only did the rabbis hold fast to the eschatological beliefs of Judaism, but in most respects it would appear that the character of those beliefs differed little from those of the apocalypticists.[39] Our concern here has not been to write an eschatology of early rabbinic Judaism, but to show that some features taken in modern study to be characteristic of apocalyptic are also components of the eschatological beliefs of another major Jewish group of the period. In the apocalypses and in other Jewish literature we have a variety of eschatological beliefs existing alongside each other. As a result it is impossible to separate out a strand of eschatological expectation which is coherent enough to be distinguished as an apocalyptic sectarian ideology. Our brief glimpse at certain aspects of early rabbinic eschatology suggests that 'apocalyptic' eschatological elements had a fairly wide currency within Judaism and formed part of the common stock of ideas which many groups would have utilized. It is difficult to speak, therefore, of an apocalyptic eschatology existing alongside a nationalistic eschatology, the two being alternative expressions of the future hope in Judaism. Great care needs to be taken when we speak of apocalyptic in Judaism and Christianity that we do not give the impression that (a) there is a completely coherent apocalyptic eschatology, and (b) the motifs which are to be found in apocalypses are peculiar to that literature alone. No one would want to deny that the apocalypses contain some very distinctive features in all areas of their thought, but the presence of isolated, unusual features hardly seems a strong enough basis for defining apocalyptic.[40]

Transcendent Eschatology

It is true that the book of Revelation in particular offers us an example of an eschatology which is replete with fantastic features. The existence of such elements in the apocalypses cannot be ignored. The identification and explanation of these features in Jewish eschatology is a necessary task,[41] but the description of them as 'apocalyptic' elements tends to give them a label which singles out one small feature of the apocalypses and elevates it to the level of a defining principle. The danger is that mythological features in Jewish eschatology are labelled 'apocalyptic' without due consideration of whether such a label may prove to apply to an extremely restricted number of the different elements contained in the apocalypses.

The retreat from history is said to be one of the marks of the apocalyptic outlook. In the sense that the apocalypticist concerns himself with another world, its inhabitants and its secrets as a way of dealing with the vexing problems presented by history, this analysis is certainly correct. Nevertheless, the corollary of this is that the present world was considered unsuitable for the age to come. For example, W. Schmithals puts it in this way:

> In the last analysis man stands powerless in the face of the suffering and misery of the world, and, in the conviction that the new world is to be brought in only by God, the existential experience is asser-

ted that man cannot achieve salvation, but can only await it, and hence that salvation is not to be realised of and in this age at all.[42]

There is little doubt that the hope for the future in Judaism was closely allied to a pessimistic view of the state of the world in the present. After all, the economic deprivations suffered by many Jews in Palestine during the first two centuries of the Christian era encouraged utopian ideas about a glorious future for Israel.[43] Nevertheless the attitude towards the present age, such as we find it in the apocalypses, arises, not so much from the conviction that the present world was too corrupt for the establishment of God's Kingdom, but from the frank admission that without God's help the dominance of Israel and the coming of the new age could never be achieved. There is an important distinction here, which must be fully recognized in order to do justice to the character of the future hope in the apocalypses. Despite the inclusion of occasional mythological elements in the eschatological descriptions, whether it be a belief in a new creation or the intervention of supernatural beings, the apocalypses indicate a view of the future which stresses the outworking of God's purposes within history. A glance at the contents of the apocalypses reveals that other-worldly eschatology is by no means as typical as is often suggested. Indeed, when it is to be found, it is not usually at the expense of the vindication of God's ways within the fabric of history. The eschatology of the apocalypses may have looked to God at work in history as the only means of final salvation, but their authors expected a vindication of their righteousness within the world of men, not in some intangible existence beyond the sphere of history. It is no surprise, therefore, to find that in Revelation the idea of a new heaven and earth follows after the messianic period, during which the martyrs are vindicated and reign with the messiah. This, as much as anything else, is the vindication of their obedience to God in the previous world-order. In this respect Revelation is typical of the eschatology of most of the apocalypses, which tend to stress the arrival of a new age as a direct result of the divinely appointed quota of transitional 'messianic woes' which precede it.

The Qumran War Scroll and the Synoptic Apocalypse

All this leads one to wonder whether enough precision has been used in the past in the definition of eschatological ideas in Judaism and Christianity. That there is a tendency to use mythological material and supernatural agencies in the description of the last things cannot be denied, but we must ask whether inclusion of such elements automatically demands the application of the word 'apocalyptic' to a particular text.

Illustration of some of the difficulties which attend the extension of the term to cover eschatological ideas can be given by reference to two eschatological texts from the early Christian era, the War Scroll (1QM) and the so-called Synoptic Apocalypse (Mark 13 and parallels). Both are frequently called apocalyptic, because their contents concern the last things and seem to manifest some of the characteristics which appear in a work like the New Testament apocalypse: social and political unrest, cosmic disasters and the coming of supernatural agencies either to assist in the final struggle or to vindicate the elect. No one would doubt that the dominant concern of both texts is eschatological, but the question is whether it is also correct to specify further the type of hope found in the two texts, and, if so, whether the label 'apocalyptic' accurately describes their contents.

In the War Scroll we have detailed regulations for the final battle between the sons of light (the members of the community) and the sons of darkness (the *Kittim*). The form of the work is not a disclosure of divine mysteries through an apocalyptic revelation but is a list of precise details for the disposition of the hosts of light in the final struggle. What is it then that has led commentators to refer to this work as an example of apocalyptic?[44] Three points are usually made:

(i) The work takes its inspiration from apocalyptic literature and the influence of the book of Daniel is very much in evidence.[45] What is more, many would consider the detailed regulations the product of the mind of the apocalyptic fanatic rather than the practical details of the man who soberly prepares for the revolutionary struggle. This point of view is well put by Dupont-Sommer:

> The holy war is described concretely and in detail; the many regulations in the book provide, carefully and minutely, for everything that had to be done to place Israel on a war footing and to enable it to overcome the most powerful of enemies. But in reality the author

of the scroll was an enthusiastic visionary, an extraordinary Utopian: it is a grandiose and chimerical dream that he elaborates, rather than any really practicable programme.[46]

(ii) The fact that the phases of the last battle are determined in advance has led to the supposition that we have here an identical kind of outlook to that which we find in apocalyptic literature, where the whole course of history from creation to the messianic age is laid down beforehand and its fulfilment is believed to correspond exactly to the divine plan.

(iii) It is quite clear that the decisive struggle against the forces of darkness will not be fought by human beings alone. Not only are the hosts of heaven expected to join with the righteous community,[47] but also the hosts of Satan fight on the side of the sons of darkness. This outlook is well illustrated by the following quotation from 1QM 12.4–8 (1QM 1.11f., 15.14 and 17.6).

> Thou wilt muster the hosts of thine elect, in their thousands and myriads, with thy holy ones and with all thine angels, that they may be mighty in battle, and may smite the rebels of the earth by thy great judgements, and that they may triumph together with the elect of heaven . . . for our Lord is holy, and the King of Glory is with us together with the holy ones. Valiant warriors of the angelic host are among our numbered men, and the hero of war is with our congregation; the host of his spirits is with our foot-soldiers and horsemen (tr. G. Vermes).

The fact that Daniel has contributed so much to the ideas of this document does not mean that the latter is inevitably an apocalypse in form or apocalyptic in outlook. As Daniel was one of the authoritative writings at Qumran,[48] it is hardly surprising that it should have provided a basis for the speculations contained in the War Scroll. It is true that from a modern perspective such regulations do seem to have an air of unreality, but it would be wrong to conclude from this that only an apocalyptic fanatic could have conjured up a plan of campaign of this kind. Isolated the Qumran community may have been and not typical of contemporary Jewish religion in many respects, but the fervent hope of deliverance runs like a thread throughout the eschatology of all groups during this period. Thus the details of the final preparations may have been lacking in the eschatology of other groups, but the debate would have been about detail and not about the conviction concerning future redemption.

Secondly, in any eschatological description a certain degree of determinism is inevitable. Jewish belief in the sovereignty of God meant that the military dispositions which we find in 1QM would result from God's care for his people and his knowledge of that which was to come. Just as God knows the name of the messiah before the creation of the world (b. Pesaḥim 54a), so too the whole of history, including the stages leading up to the new age, are known to him. We saw that there is evidence from the early rabbinic literature that a similar belief is to be found there also. Thus we are dealing here with a belief which was held in common by many groups which had eschatological interests at this time. There is, however, one important distinction between the War Scroll and the apocalypses. Whereas the latter stress that the unfolding of the details of history, whether eschatological or not, comes by means of revelation, there is no suggestion that the War Scroll offers the results of divine revelation about the dispositions of the hosts of light in the new age. Although the authority of the War Scroll for the sect cannot be doubted, there is nothing to justify the label 'apocalyptic' being attached to this document.

Thirdly, the intervention of the heavenly hosts is taken to be symptomatic of that trend in apocalyptic eschatology which looked to supernatural intervention into history to bring about the glorious future foretold by the prophets. But there is no suggestion that the battle mentioned here takes place anywhere except within the framework of history. The theme of the divine assistance is not one that is to be found only in apocalypses. It is already very much part of the biblical narratives which speak of the deliverance of God's people. For example, both Joshua 5.13ff. and 2 Kings 6.15–17 show certain affinities with the War Scroll, in speaking of a joint effort between the people of God and the heavenly host to defeat those who are opposed to God.[49] But this emphasis on the combined efforts of the angelic armies and the elect people of God is in itself one which appears to contrast with the bulk of the apocalyptic literature. Unlike the apocalypses, where the task of the elect is to engage in renewed endeavours to remain righteous before God, the War Scroll demands of the community that they take an active part in the final overthrow of wickedness, in a manner similar to the Jewish military activists of the period, the Zealots. Zealot influence is not strong in the apocalyptic literature. A passage like 1 Enoch

90.19 (part of the 'Animal-Apocalypse') seems to indicate that at this stage of the apocalyptic tradition an armed conflict between the righteous and the sinners was contemplated:

> And I saw till a great sword was given to the sheep, and the sheep proceeded against all the beasts of the field to slay them, and all the beasts and the birds of heaven fled before their face.[50]

This passage can hardly be said to be typical, however, and the dominant theme throughout the apocalypses seems to be one of patient pacifism. Indeed, even in a work like 4 Ezra the picture of the messiah loses many of the warlike characteristics which are to be found in a passage like the Psalms of Solomon 17. This is quite evident in this extract from 13.37ff:

> But he, my son, shall reprove the nations that are come for their ungodliness . . . and shall reproach them to their face with their evil thoughts and with the tortures with which they are destined to be tortured . . . and then shall he destroy them without labour by the Law . . .

By and large then the apocalypses do not countenance participation in an armed struggle as part of the lot of the righteous. Often it is left unspecified how in fact the unrighteous nations will be overthrown, though one may expect that the messiah was sometimes considered to have an important part to play in the process. If the eschatological section in Syriac Baruch 24–30 is anything to go by, the tribulations which precede the coming of the messiah will have so decimated the population of the earth that they will be in no state to offer resistance to the messiah when he comes to establish God's kingdom. This issue need not detain us at the present, however. What is clear, when we compare the apocalypses and the War Scroll, is that the readiness for armed struggle, which so dominated the outlook of the author of this document and his community, is notably absent from the contemporary apocalyptic literature. All this seems to indicate that we are dealing with a text which is related to the apocalypses, but one which hardly justifies the label 'apocalyptic'. The common element between the Qumran text and the apocalypses is eschatology, but the underlying conviction that what the writer had to communicate was in fact a direct revelation of the divine purposes (the underlying conviction which we have identified as characteristic of apocalyptic) is nowhere stressed in the Qumran text.

Let us move on now to an examination of that section of the synoptic gospels which is often cited as an example of apocalyptic within the New Testament, with the result that the title, 'The Synoptic or Little Apocalypse', is often used to describe it.[51] The material in Mark 13 consists of a series of predictions made by Jesus in the setting of his final visit to Jerusalem immediately before his death. Its position in the gospel of Mark (immediately before the account of Jesus' arrest, trial and death) suggests that, like the testaments of the patriarchs, this section should be understood as the last testament of Jesus before his passion. The collection of sayings[52] is introduced by a remark by one of Jesus' disciples about the beauty of the Temple (13.1). This then provides a setting for sayings about the destruction of the Temple (13.2), the dreadful days which will precede the coming of the messiah (13.4–8 and 14–27), the imminent persecution of the elect (vv. 9–13) and their final vindication by the Son of Man (v. 26f.).

There is no suggestion here that this eschatological teaching forms part of an apocalypse.[53] Indeed, all we have is a succession of predictions about what is to come in the future. It is not impossible that some of the ideas expressed here may have originated in a revelation, whether from Jesus[54] or through a Christian prophet, but the present form of the chapter makes it difficult to justify the description of it as apocalyptic.[55] Rather than describe this chapter as an apocalypse it would seem to be more accurate to describe it as eschatological prediction in a form similar to the non-apocalyptic testament literature of Judaism (particularly the Testaments of the XII Patriarchs).

Much more akin to the apocalyptic literature, however, are the contents of this chapter, which take up some themes familiar to us from the apocalypses, such as the messianic woes and the cosmic disorders which precede the new age. That is not to suggest that Mark 13 offers us a complete eschatological picture. It seems to concentrate only on part of the traditional eschatological drama: the tribulations which precede the end and a statement of the conviction that the elect would be vindicated. Nothing whatever is said about the period of bliss which follows the tribulations or even the resurrection and final judgement, though the latter element does appear in the later development of the discourse in Matthew 25.31ff.[56] We have seen that the eschatological tribulations are not just typical of apocalyptic

eschatology but form a major part of the eschatological expectations of most Jewish groups. The presence of such ideas, and for
that matter predictions of a time of unrest and suffering for the
elect, should not be regarded as constituting evidence that this
chapter is to be regarded as an example of apocalyptic.[57]

Much more difficult to assess, however, are the passages
concerning the abomination of desolation (Mark 13.14) and the
coming of the Son of Man on the clouds of heaven (Mark 13.26).
Whatever the meaning of the former verse (and the suggestions
are numerous),[58] we have here the kind of obscure statement
familiar to us from other apocalypses. Already in Daniel 9.27;
11.31 and 12.11 the phrase occurs in various forms with reference to the outrageous desecration of the Temple by Antiochus
Epiphanes. There it already has an air of mystery, similar to the
attempt to identify the beast by means of *gematria* in Revelation
13.18. In Mark 13.14 certainty as to precise significance of the
reference is now lost, and we are left to decide which of the
various speculations is the most probable. But the fact that
Mark, or an earlier editor, included the redactional comment 'let
the reader understand' suggests that the significance of the
reference to the 'abomination of desolation' would have been
reasonably clear to his readers. Although the enigma is already
present within the scriptural passage which forms the basis of
this prediction, there can be no doubt that we have in this verse
an outlook which is akin to apocalyptic. The hidden mysteries
are a key-element in the apocalypses, and it is clear that on
occasion the unfolding of the divine secrets often involved the
disclosure of the true meaning of scripture, e.g. Daniel 9.2ff. Of
course, the quest for the true meaning of the sacred scriptures
was one which was pursued by many groups. For example,
Philo speaks in the following way about the exegetical activities
of the *Therapeutae:*

> They read the Holy Scriptures and seek wisdom from their ancestral
> philosophy by taking it as an allegory, since they think that the
> words of the literal text are symbols of something whose hidden
> nature is revealed by studying the underlying meaning (*De Vita
> Contemplativa* 28).

Such an approach also characterizes Philo's attitude to the Pentateuch, but it is also apparent in the interpretation of Scripture
at Qumran.[59] Throughout the Scrolls there is frequent use of

words like secret *(sod)*, conceal *(satar)* and mystery *(raz)* (1QS 8.18; 9.17 and 22).[60] There is one document which makes it quite clear that the true meaning of the prophetic oracles was not available to the original prophet but was available only to the Teacher of Righteousness. The Habakkuk commentary (1QpHab) is a very good example of the way in which the original setting and meaning of the text is ignored in favour of a new, deeper meaning which enshrines the import which God intended the passage to have:

> . . . and God told Habakkuk to write down that which would happen to the final generation, but he did not make known to him when time would come to an end. And as for that which he said, That he who reads may read it speedily, interpreted this concerns the Teacher of Righteousness, to whom God made known all the mysteries of the words of his servants the prophets (7.1ff.).

What we can say about Mark 13.14, therefore, is that it shares with various types of literature in the Judaism of this period the conviction that the true meaning of an obscure passage can be unfolded. The means by which this true meaning can be ascertained were various, however. The detailed interpretation of Scriptures was just as likely to offer a means of ascertaining the true meaning of the text as the disclosure of its meaning through apocalyptic revelation. Thus the similarity which exists between Mark 13.14 and apocalyptic stems from the common belief which existed in Judaism that the significance of Scripture did not rely on the meaning it had for its original writer and that subsequent generations alone were permitted to understand and experience the true meaning of the words spoken by the prophets (cf. 1 Pet. 1.12).

In the second passage which is offered as an example of apocalyptic eschatology in Mark 13 we read that the vindication of the elect is to be attended by the coming of the Son of Man with the angelic host. This seems to many to be at the heart of apocalyptic, with its description of a supernatural irruption into the historical process to rescue the righteous. There can be no question here of the future arising out of the present, for the divine will is executed, not through history, but by a direct intervention into it. Unlike the Jewish beliefs about the birth of a human messiah and a new age, in which the world would gradually be transformed into the perfection of its beginning, we have here an event whose origin is in heaven. Here is a passage which seems to confirm Philipp Vielhauer's assertion that in apocalyptic 'the new age is of a transcendent kind'.[61] A glance at the final chapters of the book of Revelation will show that it too contains passages in which the divine breaks into human history, e.g. Rev. 19.11ff. It is true that Mark 13.26 reveals certain similarities with Revelation and differs from an eschatology which stresses the origin of the redeemer in this world, but it is to be doubted whether the label 'apocalyptic' is appropriate to specify the characteristics of the eschatology of this verse and the similar passages in Revelation. Leaving aside for the moment the fact that Mark 13.26 does not form part of an apocalypse proper, there are two questions which must be asked about the justification for referring to this as an example of apocalyptic. First, how far is it possible to argue that passages like this one are typical of the apocalytic literature alone, and second, are the references to supernatural intervention typical of the apocalyptic literature as a whole?

We have already seen when dealing with the War Scroll that the idea of direct divine intervention is rooted in Scripture, and it is difficult to argue that its presence in later Jewish literature necessarily denotes a move away from a positive view of history to one which stresses the need for supernatural agencies. A reference to a supernatural agent cannot by itself be taken as an indication of a despair of history as the stage for redemption. That is not to deny the significance of the supernatural intervention mentioned in Mark 13, but its presence in the chapter needs to be set alongside the fact that the rest of the chapter is dealing with events which arise out of history, a fact which even applies to the astronomical disorders mentioned in Mark 13.24f.[62] Even if we felt justified in referring to these verses as an example of apocalyptic, the singular lack of such elements elsewhere in the chapter should make us reluctant in applying the term to the discourse as a whole.

But the main reason for doubting whether apocalyptic is an apt description of these verses is that, the New Testament apart, examples of supernatural intervention of this kind are by no means common in the apocalypses, nor, as we have seen, does the eschatology of apocalyptic literature confine itself to supernatural intervention and an other-worldly hope. The idea of a heavenly messiah coming at the end is not common in Jewish apocalyptic and is found only in the Similitudes of Enoch and perhaps also 4 Ezra.[63] This contrasts markedly with early Christian eschatology which fervently expected their messiah to come from heaven (Acts 3.19ff.; 1 Thess. 4.15ff; 1 Pet. 1.13). In the light of this difference it would be dangerous to assume that the early Christian belief, along with that found in the Similitudes, reflects the normal type of eschatology which is to be found in the Jewish apocalypses. Before attributing to the Jewish apocalypses an obsessive interest in direct supernatural intervention, which appears to be rather rare, it is imperative that full consideration be given to the possibility that the distinctive contours of early Christian eschatology may arise from the character of its own beliefs about Jesus, rather than a simple transference of a supposed apocalyptic eschatology into early Christian thought. The point is that the early Christian expectation that Jesus would function as the final agent of God's saving purposes necessitated a descent from heaven to perform this function (Acts 3.19ff.). The parousia doctrine is thus just as likely to have been the result of the distinctive beliefs about Jesus' exaltation as the importation of heavenly messianic figures from Jewish eschatology. This is not to deny the influence of apocalyptic on the thought-patterns of the early Christian writers, as we shall see in due course. Rather it is a plea that as much precision as possible should be used in describing the way in which early Christians interacted with the Jewish thought of their day. The contribution of apocalyptic and eschatology may sometimes have overlapped, as is clearly the case in Revelation, but it would be wrong to assume that this was always the case. Early Christianity drew on the traditional Jewish eschatology to express the consequences of the life, death and resurrection of Jesus. Its debt to the apocalyptic outlook is at times only loosely related to the eschatological ideas, however. While it is true that the dawn of the new age made a difference to the early Christian attitude towards revelation (e.g. Acts 2.17), the apocalyptic mode of revelation was quite independent of any eschatological system. The outpouring of the spirit may have meant that direct communion between God and man was more likely, but the nature of this communion and its modes of expression owed much to other contemporary Jewish beliefs, which are only incidentally linked with eschatology.

Our study of the relationship between apocalyptic and

eschatology has indicated that we are dealing with two separate issues in Jewish religion. The first concerns a way of apprehending the divine will and the second the character of Jewish hopes for the future. They come together precisely because the task of understanding God's will was particularly difficult as far as eschatology was concerned. Consequently it comes as no surprise that a dominant feature of the mysteries revealed to the apocalypticists is the secret of the future, particularly with regard to Israel. To say that, however, is not the same as saying that eschatology is a constitutive feature of apocalyptic. An apocalypse often does contain much eschatological material, but it need not. Secondly, we have also had reason to doubt whether such eschatological material as is to be found within the apocalypses offers us distinctive characteristics. All the indications are that the apocalypses share with other examples of Jewish literature similar eschatological beliefs. No doubt distinctive ideas emerge in the apocalypses but the eschatological elements hardly occur on anything like a large enough scale for us to speak of an apocalyptic eschatology over against other eschatological systems. This applies particularly to transcendent or other-worldly eschatology. There are certainly signs in some apocalypses of a belief that this world would be replaced by a new order of existence, but hardly ever do we find this belief replacing a hope for a period of bliss in this world. When an other-worldly eschatology does appear, as, for example, in 4 Ezra 7.31ff., it is juxtaposed with a this-worldly eschatology.[64] The character of the eschatological beliefs is too varied, and the detail in the various apocalypses insufficient, to make a clear-cut definition of apocalyptic eschatology anything but a very hazardous task. Thus there does not appear to be enough consistency in apocalyptic eschatology to speak of it as if it were a cohesive religious system in Judaism at the beginning of the Christian era.

CHAPTER 3

Apocalypse and Apocalyptic

The Apocalypse

OUR CONCERN IN the previous sections has been to identify as precisely as possible the religious perspective in Judaism and Christianity which we designate apocalyptic. The literary form in which this type of religion normally manifested itself was the apocalypse, a Jewish literary genre of a fairly fixed type. Examination of the collection of apocalyptic writings reveals not only an underlying religious conviction, the direct revelation of the divine mysteries, but also a literary genre which exhibits several common elements. In most cases we find that the apocalypse proper is not the only component of the work, and some kind of setting is normally given to the divine disclosures. If we concentrate for a moment on the book of Daniel, we find that the work as we have it consists of two major parts. The first six chapters offer us a collection of tales about righteous Jews in Babylon during the Exile, into which are inserted the interpretation of two dreams which are essentially apocalyptic in character (Dan. 2.31ff.; 4.13ff; cf. 5.24f.). These opening chapters then form the setting[1] for the subsequent revelations given to Daniel either through dream-visions and interpretations (Dan. 7–8) or direct disclosures by an angelic intermediary (Dan. 10–12). This genre is followed more or less by all the Jewish apocalypses, and one or two of the Christian documents. Sometimes there have been added to the opening legends and apocalypses admonitions by the apocalyptic seer after his vision (e.g. 1 Enoch 91ff.), an element which is absent from Daniel.[2] When we examine the apocalypses we find that, despite the variety of issues which are covered in the course of a particular document, this basic genre is more or less adhered to. The New Testament apocalypse offers a slight variation of this form, as its lack of pseudonymity makes the introductory legends found in the Jewish apocalypses superfluous. Nevertheless it resembles them in its inclusion at the end of various admonitions (Rev. 22.6ff.) and, what is more, allows this hortatory tone to intrude into the visions themselves, e.g. Rev. 2–3; 13.9f.; 14.12.

The threefold structure of legends, visions and admonitions is found most clearly in Slavonic Enoch and the Testament of Levi. Both works purport to be the reports of visions which these great men had before their final departure from the earth. In Enoch's case he is allowed to return to his house after the heavenly ascent to report to his sons what he has seen (Slav. Enoch 33.6). This gives the antediluvian hero the opportunity to offer advice to his sons about the character of their lives. Essentially the same form is to be found in Syriac Baruch. Here, however, the precise distinction between the legendary material and the apocalyptic disclosures is not so clear. Reference is made in Syriac Baruch 1—2; 6; 9—10 to the setting in which the revelations take place. Also admonitions (Syr. Baruch 31—33) are interspersed among the revelations as well as other material (e.g. Baruch's prayer in chapter 48). Nevertheless the visions and other disclosures are rounded off by an admonition by Baruch to the people (Syr. Baruch 76f) and a letter of Baruch to the nine and a half tribes beyond the Euphrates (Syr. Baruch 78ff.). As in the two previous works this document is set towards the end of Baruch's life (Syr. Baruch 43.1ff.). The contemporary 4 Ezra concentrates much more on the revelations. 4 Ezra 3.4–9, 37 consists of dialogues between the seer and an angel and includes eschatological predictions by the latter. The visions are to be found in 4 Ezra 9.38—13 end, leaving the last chapter for final instructions to the seer and certain admonitions (4 Ezra 14.27ff.). Only the briefest reference is made in 4 Ezra 3.1f. to the historical situation in which the revelations were supposed to have been received.

What is perhaps most surprising of all, however, is the fact that evidence of a coherent literary form can be discerned in that most composite of apocalypses, 1 Enoch, even in its final form. This is even more apparent if the Similitudes (1 Enoch 37—71), an amalgam of legend and apocalypse, are omitted. The opening five chapters also present something of a problem to the apocalyptic form. They consist of a prediction based on the prophecies in the Old Testament concerning the Day of the Lord (1 Enoch 1.3–9) observations concerning the natural world (1 Enoch 2—5.3) and a concluding prediction of destruction for sinners and bliss for the righteous. Apart from the opening verses there is little mention of Enoch, and it is difficult to see how this whole section fits in with the subsequent stories. It seems probable, therefore, that this is early material which has been placed here, though it has no connection with the Enoch-legends which follow.[3] If we leave the opening chapters out, we find that the stories in 1 Enoch 6—11 provide the setting for Enoch's ascent to heaven to intercede on behalf of the Watchers and then his subsequent wanderings through creation. Leaving out the Similitudes for a moment, we note that Enoch continues his revelations about the cosmos in chapter 72ff. which are then followed by eschatological visions and predictions (1 Enoch 83—90).[4] The work then concludes with extensive admonitions interspersed with further eschatological predictions. Even if we include the Similitudes, we still have, in a rather attenuated form, the structure which we have outlined, in which visions and other revelations are sandwiched between legends and paraenetic material.

Not only is this basic structure typical of most of the Jewish apocalypses which have come down to us, but, in one notable case, it would appear that precisely this structure has been taken over in a work whose contents may not lead us to suspect any connection with the apocalyptic outlook, namely the book of Jubilees.[5] This offers a rewriting of the biblical account of history from creation to the passover and exodus from Egypt. There may appear to be little here to rank it with the apocalypses, but the significant fact is the way in which this whole story is placed in the context of God's revelation to Moses on Sinai. The book starts off with the command to Moses by God to 'come up to me on the mountain' (Jub. 1.1, cf. Exod. 24.12).[6] After a long speech God commands the angel of the presence to make known to Moses the history of creation and the story of the covenant people:

> And he said to the angel of the presence: Write for Moses from the beginning of creation till my sanctuary has been built among them for all eternity . . . And the angel of the presence spake to Moses according to the word of the Lord saying: Write the complete history of the creation how in six days the Lord God finished all his works etc. (Jub. 1.27—2.1)

Thus the whole of the history of creation and the story of the beginnings of the covenant-people are said to be a revelation by God to Moses, in the same way as the revelation of the ethical and ritual regulations revealed to the law-giver on the mountain. This is exactly the kind of development which one would expect in a religion which had given authoritative status to the Torah. Jubilees thus extends to the book of Genesis and the early chapters of Exodus the status which the bulk of Exodus already claims for itself, namely a direct revelation of God (or, in this case, the angel of the presence) to Moses. The framework of an apocalypse guarantees that the earlier, historical, writing is seen to be of equal importance in the whole scheme of God's revelation to his people. Thus what at first sight appears to be an unpromising candidate for inclusion in a list of apocalyptic writings is on closer inspection a work of exactly the same type of genre as other apocalypses. As one recent commentator put it,

> It shares many of the familiar characteristics of apocalyptic and only an arbitrarily rigid notion of which 'revelations' qualify as apocalyptic can exclude it from consideration. What may be said is that it is a member of the group in which the 'historiographical' moment has the position of dominance that in some other apocalyptic works belongs to the eschatological one.[7]

So it can be said that the apocalypses present us with a fairly distinctive literary form, though apart from the claim to offer revelations, fictitious settings and ethical admonitions are features of other Jewish works of the period, particularly, of course, in the Testaments of the XII Patriarchs. Although one would not want to speak of the apocalypse as a literary genre which was rigidly adhered to, there does seem to be good evidence that the apocalyptic spirit did tend to manifest itself in a particular form.

Types of Visions

While there seems to be a degree of uniformity in the way in which the apocalypse is constructed, the same cannot be said for the way in which the divine revelations were communicated to the apocalyptic seer. Although there is an underlying theme in the apocalypses that the seer has direct access to the divine counsels, the mode of revelation appears to be influenced very much by the situation and outlook of the particular author.

All the apocalypses attributed to Enoch and Abraham take as

their starting-point the journey of the righteous man in the heavenly abode.[8] For example, in the Apocalypse of Abraham the sacrifice of Abraham (Gen. 15.17) is the setting for the ascent of the patriarch to heaven on the wings of one of the sacrificial victims:

> And it came to pass when the sun went down . . . and the angel took me with the right hand and set me on the wing of the pigeon, and set himself on the left wing of the turtle-dove . . . and he bore me to the borders of the flaming fire and we ascended as with many winds to the heaven . . . (ch. 15)

In the Testament of Abraham, on the other hand, the patriarch ascends to heaven in a chariot of cherubim (Rec. A 10). Apart from the Enochic and Abrahamic apocalypses the heavenly journey features also in the Testament of Levi, the Ascension of Isaiah and Revelation.[9] It is absent, however, in three of the major apocalypses of our period, Daniel, 4 Ezra and Syriac Baruch. The major parts of Syriac Baruch and 4 Ezra consist of dialogues between an angelic intermediary and the seer. When visions are to be found in 4 Ezra (9.38—13 end) and Syriac Baruch (36f; 53), it is quite clear that we have to do here with visions whose contents are merely a picturesque way of expressing the divine secrets which the seer has to communicate. Indeed, in contrast to Enoch and Abraham, God explicitly denies that Ezra has ever ascended into the heavenly world: 'Perchance thou wouldst have said to me: Into the deep I have not descended, nor as yet gone down into Hades; neither to heaven have I ascended, nor entered Paradise' (4 Ezra 4.8).

Not only is the heavenly ascent excluded but also the glimpse into the heavenly world, which had formed part of the prophetic experience (1 Kings 22.19). Indeed, in Syriac Baruch 22.1 we find that precisely the same stereotyped introduction,[10] which had introduced Ezekiel's vision of the divine throne-chariot, is repeated here, but without any suggestion that Baruch has the opportunity of glimpsing into the heavenly world:

> And it came to pass after these things that lo, the heavens were opened, and I saw, and power was given to me, and a voice was heard from on high, and it said unto me, Baruch, Baruch why art thou troubled?

Unlike most of the occurrences of the open heaven in Jewish literature this is not followed by a vision of heavenly things, and this despite the fact that reference is made to the opportunity which Baruch had to see into the divine world. The introduction to the divine pronouncement is a verbatim reproduction of Ezekiel 1.1 ('the heavens were opened, and I saw visions of God') but without any reference to a vision of God. Baruch merely hears the voice of God who answers his prayer. Clearly the open heaven indicates to the seer that his dealings are directly with God himself, but this directness does not appear to give the seer any grounds for a vision of God and the world above (cf. Hermas Vis. I. 1.4).

Reasons for this development are not easy to ascertain, though two pieces of evidence from 4 Ezra may be of assistance to us. Firstly, it is apparent throughout this work that man's lot is due in no small part to Adam's sin (4 Ezra 3.7) and the abiding iniquity which is to be found in every generation of Adam's descendants: 'For all the earth-born are defiled with iniquities full of sins, laden with offences' (7.68). Although the righteous Ezra is permitted to enter into dialogue with the angelic inter-mediary and even has the divine mysteries revealed to him, he is still a participant in the evil human race and as such not of sufficient holiness to enter the holy realm of God. That must wait until his final departure from the world of men at his death (4 Ezra 14.49). Secondly, we should not miss the significance of the address of Ezra to God which is to be found in the opening of Ezra's prayer in 4 Ezra 8.20 (cf. Apocalypse of Moses 33.2):

> O Lord that dwellest eternally, whose are the highest heavens, whose chambers are in the air, whose throne is beyond imagination, whose glory is inconceivable, before whom heaven's hosts stand trembling, and at thy word change to wind and fire.

Whereas other apocalypticists, including Daniel, had considered that it was possible to look upon and describe the glory of God and his throne, such a possibility is explicitly ruled out by Ezra. Despite being able to know God's will through revelation of the angelic agent, it is not possible for him to know the secrets of the transcendent God enthroned in glory far above the heavens. The nearest parallel to this in contemporary literature is a passage which we shall have to consider a little later in this study. It is the second half of the mishnah dealing with the study of esoteric subjects, particularly the first chapters of Ezekiel and Genesis. The second half of M. Hagigah 2.1 is a warning to those who would indulge in speculation about the things of God to confine themselves to matters which are within their competence.[11] Both 4 Ezra 8.20 and the second half of the mishnah seem to be products of schools of thought, which viewed with suspicion the claims of those who dared to imagine the invisible God and attempt descriptions of the one who surpassed all human language.

The book of Daniel resembles Syr. Baruch and 4 Ezra in not including a reference to a heavenly ascent. But, unlike the other two documents, Daniel does include one passage which offers the readers a clear glimpse into the character of the heavenly court. In Dan. 7.9f. the seer describes the judgement of the beasts, and in the course of this pauses to sketch a picture of the inhabitants of heaven in language whose ultimate inspiration is the first chapter of Ezekiel:[12]

> As I looked, thrones were placed and one that was Ancient of Days took his seat; his raiment was white as snow, and the hair of his head like pure wool; his throne was fiery flames, its wheels were burning fire. A stream of fire issued and came forth from before him; a thousand thousands served him, and ten thousand times ten thousand stood before him.

This passage and the related description of the heavenly world in 1 Enoch 14[13] show that at an early period (the beginning of the second century BC or before) there was not the reluctance to refer to a heavenly ascent and to unfold the secrets of the being of God himself which were ascertained during such journeys.

This essential difference between the apocalypses inevitably means that there are consequent differences in the way in which the revelation is communicated to the apocalypticist. In the revelation following a heavenly journey the seer is shown the divine secrets as they actually exist in the heavenly world (Rev. 4f., Apocalypse of Abraham 18ff., 1 Enoch 71.3f.). When he reaches heaven and has gazed upon God in glory, he is then allowed, usually guided by an angel, to see the mysteries which are concealed in heaven. These secrets are very varied and include cosmogony (Slav. Enoch 25ff.) and astronomy (1 Enoch 72ff.) as well as the course of human history past and future (Apocalypse of Abraham 21ff.). Whatever pertains to the heavens and the earth, its past or its future could be and was included in the apocalypses.

The initiation into the divine secrets in heaven is usually of two types. Either the apocalyptic seer is told directly by God or an angel (e.g. Slav. Enoch 25 and Dan. 10.20ff.); or he is *shown* heavenly mysteries. In both cases there is reflected the belief that the secrets of the universe are in some sense stored up in heaven. Heaven is a kind of repository of the whole spectrum of human history which can be glimpsed by the elect. Most common of all is the notion that the events of the future can be revealed verbally to the seer. In this case the seer could have proleptic knowledge of that which had still to be actualized in human history (cf. 4 Ezra 6.1–6). A good example of this is the plan for the future Jerusalem, which, according to Syr. Baruch 4.2ff., is already engraved on God's palms:

> Dost thou think that this is that city of which I said: On the palms of my hands have I graven thee? This building now built in your midst is not that which is revealed with me, that which was prepared beforehand here from the time when I took counsel to make Paradise, and showed it to Adam before he sinned, but when he transgressed the commandment it was moved from him, as also Paradise. And after these things I showed it to my servant Abraham by night among the portion of the victims. And again also I showed it to Moses on Mount Sinai when I showed to him the likeness of the tabernacle and its vessels. And now behold it is preserved with me as also Paradise.[14]

It is not a question here of the Jerusalem of the new age actually existing as a physical entity in heaven, though that may be the impression given by a too literal interpretation of the vision in Rev. 21.1ff. Rather we have reflected here the idea that all human history ·exists in the mind of God, or to put it in apocalyptic categories, hidden in the treasury of heavenly secrets. It is hardly surprising, therefore, that the journey to heaven offered an opportunity to learn some of the answers to some of the perplexing features of human life and history.[15]

While the majority of instances have angels revealing the secrets verbally to the seer, much more interesting are those occasions when he is offered an actual vision of these events. In these cases there is not merely a general prediction but a visual presentation of the events of history, a conviction that it was possible to *see*, not only the past events of human history, but also that which was to take place in the future. The picture which is offered to the seer is not just the vague prophecy of doom which is to be found in the prophetic literature (though some apocalyptic presentations do leave certain issues rather vague) but a clearly defined vision of the whole of human history laid up in heaven. Probably the best example of this particular feature of apocalyptic literature is to be found at the opening of Apocalypse of Abraham 22:

> And I said: O Eternal, Mighty One, what is this picture of the creatures? And he said to me: This is my will with regard to those who exist in the divine world counsel, and it seemed well-pleasing before my sight, and then afterwards I gave commandment to them through my word. And it came to pass whatever I had determined to be was already planned beforehand in this (picture), and it stood before me ere it was created, as thou hast seen.[16]

Abraham is then shown a picture of the fall of Adam as well as the glorious future which will be inaugurated by the Elect One. Here earthly events find themselves mirrored in the heavenly world. There can be no doubt that the thrust of this presentation offers a deterministic view of history: God knows the whole course of human history before the universe was created. It would, however, be a mistake to conclude from this that human action is predetermined down to the last detail. The apocalyptic view of history is deterministic as far as the direction of history is concerned. The destiny of man inevitably moves towards a final realization of the kingdom of God. It is this conviction which dominates the historical perspective of the apocalypses, not the fate of the individual, which is left unspecified within this inexorable movement towards the new age.

Other revelations are to be found in two major forms. The vision followed by interpretation normally differs from the visions which accompany the heavenly ascent, in that there is no suggestion in the former that what the seer sees in his vision actually corresponds with any reality in heaven. The various images which make up his dream or vision are merely means whereby the essential truths of the heavenly mysteries can be communicated to him.[17] An example of such a vision from a biblical apocalypse is to be found in Daniel 8. The vision of the ram and the he-goat is clearly a vivid way of communicating certain truths about the fate of various pagan kings (Dan. 8.19ff.). In most cases the symbolic character of the vision is verified by the inclusion of an interpretation, which makes it

quite clear that the earlier vision is just a way of expressing
certain facts about the course of human history in picturesque
language. In this category we should probably include all the
visions in Syriac Baruch and 4 Ezra, Revelation, chapter 17,
Daniel, chapters 2 and 8, and the Shepherd of Hermas from
early Christian apocalyptic literature. A little more difficult to
explain, but of essentially the same type, are the symbolic
visions which do not have any interpretation. The best example
in the apocalypses is the animal-apocalypse in 1 Enoch 85ff.
Although nothing whatever is said explicitly about the different
animals representing historical personages, it is quite clear from
the context that they represent different figures in the history of
the world, and particularly the history of Israel down to the
Maccabaean period. Although there is one example of a vision
followed by an interpretation in Revelation chapter 17, it is the
symbolic vision without any interpretation which seems to pre-
dominate in this work.

Finally, there is the dialogue between the angel or God and
the seer which figures prominently in 4 Ezra and Syriac Baruch.
This type of dialogue, so reminiscent of the dialogues in the
book of Job,[18] is not so common in the other apocalypses, where
the seer is merely a passive recipient of any secrets which the
angel has to offer him. Typical of the latter form of revelation is
the final series of disclosures in the book of Daniel (10—12). In
this situation the seer is often prepared to receive divine revelations (Dan. 10.2f.), and as a result an angel appears to him and
unfolds to Daniel 'what is inscribed in the book of truth' (10.21).

Apocalyptic Imagery

It will be apparent from the preceding paragraphs that certain
visions in the apocalypses contain imagery which is used by the
apocalypticist as a means of presenting a particular truth about
existence. In visions of this type there is usually no doubt as to
what the seer thinks his imagery meant, as an angelic interpretation of the dream or vision is included as well to explain the
contents of the vision. It becomes more difficult when we have a
vision which does not purport to communicate the truth about
earthly realities in symbolic form but the actual contents of the
heavenly world. How, for example, do we go about interpreting
a passage like Revelation chapter 4 which is replete with imagery

of various kinds? Consideration of the following will illustrate the point:

> And he who sat there appeared like jasper and carnelian, and round the throne was a rainbow that looked like an emerald. Round the throne were twenty-four thrones, and seated on the thrones were twenty-four elders, clad in white garments, with golden crowns on their heads. From the throne issue flashes of lightning, and voices and peals of thunder, and before the throne burn seven torches of fire, which are the seven spirits of God; (Rev. 4.3–5)

This description is typical of similar theophanies in the apocalyptic literature[19] and sets out to offer a description of the throne of God and its environs as it exists in the world above. In other words, we have here a picture of what John thought the heavenly world was like. If we were to examine parallel descriptions of the world above, we would not normally interpret the various components of that realm symbolically unless the visionary himself had given us leave to do so.

The same principle applies when we interpret a passage such as Revelation 4. In verse 5 John himself tells us that the seven torches were the seven spirits of God. He thus shows himself willing to comment on the significance of what is contained in the chapter when he feels that it is necessary. What then are we to make of the rainbow in verse 3? It is tempting to find here an allusion to Genesis 9.12–15 and God's covenant with Noah:

> This is the sign of the covenant which I make between me and you and every living creature that is with you, for all future generations; I set my bow in the cloud, and it shall be a sign of the covenant between me and the earth. When I bring clouds over the earth and the bow is seen in the clouds, I will remember my covenant which is between me and you and every living creature of all flesh; and the waters never again shall become a flood to destroy all flesh.

It is often suggested that these verses have provided the rainbow as a symbol of God's mercy in Revelation 4.[20] If this were the only Old Testament passage which illuminated this verse there would probably be a strong case for stressing its importance. But much closer to the subject-matter of Revelation 4 is the reference to the bow in the clouds which is found in Ezekiel 1.28. Here the glory of God revealed to the prophet Ezekiel on the throne-chariot is compared to a rainbow. In the light of the many similarities between Revelation 4 and Ezekiel 1, it is much more likely that the reference to the rainbow is included by John for the simple reason that this was the way in which the prophet Ezekiel set out to describe the impression made on him by the colour of the light of God's glory.

Thus it would seem that a distinction ought to be made between those passages, which speak directly of the world above and its inhabitants, and the visions which are clearly intended to be nothing more than symbolic of more profound truths. The fact is that Revelation is replete with this latter type of vision as well.[21] The vision of the two witnesses and the pregnant woman in Revelation 11—12 both use images to convey a theological message about the Church and its role. In these instances it is justified to ask why elements of the life and work of Moses and Elijah are used in chapter 11 to describe the two witnesses or why the woman is pursued by the dragon in chapter 12. We are not dealing here with glimpses of actual circumstances in the world above, or, for that matter, heavenly reflections of future historical circumstances, for the mystery which is being revealed is mediated in the imagery of the visions. Therefore, it is entirely appropriate that we should endeavour to investigate what particular message the visionary is wanting to communicate to his readers by means of the images which are included in his vision.

The major source of the imagery of the apocalypses is, of course, the Old Testament, though the reservoir of mythological ideas which was available to many religions and cultures throughout late antiquity also provided some of the ideas which are now found in the apocalypses.[22] Among the Jewish scriptures it was books like Daniel and Ezekiel which provided much inspiration for later apocalypticists. Nevertheless it would be wrong to suppose that the apocalypticists drew only on a literary or oral tradition for their visions. Some of the visions which make their appearance in the apocalypses could equally well have been inspired by the contemplation of the natural world, which then provided the vehicle for the apocalyptic message. A good specimen of such a vision is the vision of the forest in Syriac Baruch 36. In this vision the forest symbolizes the great empires of the world, all of which pass away except one tree. This tree (which represents Rome) is then cast down and burnt with a dire proclamation of judgement uttered over it. The means whereby the forest is destroyed are a fountain and a vine which represent the ultimate triumph of God and his messiah. Although the vine has a long history in the Old Testament as a symbol of the people of God (e.g. Isa. 5, Ps. 80.8f., Jer. 2.21, and Ezek. 15) and occasionally of the royal line (Ezek. 17.7; 19.10f.), the rest of the imagery is derived from an ordinary pastoral scene which then serves as a medium of the eschatological message communicated to the seer (but cf. Judg. 9.7ff.).

If we were limited to Revelation for our understanding of apocalyptic, we would probably get the impression that symbolism and extravagant imagery was one of the hallmarks of apocalyptic.[23] In this respect at least, the New Testament apocalypse is not typical of the rest of Jewish apocalyptic literature. The profusion of imagery which confronts us in virtually every chapter of Revelation is far less apparent in contemporary apocalypses. Large parts of 4 Ezra and Syriac Baruch, for example, consist of dialogues between the seer and God or his angel. The same is also true of the earlier 1 Enoch and the Shepherd of Hermas. Although the latter is replete with rambling allegorical visions, much of the work consists of a rather prosaic series of pronouncements on the subject of ecclesiastical discipline.

Pseudepigraphy

There is, however, another respect in which Revelation differs from contemporary Jewish apocalypses, namely its lack of pseudonymity. This is a device which is present in virtually all the Jewish apocalypses and forms an important element in the literary form in which the apocalyptic religion manifests itself. Some great figure from Israel's past (though the antediluvian hero Enoch is also included) is chosen as the recipient of the disclosures and visions. Pseudepigraphy was very common in the ancient world,[24] and this frequency makes it preferable to see the phenomenon in the apocalyptic literature as one of the accidents rather than the substance of apocalyptic. The origin of this literary device in Judaism is not easy to unravel. It now seems most unlikely that, as far as apocalyptic is concerned, its use can be so closely tied to the book of Daniel as Rowley once suggested.[25] This is because recent study has indicated that of the extant non-canonical apocalypses portions of the pseudonymous Enoch-apocalypse antedate the writing of Daniel.[26] Influence from the Hellenistic world cannot be ruled out as an explanation of the rise of pseudonymity within Israel,[27] but it is clear that it has a long history. The additions made to the collections of prophetic oracles, particularly the Isaianic collection, probably offer us the antecedents of pseudepigraphy within Jewish religion, though it must be stressed that the form of pseudepigraphy which we find in the apocalypses is rather different from that found in the pseudonymous oracles added to the prophetic pronouncements.[28]

The major difference to be noted in the pseudepigraphic form of the apocalypse is the use of extended accounts of aspects of the career of the supposed visionary. Nowhere is this better demonstrated than in the Apocalypse of Abraham. The ascent to heaven and the visions are preceded by an account of the patriarch's repudiation of idolatry. This legend about Abraham was well known in Jewish tradition[29] and provides the setting for the apocalypse which follows. The immediate basis for the patriarch's ascent into heaven is another story about Abraham, this time one more firmly rooted in Scripture. The sacrifice made by Abraham mentioned in Genesis 15 had, in Jewish tradition, become a moment when Abraham had been given visions of God and the future.[30] It is hardly surprising that this particular story should have been used as the setting for the visions described in the second half of the apocalypse as sleep was the setting for a divine revelation (Gen. 15.12) and later the sacrifice was the moment of a vision of a pot and a torch (Gen. 15.17). For the apocalypticist the stories about the hero, derived as they are from Scripture or tradition, provide an important framework for the revelations given to the seer.

This example from the Abraham cycle of apocalypses shows that the choice of figure from Israel's past was no arbitrary matter. It was not just a case of picking any figure as a peg upon which to hang any speculative revelations one may have. The ascent of Abraham and his vision are rooted in the interpretation of Scripture. Likewise the fact that Enoch looms so large as the supposed recipient of divine revelations is grounded in Scripture. In Genesis 5.24 there is an enigmatic reference to Enoch as a man who 'walked with God and was not for God took him'. It was the enigmatic character of this passage more than anything else which led to the various legends about him,[31] from the earliest sections of 1 Enoch to the latest rabbinic stories.[32] The fact that God is said to have 'taken' (*laqah*) (cf. 2 Kings 2.9; Ps.

49.15; 73.24) Enoch is the basis for the belief that at some point in his life Enoch had been taken to the very presence of God, either on earth (Jub. 4.20ff.) or in heaven (1 Enoch 14.8ff., cf. 1 Enoch 71.1ff.).

The vision of Isaiah in chapter 6 is justification enough for the assumption that this was a figure to whom one could attribute visions of God and the world above. Not so easily explained, however, is the reason why Levi is chosen as the recipient of an apocalypse. Presumably as a priest it was expected that his proximity to God made it likely that a vision would be granted to him, though it has to be pointed out that the heavenly ascent referred to in Testament of Levi 2f. does not take place in the setting of the cult at all. The experience attributed to Zechariah, which occurred during the exercise of his priestly duties, was not necessarily totally out of the ordinary (Luke 1.22),[33] and the choice of Levi as an apocalyptic seer is best explained by the priestly privilege of close contact with God.

A rather different explanation can be offered for the attribution of the apocalypse of Ezra and Baruch, the two heroes of Jewish history who flourished just before and after the Exile. Most scholars now recognize that both apocalypses attributed to them were written towards the end of the first century and reflect the desperate situation of Judaism after the fall of the city and the shattering consequences for the religion.[34] We note from the opening of Syriac Baruch (1.1) that the date is fixed in the reign of Jeconiah (Jehoiachin), in other words a date shortly before the capture of the city of Jerusalem and the destruction of Solomon's temple by Nebuchadnezzar in 587 BC. Indeed, the destruction of the city is explicitly described in chapter 6. So the setting corresponds exactly to that which confronted the unknown visionary who composed the work towards the end of the first century AD. The setting of 4 Ezra is slightly different. Though there is some dispute about the precise date of Ezra's mission,[35] biblical tradition puts the life of Ezra long after the destruction of the Temple and the career of Baruch, disciple of Jeremiah. According to Ezra 7.8 the mission of Ezra took place in 458 BC, roughly sixty years after the return from Exile and the rebuilding of the Temple. This situation is chosen because it reflects the need for reorganization of the religion with renewed discipline and obedience to the Law of God (Ezra 10 and Neh. 8) as a result of the fall of Jerusalem. This was clearly the situation

in which Judaism found itself at the end of the first century AD
when R. Johanan b. Zakkai established the academy at Jamnia
which was to form a rallying point for the Jewish religion.[36] Thus
in both cases the historical situations of Ezra and Baruch are
appropriate to the circumstances of the visionaries as they seek
to understand the disasters that have befallen them in their
generation, and attempt the process of rebuilding which was
accomplished so successfully by Ezra in his day.

There is, however, another side to both these characters which
may help to explain the choice of them as recipients of
apocalypses. Both Ezra and Baruch are regarded by tradition as
scribes (Ezra 7.6 and Jer. 45.1), the class within Judaism whose
task it was to write and interpret the scriptures.[37] Such an
authoritative group would be eminently qualified to receive and
pass on further revelations, which would not conflict with the
heart of Jewish religion and which their scribal activities enabled
them to understand so well. In 4 Ezra 14.38f. it is quite clear that
the same expertise which enabled Ezra to dictate the canonical
scriptures also equipped him to communicate the secret teaching
which was to be reserved for the elect. Likewise Enoch too has
been given a scribal function as the following passage from
Jubilees makes plain:

> And he was the first among men that are born on earth who learnt
> writing and knowledge and wisdom and who wrote down the signs
> of heaven according to the order of their months in a book, that men
> may know the reasons of the years according to the order of their
> separate months (Jub. 4.17, cf. 1 Enoch 12.1; Test. Abraham Rec.
> B 11; Targum Ps. Jonathan on Gen. 5.24).

Enoch is the first in the long series of wise men who were
particularly well qualified to receive visions and revelations, for
to men such as these had been given the keys of knowledge of
God's will (cf. Luke 11.52).

From what we have seen so far it would appear that there was
a degree of sensitivity in the choice of the ancient worthy under
whose name the apocalypses were written. So we find that a
vision of the heavens and a heavenly journey are linked with
those figures to whom such experiences were attributed either
by Scripture or tradition, whereas the questioning of traditional
ideas consequent upon a disaster of the magnitude of AD 70
finds a natural parallel in the similar situation facing Jews some

six hundred years before. The apocalypticist finds in the circumstances of the pseudonymous writer's day and in the experiences which have been linked with him a suitable framework for
visions which speak to the situation of the apocalypticist.[38]

This is essentially the thesis of D. S. Russell, who has argued
that the pseudonymity in apocalyptic has its origin in the Hebrew idea of corporate personality, where 'there is a fluidity of
transition from the one to the many and from the many to
one'.[39] Because of this, the writers of the apocalypses were
conscious of standing in a tradition whose origins stretched back
to the earliest days of men.[40] The close bonds which linked
God's people, past and present, Russell argues, enabled the
writer to regard his situation and thoughts as very much in tune
with those of his ancestors. Thus the apocalypticist believed
that, by virtue of using the name of some great figure of the
past, he was communicating what that hero would have
revealed had he been alive at that time.

Secondly, Russell suggests that there was the sense of common experience between the apocalypticist and earlier generations, so that 'the sameness of their respective experiences would
make it possible for them to associate, to the point of coincidence, their own circumstances with those of their worthy
predecessor and to see in them, as it were, a spiritual reproduction of their own'.[41] So, by adopting the name of some great
figure of the past the apocalypticist believed himself to be an
extension of that person. He would in fact by assuming his name,
in Russell's words, 'be sharing in his very life and character'.[42]

Of its very nature such a hypothesis is difficult to prove, for
the simple reason that it is now virtually impossible to describe
with any degree of certainty the psychology of the writers of the
apocalypses who hide behind the various pseudonyms. Whatever attractions Russell's thesis may have, doubts must be raised
about the precise form which it takes in his book. Two of the
notions on which he has placed so much weight in his attempt
to understand the mind of the apocalypticist, namely, corporate
personality and the Hebrew sense of contemporaneity, have
been subjected to critical scrutiny in recent years.[43] Consequently it is not possible to speak with so much certainty about
the distinctive Hebrew mentality which enabled a man in the
first century BC to feel some kind of deep kinship with a man
who lived centuries before.

Secondly, a distinctively Jewish interpretation of pseudonymity is difficult to uphold. It is apparent, as we have already noted, that pseudepigraphy was such a widespread phenomenon in the Hellenistic world that its presence in apocalypses is not merely the result of the Hebrew approach to life, though clearly one cannot exclude this as a contributory factor to the development of its distinctive form within Judaism. Thus doubts must be raised about Russell's presentation of the origins of pseudonymity. Nevertheless it certainly has the merit of attempting to do justice to the possibility that religious experiences are enshrined in the apocalypses, in contrast to the other dominant explanation of the phenomenon of pseudonymity, which works on the assumption that the apocalypses are purely literary productions with virtually no authentic religious experiences in them. The difficulties facing an attempt to disentangle the shreds of visionary experience should not lead to the precipitate conclusion that the claims to visionary experience are as fictitious as the authorship and setting of these texts. Russell rightly refuses to dismiss the possibility that the origins of parts of the apocalypses may have been in such circumstances, and his explanation of pseudonymity seeks to do justice to this. It is this possibility which makes it important to offer an explanation of pseudonymity which does not relegate all the material in the apocalypses to derivative forgeries in which authority is claimed for spurious revelations by this device. Modern suspicion of pseudepigraphy should not, therefore, hinder the attempt to assess whether in fact relics of authentic experiences are to be found in the apocalypses, and, if so, in what situation such experiences took place.[44]

Another factor to be considered in the rise of pseudepigraphy in Jewish apocalyptic is related to the emergence of the canon of Scripture. With the gradual formation of an authoritative body of writings there inevitably arose a tendency to make a clear differentiation between the contemporary opinions and the authoritative scriptures which were of eternal significance. Although the canon of Jewish scriptures was not formally ratified until the late first century AD, there can be little doubt that, with the exception of a handful of books, most of the documents now contained in our Old Testament already had authoritative status much earlier than this.[45] Consequently any views which were expressed subsequently needed some justification for them to be endowed with a sanctity greater than the personal opinions of some individual would possess. This is exactly what we find happening in the rabbinic tradition. The halakic pronouncements by rabbis down the centuries are invested with an importance which they do not have in their own right, by a stress on the continuity of the revelatory process down to the contemporary generation of rabbis. It is already hinted at in Aboth 1.1, where the concept of tradition is clearly enunciated as an essential feature in the study of the Torah. Nevertheless it is the later haggadah which enunciates a belief which had wide currency in rabbinic Judaism, namely that the pronouncements of the later teachers were already given to Moses on Sinai:

> How do we know that Moses did not fall asleep or even feel sleepy? It is like a king who loved his treasure and said to him: Measure out for yourself golden dinars. In his joy he had no desire to eat or drink. He felt sleepy, but he said, If I sleep, I will lose them. So also Moses, measuring out Torah, forgot to eat or drink. He felt sleepy, but he said, If I sleep, I will lose (much), because God will only speak to me for forty days. The Holy One, blessed be he, said: You are distressed, yet I swear to you that you will not lose any. On the first tables were only the ten commandments, but since you have been distressed, I will give you *halakoth midrashim* and *haggadoth* (i.e. all the rabbinic pronouncements) as it is written, Write thou these words . . . What the Holy One, blessed be he, meant was: Write thou Torah, Prophets and Writings, and they will be in writing, but *halakoth midrash* and *haggadoth* and the talmud will be 'by mouth'. (Shemoth R. 47.7)[46]

This passage is clearly very late indeed but is, for all that, symptomatic of the need to give authority to the rabbinic teaching as the body of material whose authority is binding on Jews. The *halakoth* are more than merely the pronouncements of a particular teacher but a subsequent disclosure of that which had already been communicated to Moses on Sinai. What is clear, however, is the pressing need which was felt after the closing of the canon to justify non-canonical viewpoints and endow them with a certain prestige. This may well have been a contributory factor to the pseudepigraphic style of the apocalypses, though it must be recognized that their authority derives both from the belief that divine revelations are being disclosed in these writings and from the character of the figure to whom the revelations were supposed to have been given.

There is, however, another related factor bearing on the discussion of pseudepigraphy in apocalyptic literature which is closely related to the development of the canon, namely the history of the prophetic movement after the Exile. At some point during the Persian period tradition asserts that the prophetic movement finally passed into oblivion with the last prophets Haggai, Zechariah and Malachi (Tos. Sotah 13.2).[47] Such a view can no longer be upheld. The later additions to the collections of earlier prophetic oracles show that the prophetic movement still had a very vital part to play within Israelite religion during the centuries after the Exile. That is not to say that their point of view was met with universal acceptance, despite the vindication of the eighth century prophets and the assiduous collection of their oracles during the Exile.[48] Indeed, there are hints in a late oracle like Zechariah 13.2ff. that the prophetic office gradually became one that was treated with abuse. What is more, it is most unlikely that a movement which had shown so much vitality during and after the Exile should suddenly drift into oblivion. It is more likely that the belief in the direct communication of God through the prophet was held in honour by only a small number of people. However strong the movement may once have been, it could not withstand the growing pressure which a religion based on a code of Law dictated: namely, that the Spirit which had inspired the prophets was now at work in those who interpreted the Law of Moses, or, even more radically, had departed from Israel completely.

There are, of course, enormous difficulties in sketching the character of prophetic history after the Exile, but recent study suggests that this rather simple description may not be too far from the truth.[49] The belief that the spirit had departed from Israel heralded a time without prophets, even though there did exist groups which believed that they had been called by God to speak in the same way to the people as their predecessors. For most, however, the claims to prophetic inspiration were treated with suspicion. Indeed, the return of the spirit which had inspired the prophets of old was widely believed to be a sign of the dawn of the new age.[50] Hence it comes as no surprise to read in pre-Christian texts like 1 Maccabees a passage such as the following:

They discussed what should be done about the altar of holocausts which had been profaned, and very properly decided to pull it down, that it might never become a reproach to them, from its defilement by the pagans. They therefore demolished it and deposited the stones in a suitable place on the Temple hill, to await the appearance of a prophet who should give a ruling about them (1 Macc. 4.44ff; cf. 9.27 and 14.41).

It is clear from this passage that, in the opinion of the writer, the situation in ancient Israel, where the prophet pronounced God's requirements, no longer applied. The basic authority was the Torah and the interpretations of it, and when there was an issue for which no answer could be found, the matter was deferred until such time as there was a person who would reveal the divine will on the issue.

Thus the claim to have any direct revelation from God could not be upheld, when the religion of the day viewed such revelations either as a claim that the end-time had already arrived or as entirely spurious. The only way open to those who wanted to convey to the people the communications which they believed they had received from God was to use the device of pseudonymity. By using the name of an appropriate figure from Israel's past the apocalypticists sought to ensure that the divine disclosures vouchsafed to them were treated with the same reverence as the words of those who spoke when the spirit was present and active in Israel.[51]

When we look at pseudonymity in this light, it becomes a little easier to see why the major early Christian apocalypse should lack pseudonymity. Early Christian experience was dominated by the belief that the last days had already arrived. This was indicated by the return of the eschatological spirit as a dominant feature of the lives of the early Christians. The point is made most clearly in the Pentecost speech of Peter where Joel 2.28ff. is cited. The coming of the spirit at Pentecost is regarded by the author not only as a fulfilment of Joel's prophecy, but also a sign that the last days have arrived (Acts 2.17). The words 'in the last days' are here added to the quotation from Joel to demonstrate that the barren time without the Spirit of God had now been brought to an end by the dawn of a new era dominated by the Spirit. It is, therefore, hardly surprising that pseudonymity was not such a dominant feature of the earliest Christian apocalypses (though it is to be found in Ascension of Isaiah). The necessity for its use had disappeared since direct revelation through God's spirit was considered to be a possibility within the Christian communities (1 Cor. 14 particularly v. 26f. and Rev. 22.6ff.).[52]

Thus it would appear that there were factors within Jewish religion which made it necessary to look to the past as a way of supporting the opinions and convictions of the present. In these circumstances only the most tenuous form of communication from God was permitted. The *bath qol* (lit. 'the daughter of the voice') offered the sole direct contact with the divine and even this was viewed with suspicion in some circles.[53] But nothing could compare with the Torah, which had become the dominant means of establishing God's demands for his people. Knowledge of the divine secrets was still a possibility, but the focus of revelation was not the vision or audition but the Torah. In it were all the treasures of divine wisdom which God had given to men (Aboth 6.1). They were available to anyone who was competent enough to unlock its mysteries. But however much significance was attached to the Torah and the interpretations of it, such knowledge differed radically from the way in which God had spoken to Moses and the prophets in days gone by. Those who continued to believe that such direct revelation remained a possibility for God's people had to make a deliberate attempt to give weight to the direct disclosures which continued to be received through visions and auditions. Pseudonymity offered one way of validating the deeply-rooted conviction of some that God's voice was still to be heard.[54]

Summary

In the light of the foregoing pages the main thrust of this approach to apocalyptic can be summarized in the following way:

(i) A definition of apocalyptic should not be too restricted but attempt to do justice to all the various elements in the literature.

(ii) Apocalyptic seems essentially to be about the revelation of the divine mysteries through visions or some other form of immediate disclosure of heavenly truths.

(iii) The use of the word apocalyptic to describe the literature of Judaism and early Christianity should, therefore, be confined to those works which purport to offer disclosures of the heavenly mysteries, whether as the result of vision, heavenly ascent or verbal revelations. Such a description also extends to those visionary reports which give evidence of the same kind of religious outlook as the apocalypses, even if the contexts in which they are now found cannot be said to conform to the literary genre of the apocalypse.

(iv) Although eschatology is an important component of the heavenly mysteries which are revealed in the apocalypses, it is difficult to justify the selection of this particular element as the basis of a definition of apocalyptic. The consequence of this can lead to an indifference to the fact that apocalyptic is concerned with the revelation of a variety of different matters. Any attempt, therefore, to use the term apocalyptic as a synonym of eschatology must be rejected.

However much one may be tempted to view apocalyptic as a movement which was dominated by the concern for the future it must at least be recognized that this feature cannot exclude consideration of the other components of the apocalypses, nor must it be assumed that all else in these works is necessarily merely subordinate to the apocalypticists' interest in the future. To make eschatology the key with which one can unlock all the secrets of the apocalypses runs the risk of failing to do justice to the particular contribution which the non-eschatological elements make to the phenomenon of apocalyptic as a whole.

(v) The evidence, such as it is, from literature which cannot be categorized as apocalyptic suggests that it is not easy to construct an apocalyptic eschatology which differs in any marked way from the ideas held by other writers at the time. What is more, the apocalypses themselves hardly offer enough unanimity for us to speak with any degree of conviction about a distinctive apocalyptic approach to the future hope.

(vi) Although content and form should not in the first instance be the bases for a definition of apocalyptic, it cannot be denied that apocalyptic frequently finds expression in a particular literary genre. In Judaism this is usually an apocalypse granted to some great figure from Israel's past who then reveals to subsequent generations the secrets which have been disclosed to him and gives advice to them about the sort of life which God expects of the righteous. There is some evidence to suggest that the choice of figure to act as the mystagogue was in no way arbitrary and coincided with the interests and situation of the apocalypticist.

(vii) Just as the content of the material revealed is diverse, so are the modes of revelation. Heavenly ascents, dream-visions, with or without interpretations, and angelic or divine pronouncements are all typical ways of communicating the divine will and the mysteries of the heavenly world.

Part Two

The Content of the Heavenly Mysteries

———

OUR PREVIOUS DISCUSSION has indicated that the apocalypticists were concerned with that which was beyond empirical observation and depended on the disclosure from God of the answers to questions which were impossible to elucidate by human reason alone. According to Sirach 3.21ff. these are the matters which the wise and prudent man should avoid; such speculations only lead to misguided notions:

> For great is the might of the Lord; he is glorified by the humble.[1]
> Seek not what is too difficult for you, nor investigate what is beyond your power. Reflect upon what has been assigned to you, for you do not need what is hidden. Do not meddle in what is beyond your tasks, for matters too great for human understanding have been shown to you. For their hasty judgement has led many astray, and wrong opinion has caused their thoughts to slip.

While it is not stated in so many words, the writer wants his readers to understand that the knowledge which they have already is an adequate guide for life, and there is no need to look for answers which are not readily available. One can presume that what is referred to here is the Law which man has in his possession as the source of all knowledge.[2] This was a warning which was taken up at a later period by the rabbis and applied to those who would occupy themselves on matters of a mystical kind.[3] Indeed, similar reserve is quite apparent in the mind of the author of the second part of Mishnah Hagigah 2.1, which lays down guidelines for the investigation of certain passages in Scripture. These provided the basis for speculations on the nature of God and the world which he has created. In fact the author goes much further than Ben Sirach and indicates that any one who occupied himself in such matters was in danger of imperilling his life:

> Whosoever gives his mind to four things it were better for him if he had not come into the world – what is above, what is beneath, what was beforetime, and what will be hereafter. And whosoever takes no thought for the honour of his Maker, it were better for him if he had not come into the world.

Despite such dire warnings advice such as this was not always heeded, for the quest for knowledge of matters which were too difficult to understand and which concerned the very nature of the creator himself did attract the attention of many Jews in the ancient world, including certain eminent rabbis. But, of course, this is especially true of the apocalypticists, whose work is itself a testimony to the fact that questions like these were asked, and to which, it was believed, answers were given from above. In the opinion of the writers of the apocalypses such answers were no longer a matter merely of speculation, for the content of the answers had the *imprimatur* of revelation. Most of the material contained within the apocalypses can be understood as the direct consequence of the attempts of the apocalypticists to understand God and his purpose for the world and man's place in it. The whole theme of apocalyptic is that certain individuals have been able to understand the mysteries of God, man and the universe as a whole.

When we consider the content of the heavenly wisdom revealed to the apocalypticists, it is important for us to see that the secrets of the world above and what was to come were all potentially of equal significance. The fact that some secrets receive more attention than others in the different apocalypses is, we have suggested, more a reflection of the particular situation of the writer than any indication that one element is to be regarded as the determinative factor for the understanding of apocalyptic. Although much space will be devoted in the following pages to eschatology, an attempt has been made to see it as just one part of that whole complex of subjects which was of interest to those who sought to make sense of man's existence and, in particular, the relationship of Jewish beliefs about God to the world of men. The various subjects which the apocalypses reveal can, without too much of an attempt to force the material into a rigid system, be categorized under the four topics whose discussion is proscribed in the second part of Misnah Hagigah 2.1: what is above, what is beneath, what was beforetime, and what will be hereafter. All four matters at one time or other occupied the attention of the apocalypticists, though it is particularly the mysteries of the future and the world above which tend to dominate the apocalypses.

In looking at this material opportunity will be taken not only to examine particular issues which have tended to loom large in the discussion of apocalyptic in the past but also subjects which deserve attention as examples of significant theological developments within the literature. Into the former category fall the discussions of the various messianic or saviour-figures which make their appearance in apocalyptic. As we shall see, within the whole gamut of apocalyptic ideas they have a relatively insignificant part to play (this is especially true of the heavenly 'son of man'), but students of the New Testament tend to focus on such ideas because of their value for New Testament Christology, and, as a result, they are given an importance out of all proportion to the space devoted to them in the apocalypses.

The second category only extends to two sections in this study, both of which are to be found in the chapter 'What is Above'. This is not because this marks the limit of significant theological development in apocalyptic; nothing could be further from the truth. Rather, consideration of apocalyptic angelology in particular ties in with studies in the later part of this book. There are two main reasons for examining in some detail the development of beliefs in an exalted angelic figure in Jewish apocalyptic. Firstly, it is to be hoped that it will enable us to see certain developments in rabbinic thought in a new light. Secondly, from the point of view of New Testament exegesis it illustrates a neglected aspect of Jewish doctrinal development which does not receive sufficient attention in the study of New Testament Christology.[4] In our examination of the material concerning the heavenly world some consideration will be given to the way in which the distinctive apocalyptic outlook upon the contact between God and the righteous visionary appears to have infiltrated the thought-patterns of the Qumran community.

So the major purpose of this section will be to give the student of the apocalyptic literature an overall impression of the heterogeneous nature of the material contained within it.[5] Consequently, it is hoped that the approach sketched in the first chapter may then appear more reasonable in the light of the material itself. No doubt one could spend much more time considering the various aspects of the teaching of the apocalypses. Nevertheless the major concern throughout this section will be to give as comprehensive an account as possible of the massive variety which characterises the apocalypses. What is above, what is below, what has been and what will be in the future cover the major concerns of the apocalypses, and these issues, and certain consequences of these beliefs, will form the core of our examination.

CHAPTER 4

What is Above: the Mysteries of God, the Angels and Astronomy

The Heavenly World

ONE OF THE most distinctive features of the apocalyptic literature is the conviction that the seer could pierce the vault of heaven and look upon the glorious world of God and his angels. Frequently this is expressed by the conventional expression the heavens opened (T. Levi 2.6 Greek; Acts 7.56)[1] or the belief that a door opened in heaven (1 Enoch 14.15; Rev. 4.1) to enable the seer to look and indeed at times to enter the realm above to gaze on its secrets. Already in some of our earliest apocalyptic texts the seer looks into the heavenly court. This is a feature of Daniel 7.9f., where the seer describes God enthroned on a fiery chariot surrounded by myriads of angels. There is a similar account in 1 Enoch 14.20f. though this time the seer records his description of an ascent through the heavens to reach the dwelling of God himself.

The origins of such ideas lie deep within Israel's past. Indeed, according to 1 Kings 22, 19f., Micaiah ben Imlah had seen God enthroned in glory surrounded by his heavenly court:

> And Micaiah said, 'Therefore hear the word of the LORD: I saw the LORD sitting on his throne, and all the host of heaven standing beside him on his right hand and on his left; and the LORD said, "Who will entice Ahab, that he may go up and fall at Ramoth-Gilead?" And one said one thing and another said another. Then a spirit came forward and stood before the LORD, saying "I will entice him." And the LORD said to him, "By what means?" And he said, "I will go forth, and will be a lying spirit in the mouth of all his prophets." And he said, "You are to entice him, and you shall succeed; go forth and do so." Now therefore behold, the LORD has put a lying spirit in the mouth of all these your prophets; the LORD has spoken evil concerning you.'

In this passage it is clear that Micaiah was privileged to know discussions of the heavenly court and understand why it is that the prophets should be prophesying falsely about the destiny of Ahab. The prophet of God thus knows the truth behind the historical circumstances of his day, and an explanation is offered about the apparent discrepancy between the true and false prophets; it is God's hand at work which permits the lying spirit to lead astray those who would speak words of reassurance to Ahab.

In similar vein Isaiah in his call-vision sees God enthroned in glory and the discussion within the heavenly court concerning the choice of an emissary to speak on God's behalf (6.1ff.). Indeed, the prophet himself participates in this discussion by volunteering to act as the envoy of the divine council. Likewise, at the opening of Isaiah 40 the unnamed prophet of the Exile reports a command to unspecified beings to comfort Zion. It is often assumed that this is an address to the prophet, but it is more likely that it is an address to the heavenly court of a similar type to that found in Isaiah 6; but this time concerning God's imminent act of redemption. In both passages from Isaiah the prophet is privileged to hear the divine decisions themselves and his oracles are a report of such deliberations in the heavenly court.[2] It is clear that in early Israelite religion God was pictured as one seated amidst the divine council, a view most clearly expressed in the opening words of Psalm 82 (cf. Gen. 1.26). Indeed, in this psalm God accuses the lesser gods of abuse of their authority, and as a result they are condemned for their negligence (Ps. 82.5). The background for this notion of the God of Israel as the Lord of the pantheon has been illuminated by the discovery of the Ugaritic texts in which the Canaanite god *El* acts as the dominant figure in the divine council.[3] Thus from the very beginning of Israelite religion the abode of the gods and knowledge of the discussions which took place in it had their part to play in the development of Israelite religion.

Such notions are the raw material of the later apocalyptic cosmology. The obvious difference which emerges in the later apocalyptic literature is the much sharper division which exists between the heavenly world and the world of men. The proximity which was assumed to exist between heaven and earth in earlier texts is already found to be lacking in one or two exilic texts.[4] For example, the anonymous prophet, whose words we

have in Isaiah 64, is looking at a world which seems to him to be
devoid of the divine presence. Indeed, he regards the azure
firmament above as a barrier which God must cleave in order to
redeem his people (Is. 64.1).[5] By the time we reach the apocalyptic writings of the third and second centuries BC and later,
we find that a cosmology has developed in which God is
enthroned in glory in heaven, and his activities are carried out
among men either by angelic intermediaries or other modes of
divine operation like the spirit or *shekinah*.[6] The cosmological
beliefs were such that it often became necessary for anyone who
would enter the immediate presence of God to embark on a
journey through the heavenly world, in order to reach God
himself.[7] In one of our earliest apocalyptic texts Enoch describes
his journey through the heavenly world:

> And the vision was shown to me thus: Behold, in the vision clouds
> invited me and a mist summoned me, and the course of the stars
> and the lightnings sped and hastened me, and in the vision the
> winds caused me to fly and lift me upward, and bore me into
> heaven. And I went in until I drew nigh to a wall which is built of
> crystals and surrounded by tongues of fire; and it began to affright
> me. And I went into the tongues of fire and drew nigh to a large
> house which was built of crystals and the walls of the house were
> like a tesselated floor (made) of crystals and its groundwork was of
> crystal . . . And lo, there was a second house, greater than the
> former and the entire portal stood open before me, and it was built
> of flames of fire . . . And I looked and saw therein a lofty throne: its
> appearance was as crystal, and the wheels thereof as the shining
> sun . . . and from underneath the throne came streams of flaming
> fire so that I could not look thereon. (1 Enoch 14.8ff.)

In this ascent to heaven there is very little said about the means
of ascent but elsewhere the apocalypticists describe ascents by
means of a cherubim-chariot (Test. Abraham Rec. A 10), sacrifi-
cal victims (Apocalypse of Abraham 15) or the spirit (Rev. 4.2, cf.
Ezek. 8.2). Such a need to travel to the world above to see
visions of God contrasts with the biblical visions in which the
heavenly journey plays no part.[8] Isaiah and Micaiah are allowed
to glimpse directly into the heavenly world, though mention is
made in Ezekiel's case of an open heaven before he sees the
'visions of God' (Ezek 1.1). Although nothing is said about a
heavenly journey in the case of Daniel, the setting of his glimpse
of the heavenly court (Dan. 7.9f.) is itself a dream-vision.

Just as immediate apprehension of God becomes more restricted in Jewish thought, so also his position in the heavenly world becomes more transcendent. Another feature of the developing apocalyptic cosmology is the way in which heaven was gradually divided into a series of compartments varying in number from two to seven.[9] In the cosmological section of b. Hagigah 12b we find that the existence of seven heavens appears to be a standard Jewish belief:

> R. Judah said: There are two firmaments, for it is said, Behold unto the Lord thy God belongeth heaven, and the heaven of heavens. Resh Lakish said: There are seven, namely, *Wilon, Raqia, Shehaqim, Zebul, Ma'on, Makon, Araboth.*

Nevertheless there was wide variety in the earlier literature, a fact indicated by the varying opinions of R. Judah and Resh Lakish in the passage just quoted. The Greek version of Test. Levi 3.1ff. presupposes a similar cosmology, whereas the preceding chapter offers a rival cosmology in which only three heavens are named. The latter probably represents the earlier view which, in Charles' opinion, 'has been worked up to include seven'.[10] The smaller number appears to agree with the number of heavens presupposed by Paul in 2 Cor. 12.2ff.[11] where, as we shall argue later, it is unlikely that the apostle held the belief that there were only three heavens.

There is clearly great variety in the cosmology of the apocalypses. On the one hand we have a work like Revelation which appears to have a relatively simple view of the heavenly world or chooses to ignore the more complex cosmologies which were to be found in some contemporary literature.[12] In the opening description of the heavenly world in Revelation 4, John's account of his vision contains no reference to intermediate compartments in the heavens through which he has to travel to reach God's presence. He speaks immediately of being in the presence of God himself. Indeed, the very first thing that attracts his attention in heaven is the throne of God himself. On the other hand there are works like Greek Baruch and Slavonic Enoch, which speak of five and ten heavens respectively.

Although in its present form Greek Baruch has the appearance of being a complete apocalypse, one must ask whether in fact its reference to five heavens accurately reflects the totality of its cosmology. Two points deserve attention. First of all, no mention is made of any theophany or description of the throne of God, a unique omission in accounts of heavenly journeys. Secondly, the description of the fifth heaven does seem to presuppose that there was another part of the heavenly world which is not described in the apocalypse:

> And Michael said to the angels, Wait till I learn from the Lord what shall come to pass. And in that very hour Michael departed and the doors were closed. And there was a sound as thunder. And I asked the angel, What is the sound? And he said to me, Michael is even now presenting the merits of men to God. And in that very hour Michael descended, and the gate was opened; and he brought oil . . . and while he yet spake, the door was closed, and we withdrew. (Gk. Baruch (13.5–17.2).

We read here that Michael disappears to God's presence and descends again to the fifth heaven. This significant remark indicates that what we have in Greek Baruch is in fact an incomplete cosmology and, for some reason, the author chooses not to mention the other part or parts of the heavenly world where God and his angelic attendants dwell. The absence of any theophany is at first sight rather puzzling, but its significance can probably be understood when we examine some of the descriptions of theophanies in the apocalypses a little later in this chapter.

In Slavonic Enoch the text as its stands appears to have a belief in ten heavens. There are, however, indications which may point to this being a later emendation of a text which originally knew of only seven heavens. When Enoch finally reaches the seventh heaven (Slav. Enoch 20.1ff.), he sees all the angelic host surrounding God and comes into God's presence (Slav. Enoch 21.5). Then in the next verse (Slav. Enoch 21.6) brief reference is made to the eighth and ninth heavens, and in 22.1 Enoch describes how he was brought to the tenth heaven, where he sees God's face. The tenth heaven is given the name *Araboth*, the name given to the seventh heaven in b. Hagigah 12b. It would appear that 21.6 is a later gloss, and that originally 22.1 was a continuation of the description of the theophany in the seventh heaven already started in 21.5.[13] This apocalypse, like the apocalypse of Abraham (ch. 19) and the Ascension of Isaiah, seems to presuppose that cosmology which was generally accepted in rabbinic Judaism.

The origin of the belief in a plurality of heavens in Jewish religion is not easily traced. There are signs that it may already have been known during the Exile, or just before, as passages such as Deut. 10.14, 1 Kings 8.27, Ps. 68.33 (Heb. 34) and 148.4 seem to indicate. Language about the heaven and the heaven of heavens at least provides the basis for the development of a more complex view of the heavenly world, even if there is no suggestion that a more developed cosmology is present in the mind of the original author.[14] Whatever foreign influences may have contributed to the developed cosmology of the apocalyptic literature,[15] it can be established that the conditions existed within Jewish religion for the ready acceptance of such notions. In addition to the language about the heavens and the heaven of heavens there seems to be some justification for supposing that the design of the Temple contributed to the beliefs about heaven found in the apocalypses.[16] Though the descriptions of heaven in apocalyptic literature do not always give evidence of a close dependence on the form and contents of the earthly Temple, there is enough similarity to suggest that such influence did exist. As the pre-eminent place where God's presence dwelt on earth, it is only to be expected that the earthly shrine would have the form of the heavenly. By the same token the form of the earthly would inevitably colour descriptions of the heavenly. A correspondence between the earthly and the heavenly is hinted at in Exodus 25.9 and 40.

> According to all that I show you concerning the tabernacle, and of all its furniture, so shall you make it . . . And see that you make them after the pattern for them, which is being shown you on the mountain.[17]

The description of the temple of Solomon in 1 Kings 6 shows that the Temple had two major parts, the outer sanctuary (1 Kings 6.14) and the Holy of Holies (1 Kings 6.19), into which the High Priest went once every year (cf. Lev. 16.2f.). Such a division of the parts of heaven is found in 1 Enoch 14.10ff., where Enoch speaks of two houses in heaven, an outer and an inner house, and it is in the latter that God is seated on the throne of glory (1 Enoch 14.18ff.). This distinction seems to reflect the division of the earthly Temple.[18]. An explicit cultic reference is to be found in Test. Levi 3.4, where the heavenly vestibule to God's own presence is coloured by the dispositions of the earthly shrine:

> And in the highest [heaven] of all dwelleth the Great Glory far above all holiness. In it are the archangels who minister and make propitiation to the Lord for all the sins of ignorance of the righteous; offering to the Lord a sweet-smelling savour, a reasonable and a bloodless offering.

The character of the national shrine, as well as hints already present in the scriptures, made the gradual evolution of cosmology in Judaism generally, and in apocalyptic literature in particular, quite a natural progression.

When the contents of the heavenly world are described in apocalypses, the attention of the seer is directed particularly to the immediate environs of God himself. Even a work like Revelation, which starts its description of the heavenly world with an account of God's throne, also includes references to other components of the heavenly court. Most descriptions of the heavenly journey devote attention also to the contents of the lower parts of the heavenly world through which the seer must travel on his way to God. Sometimes, as is the case with the Ascension of Isaiah, this merely takes the form of a stereotyped description of the inhabitants of the lower heavens, with most interest being devoted to the highest heaven in which God dwells. But in works like Test. Levi and Slavonic Enoch the occupants of the different layers of the heavenly realm are very diverse indeed. One feature which often stands out, and which doubtless derives from the first chapter of Ezekiel, is the fiery character of the heavenly world. In 1 Enoch 14 and the Apocalypse of Abraham 17f. the fiery character of Ezekiel's throne-chariot has contributed greatly to the descriptions of the heavens found in these apocalypses.

It is the vision of God himself which is the climax of the heavenly ascent. Despite the prohibition in Exodus 33.20 that man cannot see God's face and live, there does appear to be some readiness to offer details of the form of the all-holy God enthroned in glory. The basis for such descriptions, however circumspect they may be, had already been given in Scripture, when the prophet Ezekiel in the most tentative way had described the human figure who was seated above the living creatures:[19]

> And above the firmament over their heads there was the likeness of

a throne, in appearance like sapphire; and seated above the likeness of a throne was a likeness as it were of a human form. And upward from what had the appearance of his loins I saw as it were gleaming bronze, like the appearance of fire enclosed round about; and downward from what had the appearance of his loins I saw as it were the appearance of fire, and there was brightness round about him. (Ezek. 1.26–28.)

The willingness shown by the prophet to describe the form of a figure of God on the throne offered an opportunity to later generations of apocalypticists and mystics to indulge in speculation of varying degrees of extravagance about the form of the God of Israel. In the early apocalyptic theophany in 1 Enoch 14.20f. the impetus offered by Ezekiel 1 is evident in the willingness to speak about the form of God on the throne: 'And the Great Glory sat thereon, and his raiment shone more brightly than the sun and was whiter than any snow.' In the short passage describing the heavenly court in Daniel 7.9f. the description is even more daring, for the physical features of the Ancient of Days are here mentioned by the seer (cf. 1 Enoch 71.10). Among the apocalyptic theophanies nothing can compare with the detailed description of the form and person of God given in Slavonic Enoch. Unfortunately the English edition does not contain the important section, which is, however, to be found in Vaillant's edition:[20]

You see my face, the face of a man created like yourselves, but I have seen the face of the Lord, which is like a very hot fire. You yourselves now look upon the eyes of a man, created just as you yourselves are, but I have looked upon the eyes of the Lord shining like the sun's rays and terrifying the eyes of man. You, my children, now see my right hand, the hand of him who helps you, but I have seen for myself the right hand of the Lord, filling the heaven, the hand of him who made me. You now see the extent of my body, similar to your own, but I have seen the extent of Lord, who is without measure or comparison.

In this passage we come nearest of all to the extravagant descriptions of the limbs of God, the *shi 'ur komah* speculation, which had such an important part to play in later Jewish mysticism inspired by the first chapter of Ezekiel.

Such explicit descriptions of the form of God are not typical of all the apocalypses. We have already noted that in Greek Baruch the seer's ascent to heaven does not reach its climax in a

theophany, and the absence of such a description could be taken
as an indication of reluctance on the part of the apocalypticist to
indulge in the kind of speculation found elsewhere in the
apocalypses. That there was a gradually increasing reluctance to
speak of God's form is in fact indicated by an examination of
other descriptions of the heavenly world in the apocalypses.

Although the vision of God appears to be similar in its basic
outline to the parallel versions in other apocalypses, the visions
of God in Enoch 14 and Daniel 7 are really quite distinctive.
Whereas these two passages speak in varying degrees of detail
about the form of God, John of Patmos is quite content to leave
his statement about God with a simple reference to the fact that
there was one seated upon the throne (Rev. 4.2). This is a move
away from Ezekiel 1.27 as well where, as we have already seen,
vague reference is made to the figure. Compared with Revelation 4, however, the next two passages show an even greater
reluctance to speak of God enthroned in glory. In the short
reference to the divine throne-chariot in a fragment from Cave 4
at Qumran there is a brief mention of the throne, though the
main interest of the author is in the movement of the chariot and
its angelic attendants: 'The cherubim bless the image of the
throne-chariot above the firmament, and they praise the
(majesty) of the fiery firmament beneath the seat of his glory.'
From what is now extant it would appear that nothing whatever
is said about the one seated upon the throne. Either the writer
considered that the heavenly throne was empty or he accepted
the description of passages like Ezekiel 1.26f. but did not see fit
to include a reference to the human figure in his description of
the theophany. The trend away from anthropomorphism is even
more apparent in the Apocalypse of Abraham 18:

> And as I stood alone and looked, I saw behind the living creatures a
> chariot with fiery wheels, each wheel full of eyes round about; and
> over the wheels was a throne; which I saw, and this was covered
> with fire, and fire encircled it round about, and lo, an indescribable
> fire environed a fiery host. And I heard its holy voice like the voice
> of a man.

There are many similarities here with Ezekiel 1, though there is
the occasional change. Perhaps the most significant change of
all, however, is the abrupt termination of the description of the
throne. This is all the more significant, because, as Box has

pointed out,[21] there is some affinity in the order in which the various elements occur in Ezekiel 1.26f. and the Apocalypse of Abraham. This relationship can best be seen by comparing the appropriate sections in synoptic form:

EZEKIEL
And above the firmament over their (the creatures) heads there was the likeness of a throne, in appearance like a sapphire; and seated above the likeness of the throne was a likeness as it were of a human form . . . and there was brightness round about . . . And I heard the voice of one speaking . . .

APOCALYPSE OF ABRAHAM
Over the wheels was a throne . . . this was covered with fire, and fire encircled it round about, and lo, an indescribable fire environed a fiery host. And I heard its holy voice like the voice of a man . . .

There appears here to have been a deliberate attempt made to exclude all reference to the human figure mentioned in Ezekiel 1. Similar restraint is to be found in two other 'theophanies', both of which avoid speaking directly to God himself and give the reader to understand that the seer had gained access to the divine presence by use of language concerning fire and the fiery stream associated with a theophany rather then speaking directly of God himself:

1 ENOCH 71.2
And I saw two streams of fire, and the light of that fire shone like hyacinth, and I fell on my face before the Lord of spirits.

APOCALYPSE OF ZEDRACH
And stretching out his wings he took him (Zedrach) up into heaven to the very flame, and he set him as high as the third heaven, and in it stood the flame of divinity.

Tendencies such as these within the apocalyptic theophanies suggest that there was a definite trend within apocalyptic thought away from the direct description of God and his throne. In fact we noticed a similar kind of development, which was even more radical, within 4 Ezra and Syriac Baruch.[22] In both these apocalypses all claim to heavenly ascent is discounted, and nothing whatever is said about a theophany. The fascination with the world above was clearly matched by a growing reluctance to speak about matters which were beyond the wit of man to comprehend fully.

In close proximity to God and his throne were the living creatures (*ḥayyoth*), which are mentioned in Ezekiel 1.5ff. and are identified with the cherubim in Ezekiel 10. Together with Isaiah 6.2, which is frequently conflated with Ezekiel 1 and 10, these passages make an important contribution to the angelology of the apocalypses. For example, when John of Patmos describes the throne-room of God, it is the living creatures of Ezekiel, the description of which is subtly interwoven with elements from Isaiah 6, which surround the throne of God. The situation is the same in the Apocalypse of Abraham 18, where the detailed account of the creatures and their activities reflects Ezekiel 1, though with a number of differences:

> . . . under the throne four living creatures singing, and their appearance was one, each one of them with four faces. And such was the appearance of their countenances, of a lion, of man, of an ox and of an eagle: four heads were upon their bodies . . . and each had six wings; from their shoulders, and their sides and their loins. And with the two wings from their shoulders they covered their faces, and with the two wings from their loins they covered their feet, while the two middle wings they spread out for flying straight forward. And when they had ended their singing, they looked at one another and threatened one another.

The living creatures have an important part to play in Jewish and Christian angelology. In later Jewish works we find that angelic status is also given to other parts of the divine throne-chariot. Thus, for example, the hubs (*ophannim*) of the chariot have become a class of angels in the heavenly world. This has happened already in 1 Enoch 71.7, where the *ophannim* along with the *cherubim* and *seraphim* guard the throne of glory.[23]

Also in the immediate presence of God are archangels, whose creation is mentioned in Jub. 2.2. The belief in exalted angelic mediators of God's will has a long history in Israelite religion, and, whatever foreign influence there may have been, there can be little doubt that belief in angels lies deep at the heart of Israel's religion and is not simply a later accretion, however much it may have developed in later Judaism and especially in apocalyptic literature.[24] According to 1 Enoch 40.2 (cf. 9.1, 54.6ff. and 71.8ff.), there are four archangels who stand on the four sides of God's throne. In the book of Daniel two exalted angels are mentioned, Michael and Gabriel. The former has the important function of acting as guardian angel of the people of God (Dan. 12.1), whereas the latter functions as an interpreter to the seer of the significance of his visions and a communicator of the divine secrets (Dan. 8.16f. cf. Dan. 10.10ff.)

Already in the visions which are to be found in the opening

chapters of Zechariah an angelic intermediary explains to the prophet the significance of his visions.[25] The identity of the angel who accompanies the seer varies enormously. It is the archangel Uriel in 4 Ezra 4.1 (cf. Life of Adam and Eve 48.4ff.), whereas in the Apocalypse of Abraham it is the angel Jaoel who accompanies the patriarch to heaven, and in the Testament of Abraham it is Michael. Whether the seer ascends to heaven or not, an angel who stands in close proximity to God usually appears to help in the unfolding of divine secrets to the seer. In Slavonic Enoch 22.11f. the angel Pravuil shows Enoch the divine secrets after his ascent to heaven and his vision of God. In Daniel and 4 Ezra, however, the angels come to the seers and unfold the divine secrets, either by interpreting the significance of a dream-vision or answering the questions which the seer puts to God in his prayers.

The role of Michael as the heavenly representative of Israel clearly played an important role within Jewish theology[26] and is well illustrated by the following passage from the War Scroll (1QM):

> This is the day appointed for the defeat and overthrow of the prince of the kingdom of wickedness, and he will send eternal succour to the company of his redeemed by the might of the princely angel of the kingdom of Michael. With everlasting light he will enlighten with joy (the children) of Israel; peace and blessing shall be with the company of God. He will raise up the kingdom of Michael in the midst of the gods, and the realm of Israel in the midst of all flesh (1QM 17.5ff.).

The triumph of Michael in heaven is a sign of hope for the dominance of the people of God on earth (cf. Rev. 12.7). This notion of the guardian-angel of Israel has its parallels elsewhere in apocalyptic literature, where we find the notion that all the nations of the world have their guardian angels in the heavenly world. In Daniel's discussion with the exalted angel in chapter 10 he is told that the angel has been prevented from visiting him because of his involvement with 'the prince of the kingdom of Persia' (Dan. 10.13). It is clear from the context (Michael is referred to as one of the chief princes in the same verse), that the prince here is no human king but the angelic representative of the Persian kingdom. That the nations have their angelic representatives is at least as old as the LXX version of Deuteronomy 32.8: 'When the Most High divided up the nations . . . he set the boundaries of the nations according to the number of the angels of God' (my translation). By the second century BC this notion has an important place within Jewish thought. In Jub. 15.31f. we find that, whereas the nation of Israel is ruled by God alone, the nations of the world are consigned for their government to the (angelic) spirits:

> And he sanctified it (Israel), and gathered it from among all the children of men; for there are many nations and many peoples, and all are his (God's) and over all hath he placed spirits in authority to lead them astray from him. But over Israel he did not appoint any angel or spirit, for he alone is their ruler . . .

The following passage from 1 Enoch also makes a similar point. In 1 Enoch 89 we find that a period of Israel's history is under the dominance of 'shepherds', who, in the Animal-Apocalypse, represent the angels of the nations:[27]

> And he called seventy shepherds and cast those sheep to them that they might pasture them, and he spake to the shepherds and their companions: Let each individual of you pasture the sheep henceforward, and everything that I shall command, that do ye. And I will deliver them over to you duly numbered, and tell you which of them are to be destroyed – and them destroy ye. And he gave over unto them those sheep. And he called another and said unto him: Observe and mark everything that the shepherds will do to those sheep; for they will destroy more of them than I have commanded them. And every excess and the destruction which will be wrought through the shepherds, record, (namely) how many they destroy according to my command, and how many according to their own caprice: record against every individual shepherd all the destruction he effects (1 Enoch 89.59–62).

The significance of this type of belief within the whole gamut of apocalyptic thought is considerable. As we shall see later, one of the distinguishing features of the view of history in apocalyptic is the belief that the whole course of history is under God's control and conforms to the plan laid down by God before the foundation of the world. There can be no suggestion that the doings of men, however contrary they may appear to the divine will in the present, are in any way outside the control of the omnipotent God (cf. 1 Enoch 89.58). The nations of the world triumph and Israel suffers, because God has temporarily allowed the angelic representatives of the nations to exercise dominion in the heavenly world. The picture emerges here of earthly events being reflections of heavenly realities. The dominance of one group in heaven is reflected in the dominance of their counterparts on earth. Likewise, the fall of one world-power is presaged by the demise of the heavenly representative of that kingdom. Not only does this kind of outlook allow the readers of the apocalypses to see the transitory nature of the dominant world-powers but also demands that they accept that the present hardship is in fact divinely ordained. This makes the task of the righteous merely one of waiting until the time which God has ordained for the triumph of Israel's angelic representative to inaugurate a time of victory for his people on earth. We thus have a picture here of God, as it were, voluntarily surrendering his sovereignty to lesser divine beings for a period, until the time comes for the final vindication of God's ways in earth and heaven. This point is put in a most graphic form in the late Hebrew Enoch 48, where R. Ishmael tells of the sight of God's right arm temporarily inactive, with the result that God's ways are not vindicated in the world. He tells also, however, of the temporary nature of his inactivity and the way in which God will in the future raise his right arm and work on behalf of his people:

> In that moment will the Holy One, blessed be he, reveal his great arm and show it to the nations of the world . . . forthwith Israel will be saved from among the nations of the world. And the Messiah will appear unto them and he will bring them up to Jerusalem with great joy. (Heb. Enoch 48.9f.)

We can see from the quotation from 1 Enoch 89 that the apocalypticist reckons with the fact that some at least of the angels will abuse the power given to them by God and as a result fall under divine judgement. One figure in particular emerges as the representative of all that is opposed to God, namely Satan.[28] Jewish apocalyptic literature never really loses the view of Satan which we find in passages like Job 1—2 and Zech. 3.1ff., where Satan appears as an accuser of man before the divine tribunal, and whose power is ultimately limited by God himself. However much the apocalypticist may be tempted to regard the present age as under the control of an alien power (and that evidence is by no means as strong as is often suggested),[29] the dominance of the power opposed to God is only a temporary phenomenon. While language which is extremely dualistic can at times be used to talk about the power of the being opposed to God (Asc. Is. 2.4; 4.2), the control of God over the works of darkness is always held firm by the apocalypticists. This control is well illustrated by the book of Revelation. Despite the close link between the powers of darkness and the dominant world-power of the day (Rev. 13.1f.), the final triumph of God is shown to be assured, not least because the decisive victory has already been won in the world above (Rev. 12.7). The activities of Satan in the world are allowed by God for a short time only (Rev. 13.5), which will end when the overthrow of his power in the world above is matched by the overthrow of his power on earth. Even the exercise of the destructive power is under the divine providence, as his release from bondage after the messianic kingdom seems to indicate (Rev. 20.7f.).[30]

The monistic outlook of the bulk of apocalyptic literature is also evident in the attitude which we find with regard to the world of darkness. Only occasionally do we find the realm of darkness relegated to a completely different sphere from heaven. It is particularly in 1 Enoch that we find reference to an underworld of punishment (1 Enoch 10.13; 18.11; 21.7; 88.1ff.; 90.23ff.). Of these references, the majority refer to the place reserved for the impious angels whose descent to earth brought about the judgement of God in the days of Noah (1 Enoch 6ff.). More often than not, however, the place of darkness is part of the heavenly world. In Slavonic Enoch 18, for example, Enoch is said to see the 'Grigori who with Satanail rejected God', while in the second heaven he sees a place of great darkness reserved for the apostates (cf. Test. Levi 3.2 and Slav. Enoch 42). The picture of heaven as a realm containing both the powers of light and the powers of darkness is particularly apparent in the Jewish-Christian apocalypse, the Ascension of Isaiah. Here the lower realms, particularly the firmament, where a great struggle was taking place between the angels of Sammael and Satan (Asc. Is. 7.9), are opposed to the highest part of the heavenly world where God himself dwells.[31] Although this work is perilously close to the kind of gnostic dualism familiar to us from the gnostic systems of the second century AD, its portrayal of the heavenly world as the abode of good and evil powers derives from the earlier apocalyptic emphasis on the ultimate control of God over the universe, and the refusal to see the present triumph of evil as the result of the inability of God to deal with the evil forces at work in the world.

Another aspect of angelology which comes to the fore, especially in the early traditions about Enoch, is the series of legends about the fallen angels. Taking its inspiration from Genesis 6.1, 1 Enoch 6–11 tells of the way in which the *bene elohim* or 'Watchers', as they are called in 1 Enoch, came down to earth to seduce the beautiful human women (1 Enoch 6.1).[32] The crime of these angelic beings involved not only sexual misdemeanours but also revelation to men of various secrets including 'charms and enchantments and the cutting of roots' (1 Enoch 7.1f.), as well as the secrets of astronomy (1 Enoch 8.3). All this knowledge only brings about great unhappiness in the world, which is reported by the archangels to God himself (1 Enoch 9.4). This act leads to the damnation of the angels, who are not allowed any mercy, despite the fact that Enoch intercedes on their behalf (1 Enoch 12–16). Although the stories take up a considerable section of the early part of 1 Enoch, there is no evidence to suggest that they were coined specifically for this context.[33] The parallels to them from other sources (e.g. Jub. 4.22) indicate that we are dealing here with legends well known in Jewish tradition and used here in a way similar to the way in which other tales are used, namely as a backdrop to the revelations given to the seer. The stories provide a setting for the introduction of the hidden Enoch in 12.1 and his journeys to heaven and other parts of the cosmos (cf. 1 Enoch 14–36). As far as one can see, therefore, the stories do not appear to be intended to function as an explanation of the problem of evil in their present context,[34] though such an interest may go some way to explaining the development of these legends at an earlier time.

There does appear to be a contrast between the Watchers and Enoch. One of the great sins of Azazel is that he has 'revealed the eternal secrets which were in heaven, which men were striving to learn' (1 Enoch 9.6). This charge seems a strange one in an apocalypse which sets out to do precisely that for which the angels were condemned. Indeed, in Jub. 4.18ff. Enoch's fame is based on the fact that he introduced many secrets, including astronomy (cf. 1 Enoch's 8.3), which the angels are said to have done. One can only assume that the major difference between Enoch and the angels is the fact that man receives the heavenly mysteries by means of revelation, whereas the angels are guilty of exposing the heavenly mysteries to man without God's permission. Enoch reveals exactly what he is told to reveal, and, as a result, God only allows man to know sufficient for man's well-being. The angels, however, usurp God's right to reveal his mysteries and indulge in a profligate disclosure of the secrets of God. It may be, therefore, that there is an implicit contrast in these legends with the figure of Enoch who is presented as the archetypal mystagogue, whose disclosures correspond totally with what God wills man to know.

The Development of an Exalted Angel in Apocalyptic Literature

We have examined different facets of Jewish angelology in the Jewish apocalypses and noted the way in which angelic intermediaries have a significant role within the apocalyptic literature. There is, however, one aspect of angelology which particularly demands our attention. Although it cannot be said to be a typical feature of all the apocalypses under consideration, there does seem to be evidence that the developing angelology had produced an angelic figure of considerable status, whose position in the heavenly hierarchy set him apart from the rest of the angels. One recalls the special position of Michael and other archangels, as is particularly seen in a passage like Slavonic Enoch 24.1, where Gabriel appears to sit on God's left hand. But there are other passages also which will demand our attention, particularly that concerning the angel Jaoel who acts as guide to the patriarchs in the Apocalypse of Abraham, as well as the more familiar passages about the son of man in Daniel 7.13f. and the Similitudes of Enoch. The similarities which exist between these figures, their origin and theological significance for Judaism will demand our attention in the following section.

Angelophanies have a long history in Israelite religion and are already found in the earliest strands of the pentateuch, e.g. Gen. 16.7ff.[35] The angel of the Lord (mal'ak YHWH) who appears to various figures in the early books of the Old Testament acts as God's representative and can even be thought of as God himself (e.g. Judg. 13.3ff. and Gen. 16.13). W. Eichrodt has recognized the significance of such angelophanies and has commented on them in the following way:

Among the narratives relating to the angel one particular group stands out because it describes an emissary of Yahweh who is no longer clearly distinguishable from his master, but in his appearing and speaking clothes himself with Yahweh's own appearance and speech . . . Consequently when the words of the *mal'ak* in Gen. 21.18 and 22.11 make use of the divine 'I', this is not to be regarded as a naive self-identification on the part of the emissary with the one who has given him the orders but as a sign of the presence of God in the angel-phenomenon.[36]

Although little detail is given about these angelophanies, it appears that there was an angelic being who in some sense was regarded as communicating the appearance of God himself and who sometimes appeared in the form of a man (Gen. 18.2). This being was called by the name of God (Gen. 31.11–13), even though this attribution was derived from his function as God's representative. Our purpose in mentioning the *mal'ak YHWH* is merely to show that the ideas which we shall be looking at in the apocalypses were no innovation in Jewish religion, whatever the contribution in details may have been from other sources, but have their origin within the ancient traditions of Israel.

At the end of his vision of the divine throne-chariot Ezekiel sees the appearance of God in human form (Ezek. 1.26f.), which, despite all the qualifications offered by the prophet, clearly gives the reader the impression that the prophet pictured God in this way. What is most interesting, however, is that the figure described in this vision appears again to the prophet in chapter 8.2, but this time without the throne-chariot.[37] A comparison of this verse with Ezekiel 1.26f. shows how close they are:

EZEK. 1.26–27	EZEK. 8.2
. . . and seated above the likeness of a throne was a likeness as it were of a human form. And upward from what had the appearance of his loins I saw as it were gleaming bronze, like the appearance of fire enclosed round about; and downward from what had the appearance of his loins I saw as it were the appearance of fire, and there was brightness round about him.	Then I beheld, and, lo a form that had the appearance of a man;[38] below what appeared to be his loins it was fire, and above his loins it was like the appearance of brightness, like gleaming bronze.

The independence of the human figure from the throne-chariot is probably not new to Ezekiel. Already in cultic acclamations such as we find in Psalm 99.1 we find the belief that God was enthroned above the cherubim, and, despite the important position of the national shrine in Jewish theology, it is probably correct to assume that God's presence was not always confined to the position above the ark, even if it was the circumstances of the Exile which brought this conviction to prominence.[39] In any case Ezekiel himself knows of the independence of God's *kabod* from the throne-chariot. In the second appearance of the chariot in chapter 10 the prophet sees the *kabod* moving from above the cherubim to take up a position in another part of the Temple:

> And the glory of the LORD went up from the cherubim to the threshold of the house; and the house was filled with the cloud, and the court was full of the brightness of the glory of the LORD.[40] (Ezek. 10.4.)

The significance of Ezekiel 1.26f. for Jewish theology has not gone unnoticed.[41] H. R. Balz, for example, thinks that ultimately this passage lies behind the theological scene in Daniel 7.13f. He explains the connection by pointing to the gradual separation of divine functions which appears to be taking place in the book of Ezekiel which results in Daniel 7.13f. where there are two divine figures.[42] He fails to notice the real importance of the separation between the human figure and the throne in Ezekiel 8, however, and concentrates most of his attention on the angelic scribe who appears in Ezekiel 9.2ff.[43] There would seem to be no evidence to connect the human figure referred to in chapter 8 whom we have already had reason to link with chapter 1 and the scribe of chapter 9. Unlike the figure in chapter 8 the angelic scribe can in no sense be considered especially close to God, despite the permission granted to the angel to draw near to the cherubim-chariot (Ezek. 10.2), for he is not the bearer of divine characteristics in the way that the figure in chapter 8 is. Balz is right to point to the fact that there is a gradual splitting in the way in which the divine functions are described, but omits detailed consideration of the most significant development, the relationship between Ezekiel 1.26f. and 8.2.[44]

Consideration of these verses only permits us to conclude that the human figure on the throne is not tied to the throne and could appear apart from it. According to chapter 8 this separability enabled the figure to act as an agent of the divine purpose, in so far as he was the means whereby the prophet was removed to

Jerusalem (Ezek. 8.3).[45] How far Ezekiel 8 can be connected with the appearance of the *mal'ak YHWH* who speaks and acts as though he were God himself is by no means clear. What is not in doubt, however, is that the figure who appears in Ezekiel 8.2 is intimately linked with the glory of God which appeared to the prophet by the banks of the river Chebar. What has happened here is not so much the splitting up of divine functions among various angelic figures but the separation of the form of God from the divine throne-chariot to act as quasi-angelic mediator.

There are good reasons for supposing that parts of Daniel 7 can be explained by reference to Ezekiel 1. Clearly Daniel 7.9f. owes much of its imagery either to Ezekiel 1 or, more likely, to traditional developments of that chapter.[46] Possible examples of such borrowing, apart from the reference to the throne of God, include the four winds (Dan. 7.2f., cf. Ezek. 1.4), and the four beasts (cf. the four living creatures in Ezek. 1.5ff.), but how far this extends to the description of God as the Ancient of Days and the human figure of Daniel 7.13 is more difficult to assess.[47] It would appear to be difficult to explain the presence of two divine beings in Daniel 7 from Ezekiel alone, and it is not surprising that suggestions about possible Canaanite influence have been prominent in recent discussions of the chapter as a way of explaining the phenomenon of a divine being taking over authority from another (older) figure.[48] Whatever we make of the Canaanite hypothesis (and however attractive the parallels may appear, the difference in date between the Jewish works and the Ugaritic parallels cannot be ignored), there may well have been ideas inherent in Israelite theology which made reception of the details known to us from the Canaanite picture more easy to explain. The picture which we have in Daniel 7.13 is of one heavenly being acting in place of another. It is not that the God of Israel abdicates his position but allows another divine being to act in his stead. The similarity which exists between Ezekiel 8.2 and Daniel 7.13 lies in the fact that both verses refer to heavenly figures and speak of them in quasi-divine terms. [49] In the Ezekiel passage this divine status is determined by the similarity which exists with the theophany in chapter 1.26f., whereas in the latter the bestowal of universal rule on the Son of Man is an indication of the fact that he acts as God's vice-regent. The difference between the two verses is that the Danielic figure stands alongside God, the Ancient of Days, and is in some sense the representative of the latter's kingly power. The figure in Ezekiel 8 on the other hand is to be regarded as the deity himself described in human form. [50]

Although we shall have more to say at a later stage about the meaning of Daniel 7, we have said enough thus far to indicate that in this chapter we have a scene in which God's power and authority are given to another heavenly figure. The divine status of the human figure of Daniel 7.13 is even more apparent in the LXX version, however. Whereas Theodotion follows the Hebrew and translates 'and he came to the Ancient of Days', the LXX translates the same Hebrew phrase in the following way, 'he came as the Ancient of Days',[51] a variant which was probably known to at least two Jewish writers (Rev. 1.14 and Apocalypse of Abraham 11).[52] This variant suggests that the Son of Man is in fact the embodiment of the person of the Ancient of Days. In other words the original scene in Daniel 7, where two figures exist alongside each other in heaven, is changed so that the vice-regent, the Son of Man, takes upon himself the form and character of God himself.

We noted that in the reference to the *mal'ak YHWH* in the Old Testament the recipients of the theophany frequently refer to the figure as if it were God himself. Similar confusion is found in Ezekiel 8.2 where the being who transports the prophet is the human figure who is seated on the throne in the call-vision. Nowhere is this confusion better illustrated than in the angelophany which is described in Daniel 10.5ff. Commentators tend to assume that this must be a reference to the angel Gabriel who appears to the prophet earlier, and is there also described in human form (Dan. 8.15f.), though apart from exclusion of any identity with Michael (cf. Dan. 10.21) there is nothing to suggest that this is the case in the passage itself.[53] The overall impression which the angelophany gives is not dissimilar to Ezekiel 1, and the similarities which exist can best be appreciated after the passage itself has been quoted:

> On the twenty-fourth day of the first month, as I was standing on the bank of the great river, that is, the Tigris, I lifted up my eyes and looked, and behold, a man clothed in linen, whose loins were girded with gold of Uphaz. His body was like beryl, his face like the appearance of lightning, his eyes like flaming torches, his arms and legs like the gleam of burnished bronze, and the sound of his words like the noise of a multitude . . . when I heard the sound of his

words, I fell on my face in a deep sleep with my face to the ground. (Dan. 10.4–9.)

The first four words of Daniel 10.5 reveal very close contact with Ezekiel 9.2, though the overall impression given by the vision is of a closer connection with the first chapter of Ezekiel. The phrase 'his loins' is found in Ezekiel 1.27 to describe the human figure, and the more explicit references to the different parts of the angel's body in Daniel 10.6 seems to be a development of the more reserved outlook of Ezekiel. In the same verse the eyes of the angel are said to be 'like flaming torches'. A similar phenomenon is said to be in the middle of the living creatures in Ezekiel 1.13. Whereas in Ezekiel 1.16 the wheels of the chariot are said to be 'like the gleaming of a chrysolite', in Daniel the word *tarshish* (chrysolite) is now transferred to the description of the body of the angel. The body and feet can be paralleled in Ezekiel 1.23 and 1.7 respectively, and the voice of the angel (Dan. 10.6) bears some resemblance to the phrase 'a sound of tumult like the sound of a host' in Ezekiel 1.24. The phrase 'like the gleam of burnished bronze' is quoted verbatim from Ezekiel 1.7, where it is used of the legs of the living creatures.[54]

Another source for the description of the angel in Daniel 10 is the portrayal of the glory of the primal man in Ezekiel 28.13. In that passage the words like *tarshish* (beryl), *zahab* (gold cf. Dan. *kethem 'uphaz*) and *barquat* (lightning cf. Dan. *baraq*) are used. The description of the man seems to have contributed to the portrait of the one seated upon the throne in Revelation 4.3. While there are no direct parallels between Revelation 4.3 and Daniel 10.5f., common indebtedness to Ezekiel 28.13 suggests that this passage was an important feature of the development of the heavenly man tradition and at the same time is an indirect link between Daniel 10.6 and the human figure sitting on the throne of glory.

What we find in Daniel 10.5f. then is a broadly based dependence on Ezekiel and especially on the first chapter. It would seem that either Ezekiel 1.26f. or 8.2 has been interpreted and influenced by other aspects of the first chapter of Ezekiel. Such a transference of images to the human figure could well have taken place during a vision when the precise identification of various words and phrases was confused by the overwhelming impression of glory upon the seer. What does emerge from this study of the angelophany in this chapter is that we are dealing

here with no ordinary angelic being. It is true that he was sent
by God to fulfil a particular function, namely to communicate to
Daniel the historical events which are to take place. But the fact
that he acts as a divine emissary cannot disguise the exalted
language used to describe the angel. R. H. Charles has pointed
out the theological complexities which are to be found in these
verses, and which are admirably epitomized by the impact
which the angelophany makes upon the seer (Dan. 10.9, cf.
Ezek. 2.1, 1 Enoch 71.11, Matt. 17.6, and 3 Enoch 16).[55] What we
have here is the beginning of a hypostatic development similar
to that connected with divine attributes like God's word and
wisdom.[56]

> Later tradition is divided over the identity of the angel in Dan. 10.
> The Syriac of Dan. 10.6 gives a hint of a more profound understand-
> ing of this verse by stating that the angel 'had no form', a sentence
> which replaces 'his body was like beryl'. There seems to be some
> reluctance to describe or even mention the body of the angel, an
> omission which is to be found also in Rev. 1.13ff.[57] Such a refine-
> ment would hardly be necessary if the angel was not an exalted
> figure and recalls the reserve expressed by the targum on Ezek.
> 1.26f. Also in the MS. H.P. 34 the river by which Daniel is said to
> have his vision (10.4) is explicitly linked with Ezek. 1 by insertion of
> the name Chebar.[58] The treatment of Dan. 10 in later Jewish tradi-
> tion does not appear to mark this angel off from others as being in a
> special position in the angelic hierarchy. Shemoth R. 28, b. Megillah
> 3a, b. Ḥullin 91b and 3 Enoch 35.2 all quote from Dan. 10.5f. but in
> connexion with quite ordinary angelic beings. More significant,
> however, is the way in which Metatron, the lesser Yahweh, is
> described in 3 Enoch 15 and 48c in language reminiscent of Dan. 10,
> even though there do not appear to be any direct quotations from
> that chapter.

Evidence of the continued influence of this exalted figure can be
found in the appearance of the Risen Christ described in Revelation 1.13ff. This christophany is most significant because it is one
of the few passages from early Christian literature which allow
us to ascertain the way in which the early Christians visualized
the exalted Lord. The extensive use of Daniel. 10.5f. in the
description of the Risen Christ, as the following synopsis shows,
suggests that the seer of Patmos considered that the appearance
of the angel in Daniel 10 was a natural quarry for imagery to
describe his Lord.[59]

REVELATION 1.13–17

. . . and in the midst of the lamp-stands one like a son of man, clothed with a long robe and with a golden girdle round his breast; his head and his hair were white as white wool, white as snow; his eyes were like a flame of fire, his feet were like burnished bronze, refined as in a furnace, and his voice was like the sound of many waters; in his right hand he held seven stars, from his mouth issued a sharp two-edged sword, and his face was like the sun shining in full strength. When I saw him, I fell at his feet as though dead. But he laid his right hand upon me . . .

DANIEL 10.5–10

I lifted up my eyes and looked, and behold, a man clothed in linen, whose loins were girded with gold of Uphaz. His body was like beryl, his face like the appearance of lightning, his eyes like flaming torches, his arms and legs like the gleam of burnished bronze and the sound of his words like the noise of a multitude . . . and when I heard the sound of his words, I fell on my face in a deep sleep with my face to the ground. And behold a hand touched me . . .[60]

The synopsis shows how indebted Revelation is to Daniel 10, though Daniel 7.9 and 13 and Ezekiel 1.24 have also contributed to the christophany. The divine status of the risen Christ is evident from the way in which a characteristic of the Ancient of Days is here used to describe the heavenly Son of Man, in all probability an idea which derives from the LXX variant which we have already mentioned. As far as John is concerned, there is no incongruity for him to describe the exalted Christ in this way because there was a very close connection in his mind between this angel and God himself. So close was the relationship in fact that the attributes of God are used to describe the heavenly being which appears to him (cf. 7.17).

An angelophany which has many similarities with the description of the glorified Christ in Revelation 1 appears in the Apocalypse of Abraham. In this work the patriarch's guide to the presence of God is an angel called Jaoel, whose appearance is described in chapter 10f.

And the angel came, whom he (God) had sent to me, in the likeness of a man, and grasped me by my right hand, and set me upon my feet, and said to me: Stand up, Abraham, friend of God, who loveth thee; let not the trembling of man seize thee. For lo, I have been sent to strengthen thee and bless thee in the name of God – who loveth thee – the creator of the celestial and the terrestrial. Be fearless and hasten to him. I am called Jaoel by him who moveth that which existeth with me on the seventh expanse of the firmament, a power in virtue of the ineffable name that is dwelling in me . . .[61]

> And I rose and saw him who had grasped me by my right hand
> and set me up upon my feet; and the appearance of his body was
> like sapphire, and the look of his countenance like chrysolite, and
> the hair of his head like snow, and the turban upon his head like the
> appearance of a rainbow and the clothing of his garments like
> purple; and a golden sceptre was in his right hand.

Apart from the exalted status bestowed on the angel by possession of the divine name, the description of Jaoel is similar
enough to the other angelophanies which we have examined to
see here a link with that tradition. The description of the figure
owes its origin to several sources. The body of the angel resembles Daniel 10.6 but the mention of sapphire derives from
Ezekiel 28.13. This is also true of the reference to chrysolite, but
a link with Daniel 10.6 must not be ruled out.[62] The possession
of a turban is an unusual feature and may indicate the priestly
function of Jaoel (cf. Ex. 28.4).[63] The mention of the rainbow is
reminiscent of Ezekiel 1.28 (cf. Rev. 4.3), where God's glory is
compared to the bow in the clouds. An angel with a rainbow
around his head appears also in Revelation 10.1, and it is not
easy to differentiate between this angel and the risen Christ who
appears to John on the island of Patmos.[64] As in Revelation 1 the
description of the angel takes up the reference to the Ancient of
Days in Daniel 7.9. Once again there would appear to be a
strong indication that this angel is closely linked with God
himself. The purple colour of Jaoel's garment may derive from
the use of the colour in the description of the furnishing of the
tabernacle (Ex. 25.4 and 26.1), but more intriguing is the
possibility that we may have here a link with the thread of blue
in the tassels, prescribed by Numbers 15.38f. According to R.
Meir (b. Menahoth 43b) the colour of the thread of blue is in fact
the colour of the throne of glory itself.[65] The sceptre in Jaoel's
right hand is similar to Revelation 1.16, where Christ holds in
his hands, not a sceptre but seven stars. In the Apocalypse of
Abraham the sceptre is a symbol of authority and power (cf. Ps.
45.6). In this respect the angelophany bears some resemblance to
a passage from Ezekiel the Tragedian, where God places Moses
on a throne with a diadem upon his head and a sceptre in his
hand.[66]

The description of God's throne in the Apocalypse of
Abraham (ch. 18) is notable for the absence of any reference to a
figure sitting on the throne. As we have seen, the description of

the throne-chariot clearly owes much to Ezekiel 1, which makes the lack of any figure on the throne all the more significant. It is clear that Jaoel is the companion of the throne of glory. This close link between the two is confirmed by the words of the angel: 'I am called Jaoel by him who moveth that which existeth with me . . .'. We know from chapter 19 that it is the throne that Abraham sees on the seventh firmament, and one must assume that this is what the angel is referring to when he speaks rather obliquely of 'that which existeth with me'. Such an identification may be confirmed by reference to Ezekiel 1.12, where movement is one of the characteristics pointed out by the prophet, as it is also in the throne-chariot firmament from Cave 4 at Qumran. At the very least it seems that Jaoel, like Wisdom (Wisd. 9.4) was the companion of God's throne. While there is no explicit evidence from the Apocalypse of Abraham to suggest that Jaoel was the one whose seat was on the throne of God, it is not impossible that we have a theological description here which reflects that found in Ezekiel 1 and 8, where the human figure on the throne leaves the throne to function as the agent of the divine will.

Revelation 1.13ff. and the angelophany in the Apocalypse of Abraham show some affinities with developments of Ezekiel 1.26f., particularly as they are found in Daniel 10.5f. The result is a theology of some complexity. Both works clearly think of the angelic figure as one who possesses divine attributes, but in the case of the Apocalypse of Abraham the figure is clearly an angel as well. There is a little more reserve in Revelation about describing the risen Christ as an angel,[67] but his function is not too different from the angelic intermediaries, who guide the apocalypticists on their heavenly journeys and reveal to them the secrets of God (cf. Rev. 1.1 and 22.16).

So far we have dealt with angelological passages in Jewish apocalyptic literature which seem to derive from the separation of the human figure on the throne of glory from the cherubim-chariot, such as we find in Ezekiel 8.2. We have argued that within the tradition of the throne-theophany there was a tendency to continue this separation, with the result that an angelic figure developed who embodied the attributes of the glorious God whom the prophet Ezekiel had seen by the river Chebar. There is, however, another development which is related to this but which takes a rather different form. In it we find once again an interest in the divine throne. Instead of the splitting of the human figure from the throne, there would appear to be an attempt to reinterpret the throne-theophany by identifying the figure on the throne, not with God but with a man exalted to heaven by God. This phenomenon is to be found particularly in the Similitudes of Enoch and the Testament of Abraham.

The significance of the Similitudes of Enoch (i.e. 1 Enoch 37–71) for the theology of Judaism has for a long time been a hotly disputed issue. The fact that they are the repository of the heavenly Son of Man ideas, so important for New Testament christology, means that they assume a place of disproportionate significance among relevant 'background' texts for the understanding of the New Testament. The use of the title Head of Days and the description of God in these terms (particularly in a passage like 1 Enoch 46.1f.), seems to indicate clear dependence on Daniel 7.9 and 13.[68] What is most interesting, however, is that the Son of Man/Elect One is said to sit on God's throne of glory (e.g. 1 Enoch 61.8; 69.29), an idea which may be implied in Daniel 7 but certainly never explicitly stated. This belief demands some consideration in the light of the angelic ideas which we have just examined.[69]

A cursory glance at the material in chapters 37—71 shows that two principal titles are used for God, namely Head of Days and Lord of Spirits. Of these two titles Lord of Spirits is by far the more frequent, occurring no less than one hundred and four times in the work.[70] The title Head of Days occurs only at 46.2, 47.3, 48.2, 55.1, 60.2, and 71.10, 13, and 14. The other title, Lord of Spirits, is rare in Jewish literature. Charles points to precedents to the title in Numbers 16.22 and 27.16 and in 2 Maccabees 3.24, which is the only explicit reference known to him.[71] A similar phrase does occur in Hebrews 12.9 ('the father of spirits'). Also in 1QH 10.8 there is a reference to God which is very close to the title used in the Similitudes. The phrase in question is 'Lord of every spirit' *(adon l'col ruaḥ)* and is similar enough to suppose that we are dealing in the Similitudes with a title for God which was known to Jews at the start of the Christian era.

Even though the occasional parallel can be offered for this title, what is quite remarkable is the frequency with which the title is used in the Similitudes. This dominance raises the question whether the title reflects a view of God which the author wanted to enunciate in his writings. Our suspicion that this may in fact be the case is confirmed when we realize that nowhere in the Similitudes is the Lord of Spirits said to sit upon the throne of glory.[72] There are, however, two references to God as Head of Days sitting on the throne of glory (1 Enoch 47.3 and 60.2). It would appear that when the throne-theophany is described it is the title Head of Days which is used to speak of God rather than Lord of Spirits. In all likelihood the fact that in Daniel 7.9 the Ancient of Days not only sits upon the divine throne but also is described in anthropomorphic terms has been responsible for the two references which we do have to God sitting on the throne' of glory. The paucity of reference to God sitting on the throne, together with the fact that the title Lord of Spirits is never linked with the throne, seems to point to the fact that we have here at least the beginnings of an understanding of God which played down the anthropomorphisms found in the biblical theophanies.[73]

When reference is made to the throne of glory, one is probably right in assuming that this is the throne of God himself,[74] and it is this throne upon which the Son of Man/Elect One sits in judgement over the kings of the earth. The fact that there is a transference of the throne of glory from God to another figure indicates a development of some significance. With the exception of the two references to the Head of Days sitting on the throne, God is hardly linked with the throne, with the result that there is an emphasis on the spiritual nature of God. Indeed, when the author describes the messianic bliss in the future in 1 Enoch 62.14 God's presence is at the messianic banquet but, unlike the Son of Man, he plays no part in the actual meal: 'And the Lord of Spirits will abide *over* them, and *with* that Son of Man shall they eat and lie down and rise up for ever and ever.' What is equally remarkable are the occasions when the author comes nearest of all to describing a theophany in which the Lord of Spirits is mentioned. In 40.2 Enoch describes the angels around God. The whole scene is reminiscent of theophanies such as those in Daniel 7.9f. and 1 Enoch 14, but while the angelic attendants are described nothing at all is said about the throne or the figure on it:

And after that I saw thousands of thousands and ten thousand times ten thousand, I saw a multitude beyond number and reckon-

The Open Heaven

ing, who stood before the Lord of Spirits. And on the four sides of the Lord of Spirits I saw four presences, different from those that sleep not, and I learnt their names: for the angel who went with me made known to me their names and showed me all the hidden things.

In the first part of the account of Enoch's ascent, which is probably to be separated from the other description of the ascent in the second half of the chapter (1 Enoch 71.5ff.),[75] Enoch describes what he sees when he arrives in God's presence (71.1f.). The fiery stream is normally closely linked with the throne of God (1 Enoch 14.19, Dan. 7.10 and 4QS1), but here the reference to the throne and its occupant is absent and one is left to conclude from the context that Enoch is in the presence of God:

> And it came to pass after this that my spirit was translated, and it ascended into the heavens: and I saw the holy sons of God. They were stepping on flames of fire: their garments were white and their raiment, and their faces shone like snow. And I saw two streams of fire, and the light of that fire shone like hyacinth, and I fell on my face before the Lord of Spirits. And the angel Michael seized me by my right hand, and lifted me up and led me forth into all the secrets, and he showed me all the secrets of righteousness.

The transference of the session on the throne of glory is not the only attribute of God taken over by the Son of Man/Elect One. The role of judgement is now exercised by the Son of Man/Elect One (though God still has a part to play in chapter 62.10ff.). He it is who 'raises the kings and mighty from their seats . . . and breaks the teeth of sinners' (1 Enoch 46.4, cf. 1 Enoch 62.10ff.). But this transference of divine functions becomes all the more significant when we look at it in the context of the work as we have it. The final chapter of the Similitudes (1 Enoch 71) concludes by identifying the heavenly Son of Man with the righteous man of primeval times, Enoch. Some have seen fit to discount this final chapter as an addition to the Similitudes, which should have no part in establishing the theological perspective of the earlier chapters. Whether the chapter is a later addition or not, its significance lies in the insight it offers us into the mind of the man who actually placed this passage at the end of chapters dealing with the heavenly Son of Man.

In their present form the Similitudes not only give evidence of the transference of divine attributes to another heavenly figure but also identify this heavenly figure with Enoch, who, it was thought, had been taken up to heaven by God without seeing death.[76] Thus the problem of anthropomorphism inherent in the divine throne-theophany is neatly side-stepped by separating the throne of glory from God and making its occupant the glorified Enoch.

A similar phenomenon confronts us in the Greek version of the Testament of Abraham. This work is not easy to date, but it does not appear to give evidence of any extensive Christian editing. The fact that it exists in a variety of different recensions is probably a strong indication of its antiquity. It may not be too far from the mark to suppose that we are dealing with a document which was written round about the beginning of the Christian era.[77]

In chapter 11ff. of Recension A we have the description of a rather elaborate judgement-scene in heaven, witnessed by the patriarch. The first part of this consists of two ways leading to two different gates, along which souls were being driven. Outside the gate sat Adam, mourning the fact that so few souls were going through the gate which led to life and countless were being driven along the way which led to perdition:

> So Michael turned the chariot, and brought Abraham to the east, to the first gate of heaven. And Abraham saw two ways, the one narrow and compressed, and the other broad and spacious; and there also he saw two gates, one gate broad on the broad way, and one gate narrow on the narrow way. And outside the two gates there I saw a man seated upon a golden throne, and the appearance of that man was terrible like unto that of the Lord. And I saw many souls being driven by angels and led in through the broad gate; and other souls I saw, few in number, that were being borne by angels through the narrow gate.

Inside the broad gate there stood another throne, the centre of a heavenly tribunal, where the fate of the souls of men was decided, and particularly those whose righteous deeds were equally matched by the evil deeds they had committed during their lives. Before describing the process which arose from the peculiar problems presented by one particular soul the patriarch pauses to describe the glorious judge who presided over the tribunal:

> So we also followed the angels, and came within that broad gate, and in between the two gates stood a throne, dread in appearance, of dread crystal, flashining like unto fire, and and upon it sat a wondrous man, shining as the sun, like unto the Son of God. Before him stood a table like crystal, all of gold and fine linen. And upon the table was lying a book, the thickness thereof six cubits, and the breadth thereof ten cubits, and on the right hand thereof and on the left stood two angels, holding paper, and ink, and pen.

The picture of the throne and its occupant bears some resemblance to other Jewish theophanies, but the major difference about this judgement-scene is that it is not God who sits on the throne but the righteous Abel.

In most respects the form of this work resembles other apocalypses. There is the description of the heavenly journey in a heavenly chariot.[78] But on entering the heavenly world Abraham is confronted by the throne of Abel and not the throne of God. This difference should not disguise the fact that there are certain similarities between this throne-scene and other theophanies. The description of the throne of Abel ('of dread crystal') resembles the description of God's throne in 1 Enoch 14.18 ('I saw a lofty throne and its appearance was as crystal'). The fact that the heavenly man is said to be shining like the sun has some affinities with 1 Enoch 14.20 (cf. Rev. 1.16), where the garment of God is compared to the light of the sun. The book of judgement can be compared with judgement-scenes like Daniel 7.10f. and Revelation 20.12. We have also the transference (albeit temporary in Rec. A.) of the right to judge, and the picture emerges of a theophanic scene which does not mention God. Instead of God Abel, the son of the first man, is the one who sits on the throne like God's throne exercising judgement over the souls of men.[79] Thus we appear to have an essentially Jewish scene,[80] which draws upon imagery usually connected with the throne of God, but here linked with Abel to avoid the need to describe the 'invisible God' (Rec. A 16).

It would appear that the throne of God has been separated from God himself and linked with Abel, just as in the Similitudes it is the Son of Man/Elect One who sits on the throne of glory. This seems to be confirmed by the fact that there appears to be a clear distinction in the heavenly hierarchy between Abel and the other angels, exactly what one would expect if Abel has been identified with the figure on God's throne. It is true that similar adjectives are used to describe Adam and Michael as well as Abel. But despite this Abel alone is the judge and he alone is said to be 'like a son of God'.

Thus the theophany, familiar to us from other Jewish texts, and the judgement-scene in both apocalypses have been linked with another figure; God is no longer directly connected with the throne. Added confirmation that this was a development which was taking place in Jewish theology is provided by the extremely fragmentary Melchizedek document from Cave 11 at Qumran.[81] In similar vein to the Testament of Abraham and the Similitudes this document describes the way in which Melchizedek acts as judge in the heavenly court. What is most interesting about this fragment is the fact that Psalm 82.1 is applied to Melchizedek, thus portraying him as the divine being who sits in judgement over the heavenly court. Though the text as a whole is rather fragmentary, the section which most concerns us is relatively straightforward:

> For this is the moment of the year of grace for Melchizedek. And he will, by his strength, judge the holy ones of God, executing judgement, as it is written concerning him in the songs of David, who said, ELOHIM has taken his place in the divine council; in the midst of the gods he holds judgement. And it was concerning him that he said, (Let the assembly of the peoples) return to the height above them; El will judge the peoples. As for that which he said (how long will you) judge unjustly and show partiality to the wicked? Selah, its interpretation concerns Satan and the spirits of his lot (who) rebelled by turning away from the precepts of God . . . And Melchizedek will avenge the vengeance of the judgement of God . . .[82]

Not only is Melchizedek seen as the divine judge, but a citation from Scripture originally referring to God has now been applied to the enigmatic figure of Melchizedek, who, like Enoch, makes a brief but suggestive appearance in Scripture in Genesis 14.[83] In this passage Melchizedek is thought of as the *Elohim* who sits in judgement over other angelic beings. While no reference is made to the throne of glory, the implication is that Melchizedek both sits on God's throne and exercises the divine right of judgement. As in the Testament of Abraham and the Similitudes descriptions of God as judge enthroned in glory are here transferred to a human figure, who, like Enoch (Gen. 5.24) and Abel (cf. Heb. 11.4), was renowned for his righteousness (cf. Heb. 7.2).[84]

Finally, mention must be made of the much later example of

the Enoch-tradition, so called Hebrew Enoch. Here the metamorphosis of Enoch into the angel Metatron is described,
together with his coronation in the heavenly court. It offers us
the final development of the tradition about Enoch's exaltation
with a description of his apotheosis, which, while it is not
unique in Jewish literature, certainly exhibits several unusual
features. Enoch/Metatron is bestowed with divine honour and
glory. He is given the position of vice-regent in the heavenly
realm and even the name of God himself, so that he is known as
the 'lesser YHWH' (Heb. Enoch 12.5). The following quotation
from Hebrew Enoch 10 enables one to see how extraordinary are
the qualities which are bestowed upon this angel:

> R. Ishmael said: Metatron, the Prince of the Presence, said to me: All
> these things, the Holy One, blessed be he, made for me: He made
> me a Throne, similar to the Throne of glory. And he spread over me
> a curtain of splendour and brilliant appearance, of beauty, grace,
> and mercy, similar to the curtain of the Throne of glory; and on it
> were fixed all kinds of lights in the universe. And he placed it at the
> door of the seventh hall and seated me on it. And the herald went
> forth into every heaven, saying: This is Metatron, my servant. I have
> made him into a prince and a ruler over all the princes of my
> kingdoms and over all the children of heaven . . .

There can be little doubt that the work as we have it is post-
Christian, and probably comes from a period as much as four or
five hundred years after the life of Jesus.[85] Inevitably, the question of Christian or even gnostic influence arises in the picture of
Metatron found here.[86] Certainly some influence from both these
movements cannot be ruled out at this period, but the significant
thing about Hebrew Enoch is that it merely reinforces ideas
which were already present in Judaism before the Christian era.
It would, therefore, be a mistake to suppose that theological
developments of the kind found in Hebrew Enoch mark a stage
when Judaism needed to react to excessive claims by gnostics
and Christians. The exalted language about Enoch may well
have offered convenient polemic against Christians, but the
point is that the raw material for such ideas already existed
within Judaism and was not specifically coined to meet the
threat of Christian affirmations about Jesus.

Hebrew Enoch resembles the Similitudes in their final form in
stressing that an exalted man of antiquity exercises divine pre-

rogatives and sits on a throne like God's throne. Unlike the Similitudes, however, it is not a question here of a figure taking over the throne of God himself. The heavenly scene in this work clearly presupposes that Metatron only has a throne which *resembles* the throne of God and which is situated outside the seventh heavenly hall. But the end result is the same in both cases. Metatron is the figure who commands attention, and to whom God has given the right to exercise jurisdiction over the heavenly potentates. Indeed, so similar is Metatron to God and so alike the trappings of his authority and power, that one is left with the impression that we have a figure here who is so like God that he virtually acts as the very embodiment of divinity. Metatron's position at the door of the seventh heavenly hall makes him the focal point in heaven rather than God. God may be enthroned in glory within the inner sanctum of heaven, but it is Metatron who exercises the divine power and is visible as king over the heavenly world. What is more, apart from the brief reference to R. Ishmael seeing the right hand of God tied behind his back awaiting the deliverance of Israel (chapter 48), no mention is made in this work of a theophany. One is left with the impression that, despite the presence of the invisible God within the sanctum of heaven, throned in glory, the character of God's majesty is made manifest through the portrayal of the enthroned Metatron, whose garb and character closely correspond to the characteristic features of God himself.

This survey of various apocalyptic passages suggests that Jewish religion had produced a belief in an exalted angel, which owed much to the developments of the throne-theophany already inherent in the book of Ezekiel itself. Whether we can yet speak of this angel being a second power in the heavenly world must be doubted.[87] In all the passages which we have been examining there seems to be no doubt at all that the power and authority of the second figure derive entirely from the God of Israel. It is God's throne on which the heavenly Son of Man sits and the name of God which indwells the angels Jaoel and Metatron. Even in Hebrew Enoch, where the language is more extreme than elsewhere, a firm grip is kept on the fact that the origin of the angel's power is God himself. But having said all this, it is difficult to resist the impression that beliefs like this were susceptible of complete misunderstanding. Once a religion had notions like this as part of the fabric of its belief, it is not difficult to see how circumstances could so affect those beliefs that the monotheistic thread, which runs through the whole of this angelic doctrine, could rapidly disintegrate, leaving either the danger of a dualistic theology or the need to show how the disparate parts of this theological system could be made to relate to each other. This aspect of apocalyptic theology is one that has great significance for our understanding of Jewish theology as a whole at this critical period in the history of religious ideas. Not only did the first century see the need for Judaism to reinterpret its past in the light of catastrophic historical events, but it also had to understand its own position over against that of its offspring, the early Christian movement.

This is an area in which developments such as those which we have noted in the previous pages may be relevant for understanding early Christian thought. The fact that we have drawn upon one passage from an early Christian apocalypse indicates that at least one writer drew upon this angelological tradition in the formation of his Christology. It is obvious that early Christians drew extensively on a vast range of contemporary Jewish ideas to express their convictions about Jesus of Nazareth. While it is true that they may have adapted some of the Jewish doctrines to fit their distinctive appreciation of the character of Jesus, it is usually quite possible to trace the origins of many of the notions which form the basis of early Christian christological doctrine. A glance at any recent contribution to New Testament Christology will reveal the extent of the debt which modern scholarship believes that Christianity owed to its Jewish heritage. What most modern discussions of early Christology fail to include, however, is discussion of the extent of the influence of angel-christology on primitive Christian doctrine. It is not just a question here of the rejection of angel-christology as an important factor in christological development; there is an almost total lack of any discussion of the topic at all.[88]

Evidence from the letter to the Hebrews indicates that in the community addressed some were having difficulty separating Christ from other angelic beings.[89] The opening chapters of the letter give evidence of the author's attempt to show his readers the distinctive position of Christ in relationship to other angelic beings. This is not the place to go into the detailed exegesis of this letter. Suffice it to say here, however, that the developments in angelology which we have noted earlier would have made it difficult for early Christians to differentiate precisely between Jesus and other prominent members of the heavenly hierarchy. That is not to say that such ideas were a positive hindrance to early doctrinal reflections. The notion about the apotheosis of a righteous individual offered an idea which would enable Christians to express their convictions about the exaltation of Jesus. What is more, we find the author of the letter to the Hebrews borrowing at least one notion from Jewish angelology to explicate his Christology. In the opening verses of the letter, after making the point about the decisive revelation of God in the Son (Heb 1.1f.), the writer speaks about the exaltation of Jesus. Of central importance for him is the fact that this exaltation comes as a direct result of the sacrificial death of Jesus (Heb. 1.3, cf. 9.11ff.). But the decisive point of separation from other angelic beings is the fact that Christ has inherited 'a more excellent name than theirs' (Heb. 1.4). This is probably a reference to the name of God which the exalted Jesus has been given at his exaltation (cf. Phil. 2.11).[90] The possession of the divine name, not to mention sitting alongside God, is the privilege of other prominent heavenly figures also. It would appear that in his quest to demonstrate the superiority of Jesus the author of Hebrews is drawing on precisely those angelic traditions which have begun to give a position of importance to one angelic being. This hint, if nothing else, suggests that Jewish angelology and angel-christology, is still a field which requires further consideration, in order that a complete elucidation of the complex development of early Christian beliefs can be fully understood.

Man and the World Above:
the Community and the Glory of Heaven in the Qumran Scrolls

The very essence of apocalyptic is the privilege granted to an individual to have direct contact with the heavenly world and its secrets. In the apocalyptic literature this takes the form either of direct appreciation of the heavenly secrets after a journey to the presence of God in heaven or disclosure of them by an angel. Temporarily the apocalyptic seer enjoyed the lot of the angels and witnessed the glory which was to come, though, as we have argued, the latter theme does not in any way exhaust the content of the apocalypses.[91] Although the apocalyptic seer usually acts as a witness of events and secrets in heaven, there are occasional pieces of evidence that the apocalypticist believed that the glory of heaven was his to share temporarily. In the Apocalypse of Abraham, for example, the patriarch's ascent to the world above is marked by his participation in the song of the angels which Jaoel teaches him (chapter 17). Abraham is not merely a spectator of the heavenly paean of praise, unlike John of Patmos, who according to Revelation 4 stands on the periphery of the heavenly liturgy and does not himself participate in it.

In a rather different way the ascent of Enoch, according to Slavonic Enoch, brought about a change in the character of the exalted man of primaeval times. In chapter 22.8ff. we are told that Enoch was transformed:

> And the Lord said to Michael: Go and take Enoch from out his earthly garments, and anoint him with my sweet ointment, and put him into garments of my glory. And Michael did thus, as the Lord told him. He anointed me, and dressed me, and the appearance of that ointment is more than the great light, and his ointment is like the sweet dew, and its smell mild, shining like the sun's ray, and I looked at myself, and was like one of his glorious ones.

His glorious appearance cannot be left as it is when Enoch returns to his children, and so it has to be transformed for a time in order that his children may be able to look upon his face (Slav. Enoch 37.2). Although it is not stated in so many words in Slavonic Enoch, we are probably right to assume that Enoch here receives the garments of glory which are laid up for the righteous in heaven and which they will receive only in the new age (cf. 1 Enoch 62.15 and 2 Cor. 5.1f.). Similarly Isaiah's departure from the world of men to the highest heaven means leaving behind the body of flesh (Asc. Is. 7.5) and becoming like an angel (9.30 cf. Mark 12.35). It would appear from Ascension of Isaiah 11.35 that Isaiah has been temporarily given those garments reserved for the last days to enable him to ascend into the presence of the most holy God (cf. Asc. Is. 9.2). His return to earth means putting aside the garment of glory until he receives it again at death.

The significance of such participation in glory, such as we find it in several of the apocalypses, has been obscured somewhat by the pseudepigraphic form of the writings. The attribution of such experience to men of the past appears to indicate an unwillingness on the part of the anonymous apocalypticist to allow the possibility that knowledge of such glory could be appreciated in the present. The question thus arises whether the pseudepigraphic apocalypses give evidence of nothing more than a literary device or whether the apocalypticists themselves believed that communion with the heavenly world was not only a phenomenon of Israel's past experience but also a possibility in the present. This is a topic to which we shall have to turn our attention later. Suffice it to say for the present, that the evidence would suggest that we cannot exclude the possibility that in the apocalypses we possess the actual experience of the heavenly world and its inhabitants in the present. It would, for example, be a mistake to suppose that the glimpse of the heavenly world and its worship, which we find in the New Testament apocalypse, is a unique expression within first century Jewish and Christian religion of the belief that the knowledge of the world above was a possibility for the contemporary generation as well as for those of the distant past. There can be no doubt that different factors were operating within the early Christian movement, which made the device of pseudonymity unnecessary, but it is difficult to believe that the experience of John of Patmos differed in any marked way from earlier or contemporary apocalyptic visionaries. That such convictions did exist within contemporary religion can be demonstrated by a consideration of certain passages from the Qumran scrolls.

Knowledge of the divine secrets formed an important part of the doctrinal convictions of the Qumran sect.[92] But the means whereby these secrets were ascertained were certainly not confined to apocalyptic revelations. Indeed, the understanding of Scripture itself was intimately bound up with the unfolding of the divine mysteries.[93] The community believed that it was to the Teacher of Righteousness that God had made known all the mysteries of the prophetic teaching (1QpHab 7.1ff.). The attempt to give divine authority to the interpretation of Scripture adopted by the sect is not an uncommon device in Judaism,[94] though it is clear that the degree of flexibility which is normally apparent in the diversity of rabbinic opinion is almost totally absent from the Qumran exegesis. Because the true meaning of the words of Scripture had been revealed to the Teacher of

Righteousness, there could be no question of offering a rival opinion. Nevertheless our main concern here is not with the community's belief that their hermeneutical activity was the process of uncovering the divine mysteries, which is still an indirect means of appropriating the divine counsels. Rather our interest centres on the convictions held by the community about their relationship with the heavenly world. The point is hinted at in the hymnic passage in 1QM 10.8ff.:

> O God of Israel, who is like thee in heaven or on earth? Who accomplished deeds and mighty works like thine? Who is like thy people Israel which thou hast chosen for thyself from all the peoples of the lands; the people of the saints of the covenant, instructed in the laws and learned in wisdom . . . who have heard the voice of majesty and have seen the angels of holiness, whose ear has been unstopped and who have heard profound things.

Two facts emerge in this passage. Firstly, the community believes that it has been privileged to hear the voice of God himself. This need mean no more than that the community had ascertained the true meaning of Scripture through the inspired interpretation of it. But the second feature of this passage would seem to indicate that we have to do here with more than merely an indirect apprehension of the divine will: the reference to the community as those who have seen angels. The juxtaposition of hearing God's voice and seeing angels looks remarkably like the kind of visions of the heavenly world familiar to us from the apocalypses. H.-W. Kuhn has pointed out the significance of certain passages in the scrolls which appear to speak not only of a present experience of the world above but also of a proleptic participation in the glory of the future.[95] Since heaven is regarded as in some sense the repository of the glorious gifts of the new age, communion with the world above inevitably offers the opportunity of participating in the glory which is to come. Nevertheless in our examination of the central passages from the Qumran scrolls, which have a bearing on these ideas, our interest will centre only on sections where the community's relationship with the inhabitants of the world above is being discussed. Particularly important are 1QH 3.20ff., 11.13f. and 1QS 11.7f.

In 1QH 3.20f. the psalmist speaks in the following way about his experience, as a result of his participation in the life of the community:

Thou hast raised me up to the everlasting height. I walk on limitless level ground, and I know there is hope for him whom thou hast shaped from the dust for the everlasting council. Thou hast cleansed a perverse spirit of great sin that it may stand with the host of the holy ones , and that it may enter into community with the congregation of the sons of heaven.

Whereas hitherto the psalmist was destined to death, he has now been raised to the heights and participates with the holy ones. Most commentators agree that life in the holy community meant a very close fellowship with heaven. The reference to the holy ones in this passage is a reference to angels.[96] The language used to express the basis of the psalmist's joy is quite remarkable. He speaks about being raised to the everlasting height. Kuhn has offered sufficient evidence to show that this is probably a synonym of heaven.[97] Here then the language such as we have in apocalyptic literature about the rapture of the seer to heaven has been taken over and applied to the experience of the member of the holy community. Not only does the community have the privilege of angelic beings sharing their life in the present as well as the future (1QM 12.8ff.), but also the members are able to take their stand with the angelic host in the very presence of God himself. Such a belief is reflected in the use of a stereotyped expression ('to stand before') to refer to the privilege of standing in the divine presence.[98]

In a similar vein 1QH 11.10ff. stresses that purification by God enables the members of the community to enjoy the lot of the angels:

> For the sake of thy glory thou hast purified man of sin,that he may be made holy for thee, with no abominable uncleanness and no guilty wickedness: that he may be one with the children of thy truth and partake of the lot of thy holy ones; that bodies gnawed by worms may be raised from the dust to the counsel (of thy truth) and that the perverse spirit may be lifted to the understanding which comes from thee: that he may stand before thee with the everlasting host and with thy spirits of holiness.

Leaving aside the question whether this passage presupposes some kind of belief in immortality[99] there seems to be little doubt that once again entry into the community is regarded as a participation in the glory of the heavenly realm. Unlike the previous passage nothing explicitly is stated about the exaltation of the members of the community to participate in the heavenly company, though there is a close link between the purification of the initiate and the resulting experience of heavenly bliss.

In rather different language, though once again in hymnic style, the writer of the Manual of Discipline betrays his conviction that life in the Qumran community was closely linked with the glory of the heavenly world (1QS 11.6ff.):

> My eyes have gazed on that which is eternal, on wisdom concealed from men, on knowledge and wise design (hidden) from the sons of men; on a fountain of righteousness and on a storehouse of power, on a spring of glory (hidden) from the assembly of flesh. God has given them to his chosen ones as an everlasting possession and has caused them to inherit the lot of the holy ones. He has joined their assembly to the sons of heaven, to be a council of the community, a foundation of the building of holiness, an eternal plantation throughout all ages to come.

Participation with the glory of the angels is presupposed in this passage as in the passages from the Hodayoth.[100] But the evidence of this passage suggests that the life of the elect community was an extension of the heavenly world. God has, as it were, extended the boundaries of heaven to include this haven of holiness.[101] This passage tends to shed a rather different light on the hint which we had in 1QH 3.20 that entry into the community involved a heavenly ascent. What appears to have been the case is that language more appropriate to the apocalyptic ascent has been taken over to describe the character of life in the community. The man who enters the community can be said to have been taken on high precisely because the quality of life in the world above is extended to include the community. This was no temporary exaltation such as we find in the apocalypses, for the knowledge of the heavenly world and fellowship with its inhabitants is the abiding characteristic of life in this esoteric community.

One may speculate about the origins of this language, but the clear indications from the Qumran scrolls about the priestly influence on the ideas of the community makes cultic influence an important element in the explanation for the extravagant claims made by the writers of these documents.[102] Of course, the Temple was the place of God's particular manifestation of his presence in the world, and in that sense the place where heaven and earth coincided. The separation of the Qumran community from the activities of the Temple in their own day makes it easy to see why they should have seen their own communal life as the place of the coming together of things earthly and heavenly. Although they were apart from the physical Temple, they believed that the quality of life lived by them qualified their community to be at least on the same level as the Temple in Jerusalem. They were the true remnant who preserved the ways of God and it was entirely appropriate for them to transfer to their common life ideas connected with the rites and theology of the cult. Elsewhere in the Manual of Discipline we find the community interpreting its life in sacrificial terms (1QS 8.5ff. and 11.8).[103] Thus, not only was the obedience of the members of the community interpreted in sacrificial terms, but also their gathering was itself the place where the heavenly realm came into closest contact with the world of men.

Nevertheless it would be a mistake to see here a point of view which has little or no connection with apocalyptic. As we have already seen, there is some evidence to suggest that in apocalyptic the seer was not merely a spectator of the heavenly glory but also participated in it, albeit temporarily, and on occasion even had a foretaste of the glory of the future. While the extent to which heavenly bliss was enjoyed by the Qumran sectarians goes beyond anything we know from Jewish apocalyptic, what we have in the apocalypses is essentially the same type of religion as is evident in these passages from the Qumran scrolls.[104] No doubt the scrolls have a much more sophisticated view of their relationship with heaven, but implicit within apocalyptic literature is the view that for a limited amount of time certain individuals also could be transported from the world of men to share in the lot of the angels and witness the activities of the angels who surrounded God. Only by orientating apocalyptic solely towards the future can such a sharp distinction be made between the scrolls and apocalyptic. If anything, we have a coming together in these passages of priestly and apocalyptic ideas, which may themselves be related,[105] in order to express the distinctive belief of the community about the relationship to God. One need not look any further than the hymns themselves for evidence of the fact that apocalyptic and priestly ideas have come together. The 'vertical' relationship with the heavenly world which is enunciated by certain parts of the apocalyptic tradition is here linked with distinctively priestly ideas about the present relationship with God which is enjoyed in the cult.

Knowledge of the world above as it already exists in the present has been taken up and made into a characteristic of the life of the community, whose holiness means that the temporary privilege of the apocalyptic seer has now become a permanent feature of the corporate life of the group.[106]

Astronomy

Discussion of the interest in the world above in the apocalypses would not be complete without reference to the small, but none the less significant, part which revelations about the details of the movements of the heavenly bodies play in the Enochic literature. We would expect the encyclopaedic concerns of the apocalypticists to include an interest in the movements of the stars, and particularly the sun and the moon. Thus it comes as no surprise that a long section is devoted to the subject in 1 Enoch 72—75 and 78—79[107] and much smaller sections in Slavonic Enoch 16 and 1 Enoch 41, 43. Such a close identification of astronomical material with Enoch is not surprising in the light of the reference to his interest in this subject in Jubilees 4.17, not to mention the fact that the length of his life corresponds with the number of days in the year (Gen. 5.23).[108] An interest in the movements of sun and moon which we find in the Enochic apocalypses is not merely the result of an interest in all things connected with the universe. Precise computation concerning their movements was vitally important for the construction of the Jewish calendar. In Judaism the exact calculation of the dates of the various festivals was a matter central to religion.[109] Nowhere is this more evident than in Jubilees 6.32ff., a work which as a whole sets out to link the observance of various festivals with the patriarchal age:

> And command thou the children of Israel that they observe the years according to this reckoning – three hundred and sixty four days, and these will constitute a complete year, and they will not disturb its time from its days and from its feasts; for everything will fall out in them according to their testimony, and they will not leave out any day nor disturb any feasts. But if they do not neglect and do not observe them according to his commandment, then they will disturb all their seasons, and the years will be dislodged from this order . . . and they will neglect their ordinances. And all the children of Israel will forget, and will not find the path of the years,

and will forget the new moons and the seasons, and sabbaths and will go wrong as to all the order of years. For I know and henceforth will I declare it unto thee, and it is not of my devising; for the book lies written before me, and on the heavenly tablets the division of days is ordained . . . For there will be those who will assuredly make observations of the moon – how it disturbs the seasons and comes in from year to year ten days too soon. For this reason the days will come upon them when they will disturb the order . . . and they will confound all the days, the holy with the unclean.

Here a calendar is presupposed, observed by the patriarchs (Jub. 45.16) and revealed to Moses by the angel of the presence, which has only 364 days in the year. If anyone used this calendar, it would enable him to observe the festival on the same day of the week every year. The official Jewish calendar which passed on into rabbinic Judaism is based on twelve lunar months of twenty-nine or thirty days forming a year of three hundred and fifty-four days. The gap between the lunar and the solar year is rectified by the insertion of an intercalated month every three years. These different methods of computation are reflected in the quotation from Jubilees, which inveighs against those who would pay more attention to the phases of the moon and base their calendar on the moon rather than the sun. With two such different methods of computation it is hardly surprising that there was profound disagreement over this issue within Judaism.[110]

The invective of Jubilees finds an echo in the astronomical section of 1 Enoch (82.4), where the righteous are specifically linked with those who espouse the solar calendar rather than a different calendar. The truth of the former point of view is vouchsafed by placing the detailed computations concerning the phases of sun and moon within the framework of an apocalypse. Moses in Jubilees reveals that the secrets of the calendar are not the result of his own devising but the disclosures of that which has been written on the heavenly tablets. In other words, this is no mere opinion but the regulations for the seasons laid down in heaven (cf. 1 Enoch 82.3). The point is made even more strongly in Jubilees, for it is stated that God keeps the sabbath in heaven with his angels (Jub. 2.17f.). It is, therefore, imperative that Israel should observe the sabbath and other festivals at the same time as they are observed in heaven, and that there should be no discrepancy between earthly and heavenly observances.

The life of the people of God is thus expected to reflect the pattern of existence in the world above. For this reason, any different approach to the calendar from that which was set out in heaven meant that there would be a complete breakdown in the relationship between the world above and the people of God on earth. Mistaken notions about the organization of the calendar may seem fairly insignificant in themselves, but when they are seen as a transgression against the divine order, it means that the whole of the people are led astray, In the light of the importance which was attached to the observance of festivals throughout the year in Judaism, a calendrical irregularity was believed to bring about the complete upheaval of the obedience of Israel to God.

What is most important in examining the views on the calendar in the apocalypses is the fact that the solar calendar favoured in these documents is given weight and authority by virtue of its context within an apocalypse. The complexities and the detail of this astronomical material are testimony itself to the seriousness with which this issue was approached by the apocalypticists. For them the crowning argument for their particular approach to the calendar was the fact that this was the one which corresponded to the divine plan for the universe. Consequently revelation demanded that this is the only proper option open to the people of God in the process of working out the dates of festivals and sabbaths. Herein we have one of the few occurrences in the apocalypses where the apocalyptic framework is used to justify a particular point of view in the face of contrary opinion from fellow Jews. Needless to say, such a technique was not without its dangers. All too easily the validity of claims to divine revelation came under suspicion, especially in the face of the impossible task of separating out the authentic from the spurious. One of the interesting things about the astronomical material is the obvious feeling that the apocalyptic framework justifies a point of view which would otherwise be looked on with some suspicion by the majority. It is a technique to which this type of religion could, and did all too easily, succumb, and it inevitably provoked a reaction from the majority against those who made audacious claims that their position had the backing of heaven itself.[111]

Our consideration of the visions of the heavenly world in the apocalypses indicates that we are faced with material which is in no way stereotyped and shows some variety in its different elements and certain significant theological developments. Similar elements tend to turn up in several of the apocalypses; but there is nothing here to suggest anything other than the common background in the Jewish scriptures. The space and attention devoted to the various inhabitants of the heavenly world point to a more than passing interest in the apocalypses in the nature of heaven. This material is not merely a necessary prelude to the eschatological disclosures but is of interest to the seer in its own right. However much the apocalyptic pronouncements about the movements of sun and moon may look like special pleading to the modern reader, there is clearly a sense in which what heaven itself decreed was of vital importance to the apocalypticist on all matters. Even if the information in the heavenly tablets did happen to agree with the opinion of the apocalypticist, the need to justify that particular opinion by reference to divine revelation gives evidence of an outlook which was not in any way directed solely towards the future. If anything, it is a sign that the apocalypticists directed their attention to the world above as a means of justifying actions and attitudes in the present. Knowledge of the fact that their views corresponded with the divine order was one means of continuing to support a particular line in the face of adverse reaction from opponents. To know what is above, and particularly the God who was enthroned above, was a desire of every Jew, but when this knowledge also served to support the way of life lived in the present, interest in the heavenly world can be seen to be an important component of the apocalyptic outlook.

CHAPTER 5

What is Below:
Man and his World

Enoch's Journeys through the Universe

WE SAW IN the previous section that 1 Enoch offers us an example of detailed interest in the dispositions of the heavenly bodies. In the same apocalypse we find also space devoted to the journeys of Enoch through parts of the world of men.

After Enoch has been up to heaven and received God's refusal to accept his attempt to mediate on behalf of the Watchers (1 Enoch 14–16), he embarks on a journey which takes him to various parts of the world (ch. 17–36) and the underworld (ch. 22). There is little attempt to offer any precise geographical locations. Jerusalem and its environs are referred to in chapter 26f., but apart from this passage the material included in the account is there for religious reasons. Enoch is shown the place of imprisonment of the fallen angels (1 Enoch 21.10) as well as the location of Paradise, which in this early literature is still located on earth (1 Enoch 25.1ff., 32.3, cf. Jub. 4.23). The absence of references to familiar places in the world is probably to be explained by the fact that Enoch is being shown those parts of the universe which are unknown to men. With the exception of Jerusalem, the character of the abode of the dead (1 Enoch 22), the origin of the winds (1 Enoch 18.3) and the ends of heaven and earth (18.12ff.), not to mention Paradise, are all locations about which normal perception of the universe would not be able to give any information. In other words, in this section we are still aware of the apocalyptic outlook. That which is beyond man's ability to investigate for himself is here revealed to the wandering Enoch, who has the archangels for his guides (e.g. 1 Enoch 19.1ff.).

After the description of Jerusalem the opportunity is taken to expand on the legend of Gehenna (ch. 27).[1] The valley of

Hinnom was a place with foul associations in the Old Testament (e.g. 2 Kings 23.10) and by the time of 1 Enoch was regarded as a place of punishment and torment. The notorious reputation which the valley had in Jewish folklore is echoed here and the role which it would play in the future emphasized. The eschatological significance of other sites visited by Enoch is also pointed out. For example, when he visits a lofty mountain (ch. 24f.) he is told that this is the mountain upon which God will descend in the future (1 Enoch 25.3). It is not easy to decide exactly which mountain the writer has in mind, though its location in the north-west may give us reason for supposing that the traditions known to us from the Bible about God's dwelling on a mountain in the north (cf. Ps. 48.2) may have contributed to the location of this site for God's future manifestation of himself.[2]

If this passage deals mainly with places in the world which men would long to have more information about, the same is not true of the whole of the geographical section in 1 Enoch 76—77. Although material similar to that found in the earlier chapters of 1 Enoch is taken up again, particularly the origins of the winds and the different climatic conditions, chapter 77.4ff. gives evidence of a more precise geographical knowledge:

> I saw seven high mountains, higher than all the mountains which are on earth: and thence comes forth hoar-frost, and days, seasons, and years pass away. I saw seven rivers on the earth larger than all the rivers; one of them coming from the west pours its waters into the Great Sea. And these two come from the north to the sea and pour their waters into the Erythraean Sea in the east. And the remaining four come forth on the side of the north to their own sea, (two of them to) the Erythraean Sea, and two into the Great Sea and discharge themselves there . . . Seven great islands I saw in the sea and in the mainland: two in the mainland and five in the Great Sea.

Milik has suggested that the material in this section, though rather scanty, is an attempt to embark upon a real rather than a mythological geography.[3] Though no names are given to the seven mountains, their location in the north could be a reference to the Caucasus range in northern Turkey. Of the rivers the Nile is the river which 'pours its water into the Great Sea', (1 Enoch 77.5). The two rivers which come from the north and flow into the Erythraean Sea are the Tigris and the Euphrates. The knowledge of geography is rather general, to say the least, but this small section does indicate that apocalyptic literature did have an interest in the world as it was, even if it was merely the repetition of conventional wisdom on the subject and not the result of the individual's observation of it.

Quite incidentally, a more complicated geographical picture is to be found in Jubilees 8.12ff. In this chapter there is described the dividing of the earth after the flood among Noah's sons. Although once again the interest centres on those lands which border Palestine, there does appear to be reference to Asia Minor (v. 27), and in verse 12 knowledge of the countries on the northern side of the Black Sea and the Caspian Sea. Nevertheless this section is rather different from the verses in 1 Enoch 77.4ff., which we have already examined. There is no question here of the geographical information being part of the disclosures about the universe which are given to the apocalyptic seer. The geography comes in quite incidentally as part of the story of the aftermath of the Flood. The fact that such an interest only emerges in one apocalypse should be indication enough that we are not dealing here with a subject which loomed large on the horizon of the apocalypticists. But the very fact that we do have passages, which attempt to give a comprehensive picture of the world as it is, demonstrates the potentially numerous and varied interests of the apocalypticists. It should also make us wary of assuming that apocalyptic was always tied to particular historical circumstances in which the people of God faced a crisis of faith. The interest in the world as it is speaks more of reflection and the quest for knowledge than the urgent expectation of the end of the world, where such interests would be superfluous.

The Lot of Man

It is well known that Jewish apocalyptic was concerned with the fate of mankind in the future, and particularly the destiny of the people of God. There is, however, a related issue which makes its appearance in the apocalypses, namely the lot of man in the present and the reasons which have led to his present, unhappy state. These issues emerge particularly in three documents which are usually dated towards the end of the first century AD, the Apocalypse of Abraham, 4 Ezra and Syriac Baruch, though there are occasional signs of its presence in other apocalypses.

For example, in the passage dealing with creation in Slavonic Enoch 30.13ff. there are indications that some attempt is being made to justify God's judgement on Adam by stressing a doctrine of free will. The concern with man's lot has some affinities with the meditations of part of the Wisdom-tradition.[4] Of central importance for this, of course, is the book of Job, which explores the reasons for innocent suffering and examines critically the traditional explanations for it. It is the problem of suffering which particularly dominates the opening dialogues between Ezra and the angel Uriel in 4 Ezra, though here it forms part of a very profound exploration of the character of human nature and the consequences of it for human existence. It is this concern as it manifests itself in these three apocalypses which will occupy our attention in this section.

In Apocalypse of Abraham 20, the apocalypse's version of the promise to Abraham, we have the setting for the debate about the reasons for human sinfulness and the oppression of Israel. In his promise to Abraham, God predicts that Abraham's seed will be 'set apart for me in my heritage with Azazel', implying that God in the present shares power over the world with the forces of darkness. This divine statement naturally horrifies Abraham, who is compelled to ask God how he can be yoked together with one who has been such a vehement opponent in the past of Abraham, the friend of God (cf. ch. 13). God's answer to Abraham's question is to show him a vision of the scene in the Garden of Eden and the fall of man. This event is then explained by God as the direct result of his desire to do evil and be under the power of the Evil One:

> And I said: O Eternal Mighty One, why hast thou given to such [Azazel] power to destroy the generation of men in their works upon earth?
> And he said to me: They who will [to do] evil – and how much I hated [it] in those who do it – over them I gave him power and to be beloved of them. (Apoc. Abr. 23.)

Abraham persists in his questioning, however, and asks why it is that God has allowed evil to be desired by men. The answer to this question is closely connected with the oppression of Israel by the nations of the world. Because God foresees this oppressive attitude, he permits man to desire evil, so that the nations can be punished for their deeds. Abraham is still unsatisfied with God's answer, however, and he puts a further question concerning the reason for his willingness to allow evil in the world. God's reply merely stresses his right to act in any way he pleases. Just as man is free, whether to serve God or bow down before idols, so also God is free to act as he thinks fit:

> Hear Abraham. As the counsel of thy father is in him, and as thy counsel is in thee, so also is the counsel of my will in me ready for the coming days, before thou hast knowledge of these, or canst see with thine eyes what is future in them.

Thus what appears to be unjustified in the patriarch's eyes is merely a short-term view, which ignores the eschatological perspective with which God views history. It is only when Abraham sees the glorious future unfolding in his vision that he will be able to see the rectitude of the divine counsels. In the opinion of the apocalypticist the judgement of the heathen nations who oppress Israel and the vindication of the elect could not have taken place without God allowing the possibility of evil to dominate man.

The concern with man and his destiny is even more pressing in 4 Ezra 3.4ff.[5] Ezra recites the terrible lot of mankind, afflicted as he is by 'the evil germ' (4 Ezra 3.22), which so hinders his proper service of God. But what particularly concerns the seer is the lot of Israel. The deeds of the people of God appear to be no worse than the inhabitants of a city like Babylon which has triumphed over them (4 Ezra 3.28, cf. 5.23ff.; 6.38–59). The angelic messenger explains to Ezra that the ways of God are inscrutable (4 Ezra 4.11, cf. 4.21; 5.34ff.). Nevertheless the bitter experience of Israel causes the seer to lament once again the lot of Israel. The answer is yet again an eschatological one. The present age is hastening fast towards its end (4 Ezra 4.26), and it is, therefore, up to Ezra and others like him to make sure that they survive until the end when the perplexities of the present will vanish away. The present holds out the opportunity to make sure of one's final destiny, for the constraints upon the righteous in the present are merely a temporary phenomenon, which have to be endured in order to achieve the glory which is to come. The point is made in this following extract from the beginning of chapter 7:

> There is a builded city which lies on level ground, and it is full of good things; but its entrance is narrow . . . having fire on the right

hand and deep water on the left; and there is only one path lying between them both, that is between the fire and the water, (and so small) is this path, that it can contain only one man's footstep at once.[6] If, now, this city be given to a man for an inheritance, unless the heir pass through the danger set before him, how shall he receive the inheritance? . . . Even so also is Israel's portion; for it was for their sakes I made the world; but when Adam transgressed my statutes, then that which had been made was judged, and then the ways of the world become narrow and sorrowful and painful, and full of perils coupled with great toils. But the ways of the future world are broad and safe, and yield the fruit of immortality. If then, the living shall not have assuredly entered into these narrow and vain things, they will not be able to receive what has been reserved for them.

After having been given a description of the new age (4 Ezra 7.26–44) Ezra laments the fact that by his very nature man is prone to sinfulness, and therefore the number of those who can reach the new age is going to be few (4 Ezra 7.47f.). Once again the answer of the angel is very uncompromising, and Ezra is forced to see that there can be no possibility of salvation for those who do not deserve it. This provokes the seer to lament man's lot and compare it with that of the animals, but the superiority of man is pointed out and his capacity to follow the ways of God (4 Ezra 7.72). He has the advantage over the animals of understanding and being able to obey the Law of God, yet this is what he has consistently refused to do. Therefore, he has to pay the penalty for the abuse of his freedom. The obligation upon each individual to seek after God and follow his ways means that there can be no shirking the necessity for moral endeavour on the part of the individual. No man is able to rest on his special status, even as part of the covenant people, nor to avail himself of the divine promises unless the character of his life justifies the fulfilment of these promises in his case.

This issue is dealt with in the section concerning imputed righteousness: is it possible for the prayers of the righteous to have benefit for the ungodly (4 Ezra 7.102ff.)? The doctrine of merits was one which was firmly rooted in Jewish thought[7] and looked to the steadfastness of God's promises to his people as the basis of their ultimate redemption. Intercession of the righteous on behalf of the impious is something which occasionally appears in apocalyptic literature. For example, in the Testament of Abraham (Rec. A) 14 Michael and Abraham pray on behalf of the soul whose destiny is in doubt, and their intercession effects the salvation of that soul. The attitude taken in 4 Ezra is completely different; there can be no intercession on behalf of the impious. The salvation of the individual is based on the readiness of each to obey the commands of God.

With some justification Ezra then turns to the biggest problem of all: the fact that man's circumstances have been so much dictated by the results of Adam's sin (4 Ezra 7.118). He questions the value of the idea of eternal bliss to come when so many inhabitants of the earth will perish, who have done nothing to merit their inclusion in the new age. This in turn leads into a questioning of the traditional understanding of God's character (4 Ezra 7.132ff.). How can the merciful God allow so few to be saved and permit his own creature to be destroyed eternally (4 Ezra 8.4ff.)? Ezra's pleas are, however, in vain. In the end he finds himself rebuked for dwelling too much on the fate of sinners (4 Ezra 8.37ff.). Because he has shown himself to be righteous, he is promised a place in Paradise (4 Ezra 8.52). It is this promise which is offered as consolation for the righteous. They should concern themselves with making sure that the future bliss does not pass them by and not concern themselves too much with those whose evil deeds have made it impossible for them to achieve this goal. Ezra sees that the history of Israel does indicate that the position of God is in fact the correct one, as his final pronouncement before the visions indicates:

> But our fathers, who received the Law, observed it not, and the statutes they did not keep, and yet the fruit of the Law did not perish, nor could it – because it was thine; but they who received it perished, because they kept not that which was sown in them. Now it is a general rule, that when the ground has received seed, or the sea a ship, or any other vessel food or drink, and when it happens that what is sown, or what is launched, or the things that have been taken in come to an end – these come to an end, while the receptacles remain: but with us it has not been so. We who have received the Law and sinned must perish, together with our heart, which has taken it in: the Law, however, perishes not but abides in its glory. (4 Ezra 9.32ff.)

The bulk of this apocalypse consists of a dialogue between Ezra and the angel concerning the nature and destiny of man, but the final chapters of the work contain visionary material whose theme is essentially eschatological. Although at several places earlier in the dialogues mention has been made of the future (e.g. 4 Ezra 7.26ff.), the final visions offer reassurance that the way of righteousness will ultimately be vindicated.[8] The work may end on a note of hope and promise, but there is nothing in these final visions which reverses the pessimistic tone of the earlier part of the book. The promise of the new Jerusalem (4 Ezra 10.46ff.), the overthrow of pagan Rome (4 Ezra 11–12) and the coming of the messiah are all part of the apparatus of the eschatology of Judaism, but the hope is reserved for the righteous alone. There is no relaxation of the rigorous attitude taken by the angel in the dialogues. The great multitude which assembles on Mount Zion (4 Ezra 13.40ff.) is there, not because it happens to be the elect people but because it has kept the statutes of God.[9] The future glory is for the righteous alone, and no one who has acted impiously, whatever his religious affiliation, can escape the coming wrath.

The issues which are raised in the opening chapters of the apocalypse are precisely those which we would expect the Jewish people to ask after it had undergone the traumatic consequences of the spoliation of their religious inheritance in AD 70.[10] The reorganization of Judaism at Jamnia saw a reappraisal of attitudes towards those who did not accept the interpretation of the Scripture espoused by the dominant group in the academy. The need for more precise definition of what constituted the people of God appears to have been an important factor in the discussions which took place there.[11] Although thinking more in terms of those who would finally achieve salvation, the author of 4 Ezra is occupied with a similar question. That is not to say that the gloomy attitude prevalent in this apocalypse necessarily coincides with the view of the rabbinic authorities at Jamnia on this issue.[12] Rather we have manifested in 4 Ezra that kind of concern which was occupying the attention of Jews at this time and an attempt to move towards some kind of solution of the precise delineation of the identity of the religious community.

Similar questions come to the surface in the contemporary Syriac Baruch,[13] though there is rather less concern with man in general and more references to the special position of Israel (e.g. Syr. Baruch 3 and 14). Emphasis is placed here also on man's deliberate transgression of the Law as the reason for his damnation (Syr. Baruch 15.5f.), but the righteous deeds of man will be rewarded (14.7) in the age to come (15.7f.). As in The Wisdom of Solomon 2—4 the joys of the present age are rejected as a criterion of divine acceptance and reward:

> With the Most High account is not taken of much time nor of a few years. For what did it profit Adam that he lived nine hundred and thirty years, and transgressed that which he was commanded? Therefore the multitude of time that he lived did not profit him, but brought death and cut off the years of those who were born from him. Or wherein did Moses suffer loss in that he lived only one hundred and twenty years, and, inasmuch as he was subject to him who formed him, brought the law to the seed of Jacob and lighted a lamp for the nation of Israel. (Syr. Baruch 17.1ff.)

Like Ezra, Baruch sees that the consequences of Adam's sin are overwhelming in their effects on the human condition (Syr. Baruch 48.40–42; 56.6), but the terrible mistake of Adam is not allowed to excuse mankind in general whose existence has been a continuous repetition of the initial transgression:

> For though Adam first sinned and brought untimely death upon all, yet of those who were born from him each one has prepared for his own soul torment to come, and again each one of them has chosen for himself glories to come . . . Adam is therefore not the cause, save only of his own soul, but each of us has been the Adam of his soul. (Syr. Baruch 54.15 and 19)

Excessive interest in man's fate and his misdemeanours can detract from the real issues. It is the task of man to respond in the present to the challenge to accept either the way of life or death and not to be too concerned about apparent injustices or the difficulties of the present age, for the present must at all times be viewed in the light of God's future redemption:

> Now regarding everything that is, it is I that judge, but do not thou take counsel in thy soul regarding these things, nor afflict thyself because of those which have been. For now it is the consummation of time that should be considered . . . and not the beginning thereof. Because if a man be prospered in his beginnings and shamefully entreated in his old age, he forgets all the prosperity he had. And again, if a man is shamefully entreated in his beginnings, and at his end is prospered, he remembereth not again his evil entreatment. And again hearken: though each one were prospered all that time – all the time from the day on which death was decreed

against those who transgress – and in his end was destroyed, in vain would have been everything. (Syr. Baruch 19.4ff.)

It can be dangerous for the righteous to become so infatuated with the desperate situation in which they find themselves; they become so bound up with the misfortunes of the present, the apparent injustices of God and the terrible fate awaiting mankind, that they lose the historical perspective which would enable them to look forward to a time of bliss on the other side of the terrors of judgement which seem to dominate the horizon of the apocalypticist (Syr. Baruch 55.1ff.).

This attempt to enable the apocalypticist to see present circumstances within a much broader framework is seen particularly in chapter 20. The disaster of the destruction of Zion was in fact a blessing in disguise. For one thing the earthly city was not the one which was engraved on the divine palms (Syr. Baruch 4.2ff. cf. 4 Ezra 9.38ff.). The destruction of the city thus cleared the way for the establishment of the heavenly Zion. This point is made explicitly in this chapter, where the destruction of the city is shown to be a sure sign of the imminence of God's eschatological action:

> Therefore behold the days come, and the times shall hasten more than the former, and the seasons shall speed on more than those that are past, and the years shall pass more quickly than the present. Therefore have I now taken away Zion, that I may the more speedily visit the world in its season. (Syr. Baruch 20.1ff.)

The historical circumstances of the present are thus given meaning and significance by the divine pronouncement. Despair over the fulfilment of the divine promises is forced to give way to hope. The very event which has called the reality of God into question, and apparently made a mockery of the statements in Scripture concerning God's holy city and the promises for the future, is shown to be the turning point in historical process. The moment of greatest dereliction is, paradoxically, the moment when the flame of hope is rekindled.

The theological contribution which this material from 4 Ezra and Syriac Baruch makes to Jewish theology is considerable. Our interest in this material is not, however, as a reservoir of Jewish theology but as a way of seeing the kind of interests which dominated the consciousness of the apocalypticist. There can be no doubt that eschatology has its part to play in both works, but one cannot resist the impression that in both cases it functions as a kind of final justification of God in the face of insoluble problems presented by existence. The burning question in both apocalypses is not 'When will the end be?', but 'How can one make sense of the present and the promises of the past when history seems to contradict all that was originally sacrosanct?'. It is true that occasionally the curiosity about the future has to be satisfied, and the question about the resurrection-body in Syriac Baruch 49ff. indicates this. But the setting of both works and the dominant position given, particularly in 4 Ezra, to the discussion of human existence points to the major issues which are confronting the apocalypticists at the end of the first century AD, the decimation of Judaism and the position of the divine promises. In this respect it is interesting to note that eschatological matters are usually the result of the divine reply to existential questions, whereas the thoughts which are on the mind of the apocalypticists are more concerned with the situation as it is.

In this situation the function of the apocalyptic framework is most important. Firstly, the apocalypticist is allowed to see the present in the framework of the divine plan. Present circumstances cannot be viewed in isolation, and the rectitude of the divine attitude has to be seen in the light of the final outcome of history. Secondly, apocalyptic guarantees that the viability of the promises has added support. Trust in God is based not only on the fact that tradition has stated that certain beliefs are true but on the basis of the divine pronouncement. Thus the answers to man's most pressing questions are not products of hopeful speculation, but, as far as the apocalypticists are concerned, they come with the full authority of God himself. In the light of this the frightening demands made upon man in 4 Ezra have all the ingredients of a final challenge to do all that is humanly possible to overcome the disability caused by Adam's sin and to pursue the ways of God as they are set out in the Law. The apocalyptic framework allows God, as it were, to cast down the gauntlet before his people to spur them on to renewed endeavours so as to ensure that they are among the few who are to be saved. Here is an example of that 'interim ethic' which Albert Schweitzer thought was characteristic of the teaching of Jesus.[14] In addition, the emphasis on the revelatory dimension allows those novel aspects of the teaching of the apocalypse to receive that authority which other literary forms would not have given them.

Thus it would appear that in the apocalypses written towards the end of the first century AD the interest in eschatology is matched by another issue, the nature of man and the reason for the desperate straits in which the people of God found themselves. It is wrong to see these concerns as merely a prelude to the hope for the future. The pessimistic attitude with regard to man and the lot of Israel does not necessarily lead to a despair of this world-order and a concern only with that which is beyond history. The evidence from 4 Ezra and Syriac Baruch suggests that what we are dealing with in these works are questions which arise from the perplexities caused by history, in other words, with real human responses to particular historical events. They are not simply a convenient opportunity to trot out a particular eschatological belief but represent part of that process whereby Jews sought to make sense of their beliefs and their history, aided by the conviction that even in the most terrible circumstances God still allowed men glimpses of his purposes and thus assurance of the divine dimension to human experience.

CHAPTER 6

What Had Happened Previously: the Interest in Past History in Apocalyptic

The History of Israel

AS WE HAVE already noted, one of the features of the apocalypses is that they are pseudonymous. This makes them have the appearance of divine pronouncements which are peculiarly apposite to much later generations. Nowhere is this more the case than in those sections of the apocalypses which recite the details of history. Several of the apocalypses evince a concern with the totality of human history and particularly the history of Israel[1] (Dan. 2; 7; 8—9; 10—12; 1 Enoch 85—90; 91.12–17; 93; 4 Ezra 11—12; Syr. Baruch 36—40; 53—74; Apoc. Abraham 27ff., cf. Life of Adam and Eve 25ff.; Ass. Moses 2—10). From the point of view of the apocalypticist himself the events recorded are all in the past. Indeed, the story of Israel is usually told with considerable precision until the writer's own day, when predictions about the future become more vague (e.g. Dan. 12.1ff.). The fact that these detailed historical accounts are said to have been revealed to men of old gives the impression that the whole of human history has been foreseen by God and its conclusion determined. Not only is the whole course of human history set out before God, but also that plan can, in whole or in part, be made known to the wise through the revelation which comes from God. Although the prophets had in no way been parochial in their interests, as the numerous oracles against foreign nations indicate (e.g. Isa. 13—19; Ezek. 25—32: Amos 1.3—2.3), there is little in the prophetic literature which resembles the interest in the totality of history which we find in the apocalypses. The nearest we get to it in the prophetic literature is a passage like Ezek. 20 (cf. Sirach 42.15—50.23), where the history of Israel is used as the basis of a condemnation of the character of the people of God from the very outset of God's relationship with them. But the absence of this type of historiography from the prophetic literature should not obscure the fact that, from the Exile on, there had been a keen concern for history as a vehicle for establishing contemporary attitudes and vindicating the righteousness of God, by demonstrating the consequence of disobedience and the veracity of the divine word to Israel through the prophets.[2]

The amount of space taken up by presentations of past history makes it difficult to see in this phenomenon merely a device to justify the validity of the speculations about the future contained in the apocalypses. It has been argued that the records of past history are included mainly to show that, if the information about the history up to the present has been correct, the same is also likely to be true about the future predictions as well.[3] The detail which is often included in the review of the past suggests more than a mere device to bolster eschatological teaching. As with the other aspects of the apocalyptic literature which we have examined so far, there appears to be an interest in history for its own sake and not merely as a backdrop for the eschatological predictions which were to follow. The character of this interest in the past must now be illustrated by reference to some of the historical accounts in the apocalypses.

In Daniel 2.31ff. and 7.1–14 we have two visions; the first of these is Daniel's report concerning a vision of Nebuchadnezzar and the second, a dream-vision, which Daniel himself had. The first vision concerns the statue made of different materials, which was shattered by a stone, and in turn became a huge mountain which filled the earth (Dan. 2.35). The second concerns the rising from the sea of four different beasts, all of whom are eventually judged by God and replaced by a human figure, who is given divine authority. It is clear from the interpretations offered of both visions that the message concerns the fate of the four world-empires dominant until the second century BC (Dan. 2.36–45; 7.17–27). In other words, the concern here appears to be almost exclusively with secular history. Nevertheless it is apparent from the message of both chapters that there is also interest in the fact that ultimately God's kingdom will triumph in the world of men, which will mean the triumph also of God's people, a point clearly brought out in Daniel 7, if not in the earlier vision. Thus the interest in secular history forms part of the interest of the apocalypticist here in so far as it impinges on the history of Israel. It is generally agreed that the world-empires presupposed in both visions are precisely those which had had an impact on Israel after the Exile.[4] So the attention devoted to the fourth beast in Daniel 7, the origin of Israel's present oppression (v. 8), is an indication that the interest in history is not in this case evidence of a dispassionate interest in human history, for, as in most parallel passages in the apoca-lypses, it is the impact of human history on the people of God which conditions the outlook of the writer.

Whereas in Daniel 2 and 7 the past history is sketched in the most vague fashion, with particular attention only being devoted to the issue which most concerned the readers of the apocalypse (Dan. 7.25), other parts of Daniel show a more detailed (if at times inaccurate) concern with the past. Throughout Daniel 8—12 there are different presentations of Israel's past starting from the Exile and going down to the middle of the second century BC, given in the form of prediction (ch. 10ff.), by means of the dream-vision and interpretation (ch. 8), and the offering of the correct interpretation of the scriptures (ch. 9). In all cases the predictions offered by the seer go down to the generation of the apocalypticist and his readers, which is seen to be the decisive point in the history of mankind when the plans of God for the coming of his kingdom and the vindication of his people will be brought to fruition. In Daniel 8.9, for example, the climax of the vision comes with the triumph of the 'little horn', repre-senting Antiochus Epiphanes, who meets his match when he tries to put himself on the same level as God (cf. Dan. 8.25). Similarly in 11—12 the extended description of the activities of Antiochus (11.21ff.) are brought to an end (v. 45) and are then followed by references to resurrection and judgement on those opposed to God (Dan. 12.1ff.). Throughout these chapters inter-est centres on the fact that God watches over the history of man, and nothing happens without his knowledge. The rise and fall of the world-empires are shown in the apocalypse to be part of the divine plan for human history. The dominance of one world power has to be seen in the light of the demise of earlier empires as well as in the framework of God's ultimate triumph. Throughout Daniel there is little interest on the character of the future kingdom and the way in which the righteous will reign over the nations of the earth. The focus of the book is not so much on the future as on the divine control of the totality of human history. Only the prediction of resurrection, a source of hope for the martyrs (Dan. 12.2), is allowed to intrude into this dominant concern with the totality of human history.

Whereas the interest in history in the book of Daniel had tended to concentrate on the history of Israel since the Exile, and particularly since the rise of Alexander, a much broader perspective emerges in the roughly contemporary 'Animal-Apocalypse' in 1 Enoch 85ff.[5] Here the story starts with creation itself and includes the story of Israel before the Exile (1 Enoch 89.10–67). The story is taken down to the Hellenistic period and the inauguration of the last things is said to follow immediately after the Maccabaean crisis (1 Enoch 90.13ff.). The story is told in symbolic form, with the different characters being represented by animals and birds. In the following extract the shepherds represent the angels of the nations, the sheep are the people of God, the birds of prey the Greek rulers of the Seleucid and Ptolemaic dynasties and the lambs the *hasidim* who held out against hellenization in the first half of the second century BC:

> And I saw till that in this manner thirty-five shepherds undertook the pasturing, and they severally completed their periods as did the first; and others received them into their hands to pasture them for their period, each shepherd in his own period. And after that I saw in my vision all the birds of heaven coming, the eagles, the vultures, the kites, the ravens; but the eagles led all the birds; and they began to devour those sheep, and to pick out their eyes and to devour their flesh. And the sheep cried out because their flesh was being devoured by the birds, and as for me I looked and lamented in my sleep over that shepherd who pastured those sheep. And I saw until those sheep were devoured by the dogs and eagles and kites, and they left neither flesh nor skin nor sinew remaining on them until only their bones stood there: and their bones fell to the earth and the sheep became few. And I saw until that twenty-three had undertaken the pasturing and completed in their several periods fifty-eight times. But behold lambs were borne by those white sheep, and they began to open their eyes and to see, and to cry to the sheep . . . (1 Enoch 90.1–6.)

Together with the vision of the cloud with black and bright waters in Syriac Baruch 53ff. this dream-vision offers the most extended historical review in the whole of the apocalyptic literature. There is a similar, if less prolix, account of biblical history in the so-called Apocalypse of Weeks, Enoch 93 and 91.12ff., which makes its start with Enoch's generation and takes the story down to post-exilic times.[6] The precision about historical details becomes much less pronounced here after the reference to the Exile (93.8). Indeed, the beginning of the new age is closely related to the post-exilic situation and so does not appear to be in any way related to the events in Palestine during the reign of Antiochus Epiphanes. If we are to see here any indication of the date of this material, it would imply that we have here a historical review with predictions about the future which antedates the material in Daniel and the other parallel passage in 1 Enoch 85ff.

We have already seen that the retelling of the account in Genesis and the beginning of Exodus in Jubilees is framed within the context of an apocalypse. This work represents exactly the same type of outlook as we find in the historical sections of Daniel and 1 Enoch, even if the story does not reach its climax here with the description of the arrival of a new age and the events which precede it. The retelling of biblical history is not confined to the apocalypses, however. In the Assumption of Moses, for example, the dying words of Moses are taken up almost completely by a prediction of Israel's history from its entry into the promised land to the coming of God in the last days (2—10). The early period down to the Exile is covered in summary form, there then follow chapters which deal with the Exile and the period down to Antiochus (3—4), then the history of Israel during the rise of Roman rule with predictions about the reign of Herod (6.2) and the destruction of the Temple (6.8). There is a period of persecution for the elect with the warning that those who confess to being circumcised will be crucified, a reference to the dire consequences for those practising Judaism consequent upon the failure of the revolt of Simeon b. Koseba in the reign of Hadrian.[7] The prelude to the coming of the new age here is the coming of a levite called Taxo who exhorts Israel to stand firm (9.1ff.). In its detail, the account of Israel's history is in most respects similar to that found in the apocalypses. The important difference is the absence of the apocalyptic framework of divine revelation. Though the work is said to derive from Moses, nothing whatever is said about Moses receiving the information which he divulges to Joshua directly from God on the mountain. The value of the words comes from the importance of the figure who speaks rather than being the result of their divine origin. Indeed, it is interesting to compare the Assumption of Moses with Jubilees in this respect. In the latter we are left in no doubt that the material included is not merely a series of inspired guesses by the Law-giver but the revelation to him of the history of the world by the angel of the presence. The presence of such an interest in history is thus not a distinguishing mark of apocalyptic alone, as it is just another example of the way in which the belief in God's sovereignty manifested itself throughout the pseudepigrapha and indeed in contemporary Jewish thought generally.

It is in the two major examples of apocalyptic literature from the late first century that we find the other examples of historical reviews. In 4 Ezra 11—12 (the vision of the eagle) we have interest, not in history as a whole, but in that part of it which had most impact on first century Jews, the history of Rome.[8] As in 1 Enoch 85ff. the climax of the vision comes with the coming of the messiah and the judgement of that world-power which had inflicted such dreadful humiliation on the Jewish people (4 Ezra 12.30ff.). In Syriac Baruch 36—40 as with the four world empires of Daniel, all interest lies in the final power, in this case Rome (Syr. Baruch 36.5, cf. 4 Ezra 12.13f.). Here too the climax of the vision comes with the destruction of Rome (Syr. Baruch 36.8f.).

Much more extensive than either of these two visions is the vision of the cloud with black and bright waters in Syriac Baruch 53—74, which describes history from Adam to the coming of the new age.[9] Because the interpretation of the vision is much more explicit than is usually the case, there is no doubt whatsoever about the meaning of the different features which the seer has seen. Events in Israel's past and the dominant figures of her history are referred to quite explicitly in the interpretation. The history is quite detailed and precise down to the Exile, in other words down to Baruch's own day, then it becomes rather vague. The destruction of Jerusalem is mentioned (Syr. Baruch 67.6) as also is the rebuilding of Zion (Syr. Baruch 68.4f.). Precise historical references merge into indefinite predictions about catastrophic events (69f.), all of which lead into the messianic age (72—74). It is much more difficult to offer any kind of explanation of the relationship of the coming of the new age with the

historical events of the author's own day. If it had been a case of
the destruction of the first Temple being a herald of the last
things we may be justified in suspecting that the circumstances
of Baruch's day were regarded by the apocalypticist as a type of
his own. In this instance this does not appear to be true. The
end of the Temple does not immediately precede the arrival of
the messianic woes. Indeed, the rebuilding of Zion and the
restoration of the sacrificial system, not to mention a time of
'much joy' (68.4), follow the destruction. Such an interval
between destruction and the dawn of the new age hardly justifies the assumption that the end of the first Temple and its
circumstances were merely being used as a vehicle for the
message of hope in the author's day.[10] Indeed, if there is
intended to be any correspondence between the two situations it
would appear that the apocalypticist is, if anything, playing
down any imminent expectation by affirming that the Temple
must be rebuilt before the final chapter in the history of man can
be unfolded.

This vision should warn us, however, not to see in these
historical reviews merely a device to communicate the eschatological message of apocalyptic. Although the review in Syriac
Baruch reaches its conclusion with a description of the messianic
age, this period is given no more prominence than any other
part of Israel's history. What is more, there is no evidence to
suggest that the inauguration of the Last Things within a short
time is the issue to which the whole of history has been leading.
There seems here, and for that matter in the similar reviews in
other apocalypses, an interest in history in its own right. The
details of the past seem hardly appropriate to the simple purpose of communicating an eschatological message. Indeed, if
careful consideration is given to the extent of the eschatological
material in these passages, it will be found to add up to a small
fraction of the accounts. As we have already mentioned, in
Daniel virtually nothing is said about the future, and in the other
passages there is very little detailed prediction about it, just
sufficient, in fact, to give a general outline of what was hoped
for. In the light of this it seems to me that we should not confine
the significance of these passages to the realm of eschatology but
seek to place them within the total framework of apocalyptic.

While it is not clear that the apocalypticist sets out to draw
lessons from history in quite the same way as, say, we find in

the Deuteronomic history (e.g. 2 Kings 18.9–12), the revelation of the whole of history to the seer found in these 'predictions' seems to have a theological point. The readers of the apocalypses are permitted to see that the experiences of the present must be related to the totality of human history, whose course is entirely directed by God. The interest of the apocalypticists in human history indicates that all the vicissitudes of Israel's experiences from creation to the last days are shown to have been foreknown by God. Its course is mapped out for the seer, and he is made to see that even the most catastrophic events in Israel's history have been permitted by God (cf. Syr. Baruch 6). Nothing takes place without God's foreknowledge, and his control over the destinies of the most powerful nations of the world and is complete. There is no suggestion that God has in any way lost control of the world and its inhabitants, and all the disasters which befall God's people are the result of the divine will. He it is, for example, who hands Israel over to the angelic 'shepherds' (1 Enoch 89.59), in the light of which there can be no justification for the people of God to question God's ability to vindicate his people. But that event can only come in God's own time, and according to the plan for history laid down before the foundation of the world. In a similar way the eschatological predictions with which the historical reviews conclude is a way of affirming the divine control over history. The overall presentation averts the attention of the people of God from the distressing situation of the present and encourages a view of history which looks at it from the divine perspective. Thereby, meaning could be given to apparently futile and apparently godless acts. The revelation that God had in fact allowed for such developments is just one way of encouraging a religious group to see that their theological convictions were in fact to be trusted. It was not sufficient for the Jew merely to reveal the existence of God enthroned in glory far above the heavens. Jewish religion was intimately linked with God's work in history, a belief encouraged year by year with the Passover celebrations.[11] The Jew needed to be shown that the God who existed in glory in the world above had not abandoned his creation or his people and that the present, just as much as the past and the future, fitted into the overall pattern of God's purposes for mankind.

The view of human history with its many epochs which emerges in the apocalypses can be compared to a play with many scenes which have been written but not all acted out on stage. Only part of the number of scenes has been portrayed on stage; the rest is still to come. The apocalyptic seer, however, is privileged to have a total view of the play, including that which is still to be actualized on the stage of history. Such an understanding of history is most clearly seen in a passage, to which we have already had reason to refer, the Apocalypse of Abraham 21—22:

> And he said to me: Look now beneath thy feet at the firmaments and understand the creation foreshadowed in this expanse, the creatures existing on it and the age prepared according to it . . . Whatever I had determined to be, was already planned beforehand, and it stood before me ere it was created, as thou hast seen.

Abraham here sees the whole of the drama of human history before it is presented on the world-stage, and, of course, in the case of Adam and Eve, a scene which has already taken place. This panoramic view directly opposes any tendency to relegate God to the beginning and the end only and to see the rest of history as an aberration, which has to be corrected by the cataclysmic intervention of God in the last days. The apocalypses keep a very firm grip on the divine control over events in the world, and there is no suggestion that the present age is in any sense abandoned by God, however much God's people may suffer and however obscure the signs may be of divine control and activity.

The theological consequences of such a view may appear to be very far-reaching. After all, with the whole of history already mapped out by God, it would be tempting to conclude that the position of the individual within such a deterministic framework was insignificant. It would appear, however, that the main concern of the apocalypticist in viewing human history in this way was not because of a rigid predestinarian theology, though such views are sometimes encountered in Jewish writings of this period. The rigidity of the determinism of the apocalyptic view of history is more apparent than real. What concerns the apocalypticists is the movement of history as a whole towards its final goal, the establishment of God's kingdom. There is no suggestion that the deeds of men can in any way alter the inexorable tread towards this goal. The repentance of a Roman emperor, for example (should a Jewish writer have been able to countenance such an act!) would not have meant that the divine plan had been altered in any way, merely that the possibility now existed in the present for the reflection of that relationship with God which was to come in the future.[12] For the individual, and for the apocalypticist, this meant usually only a very select group, who knew the divine secrets. The challenge was whether they aligned themselves with God's way or the way of the world. Even though God may know the ways of man (Slav. Enoch 53.2), the opportunity is open to each to decide for or against the divine will in the present (Slav. Enoch 30.15, cf. Syr. Baruch 85.7). The function of the revelation of history is one way of showing readers who may be tempted to desperate action in the present the value of abiding patiently in a pattern of religious obedience, which apparently serves no useful end in the short term. The divine control of history is both an encouragement in adversity as well as a remedy for despair. World-history is on a particular course leading to the ultimate triumph of God, and, by the same token, the triumph of those who have allied themselves to him. The apocalypse does not tell its readers that a change of heart is out of the question. Indeed, the pastoral significance of the apocalyptic form lies in precisely the opposite direction. The function of revealing the divine plan of history is to encourage readers to move in the opposite direction from that which they had hitherto decided upon (cf. Rev. 2—3). By better understanding of the position of their own circumstances within the overall purposes of God, the readers of the apocalypses will be prevented from precipitate action arising from an inadequate conception of the totality of the divine will.

Thus apocalyptic, whose main concern was the revelation of the divine mysteries, could in no sense be complete without offering some kind of total view of history. An orientation towards the future alone would have given a theological picture which minimized divine control of history in the present. The extent of apocalyptic's debt to the past is manifested in the way in which the divine activity through history is so consistently portrayed in the historical reviews contained in the apocalypses. To that extent the mantle of earlier historiography has fallen on the apocalypticists. But what was inherent in the prophetic attitude to history, as well as the attitude of the Deuteronomist, namely the hidden meaning of events which seemed to fit so ill with Israelite traditions, is clearly enunciated in apocalyptic. The world has become a difficult place to understand; circumstances are not susceptible of an explanation merely on the basis of observation. It thus becomes necessary for God to reveal to the apocalypticist the mystery of historical events and the relationship of the present to the past and the future. This is already to some extent the case in the prophetic writings. The position of the surrounding states and their relationship to Israel have to be explained to the prophet by the word of God. In other words, the understanding of history could not depend alone on the application of ancient beliefs to historical circumstances. The divine word to the prophets itself presupposes that there was a whole dimension to existence which would be missed without the intervention of God to speak to his people. In the same way the apocalypticist stresses that the disclosures to him put Israel's history in a completely different light, by examining the unsatisfactory nature of the present from the divine perspective.

The Creation of the World

An interest in the past which offers a rather different view of apocalyptic is the occasional evidence of concern with cosmogony. We have already seen that the apocalypticists were very anxious to know about the cosmos as it is. There is a limited amount of evidence to show that this extended to geographical interests, but far more important were the visions which disclosed that which was not so easily understood, the obscure character of the world above and its inhabitants. Despite the impression of man's puny nature, so eloquently stressed by Job 38f., it is clear that man's inability to comprehend the secrets of the heavens and the earth and their origins did not stop him being fascinated by such questions. After all, the interpretation of Scripture brought the exegete face to face with those matters, which were difficult, if not impossible, to understand. The very first chapter of the Torah gives a cursory description of creation, and questions on this chapter inevitably led the interpreter into the whole area of cosmogony. The interest of the apocalypticist in matters which proved difficult to understand naturally led him at times to occupy himself with this subject.[13]

As we would expect in a book of this character, Jubilees devotes quite a long section to the subject of the creation of the world (Jub. 2.2ff.).[14] The tendency to incorporate contemporary

Jewish ideas, which is apparent throughout the book, is evident here also, though in a slightly attenuated form, in the section on creation. Although the bulk of the account keeps fairly close to the biblical text, occasional diversions reveal the interests of the author. For example, Genesis 1 says nothing whatsoever about the creation of the angelic hosts. This omission is remedied in Jubilees 2.2:

> For on the first day He created the heavens which are above and the earth and the waters and all the spirits which serve before him – the angels of the presence, and the angels of sanctification, and the angels of the spirit of fire, and the angels of the spirit of the winds, and the angels of the spirit of the clouds, and of darkness and of snow and of hail and of hoar-frost, and the angels of the voices and of the thunder and of the lightning, and the angels of the spirits of cold and of heat, and of winter and of spring and of autumn and of summer, and of all the spirits of his creatures which are in heaven and on earth.

The lack of any mention in the opening words of Genesis 1.1 of the creation of the water is rectified, thus preparing the reader for the second half of Genesis 1.2 and the reference to the firmament in the following verses. Similarly, the absence of any reference to the Garden of Eden in Genesis 1 has compelled the author of Jubilees 2.7 to include the Garden of Eden among those things which were created on the third day (cf. b. Pesaḥim 54a).

Even 4 Ezra, which resists any kind of cosmological and theological speculation, has a lengthy account of the act of creation. Admittedly this forms part of a much longer discussion dealing with the unfortunate position of Israel among the nations of the world (4 Ezra 6.38ff.), but in the process the author offers an account of creation which shows some differences from the biblical version. Of particular interest is the opening section dealing with the first acts of creation:

> Let heaven and earth be made, and thy word perfected the work. Then was the spirit hovering; darkness and silence were on every side; the sound of man's voice was not yet before thee. Then thou didst command a ray of light to be brought forth out of thy treasuries, that then thy works might become visible. Upon the second day thou didst create the spirit of the firmament and didst command it to make a division between the waters that one part might go up, the other remain beneath.

Two matters in particular call for attention here. First of all, the seer says that God brought forth light from his treasuries (4 Ezra 6.40). In other words this is not so much an act of creation but the bestowal on the cosmos created on the first day of that which already existed with God.[15] The biblical command 'Let there be light' is taken, therefore, not as a creation of light but the manifestation of that which was pre-existent. Secondly, the creation of the spirit of the firmament is said by Box to presuppose an angel of the firmament to whom the command to produce the firmament in Genesis 1.6 was addressed.[16] Here there appears to be evidence that God shares his act of creation with another being, for the division between the waters is said to take place as a result of the delegated act of the spirit of the firmament. Such mediatorial activity in the process of creation is already found in the Wisdom-tradition, where personified Wisdom has a share in the creative process (e.g. Wisd. 8.6). Of course, it is in Philo that the clearest evidence is to be found of the participation of the Logos in the whole act of creation (e.g. *Leg. Alleg.* iii, 96; *Sacrif. Abelis et Cain.* 8; *Quod Deus sit immut.* 57; *De Fuga* 94; *De Spec. leg.* i, 81; *Opif. Mundi* 20; *De Cher.* 127f.). In all this material the Alexandrian Jew leaves us in no doubt that the divine Logos is nothing more than an attribute of God and functions only as the means whereby God creates rather than having any creative function in its own right. Indeed, in *Op. Mundi* Philo is quite adamant in his insistence on the fact that God is creator, and that it is only in the case of the creation of man that God co-operates with other divine beings (72). In this respect the view of creation which emerges in 4 Ezra 6 is not far removed from that found in Philo.[17]

Much more elaborate and speculative than either of the two passages already mentioned is the account of the revelations given to Enoch by God concerning the mystery of the creation in Slavonic Enoch 24—33.[18] In this section more detailed consideration is given to the situation at the very beginning of creation. Despite the suggestion of creation *ex nihilo* in 24.2, it would appear that we have here a belief that God gave form to the pre-existent, formless matter (Slav. Enoch 25.1). In the words of the apocalypticist God creates the 'visible creation from the invisible', and so that which always existed with God becomes part of the visible created order. The first act of creation follows the account in Genesis, in so far as it speaks of the creation of light (Slav. Enoch 25.1ff.). But the account in Slavonic Enoch parts company with the biblical narrative in speaking of the creation of light as the result of its origin from an angelic being, Adoil, from whose stomach light comes forth. This being and the other being, Archas, mentioned in 26.1f., probably are intended to depend on *tohu* and *bohu* of Genesis 1.2.[19] In the biblical account the situation at the beginning of creation is of the earth being 'without form and void' *(tohu wabohu)*. So here God exists with Adoil and Archas, from whom the components of heaven and earth are produced.

After the creation of light comes the establishment of the throne of God. In Jewish tradition there was the belief that several things were created before the world was created. Among these, in the *baraitha* in b. Pesaḥim 54a is the throne of God. Clearly in Slavonic Enoch the establishment of the throne takes place *after* the creation of light, and one must presume that this means that the throne itself was fashioned only after the first act of creation.

In Judaism at this period there was much debate concerning the priority of various pre-existent things. This uncertainty is reflected in a saying of R. Aba b. Kahana (*c*. AD 300) in Ber. R. 1.4, who speaks in the following way about the relative priority of the creation of the Torah and the throne of glory:

> I still do not know which was first, whether the Torah preceded the throne of glory, for it says the LORD made me in the beginning of his ways, before his works of old, which means before that of which it is written Thy throne is established of old . . .

Such uncertainty is probably reflected in the LXX text of the second half of Proverbs 8.27. Here the MT reads quite simply, 'when he drew a circle on the face of the deep'. The whole section stresses the presence of Wisdom at creation, and it was Wisdom, of course, which later came to be identified with the Torah itself (Sirach 24.23ff.; Sifre on Deut. 9.10; Ber. R. 1.1 and Midrash Conen).[20] For the author of the LXX version of Proverbs there was no doubt that God's Wisdom, which had been his constant companion in all his acts of creation, was also present when the throne of God itself was brought into being. Thus we find in the second half of the LXX of 8.27 the words 'when he separated his throne on the wind'. The position of the throne as one of the first acts of creation is precisely what we find in the account of creation in Slavonic Enoch.[21]

The light forms the circumference of heaven (Slav. Enoch 25.4), and the stage is set for the creation of the lower parts of the cosmos. As in 4 Ezra 6 the creation of the lower things is the result of the production from a heavenly being, named Archas, of the lower things which provide the foundation for the universe. Then the waters are created and the division between sea and earth. Only then are the angelic beings created (Slav. Enoch 29.1ff.). The account then follows, with only slight variations, that in Genesis 1, until the creation of man is described (Slav. Enoch 30.8ff.). As one might expect in an account of this kind, opportunity is taken to discuss man's sinfulness. Although every emphasis is put on the glory of man (Slav. Enoch 30.11f.), Adam from the very start has the ability to distinguish between good and evil (Slav. Enoch 30.15, cf. Gen. 2.16f.). The reason for God giving man the ability to distinguish between good and evil is itself explained. God did not create man simply as a being who would do only that which was acceptable to him. The reason for this is that God wished to ascertain whether the man whom he had created did in fact have love and obedience towards himself. Thus the responsibility for the human plight is placed fairly and squarely on man, and God is in no way held responsible. The opportunity for obedience and disobedience was given to man by God, and there was no reason why man should not choose to follow the ways of God of his own volition. But in order to make this a real choice God gave man knowledge of good and evil, so that he could prove his devotion to God by choosing the path of light rather than darkness.

Here then we have an extended rewriting of the Genesis account with every chance being taken to remedy the deficiencies of the original. Apart from the creation of man the obvious source of interest to the apocalypticist is the opening verses of the account of creation. Many matters are left unanswered by these verses, which would interest a later investigator. When, for example, were the angels created, and what were the means by which the created world came into being? Already the LXX text of Genesis 1 had attempted in its translation to answer some questions,[22] but the curiosity which the creation account stimulated clearly continued, and it should be no surprise that the apocalypse offered one way of filling in those significant gaps which were left by the biblical original. The fact that the seer receives his answers directly from God himself is yet another indication that we should see here an attempt to give to the speculative account of the beginning of creation contained in these verses precisely that authority which was normally attributed to the sacred writings of Moses. What is offered here then is no mere supposition but the authentic word from God, never before revealed to angels (Slav. Enoch 24.3f.).

There is another passage which must now be considered which exhibits many unusual characteristics and which like the three previous passages also concentrates on the act of creation. This is the strange vision of Cenez, which is contained in Pseudo-Philo's Biblical Antiquities 28. Although the vision does not give an account of the whole of creation in the way in which the passages already mentioned do, there can be little doubt, despite the peculiarities of the account, that this is what the vision is about:[23]

Now while they were seated, the holy spirit that dwelt in Cenez leapt upon him and took away from him his sense, and he began to prophesy, saying: Behold now I see that which I looked not for, and perceive that I knew not. Hearken now, ye that dwell on the earth, even as they that sojourned therein prophesied before me, when they saw this hour, even before the earth was corrupted, that ye may know the prophecies appointed aforetime, all ye that dwell therein. Behold now I see flames that burn not, and I hear springs of water awakened out of sleep, and they have no foundation, neither do I behold the tops of the mountains, nor the canopy of the firmament, but all things unappearing and invisible, which have no place whatsoever, and although my eye knoweth not what it seeth, mine heart shall discover that which it may learn. Now out of the flame which I saw, and it burned not, I beheld, and lo, a spark came up and as it were builded for itself a floor, and the likeness of the floor thereof was as a spider spinneth, in the fashion of a shield. And when the foundation was laid, I beheld, and from that spring there was stirred up as it were a boiling froth, and behold it changed itself as it were into another foundation; and between the two foundations even the upper and the lower, there drew out of the light of the invisible place as it were forms of men, and they walked to and fro: and behold a voice saying: These shall be for a foundation unto men and they shall dwell therein 4000 [7000] years, And the lower foundation was a pavement and the upper was of froth, and they that came forth out of the light of the invisible place, they are those that dwell therein, and the name of that man is . . .[24] And

> it shall be, when they have sinned against me and the time is fulfilled, that the spark shall be quenched and the spring shall cease, and so they will be changed.
>
> And it came to pass that after Cenez had spoken these words that he awakened and his sense returned unto him: but he knew not that which he had spoken neither that which he had seen . . .

With the vision of Cenez we move away from the close connection we find in the previous examples between the later interpretation and the scriptural original to a daring attempt to describe part of the process of creation which is unique in the extant literature. Although it is not immediately apparent at the beginning of the vision, it soon becomes clear that Cenez sees primaeval chaos (28.7) and the creation of the universe out of it. At first he sees only flames and springs of water. These two substances are already in existence before the process described by Cenez begins to take place (cf. Slav. Enoch 25.1ff.; 27.1). A spark from the flame becomes the basis for the lower foundation, whereas it is the spring which forms the froth which makes the upper structure. Similar constituents of the firmament of heaven are mentioned in a passage in b. Hagigah 12a. Here the Hebrew *shamaim* is explained etymologically as a conflation of *'esh* (fire) and *maim* (water), so it can be said that a mixture of fire and water produced the firmament. Into the space between the two foundations come beings who appeared to be men, and it is said that this space was created for men to dwell in. When these men have sinned, however, then the spark and the spring which have been instrumental in bringing about the process of creation will peter out, and then all will be changed.

Perhaps the most obvious way to interpret this passage is as a reference to the vault of heaven above and then the foundations of the earth. Thus the lower foundation, created by the spark, was the basis of the earth, whereas the upper was the firmament which separated God from the earth.[25] Into the gap between the two structures comes mankind, which inhabits the world for a period of four thousand years until the time determined by God (Pseud. Philo 28.9). Such a cosmology would coincide with the passage in 60.2, where the context of David's soothing song to the troubled Saul provides the setting for a further passage of this kind:

> There were darkness and silence before the world was, and the silence spake, and the darkness became visible. And then was thy

name created, even at the drawing together of that which was
stretched out, whereof the upper was called heaven and the lower
was called earth. And it was commanded to the upper that it should
rain according to its season, and to the lower it should bring
forth food for man that should be made. And after that was the tribe
of your spirits made.

Here the reference to the upper and lower parts of the cosmos
are explicitly identified with heaven and earth. If we are to
suppose that the author of the Biblical Antiquities intended any
connection between these two passages, it would be natural to
suppose that he thought of a similar cosmology in chapter 28
also.[26] Finally, it seems natural to suppose that the reference in
28.8 to the forms of men is to be understood as an allusion to the
inhabitants of the earth, who sin against God and will at the end
of time be transformed.

There are, however, certain difficulties with this interpretation. First of all it seems natural to suppose that the foundation
mentioned in verse 8 is the vault of heaven. The similarity of the
floor to a spider's web is better understood of heaven than earth.
The similarity with Ezekiel 1.22, where the firmament is
stretched out over the heads of the living creatures, is not too far
away from the resemblance to the curve of a shield mentioned
here. Also worth mentioning is the discussion of the firmament
in the late document, Pirke de R Eliezer, where the firmament
which stretches over the earth is compared to a tent:

The dome of the heavens ascends upwards like a tub, like a tent
which is spread out with its extremities [fixed] downwards and its
dome stretching upwards so that people can sit beneath it and their
feet stand on earth, whilst all of them are inside the tent; in like wise
are the heavens, their extremities are fixed [downwards] and their
dome stretches upwards and all the creatures beneath them as in a
tent . . . .(PRE 3)[27]

If we follow the first interpretation of this passage set out above,
the structure brought into being by the spark cannot be a
reference to heaven but to the earth, which according to this
passage would come into being before the vault of heaven.[28] If,
however, we want to see the lower pavement (cf. Exod. 24.10) as
a lower firmament of heaven, then the upper structure must be a
reference to a higher firmament in heaven. This would then
correspond to the sort of cosmology attributed to R. Judah as
quoted in b. Hagigah 12b: 'R. Judah said: There are two firma-

ments, for it is said: Behold unto the Lord thy God belongeth heaven, and the heaven of heavens.'

The problem with this interpretation, however, is how one explains the reference to the forms of men who dwell in the space between the two structures for four thousand years. The question is whether it is right without further ado to identify these beings with men. The first point to note is that the apocalypticist says that these beings come forth from invisible light. This can hardly be a reference to the creation of man as a number of beings are seen in the vision. If this is a reference to human beings, it must presuppose a belief in the pre-existence of human souls. Their coming from a place of light suggests that these beings have been with God. While this is by no means an impossible belief in a Jewish document,[29] one must inquire about other possible interpretations before resorting to this one. It would appear that the most natural way to take the reference in Biblical Antiquities 28.8 is as a reference to angelic beings. When first mentioned they are referred to as the forms of men (*imagines hominum*). The most natural way of interpreting this phrase would be as a reference to angels. According to the Apocalypse of Abraham 15.6 the patriarch sees 'in this light . . . many people of male appearance all (constantly) changing in aspect and form', and angels are often compared to men, e.g. Daniel 8.15.[30]

But how does a reference to angels here coincide with the mention of their dwelling between the two foundations and the sin mentioned in Biblical Antiquities 28.9? Both these verses seem to point against such an identification. If, however, we suppose that the angels referred to here are those first mentioned in Genesis 6.1 and who form the cornerstone of the legends in 1 Enoch 6.1ff., these verses would be equally applicable to fallen angels as to human beings. They await the final judgement for their punishment, and in the later Enochic literature a place is appointed for them to wait in the second heaven (Slav. Enoch 7.1ff. cf. 18). Thus the sin mentioned here is not Adam's sin but that of the fallen angels who are situated at a particular point in the cosmos waiting for the final judgement, when the heavens would be changed.

Most difficult of all for this explanation, however, is the brief, if enigmatic sentence 'and the name of that man is . . .'. Whichever reading we adopt, it is hard to see this as any other than a reference to Adam. As far as the second interpretation of the chapter is concerned, the only way round this problem is to explain the sentence as a later gloss offering an explanation of the identity of the strange figures who appear in 28.8. There are good reasons for supposing that this in fact may be the case. First of all, the sudden introduction of a reference to one man, when the previous (and following) references are in the plural, makes one suspicious about the originality of the sentence. Secondly, the MS tradition shows some variation in the way in which it punctuates the sentence as well as textual variants. Although no MS omits the sentence, the difficulties which scribes found with it suggest that it probably did not form part of the original.

On balance it would seem that the second alternative has more to commend it, even if it means accepting the need to regard one sentence as a redactional gloss. But whichever explanation we prefer, there can be no doubt that this passage offers remarkable testimony to the existence of a highly creative form of speculation on the creation-account in Genesis which takes the form of a vision of that event.

CHAPTER 7

What is to Come

The Last Stages of the Present Age

ALTHOUGH THE APOCALYPTIC literature offers us considerable variety in its angelology, it makes few concessions to the belief that God is not ultimately in control of his creation. Similarly in its eschatology the lordship of the God of Israel is maintained, not only by his final triumph over the powers of darkness, but also in the belief that God influenced historical events, even when the divine will seemed to be furthest from fulfilment. Nowhere is this notion better seen than in the 'birth-pangs' of the new age, which are typical features of much Jewish eschatology of the period.[1] These are the various disasters which, it was believed, would have to take place throughout the universe before the new age could finally arrive. Included among them are intensified human suffering through war and natural disasters, and disturbances which upset the normal pattern of planetary behaviour. A good example of such notions can be found in the sequence of seals, trumpets and bowls (Rev. 6; 8–9 and 16), where a series of terrible disasters unfolds, which must take place before the new age finally dawns. In so far as apocalyptic literature shares many of the eschatological beliefs of Judaism it is only to be expected that they should make their appearance in this literature too.[2]

There is a slight hint of the time of great distress in Daniel 12.1 ('and there shall be a time of trouble, such as never has been since there was a nation till that time'), but it is the other early apocalypses which afford better evidence of it. In the Apocalypse of Weeks (93; 91.12–17) the seventh period of world history, which precedes the coming of God's justice, is characterized by a time of rebellion against God and his ways. Similarly also in Jubilees 23.13ff. we find that a variety of calamities precedes the last days:

And in those days, if a man live a jubilee and a half of years, they shall say regarding him, He has lived long and the greater part of his days are pain and sorrow and tribulation, and there is no peace: For calamity follows on calamity, and wound on wound, and tribulation on tribulation, and evil tidings on evil tidings, and illness on illness, and evil judgements such as these, one with another, illness and overthrow, and snow and frost and ice, and fever, and chills, and torpor and famine, and death, and sword, and captivity, and all kinds of calamities and pains. And all these shall come on an evil generation which transgresses on the earth: their works are uncleanness and fornication, and pollution and abominations.

Sometimes these calamities are directed particularly against Jews, when, as in 1 Enoch 90.13ff., one of the first acts in the climax of history is the final assault of the Gentile nations upon the Jews.[3] In the later apocalypses we find that the evil days before the coming of the messianic kingdom play a significant role within the eschatological scheme. 4 Ezra 5.1 (cf. 9.1 and 13.29) gives a list of the signs which must take place before the new age is near. But the most coherent eschatological scheme of its kind is that found in Syriac Baruch 25ff. Here the signs of the end precede a carefully planned quota of disasters which have to take place in their entirety before the age of righteousness finally comes:

When a stupor shall seize the inhabitants of the earth, and they shall fall into many tribulations, and again when they shall fall into great torments. And it will come to pass when they say in their thoughts by reason of their much tribulation: The Mighty One doth no longer remember the earth – yes, it will come to pass when they abandon hope, that the time will then awake . . . Into twelve parts is that time divided, and each one of them is reserved for that which is appointed for it. In the first part there shall be the beginning of commotions. And in the second part there shall be slayings of the great ones. And in the third part the fall of many by death. And in the fourth part the sending of the sword. And in the fifth part famine and the withholding of rain. And in the sixth part earthquakes and terrors. And in the eighth part a multitude of spectres and attacks of the Shedim. And in the ninth part the fall of fire. And in the tenth part rapine and much oppression. And in the eleventh part wickedness and unchastity. And in the twelfth part confusion from the mingling together of all those things aforesaid.[4]

The purpose of such a strictly formulated prediction is essentially twofold. It stresses the sovereignty of God even over events which seem to accord ill with his revealed will, and it enables the elect who read the apocalypse to see that the present chain of disasters was only a temporary phenomenon which presaged something better (cf. Mark 13.13 and 20). In this way the eschatological woes function in much the same way as the disclosures concerning human history already discussed. The placing of the readers' generation near to the climax of the inexorable progress towards the final consummation enables the harassed people of God to wait with patience for their final redemption.

The descriptions of judgement found in some of the prophetic oracles in the Old Testament include some of the horrific events referred to in the eschatological woes in the apocalypses. Ezekiel 14.21, for example, speaks of 'God's four judgements, sword, famine, evil beasts and pestilence' (cf. Jer. 14.12; 21.7; Ezek. 13.11). The cosmic disorders can be paralleled in Isaiah 13.10 and 34.4, and earthquakes are often mentioned in connection with a theophany (e.g. Isa. 13.13; Ezek. 3.12; Hag. 2.7; Zech. 14.4; Ps. 18.7ff.). Originally such events exhausted the extent of the divine judgement upon the world and its inhabitants, but in later Jewish eschatology there is sometimes an additional reference to a last assize when God metes out justice to all mankind. This is particularly true of a passage like 4 Ezra 7.33ff. where the messianic woes (described in 6.28ff.) and the messianic age are followed by the resurrection and the final judgement. Likewise also the New Testament apocalypse has a series of acts of judgement on the world, together with a final assize after the messianic kingdom (Rev. 20.11ff.). In a similar vein the eschatological portrait in 1 Enoch 90.13ff. makes mention of an intense struggle with the enemies of God's people followed by the advent of God and the judgement of the unrighteous angels who have allowed God's people to be persecuted by the nations of the world (90.20ff.). But sometimes judgement upon man is centred more on the disasters which precede the new age rather than any final assessment as in the prophetic literature. In Jubilees 23.27ff. the calamities are followed, not by a last assize, but by a situation in which all the children learn the Torah and the world returns to perfection.[5] Similarly in the eschatological scheme in Syriac Baruch 24ff. the judgement of God on his rebel subjects takes place through the eschatological woes which lead directly into the messianic age rather than a final tribunal.

There is obviously a certain discrepancy in the eschatological accounts of the apocalypses. In some, much more weight is given to the messianic birth-pangs as an essential part of the way in which God judges man. In Jubilees and Syriac Baruch they are a necessary prelude to the messianic age, for they clear the way for the establishment of God's kingdom. Only by means of such events could a situation be created where the reign of God could come into being. Certainly there is implicit in such descriptions a despair that man is unable to reform himself or his institutions, but there is an equal insistence on the working out of God's will through the processes of history. The disasters which take place are themselves the divinely ordained means of overwhelming all which sets itself against God and his will. The revelations to the apocalypticists concerning the messianic woes are a way of stressing that the ungodly present as well as the terrific upheavals needed to get rid of the present order are all part of God's plan for the unfolding of the divine will on the stage of human history. The centrality of Israel's hope that their way of looking at the world would ultimately triumph necessitated the removal of all rival interpretations if the true reflection of God's sovereignty was to be seen in the world. Thus there are signs in some of the apocalypses that the messianic woes played an important role in preparing the world for the coming of the kingdom of God, even though at times this process was lost sight of as the judgement came to be more closely identified with a single act of divine retribution when the new age arrived.

In addition to the cathartic effect of the messianic woes, we find in Revelation that the tribulations of the last stages of the present world order are intended to have a didactic purpose as well. Repeatedly after the description of the catastrophes afflicting mankind we find John appending the comment that mankind refused to repent:

> The fourth angel poured his bowl on the sun, and it was allowed to scorch men with fire; men were scorched by the fierce heat, and they cursed the name of God who had power over these plagues, and they did not repent and give him glory. (Rev. 16.8, cf. 9.20.)

In other words man could not see the ineffectiveness of his puny attempts to organize his life without any reference to God, a fact which was demonstrated by the havoc wrought by the final disasters which came upon the world. Instead of acknowledging that in fact he had been wrong all the time mankind could not see that the woes were a means of showing up his utter folly, and instead he simply cursed God and refused to see the inadequacy of human existence without reference to him.

What we find in the various endeavours to portray the introduction to the new age by means of a series of natural disasters is yet another attempt by the apocalypticists to understand the whole of history and its relationship with the sovereignty of God. We saw that in describing the past apocalyptic had demonstrated that the whole of the history of man followed a pattern already known to God. The apocalypses also show that the disasters which are to take place are just as much a part of the divine plan as the period of bliss which is to follow them. While the prophetic oracles of judgement had offered glimpses of the imminent judgement and the glory to come, the apocalypticists set out to indicate how that central belief in the lordship of the God of Israel was not merely confined to a future divine irruption but was even now manifest, albeit unseen, in the perplexing circumstances of the present and the gradually unfolding horrors to come. The greater the insignificance of Israel within the political scene of the present, the more dramatic was the upheaval needed to initiate the time of vindication. The messianic woes or birth-pangs were just one way in which the hopes for the future which Jews cherished so dearly could come to fruition.

The Climax of History

For many interpreters the distinguishing feature of the apocalypses is their teaching about the new age. While it has been our intention to stress that eschatology is but one component of the mysteries revealed to the apocalyptic seers, there can be no denial of the significant role which eschatological mysteries do play in these writings. It is not my intention here to offer a detailed discussion of all the various beliefs concerning the future contained in the apocalypses, a task which has been carried out in great detail elsewhere.[6] Instead some attempt will be made to look at the various pictures of the climax of human history which are to be found in the apocalypses.

In the early chapters of 1 Enoch (1—36) we have little more

than the occasional hint about eschatological matters. The opening verses of the work (1.3ff.) offer a prediction of the coming of
God to his holy mountain, Sinai. This theophany has its roots in
Old Testament theophanies like Deuteronomy 33.2. The reaction
of the created world to God's coming reflects the mythological
language of some of the psalms (Ps. 18.7ff.; 97.5; cf. Exod.
19.16ff. and Mic. 1.4). God's coming initiates a period of peace
and blessing for the righteous (1 Enoch 1.8), whose vindication
comes about with God's advent and his judgement upon the
wicked (v. 9). As far as one can ascertain, this passage is merely
a prediction of future bliss for the righteous who happen to be
alive at the time of God's appearance. Its function is clearly not
to give anything but the most general encouragement to the
righteous to persevere in their way of obedience, in order to
receive God's reward when he comes in glory.[7]

In 1 Enoch 10.17 the picture of the first judgement in the days
of Noah provides an opportunity for the apocalypticist to predict
the future time of bliss after the flood, when the fallen angels
have been removed and the righteous will be able to enjoy a
time of great plenty. It is quite evident from the context that the
writer is setting out to describe the situation on earth after the
flood and not to predict the glory of the new age, a fact well
illustrated by the language of chapter 11.2. Nevertheless the
prediction of bliss for the survivors of the first world-judgement
is probably to be regarded as a paradigm of the ideal situation
which was in prospect for those who were fortunate to participate in the future world, purged as it would be of all that was
contrary to God's will.[8] As such the prediction of happier times
after the flood represents the hope for the world in the writer's
day, when evil had once again appeared to triumph among
men.

During his journeys through the created world Enoch is taken
to the underworld, where he sees the places prepared for the
souls of men awaiting the final judgement (1 Enoch 22.4). Enoch
is shown that the character of man's life will influence the sort of
temporary rest awaiting the dead until the day of judgement.
The righteous have a spring of water to refresh them (22.9),
whereas sinners will receive some of the retribution which may
have eluded them during their lives (22.10f.). According to
chapter 24f. Enoch is taken to seven mountains, the seventh of
which is surrounded by fragrant trees. He is told that this

mountain is the site of God's advent 'when he shall come to visit the earth with goodness' (25.3). Of the trees which surround the mountain one in particular attracts Enoch's attention. This is said to be for the righteous and holy in the new age, when it will be transplanted to Sion (25.5). The eschatology of this section is quite unequivocally centred on a hope for this world, and the return of God to earth to dwell with his people as he had in the beginning.

Much more extensive eschatological material is to be found, however, in the later chapters of 1 Enoch. The first important passage comes at 1 Enoch 85—90, the long record of biblical history from the creation down to the Maccabaean period (90.6). This takes the form of a dream of Enoch (85.1f.), in which the leading characters of the story are symbolized by animals and birds. The history of the people of God comes to an end with the Maccabaean struggle which serves as a prelude to the dawn of the new age. The rise of the *ḥasidim* (90.6) is a prelude to a final attack of the heathen nations upon the people of God (90.13ff.). But the people of Israel triumph (90.15), and the act of judgement on their enemies is carried out by the righteous (90.19).[9] There then follows the judgement of God, which takes place on earth, 'in the pleasant land' (90.20), presumably a reference to Israel. Included in this judgement are the seventy 'shepherds', the angelic representatives of the nations (vv. 22–25), into whose hands Israel had been committed. The fact that they had exceeded the authority given to them by God is duly punished (v. 22), as also is the apostasy of those members of Israel who have forsaken the paths of God (v. 26f.). After the judgement comes a process of rebuilding:

> And I stood up to see till they folded up that old house; and carried off its pillars, and all the beams and ornaments of the house were at the same time folded up with it, and they carried it off and laid it in a place in the south of the land. And I saw till the Lord of the sheep brought a new house greater and loftier than that first, and set it up in the place of the first which had been folded up: all its pillars were new, and its ornaments were new and larger than those of the first, the old one which he had taken away, and all the sheep were within it.

The reference to the old and new house is taken by both Charles and Russell to be the Jerusalem below and the Jerusalem above,[10] but it would appear that, in the light of the reference to pillars, beams, and ornaments reference to a new or renovated Temple, appropriate for the new age, is more likely to have been in the author's mind.

Whatever the precise significance of the reference to the house, a situation in the vicinity of Jerusalem for the consummation seems to be intended. Here the righteous dwell at peace, and the nations of the world acknowledge the sovereignty of Israel (1 Enoch 90.30ff., cf. Zech. 8.20). What is more, v. 33 seems to predict a full share in the future glory not only for 'all that had been destroyed' (an implicit reference to resurrection) but also for all the nations of the world, symbolized by the beasts of the field and the birds of heaven.[11] There then follows a time when God's people no longer wield arms to control the nations (cf. 1 Enoch 90.19) and a time of great blessing is foretold (v. 35). Even this blissful situation is subject to further transformation; the whole community is gradually transformed into perfect humanity as God intended it (90.37f.). Such a notion can be detected by comparing this section with the very beginning of the dream-vision, where Adam is symbolized by a white bull (1 Enoch 85.3). The picture in 1 Enoch 90.37f. is of the metamorphosis of humanity to reflect the glory of the first man. The crowning glory of the vision is the birth of the messiah, symbolized by a wild ox,[12] who emerges from the community. It is interesting to note that the messiah here plays virtually no role at all in the establishment of the messianic kingdom, unlike the rather aggressive role attributed to the son of David in a work like the Psalms of Solomon 17 (cf. Test Jos. 19.1ff.).

The final admonitions of Enoch conclude a variety of eschatological predictions of a more general kind concerning social unrest in the last days (1 Enoch 91.5ff.; 102), predictions of destruction for sinners (1 Enoch 94.6—95.7; 97—100; 103) as well as bliss for the righteous (1 Enoch 96). But there is another extended eschatological section in the so-called Apocalypse of Weeks (1 Enoch 93; 91.12–17), which is said to have arisen as a result of Enoch's activities with the angels.[13] In this eschatological prediction the history of the world is divided into a period of ten weeks. The first seven weeks take the history of Israel down to the post-exilic period, which is then followed by the description of the last four weeks, which describe the last stages leading up to the coming of the new age:

And after that in the seventh week shall an apostate generation arise, and many shall be its deeds, and all its deeds shall be apostate. And at its close shall be elected the elect righteous of the eternal plant of righteousness, to receive sevenfold instruction concerning all his creation. And after that there shall be another, the eighth week, that of righteousness, and a sword shall be given to it that a righteous judgement may be executed on the oppressors, and sinners shall be delivered into the hands of the righteous . . . And a house shall be built for the great King in glory for evermore. And after that in the ninth week, the righteous judgement shall be revealed to the whole world . . . and after this in the tenth week in the seventh part, there shall be the great eternal judgement, in which he will execute vengeance amongst the angels. And the first heaven shall depart and pass away, and a new heaven shall appear, and all the powers of the heavens shall give a sevenfold light. And after that there will be many weeks without number for ever, and all shall be in goodness and righteousness, and sin shall no more be mentioned for ever (1 Enoch 93.9f.; 91.12–17).

Here we find that the rise of the apostate generation is the prelude to the dawn of a new order. The means by which this comes about is the execution of judgement by the righteous on those who had oppressed them. As in 1 Enoch 90.19 righteous Israel has its part to play in the inauguration of the last things. The culmination of this process is the building of a house for God (1 Enoch 91.13). Destruction of the old temple is mentioned in chapter 93.8. This can only be a reference to the temple of Solomon which is to be replaced by a new and glorious building.[14] The triumph of the righteous during the eighth week seems to be a local affair, confined to the land of Israel. In the ninth period, however, the righteous judgement of God becomes universal with the destruction of the impious and the acknowledgement of the supremacy of God's ways. Finally, there is judgement for the angelic world together with the destruction of the old heaven and the advent of a new one.

It would be dangerous to suppose that this passage looks forward to a state of bliss in heaven alone. It is not justified to conclude from the absence of a reference to the renewal of the earth that this realm had no part to play in the new age.[15] The concern in verse 15 had been with the rooting out of impiety from the heavenly world. Indeed, the sin of the fallen angels had occupied the attention of the writers of the Enochic tradition, and, as a result, it comes as no surprise that their deeds should be judged and the consequences of their actions duly removed. Because of the gravity of the angels' misdemeanours one must suppose that nothing short of a completely new heavenly world could be contemplated to rectify the evil with which the angels had contaminated the world above. In the eyes of the apocalypticist removal of the evil from the world by the activities of the righteous was sufficient to make the earth conform to God's eternal purposes.

Finally, in our survey of the eschatological material in 1 Enoch mention must be made of the ideas contained in the Similitudes (1 Enoch 37—71). Our attention will be given to one of the more distinctive aspects of the eschatology of the Similitudes, the heavenly Son of Man, a little later. There is a great variety of eschatological statements in the Similitudes with little attempt made to work out any coherent eschatology from the disparate elements contained in these chapters. The following passage, however, is typical of several in which the eschatological agent comes to execute judgement and bring refreshment for the righteous:

> And all the kings and the mighty and the exalted and those who rule the earth shall fall down before him on their faces and worship and set their hope upon that Son of Man, and petition him and supplicate for mercy at his hands . . . and the righteous and the elect will be saved on that day, and they shall never thenceforward see the face of the sinners and unrighteous. And the Lord of Spirits shall abide over them, and with that Son of Man shall they eat and lie down and rise up for ever. And the righteous and elect shall have arisen from the earth, and ceased to be of downcast countenance. And they shall have been clothed with garments of glory and they shall be the garments of life from the Lord of Spirits . . . (1 Enoch 62.9, 13–16).

The distinctive feature about the act of judgement in many passages in the Similitudes is the fact that the agent of judgement is the heavenly Son of Man or the Elect One (e.g. 1 Enoch 46.4ff., cf. 1 Enoch 45.3f.; 61.8ff.).

The composite character of the Similitudes is seen in the way in which different eschatological pictures stand alongside each other. In chapter 41, for example, Enoch is shown the place in which man's deeds are weighed in the balance (cf. 1 Enoch 61.8), and then the act of judgement is carried out immediately rather than delaying until a final assize. The idea implicit in this chapter is found in an amplified form in the Testament of

Abraham (Rec. A) 11f., where interest in the last judgement virtually disappears from sight. Elsewhere, however, it is the revelation of the Son of Man/Elect One who brings about judgement. Traditional elements of Jewish eschatology are to be found, including the transformation of the cosmos (1 Enoch 45.4), the rise of heathen powers against Israel (1 Enoch 56.5ff.), and the resurrection of the dead (1 Enoch 51.1; 62.15). The hope for the future seems to be for a renewed world in which 'the earth shall rejoice, and the righteous shall dwell upon it, and the elect shall walk thereon' (1 Enoch 51.5; cf. 58.1–6). As far as Israel is concerned, her future includes the gathering of the scattered people of God as well as the pledge of future glory for the righteous, which has been guaranteed by the presence of the righteous Enoch in God's presence (1 Enoch 71.15f.). Thus, with the exception of the prominent position given to the part played by the Son of Man/Elect One in the final judgement, the material in the Similitudes seems to correspond with the eschatology which we find in the other apocalypses: a hope for the future which is centred in this world, but which necessitates the subjugation of all that is opposed to God before it can be fully realized.

In the book of Daniel passages which have anything to say about the character of the new age are minimal. There is much historical 'prediction' by the angelic mediator in Daniel chapters 8—11, but the bulk of this concerns the events leading up to the desecration of the Temple by Antiochus Epiphanes rather than predictions concerning the aftermath of this event. What we have in Daniel are either rather general predictions about the future kingdom of God or the odd hint about the sort of thing which may be expected to happen at that time. In Daniel 2.31ff. the end of the dominance of the great kingdoms of the earth is predicted and in their place God is to set up a kingdom which can never be destroyed, in which the people of God will have the dominant role to play (Dan. 2.44). While it is clear that God is responsible for the coming of the kingdom (Dan. 2.34), the means whereby he effects his purposes are not spelt out. Similarly in Daniel 7 the four beasts appear in the seer's vision, the fourth of which is destroyed and the rest have their power taken from them (Dan. 7.11). In the interpretation of the vision we learn that the beasts symbolize four kings. The interest of the seer centres on the fourth king and his descendants, the activities of one of whom have been particularly hurtful to the people of God (Dan. 7.25). In place of the dominion being exercised by this king and his descendants (7.26) 'the kingdom and the dominion and the greatness of the kingdoms under the whole heaven shall be given to the people of the saints of the Most High' (7.27). It seems that the author has in mind here an earthly dominion in which the people of God act as his vice-regents on earth. But the eternal dominion of God and his people is not to be confined merely to those who survive when the dominance of the world-powers has come to an end. In Daniel 12.2 the time of great trouble which is to afflict the whole universe is to be followed by the resurrection of the dead, when the righteous dead will be able to share the glorious kingdom while the impious will be punished.[16]

In the book of Jubilees there are two main passages dealing with the question of eschatology.[17] In the opening chapter God reveals to Moses that a new character will be given to the people, which will enable them to keep God's commandments (Jub. 1.23ff.). There is then the prediction that God will dwell with his people in the sanctuary in the holy city for ever (Jub. 1.27). There is a much more extended eschatological section in Jubilees 23.11–31, where the death of Abraham provokes a discussion of the way in which longevity has become less prevalent and the life of men attended by a variety of disasters (vv. 13–23).[18] The culmination of the deteriorating situation comes with great slaughter and the premature ageing of children (v. 25). This is followed by a period of great happiness, when children study the laws of God again (v. 26), and the long life which characterized man's life at the beginning of creation returns (cf. Jub. 23.9). This period will be marked by an age free from the ravages of Satan (v. 29, cf. Rev. 20.2), when the righteous will have great peace. Whether there is a belief in immortality reflected in the words of Jubilees 23.31 is much disputed.[19] In the light of v. 27 which seems to envisage a long life for mankind the fixed duration makes a belief in immortality unlikely. The future hope in Jubilees is thus entirely concerned with the renewal of this world and the return to a situation where man can live in obedience to God, unhindered by the ravages of evil and the deprivations of all that caused life to be so unbearable in the previous world-order.

Among all the questioning of the seer in 4 Ezra and the

answers of the angel are various eschatological passages. In chapter 7.26ff. Ezra is told of the appearance of the heavenly Jerusalem which ushers in a messianic age of four hundred years. During this period those who have been fortunate enough to survive will experience a time of great rejoicing (v. 29). This idyllic situation is, however, only a temporary phenomenon and comes to an end with the death of the messiah and the rest of humanity. The world then returns to its primaeval silence for 'seven days' (4 Ezra 7.30). After this there is the resurrection and the last judgement followed by 'delight and refreshment' for the righteous and 'fire and torments' for the wicked (7.38). Here there is a definite distinction between the old age and the messianic kingdom which arises out of it on the one hand and the new age on the other. Such a distinction had already been hinted at in a passage like 4 Ezra 6.7 and enunciated in the following way in chapter 7.50: 'For this cause the Most High has made not one age but two.' As far as the future age itself is concerned, the apocalypticist speaks only about the contrast which exists between the place of torment for the impious and the place of rest for the righteous, though these are further identified with Gehenna and Paradise respectively (v. 36). The absence of any detailed description of the places of bliss and torment is probably indication enough that the recitation of the eschatological beliefs in this section has not arisen to satisfy the curiosity of those who would know what the world to come was like. Throughout 4 Ezra eschatological teaching must be seen as part of the overall plan of the writer to attempt to offer some kind of justification of the divine will to refuse salvation to all but those who have been obedient to the Law of God.[20] This eschatological material, therefore, is intended to present to the readers of the apocalypse the alternatives which face them in this life. Either they accept the Law and obey it, with the possibility of Paradise in the age to come, or they neglect the Law and face consequences in the final judgement (4 Ezra 7.20f.; 7.129).

The question of man's fate at death is discussed further by Ezra and his heavenly interlocutor in chapter 7.75ff. Once again the stark contrast is put forward between torture of various kinds for the wicked (vv. 80ff.) and the sight of God's glory for those who have been faithful to God (v. 90ff.). In the following chapter the righteous individual, Ezra, is promised eternal life because of his obedience. This consists of a place in Paradise (4 Ezra 8.52), where the holy city has been rebuilt. In this situation the deeds of men will be characterized by their goodness. No longer will death have any part to play, and that aspect of man's nature which tended to lead him astray in the past will have been rooted out (4 Ezra 8.53). The picture here is much more that of the temporary messianic kingdom of chapter 7.20ff. than the new aeon which comes after it. The references to the plenteousness of the last days and the new Jerusalem (v. 52) suggest the this-worldly kingdom familiar to us from other apocalypses.

In the first of the three visions with which the work concludes Ezra sees a vision of a woman in great mourning for the loss of her son (4 Ezra 9.38ff.). The sorrow of Ezra at the fate of Zion prompts him to rebuke the woman for grieving over one son, when the inhabitants of the holy city have greater reason to mourn (4 Ezra 10.5ff.). After this outburst Ezra then sees the woman in a brilliant form transformed into a city (vv. 25ff.). The interpretation of the vision by the angel reveals that the woman symbolizes the heavenly Zion. She remained childless for a period (4 Ezra 10.45), representing the time until the building of the Temple under Solomon. The woman's child, the earthly temple in Jerusalem, was, however, eventually destroyed. Nevertheless the woman is dramatically transformed into a city, and it is this which will be one of the components of the new age. Ezra is allowed to investigate the city (4 Ezra 10.55), but, unlike John on Patmos, he has nothing to say about the various features of the new Jerusalem (cf. Rev. 21.10ff.).

Here is a promise then to Jews bereft of their national shrine that the earthly building, which has hitherto existed, is merely a replica of something greater (4 Ezra 10.48f.). The message of the vision is to look beyond the earthly shrine to its heavenly counterpart, which in due course will be actualized on earth. In the light of the fact that the apocalypticist believes that the history of the world is moving rapidly towards the accomplishment of the divine plan for it (4 Ezra 14.10f.), there is probably little doubt in his mind that the glory of the heavenly counterpart to the earthly Zion will not be long delayed in being realized on earth.

In the night after the vision of the woman in mourning Ezra has a dream concerning an eagle with three heads coming up from the sea (4 Ezra 11.1, cf. Dan. 7.2). This strange bird is said to reign over the earth and its inhabitants (11.6). After an extended description of the wings and heads of the eagle (vv. 11–35) Ezra sees a lion making the pronouncement of judgement upon the eagle (vv. 36ff.).[21] The interpretation of the vision concerns the fate of the Roman empire. The lion who finally reproves Rome is said to be the messiah (4 Ezra 12.31ff.). Only the briefest reference is made to judgement and other eschatological matters (4 Ezra 12.33ff.), for the interest in this vision is on the overthrow of Rome. Here is further encouragement to those who seek to persevere in their obedience to God. The all-powerful might of Rome, which seems an insuperable obstacle to the fulfilment of God's promises, is shown to be only a temporary phenomenon on the stage of world-history.

The final vision in 4 Ezra is the most familiar of all. In it Ezra sees a man coming up from the sea, flying with the clouds of heaven (4 Ezra 13.3). This man placed himself upon a great mountain (v. 7) and destroyed all those who had gathered against him with the fiery breath of his mouth (v. 10). After this the man comes down from the mountain and is surrounded by many different people (vv. 12ff.). In the interpretation of the vision (vv. 25ff.) Ezra is told that 'this is he whom the Most High is keeping many ages'. He slays those ranged against him by the Law (v. 38) and gathers the ten tribes, which had been dispersed in 722 BC, and those are then defended by the messianic envoy. This eschatological vision concentrates on the work of the messiah and his part in the opposition to the forces opposed to God and in gathering the people of God scattered throughout the world. The interest again is not on the character of the new age but is concerned to stress the overthrow of evil and the promise of future redemption to the repentant members of the ten tribes (vv. 40–43). The vision is thus an affirmation of the promise of future redemption to those who have been obedient to God.

In the contemporary Syriac Baruch there are several eschatological ideas similar to those in 4 Ezra. As in the latter there is the notion of the heavenly Jerusalem (Syr. Baruch 4.2–7). Likewise the Garden of God, which in earlier literature is said to be situated on earth (e.g. 1 Enoch 32.3; Jub. 4.23), is now found in heaven. Although we do not find an explicit doctrine of the two ages, such as is the case in 4 Ezra, Syriac Baruch 15.7ff. does make a sharp contrast between the present world of travail and the glorious future. The setting of the apocalypse in the difficult days just before and after the destruction of the First Temple enables the writer to stress that the uncertainties and difficulties of the present are signs that the hoped for future is imminent. The destruction of Zion is shown by God to be a sign of the nearness of the end rather than a cause for despair (Syr. Baruch 20.1ff.).

The first extended eschatological passage is to be found in Syriac Baruch 24—30. We have already had reason to mention this section on several occasions in other contexts, but we must concentrate on its ideas concerning the new age. The messianic woes are followed by revelation of the messiah and the establishment of God's reign on earth, during which the monsters Behemoth and Leviathan will be food for those who are left (Syr. Baruch 29.3ff.). This period will be marked by a time of great plenty, when harvests will be plentiful and the manna reserved in heaven will be provided for those fortunate enough to participate in this time:[22]

> And it shall come to pass in those parts, that the Messiah shall then begin to be revealed. And Behemoth shall be revealed from his place and Leviathan shall ascend from the sea, those two great monsters which I created on the fifth day of creation, and shall have kept until that time; and then they shall be for food for all that are left. The earth shall yield its fruit ten thousand-fold and on each vine there shall be a thousand branches, and each branch shall produce a thousand clusters, and each cluster produce a thousand grapes, and each grape a cor of wine. And those who have hungered shall rejoice: moreover, also, they shall behold marvels every day. For winds shall go forth from before me to bring every morning the fragrance of aromatic fruits, and at the close of the day clouds distilling dews of health. And it shall come to pass at that self-same time that the treasury of manna shall again descend from on high, and they will eat of it in those years, because these are they who have come to the consummation of time.

The period of the messiah's reign is only temporary, as in 4 Ezra 7.29f. There then follows the resurrection, which heralds the time of judgement (Syr. Baruch 30.4f.). Nothing whatever is said about the character of the age which is to follow the temporary messianic kingdom. Presumably the needs of the author were satisfied with the fact that there would soon be a time of bliss for the survivors on earth (cf. Syr. Baruch 85.10), and those who were unfortunate enough to die before this period of joy at least had the resurrection to look forward to. Clearly the apocalypticist's interest is dominated by the conviction that there would be a new age on earth, and his situation did not demand any speculation about existence after it.

In the first of Baruch's dream-visions the seer sees a forest with a vine beside it and a fountain under the vine (ch. 36). The forest is gradually submerged in the water from the fountain, with the exception of a solitary cedar. Eventually this too is destroyed, and there is said to be peace and tranquillity. After the demise of the cedar the vine pronounces a condemnation on the cedar (Syr. Baruch 36.7ff.) and justification for the adverse judgement upon it. In the interpretation (Syr. Baruch 39f.) it becomes clear that the forest symbolizes the great world-powers, which are gradually overcome (vv. 3–5). The fourth and last empire emerges (v. 6), which is to be identified with Rome (cf. 4 Ezra 12.11ff.). During this time there will be great trouble in the world (v. 5) but its leader will eventually be judged by the Jewish messiah (Syr. Baruch 40.1ff.).

The vision is typical of Jewish eschatology of the period, not only in concentrating on Rome as the arch-enemy of God and his people, but also in seeing the messianic age as one which was to be preceded by a period of turmoil. As in the Psalms of Solomon 17.24ff. the messiah is here pictured as a warrior-like figure, whose task it is to overcome the last great world-power opposed to Israel. As elsewhere the interest of the apocalypticist ceases once the triumph of God's representative over the heathen power has been promised. We have to do here not with messianic or eschatological speculation but with the fate of Rome and the means of its overthrow.

Further eschatological revelations are to be found in chapters 49—51 dealing this time with a particular eschatological problem, namely the character of the resurrection-body. This is an issue which resembles that discussed by Paul in 1 Corinthians 15. Baruch is told that the earth will restore to life the dead exactly in the form in which they were put into the earth (Syr. Baruch 50.2). After the judgement (51.1) those who have done evil will become more horrific in their looks, whereas the splendour of the righteous will become ever more glorious (51.3). To these will the age to come be revealed (51.8) and the glory of Paradise and God's own presence (51.11). In the new age the righteous will appear in glory as the angels (v. 10).

It has been argued that we have here an example of a hope for the righteous in the heavenly world.[23] It is the sentence 'in the heights of that world shall they dwell' which particularly indicates a belief in a life in the future in a world beyond the present one. Such an expression need not in any way suggest another sphere of existence for the righteous but could merely be a hyperbolic way of referring to the exalted position which they would have in the new world-order. It is a world, it is true, which is no longer subject to corruption (cf. Syr. Baruch 44.12), but it is still in essential continuity with the previous creation, albeit suitably sanctified as befits an age of perfection.

Immediately following this disclosure about the fate of the righteous and wicked Baruch reports another vision, this time of a cloud with black and white waters:

> And when I had said these things I fell asleep there, and I saw a vision, and lo, a cloud ascending from a very great sea, and I kept gazing upon it, and lo, it was full of waters white and black, and there were many colours in those self-same waters, and as it were the likeness of great lightning was seen at its summit. And I saw the cloud passing swiftly in quick courses, and it covered all the earth. And it came to pass after these things that the cloud began to pour upon the earth the waters that were in it. And I saw that there was not one and the same likeness in the waters which descended from it. For in the first beginning they were black and many for a time, and afterwards I saw that the waters became bright, but they were not many, and after this again I saw black waters, and after these things again bright, and again black and again bright. Now this was done twelve times, but the black were always more numerous than the bright. And it came to pass that lo, at the end of the cloud it rained black waters, and they were darker than had been all those waters that were before, and fire was mingled with them, and where those waters descended, they wrought devastation and destruction. And after this I saw how that lightning which I had seen on the summit of the cloud, seized hold of it and hurled it to the earth. Now that lightning shone exceedingly, so as to illuminate the whole earth, and it healed those regions where the last waters had descended and wrought devastation. And it took hold of the whole earth and had dominion over it. And I saw after these things, and lo, twelve rivers were ascending from the sea, and they began to surround that lightning and to become subject to it. (Syr. Baruch 53.1–11)

In the interpretation of the vision which follows (Syr. Baruch 56—74) we are told that the cloud represents the present age. The first black waters represent Adam's transgression (Syr. Baruch 56.5), whereas the first bright waters symbolize Abraham and his descendants who fulfilled God's commandments (57.1). Then the story of the history of Israel is told as one which alternates between times of obedience or disobedience, corresponding to the bright and black waters respectively (Syr. Baruch 58—66.) The history of Israel is told down to the destruction of the first Temple (Syr. Baruch 67.1ff.). This is then followed by the rebuilding of Zion and a time of great joy for God's people (Syr. Baruch 68.4). Finally the last black waters come which represent the calamities which are to come on the earth (ch 69f.). The coming of the lightning, however, brings to an end the domination of the black waters, and here we have a reference to the advent of the messiah (Syr. Baruch 72.2). This ushers in the new age when freedom from disease and premature death will epitomize a world such as God intended (Syr. Baruch 73.1—74.3). Although the Gentile nations who have opposed Israel will be punished (Syr. Baruch 72.4 cf. 82.3), those who have not been guilty of this crime will be spared and be allowed to participate in the new age. The description of the new age shows many affinities with that already discussed in Syriac Baruch 29.3ff. The emphasis throughout is on the restoration of things in this world with the subjugation of animals to men (Syr. Baruch 73.6) and the removal of all those evils which had made the previous world such an unhappy place for man to live in (Syr. Baruch 73.2f.).

In the two Abrahamic apocalypses very different eschatologies emerge. In the Testament of Abraham there is virtually no interest in the future of the world, with only the occasional reference in the longer Greek recension (A) to the divine assize at the end of history. In this document the process of judgement takes place at death. As soon as a man dies he is taken off to Paradise or Hades depending on whether his good deeds or his evil deeds are more numerous (Rec. A 11f.). In certain doubtful cases where good deeds and evil deeds are finely balanced Abel acts as adjudicator of the fate of the individual soul (Rec. A 12).

Much more akin to the traditional eschatological beliefs is the eschatology of the Apocalypse of Abraham. After his vision of the divine throne-chariot Abraham then receives visions about the future (ch. 20—31). The promise to the patriarch of a mighty nation descended from him (cf. Gen. 15.5) is found in an unusual form,[24] but the eschatological section proper begins in chapter 27.

In chapter 21f. Abraham has been shown mankind divided into two parts. On the left are the heathen nations and on the right God's own people. The eschatological events begin with representatives of the heathen nations treating God's people badly and burning their temple (ch. 27). God explains this suffering as the consequence of Israel's idolatry (ch. 25). Abraham then inquires of God how long it will be before the deliverance of his descendants is accomplished. Unlike some apocalypses, which allow us to decipher the time of writing from the chronological allusions, it is by no means easy to decide exactly what time-scale is presupposed here. According to chapter 30 the coming of the messianic woes takes place at the end of the twelfth hour. Since each hour is equivalent to one hundred years this gives a period of twelve hundred years for the duration of the ungodly age, but when we should start the twelve hundred year period is difficult to say. Box suggests that if we begin our reckoning with the building of Solomon's Temple we would have a period of roughly two thousand years until the destruction of the Temple by Titus in AD 70,[25] assuming, that is, that we date the apocalypse at the end of the first or at the very beginning of the second century AD. This is then followed by a long Christian interpolation,[26] after which we have a description of the period of judgement on the heathen midway through chapter 29. This is to be a series of plagues (ch. 30), which are followed by a trumpet blast and the mission of the Elect One to gather God's scattered people, when God will punish those who have badly treated the people of God in this age (ch. 31). The destiny of the people of God is set out briefly in chapter 29:

And then shall the righteous men of thy (Abraham's) seed be left in the number which is kept secret by me, hastening in the glory of my name to the place prepared beforehand for them, which thou sawest devastated in the picture (i.e. Jerusalem); and they shall live and be established through sacrifices and gifts of righteousness and truth in the age of righteousness and shall rejoice in me continually; and they shall destroy those who have destroyed them, and shall insult those who have insulted them.

Once again we have a picture of a world dominated by God's truth, when the holy nation, freed from all oppression, will worship God in a restored temple. The eschatology here is relatively complete, though, as in other apocalypses, more detailed consideration is given to human history leading up to the final messianic age than to that period itself.

Messianic Belief

Because of the importance of the title messiah for New Testament Christology it is perhaps natural that interest should focus on occurrences of the term in contemporary Jewish literature.[27] If, however, we confine ourselves to occurrences of the word messiah in apocalyptic literature, our study could be finished in a few sentences. Though the title messiah is not often found, there is evidence in the apocalypses of a messianic idea concerning a (usually human) figure who has some part to play in the eschatological process. That is not to say, however, that the apocalypses have any profound interest in messianism.[28] Indeed, the majority of references to such a figure contain the minimum of detail about his character and origin, and it would be true to say that the figure of the messiah hardly dominates the eschatological accounts which we find in the apocalypse. By comparison other Jewish texts of the period offer a slightly more productive quarry for information concerning messianic beliefs at this period (e.g. Ps. Sol. 17—18; Sib. Or. 3.652ff.; T. Levi 2.11; T. Judah 24; 1QSa 2.18f.; 1QS 9.11; 4QFlor; CD 14.19).

Clearest evidence of belief in the Messiah is to be found in the Similitudes of Enoch where, in a unique juxtaposition, the messianic title is joined with the heavenly Son of Man figure (1 Enoch 48.10; 52.4). In addition, there may be some indications that royal terminology, particularly Psalms 110 and 2 and Isaiah 11 have influenced the picture of the Son of Man as it emerges in the Similitudes.[29] For example, the judgement of the Son of Man on the kings of the earth (1 Enoch 46.5f.) is reminiscent of language used about the king in Psalm 2.9, and the attribute of wisdom bestowed upon the Elect One according to 1 Enoch 49.3 brings to mind the picture of the ideal ruler in Isaiah 11.2. Outside the Similitudes we have the briefest of references to the messiah in the Animal-Apocalypse in 1 Enoch 90.37. He is symbolized by a wild ox with great black horns on his head. All we can conclude from this reference is that he is a human figure, who is not said to be actively engaged in the inauguration of the new age.[30]

It is only with 4 Ezra and Syriac Baruch that we find the term messiah being used in an absolute sense to denote the eschatological deliverer (4 Ezra 12.32, cf. Syr. Bar. 29.3), though we find the expression 'my messiah' in several places in Syriac Baruch (39.7; 40.1; 70.9; 72.2).[31] Certain differences emerge between the picture of the messiah in chapters 29 and 72 (cf. 4 Ezra 13) on the one hand and chapter 39.7 on the other. In the first two passages the messiah plays a purely passive role, much the same as in 1 Enoch 90.37, whereas in the latter he has a decisive part to play in the judgement of the nations. Indeed, chapter 40.1 actually speaks of the messiah as one who will put the godless to the sword. Despite the language about the 'revelation' of the messiah in chapters 29.3 and 39.7 and his rapture to heaven (Syr. Baruch 30.1) it would be wrong to suppose that there is sufficient evidence from Syriac Baruch to suggest that the messiah was a pre-existent figure. The 'revelation' of the messiah may reflect the notion of the hidden messiah which had a certain currency at this period.[32] The one whose identity is hidden from human gaze and known only to God and to those to whom he wishes to reveal his secrets will, in the future, be revealed to mankind as the agent of salvation.

The same, however, cannot be said so unequivocally about 4 Ezra, where the messianic references clearly stress his humanity (4 Ezra 7.29) but at the same time his pre-existence (4 Ezra 14.9).[33] It is probably also tempting to find pre-existence presupposed in the brief messianic reference in the Apocalypse of Abraham 31, where it is stated that God will send his Elect One. It is not to be supposed, however, that this is a mission from the world above to the world below but a commissioning by God of the individual whom he has chosen to fulfil the messianic office.

The few references which we do possess to messianic figures in these texts point to a fairly standard belief. With the exception of the Similitudes (and possibly 4 Ezra 13 which will be discussed in the next section) the picture of the messiah which we find in the apocalypses is of a figure who plays a role of varying importance and who, without exception, seems to be a human being. The apocalypses, however, show a complete lack of interest in the character of the messiah. The contemporary debates which appear to be reflected in John 7.27 and 41 (cf. b.

Sanhedrin 98a) about the origin of the messiah are not even echoed in the apocalypses. Clearly the quest for knowledge which is so evident in the apocalypses did not extend to the identity of the messiah and his task.

The Son of Man

When dealing with the eschatology of the apocalyptic literature it is inevitable that some consideration be given to the vexed question of the Son of Man figure, and in particular whether the apocalypses allow us to conclude that there existed at the time of Jesus a belief in a heavenly figure who would come at the climax of history and who was called by the title Son of Man. Because of the significance of this phrase for the Christology of the New Testament this issue has, for some time, been a matter for considerable discussion and has, as a result, occasioned a great deal of secondary literature.[34] This is despite the fact that the Jewish evidence for the existence of such a figure is scanty in the extreme. Apart from the enigmatic Similitudes of Enoch (1 Enoch 37—71), where the Son of Man appears several times, we have only the briefest of references in Daniel 7.13 and a possible allusion in 4 Ezra 13.[35] Much of the recent discussion on the matter has centred on the value of the Similitudes for the study of Christian origins and, more particularly, on whether Daniel 7 gives us evidence of the existence of a heavenly Son of Man figure. Our concern in this section will be to review the evidence for the existence of such a figure by an examination of three texts.

Recent discussion of Daniel 7 from a New Testament perspective has centred on the significance of the reference to the Son of Man in Daniel 7.13. On the one hand there are those who argue that we have here the beginnings of a belief in a heavenly saviour-figure, which contributed to the developing belief in a supernatural messiah in Jewish religion.[36] On the other hand, there are those who dispute this interpretation, arguing instead that the Son of Man in Daniel 7.13 is in no way a heavenly figure but merely functions as a symbol of the saints of the Most High, who are mentioned in the interpretation of the vision (e.g. v. 18).[37] In other words, this second group argues that the Son of Man has no independent existence in the world above and acts merely as a symbol of the righteous people of God in exactly the same way as the four beasts symbolize four kings (v. 17). In order to adjudicate between these two very different interpretations of the significance of the reference to the Son of Man in Daniel 7.13 we must glance briefly at the chapter as a whole.

Daniel 7 falls into two very clearly marked sections. The first fourteen verses offer an account of a dream-vision of Daniel, in which he sees four beasts rising from the sea (v. 2). Attention is devoted in particular to the fourth beast with its horns, in one of which were 'eyes like the eyes of a man, and a mouth speaking great things' (v. 8). After this the heavenly throne-room is described, with God, the Ancient of Days, sitting in judgement (v. 9f.). Judgement is then passed against the fourth beast, and it is destroyed. The other three then have their dominion taken away from them (v. 11f.). After this there appears a human figure ('one like a son of man'), who comes with the clouds of heaven to the Ancient of Days and is given authority and power over all the nations (v. 14). When the vision is interpreted for Daniel, he is told that the four beasts represent four kings, but it is the significance of the fourth beast which particularly attracts the seer's attention (vv. 19ff.). He is told about its activities (v. 23) and those of its horns (v. 24f.) and learns that the dominion which it exercises is only temporary (v. 26). By contrast the present suffering of the Saints of the Most High[38] (vv. 21 and 25)[39] will ultimately lead to their vindication by God and the possession of 'the kingdom and the dominion and the greatness of the kingdoms under the whole heaven' (v. 27).

Most commentators agree that the fourth kingdom is the dominion of Alexander, and the ten horns which sprout from his head his successors. The horn which attracts so much attention in verse 24 is to be identified with Antiochus Epiphanes who afflicted the Jewish people in the middle of the second century BC. Few would dispute that the chapter is a message of hope to the persecuted people of God, who are undergoing the ravages of Antiochus Epiphanes' measures, to convince them that the dominion of the barbarian power will only be temporary and the vindication of the righteous assured. But if there is agreement over the overall purpose of the chapter there is considerable divergence over the interpretation of individual elements and, in particular, the identity of the human figure in Daniel 7.13.

It is not our intention here to enter into a detailed exegetical investigation of the chapter, but the following points should be noted in coming to some conclusion about the interpretation of the different parts of it. Firstly, it would appear that the beasts represent the four great kings and the ten horns other kings who would come after them. Whether they are merely symbols of the kings and therefore have no independent heavenly existence, or are to be regarded as demonic representatives in the world above of the earthly kings, cannot be decided precisely. The tendency has been to see them merely as symbols of the human kings,[40] but much will depend here on other aspects of the vision. In contrast to the interpretation of the significance of the beasts (v. 18), *nothing whatever is said in the interpretation about the significance of the Son of Man.* If the Son of Man figure had merely been a symbol of the Saints of the Most High, we might have expected to find the same kind of identification between the Son of Man and the saints which we find in respect of the beasts and the kings in v. 18, but this is lacking.

Secondly, we do not have in the opening vision one whose elements are merely symbolic of earthly events and persons.[41] Daniel 7.1–14 differs in this respect from the vision in chapter 8 and the dream-visions found in 1 Enoch 89ff., in 4 Ezra 9ff. and in Syriac Baruch 36 and 53. It could be argued, as we have seen, that the beasts are merely symbols of human kings, but the same cannot be said for other aspects of Daniel 7. Unlike other visions which include interpretations, the vision in Daniel 7 clearly has at least one component which purports to be a description of the reality in the heaven above. In Daniel 7.9–10, we have a theophany which has many similarities with visions of the heavenly world in other apocalyptic writings (e.g. 1 Enoch 14.8ff.; Rev. 4), deriving ultimately from Ezekiel's vision of God's throne-chariot.[42] These verses cannot be said to be symbols, for the author clearly believes that he is describing here the scene in the court of God himself. This passage makes it impossible to interpret the whole of the vision merely as a symbol of earthly events and persons. In this respect it differs completely, say, from Baruch's vision of the forest and the vine in Syriac Baruch 36, where, of course, there is no suggestion that these are anything but symbols of earthly happenings. All we have in the latter is the use of certain images in a vision to communicate the divine truth concerning God's plan for human history. Daniel 7 also has a message concerning human history, but this message arises out of the disclosure of certain important happenings in the heavenly world which have consequence for the history of mankind and, in particular, the people of God.

Thirdly, in the light of this, the coming of the Son of Man to the Ancient of Days must be regarded as a coming to the presence of God in heaven of a real figure. The seer believes that he is describing an event which took place in the heavenly world above, and not merely describing the divine truth in picturesque language. It is a figure who exists in the world above and who comes to the divine tribunal. As we have seen, nowhere in the following interpretation is the Son of Man identified with the saints of the Most High. The nearest we get to a link between them is the fact that both receive divine sovereignty (Dan. 7.14; cf. Dan. 7.18, 22, 27). The parallelism between vision and interpretation is between the bestowal of divine authority and dominion on the Son of Man and on the saints of the Most High. We are probably justified, therefore, in assuming that the receiving of divine sovereignty by the human-looking figure in the heavenly court is an indication that the saints too will receive dominion. It is not necessary to say that the Son of Man and the saints are, therefore, in some way to be identified. The message of the chapter is simply this: just as the Son of Man triumphs in the divine court, so the saints of the Most High will triumph in the face of the kings of the earth. The triumph of the Son of Man in heaven over the heavenly counterparts of the earthly kings is a sign that the dominion of those kings cannot be continued for much longer. It is this which is a mark of hope for the persecuted people of God.

Perhaps the best commentary on Daniel 7 can be offered by the passage from the War Scroll,[43] quoted earlier: 'He will raise up the kingdom of Michael in the midst of the gods, and the realm of Israel in the midst of all flesh.' (1QM 17.7f.). Just as in this passage Michael's triumph in the heavenly realm is paralleled on earth by the triumph of the people of God, so the triumph of the Son of Man in the vision in Daniel 7 is paralleled by the dominion of the saints on earth.

Fourthly, the question inevitably arises of the identity of this figure. The use of the phrase to describe him may suggest that he is in fact a human being who is exalted to God's presence, like Enoch or Elijah.[44] Two facts seem to point against this, however. First of all, the reference to the clouds suggests that he is a divine being, as usually in the Old Testament clouds are a sign of the divine presence.[45] Secondly, the description of the figure as 'like a (son of) man' need not indicate a human being. Elsewhere in Daniel we find that angelic beings are described in a similar way: 'When I, Daniel, had seen the vision, I sought to understand it; and behold, there stood before me one having the appearance of a man.' (Dan. 8.15).

It becomes clear from the following verses that this figure, who has the appearance of a man, is none other than the angel Gabriel. Likewise in the story of the fiery furnace in Daniel 3 Nebuchadnezzar sees four men in the furnace, one of whom was 'like a son of God' (3.25).[46] In the vision of the angel in Daniel 10.5ff. the first thing which strikes the seer as he sets out to describe the angel is his resemblance to a man. In the light of this we should probably explain the human figure in Daniel 7 as an angelic being. The close connection with the people of the saints of the Most High in the following interpretation makes closer identification possible, however, as we know from Daniel 12.1 that Michael is the guardian angel of the people of God. It is only to be expected that his dominion in the world above would be followed by the vindication of the people whom he represents.[47]

The identification of the Son of Man of Daniel 7.13 with an angel makes the attempt to find here a reference to the messiah rather difficult to support.[48] As far as one can ascertain from the chapter, there is no suggestion that the Son of Man comes as an eschatological judge. He is merely a vice-regent, exercising the divine sovereignty on God's behalf. Unlike the Son of Man in the synoptic gospels nothing is said about his coming to vindicate the elect (cf. Mark 13.26). His dominion in heaven is a sign for the saints that their vindication is assured. Nor is the title messiah mentioned in the chapter. There is a complete absence of those attributes of the messiah which can be ascertained from the Jewish literature written round about the beginning of the Christian era.

Finally, Daniel 7 gives us no leave to suppose that any Son of Man concept is presupposed by the seer. The phrase 'son of man' is used here in a merely descriptive sense in precisely the same way as the reference to the human form of the angel is in Daniel 8.15. Although Daniel 7 may have provided the material for later speculation on heavenly redeemer-figures,[49] there is no suggestion that this chapter provides us with a Jewish Son of Man doctrine. All we can say is that we have a reference to a heavenly, angelic figure, who is compared to a man and whose receiving of dominion over the universe heralds the ultimate glory of God's people.

The brief reference to the Son of Man in Daniel 7.13 contrasts with the comparatively numerous references in the Similitudes of Enoch, some of which appear to take Daniel 7.13 as their starting point[50] and develop a picture of a heavenly figure who has a significant role to play in the coming judgement of the nations. Since the discovery of the Ethiopic version of Enoch, the central chapters of this version (37—71) have attracted considerable attention from scholars, because they appear to offer a picture of the Son of Man with many affinities with the canonical gospels. Nevertheless opinion concerning the value of this material is divided. There are those who set great store by it as a repository of messianic belief at the time of Jesus, whereas others point to the absence of these chapters of 1 Enoch from the Enoch fragments found at Qumran and conclude that we have in the Similitudes a product of a later period, probably from a Christian hand.[51] Our concern here, however, is not with the beginnings of New Testament christology but the existence of speculative developments of Daniel 7.13 in later texts. Whether Jewish or Christian (and I for one find it difficult to believe that we have a Christian production in the Similitudes, whenever we date them) they do offer us evidence of the way in which Daniel 7.13 was taken up and interpreted at a later period. Therefore, along with the future Son of Man sayings in the gospels, some of which make clear reference to Daniel 7.13 (e.g. Mark 13.26; 14.62), they offer us at the very least a development of Daniel 7.13, which indicates the use which could be made of that chapter.

A glance at 1 Enoch 37—71 reveals that it is a composite work containing very varied types of material ranging from an isolated Wisdom piece in chapter 42 to legends about Noah similar to those found in the opening chapters of 1 Enoch. It is no surprise, therefore, to find that many studies of the Similitudes have felt the need to disentangle the various sources which are used in this section.[52] In the sections dealing with the Son of Man two problems immediately present themselves. First of all, reference is made to another title in the Similitudes along with the Son of Man, namely the Elect One. This title is used in much the same way as the Son of Man, e.g. 1 Enoch 45.3f; 61.8f; cf. 1 Enoch 46.4; 69.27. Secondly, the final chapter of the Similitudes has a description of the ascent of Enoch to heaven and the announcement that Enoch himself is the heavenly Son of Man. This identification of Enoch with a figure, whom the seer had described in some detail in the preceding chapters, has proved so difficult to explain that R. H. Charles felt compelled to emend the text to avoid the impression that the writer of the final chapter had in fact offered such an identification.[53]

The two principal titles, the Elect One and the Son of Man, have occasioned much speculation about different sources standing behind the two titles.[54] Such a quest seems to be fruitless, however, because there appears to be considerable overlap between the characteristics linked with the two titles,[55] and so, whatever the background of the two titles they have now merged completely in the Similitudes as we have them. As far as the relationship between the final chapter (ch. 71) and the rest of the Similitudes is concerned, the majority of commentators assume that we have in the former a later addition to the work, solving the problem of identification of the Son of Man.[56] Nevertheless there are some reasons for supposing that chapter 71 may not be dependent on the rest of the Similitudes and may in fact be an earlier passage altogether, which has influenced some of the ideas contained in the earlier chapters.

It is entirely correct to assert that the Similitudes offer evidence of an identification between the heavenly Son of Man and the title messiah. Not only are passages usually linked with the Davidic king transferred to the Son of Man/Elect One, but on two occasions the word messiah is actually used to describe this figure. Notwithstanding 4 Ezra 13 the Similitudes seem to be the only unambiguous application of the title messiah to a heavenly figure, and so we find here a confluence of two doctrinal streams which had probably hitherto remained separate. What is more, there are good reasons for supposing that the author intended his readers to understand that the Son of Man/Elect One existed in heaven long before his revelation as eschatological judge. Whether this also involved pre-existence, in the sense that Wisdom is pre-existent in a passage like Prov. 8.22ff., is difficult to ascertain. Clearly at one point reference is made to the name of the Son of Man being named before the creation of the world:

And that hour the Son of Man was named in the presence of the Lord of Spirits, and his name before the Head of Days. Yea, before the sun and the signs were created, before the stars of heaven were made, his name was named before the Lord of Spirits (1 Enoch 48.2f., cf. 62.7).

It will be seen that this passage speaks only of the pre-existence from before creation of the name of that Son of Man. Consequently it seems likely that we have here essentially the same kind of belief as that reflected in b. Pesahim 54a, where the name of the messiah is listed as one of the seven things which preceded the creation of the world.[57] Thus, although the name of the Son of Man was named before God from eternity, there is nothing in the Similitudes to suggest that the Son of Man/Elect One existed in heaven before his revelation as judge at the consummation.

Whatever our view of the relationship between chapter 71 and the earlier part of the Similitudes, the final form of the text presents us with the identification of a human being (Enoch) and a heavenly figure. As such it offers identification of the heavenly Son of Man as well as offering evidence of the existence of speculation about a heavenly man in a Jewish text.[58] Nevertheless it must be doubted whether we have in the Similitudes the phrase Son of Man used as a messianic title. It has often been pointed out that the phrase Son of Man in Charles's English version covers no less than three Ethiopic expressions,[59] and the evidence would seem to point against the use of a stereotyped expression which functions as a christological title.[60] But even if one cannot use the Similitudes as evidence of a Son of Man doctrine in Judaism, they do offer us a distinctive eschatological picture. Belief in a heavenly saviour was not widespread in Judaism.[61] Indeed, one could argue that the view of the Similitudes with regard to the heavenly Son of Man and the fragmentary Melchizedek document from cave 11 at Qumran offer us an eschatological picture of a rather idiosyncratic type. In both cases an exalted man of antiquity acts as judge in place of God. As far as the writer of the Similitudes was concerned, the problem of the identity of the Son of Man in Daniel 7.13 has been solved by identification with Enoch. Once Enoch becomes the heavenly judge, it becomes easy to see why the title messiah should have been transferred to him. The fact that the heavenly

Son of Man had been identified with the man Enoch made it possible to transfer to this figure a title which was normally linked only with a human being. Thus the Similitudes may show interest in a heavenly man and his identity but hardly provide evidence of a Son of Man doctrine in Judaism.

We have argued that in Daniel 7 and the Similitudes there does seem to be evidence of a heavenly figure who resembles a man, though the evidence for the existence of a coherent Son of Man concept does not seem to be supported by the texts. We come now to the discussion of another passage, which is usually linked with the others in any discussion of the Jewish background to the phrase Son of Man in the New Testament, 4 Ezra 13. As is the case with the Similitudes, it is quite apparent from the opening words that the passage is closely linked with Daniel 7:

> And it came to pass after seven days that I dreamed a dream by night: and I beheld, and lo, there arose a violent wind from the sea, and stirred all its waves. And I beheld, and lo, the wind caused to come up out of the heart of the seas as it were the form of a man. And I beheld, and lo, this man flew with the clouds of heaven.

The similarities with Daniel 7, not only with the description of the Son of Man in verse 13 but also with the opening verse of the chapter ('the four winds of heaven were stirring up the great sea' v. 2), are most marked. It would appear that the author of 4 Ezra was considerably influenced by this chapter in his visions, as 12.11 shows. The question is, however, whether this chapter also offers us evidence of the existence of a belief in a heavenly man like Daniel and the Similitudes.

In the chapter as we have it, the vision of the man from the sea is followed by an interpretation, but this time, unlike Daniel 7 but like the dream-visions elsewhere in 4 Ezra, the seer does not pretend to reveal the contents of heaven. He may have drawn the inspiration for this chapter from Daniel 7 but has not followed the writer of that vision in offering a vision of the heavenly world. The vision in chapter 13 is one in which the images contained in it have no independent reality in heaven but are merely symbols of events which are to happen on earth in the future. Thus the man who comes up from the sea is not a heavenly being and is merely a symbol of the messianic figure who effects judgement and deliverance in the future. In other words, the Son of Man figure in Daniel 7 has been used by the author of 4 Ezra, not as the original writer intended but as a mere symbol of the messiah. In this respect it is significant that the theophany of Daniel 7.9f. makes no appearance in the vision in 4 Ezra 13, and, with the exception of the reference to the fact that the man comes with the clouds of heaven, there is nothing to indicate that the scene takes place in the world above. Indeed, this reference to heaven here is probably to be explained as a direct borrowing from Daniel 7.13 rather than any indication by the apocalypticist that the man was a heavenly being. It becomes clear when we examine the interpretation of the vision that what the seer has seen is a picturesque way of describing certain eschatological events. Just as the great mountain which the man cut for himself (v. 6f.) is identified with Mount Zion (v. 35), and the fiery breath of his mouth (v. 10) with the Law (v. 38), so the man himself is said to be 'he whom the Most High is keeping many ages' (v. 26).

Even if the vision of the man coming with the clouds is not intended by the author to be a heavenly figure, the reference to this figure, quoted at the end of the previous paragraph, does superficially look like a reference to a pre-existent messiah. By itself this need mean no more than that the divine plan for the mission of the messiah has been laid down long ago, and therefore nothing is said with regard to the nature of the messiah at all. Indeed, the indications from chapter 7.28f. are that the messiah was regarded by the author of 4 Ezra as a man who would eventually die like other men, a belief which is hardly consistent with the idea of a heavenly figure. Thus it would appear that all the references in 4 Ezra to the messiah are susceptible of an interpretation which denies the personal pre-existence of that figure. That would, however, ignore chapter 14.9, which it is difficult to interpret in any other way than as a reference to the personal pre-existence of the messiah in heaven: 'For thou shalt be taken up from among men, and henceforth thou shalt remain with my son, and with such as are like thee, until the times be ended.'

The presence of this passage seems to suggest that the author of 4 Ezra did in fact acknowledge a belief in the pre-existent messiah, who would only be revealed to men in the new age.[62] Nevertheless the nature of this figure could not have exercised his mind greatly, as there is clearly a contradiction between the humanity presupposed by 7.29 and the pre-existence pre-supposed in a passage like this. This evidence does not, however, affect the validity of our interpretation of 4 Ezra 13. The vision of the man rising from the sea is not a vision of a man in heaven, even though the interpretation may be taken as an indication that the author had in mind a pre-existent messiah.

Where does this leave us as far as the question of the Son of Man is concerned? The evidence suggests that: (a) there is reason to suppose that there were beliefs in a heavenly man figure in Judaism and also an emerging belief that the messianic agent was pre-existent, but (b) there are virtually no grounds for supposing that there existed a Jewish Son of Man concept with the coherent outlines which can be sketched of contemporary expectations concerning the descendant of David or a prophet like Moses. It is tempting to find the antecedents of Christian ideas laid out for us in Jewish texts, but, even assuming that we are justified in using a work like the Similitudes to assist with the interpretation of the New Testament,[63] the evidence of this text, like the rest, gives little support for the existence of a clear-cut and readily understood Son of Man doctrine in Judaism.

In this sketch of the eschatological teaching of the apocalypses it will be apparent that we are not dealing with a subject which was the all-consuming interest of the apocalypticists. Eschatological teaching is certainly to be found in most apocalypses, but it did not demand the close attention from the writers which we are often led to believe. The point is well illustrated by the paucity of evidence concerning the nature of the future age. For a movement whose *raison d'être* is supposed to have been the promotion of a science of the end, the apocalypses offer meagre evidence for a reconstruction of the details of Jewish beliefs about the new age, let alone a distinctively apocalyptic belief concerning it. Most eschatological passages content themselves with only passing references to the eschatological bliss. This is hardly the stuff of which utopian dreams about the ideal society are made. In the light of this the description of the new Jerusalem in Revelation 21 stands in stark contrast to other apocalypses, which can offer nothing remotely parallel to its extensive description of the new Jerusalem. In this respect, the brief reference to the messianic kingdom in the previous chapter of Revelation is much more akin to the restraint shown by the Jewish apocalypses.

What seems to have interested the apocalypticists more than extravagant speculations about the character of the new age was the interest in human history which led up to it. The birth-pangs of the age to come, which enable the community to identify the transition to something greater and to avoid despair about the apparent absence of God from human history, are much more important; the need to understand human history from the divine perspective and in the light of the divine purposes is of far greater significance than the mere promises of glittering prizes at the end of the road for those who persevere. To know that the unsatisfactory situation which faces man in the present is a transitory phenomenon is one way of reaffirming the viability of religious belief. Ultimately the only test of that belief is an eschatological verification, but the eschatological disclosures, like other revelations in the apocalypses, brought forward the moment of verification to enable the distressed and downtrodden to stand firm in their convictions.

Apocalyptic is concerned to understand how the present relates with both the past and the future. The absence of any concern with the details of life in the future and the rather prosaic accounts of the whole of history suggest that it is not the way in which the righteous would spend their time in the kingdom but the meaning of existence in the present in the light of God's activity in the past and his hoped for acts in the future which dominated their understanding of existence. Apocalyptic certainly offers its readers a hope for the future. It is one, however, which does not persuade the righteous to faithfulness by detailed accounts of what is prepared for them but seeks to reassure them by demonstrating how the whole of history must be seen as the arena of divine activity. It is only thus that present perplexities could be properly assessed.

Part Three

Towards an Understanding of the Origins of Apocalyptic and the Dates of the Apocalypses

CHAPTER 8

A Survey of Recent Study on the Origins of Apocalyptic

I

MOST STUDIES OF apocalyptic include a substantial part on the subject of the antecedents of apocalyptic in Israelite religion.[1] Recently this has tended to concentrate on the centuries immediately after the Exile and the attempt to isolate and interpret the literature produced during this period. This is a singularly difficult task because our knowledge of religious currents at this time, not to mention the history of the Jews at this time, is extremely scanty.[2] Although scholars are prepared to use several parts of the Old Testament canon as a means of throwing light on this period, particularly the books of Chronicles and certain prophetic oracles, the evidence is so small that it is by no means easy to obtain anything like a complete picture of religious currents during the Persian period. What is more, research into the vexed question of apocalyptic origins is still at a comparatively early stage. Accordingly, it would be singularly inappropriate to do anything more at this stage than to offer a sketch of the various approaches to this question in recent study and to examine a few sections of the apocalypses themselves in the hope that it may be possible to identify some of the ways in which they came into existence.

Because the eschatological element in apocalyptic literature has tended to attract most attention in the study of this literature, it is the biblical antecedents of this particular feature which have tended to dictate the course of the study of apocalyptic origins. The reason for this, in part at least, is the way in which the book of Daniel has figured so prominently in the discussion of the issue. Indeed, this document is crucial for Rowley's thesis that the publication of Daniel marked the decisive breakthrough in the evolution of the apocalypse.[3] Concentration on the book of Daniel tends to lead a commentator to suppose that the one element for which he needs to find antecedents in the Old Testament is the eschatological interest which appears in the second half of the book. While there has been a recognition that the underlying theme of Daniel is not simply eschatological,[4] it is clear that it is to the prophetic books in particular that scholars turn to explain the origin of this feature of the book of Daniel.

The prophetic oracles are replete with judgements of doom and promises of hope, and the common future perspective found in both prophecy and apocalyptic makes the supposition of some kind of contact between prophecy and apocalyptic certain. Nevertheless scholars have not been slow to point out the differences which do exist between the two.[5] For example, it is the concern in apocalyptic to view history as a whole and not merely isolated events in the present or future. The prophetic promise of redemption has become in the apocalypses part of an elaborate plan for the whole of human history laid down in the divine counsels before the creation of the world. But it is not merely the question of the contribution of prophecy to apocalyptic which has been of interest to scholars, but whether the prophetic movement itself formed the soil within which apocalyptic of a later period flowered.

The point has been most clearly made in a recent study of certain exilic and post-exilic prophetic oracles which could be said to offer examples of 'proto-apocalyptic' eschatology. In the opinion of P. D. Hanson[6] certain oracles from the later chapters of Isaiah as well as Ezekiel 40ff., Zechariah and Haggai give us evidence of a conflict within the post-exilic community between a visionary group, who saw themselves as the true inheritors of the traditions of Second Isaiah on the one hand, and a priestly group on the other, both of whom sought to put into practice their plan for the restoration of Zion. Hanson argues, on the basis of detailed exegesis of the oracles, particularly from Third Isaiah, that the visionaries lost the struggle and became so disillusioned with what they found in Jerusalem (Isa. 59.2ff.) that they despaired of seeking any kind of restoration by human initiative and began to look to a direct intervention from God as the only basis for hope (Isa. 63.1ff.). Linked with this was their gradual despair of history as the arena of divine activity and their conviction that the new age would have to be on a higher plane than the mundane realities which caused them so much despair (Isa. 65.17ff.). In their hopes for the future Hanson argues that there is a dissolution of the fine balance which exists between history and mythology in Second Isaiah. Instead of using myth as a way of speaking about divine activity within history, as their predecessor Second Isaiah had done, the visionaries took the mythological language and saw in it the reality of their hope which was now centred on direct intervention rather than on the action of God through the historical process. A good example of this is to be found in the use of the divine warrior-myth in Isaiah 59.14ff. to express the hope of the visionary group that their God would manifest himself directly to put right all the wrongs which had been committed:[7]

> . . . Justice is turned back, and righteousness stands afar off; for truth has fallen in the public squares, and uprightness cannot enter. Truth is lacking, and he who departs from evil makes himself a prey. The LORD saw it, and it displeased him that there was no justice. He saw that there was no man, and wondered that there was no one to intervene; then his own arm brought him victory, and his righteousness upheld him. He put on righteousness as a breast-plate, and a helmet of salvation upon his head; he put on garments of vengeance for clothing, and wrapped himself in fury as a mantle. According to their deeds, so will he repay, wrath to his adversaries, requital to his enemies; . . . (Isa. 59.14–18).

It is apparent from this passage that the prophet looked to God alone for deliverance, for the simple reason that there was no one else to whom to turn. Therefore, it was God himself who would come to execute judgement on the wicked and deliverance for the elect, not the kings of the earth who would function as the rod of his anger (cf. Isa. 10.5). Hope is thus transposed to another plane, and the stuff of history gradually appears to be inadequate as a vehicle for the exercise of the divine will. We thus have an emerging pessimism with regard to the present age and a consequent dualism as hope is centred on the future glorious intervention of God, as well as the belief that only in the world beyond could proper recompense be received.

Hanson's exegesis of the prophetic oracles is fascinating, and the reconstruction of the situation after the Exile, though necessarily hypothetical, one that brilliantly makes sense of the texts. Two points have to be made, however. One recent commentator has pointed out how difficult it is to posit a precise setting for many of the oracles of the later chapters of Isaiah.[8] But even if it is granted that Hanson has offered a reconstruction of the situation in which these oracles were produced, the question arises whether he has in fact offered us any illumination of the apocalyptic movement as it is to be found in the material which has occupied our attention so far in this study. Hanson has provided evidence for the existence of a prophetic group in post-exilic Judaism whose hopes for the future were considerably influenced by earlier prophetic oracles. He has thus raised the important question of the development of prophecy after the Exile, but he has deliberately concentrated in his study more on the developments in eschatology than on the character of the prophecy itself, though considerable attention is given to the changes which were taking place in the form of the prophetic oracles. What is perhaps more important is to ascertain whether the character of post-exilic prophecy was moving in an apocalyptic direction in the way in which it apprehended the divine truths proclaimed in the oracles.

Two important questions remain, however. Firstly, can we trace links between the disillusioned visionaries of the immediate post-exilic period and the writers of the later apocalypses? Secondly, is it possible to discern in the beliefs of these oracles the essence of later apocalyptic and particularly its eschatology? An answer to the second question is clearly going to be easier than the attempt, which must inevitably rest on much hypothetical reconstruction, to establish the contribution of a group which existed at least two centuries before the full flowering of apocalyptic in the second century BC and later. That some kind of contact can be established between the eschatology of these oracles and that found in apocalyptic literature cannot be denied. The picture of the consummation in Revelation 19.11ff. has many affinities with the divine warrior passage quoted above. Nevertheless it would be wrong to suppose that, by recovering evidence of the resurgence of certain myths in the eschatology of the visionary group which produced some of the oracles in Third Isaiah, one has necessarily uncovered the essential ingredient in apocalyptic or even, for that matter, in apocalyptic eschatology. The problem is, as we have already pointed out, that apocalyptic eschatology is not susceptible of simple definitions. The direct intervention of God or his envoy into a world of sin to right all wrongs hardly characterizes the variety of apocalyptic expectation. What is more, we have here only one feature of the many which make up the phenomenon which we know as apocalyptic. The underlying theme which we sought to expound in the opening chapter, namely, that apocalyptic was concerned essentially with the disclosure of the divine secrets in a clearly defined form, is not to be found in the oracles of Third Isaiah. That is not to deny that this literature furnished important ideas which were to be taken up in later Jewish eschatology, but it is not so clear that a movement orientated towards redemption by God in some supernatural sphere is really the key to apocalyptic. There is much to agree with in Hanson's attempt to understand the apocalyptic mentality, but it is a pity that the concentration is too greatly weighted towards eschatology to do justice to the way of looking at the world which manifests itself in the non-eschatological sections of the apocalypses.[9]

While the oracles of Third Isaiah have only infrequently been cited as examples of the kind of material which offers us evidence of the transition from prophecy to apocalyptic, the same cannot be said of passages like Isaiah 24—27 and the book of Joel, which figure prominently in discussions of apocalyptic origins.[10] In both Isaiah 24—27 and Joel we find elements which show some similarities with the eschatological beliefs of later Jewish writings. In the former the prophet predicts desolation on earth and events taking place of an earth-shattering nature (Isa. 24.19–23):

> The earth is utterly broken, the earth is rent asunder, the earth is violently shaken. The earth staggers like a drunken man, it sways like a hut; its transgression lies heavy upon it, and it falls, and will not rise again. On that day the LORD will punish the hosts of heaven, in heaven, and the kings of the earth, on the earth. They will be gathered together as prisoners in a pit; they will be shut up in prison, and after many days they will be punished. Then the moon will be confounded, and the sun ashamed; and the LORD of hosts will reign on Mount Zion and in Jerusalem and before his elders he will manifest his glory.

Events like these are the prelude to the eschatological banquet on Mount Zion (Isa. 25.6), the resurrection and the final judgement (Isa. 26.19—27.1). Here we have in short space the essence of later Jewish eschatology, with the horrors which must precede the new age followed by the judgement and bliss for the righteous. Likewise in the book of Joel the horror of the day of the Lord (Joel 2.10f.) is the prelude to a new age when God will judge the nations and bring about a prosperous future for Israel (Joel 3.18ff.). This is the stuff of which later Jewish eschatology was made. Yet it has to be noted that, as in the oracles of Third Isaiah investigated by Hanson, we are dealing here with just one element which contributed to the total apocalyptic phenomenon. There is not enough in these passages, apart from the eschatological material, to be able to designate this material as an important link in the chain which connects the apocalypses with prophecy. Certainly here is a quarry for Jewish eschatology and evidence of the development of prophetic eschatology in the direction of those ideas which become part of the stock of Jewish eschatological belief round about the beginning of the Christian era. Nevertheless there are not enough indications here that we have the origin of apocalyptic, even if certain features of its eschatology are to be found.[11]

When we compare the book of Daniel with these so-called 'proto-apocalyptic' fragments, there are many differences. Although it would be generally agreed that Daniel and Isaiah 24—27 are pseudonymous (there is more uncertainty with regard to Joel),[12] many of the features which are so characteristic of Daniel are completely absent in both passages. The total view of history, which makes its appearance in the second part of the book, the visions and interpretations as well as the extensive legends about the seer are all lacking in these prophetic works. By contrast, Daniel lacks completely the more extended description of the future age which figures so prominently in both works. All this leads one to suppose that acknowledgement of the debt of the apocalypses to the developing eschatology of the later prophetic oracles is insufficient to explain the apocalypses as we have them. This eschatological material is a contributory factor to the development of later Jewish theology, on which the writers of the apocalypses inevitably drew, but it cannot be used to explain the origin of the apocalyptic movement, whose distinctive outlines are not paralleled in this literature. The continuation and development of eschatological ideas in Judaism after the Exile is not in itself enough to explain apocalyptic, whose outlook is much broader than the mere interest in the things of the last days.

If one is to look anywhere in the prophetic writings for material which may help us to understand the origins of apocalyptic, it should surely be found in the various glimpses into the heavenly world vouchsafed to the prophets (Isa. 6.1ff.; 1 Kings 22.19; Ezek 1.1ff.) and the visionary material which is to be found at the end of Ezekiel (ch. 40ff.) and in the first six chapters of Zechariah.[13] In the former we have a much more primitive version of the notion, which we find in several of the apocalypses, of the ascent to heaven in order to gain access to the divine presence and to receive knowledge of the divine secrets. In all the cases cited above from the Old Testament we find that a vision of God and his court is followed by the commissioning of the prophet (Isa. 6.9 and Ezek. 2.1) and his insight into the divine plan (1 Kings 22.20ff.). The commissioning of the apocalyptic seer after the ascent to heaven is to be found in 1 Enoch 15.1ff., where Enoch is told by God to go to the Watchers, who had asked him to intercede on their behalf, to tell them that there was no possibility of their act of repentance being accepted by God (1 Enoch 16.4). Elsewhere in the apocalypses the ascent to the throne of God is the prelude to the disclosure of the divine mysteries. In the Apocalypse of Abraham, for example, the vision of God's throne is a prelude to the disclosure of the way in which God's promise to Abraham would be fulfilled (Apoc. Abra. 20ff.).

In Ezekiel 40 the prophet is shown a vision of the Temple and the land which God has planned for the future. The parallel with the belief which is found in the apocalypses of the details of the Jerusalem of the new age being already prepared by God in heaven immediately springs to mind. The situation is not quite the same in the book of Ezekiel. Here the prophet is said to see the form of the city in a vision, but it remains unclear whether this is supposed to be the heavenly plan for the future of the land of Israel (Ezek. 40.2). What is not in doubt, however, is the fact that the plan for the reconstruction of the city is offered to the prophet as a disclosure of the divine will. It is the result of 'visions of God' (Ezek. 40.2, cf. 1.1) that enable the prophet to see the form of the city and the detailed structure of its buildings. Also of relevance for the later apocalyptic vision is the fact that Ezekiel does not merely report the details of his vision on his own initiative. He is accompanied throughout his excursion through the restored city by a man (Ezek. 40.3). Nothing whatever is said about the nature of this man, but even if we cannot be certain that he is an angel,[14] the significant thing is that there emerges here that form which was to prove so important within the apocalyptic literature: the vision followed by an angelic interpretation (Dan. 8.15f.; 1 Enoch 19.1; 40.8; Rev. 17.1). In his perambulation the prophet remains silent and a passive recipient of the information communicated to him by the angel, just as Daniel in chapter 8.19ff. merely listens to the interpretation of the dream and the other disclosures which are offered to him by the angelic envoy (ch. 10—12).

Even more important for our understanding of the origin of the outlook of apocalyptic are the visions of Zechariah. Once again we have not yet reached a stage where the prophet has ascended into heaven to receive the visions of God, but there are significant developments, even compared with Ezekiel 40ff., which make these chapters an important stage in the evolution of the prophetic experience in the direction of apocalyptic. For one thing there can be no doubt that we have here the angel of God playing an important role in the visions (Zech. 3.1ff.) and acting as a guide to the prophet (Zech. 1.19; 4.2ff.).[15] What is more, the dream-vision followed by the interpretation, which plays such an important role in apocalyptic, is found here in almost exactly the form in which we find it in the apocalypses. In chapter 4.1ff. the prophet sees a bowl with two olive-trees standing by it. This vision is then interpreted by the angel as the 'two anointed who stand by the Lord of the whole earth' (Zech. 4.14). In the opening chapters of Zechariah we find the prophetic experience moving away from the more 'normal' mode of presentation of the communication of God to his people. We still find the communications of God prefaced with the words 'Thus says the LORD' (e.g. Zech. 1.2f.; 6.9ff.). But alongside this there exists a more exotic means of understanding the divine counsel and promulgating it, through vision and interpretation. Here the divine mystery is becoming more difficult to ascertain and even more difficult to understand. It has become necessary for an angel to assist the prophet in making sense of his visions, so that he will be in a position to communicate the will of God to the people.

Earlier we raised the question of the direction in which the prophetic movement was going after the Exile. We saw how Hanson argued for a significant section of it moving off into an isolated position over against the religious establishment in Jerusalem. The character of the prophetic material in Zechariah, however, also raises other questions with regard to the nature of prophecy at this period. There are already indications in the prophecies of Ezekiel that there was a return to a more ecstatic type of prophecy, characterized by experiences of translation (Ezek. 8.2; 3.12), which probably extended to severe psychological states (3.25ff.). Also the eccentric symbolism which makes its appearance in Ezekiel (e.g. ch. 4—5) points to a resurgence of primitive prophetic elements in this pre-exilic prophet (cf. 1 Sam. 15.27).[16] What most interests us, however, is the emergence of a visionary element in later prophecy which is found in embryonic form in the concluding chapters of Ezekiel and in more developed form in Zechariah 1—6. The indications, such as they are, point in the direction of a significant visionary component in the post-exilic prophetic movement. The question is whether this continued to characterize parts of the prophetic movement during the Persian period. The answer to this question demands more detailed study than is possible here, but there do appear to be indications that this particular characteristic of prophecy continued to have currency for some considerable period.

The main reason for thinking this is the oracle contained in Zechariah 13.2–6, which speaks of the conditions which will arise in the land 'on that day':

> 'And on that day, says the LORD of hosts, I will cut off the names of the idols from the land, so that they shall be remembered no more; and also I will remove from the land the prophets and the unclean spirit. And if any one again appears as a prophet, his father and mother who bore him will say to him, "You shall not live, for you speak lies in the name of the LORD"; and his father and mother who bore him shall pierce him through when he prophesies. On that day every prophet will be ashamed of his vision when he prophesies; he will not put on a hairy mantle in order to deceive, but he will say, "I am no prophet, I am a tiller of the soil; for the land has been my possession since my youth". And if one asks him, "What are these wounds on your back?" he will say, "The wounds I received in the house of my friends".'

The dating of this oracle is uncertain,[17] though it probably was written some considerable period after the oracles contained in the first part of the book. In other words, the gap between the latest of the prophets and the first apocalypses is gradually being narrowed, and in this, one of the latest biblical accounts of prophecy, we have a view of it which is far from complimentary. In this oracle the prophet looks forward to the messianic age when the land will be as free of prophets as of idols. It will be a time when no one wants to acknowledge his prophetic office and families will want to repudiate in the most brutal way possible any suggestion that any of their children claim prophetic inspiration. The oracle tells us something about the character of the prophetic office: it involves visions (*hizayon*), the wearing of a hairy mantle, and a form of mortification or self-inflicted wounds during ecstasy (v. 6). What is not clear is whether these references characterize prophecy in the prophet's day.[18] If they do, then we must suppose that some of the more eccentric characteristics found in connection with prophets in earlier times had reappeared (cf. 2 Kings 1.8; Isa. 20.2, cf. Jer. 16.6; 14.4).

The repugnance connected with the prophetic office becomes much more understandable if such activities characterized prophetic activity at that time. But the point which most interests us is the fact that the prophet says that in the messianic age the prophet will be ashamed of his vision (v. 4). The question is whether this reference accurately characterises the type of prophetic experience known to the writer of this passage. The problem is that the word *hizayon* can be used generally of prophetic oracles, irrespective of whether they are in fact actual visionary experiences or not.[19] If we could take *hizayon* in the sense of a vision which a prophet saw,[20] this would be valuable confirmation that the kind of developments which are to be found in Zechariah continued in the gradually degenerating prophetic movement. What is not in doubt, however, is that at the time of this oracle there was so much distaste for the prophetic office that the hope for the future was marked by the abolition of such an office, a far cry from the expectations of a later period when the coming of the new age marked the return of the prophetic spirit to Israel.[21]

The history of prophecy after the Exile clearly has an important role to play in the ongoing discussion of the origin of apocalyptic, not only with respect to the various elements which make up the apocalypses but the distinctive form in which these ideas were supposed to have been communicated to the apocalyptic seers. The link between prophecy and apocalyptic has not been the only approach to this subject, however. Indeed, as one recent commentator has pointed out: 'the obvious instances of not only sapiential material, but of materials deriving from Greek, Hellenistic and various Eastern sources disallow apocalypticism as a simple rectilinear development out of prophecy.'[22] The first element is the one which must occupy our attention: the relationship of apocalyptic to the Wisdom traditions of Judaism.

Although the connections between the apocalypses and the Jewish Wisdom literature have been noted several times[23] in the past, it is the name of G. von Rad in particular which has been linked with the thesis that, far from being the child of prophecy, the apocalypses betray exactly the same kind of outlook as the Wisdom literature. The concern with the totality of human history, as well as the created world and the world above, is of a piece with the curiosity evident in the Wisdom literature:

> Once it is realised, however, that knowledge is thus the nerve-centre of apocalyptic literature, knowledge based on universal Jahwism, surprisingly divorced from the saving history, it would not be difficult to determine the real matrix from which apocalyptic literature originates. This is Wisdom, in which, as we have already noted . . . exactly the same characteristics appear. We understood Wisdom as the effort made by the people of Israel to grasp the laws which governed the world in which she lived, and to systematise them. In course of time this developed into a really encyclopedic science which applied itself not only to matters of natural philosophy but also to questions of history . . . and are not the matters with which apocalyptic literature is occupied expressly those of wisdom and science? . . . Certainly they were aware that all human striving after knowledge, especially where it is directed upon the things of God, the future, and what lies beyond the end, requires revelation, and that it can only exist as charismatic knowledge. This, however, is far from making them prophets . . .[24]

Whatever may be the polemical note in his attack on apocalyptic and its position within biblical theology,[25] one cannot doubt that von Rad has put his finger on something very central to apocalyptic when he seeks to characterize it as an offspring of Wisdom. It is true that the apocalypses do evince a thirst for knowledge about a variety of subjects, a fact which may elude us if we confine the study only to their interest in eschatological matters. As one would expect, von Rad's theories have not been

without their critics.[26] Indeed, the rather bald way in which von
Rad outlines his thesis tends at times to gloss over some of the
difficulties in positing such an origin for apocalyptic.[27] Particularly difficult is the obvious lack of eschatological material from
the major Wisdom documents of the Old Testament and Apocrypha,[28] a fact which becomes more difficult to explain when we
find that what can only be termed an 'anti-apocalyptic' stance is
to be found in Sirach. Not only do we find a warning against
speculation on matters which are beyond human comprehension
(Sir. 3.20ff.); but also a direct repudiation of the value of dreams
(Sir. 34.1ff.). Such evidence is hardly conducive to the view that
a Wisdom document like Sirach and the apocalypses share a
common background. If one compares Proverbs and Sirach with
the apocalypses, the experiential wisdom of the former finds few
parallels in the latter, though the observations concerning the
natural world in 1 Enoch, together with the astronomical sections, offer some parallels. But even here one cannot overlook
the fact that Enoch gives his information about the movements
of sun and moon, and possibly also his journeys through the
universe, *as the result of revelation* and not as a result of the
exercise of human reason. Thus despite the common quest for
knowledge there do appear to be certain profound differences
which make a direct relationship between the two unlikely.

Von Rad's suggestion about the contact of apocalyptic with
Wisdom has not remained undeveloped, however. Even if the
type of Wisdom which we find in Proverbs, Ecclesiastes and
Sirach seems far removed from the apocalypses, similarities
have been pointed out between apocalyptic and mantic Wisdom.[29] This type of Wisdom is rather different from the
experiential Wisdom of Proverbs and includes the interpretation
of dreams and the receipt of visions, in other words, exactly
what we find in the apocalypses. Indeed, the figure of Daniel as
he confronts us in the opening legends of the book of Daniel is
very much the ancient seer who interprets dreams and makes a
sense of portents (Dan. 2.31ff.; 4.19ff; 5.13ff.).[30] Like Joseph in
the book of Genesis, Daniel is one who is able to interpret the
dreams of foreign kings, and as one who is inspired with the
spirit of the holy gods and who can solve all kinds of problems
(Dan. 5.14 and 16), and it is not surprising therefore, that he
should be the recipient of further divine disclosures in visions
which he himself experiences (Dan. 7ff.). We are thus faced here

with a possible background to the apocalyptic literature which does justice to the elements which are contained in it.

Nevertheless this particular development should not obscure the value of von Rad's suggestion that there is a kindred spirit to apocalyptic in the Old Testament Wisdom tradition. The similarity between the two lies in the fact that both Wisdom and apocalyptic concerned themselves with consideration of this world and the problems which human existence presented to man. The Wisdom literature was not merely content to record the world as it found it but also sought explanations for certain perplexing phenomena which were to be found in it. The bulk of the apocalyptic literature sets out to satisfy man's curiosity about certain matters, and in particular those things which Ben Sirach had considered it a fruitless task to investigate (Sir. 3.20ff.). But even if apocalyptic occupied itself with those matters which were not susceptible of a solution merely by rational reflection, the difference from the approach of Wisdom in this respect is one of degree and not kind. The point can best be illustrated by reference to Job and Ecclesiastes on the one hand and 4 Ezra and Syriac Baruch on the other. In Ecclesiastes the author looks at the world and sees no rational explanation for the situations he finds in it, the suffering of the wise man (Eccles. 2.14f., cf. Wisd. 3—4) and the uncertainty of human existence (Eccles. 3.11). He offers only practical advice to the reader (Eccles. 9.9f.) but no answer to an unpredictable and irrational world.

Parallel issues emerge in the book of Job, this time in the context of a discussion of innocent suffering. Job is a supremely righteous man who becomes the victim of disasters of a personally debilitating kind (Job 1.18; 2.7). The story consists of various attempts by his friends, the 'comforters', to explain the cause of Job's unhappy state (Job 4ff.). The various explanations which are offered are obviously not suitable and are matched by Job's complaint to heaven. Unlike Ecclesiastes, which cannot begin to offer an answer to the perplexities facing man, the book of Job moves tentatively towards an answer, not only in the speeches of Job (e.g. Job 19.25ff.), but particularly in the final, dramatic intervention of God to answer Job (Job 38ff.). It is hard to call the divine reply an answer to Job's questions in any direct sense, but the consequence of these final chapters is that puny man is made to see that his investigation of the world and its inhabitants may lead to misguided conclusions, for the simple reason that the divine perspective is unavailable to him. It is significant that, as a result of the divine reply, Job can meekly accept the omnipotence of God and the futility of seeking answers to questions whose answers were beyond human comprehension. But what is most significant of all is the fact that Job speaks in the following way to God (Job 42.5–6):[31] 'I had heard of thee by the hearing of the ear, but now my eye sees thee; therefore I despise myself, and repent in dust and ashes.'

God's self-revelation in the whirlwind had enabled Job to see that his experiences were in fact no reason for cursing God and denying his existence, and, what is more, made him realize that what people had told him about God in fact corresponded with reality. In other words, Job is offered as an example of a victim of innocent suffering, who is shown that his traditional belief about God need not be adversely affected by what he experiences. Job is not told why there is so much unrighteousness in the world, but the divine revelation and the intimations of the divine sovereignty enable him to see that a view from the human perspective alone would lead to a distorted view of the nature of human experience.

There are two aspects to the book of Job which are of some importance for the study of apocalyptic. The first is the matter which we have just touched upon. The divine reply inevitably transforms the book of Job from a document full of human speculation about the reason for human misery into one in which the main character and the reader are shown that there is another dimension to human experience. Thus man would be totally misguided if he were to concentrate solely on what he sees without taking into account the totality of the divine purposes. The second point is related to this and involves the significance of the first two chapters. The reader of the book of Job is not allowed to remain at the level of human speculation in this story, because the explanation for Job's unfortunate experience is shown to him. The description of the debate between God and Satan in the heavenly court gives a framework to the story which was not available to Job. The reader knows that in fact all Job's suffering happened by God's permission (Job 1.12). That is to say, the following story must be viewed in the light of the fact that God is involved from the beginning in Job's experiences, and there can be no question that the afflictions of Job are samples of God's lack of involvement in human history as the whole sequence of events started in the divine presence.

The whole structure of the book of Job offers an embryonic form of the later apocalypse. The reader is allowed to see the totality of the situation by means of the description of the activities in the heavenly court. What is more, the main character in the story himself is not left without any answer to his questions, as the divine reply enables Job to see that his questioning did not take into account the divine dimension in human experience. The folly of his failure to recognize this is an important factor in the understanding of man's lot (cf. Wisd. 2.22). In this respect the book of Job is an obvious antecedent to the questionings which emerge in the apocalypses, 4 Ezra and Syriac Baruch.[32] These works devote considerable space to the laments of both apocalyptic seers about man's plight, though the dominant concern in both apocalypses tends to be with the fate of Israel rather than with mankind generally, even if the latter does tend to emerge when the nature of man and his sinfulness is raised (e.g. 4 Ezra 3.21ff.). Nevertheless both reflect the same kind of questionings as we find in the book of Job, and, what is more, the form and the character of the answers are so often the same. As in Job, either God or his angelic representative comes to offer an answer to the question of the seer. This often takes the form of an emphasis on man's inability to understand the ways of God (4 Ezra 4.3ff., cf. Job 38ff.) and the need to look at the present in the light of future redemption. The latter option was not taken up in the book of Job, but the use of such eschatological ideas is part of the attempt to get the reader to understand that the human view of a situation is too narrow, whereas the divine takes account of the future as well as the past. This is a point well made in the Apocalypse of Abraham 24 where, as we have seen, the explanation of the judgement of the nations in the future is closely related to the situation of Israel in the present.

Thus in both Job and in certain apocalypses questions regarding man and his lot arise from observation of the world. In both cases the final answers to the question only come as the result of divine revelation. It is in this respect that the apocalypses go beyond the bulk of the Wisdom literature in allowing for the possibility that the answers to such questions can be obtained by direct revelation. In a sense, one can argue that apocalyptic is an attempt to solve the problem of the dire scepticism which we find in Ecclesiastes. This comes by acknowledging the inability of man to make sense of his world from his own resources and resorting to divine revelation alone as the means whereby the obscurities of the present circumstances, as well as the mysteries of God himself, could be properly ascertained. In this respect at least there seem to be good reasons for supposing that von Rad has grasped the significance of one of the constituents of apocalyptic, indeed probably the most important of all, the quest for knowledge and the belief that some answers at least could be found.

II

Our concern so far has been with the theological streams in Jewish religion which contributed to the emerging apocalyptic outlook. Some consideration must now be given to the question of the *Sitz im Leben* of the apocalypses themselves. Obviously much will depend on whether we stress a Wisdom or prophetic background for the origin of apocalyptic ideas, as this could dictate the likely setting for the apocalypses themselves. Nevertheless the acknowledgement of influences from both prophetic and Wisdom sources need not mean that one rather than the other was the setting for the apocalypses. Indeed, recent writing on the subject has tended to stress that there was probably considerable overlap between these various streams at this period.[33] The prophetic visionary, just as much as the wise man, wanted answers to the problems which beset him. Indeed, as we have seen, this is precisely the point which Hanson is making about the later prophetic movement. The situation in the world engendered a reaction against traditional institutions and a retreat into a world of vision. One does not have to agree with this analysis to realize that the impact of the world upon the religious consciousness of the individual was such that, whatever his religious background, he would be working towards solutions to the perplexities which surrounded him. At times, this attempt to explain man's situation led to a confluence of different religious streams in the quest for the meaning of human existence.

In recent study there has been an attempt to relate apocalyptic to the various movements in emerging Judaism. Consequently we find that the apocalyptic literature of the Old Testament and the intertestamental period is used as evidence of a particular position within an ideological conflict, whether it be between theocracy and eschatology, or between universalism and exclusivism.[34] It is the former issue which has perhaps attracted more attention as the setting for the growing apocalyptic movement. It is the opinion of Plöger, for example, that post-exilic Judaism can be characterized by the tension between those who saw in the rebuilt Temple and the situation in Jerusalem the fulfilment of God's will and those who still looked to the future for the decisive demonstration of God's sovereignty. The former group is said to be represented by the book of Chronicles[35] and the latter by various late prophetic oracles (Isa. 24—27, Third Zech. and Joel) and the book of Daniel. For the Chronicler the existence of the Jerusalem Temple is itself the fulfilment of the aspirations of previous generations. Plöger puts it in the following way:

> . . . one has to proceed from the assumption that the Chronicler was indifferent, if not hostile, to an eschatological expectation which must still have had formative influence on the life of the community of his day. This is certainly not due to a desire on his part to minimise the great significance of the prophets; the Chronicler's description of the monarchical period contains frequent reference to the considerable influence of the prophetic word. But he prefers to regard prophecy in a manner which could be called almost purely historical. In this form prophecy performed a valuable guardian role until the community based on the Law of Moses received its final shape. The kings, priests and prophets, who strove for the erection of the Temple, true cult and proper obedience, and who represent the great offices of Israel at the time of the monarchy, made a valuable contribution to the constitution of the new community and were thus concerned to ensure the continuity of this community with the Israel of the Mosaic period. Now, however, what they contributed has been taken up in the theocracy which now represents Israel.[36]

On the other side there were the eschatological groups, who were the ancestors of the later apocalyptic conventicles. They were particularly open to Iranian influence, which infiltrated the apocalyptic literature.[37] They were the ones who collected the prophetic writings and thought of themselves as the true interpreters of the prophetic theology. For them the true meaning of the prophetic oracles meant that a static view of society, such as was propounded by the hierarchy in Jerusalem, did less than justice to promises contained in the oracles which they cherished.

The study of the later prophetic oracles has given some support to Plöger's hypothesis that there continued to be an eschatological hope during the Persian period, which was gradually evolving into the elaborate eschatology of later Judaism.[38] It is not so certain, however, whether we can speak of such a sharp difference of opinion within post-exilic Judaism, nor is it certain that there is any direct link between the writers of oracles like Isaiah 24—27 and the earliest apocalyptic conventicles. Indeed, as we have already seen, it is by no means clear that any direct line can be drawn between the book of Daniel and passages like Isaiah 24—27. Both passages may speak of the resurrection from the dead, but some of the distinctive characteristics and concerns which emerge in Daniel are absent from the earlier prophetic material. As far as the conflict in the post-exilic community is concerned, doubts must be raised about the opposition to eschatology in the books of Chronicles.[39] That is not to say that we can speak of a unified Judaism at this time, but the radical cleavage which Plöger wants to make does not seem to receive full support from the texts themselves. It would appear that the Chronicler may have continued to hold on to some eschatological hopes, but, of course, such an affirmation does not mean that they loomed at all large on his theological horizon. In this respect it is possible to speak of a difference of emphasis within the history of the post-exilic community, but the evidence does not appear to be available for the sort of split which Plöger presupposes. All this seems to get us no further with the question of the origin of apocalyptic. What Plöger has succeeded in achieving is much the same as what we find, more recently, in Hanson's work, namely the unravelling of the origins of Jewish eschatology. This may well have been a contributory factor to apocalyptic but it clearly does not explain the totality of the phenomenon.

When we come to the second century BC we find that apocalyptic has often been linked with the *hasidim*, who make their appearance round about the beginning of the second century but whose origin goes back much earlier than this.[40] This group, if we can call them that, had a significant part to play during the crisis in the middle of the second century when Antiochus IV (Epiphanes) sought to impose his religious practices on the

Jewish nation. For a time at least they appear to have made common cause with the Maccabaean rebels (1 Macc. 7.13, cf. Dan. 11.34f.). Their theological position is hinted at in 1 Maccabees 2.42, where they are said to be strict observers of the Law, and their concern seems to have been to resist the infiltration of Hellenism and to ensure that a valid high priest officiated in the Temple (cf. 1 Macc. 7.13).

It is now impossible to know what connection, if any, existed between the *hasidim* and the writers of the prophetic oracles of the later Persian period,[41] for we are told very little about their theology. There may, however, be some evidence to suggest that there are links between them and the apocalyptic visionaries of the early second century BC. It seems likely that the rise of the *hasidim* is hinted at in the animal-apocalypse in 1 Enoch 90.6ff. The lambs who open their eyes and cry to the sheep are the first of the *hasidim*, whose rise would be dated to the beginning of the Greek period (third century BC). It is apparent from what follows in this apocalypse (1 Enoch 90.13ff.) that the apocalypticist regards the rise of this group as marking one of the last stages of the present age. For the visionary the rise of the *hasidim*, their persecution (1 Enoch 90.8) and that of the people of God leads directly into the decisive struggle between Jews and the heathen. If it is correct to suppose that we have an implicit reference to the *hasidim* here (and most commentators are agreed that this is in fact the case),[42] it would indicate that this particular apocalypse sees the rise of the *hasidim* as a significant moment within Israelite history. We cannot necessarily suppose that this meant that the apocalypse was written in the circles of the *hasidim*, but at the very least it came from a visionary sympathetic to this movement.

Thus it would appear that what we are faced with in the *hasidim* is a loosely defined group, possibly related to the continuation of visionary activity found it some later prophetic oracles which looked to the future as the time when the promises made by God to the prophets would be realized. It has been suggested that there is a close link between the views of the *hasidim* and the later Essenes, and, therefore, the distinctive features of the theology of the Dead Sea Scrolls may be utilized to sketch the outlines of the theology of the *hasidim*.[43] It would, however, be dangerous to read back the theology of a group, whose ideas had developed under pressure of separation and isolation, into the early second century *ḥasidim*. This would be especially so, if, as seems likely, there is also some relationship between the *ḥasidim* and the Pharisees.[44] There is a tendency to separate the Pharisees from the outlook of Essenism and other splinter-groups, but such a radical dichotomy could obscure the many features which both have in common.

The attitudes of the later rabbis towards the speculations of apocalyptic is a subject to which we shall have to return later. Nevertheless it should be stressed that a common origin for Pharisees and Essenes in the hasidic movement of the early second century BC may go a long way towards explaining the common issues which we find in both later movements. We have already seen that apocalyptic plays an important role in the way in which the Qumran community understood its relationship to the heavenly world. In addition, the fact that several apocalypses have been found in the Qumran library points to an interest in this type of literature, and it may be correct to assume an Essene origin for some of them.[45] But this fact should not lead us to suppose that apocalyptic was simply the preserve of fringe-groups like the Qumran sect. Thus, for example, J. Jeremias has argued that the scribes, the theological inspiration of Pharisaism, also were interested in the subject-matter of apocalyptic:[46]

> But in fact, apocalyptic, preserved in the pseudepigraphical writings of late Judaism, with their descriptions of eschatological events and the cosmic topography of the celestial and the lower world, formed part of the esoteric tradition of the scribes.

It is something of an exaggeration to attribute the whole of apocalyptic to the scribes. Nevertheless what is implied in this point deserves careful consideration, namely that with apocalyptic we are dealing with a mode of thought whose impact on Judaism cannot be narrowly defined on a sectarian basis. Obviously the explanation for such common ideas would be made all the easier if we were in a position to establish that Pharisees and Essenes did have a common origin. But leaving this aside, we must guard against the tendency to relegate theological outlooks to the level of sectarian bias rather than seeing in them a way of looking at the world, which could be shared by groups which may in other respects differ markedly on points of doctrine. It is certainly possible to point to differences between Pharisees and

Essenes on halakic issues. For example, certain aspects of the Pharisaic sabbath *halakah* differed markedly from that of the Essenes.[47] But such differences over the way in which Scripture was interpreted in no way precludes the sharing of a common belief about God and the mysteries of the world above, as well as the means whereby knowledge of them was achieved.[48]

CHAPTER 9

An Attempt to Elucidate the Origins of Apocalyptic Visions

OUR DISCUSSION SO far has been at a rather general level concerning the possible background of the apocalyptic movement and its setting within Judaism at the beginning of the Christian era. Nevertheless the fact has to be faced that, however detailed the investigation of the texts may be, we are confronted by the problem of paucity of evidence for establishing the character of the religious currents in Judaism in the Persian and early Greek periods of Palestinian Judaism. This means that greater emphasis should be placed on an approach to the question of apocalyptic origins which starts with the apocalypses themselves. The previous survey shows how much the investigation of this subject has concentrated on similarity of ideas in earlier texts as a means of tracing links between apocalyptic and various religious traditions. But sooner or later in the study of apocalyptic the question has to be faced concerning the production of the apocalypses themselves. What kind of works are they? Are we to treat seriously their claim to visionary experience or merely explain this claim by the apocalyptic literary form? The question arises, therefore, whether this literature had its origin in the experiences of unknown visionaries. Clearly some are quite happy to ignore the apocalyptic framework as merely a convenient device for the message of the writer, and, as a result, attach no significance whatsoever to the visionary claim.[1] Certainly pseudonymity seems *a priori* to make it unlikely. that we have the remnants of actual experience contained in these documents, but the reluctance of commentators to write off the apocalypses as testimonies to the religious experience of Jews suggests that the matter of the evolution of the visionary material demands further attention.[2] It is clear from some recent studies that this issue is being taken much more seriously, for the contents of the apocalypses themselves are now becoming a subject for examination in their own right as a basis for ascertaining the setting of the writer and the development of the material included in them.[3]

A starting-place for an investigation of the way in which the apocalypses came to be produced is the recognition of the fact that many of the visions contained in the apocalypses do not arise spontaneously. Frequently the visionary experience of the apocalypticist is the result of some kind of preparatory meditation, and it is apparent that the meditation upon Scripture has a large part to play in this process.[4] In Daniel 9.1ff. the immediate cause of Daniel's vision of Gabriel is his meditation upon Jeremiah 25.11f. The fictitious setting of the book of Daniel places this meditation on these words of Jeremiah during the Exile when the promise of restoration has yet to be fulfilled. But from the perspective of the writer living in the mid-second century BC there is the need to know what this promise meant to his own generation. Clearly if the oracle was understood at its face value, it would apply only to the length of the Exile in Babylon, and as a result, have nothing to say to the persecuted people of God in a later age. It comes as no surprise, therefore, that the true meaning of the reference to the seventy years in Jeremiah 25.11f. is reinterpreted as seventy weeks of years (Dan. 9.24). It is not easy to make the seventy weeks of years cover the period from the time of Jeremiah to the desecration of the Temple by Antiochus Epiphanes, which most would agree is hinted at in Daniel 9.27, but the problems of exegesis need not detain us at this point.[5] It is sufficient to point out the way in which Scripture, and in particular a puzzling aspect of it, has provided the basis for the angelic disclosure concerning the true meaning of the text. The result of this reflection on Scripture is not just one possible interpretation but the authentic interpretation of the divine oracle. This is guaranteed by the fact that it is the result of revelation, in this case mediated by an angel. Whether the reference to the angel is merely a literary device, or as seems preferable to suppose, reflects the belief of the apocalypticist concerning the means of the divine disclosure, one thing is not in doubt: the writer thought that the meaning of the passage which he was considering was that which God himself intended it to mean.[6]

We find a similar situation emerging in 4 Ezra. As we have

already seen, in chapter 6.38ff. Ezra recounts his own version of the story of creation, one which is clearly based on the biblical version. The function of this occupation with the first chapter of Genesis is quite clear and is set out in verses 55ff.[7] According to the biblical account Adam is said to be the lord over the whole of creation and the world created for the sake of Israel (v. 55), whereas the other nations are of no account. The fact is that, as far as the apocalypticist is concerned, the lordship of Adam is an example of what Israel's own position should be, and yet the reverse is the case (cf. Syr. Bar. 19.6ff.). Instead of dominion Israel experiences oppression, and the seer longs to know how long she must endure such a state of affairs. The statement of the theological problem by the seer arises directly out of the meditation upon the first chapter of Genesis, which leads him to the conclusion that the promise of Scripture as set out in Genesis 1.26 concerning man's dominion, and applied in particular to Israel, has not been fulfilled. Once again this leads directly into an angelic vision, where some attempt at an answer is offered. Unlike Daniel 9, where Gabriel responds directly to Daniel's uncertainty about the meaning of the oracle of Jeremiah, the reply of the angel does not at first appear to have any connection at all with the problem which the seer has propounded. Nevertheless after the opening parables (4 Ezra 7.1–9), it becomes clear that the angel is setting out to show Ezra that the way to the new age is a difficult one which has to be endured in order to attain to that which is to come (4 Ezra 7.14). There can be no question that the divine promise is in any way mistaken (v. 11), but Ezra has reckoned without Adam's sin which had terrible consequences for life in the world (v. 12) and meant that the fulfilment of the promise was postponed to the future.

In a similar vein a brief survey of the biblical history from the creation down to the destruction by the Babylonians in 4 Ezra 3.4ff. is the basis for the apocalypticist's meditation. The purpose of this recitation is twofold. First, the author compares Israel with other nations, and while admitting her unrighteousness, questions whether her misdemeanours are any greater than those of her oppressor (4 Ezra 3.29ff.). Secondly, as in 4 Ezra 7.62ff. the biblical account of the Fall provides the basis for reflection on man's inability to keep God's commandments (4 Ezra 3.20) and the consequent inevitability of sinfulness in the world. Elsewhere it is the scriptures which provide the launching-pad for the discussion on intercession for the ungodly. In 4 Ezra 7.106ff. the seer offers examples from Scripture to justify the viability of a belief in intercession, but such examples are not considered to be valid as justification for the doctrine which Ezra is wanting to espouse. The reason is that the analogous situations which Ezra has offered are concerned with this age whereas the kind of intercession which he wants to justify will have consequences for man's eternal destiny (vv. 112ff.).

In the last two visions of 4 Ezra the book of Daniel itself appears to have been the basis of the visions. In the vision of the eagle which rose from the sea (ch. 11) it is quite apparent in the interpretation (4 Ezra 12.11f.) that the starting point for the vision is the ascent of the four beasts from the sea in Daniel 7.2f. In Ezra's case the purpose of the vision was probably dictated by the need to update the relevance of the scriptures in a way similar to that which we find in Daniel 9.24. Since Daniel was written before the might of Rome was involved in Jewish political life, the significance of Daniel's vision had to be more closely integrated with the political realities of the apocalypticist's day. That is not to suggest that the vision was necessarily a deliberate literary formulation in order to make the fourth beast of Daniel correspond with Rome. What we have is the Scripture used as a basis for a vision, though subsequent reflection on the vision is evident in the rather tortuous explanation which is offered and certain aspects of the vision itself (4 Ezra 11.12ff.).

But further evidence can be offered to show that this use of Scripture may not have been merely an artificial construction by the writer which has subsequently been given a visionary framework.

The last vision in 4 Ezra of the man coming from the sea also looks like an allusion to Daniel 7 and in particular, verse 13. The point is, however, that the reference to the man flying with the clouds is juxtaposed with a reference to the fact that he arose from the sea. This can only be an allusion to Daniel 7.2, where the beasts are said to arise from the sea. This linking of the sea with the man has caused some surprise among commentators,[8] but the strange combination of the man with the sea, which in the original vision was linked with the beasts, could easily have arisen within the situation of an actual vision. With a passage like Daniel 7 as the basis for his understanding of eschatological matters it is not beyond the realms of possibility that elements which existed separately in that chapter were, in the circumstances of a vision, reorganized to bring about the combination which we find in the opening verses of 4 Ezra 13.[9] It is most unlikely that a careful interpreter of Daniel 7 would have linked the divine envoy with the home of the beasts and thereby deliberately linked the divine with the demonic in the way in which we find it in this chapter.

Thus there are indications from this final vision that the meditation upon Scripture may have been the basis for a subsequent vision.

This is more difficult to prove with regard to the other passages where the consideration of Scripture led to an angelic announcement. But it seems fair to say that at the very least the person who wrote them either claimed to have, or believed that he had, the authority of divine revelation when he put forward the solutions to the questions which were occupying his attention. There are, therefore, indications that the author of 4 Ezra may have used Scripture as the basis for subsequent visionary experience. It is possible to test the validity of these hints a little further by a glance at some other visions in the corpus of apocalyptic writings.

Of prime importance in this respect are those accounts of visions of God and/or his throne, which occur from time to time in the apocalypses. There are connections between these various passages, because the inspiration of the various elements contained within them is the first chapter of Ezekiel, where the prophet sees the glory of God in the form of a vision of a celestial chariot surrounded by strange living creatures. As we shall see later, this chapter had an important part to play in later Jewish speculation about the nature of God and heaven. Already in the apocalypses there are signs that interest in the first chapter of Ezekiel formed a part of the framework of apocalyptic. Some elements of this material have already been touched on in our consideration of the heavenly world, and there is no need to cover the same ground again. What particularly concerns us here is the extent of the relationship with the first chapter of Ezekiel. Our special interest will be to ascertain whether the vision of God in the apocalypses is merely a description of God which is a repetition of material in Ezekiel 1 and Isaiah 6 or shows signs of being a subject of interest in its own right which may have involved the writer in actually seeing again the vision of Ezekiel. Two passages only will be considered in detail, the theophany found in 1 Enoch 14.8ff. and the vision of God's heavenly court which is the prelude to John's vision of the future in Revelation 4.[10]

Although the immediate impression one gets when reading the account of Enoch's ascent to heaven and vision of God in 1 Enoch 14.8ff. is of a close link between the theophany and Ezekiel 1, there are in fact few precise contacts. Apart from the reference to the throne, which is much influenced by Isaiah 6.1 (1 Enoch 14.18, 'a lofty throne'), the frequent mention of fire (1 Enoch 14.9, 12, 15, 17, 19, 22) does parallel the prominent part which it plays in Ezekiel's vision (e.g. Ezek. 1.4). Also certain words found in Ezekiel 1 are also found in 1 Enoch 14, e.g. 'lightning' (1 Enoch 14.11, 17, cf. Ezek. 1.14) and 'crystal' (1 Enoch 14.10, 18, cf. Ezek. 1.22). Most obvious of all is the brief reference to the wheels in chapter 14.18, which indicates that what Enoch saw was in fact the throne-chariot of God.

Despite this, however, some clear differences emerge in the later vision. Unlike Ezekiel 1 the living creatures are not mentioned by name, and the prominent position which they have in the latter chapter completely disappears here, as also Ezekiel's interest in the movement of the chariot (Ezek. 1.19ff.).[11] The fiery cherubim which form part of the roof of heaven (1 Enoch 14.11) doubtless have their origin in the description of the Temple in 1 Kings 6.29, where the walls are said to be full of carved figures of cherubim, palm trees, and flowers. In addition to the cherubim as part of the decoration of the heavenly world there is only passing reference to them as attendants of the throne-chariot at the end of 1 Enoch 14.18.[12] Though no mention is made of cherubim in Ezekiel 1, it becomes clear from a comparison between the call-vision and the parallel vision in Ezekiel 10 that the cherubim and the living creatures described in so much detail in the opening chapter are in fact identical (cf. Sir. 49.8f.). Thus, although the cherubim are mentioned immediately after the reference to the throne in 1 Enoch 14.18 and form part of the divine entourage, it is quite remarkable that they are mentioned only in passing here.

Much attention is devoted in 1 Enoch 14 to the character of the heavenly dwelling which Enoch enters. Despite its fiery appearance the walls and the floor of the house are said to be made of crystal (1 Enoch 14.9f.).[13] This characteristic owes much to Ezekiel 1.22 and Exodus 24.10. In the former the firmament of heaven is said to resemble crystal *(qeraḥ)*. This is the only place in which the consistency of the framework of heaven is mentioned. It is, therefore, only to be expected that it should have been transferred to the walls and the floor of God's palace when the original vision had been extended to include references to the environs of the heavenly palace as well. The second passage describes the sapphire pavement underneath the feet of God in the theophany in Exodus 24.[14] The icy brilliance of crystal clearly has affinities with the limpid appearance of the sapphire of which the pavement is made. This would tend to confirm the impression that the foundations and walls of the heavenly world were made of a substance which was like crystal. The limpid appearance of the sapphire pavement may also explain why heaven is said to be watery in its appearance in 1 Enoch 14.11.

The comparison of heaven (or at least part of it) with water is a feature which we shall have to investigate further when we consider Revelation 4.6, where something resembling a sea of crystal stands before the throne of God. No doubt Genesis 1.7 had its part to play, with its reference to the heavenly waters, but the comparison of heaven to water is a feature which is to be found in the dangers encountered by later Jewish mystics during their ascent to heaven. In particular it calls to mind the addition to the story of the four who entered *pardes* in b. Hagigah 14b. In a short sentence R. Akiba is said to have warned his fellow-travellers to heaven not to be deceived by a substance in heaven which may lead them to exclaim that water is confronting them. Akiba tells his companions that this in fact is pure marble.[15] Scholem has conjectured that what we have in this story and in the later developments of it reflects a real danger encountered by the mystics during their ascent to the highest of the heavens.[16] The basis of later speculation concerning the nature of heaven seems already to have existed in one of the earliest apocalyptic visions.

The heavenly world in 1 Enoch 14 is divided into two parts.[17] The most plausible explanation of this is the division of the central part of the Temple into two major sections. Apart from this isolated comment the chapter as a whole does not give enough indication to suppose a close dependence on layout and furniture of the cult. The lack of interest in important cultic objects, like the cherubim and the veil, makes it difficult to conclude that the origin of the chapter must have been within priestly circles. Indeed, the links which we do have with the cult hardly justify any but the conclusion that the outline of the Temple has been used as a basic plan for this excursion into uranography.

When Enoch enters the inner sanctuary of heaven (1 Enoch 14.17), he finds an even more glorious sight confronting him. Fire once again dominates the description, though its link with the floor of the inner house may have been inspired by the golden covering of the floor of the Temple (1 Kings 6.21). At last Enoch sees God and his throne. The throne here is said to be made of crystal, an attribute which is linked with the firmament in Ezekiel 1.22, whereas Ezekiel 1.26 compares the throne to sapphire. How and why such a transference took place is not clear. Once again it could be argued that the sapphire pavement in Exodus 24.10 may offer a bridge between Ezekiel 1.22 and 26. Like Ezekiel 1.26, sapphire is mentioned but in connection with the pavement, whereas its clarity resembles more the crystal in Ezekiel 1.22, but the existence of such connections is inevitably very conjectural. When the wheel of the throne-chariot is described,[18] the description of Ezekiel 1.16 which compares them to bronze (*tarshish*) is omitted in favour of a more general comparison to the sun. A move away from the identification with a specific colour can be found also in Daniel 7.9, where the wheels are said to be of fiery hue.

An obvious development of Ezekiel 1 is to be found in 1 Enoch 14.19 in the inclusion of the reference to the rivers of fire, an image to be found also in Daniel 7.10 and the *merkabah* fragment from Qumran (4 Q S1)[19]

1 ENOCH	4Q S 1	DANIEL
And from underneath the throne came streams of flaming fire	. . . about them seeing rivulets of fire, like gleaming bronze . . .	A stream of fire issued and came forth before him

This is a feature of other theophanies and became an important element of the later Jewish speculation on the throne of God.[20] The origin of this imagery is not easily explained, though a verse like Ezekiel 1.13 ('. . . out of the fire went forth lightning') could easily have provided the basis for this development within the throne-chariot vision itself. Also the description of the theophany at Sinai in Exodus 19.16 provided material which could form the basis of the belief in the fiery elements which proceeded from God's immediate presence. Indeed, in Revelation 4.5 an allusion to Exodus 19.16 replaces the reference to the fiery stream.

In the description of God (1 Enoch 14.20) there is continuation of the veiled anthropomorphism of Ezekiel 1.26f. The qualifying nouns of Ezekiel 1.26b disappear, but the author proves to be more reluctant than the prophet Ezekiel in speaking of the body of God (Ezek. 1.27). Nevertheless, there is no doubt that the author of 1 Enoch 14 sees a human figure on the throne, though the precise outlines of the figure are left unexpressed. Unlike in Ezekiel God is said to be clothed in a glorious garment ('his raiment shone more brightly than the sun and was whiter than any snow'). The reference to God's garment doubtless derives from Isaiah 6.1, where the lower part of God's robe fills the Temple. This brief allusion in Isaiah 6, however, is filled out somewhat here. The impression one gets from this section is that the seer is said to see God himself and, despite his prostrate position before God (1 Enoch 14.14), he is able to catch a glimpse of God in his glory as he looks up to the enthroned figure before him.

The examination of this vision suggests that already, in what is probably the earliest extra-canonical evidence of a theophany,[21] there is no mere repetition of the details of Ezekiel 1 and Isaiah 6, though the indebtedness to both chapters is not in doubt. The vision offers us indications of the growth in the interest in subjects which were not mentioned in the biblical visions as well as neglect of elements which featured prominently there. It is thus justifiable to speak here of the beginnings of a speculative interest in Ezekiel 1 at the beginning of the second century BC or earlier.

In the New Testament the only example of a vision of God and his heavenly court is to be found in Revelation 4. This chapter shows no evidence at all of Christian influence, and, treated in isolation, it is evident that it is entirely Jewish in its inspiration. Indeed, the author obviously intends a deliberate contrast between the description of the divine court in Revelation 4 and the transformation which takes place as the result of the exaltation of the Lamb.

In Revelation 4 there are obvious omissions as compared with

Ezekiel 1. Thus, for example, there is no mention made of the wheels of the chariot, but the links with that chapter are never in doubt, with the inclusion of the rainbow, and, particularly, the detailed description of the living creatures (Rev. 4.6b ff.). This owes much to Ezekiel 1 but contains some differences.[22] Firstly it will be noticed that each living creature has been identified with one of the four faces of the creatures of Ezekiel 1. 10f.:

EZEKIEL 1	REVELATION 4
And as for the likeness of their faces, each had the face of a man in front; and the four had the face of a lion on the right side, the four had the face of an ox on the left side, and the four had the face of an eagle at the back.	. . . on each side of the throne are four living creatures; full of eyes in front and behind; the first living creature like a lion, the second living creature like an ox, the third living creature with the face of a man, and the fourth living creature like a flying eagle.

As a result Ezekiel's description is considerably simplified in Revelation by having four completely different creatures rather than Ezekiel's four creatures, each with four different faces. Secondly, in Ezekiel 1.18 it is the rims of the wheels of the chariot which are full of eyes, but this particular characteristic is now transferred to the creatures themselves. Thirdly, the order in which the creatures are mentioned differs from Ezekiel. Whereas in Ezekiel the face of the man is mentioned first of all, in Revelation it is placed third in the list.

Despite its obvious debt to Ezekiel 1 Revelation 4 also derives some of its imagery from Isaiah 6, a feature which we found also in 1 Enoch 14 (cf. Apoc. Abr. 18). This is particularly evident in verse 8. First of all, the four living creatures of Ezekiel do not have four wings, as they do in Ezekiel 1, but six, just as the seraphim do in Isaiah 6.2. Secondly, the song which the living creatures sing is also that of the seraphim, the *trisagion*. Verse 8 offers evidence of a feature of Ezekiel 1 being modified by the addition of a whole verse from Isaiah 6. In Isaiah we find that, as in Revelation, the description of the wings of the seraphim is followed immediately by the reference to the song which they sing to God.

As with Enoch, John of Patmos appears to be taken up to heaven,[23] and the first thing which he notices in heaven is a throne. There is no attempt made to describe the throne itself, and John contents himself with stating that there was one seated upon it, whom he described by reference to the stones 'jasper and carnelian' (Rev. 4.3), words which occur in Ezekiel 28.13. The reference to the rainbow in the same verse in all probability derives from Ezekiel 1.28, though its resemblance to an emerald may once again mark its indebtedness to Ezekiel 28.13. In God's immediate presence there are other thrones (Rev. 4.4). This heavenly scene can be paralleled in the Ascension of Isaiah 9.9f., where, in the seventh heaven, the righteous are said to be clad in garments of glory and have thrones and crowns. It is unlikely that we have a reference to the righteous in Revelation 4.4 (cf. Rev. 6.9ff.), and probable that these are the angelic attendants who surround the throne of God (cf. Dan. 7.10). The origin of the number of the elders, a peculiar feature of Revelation 4, is not clear, but many have suggested, with some degree of plausibility, that it is derived from the twenty-four priestly orders of 1 Chronicles 24.7–18.[24]

From God's throne proceed lightnings, voices, and thunders, but, as we have already seen, there is no mention of the fiery stream which we found in 1 Enoch 14. We suggested that this fiery phenomenon replaces the stream of fire in Revelation 4.5, but there is an indication that John does know of the fiery stream, as we find in Revelation 22.1 a reference to 'a river of living water as clear as crystal' coming out of God's throne. Despite the pastoral setting, and whatever the influence of passages like Ezekiel 47.1 and Zechariah 14.8, the river is to be connected with the fiery stream because of the close link which exists between it and the throne of God. What has happened here is that the threatening aspect, which the fiery stream presents to those who enter the divine presence (Rev. 15.2ff.), has been replaced with the life-giving water which flows through the new Jerusalem and renews the inheritors of the new age. The barrier which had hitherto existed between God and man has now been removed (Rev. 21.3), and so it is entirely appropriate that all that might appear to separate man from God should be removed.

The seven lamps which stand before God (Rev. 4.5) have their origin in Ezekiel 1.13 (cf. Exod. 26.35; 2 Chron. 4.7), where the burning fires in the middle of the living creatures are compared to torches. Some influence from Zechariah 4.2 is certain here also, not least because the interpretation of the seven lamps as the seven spirits of God resembles the pattern of Zechariah 4.2 and 10, where the lamps too are interpreted, but in this case, as symbols of the seven eyes of God.

Perhaps the most distinctive feature about the vision of God's heavenly dwelling in Revelation is the reference to the sea of glass (4.6).[25] Unlike the Testament of Levi 2.7, Slavonic Enoch 3.3 and Test. Abraham Rec. B 8, in all of which some form of water or sea is said to be in heaven, Revelation merely indicates that in the immediate vicinity of God's presence there was something which resembled a sea of glass. Although the influence of cultic ideas cannot be discounted (1 Kings 7.23, cf. Josephus *Ant.* viii, 79), the more likely origin is Ezekiel 1.22, where the firmament which separates the creatures from God is likened to crystal. The sea of glass in Revelation 4.6 likewise serves to separate the throne from the rest of heaven. Unlike Ezekiel 1, however, where the living creatures are set apart from God's throne (Ezek. 1.22), the creatures in Revelation are said to be in close proximity to the throne itself (Rev. 4.6b). Of course, Genesis 1.7 speaks of the upper and lower waters being separated by a firmament. The reference to the firmament in Ezekiel and Genesis could easily have led a later reader to combine the two verses and as a result water would play a part in the cosmology, whose appearance would be like the crystal which characterized the firmament in Ezekiel 1.22.

A feature of this chapter and indeed the apocalypse as a whole, is the way in which hymnic material is introduced. We have seen how the *trisagion* from Isaiah 6.3 has contributed to the hymn of the living creatures, but the whole of the heavenly court praise the creator of the universe in the final scene in Revelation 4.10f. The recitation of hymns extolling the attributes of God is a feature of later Jewish mysticism.[26] Some of the extant mystical texts devote much space to such hyms of praise, especially to God as the creator. There is another, even more extensive example of such a hymn, in the account of Abraham's ascent in the Apocalypse of Abraham 17. The patriarch joins in this celestial hymn before he finally reaches the throne of God in the highest heaven. Clearly the brief reference to the song of the seraphim in Isaiah 6.3 has become the basis for the composition of much more elaborate hymns of praise to God, doubtless owing much to contemporary liturgical practice,[27] early examples of which are to be found in Revelation and the Apocalypse of Abraham.

This short chapter in the New Testament apocalypse resem-

bles 1 Enoch 14 only in offering further evidence of the way in
which a passage like Ezekiel 1 has provided the basis for further
developments in the understanding of the nature of God and his
world. In many respects, considering that both passages owe
their inspiration to Ezekiel 1 and Isaiah 6,. the differences between them are remarkable.[28] The question is, however,
whether these idiosyncratic developments which we find in
these two apocalypses have their origin in something more
experiential than the speculative exegesis of Scripture of certain
individuals. Points of contact do certainly exist between these
visions and biblical passages, but we cannot speak of a uniform
type of speculation on Ezekiel 1. Nor is there anything resembling a systematic exposition of that chapter in these visions. If we
were dealing with an exegetical tradition which has been put in
the form of a vision, we would surely expect signs of an ordered
discussion of the various elements of Ezekiel's vision. Of this
there is no sign, however. The way in which hitherto disparate
elements in the chariot-vision have been combined in these
passages shows no sign of a deliberate attempt by the authors to
justify juxtaposition of these ideas on the basis of rational
exegesis. Likewise the visions are completely devoid of any
self-conscious desire to offer a pastiche of various appropriate
scriptural passages. The precise biblical language is only rarely
adhered to, and the changes of the original which can be found
all suggest that we have to do here with more than a mere
interpretation of the biblical original. The variety which we find
in the contents of the visions suggests that, while Ezekiel may
have been the starting-point for what we have in these chapters,
the order and detail of the original have been left behind in
favour of a more elaborate view of the nature of God's dwelling
in heaven. It seems, therefore, a reasonable hypothesis to suppose that the visions in these apocalypses are in fact what they
purport to be: the descriptions of visions of . visionaries who
believed that it was possible for them to pierce the vault of
heaven and be shown the most intimate secrets of God and his
world. The visions would have arisen within a situation, where
an individual started with the scriptural description of God's
glory in Ezekiel 1 and, on the basis of this passage, believed that
he saw again the vision which had once appeared to the prophet
Ezekiel by the banks of the river Chebar. Thus although the
details of Ezekiel's vision marked the launching-pad for this new

vision, the imagination of the visionary enabled him to transcend the original, for other elements colour his reflections, notably, of course, relevant scriptural passages, so that an entirely new view of the character of God and his world is produced.

If a man believes that the God who had appeared to Ezekiel had been seen by him also, it is not too difficult to see how he could then go on to take the next step of supposing that the revelation of the divine purposes which followed on from Ezekiel's call-vision should also follow his experience. In this respect Revelation is typical of many apocalypses of a similar type in having the revelation of divine secrets as a direct consequence of the appearance of the seer before God (cf. Apoc. Abr. 17ff.). After all the entrance into the divine presence offered the opportunity to inquire into those mysteries which were hidden in the very presence of God. Indeed, according to the later Jewish mystical text Hebrew Enoch 45, it was believed that all the divine secrets were engraved in the celestial veil. Thus any individual who was fortunate enough to reach the court of God might also expect to know also about God's eternal purposes:[29]

> R. Ishmael said: Metatron said to me: Come and I will show you the curtain of *Maqom* which is spread before the Holy One, blessed be he, whereon are engraven all the generations of the world and all their doings, both what they have done and what they will do until the end of all generation.[30]

Already in the earlier apocalyptic literature access to the divine presence is the means whereby the mysteries are ascertained (1 Enoch 71.3f.; 93.2; Slav. Enoch 23.1). Thus it would appear that any one who believed that he had experienced a vision of this kind could also expect to look into the divine secrets. While in some instances this may have involved further speculative activity on prophetic oracles of promise, the norm tends to be that current eschatological expectation in one form or other and cosmological beliefs were taken up and clothed with the aura of direct revelation (Rev. 6ff.; Apoc. Abr. 20ff.; Slav. Enoch 23ff.). For the apocalypticist it was not the details of eschatology which most concerned him but the affirmation of their verisimilitude by means of heavenly authentication. Thus the mode of revelation was more important than the precise contents, for the knowledge of the innermost recesses of heaven was a means of confirming the validity of those beliefs which the readers of the apocalypses held dear. In a way such as this, therefore, some of the eschatological speculations which follow the vision of God could have arisen, as the result of the seer's belief that his privileged glimpse into the world above opened up for him the treasuries of God's purposes.

Our study so far has led to the assumption that we should reckon with the possibility that some at least of the apocalyptic visions arose in a situation where the reflection on Scripture led to a revelation of God or a disclosure concerning the problems which the study of Scripture had presented to the apocalypticist. Apart from the claim which the apocalypses themselves make to incorporate visionary experiences of various kinds, albeit under the disguise of a pseudonym, there are certain passages which lend some support to the view that some of this literature may have arisen in the actual religious experiences of apocalyptic seers.[31] I refer to the mention made in some apocalypses of the preparations needed for the reception of the revelations. As early as the book of Daniel, the seer mentions the fact that he undertook a period of fasting before the angel came to him from God:[32] 'In those days, I, Daniel, was mourning for three weeks. I ate no delicacies, no meat or wine entered my mouth, nor did I anoint myself at all, for the full three weeks' (10.2f.).

Although it is not stated explicitly that the purpose of these ascetic practices was to enable him to achieve a sufficient state of preparedness to receive divine enlightenment, the words of the angel (Dan. 10.12) suggest that the seer had been setting out to receive further information from God about those issues which were particularly troubling him. The point is made explicitly in chapter 9.3, where Daniel puts on sackcloth and begins to fast in order to ensure an answer to his earnest entreaties. References to fasting are found in several places in the apocalypses (Apoc. Abr. 9; 4 Ezra 9.23ff.; Syr. Bar. 5.7; 9.2; 12.5; 21.1; 47.2). One of the clearest references to the fasting which was necessary as a preparation for the communication of God's word is to be found in Hermas Vis. 3.10. Hermas is perplexed by the way in which the lady who appears to him in his visions takes different forms:

> Now she had appeared to me, brethren, in the first vision in the former year as very old and sitting on a chair. But in the second vision her face was younger, but her body and hair were old and she spoke with me standing; but she was more joyful than the first

time. But in the third vision she was quite young and exceeding beautiful and only her hair was old; and she was quite joyful, and sat on a couch. I was very unhappy about this, and wished to understand this revelation, and in a vision of the night I saw the ancient lady saying to me, 'Every request needs humility [*tapeino-phrosyne*, cf. Col. 2.18]: fast therefore and you shall receive what you asked from the Lord. So I fasted one day and in the same night a young man appeared to me. . . . (Vis. 3.10.3ff.).

The necessary prerequisite for Hermas's understanding of the differences between the various appearances of the lady depends on his own preparation of himself to receive the divine answer to his questions.

More intriguing than any of these references is the preparation mentioned in the last chapter of 4 Ezra (14.38ff.). Here Ezra is preparing to restore the scriptures (14.18ff.). He prays for the Holy Spirit to enable him to write down the law of God. In response to this God promises him 'the lamp of understanding', but when we learn more precisely what is involved in this enlightenment we find that the mode of inspiration is quite unusual:[33]

And it came to pass on the morrow that, lo, a voice called me saying: Ezra open thy mouth and drink what I give thee to drink. Then I opened my mouth, and lo, there was reached unto me a full cup, which was full as it were with water, but the colour of it was like fire. And I took it and drank; and when I had drunk, my heart poured forth understanding, wisdom grew in my breast, and my spirit retained its memory. (cf. Ezek. 3.2f.)

Of course, this passage could represent a rather strange way of affirming that Ezra's dictation of the scriptures was inspired, but it is more likely that at the very least we have reflected here a current notion of the way in which inspiration could be brought about. It is, therefore, possible that we have in this a relic of a technique whereby a visionary can be in that correct frame of mind which will make him most receptive to God and will retain the things told him in his ecstatic state.[34]

We turn now to those passages where mention is made of the state of the visionary and his attempts to describe the character of his experience during the course of his vision. In the Ascension of Isaiah we have a description of the visionary's state which has few parallels in the early apocalyptic literature:

And while he (Isaiah) was speaking by the Holy Spirit in the hearing of all, he (suddenly) became silent and his consciousness was taken from him and he saw (no more) the men who were standing before him: his eyes were open, but his mouth was silent and the consciousness in his body was taken from him; but his breath was still in him, for he saw a vision . . . And the people who were standing around, with the exception of the circle of the prophets, did not think that the holy Isaiah had been taken up. And the vision which he saw was not of this world, but from the world which is hidden from all flesh. And after Isaiah had beheld this vision, he imparted it to Hezekiah, his son Jasub, and the remaining prophets . . . but the people did not hear for Micaiah and Jasub his son had caused them to go forth, when the knowledge of this world was taken from him and he became as a dead man. (Asc. Isa. 6.10ff.)[35]

Occasionally an apocalyptic seer makes mention of the fact that a vision causes him to fall down and be like a corpse, e.g. Revelation 1.17, but this passage offers us an account of the way in which a vision affected the consciousness of a seer and how he appeared to those who happened to be present during his heavenly ascent.[36] The seer's own understanding of his ascent is said to be in terms of a separation between body and soul. Isaiah describes how he is led away by an angel through the heavens (Asc. Isa. 7.1ff.) and is told that he has left behind his own body temporarily to return to it when the vision has ended (Asc. Isa. 7.5, cf. 8.11).[37] The situation, in which the visionary is surrounded by his disciples as he makes his ascent through the heavens, is reminiscent of the story of R. Nehuniah b. Hakanah in Hekaloth R. 18, who is surrounded by a group of his disciples waiting expectantly as their teacher reveals to them what he sees as he journeys through the celestial spheres.[38] At one point in this ascent he speaks of a matter which his hearers cannot understand. So, in order to gain further enlightenment on the matter, Nehuniah is brought out of his trance by being brought into contact with an impure object, so that his disciples can learn more accurately the things pertaining to the realm above. Whether this story is a legend or not need not detain us here. The fact is that it shows the kind of situation in which the writer of this passage believed a man was wont to experience the secrets of the world above. The mystic would be surrounded by his disciples, who would listen attentively to the disclosures which the ecstatic would make during his ascent through the heavenly spheres. Despite the fact that this legend about R. Nehuniah is from a much later text, it bears out the implications of the passage in the Ascension of Isaiah concerning the situation in which such ascents took place. What is more, both give evidence, despite their fictitious settings, that fragments of actual reminiscence concerning the precise situation of ecstatic ascents to heaven could be preserved in the pseudepigrapha.

Apart from this description of the physical state of the apocalyptic seer and the situation in which the ascent took place, there are other passages which demand our consideration as examples of the way in which the mystic would describe the impact of the vision upon himself. Already among the prophetic oracles the enigmatic 'oracle of the desert' in Isaiah 21.1ff. appears to offer us an account of the emotional upheaval caused by a vision (cf. Jer. 4.19ff.).[39] The complete subjection of the prophet to the force of his experience (v. 1) and the physical effects of it (v. 3,cf. 1 Enoch 71.11) indicate that the emotional impact of such prophetic experiences was quite overwhelming. Apart from the many references to the prostration of the apocalyptic seer and his feeling of great fear in the face of an angelophany or theophany (Dan. 10.9; 1 Enoch 14.13f.) there are occasional hints of the overwhelming character of some of these experiences. In 4 Ezra 6.29 the seer speaks in the following way about the impact of the divine pronouncement upon him: 'And it came to pass, while he spake to me, behold by little and little, the place whereon I stood rocked to and fro.'

If this had been merely an attempt to convey the accompaniment of a theophany in traditional terms, we might have expected reference to an earthquake or other supernatural manifestations. Nothing so dramatic is found here. The seer merely speaks of his unsteadiness during the vision. Likewise in the Apocalypse of Abraham 18 the seer experiences a feeling of great unsteadiness during his journey through heaven:[40]

> And while he yet spake and lo, fire came against us round about, and a voice was in the fire like a voice of many waters, like the sound of the sea in its uproar. And the angel bent his head with me and worshipped. And I desired to fall down upon the earth, and the high place, on which we stood at one moment rose upright but at another rolled downwards.

On any showing this last sentence is a remarkable statement, and it makes it difficult to see how we can suppose that the apocalypses are devoid of relics of actual experience. Even the attempt to add verisimilitude to the fictitious account of a heavenly ascent by the use of comments like these may reflect something of what visionaries actually underwent during the heavenly ascent. But such a deliberate attempt to add colour to a fictitious account seems a less convincing explanation of a comment like this than that it is the relic of what was actually experienced during the heavenly ascent.

Physical sensation either of heat or coldness is a feature of various mystical texts. For example when she describes her own rapture St Teresa of Avila speaks in the following way about the physical consequences of the experience:

> In these raptures the soul no longer seems to animate the body; its natural heat, therefore, is said to diminish and gradually gets cold, though with a feeling of great joy and sweetness. (*Life of St Teresa* 20)[41]

There is a brief comment in 1 Enoch 14.13, where the seer speaks of his inability to determine accurately the sensations of heat and cold while he is in heaven: 'And I entered into that house, and it was hot as fire and cold as ice: there were no delights of life therein: fear covered me, and trembling gat hold upon me.' The inability of the seer to decide exactly what sensation he felt may have been the result of the impossible combination of extremely hot and cold features, in the form of fire and crystal, which confronted him in the heavenly ascent. Equally possible, however, is the fact that we may have here the physical result of his experience. The link between feelings of great fear and the inability to distinguish whether one is either hot or cold could well be symptoms of the physical changes to the body which could arise from the frightening situation which faces the visionary as he believes that he is going to be confronted by the all holy God. One of the symptoms of shock, induced by great fear, is a feeling of cold, which can in certain instances manifest itself in the form of a cold sweat. Such symptoms, induced by the fear of what was to come as the seer went further into the heavenly world, may well account for this comment.[42]

In certain places mention is made of the impact which the heavenly ascent made on the visionary. In 1 Enoch 14.8, for example, the visionary describes his ascent in the following way:

> And the vision was shown to me thus: Behold, in the vision clouds invited me and a mist summoned me, and the course of the stars and the lightnings sped and hastened me, and the winds in the vision caused me to fly and lifted me upward and bore me into heaven.

In the Apocalypse of Abraham 15 the patriarch describes his ascent into heaven as follows:

> And the angel took me with the right hand and set me on the right wing of the pigeon, and set himself on the left wing of the turtle dove, which birds had neither been slaughtered nor divided. And he bore me to the borders of the flaming fire . . .

Both these images are used by St Teresa as she seeks to express the way in which the soul is taken up to God:

> The Lord catches up the soul, just as one might say the clouds gather up the mist of the earth and carries it right out of itself, just as I have heard it said that the clouds or the sun actually do catch up the mists. Then the cloud rises to heaven taking the soul with it . . . I do not know whether this is in fact an accurate comparison but in point of fact this is how it happens . . . You see and feel this cloud, or this powerful eagle raising you and bearing it upon its wings. (*Life of St Teresa* 20)[43]

Teresa's comparison of the ascent with a bird lifting up the soul on its wings is precisely what we find in the Apocalypse of Abraham. Her use of clouds and mists, however, is somewhat different from the way in which these images are utilized in 1 Enoch 14. There, both are said to be the things which called the seer from earth, though in fact it was the wind which caught him up and took him to heaven. The point is that these images are used by another mystic, though of another era, in an attempt to describe the way in which she experienced the rapture to God.

A comment on the way in which the ascent to heaven took place is to be found also in the vision of Satyrus in the *Passio Perpetuae* 4: 'And we floated not supine, looking upwards, but as if ascending a gentle slope' (Translation from *The Ante-Nicene Fathers*). In this instance the visionary does not experience the ascent as a form of levitation (*non supini*) but as a gentle ascent up an incline. Whether he expected his ascent to involve the 'floating' sensation of levitation is not clear, but he does reject this in favour of an ascent which involved a different kind of sensation.

The significance of these occasional references to the experience of the apocalyptic seers, like the references to fasting, have implications for our understanding of the apocalypses as a whole. If it is thought that the apocalypses are merely repositories of a particular message, with no evidence of religious experience at all, why should these brief comments find any place within them? They seem to be completely superfluous to the needs of an author who was wanting to communicate only a particular message by means of the apocalyptic framework. It is hard to believe that they are deliberate attempts to add a touch of realism to the account, especially when several of the elements actually do coincide with the way in which mystical experiences were described in later mystical writings. But even if the supposition that the apocalypses contain relics of mystical experience is rejected, such touches as these probably give evidence of the physical effects which were believed to accompany the heavenly ascent or the experience of the divine. The likelihood is, however, that we have indications here of the experiences of early Jewish visionaries.[44]

That is not to suggest, however, that *all* apocalyptic literature can be explained in this way. There are clear signs that some of the visionary material now found in the apocalypses has been subject to considerable redactional activity (e.g. 4 Ezra 11—12), so that often it is impossible to discern the character of an original vision. Indeed, in some instances one must suppose that what purports to be a vision is in fact an artificial construction which has been put together to coincide exactly with the message which the seer wants to get across to his readers. But the point should be made that it cannot be assumed without further investigation that all the visions in the apocalypses arose in this way. It is necessary, therefore, to judge each vision on its merits. We have suggested that a comparison of visions which are clearly inspired by scriptural passages may offer one means of deciding whether a vision is the result of the apocalypticist's own experience or an artificial construction. Unfortunately not all the visions contained in the apocalypses can be shown to be the direct consequence of scriptural meditation. This is particularly true of certain of the dream-visions in Syriac Baruch as well as some of the visions in Revelation. It is important, therefore, to try to work towards some kind of criterion for separating out the authentic visions which are contained in the apocalypses.

Consideration of this question has concentrated particularly on the visions in the book of Revelation. Obviously these have a much stronger claim to be considered as the products of the actual experience of an apocalyptic seer for the simple reason that consideration of them is not complicated by the pseudonymous form which complicates consideration of Jewish apocalypses. The fact that we can be almost certain that we have the writing of an individual who lived in the first century AD rather than the fictitious claims of the Jewish apocalypses that they contain the experiences of men who lived long ago makes Revelation a natural place to start in our discussion of this issue. Denial of the claim of the book to contain actual visionary experiences has been widespread, but there have been those who have been prepared to support its claim to incorporate the products of visionary experience.[45] To say this does not mean, of course, that one turns a blind eye to the considerable amount of later reflection which has gone on in the construction of the book. The many attempts to offer some account of the arrangement of the book is testimony in itself to the fact that the apocalypse exhibits a degree of order which makes such an enterprise necessary.[46] Nevertheless the sophistication of the structure need not exclude the possibility that the starting-point for the eschatological sequence which we find in the book was in fact a series of visions which John of Patmos had.

J. Lindblom in particular has turned his mind to this question.[47] On the basis of certain criteria which he lists as the characteristic marks of authentic visions he finds evidence of actual visionary experience in a small number of passages in Revelation (Rev. 1.9–20; 4.1–5; 8; 11.19; 12.13–18; 15.1–4; 15.5–8; 19.9–10; 19.11–16; 19.17–18; 22.8). The rest of the material he thinks is the result of more conventional literary activity.[48] The characteristics of authentic visionary experience he suggests are as follows: (i) spontaneity; (ii) concise visions which are only expanded later; (iii) dreamlike character of the experience: the vision may be clear in its detail but as a whole has an unreal and fantastic quality; (iv) the vision is entirely fresh and unsophisticated in its form and content; (v) the vision concerns things on an other-worldly plane; (vi) there are difficulties in expressing the experience in words; (vii) the experience has emotional side-effects, and (viii) mention is made of the date and place of the vision.

Of these characteristics of the authentic vision only the first and the fifth must be questioned. The evidence of preparation for spiritual experience is so overwhelming, that it is difficult to see how one can suppose that only those visions are authentic which come upon the recipient unawares. The occurrence of visions is in no way invalidated by the need to make certain preparations for them. The suggestion that direct revelations from God could be prepared for may seem questionable to the religious mind, but that surely does not mean that claims to visions following extensive preparation are any less authentic in the mind of the visionary concerned. Even the (probably authentic) visions of Perpetua describe the preparations which were made by her for divine revelation, in this case extensive prayer to God. What concerns us here is the authenticity of the claim to visionary experience, not the validity of that claim in theological terms, which is a completely different issue. Accordingly, spontaneity must be rejected as a mark of the authentic vision.

As far as the fifth characteristic is concerned, it seems to me that it would be wrong to exclude from consideration as authentic visions those which contain predominantly ordinary images. Consideration of the prophetic literature shows how easily an everyday object can become the nucleus of a prophetic vision (e.g. Jer. 1.11ff.; Amos 8.1ff.).[49] We may expect these everyday objects to function in the vision in unusual and bizarre ways, but the inclusion of them in the vision should be no barrier to consideration of the authenticity of those visions which contain them.

Apart from these two points the list set out by Lindblom is a useful basis for further attempts to define more precisely which visions are the result of actual experience. Nevertheless in the interests of further precision it seems to me to be necessary to ask the following questions of the material under consideration:

(i) In the light of the earlier investigation of the visions based on Ezekiel 1, one must ask whether there is evidence in a vision to suggest that the way in which hitherto familiar images are used moves away from the original, resulting in new combinations of ideas, as well as the inclusion of new elements.

(ii) If the answer to the first question is positive, one must then ask the following question: is the juxtaposition of the various elements free from any sign of exegetical activity or any conscious attempt to reformulate originally disparate ideas? If this is the case, then the possibility must be faced that we have the result of visionary experience.

With regard to those visions which do not purport to offer disclosures about the world above the following questions should be asked:

(iii) Does the vision contain superfluous material which has little or no significance for the apocalypticist either when he comes to reflect on the meaning of what he has seen or in the interpretation which follows the vision?

(iv) Does the vision contain a series of complicated images whose presence seems to be dictated by their significance for the later interpretation?

As far as the visions of Revelation are concerned, the obvious example of a vision which has been subject to later reflection is that concerning the great harlot in chapter 17. This vision is interpreted very carefully, so that the reader is left in no doubt as to the significance of various elements which are to be found in the vision (Rev. 17.8ff.). The question is whether the vision (vv. 3–6) contains within it an experience of the seer. In the light of (iii) and (iv) above a comparison between vision and interpretation is required:

Details of vision	Where interpreted
1. The woman	v. 18
2. Scarlet beast	v. 8
3. Seven heads and ten horns on beast	vv. 9ff.
4. Dress of the woman	
5. Golden cup	
6. Name on her forehead	

It would appear that there are elements in the vision which remain without any parallel interpretation in verses 8ff. The various aspects of the woman's dress and appearance are not interpreted in the vision, nor for that matter is the colour of the beast (v. 3), a colour which might have been expected to have led to some comment, especially in the light of the reference to the blood of the martyrs in verse 6. In actual fact consideration of the interpretation reveals that the interest of the seer centred on the beast which supported the woman rather than the woman herself, whereas the vision mentions the beast only briefly. The vision itself is relatively free from difficulties; these only arise when we come to the interpretation. A good example of such complexity is the double interpretation given of the heads of the beast (Rev. 17.9). Indeed, consideration of the interpretation reveals how much it attempts to make its particular point conform to the details of the vision without in any way altering the details of the latter. The explanation of how there could be an eighth king in the future is carried out by reference to the *Nero Rediturus* myth. In fact there are only seven heads mentioned, and there could only be another king by supposing that the eighth would in fact be one of the previous seven. Another indication that the complexities arose only at the level of interpretation can be found in verse 15. Here the significance of the waters (cf. Jer. 51.13), upon which the woman is seated, is explained. This is not an interpretation of an element of the original vision, however, and the waters are only mentioned as part of the (redactional?) introduction to the vision in verse 1.[50] There are signs therefore that we may have an original vision which has been subject to later reflection. This has not affected the original vision in any way, however, for the complications are confined to the interpretation only.

The other visions in Revelation are not so easily discussed. Revelation 17, as we have seen, is the only example in the apocalypse of a vision followed by interpretation. But the considerations which apply to Revelation 17 are equally relevant for other visions as well. If there are signs that the details of the vision have a significance which is out of all proportion to the part which they play in the vision itself, we may suspect either an artificial construction or the result of later reflection. The fact is, however, despite the attempts of commentators to find deep significance in all the details of the visions in Revelation, we are seldom faced with a situation where there are signs of a deliberate attempt to construct an appropriate image. While there are parallels to many of the images used in Revelation, one cannot fail to be impressed by the remarkable freshness of the visions and the lack of any laboured endeavours to make sure that the images say all that the author wishes them to. Bizarre and extravagant the imagery may be, but it lacks any hint of the self-conscious desire to make these images as relevant as possible.

A similar conclusion emerges when we consider a dream-vision in the apocalypses like the vision of the forest in Syriac Baruch 36. It appears that the vision is very closely related to the following interpretation (ch. 38) with the forest (36.3) representing the nations of the world (39.2) and the fountain and vine (39.3) the messiah (39.7). A closer glance will reveal that several elements of the vision do not play an important part in the interpretation, e.g. the extent and the setting of the forest (36.2). Also in the vision the overthrow of the forest is represented as one action (v. 4f.), whereas in the interpretation a series of destructions corresponds to the demise of several world-empires over a very long period (Syr. Bar. 39.2f.). There is nothing in the vision, therefore, which corresponds to the fourth kingdom mentioned in the interpretation (Syr. Bar. 39.5), though both vision and interpretation coincide in their interest in the last leader (Syr. Bar. 36.6ff., cf. 40.1ff.). Finally it should be pointed out that no less than five verses of a vision described in eleven verses are taken up with the pronouncement of condemnation on the last cedar, an idea which is only partially taken up in the interpretation (Syr. Bar 40.1). Such discrepancies as these between vision and interpretation suggest that here too an original vision has been pressed into service to yield the interpretation we now have, despite the fact that the details of the vision do not completely coincide with the message which the apocalypticist wishes to convey.

Application of a method of this sort to the visions of the apocalypses should enable us to ascertain which visions can be considered to be the result of actual experience, and, what is equally important, the way in which subsequent reflection upon the vision has enabled the seer to communicate his message to his readers. That is not to suggest that the message is often appended to a vision at the expense of the original intention of the vision. Such a supposition is most unlikely, for we must suppose that the questions facing the apocalypticist had a profound influence on the form of the visions which he received (e.g. Rev. 11—12). The later reflection on the vision, however, gave him the opportunity to draw out even more plainly the meaning which the original vision had suggested to him, even if it meant exercising a degree of latitude in the way in which the original vision was interpreted. No doubt the visionary believed that the interpretation itself was just as much under the influence of divine guidance as the original vision. Hence we find him talking about the interpretation of visions in terms of angelic revelation. Although the part which reflection played on the original vision was probably considerable, the evidence which we possess of the apocalyptic seer preparing himself to learn more about the vision which he has already seen suggests that he considered the reflective process itself and the answers which emerged equally the result of divine guidance.

Excursus: Visionary Experience and Pseudonymity

One of the major reasons why the Jewish apocalypses have not seemed to be a likely source of authentic visions is the fact that without exception all these visions are said to have been given to figures of the past. The device of pseudonymity has merely increased suspicions that we are dealing in the apocalypses with literary constructions which have little or no contact with actual experience. With the literature of later Christian mysticism one cannot doubt the intensity of religious feelings spoken of by, for example, Richard Rolle in his *Fire of Divine Love*, whatever reservations one might have about the sensuous character of the experiences which he relates. The point is that we are dealing in this later literature with a named individual who does not hide his identity under a pseudonym. In contrast, the stories of the heavenly journeys of patriarchs and prophets is so obviously fictitious that one is tempted to regard the whole corpus of apocalyptic literature as little more than the flights of fancy of certain individuals with a particular theological axe to grind. The question inevitably arises how we are to relate the phenomenon of pseudonymity to the indications that apocalyptic literature does in fact contain relics of visionary experience.

The easiest explanation of all would be to suggest that the visionaries placed their experiences in the context of the lives of some great figures of the past, who, it was believed, had been fortunate to have visions similar to their own. For reasons which we have already outlined above,[51] the communication of such visions in a literary form may have gained added weight by being attached to the name of one who had a reputation for revelations of this kind. Such a view presupposes that the visions are only loosely related to the fictitious settings in which they now appear, and it is this matter which first demands our consideration.

In the book of Daniel and the Apocalypse of Abraham it is particularly easy to divorce the visions from their setting in the lives of great figures of the past. In Daniel it is quite apparent that a distinct change comes after the end of chapter 6, when the book, though still in Aramaic, suddenly leaves behind the legends about Daniel and his Jewish companions in Babylon, and we have a series of visions (7—8) and other revelations by an angelic intermediary. Even if we suppose that the book is a unity in its final form,[52] we need not deny that the legends in the opening chapters were in existence before their incorporation into this apocalypse. They thus provide the framework and authority for the visionary material with which the book concludes. Similarly, in the Apocalypse of Abraham there is a clear distinction between the two halves of the work. The opening eight chapters consist of a long account of Abraham's turning away from idolatry, and there is no mention of visionary activity at this stage. Although, as in Daniel, the fictitious setting still pervades the second, apocalyptic, section, the bulk of this material is only loosely related to the opening legends.[53] Thus, once a setting has been provided for the heavenly ascent, the rest of this material can be seen as a series of visions which could have been linked with Abraham and a cycle of stories about him.

Unlike the two apocalypses which we have just been considering 1 Enoch does not offer such an easy task in the matter of separating the visionary material from its present context. One example of this is the account of the ascent to heaven in 1 Enoch 14.8ff. As it stands this vision is intimately related to the pronouncement of divine judgement upon the Watchers which colours the whole of chapters 15 and 16. But, allowing for the fact that this vision has been integrated into its present context there are occasional signs that it may have existed separately.[54]

Firstly, it is quite apparent that the reference to the ascent to heaven is introduced rather suddenly in 1 Enoch 14.8. Enoch has just spoken of the divine message of judgement which he had received (vv. 4ff.), and then, after reporting the result of the vision, in verse 8 he describes in more detail the vision, whose consequences he had just outlined. This may indicate that the account in verses 8ff. has been added to this brief report of a vision of Enoch at a later stage. Indeed, in the context of the story of Enoch this extended account of Enoch's vision seems rather superfluous in the light of the references to visions already in chapters 13.8ff. and 14.4ff.

Secondly, the character of the confrontation with God which is described in the account of the heavenly ascent (1 Enoch 14.13, 25) looks more like the initial ascent of a man into the heavenly realm. This hardly fits in with the picture we have of Enoch in these chapters as one who had been taken up[55] and whose life was involved with the angels and God himself (1 Enoch 12.2f.). The account of the vision in chapter 14.8ff. seems to be one which does not fit well with the context presupposed by chapter 12.2f.

Thirdly, the title used for God in 1 Enoch 14.2 contrasts with other titles. This point is of less weight, however, as there is some variety of titles used in these chapters. It may nevertheless offer a further indication that we are dealing here with a passage which may originally have had no relationship with earlier Enoch legends. Indeed, there are signs that chapters 15 and 16 themselves contrast with the earlier legends. According to chapter 16.1ff. the Watchers will not be punished until the final judgement, whereas in chapter 14.6 they are to be punished at once. The words of God in chapter 16.4 ('You have no peace') are parallel to chapter 13.1, suggesting that the whole is a parallel version to what had already been stated. Thus, although chapters 14—16 offer a fairly coherent account of an ascent to heaven and the divine message which follows from it, there are signs that they are superfluous to what has already been said in chapter 12.1—14.7. Within chapters 14—16 the extended account of the journey through heaven is unnecessary for the condemnation which follows. There is, therefore, reason to believe that the vision may have been inserted into the framework of Enoch's receipt of the divine message of judgement on the Watchers and then made part of the longer account of Enoch's intercession on behalf of the angels which already presupposed that Enoch had received visions of various kinds (1 Enoch 13.8; 14.4).

The use of such legends as an authenticating framework for an individual's visions would offer a satisfactory explanation of how pseudonymity can be related to the contemporary claims to religious experience. The question has to be raised, however, whether the use of pseudonymity may in part have arisen out of the psychology of the visionary experience itself. Lindblom has pointed to the occurrence, in visionary literature of diverse origins, of the tendency of the visionary to mark a separation between his normal experience and his visionary life by speaking of the latter as if it had happened to another person, what Lindblom calls *die Objektivierung des Ichs*.[56] He speaks in the following way about this phenomenon:

> . . . frequently the visionary distinguishes between two persons representing himself; the one being his everyday *ego*, the other the extraordinary *ego*, which is the subject of the supernatural experience. In the visionary experiences this *alter ego* replaces the everyday *ego*, this latter *ego* having so to speak been removed from its ordinary position. The extraordinary *ego* beholds the invisible things, hears the voices, receives the revelations, has intercourse with the divinities, makes journeys into supernatural regions. Everyday man does not recognize himself in such wonderful experiences. He finds his unexpected accomplishments in the blessed moments so exceptional, so surpassing his normal faculty, that he cannot help ascribing them to an alien person actually playing the role of his extraordinary and better *ego* . . . Generally the mentioning of double personalities takes place in connection with the reflection on, or the reproducing of, the vision itself . . . Of course, this doubling can in some measure be conditioned by personal humility before the supernatural powers, thanks to whom the visionary was endowed with his unexampled experiences, but there is no doubt that the feeling of being two individuals is principally derived from the visionary experiences themselves.[57]

Such a phenomenon is not unknown in Jewish religion outside the apocalypses. One of the best examples from the prophetic literature, which Lindblom himself quotes,[58] is the vision of the watchman in Isaiah 21. In this oracle, which we have had reason to mention in discussing the emotional turmoil which prophetic inspiration involved, we find reference to the watchman who is placed in a position to see the onslaught of the enemy. There has been much discussion about the identity of this figure, but the most likely explanation is that the watchman is none other than the prophet himself in his role as visionary.[59] This is the *alter ego* who acts within the vision and who is to some extent distanced from the prophet. In the opening instruction to the prophet the command comes to place the watchman at his post to tell of what he sees. The command to the prophet concerns his visionary self which will participate in the ensuing vision, while the prophet looks upon his *alter ego* giving warning of the marauding hordes (Isa. 21.9).

Precisely the same phenomenon is to be found in one of the visions in *Passio Perpetuae*. In 3.2 Perpetua sees a vision of herself transformed into a man and fighting as a gladiator in the arena, an experience clearly influenced by the prospect of her imminent death:

> . . . because I knew that I was given to the wild beasts, I marvelled that the wild beasts were not loose upon me. Then there came forth against me a certain Egyptian, horrible in appearance . . . And there came to me as my helpers and encouragers, handsome youths; and I was stripped and became a man.

The situation with 2 Corinthians 12.2ff. where Paul describes his rapture into the third heaven is rather different from the two visions just mentioned.[60] Here the apostle is reporting an experience which he had had fourteen years before. He does not, therefore, offer an account of the actual vision but merely summarizes the character of the experience as a whole. The significant point as far as we are concerned is that, when he comes to relate this experience to the Corinthian Christians, he feels the need to relate it in a rather strange way, preferring to talk of the rapture of 'a man in Christ' rather than himself (2 Cor. 12.2). Commentators rightly point to Paul's unwillingness to boast about his own achievements and to glory only in his weakness (e.g. 2 Cor. 11.30). Nevertheless his compulsion to speak of what was clearly his own experience (2 Cor. 12.7) in this peculiar way has some affinities with the tendency within mystical literature to which Lindblom has drawn attention, where the mystic distances his ordinary self from the self which experiences the visions.

The problem with Paul's account, however, is that we cannot be sure whether the apostle actually experienced the phenomenon of dual personality during the ascent itself or had only used this form when he came to report it to others. Either way, of course, the phenomenon is of interest to our understanding of the mind of the apocalypticist. Even if we suppose that Paul is merely using a literary device here (as is more likely), the fact that he feels the need to speak of his ascent in this particular way may enable us to see why a similar form was used by the apocalypticists.

Even these examples are still some distance from the way in which pseudonymity functions within Jewish apocalyptic. All offer an example of another figure, the *alter ego*, who is, without exception, anonymous. The fundamental difference in the apocalypses, of course, is that the person to whom the experiences are attributed is a named, and, as far as the apocalypticists are concerned, historical figure. What we would have in the apocalypses, therefore, would be the linking of the visionary's *alter ego* in the literary account of visions with a figure of the past, whose visionary prowess was renowned. Though we may expect that the bulk of the material in the apocalypses may have been inserted within a fictitious framework deliberately, in order to gain some authority for the visions, it seems that a case can be made for some visions at least being linked with a pseudonymous author precisely because the character of the experience itself drove the visionary to the conclusion that narrating in the name of some other person was the only way in which he could do justice to the nature of his experience.

While it would be wrong to speak of firm conclusions arising out of the foregoing survey of recent study of apocalyptic origins and the suggestions with regard to the visionary origin of some of the material, the following points can be made:

(i) There can be no disputing the fact that the prophetic oracles concerning the future had a central role to play in the formation of the various Jewish eschatologies which existed during the period of the Second Temple. The contribution of prophecy to the idea of apocalyptic, therefore, was very extensive and cannot be denied. Although there are many differences between prophecy and apocalyptic, not least the total view of history in apocalyptic, it cannot be established that apocalyptic had abandoned, or was in the process of abandoning, the conviction that the divine promises would be fulfilled in history. Of all the common elements in prophecy and apocalyptic, it is the shared conviction that knowledge of God comes through inspiration which is the most important contribution of the former to the latter.

(ii) Confirmation of the contribution of prophecy to the ideas of apocalyptic is not an indication that apocalyptic is the child of prophecy. Study of the Israelite Wisdom literature, and in particular those aspects concerned with divination, the interpretation of dreams and foretelling the future (mantic wisdom), shows many affinities with apocalyptic, and these elements probably had as significant a contribution to make to the outlook of apocalyptic as any other movement. Whether such ideas were imported from Wisdom schools or were already part of the developing prophetic movement is at present difficult to say. Nevertheless the similarity which exists between the profound questions posed in certain apocalypses and a book like Job suggests that the contribution of the Wisdom-tradition to apocalyptic is extremely important.

(iii) If one is to take the claim to visionary experience seriously, the most likely origin for apocalyptic seems to be among those prophetic circles which continued after the Exile to maintain the validity of visions as a means of understanding God's will. That is not to say that these were eschatologically orientated groups whose sole aim was to preserve intact the authentic prophetic eschatology in the face of contrary forces in Israelite society. Part of the interest of such groups may have been in eschatology, but the main similarity between such circles and apocalyptic is the claim to direct access to the divine secrets through revelation. In other words, it is the stand on behalf of the divine charisma as a continuing mode of revelation against attempts to reject such claims in favour of more indirect channels of communicating the divine will. This claim is not necessarily sectarian in its characteristics and could, in principle, be the common property of all groups.

(iv) Investigation of the material within the apocalypses suggests that they *may* contain relics of unknown apocalyptic seers. These visions, while subject to later reflection in many instances, often were inspired by the study of Scripture.[61] This led either to a belief that answers to vexing problems posed by the text could be given directly or, as in the case of the study of the first chapter of Ezekiel, led to a vision of the glory of God along the lines of that vouchsafed to the prophet long ago.

(v) The suggestion that such visions are preserved in the apocalypses should not lead to the assumption that all the apocalyptic literature arose in this way. The composite nature of many apocalypses, as well as the obvious signs of artificial construction of visions, indicate that these works cannot be treated simply as the repositories of the visionary activity of unknown seers who lived during the period of the Second Temple. Each vision must be investigated on its merits. The presence of some authentic visionary material in an apocalypse does not, therefore, guarantee that a similar origin can be posited of other visions in the same work.

CHAPTER 10

Dating the Apocalypses[1]

FRIEDRICH ENGELS' CLAIM for the New Testament apocalypse, that it could be dated with some precision in the months of late AD 67 or early 68, would not be echoed by all commentators on this work.[2] Nevertheless all commentators date it within thirty years of this date. Any attempt at precision of this sort is completely out of the question when it comes to the dating of the Jewish apocalypses. A variety of factors has made this an extraordinarily difficult subject, and the difficulties can be seen in the vast differences which are to be found between the suggestions of various commentators concerning the date of a particular document, sometimes amounting to centuries, not years! Such an issue may not be so important for the student of the history of religion, whose interest in the apocalyptic texts continues to exist irrespective of the date of the original text, though, naturally, the question of date is going to affect the way in which he attempts to relate a particular text to other apocalypses. The same cannot be said of the student of the New Testament, whose interest in the apocalypses arises out of his conviction that they may be of value for his understanding of the primary texts of the early Christian movement. If it can be shown that a text, which he would like to use to illustrate a New Testament passage, was in fact written after the first century AD, its value diminishes, because he can no longer be sure that the text is free from the influence of precisely those documents upon which the Jewish text is supposed to be shedding light. Of course, this difficulty applies to other types of Jewish literature as well as apocalyptic material. As indiscriminate use of the vast amount of rabbinic material available to the student in translation, particularly P. Billerbeck's *Kommentar zum NT aus Talmud und Midrasch,* may lead one to utilize material which was written centuries after the last NT document was written.[3] The result is that there are those who are very suspicious about using any

Jewish text which was written after the first century AD, whereas others are quite happy to use material, almost at times irrespective of date, on the grounds that the later material contains ideas which would have been current at the beginning of the Christian era.

The scholarly debate over the use of Jewish material for the interpretation of the New Testament is similar to the debate which has gone on throughout this century about the value of the later gnostic material for New Testament exegesis. There are those who see the later gnostic systems as the result of extensive Christian influence (some would say directly inspired by Christianity), and therefore of no value whatsoever for the understanding of the New Testament, being a movement which is parasitic upon early Christian ideas.[4] On the other hand there has been an influential body of opinion which has consistently maintained that gnosticism was essentially a non-Christian movement, whose origins go back well before the first century AD and that the ideas which we find in later gnostic writings, even including the much later Manichaean and Mandaean movements, are symptomatic of the sort of ideas which existed at the time when Christianity came into being. Accordingly, some are quite prepared to argue that such ideas were already available to the early Christian writers as they sought to express their convictions about Jesus of Nazareth.[5]

Thankfully, the problems posed by the Jewish literature are not as vast as those which confront anyone who seeks to elucidate the relationship between Christianity and gnosticism. Nevertheless the differences of opinion which do exist in the scholarly world over the value of certain key-texts makes the question of the relationship between early Christianity and Judaism a very difficult one. There are unfortunately no hard and fast rules which can be laid down concerning the use of Jewish material for the interpretation of the New Testament. As one might expect, it is the texts which are centrally important which have been the subject of so much debate, and, while most would concede that later material may contain earlier ideas, the value of ideas which are very much akin to early Christian notions within Jewish texts is less readily admitted. As far as the apocalypses are concerned, there are no easy ways of solving this problem. The best that can be done is to point out certain factors which need to be borne in mind when the question of dating arises.

One of the features of the apocalypses which Koch considers to be characteristic of apocalyptic as a whole is the composite character of many of the apocalypses.[6] Some of them do have a long literary history, and there are signs not only of redactional glosses on the visions already incorporated in a work but also on occasion of the addition of further visionary material. Evidence of this history is to be found in the fact that many of the apocalypses are now only extant in languages like Slavonic or Ethiopic, though in many cases a Hebrew or Aramaic original seems likely. This means that we have to reckon with the possibility that changes, sometimes of substance, took place during the translation of the work into its present form.[7] But what attracts most attention is the way in which the original visionary deposit has been added to at a later time, often giving the apocalypse the appearance of being a vast jumble of disparate material. This is the impression created by 1 Enoch, especially in its Ethiopic version. For example, the opening five chapters have nothing to do with the story of the Watchers, Enoch's intercession and its consequences which we find in chapters 6–36. But by far the most complicated section of the Ethiopic version is the Similitudes (37–71), which is a hotchpotch of visions, legends about antediluvians, eschatological predictions and astronomical secrets which are put together with little evidence of any conscious plan. This section of 1 Enoch certainly has the appearance of being a collection of material, some of which may have originally had some kind of structure, but which in the course of time, has been added to, resulting in the disparate collection we now have.

Another work which has been subject to extensive later additions is 4 Ezra, though the way in which the material has been added has left the form of the original apocalypse intact. The opening and closing chapters of the Latin version (1–2 and 15–16), which are missing in the oriental versions, usually referred to as 5 and 6 Ezra respectively, were added later in the Christian era, but they can easily be removed, (as is done, for example, in the version in Charles' *Pseudepigrapha* which starts at chapter 3), leaving behind the Jewish apocalypse.

When we decide about the date of an apocalypse we have to ask whether our dating for one section necessarily applies to the apocalypse as a whole. The Similitudes again are a good example in this respect. There are clear breaks in the subject-matter after chapters 36 and 71 in the Ethiopic version, indicating that this section may have existed as a separate unit. Also the absence of the Similitudes from the Enoch-fragments from Qumran has apparently confirmed the opinion of those who argue that a completely different explanation of the origin of this section should be offered. The fact that we can date some sections of 1 Enoch as early as the third century BC cannot be taken to imply an early date for the Similitudes. Indeed, some would say that the absence of the Similitudes from Qumran means that we should also be prepared to date this material in the post-Christian era. Even within the Similitudes the date given to one section should not necessarily be taken as indicative of the date of the composition of the rest of the material.[8] Thus the dating of the material must be carried out on the basis of an examination of the various constituent parts.

One of the easiest means of dating the material in the apocalypses is the identification of historical allusions which they may contain. Several of them reflect identifiable historical events which thus offer us a time before which a work could not have been written, though this is not to deny the probability in many cases that the works reflect earlier ideas. The best example of this process of dating is the book of Daniel. Though it was apparently written during the Exile by a Jew named 'Daniel, most scholars today accept that the book is a pseudepigraphon written during the middle of the second century BC at the height of the crisis precipitated by Antiochus Epiphanes' attempt to eradicate Jewish beliefs.[9] This can be seen in the frequent allusion to the threat to Judaism which Antiochus posed (Dan. 8.9–12, cf. Dan. 11.31ff. and 1 Macc. 1.54). The references to Antiochus' desecration of the Temple makes a date for the final form of the book impossible before 168 BC. Many would go further and suggest that the absence of any reference to the dedication of the Temple in 165 BC (1 Macc. 4.36ff.) makes a date before this event most likely. Thus we are left with a very short period of about three years during which the book was written. A date towards the beginning of this period is more likely, before the success of the Maccabees changed the prospects for the Jewish people. The tone of Daniel is one which seems to presuppose the necessity of suffering in the short term but the prospect of vindication in the future.

A little more difficult to date is the Animal-Apocalypse in

1 Enoch 85ff. We have already seen that the vision presupposes the rise of the *ḥasidim* (1 Enoch 90.6f.) and probably the Maccabaean uprising (90.11f.). The fact that there is no reference to further historical events after this, apart from those events which inaugurated the new age may lead us to suppose that the time of writing was the moment when the author leaves off writing about past history and turns his attention to the issue of God's imminent intervention (1 Enoch 90.13ff.). In the telling of Israel's history up to the beginning of the second century BC the author has been reasonably precise, but the change to interest in eschatological matters in verse 13 is surely a sign that the preceding reference marked the situation in the author's own day. The date for this vision appears to be at a time of great persecution for the Jewish people (1 Enoch 90.8), but with the promise of deliverance imminent (v. 9). For this reason the vision is probably just a little later than Daniel, round about 164 BC.[10] Such a date applies only to chapters 83—90 which appear to be a unified section. A glance at the (astronomical) material which precedes this and the break after chapter 90.42 shows that we are probably right to deal with these chapters in isolation.

Much more difficult to date are the closing chapters of 1 Enoch (91ff.). The Apocalypse of Weeks does not furnish enough chronological information to allow us to date the section with any precision. Milik argues for a date in the middle of the first century BC on the basis of the orthography of 4Q Enoch 5, giving an indication of the possible value of these finds by the study of the pseudepigrapha.[11]

One feature which is often used in the dating of Revelation is the allusion which we find in chapters 13.3 and 17.11 to the legend which was current at the end of the first century, and was known to Suetonius (Nero 57), concerning the return of Nero. Although, as we have already seen, commentators on Revelation have usually sought much more precision than a link with the currency of a legend such as this would offer, the presence of it in Revelation, clearly a first century document, is a useful guide to the dating of another document which seems to mention it. In the Ascension of Isaiah 4.2 the return of Nero may be hinted at in the following words:

. . . these are the days of the completion of the world. And after it

has come to its consummation, Beliar, the great prince, the king of
this world, who has ruled it since it came into being, shall descend;
he will come down from his firmament in the form of a man, a
lawless king, a slayer of his mother, who himself even this king will
persecute the plant which the Twelve apostles of the Beloved have
planted.

This passage appears to reflect the *Nero Rediturus* myth as the
reference to 'the slayer of his mother' indicates (Suetonius Nero
34; Sib. Or. iv. 121; v. 145). Therefore, it is difficult to suppose
that a date much later than the end of the first century can be
considered for the final form of this work, as the legend concerning Nero would not have had currency for very much longer.[12]
Alternatively the writer of this section may consider that the
incarnation of Beliar is the king who is now on the throne and as
such, it is his reign that marks the decisive transition to the new
age. Such an early date is impossible if the work is dependent
on the gospels of Matthew and Luke as the allusions to Luke
1.27 and Matthew 1.18f. in Ascension of Isaiah 11.2ff. would
seem to indicate. Its Christian elements make a date for the final
form of the work much earlier than the reign of Nero impossible,
though it is clear that parts of the work may go back to a Jewish
original.

As is often the case in dating early Christian literature reference (or lack of it) to the fall of Jerusalem in AD 70 is regarded as
an indication of date.[13] No less than three Jewish apocalypses
fall into this category. 4 Ezra is placed in the fictitious situation
after the destruction of Solomon's temple. Such a setting would
have been most appropriate for a late first century apocalypticist
who lamented the ruins of Zion at the hand of Titus and his
legions. Apart from the setting after the destruction of Solomon's temple the vision of the disconsolate woman in 4 Ezra
9.38ff. would seem to provide added support for a late first
century date.[14] If this woman symbolizes the heavenly Zion
whose earthly counterpart has been destroyed, it would appear
that the appropriateness of this image would fit in with a
situation after AD 70. Added to this, the intense questioning of
traditional beliefs as well as the urgent eschatological expectation
befits a writing of this period when severe upheaval went hand
in hand with intense hope for the coming of the messianic age.[15]
Also Ezra's function as the one who restores the Law is not
dissimilar to the position of the rabbis under R. Johanan b.

Zakkai at Jamnia, whose task it was to reorganize Judaism under the authority of the Torah.[16] The closely related Syriac Baruch has a similar setting. This time, however, the fictitious situation is not in the period after the Exile but immediately preceding the destruction (Syr. Baruch 1.1) and in its immediate aftermath (6ff.). Passages like chapters 85.3 ('Zion has been taken from us, and we have nothing now save the Mighty One and his Law') and 20.2 ('Therefore have I now taken away Zion, that I more speedily visit the world in its season') read like the views of one who had himself experienced the fall of the Temple and was seeking to understand the theological significance of this event. 4 Ezra and Syriac Baruch are unique in the corpus of apocalyptic literature in their concerns with the predicament caused by the destruction of Jerusalem. It would seem, therefore, that the setting of both apocalypses is a decisive factor in the dating of them at the end of the first or early in the second century AD.

The third apocalypse to mention the destruction of the Temple, though this time without a matching setting in the fifth or sixth centuries BC, is the Apocalypse of Abraham. In chapter 27 of this apocalypse the destruction of the Temple is described:

> And I looked and saw: lo, the picture swayed and from it emerged, on its left side, a heathen people, and they pillaged those who were on the right side, men, women and children: some they slaughtered, others they retained with themselves. Lo, I saw them run towards them through four entrances, and they burnt the Temple with fire, and the holy things that were therein they plundered.

According to chapter 28 the apocalypticist regards the present age as extending from the founding of Zion to the destruction of the Temple. This means that this apocalypse too was born in an atmosphere of expectation concerning the fulfilment of Israel's eschatological hopes, which fits the years after the fall of Jerusalem very well indeed.[17]

The Jewish War in AD 66–70 is also important for another reason. It is now widely agreed by commentators on the Dead Sea Scrolls that, in the light of the archaeological evidence, the Qumran community probably perished at the hands of the Romans in round about AD 68.[18] This means that the library of the community, which contains fragments of apocalypses like Jubilees, 1 Enoch and the Testament of Levi must have been written before that date.[19] Therefore we are dealing here with versions of works which in their final form cannot be dated later than AD 68, unlike many of the apocalypses which in their present form have a relatively late date. What is more, by study of the handwriting of some of these texts we are sometimes in a position to work out a date for the written version of the work at Qumran, which could mean that the autograph may have been much earlier. An example of this is the fragments of 1 Enoch 91—108, which Milik on the basis of the orthography would date round about 100 BC, thus making the original some time earlier than this date.[20] A good case can be made for the unity of 91—105 (with the possible exception of 105.2 which looks like a Christian addition).[21] Thus the evidence of Qumran may indicate a date during the late second century BC for the bulk of the final chapters of 1 Enoch. The fragments of the earlier chapters of 1 Enoch (1—36) found at Qumran have opened up the possibility that we should find the origin of this material in the third century BC or even earlier.[22]

These indications from the Enoch fragments receive some confirmation when the internal evidence is examined. The question of the dependence of one apocalypse on another has often been raised, particularly in relation to 4 Ezra and Syriac Baruch.[23] This issue is particularly relevant to the discussion of 1 Enoch 14.8ff., which has certain affinities with Daniel 7. The extent of the relationship between the two texts is best seen in tabulated form. The order of elements in this table follows the order of material in Daniel:

Daniel 7	1 Enoch
1. Throne and description of it (v. 9)	v. 18
2. God's raiment (v. 9)	v. 20
3. God's physical features (v. 9)	
4. The wheels (v. 9)	v. 18
5. Rivers of fire (v. 10)	v. 19
6. Thousands of angels (v. 10)	
7. Tens of thousands of angels (v. 10)	v. 22
8. Judgement (v. 10f.)	
9. Coming of son of man with clouds (v. 13)	v. 8

Some of these parallels can be explained by the common use of Old Testament imagery, particularly the first chapter of Ezekiel, but this is hardly enough to explain why in such a short space such agreement should be found. Even if we suppose that these verses in Daniel may have come from an earlier source which described a theophany,[24] the question of the relationship between that source and the vision in 1 Enoch 14 still has to be explained. Much of the debate on this question has been of a rather general nature, and the influence of H. H. Rowley's discussion of the subject has been considerable.[25] His remarks take the form of a series of criticisms of the suggestion of R. H. Charles that this section of 1 Enoch is earlier than Daniel.[26] Rowley's discussion is not based on a detailed examination of the text, however, for he considers that pointing out inconsistencies in Charles's argument[27] is sufficient to establish the priority of Daniel. The major point he makes with regard to the two texts concerns their style. He thinks that the author of 1 Enoch 14 shows little versatility or originality compared with the author of Daniel, and thus he argues that the lack of 'style, imagination and brilliance' in 1 Enoch means that 'the less original work is the dependent one.'[28]

Arguments based on style are notoriously subjective, and the urgency and drama of Daniel 7 tell us nothing about its relationship with its more prosaic companion, 1 Enoch 14, except to stress the quality of the writing of Daniel 7. Much more important is a comparison of the different elements in the two chapters. Unfortunately, this too is rather inconclusive.

The scene in Daniel is of the Ancient of Days coming to the divine court with all the trappings of a tribunal (Dan. 7.10). Despite the fact that 1 Enoch 14 also concerns the theme of judgement, such elements are lacking. The description of the raiment of God in both accounts compares its brilliance to snow, though in 1 Enoch this is an extra mode of comparison after a reference to the sun (v. 20). Daniel lacks a reference to the cherubim, whereas 1 Enoch no longer has the parallel reference to the angels, retaining only a reference to the ten thousand who stood before God (v. 22b, cf. Dan. 7.10). In his attempt to describe the throne and the wheels of the chariot Daniel is content merely to describe their fiery appearance, whereas 1 Enoch compares the throne to crystal (1 Enoch 14.18) and the wheels to the sun (ibid.). Whereas the additional comparison of the garment of God on 1 Enoch 14.20 could indicate dependence on Daniel, there are other pieces of evidence (particularly the lack of the forensic elements and the lack of parallelism with regard to the angelic attendants) which point in the other direction.

Similarly decision about originality on the basis of an examination of anthropomorphisms is difficult to evaluate. Daniel 7 is certainly more explicit in this respect in the words 'the hair of his head was white like wool'. There is nothing to compare with this in 1 Enoch 14, though the reader is not left in any doubt that an anthropomorphic view of God is implied with the reference to the raiment of God (v. 20) and the reference to his face in verse 21. In other words 1 Enoch carried on the tendency already found in Ezekiel 1 of restrained anthropomorphism but without the additional element contained in Daniel 7, which cannot be derived from the theophany in Ezekiel. In the light of other developments, which we have noted in other apocalyptic theophanies, it would be tempting to argue that 1 Enoch 14 marks a move away from the frank anthropomorphism of Daniel towards the greater restraint of the later apocalypses.[29] Such a conclusion would be based only on the reference to the hair of the deity, however, and it is this particular element which has been one of the reasons for connections of Daniel 7 with Canaanite ideas.[30]

The picture of God as Ancient of Days recalls the description of the Canaanite God El as *ab shnm*, an aged divinity with grey hair.[31] What is of even more importance are the similarities which exist between the Son of Man in Daniel 7.13 and the exaltation of Baal, who is called a 'rider of clouds',[32] and is said to take over sovereignty from the older God, El, exactly as the Son of Man does in Daniel 7.14. Although these parallels are very attractive, one of the major difficulties in supposing that there has been influence of Canaanite mythology on Daniel 7 is the enormous time-lapse which exists between the writing of the Ugaritic texts and the book of Daniel, well over a thousand years. Thus, while we can be certain that Canaanite influence on Israelite theology was extensive in the earlier period, it is not so easy to explain how these ideas could have existed within Israel and only come to the surface in a writing of the second century BC.[33]

One cannot gloss over such difficulties as these in assessing the value of the Canaanite hypothesis for the interpretation of Daniel, but, as far as our study is concerned, it makes us focus on one particular issue which may point us towards a solution of our problem. What is immediately apparent when we examine 1 Enoch 14 is the lack of precisely those elements which we might term, for the sake of convenience, 'Canaanite', viz., the description of the hair of the Ancient of Days, the use of that particular title for God, the coming of a man to God with the clouds, and the transfer of divine sovereignty from one divine being to another. When we compare Daniel 7.13 and 1 Enoch 14.8 in particular, it is much easier to suppose that Daniel is dependent on 1 Enoch than *vice versa*. In the former we have the bestowal on the human figure of dominion and authority. 1 Enoch nowhere suggests that such honour is given to Enoch. The only authority which he possesses is to intercede with God and to communicate God's decision to the Watchers. In 1 Enoch 14.8 the clouds do not carry Enoch to heaven, for it is the winds which transport him thither. The clouds in 1 Enoch are more an indication of the visionary state than a sign of the divine presence. The lack of such elements in 1 Enoch 14 makes it difficult to see how that chapter could have been dependent on Daniel 7. If he had fused Daniel 7, or even part of it, it is not easy to see how the author of 1 Enoch 14 could have avoided mentioning these distinctive elements. Thus, assuming that there is some literary relationship between these two chapters, the balance of probability would seem to favour the priority of 1 Enoch, a fact which, as we have seen, seems to be confirmed by the early date indicated for these chapters by the fragments of 1 Enoch 1–36 from Qumran.[34] Thus the tendency to date parts of other non-canonical apocalypses earlier than the second century BC makes it difficult to continue to put Daniel at the forefront of the study of apocalyptic origins. It is the relationship of the earliest parts of the Enochic literature, and the visionary material contained in it, to the later form of Israelite prophecy which should be demanding more attention in the future search for the origins of apocalyptic.

When we turn to apocalypses like Slavonic Enoch and the Testament of Abraham, the question of dating is an even more difficult issue. Arguments have been put forward for seeing the former as a mediaeval document,[35] and as such of little relevance for the study of early Jewish apocalyptic. While there are peculiar features in the book, there seems to be nothing which is inconsistent with the mainstream of apocalyptic literature which dates from the beginning of the Christian era. Thus, even if it was committed to writing at a fairly late stage, it reflects the typical features of Jewish apocalyptic thought. Charles may have been too glib in his assumption that the lack of reference to the fall of Jerusalem in AD 70 suggested a date before this event.[36]

But equally, there seems to be little justification for the suggestion that we have a basically Christian document here.[37] If anything, the picture of Enoch is more restrained than in the Similitudes, and the lack of Christian elements on any large scale is not easily reconciled with a Christian author. Thus there are no compelling reasons for denying a date round about the beginning of the Christian era for the earliest version of this apocalypse, probably within a Hellenistic (even Alexandrian) Jewish environment.[38]

A similar setting and date have been suggested for the Testament of Abraham.[39] Its preservation in a variety of different languages testifies not only the popularity of the book but also a fairly early date for the original.[40] Clearly in their final form both Greek recensions show signs of Christian scribal activity, but the place of Abel as the judge makes it virtually impossible to suppose that it is a Christian work (cf. 2 Cor. 5.10). Nevertheless these two apocalypses epitomize the problems facing the student of apocalyptic. As we have no independent evidence of the existence of a Semitic original nor fragments of the original, we have to resort to conjectures in postulating the original language and date of the document.

This brings us to what is by far the most contentious issue in the discussion of the date of the apocalyptic literature, namely the question of the extent of Christian influence on the apocalypses. This issue does not apply to the apocalypses alone but many of the pseudepigrapha, which owed their preservation to the interest of Christian scribes.[41] The question which we have to ask ourselves when we consider the extent of Christian influence is if it is merely superficial, i.e. occasional Christian glosses in an essentially non-Christian book, or if Christian theology has dictated the themes of the work as we have it. That Christian scribes did tamper extensively with Jewish documents cannot be doubted. A glance at the Testaments of the Twelve Patriarchs reveals unmistakable signs of the distinctive influence of the Christian kerygma. The following quotation from the Testament of Levi 18.5ff., which presupposes the account of Jesus' baptism, will indicate the character of this influence:

> The heavens shall exult in his days, and the earth shall be glad, and the clouds rejoice; and the knowledge of the Lord shall be poured

forth upon the earth, as the water of the seas; and the angels of the
glory of the presence of the Lord shall be glad in him. The heavens
shall be opened, and from the temple of glory shall come upon him
sanctification, with the Father's voice as from Abraham to Isaac.
And the glory of the Most High shall be uttered over him, and the
spirit of understanding and sanctification shall rest upon him in the
water.[42]

Unfortunately not all the supposed examples of Christian influence are as obvious as this one. This means that evidence of
such influence is not merely confined to the inclusion of references to the life of Jesus but also to ideas which have affinities
with notions found in the New Testament. Thus, discussion of
the subject cannot be confined to those passages, which are
clearly based on the Christian kerygma, but must extend to
those apocalypses whose leading ideas are closely related to
Christian beliefs. Accordingly our survey will be in two parts:
first of all an examination of those works which betray little
Christian influence (the Apocalypse of Abraham, the Testament
of Abraham and Slavonic Enoch) and then those where extensive Christian influence has been supposed, whether of an
explicit or implicit kind (the Testaments of the Twelve Patriarchs, the Ascension of Isaiah, and the Similitudes of Enoch).

Sometimes the only evidence of Christian influence in an
apocalypse comes when a Christian scribe appends a doxology
to a Jewish pseudepigraphon, such as is evident in chapter 14 of
the shorter Greek recension of the Testament of Abraham (Rec.
B). In some manuscripts of the longer Greek recension (Rec. A)
some scribes have obviously felt dissatisfied with the purely
Jewish notion of judgement which they are purveying. In chapter 13, where the longer recension makes mention of the judgement of God in the future as well as that exercised by the twelve
tribes of Israel, some manuscripts include reference to the fact
that the twelve tribes of Israel will themselves by judged by the
apostles.[43] Apart from the ending and the occasional additions in
some manuscripts, however, it is difficult to see how any kind of
case can be made for a Christian origin for this text.

The Apocalypse of Abraham, however, shows signs of greater
influence, though this is confined to one long passage in the
eschatological section (ch. 29):

And I looked and saw a man going out from the left side of the
heathen; and there went out men, women and children, from the

side of the heathen, many hosts, and worshipped him. And while I still looked, there came out from the right side (many), and some insulted that man, while some struck him; others, however, worshipped him. And I saw how these worshipped him, and Azazel ran and worshipped him, and having kissed his face he turned and stood behind him.

And I said: O Eternal, Mighty One, who is this man insulted and beaten, who is worshipped by the heathen with Azazel?

And he answered and said: hear Abraham: The man whom thou sawest insulted and beaten and again worshipped – that is the relief (granted) by the heathen to the people who proceed from thee, in the last days, in this twelfth hour of the age of ungodliness. But in the twelfth year of my final age I will set up this man from thy generation, whom thou sawest (issue) from my people; this one all will follow, and such as are called by me will join, those who change in their counsels. And those whom thou sawest emerge from the left side of the picture – the meaning is: there shall be many from the heathen who set their hopes on him; and as for those whom thou sawest from thy seed on the right side, some insulting and striking and others worshipping him – many of them shall be offended at him. He, however, is testing those who have worshipped him of thy seed, in that twelfth hour of the end, with a view to shortening the age of ungodliness.

Box's suggestion that these words are a Jewish–Christian interpolation of an idiosyncratic type into an essentially Jewish apocalypse is almost certainly correct. If we leave out the section just quoted, the account of the last things reads very well without it. Indeed, a reference to the messianic figure at this stage before the woes of the end-time is singularly out of place. Thus, in the case of this apocalypse we have an easily identifiable section whose exclusion does not radically affect the form of the work. Christian influence can, therefore, in the case of this apocalypse be easily identified and confined to one small section.

Slavonic Enoch is more difficult to assess, for the simple reason that there do not seem to be any obvious Christian interpolations. This has led to the supposition that we have to look for subtle hints of Christian theology in the language of the apocalypse.[44] Convincing evidence of such influence is, however, lacking. As an example one may quote the opinion of Daniélou that 'the concept of the corporeal ascension of the just to Paradise before the Judgement . . . is not found in the old

Jewish apocalyptic, where the ascensions are only temporary journeys.'[45] He points to Slavonic Enoch 36.2 which speaks of Enoch's final departure from earth. Apart from 1 Enoch 70–71, where traditions about Enoch's final departure are mentioned, the text of Genesis 5.24 itself must have led interpreters to conclude that Enoch's removal, just like that of Elijah's later, involved the translation of the righteous into the world above in bodily form.[46] It is hard to see how this idea can be considered the result of Christian theology when it is so intimately related to the traditions about Enoch. Sometimes it could be argued that the belief in the apotheosis of certain righteous men of the past could have been the result of an attempt to counteract Christian beliefs about Jesus. But while Enoch is given many privileges in this work, the picture of him is hardly an advance on other Jewish views of him. He is still the typical apocalyptic seer to whom God has revealed the mysteries of heaven and earth. Unless we conjecture that this pseudepigraphon was written by a Christian group, content to leave out any reference to their Master, there seems to be no good reason for conjecturing a Christian origin when virtually all signs of Christian influence are absent.[47] There is nothing parallel to the sort of interpolation which we found in the Testament of Abraham and the Apocalypse of Abraham. When we know the sort of additions which were made to a Jewish text, it seems to show excessive caution to suspect Christian influence when there are so few signs of it.

Such confidence, however, cannot be maintained when we turn to the other three works mentioned above, which, it has been suggested, have been subject to more extensive Christian redaction. There can be little doubt that the Ascension of Isaiah is in its present form a Jewish–Christian apocalypse. The concluding part of Isaiah's heavenly vision describes the descent of the redeemer with more than one allusion to the gospel-traditions (Asc. Isa. 11.2ff.). In the light of this it would obviously be wrong to cite the account of the descent of the redeemer through the heavens as an example of Jewish belief, though the origin of it may ultimately be derived from Jewish sources.[48] But the question is whether we should reject this work completely as a source for Jewish theology and find in it an example only of early Christian thought. While there does need to be a considerable degree of caution in this matter, it seems to me that a case can be made for the use of a document of this sort, not only to illuminate Jewish theology but also the New Testament material. While one must clearly admit that the distinctive soteriology may derive its inspiration from the Christian gospel, the case for supposing that the whole of its conceptual framework derives from that source is nothing like as strong. How far, for example, is it possible to derive the cosmology of this work from early Christian theology? Parallels from non-Christian sources suggest that the Jewish cosmology was gradually moving towards a belief in seven heavens.[49] Accordingly, it is entirely possible to distinguish between the Christian contribution made by the notion of the descent of the redeemer and the cosmological framework, which Christian belief had no reason whatever to modify substantially.

We have already noted that the Testaments of the Twelve Patriarchs has been subject to Christian redaction. Charles thought it was possible to identify these passages with some precision, and by removing them, leave behind a Jewish document untouched by Christian ideas.[50] This hypothesis was challenged by M. de Jonge, however, who argued that the Testaments in their Greek form are the product of Jewish–Christianity, though based on earlier Jewish traditions.[51] The discovery of Aramaic fragments of the Testament of Levi in Caves 1 and 4 at Qumran, a Hebrew version in the Cairo Geniza as well as a Hebrew version of the Testament of Naphtali, suggests that parts at least of the Testaments did have a non-Christian origin. Comparison between the Aramaic fragments of the Testament of Levi and the Greek version reveal several differences, and this would tend to support the view that the work as we have it in Greek is the product of considerable revision. The present uncertainty which exists concerning the Greek version of the Testaments makes it necessary to be cautious in using them as a source for the reconstruction of Jewish theology.

Two points can be made in this regard. First of all, they should only be used as supporting evidence for the existence of a particular Jewish idea. For example, the Testaments make frequent reference to two eschatological figures, one priestly, the other Davidic (e.g. T. Simeon 7.1ff.; T. Levi 2.11; T. Dan. 5 and T. Naphtali 8). The fact that a similar idea is to be found at Qumran (e.g. 1 QSa 2.19f, and 1 QS 9.11) makes it possible to see that this particular belief is the product of a Jewish rather than a Christian background. Secondly, as we saw in the case of the Christian Ascension of Isaiah, there seems to be little reason to suppose that the literary and conceptual framework are the result of distinctively Christian ideas. The cosmology which is found in Testament of Levi 3ff. cannot be said to be Christian in any way, though the differences which exist between the various versions suggest that the subject has been open to further developments.[52] But even if we admit that the whole of this section in its present form is the product of a Christian writer, there seems to be no reason to suppose that he is doing anything more than reproduce the type of Jewish cosmology which he had inherited and which was unlikely to have been altered to any great extent by his Christian beliefs.[53]

In fact, the amount of parallel material which is peculiar to the Testaments is not very extensive, and there is not going to be much difficulty in using the bulk of them as sources for Jewish theology. The same cannot be said, however, with regard to the Similitudes of Enoch. We have already had reason to mention this section of 1 Enoch when we looked at the composition of the apocalypses and saw that the absence of this section of the Ethiopic version from the fragments of Enochic literature found at Qumran has strengthened the argument of those who doubt the relevance of this material for the study of early Christianity. It speaks volumes for the importance of this material for New Testament christology that this hybrid collection continues to attract so much attention. The fact is, of course, that these chapters offer us unequivocal evidence of the existence of a belief in a heavenly man, who could be described as the Son of Man, not to mention the identification of this figure with the messiah. There can be no doubting the similarities which exist between the picture of the heavenly son of man in this work and certain of the Son of Man sayings in the canonical gospels, e.g. Matt. 25.31.[54]

In the light of this apparently unique position it becomes imperative to answer the following questions: can we justify the use of a text of uncertain date and origin to illustrate the New Testament? Secondly, how can we be sure that this supposedly Jewish material is free from the influence of precisely those texts which it is supposed to illuminate? There has been a growing tendency to cast doubt on the value of the Similitudes among New Testament scholars,[55] but there are reasons for supposing that the complete neglect of this material is a rash step for the following reasons.

Despite the absence of this section of the Ethiopic version from Qumran it would be wrong to conclude that they could not have been written by a Jewish writer either before or during the first century AD. There is no justification for supposing anything other than that the Qumran community did not know of this section of 1 Enoch, and that it was only added to the corpus of Enochic literature at a later time. The Similitudes themselves betray no sign of any Christian influence. Indeed, the conclusion of the work shows that the group saw *Enoch* as the one who was to be the eschatological deliverer, hardly the conclusion a Christian writer was likely to reach. Of course, it is not impossible that this belief could have arisen in direct opposition to early Christian claims for Jesus among heterodox non-Christian Jewish groups,[56] but the lack of any evidence for the persistence of a 'Son of Man' christology in early Christianity makes this supposition unlikely.

The uniqueness of the Similitudes as evidence for a particular type of mediatorial figure will depend greatly on the interpretation of Daniel 7.13f. The position of the Similitudes becomes all the more isolated within the corpus of Jewish apocalyptic literature if no evidence is found in Daniel of a heavenly man. If, on the other hand, the Son of Man in Daniel 7 is considered to differ from the Son of Man in the Similitudes only in respect of details the latter cease to be quite so important. The interpretation of Daniel 7 outlined above rejected this chapter as evidence of a heavenly Messiah, but saw in the human figure of Daniel 7.13 the angelic representative of the people of God. If this is the case, both Daniel 7 and the Similitudes offer evidence of a belief in a heavenly figure, who can be likened to a man and who is a guarantee of the future glory of the righteous (cf. 1 Enoch 71.16).

To Daniel 7 must be added the material which we discussed earlier, which suggests that there did exist a belief in Judaism in a heavenly man who was on occasion identified with some righteous figure from the past. Prominent in this respect are the Testament of Abraham and 11Q Melchizedek. The figure of the Son of Man fits well into this type of belief.[57] For this reason there is no reason why the Similitudes should be regarded as in any way eccentric in their doctrine, even if it would be wrong to suppose that we have an example of mainstream thought in them. To say this is not the same as supposing that there is direct dependence of the Son of Man sayings in the gospels on them. Indeed, apart from Matt. 25.31 and John 5.27 the links are rather tenuous. Rather, the value of the Similitudes lies in the fact that they are indicative of a particular theological climate within first century Judaism in which the first Christian theologians moved. As such they may be considered important indications of the way in which Jewish thinkers could develop their understanding of mediatorial figures and as such throw light on the similar process which was taking place within the Christian movement.

The result of this discussion has surely been to show how difficult it is to date with any degree of precision the majority of apocalypses. Occasionally, as with the book of Daniel, we are in the fortunate position of being able to offer a date within a matter of years. In most instances, however, if we leave aside external attestation, the internal evidence hardly allows us to decide with any degree of conviction. So, taking due account of the difficulty of dating the apocalypses accurately, the following table is only offered as a general guide to the dates of the major texts:

250 BC	1 Enoch 1—36
200 BC	Daniel (c. 167)
	1 Enoch 83—90 (c. 165)
	1 Enoch 91—105 (c. 140)
	Jubilees
100 BC	Aramaic T. Levi
	4 Q S1
AD 50	Similitudes of Enoch
	Slavonic Enoch
	Testament of Abraham
	Revelation
AD 70	4 Ezra
	Apocalypse of Abraham
	Syriac Baruch

AD 100	Ascension of Isaiah
	Greek Baruch
AD 150	Greek Versions of Testaments of XII Patriarchs
	Shepherd of Hermas

Part Four

The Esoteric Tradition in Early Rabbinic Judaism

IN CONSIDERATIONS OF the rise and development of apocalyptic in Judaism at the beginning of the Christian era very little attention is devoted to the part it played in rabbinic thought. This is in part due to the fact that a work like the Mishnah has very little to say about such matters. Nevertheless, reliance on the Mishnah as a guide to the attitudes of the rabbis towards apocalyptic would give an inaccurate impression, for this collection is not intended as a complete guide to rabbinic theology, not least because its prime function is a codification of legal decisions. It cannot, therefore, be taken as a complete statement of rabbinic beliefs. The absence of the distinctive marks of the apocalyptic literature from the Mishnah has led many to assume that rabbinic thought was at the other end of the religious spectrum from apocalyptic.[1] Nevertheless, we have already seen that eschatology is only one part of apocalyptic literature, and that it is a dangerous oversimplification to think of apocalyptic merely as a brand of eschatology. What we are confronted with in the apocalyptic literature is a particular way of looking at the world which need not necesarily be confined to those groups who interested themselves in eschatological matters. If we refrain from confining ourselves to a search for the fantastic imagery typical of a few apocalypses and see apocalyptic as a religious phenomenon which is interested in what is usually hidden from normal human perception, then we shall see that such concerns are not at variance with certain rabbinic interests.

We have argued that apocalyptic is concerned with 'what is above, what is below, what has been beforehand and what is to come' (M. Hagigah 2.1). All these issues were of some importance to rabbis of the first and second centuries AD. Indeed, such matters were so exercising the imagination of some that warnings had to be given about the dangers inherent in excessive interest in such issues. When we view apocalyptic as essentially the concern with the revelation of the divine mysteries we are not too far away from issues which had a significant role to play within early rabbinic theology.

The quest for knowledge of secret matters was something which a rabbi came up against in his study of the scriptures. In other words, those same scriptures which provided the launching-pad for the visions of the apocalypticists drove the rabbis to seek after answers to the same questions. Despite the reserve which was often expressed towards such speculative matters, 'the Torah is . . . an envelope for the mystery of the divine creation which underlies it and all being and to which one must seek to penetrate in mystical interpretation'.[2]

Mysticism may seem to be a rather inappropriate word to use in connection with rabbinic Judaism. The religion of the rabbis, with its emphasis on the practical side of religion, seems to be poles apart from mystical matters. Yet if we use the term mysticism in the sense of concern with hidden truths, then there is evidence from rabbinic literature to show that there was indeed considerable interest in such matters from a very early period.[3] The scriptures themselves were full of the secrets of God, which the student may expect to ascertain as he studied the sacred text, a point made very clearly in Aboth 6.1:

> He that occupies himself in the study of the Law for its own sake merits many things, and still more, he is deserving of the whole world. He is called friend, beloved of God, lover of God, lover of mankind; righteous, saintly, upright, and faithful . . . it gives him kingship and dominion, and discernment in judgement; to him are revealed the secrets of the Law . . .

This passage presupposes that the Torah, because it is the revelation of God himself, inevitably contains many of the secret things of God, which will become apparent when the sacred text is studied. Since the Torah is the repository of the secret things of God, it is hardly suprising that we come across a passage like the following one in b. Megillah 3a, which stresses the need to keep the knowledge of the Torah within the confines of Israel:

> R. Jeremiah [early 4th century AD] – or some say R. Hiyya b. Abba [late 3rd century AD] – also said: the targum of the Pentateuch was composed by Onkelos the proselyte under the guidance of R. Eleazar and R. Joshua. The targum of the Prophets was composed by Jonathan ben Uzziel under the guidance of Haggai, Zechariah and Malachi; and the land of Israel quaked over an area of four hundred parasangs by four hundred parasangs, and a *bath qol* came forth and exclaimed, Who is this that has revealed my secrets to mankind? Jonathan ben Uzziel arose and said, It is I who have revealed thy secrets to mankind. It is fully known to thee that I have not done this for my own honour or for the honour of my father's

house, but for thy honour have I done it, that dissension may not increase in Israel. He further sought to reveal by a targum of the hagiographa, but a *bath qol* went forth and said, Enough. What was the reason? – the end of the messiah is foretold in it.[4]

This legendary story about the origin of the Aramaic *targumim* reflects the Jewish tradition that Jonathan ben Uzziel was supposed to have carried out the process of translating parts of the Bible into Aramaic, a fact reflected in the names given to various *targumim*. The *targumim* are the translations of the Hebrew Bible into Aramaic, and the Palestinian *targumim* in particular offer a considerable amount of additional interpretative material at various points. It is the activity of translating the scriptures from Hebrew into another language which is censured. This is for the simple reason that it makes the divine revelation available to many more people, and thereby lets them into the secrets of God, from which they would normally be excluded by the barrier of language. This legend sees a difference between the targum to the Pentateuch and that to the Prophets. No complaint is made against the translation of Onkelos, but a protest from heaven greets the promulgation of the targum to the Prophets, because the translation into Aramaic discloses many of the divine secrets about God and the future contained in these texts. Passages like this illustrate the way in which the rabbis viewed their scriptures as an inheritance which contained the most profound mysteries which would be readily available to those who studied the texts carefully.

Nevertheless, concern with the secrets of God, whether they are part of Scripture or in the world above, must be set within the framework of Jewish piety. It is right to see the concern with cosmology and theology as a special interest reserved only for the elect few, and too great an emphasis on the particular understanding of God which such an outlook produces would give us a false impression of Jewish understanding of theology. The production of an elaborate cosmology and angelology did tend to produce a picture of God far removed from the world of men enthroned high above the heavens, accessible, after elaborate preparation, only to a few privileged individuals. The fact that access to the world of the throne-chariot was confined to the favoured few meant that a theology which looked at God solely in these terms was meaningless for the majority of ordinary people. It is true that a later mystical text (Hekaloth R. 20) can compare the opportunity for the heavenly journey to a man having a ladder in his house which gave him direct access to the world above, but this is only possible for the man who is perfectly versed in every aspect of Jewish tradition (Hek. R. 20 beginning). Such a remote view of God and his secrets contrasts with that we find hinted at in the two texts quoted above, namely, that the Torah itself offers the opportunity for every student to acquaint himself with the mysteries of God.

Knowledge of God's ways are thus not difficult to ascertain for Israel has been blessed with the gift of the Torah (Aboth 3.15). Just as possession of the divine secrets is possible through the study of the Torah, so also the presence of God with his people is something which is emphasized. According to R. Johanan b. Zakkai the exposition of the chariot-chapter of Ezekiel meant that the divine presence *(shekinah)* was present with the two rabbis. This belief, however, is nothing out of the ordinary when it is viewed in the light of other beliefs, which stress the close relationship which exists between God and the righteous. God may be enthroned in the seventh heaven, but he has not left his people without the assurance of his presence. Frequently we find references, not only to the divine presence accompanying those who studied the Torah, but also to supernatural manifestations attending such activities.[5] Typical of the former belief is the passage in Aboth 3.2:

> R. Hananiah b. Teradion said: If two sit together and no words of the Law [are spoken] between them, there is the seat of the scornful, as it is written, Nor sitteth in the seat of the scornful. But if two sit together and the words of the Law [are spoken] between them, the divine presence [*shekinah*] rests between them, as it is written, Then they that feared the Lord spoke one with another: and the Lord hearkened and heard, and a book of remembrance was written before him, for them that feared the Lord, and that thought upon his name.

The conviction that everyday religion is supported by the favour of the divine presence gives a deeper meaning to ordinary existence. It is important for the religious man to know that his acts do not go unnoticed by God.

This type of belief presupposes the acceptance of the dogma of the unseen divine presence in everyday life. In times of crisis, however, there is often need for something more convincing and direct. This is where the *bath qol* and visions are so important. The *bath qol* is the divine voice, which temporarily replaces the activity of the Spirit of God, and which may be inferior to the Spirit, nevertheless it offered the opportunity to hear directly what God's will was. This phenomenon and the visions of the mystics make man aware of another dimension to reality, which is not apparent to normal perception and which offered important means of underpinning religious practice and belief in a world which seemed to be bereft of God's presence. Both presuppose a type of experience which is more occasional and eccentric than a regular part of an individual's religious life. Herein lies the difference between the two types of religion. The belief in the immanence of God was not a special category of experience reserved for a spiritual élite. As Kadushin has put it, 'through the agency of the halakah, the gifted man shared his finest achievements with the ordinary man, the spiritual leader brought the common man up to his own level.'[6] In his ordinary religious devotion the ordinary man had exactly the same privileges as the sage. But it is the occasional, direct, even dramatic, experience of the divine which is absent from normal piety.

The Jewish mystics stress the exaltation of God in the highest heaven, and, as a result, tend to separate God from normal life. By virtue of the fact that they feel the need to communicate with this higher realm, they suggest that a normal life does not satisfy their needs and has to be supplemented by knowledge of the God who is enthroned in glory. Although most would have held to the belief in God's presence in the world, particularly in the life of the convenant-community, this belief in the immanence of God was of secondary importance to the special privileges vouchsafed to the mystic. Thus while it would be wrong to isolate interest in mystical matters in rabbinic Judaism from the totality of religious experience, one cannot disguise the impact which the opportunity of an apocalyptic or mystical form of religion was likely to have had. Theology was here confirmed by experience in a way which was not really possible by any other means. We have more here than the simple belief that man was close to God. The mystic is convinced that his theology has interacted with experience of the divine so that the authenticity of the religious traditions he has received finds its direct confirmation in the impact which his mystical insight has had upon him.

Rabbinic Judaism was no exception in the religious scene of the early Christian era in having an important, and highly developed, mystical lore.[7] Of paramount importance was the meditation on the first chapter of Genesis, called in rabbinic sources the *ma'aseh bereshith*, and the first chapter of Ezekiel, known as the *ma'aseh merkabah*. We have noted that several references to the divine throne-chariot have turned up in the apocalyptic literature (e.g. 1 Enoch 14.8ff.; Dan. 7.9f.; Apoc. Abr. 18f.; Rev. 4). Several of these have been influenced by the first chapter of Ezekiel but, by and large, are significant developments of it. This led us to conclude that already in the early apocalyptic literature there was a speculative interest in this chapter which was central to the understanding of the genesis of certain apocalyptic visions. The visions of God in the apocalyptic literature, however, do not explicitly give these parts of Scripture any special status. Often the vision of God is mentioned incidentally as part of a much longer description of heaven and the secrets of God's purposes for the universe. The situation is somewhat different in the early rabbinic texts. Already in the Mishnah we have regulations dealing with both the account of creation and Ezekiel's vision of the throne-chariot. In a passage in M. Megillah 4.10 regulations are given concerning the reading of certain passages and their translation into Aramaic *(targum)*:

> The incident of Reuben is read in synagogue but not translated. The story of Tamar is read and translated. The first account of the incident of the Golden Calf is both read and translated, the second is read and not translated. The blessing of the priests is read but not translated. The stories of David and Amnon are read but not translated. The portion of the chariot is not read as a *haftarah*, but R. Judah permits this. R. Eleazar says: the portion 'Make known to Jerusalem' is not read as a *haftarah*.[8]

This passage indicates that some authorities actually forbid the use of Ezekiel 1 as a reading from the prophets *(haftarah)*,[9] although it should be noted that this excessively strict prohibition was not accepted by R. Judah, who was responsible for the redaction of the Mishnah. It would seem that an attempt is here being made to prevent ordinary people from becoming too familiar with theologically dangerous passages, particularly that concerned with the secrets of God's heavenly chariot. It is significant that the parallel passage in the Tosefta, another Mishnah collection, indicates the importance of the first chapter of Ezekiel as a reading from the prophets and by no means excludes its inclusion in the synagogue liturgy at the appropriate point. This difference between Mishnah and Tosefta points to the fact that at an early period doubt was cast by some teachers on the wisdom of including the reading of this chapter for fear that it would be improperly used. After all the chapter did communicate one of the most profound secrets of Judaism, the mystery of God himself. Knowledge of such things was something for those who were in a position to appreciate the majesty of God and safeguard these mysteries from abuse. This point is made most clearly in M. Hagigah 2.1:

> The forbidden degrees [Lev. 18.6ff.] may not be expounded before three persons, nor the story of creation [Gen. 1] before two, nor the chariot-chapter [Ezek. 1 and 10] before one alone, unless he is a sage that understands of his own knowledge.
>
> Whoever gives his mind to four things, it were better for him if he had not come into the world – what is above, what is beneath, what was beforetime, and that will be hereafter. And whosoever does not take any thought for the glory of his creator, it were better for him if he had not come into the world.

Even from this bald statement we can see that during the second century the teachers considered that exposition and meditation on the first chapters of Ezekiel and Genesis were matters of considerable importance and no little danger. After all it is not every biblical passage about which regulations are laid down governing its study. Clearly we are dealing here with material whose content was potentially more significant than other parts of Scripture, for the simple reason that these passages offered the basis of further reflection on the nature of the universe and God himself beyond what was actually written.

Although these rules show us that there was considerable anxiety about the way in which these passages were being used by certain individuals, we should not assume that the dire warning which is to be found in the second half of the Mishnah necessarily indicates that the rabbis refused to embark on speculative interpretations of these passages. The permission in the first paragraph and the implicit prohibition in the apodictic rule in the second paragraph point to rules emerging at different periods. Whereas the first paragraph merely lays down rules for the study of certain passages, the second paragraph qualifies what are already strict regulations, by adding a rider pointing out the terrible consequences of speculative activity.[10] Nevertheless, as we shall see later, there could be no question of a complete prohibition on the study of these passages, precisely because they were at the heart of the spirituality of early rabbinic Judaism. Some kind of guidelines needed to be set out, however, because the passages were open to misunderstanding within the rabbinic schools themselves. Also, the contents of these chapters naturally meant that they were open to abuse by those whose interest in them was not as part of the revelation of God as a whole but as isolated insights into God and the universe which could be taken and used without any commitment to the ancestral customs and religion of Judaism.[11] To avoid the easy communication of these more revealing passages of the scriptures the rabbis ordered that all exposition on them should be confined to those who already had the training in the Jewish religion and the interpretation of the Torah, which would enable them to steer clear of interpretations which would be contrary to the spirit of Judaism. When we look at Genesis 1 and Ezekiel 1 today, we are struck by how little is said about God and his universe rather than the amount which the passages divulge. This means that considerable room is left to the individual as he seeks to fill in the gaps left by the scriptural accounts. It is here, above all, that care was required. A student who did not have a long background of training in rabbinic methods and Jewish beliefs could easily be tempted to provide answers to questions not given by Scripture itself by postulating concepts which in fact owed more to contemporary philosophical or religious ideas than the traditional beliefs of Judaism.

Although it is not too difficult to understand the general point of the mishnaic regulation, one has to face up to the fact that the meaning of its individual parts is by no means clear. The basic qualification of the person who is permitted to expound the chariot-chapter is that he should be wise and able to understand of his own knowledge. Wisdom in this context refers to the ability of the sage (ḥakam), the qualified exponent of the Torah. This means that the exponent of the mysteries of creation and the chariot should have already shown himself to be completely competent in his exposition of the Torah as a whole and his application of traditional beliefs and interpretations to contemporary problems. But in the passage which we shall examine a little later in which R. Eleazar b. Arak expounds the meaning of the story of the chariot before his teacher, R. Johanan b. Zakkai, the latter offers his congratulations to his pupil, because he is not only able to expound but also to understand the glory of his heavenly father. Exposition of the chapter thus had to be accompanied by a facility to understand its significance and meaning on the basis of one's own knowledge. The understanding of the meaning of the text will come in part at least from the received opinion which would form part of the pupil's knowledge received during his training.[12]

Another way in which a passage would be made intelligible would be by finding analogies to it from other parts of Scripture to explain ideas which otherwise appears to be obscure.[13] While this could follow precedent, it is likely that we have here room for the individual exponent to offer his own understanding of the text on the basis of his own construction of parallel cases to illustrate the matter under discussion. This would mean that the Mishnah itself is already reckoning with the possibility that the exponent of the chariot-chapter is utilizing his knowledge of the scriptures as a whole in the interpretation of the passage to fill out the description of the divine chariot given by Ezekiel and to offer more information about its character on the basis of the use of other material. Of course, it is exactly this process which we find in the apocalyptic accounts of God's throne, where passages like Isaiah 6 are utilized in order to extend the information available on the nature of God and his throne. It seems likely then that some degree of flexibility is countenanced here with the major safeguard being the competence of interpreter as a result of his knowledge of the Jewish traditions.

Further information about the character of the exposition is given in the additional material in the Mishnah. A dire warning is given to those who would speculate on particular matters about which there is insufficient information in the scriptures and tradition. One presumes that issues which are to be avoided include the character of heaven and hell (what is above and what is beneath) and the beginnings of the universe and God's plan for the consummation of all things (what was beforehand and what will be hereafter).[14] Like so many warnings of a similar kind, this is not an attempt to keep out patterns of thought which were alien to the rabbinic mind, but to guard against excessive interest in subjects which had been a cause of unbalanced and probably heterodox views among certain teachers of the period.

The matter which calls for particular comment, however, is profanation of God's glory. The man who takes no thought for the glory of his creator is one who does not appreciate the transcendence and the holiness of God and considers that he is able to make God's being an object of speculation.[15] This warning in particular is probably directed at those who would engage in study of the chariot-chapter, for, in addition to the detailed description of the chariot itself, the chapter closes with a reference to the human form which was seated upon the throne. However restrained the description there is no denying the fact that we have here an anthropomorphic description of God which would form the basis of later reflection on God's nature.[16] The reference to the glory of God here is probably a way of referring to the form of God seated upon the throne-chariot. The use of glory *(kabod)* as a technical term could well derive from the end of Ezekiel 1 where the phrase 'the glory of the LORD' refers not to the preceding description of the chariot as a whole but to the shadowy figure on the throne. This is confirmed by the use of the phrase in the second occurrence of the chariot-vision in Chapter 10. In 10.4 we read that 'the glory of the LORD rose from above the cherubim-chariot'. This indicates that the phrase refers in particular to the last verses of the chariot-chapter describing the form of God himself. Thus the additional warning in the Mishnah provides us with further evidence of an interest in matters of a speculative kind among the early rabbis. In particular, the subject which seems to have intrigued some, to such a degree that a warning was necessary, was speculation about the nature of God himself: interest, in other words, in the holy God, whom it was not possible for man to look upon without death (Exod. 33.20). It is hardly surprising that in a religion which prohibited images and seemed to cultivate a belief in the invisibility of God, a passage like Ezekiel 1 should quickly assume an important position as the basis for discussion about the form and character of the unseen God.[17]

If we were confined to the Mishnah for our knowledge of rabbinic interest and concern over matters of this speculative and apocalyptic kind, we would have to rest content with the conviction that there was much more to rabbinic thought than the extensive collection of legal statements in the Mishnah.[18] We would not, however, be in a position to say with any certainty whether these hints of other interests among the early rabbinic teachers were the result of external influence or told us about something much more central to rabbinic theology. We have already assumed that the warnings given in the second part of the Mishnah betoken a threat which arose as a result of the misuse of ideas which were central to rabbinic thought rather than a warning against extraneous influences.[19] Our justification for such an assumption arises from the information which we can glean from the versions of the tractate Hagigah in the Tosefta (a collection of legal precepts similar to the Mishnah but with much additional material) and the later Talmuds (Babylonian and Jerusalem). Of course the amount of material available to us is but a minute proportion of the rabbinic literature, and it would be wrong, therefore, to exaggerate its importance. Nevertheless it does extend our knowledge about the character of the speculative interest in Scripture in early rabbinic Judaism. Our task in the next two chapters will be to evaluate the significance of just two blocks of material. First of all, we shall consider the earliest evidence for interest in the chariot-chapter in rabbinic texts, the exposition of the first chapter of Ezekiel among those connected with R. Johanan b. Zakkai, particularly by Eleazar b. Arak. Because of the different versions of the exposition of Eleazar before his teacher R. Johanan b. Zakkai which have come down to us, an attempt will have to be made to get back to the earliest version of the story. The second group of texts concerns the generation of teachers who flourished in the opening decades of the second century AD. Our concern here will be the way in which speculative interests were a cause of heterodoxy, which in turn led to the dire warnings about such studies which are now to be found in the addition which forms the second part of the mishnaic ruling.

CHAPTER 11

The Meditation of Rabban Johanan Ben Zakkai and his Circle on the Chariot-Chapter

IT MIGHT BE expected that matters of a speculative kind were only peripheral to the central religious beliefs of the great teachers who flourished at the end of the first century. Any evidence of the growth of such interest, it could be argued, merely reflects a changing religious situation after the fall of Jerusalem in which non-pharisaic elements were absorbed into the emerging rabbinic Judaism.[1] But any attempt to argue that Pharisaism was only infected with an apocalyptic outlook when it became the dominant group in a reconstituted Judaism has to explain certain facets of the traditions about R. Johanan b. Zakkai. It is well known that Johanan was the architect of the reformed Jewish religion after the destruction of the Temple. It fell to him and his companions to pick up the pieces of Jewish religion. This they did at Javneh or Jamnia,[2] and the decisions promulgated by this group had considerable authority. What is most important for our investigation is that there is evidence to suggest that interest in the chariot-chapter formed a central pillar of the religious life of Johanan himself. This means that a speculative interest is to be found right at the heart of the rabbinic college at Jamnia and closely linked with none other than Johanan himself. It cannot, therefore, be assumed that this was an alien element in early rabbinic thought, resulting from the inevitable infiltration into rabbinic circles of teachers from other Jewish groups, whose influence on Jewish religion terminated with the destruction of the city.

The traditions about the exposition of the chariot-chapter do show that Johanan formed part of the chain of recognized exponents, e.g. Tos. Hagigah 2.2 (and below lines 143ff.). The fact that it goes back no further than Johanan is no indication that interest in the chariot in pharisaic circles does not antedate Johanan and the fall of Jerusalem. As far as the rabbinic schools were concerned, all that was important in tracing the pedigree of an idea was to take it back to the founding fathers of the academy at Jamnia. Apart from this fleeting reference we have an extended passage which tells of R. Eleazar b. Arak's exposition of the story of the chariot before Johanan.[3] This story is found in no less than four different versions: in the versions of the tractate Hagigah in the two Talmuds and the Tosefta (Tos. Hag. 2.1; j. Hag. 77a; b. Hag. 14b), and in one of the extant fragments of the early midrash, the Mekilta de R. Simeon b. Yohai (*Mishpatim* 21.1). There is enough similarity between the four versions to present them in synoptic form.[4]

Proper assessment of the character of the earliest evidence of rabbinic interest in the chariot-chapter depends on a careful analysis of the various accounts and their relationship to each other. There is little point in utilizing a story for the reconstruction of the idea of a particular period when it may reflect the ideas of a later age. This problem has confronted students of the New Testament gospels as they try to reconstruct the earliest form of a saying or story. The students of the gospels now have a variety of critical tools available to them, as they seek to distinguish between the different layers of tradition and get back to the earliest form of a saying of Jesus.[5] It is now apparent that we have an analogous situation facing us when we examine early rabbinic material.[6] A glance at the different versions of the story of Eleazar's exposition of the chariot-chapter indicates that our story too has been subject to revision in the course of its transmission. It is imperative for us to explain the differences which exist between the different versions of the story as an essential preliminary to our quest for the earliest form of rabbinic exposition and meditation upon the divine throne-chariot.

With the exception of the version in M(ekilta) all the accounts occur in contexts dealing with the subject of mishnaic regulation governing the exposition of the chariot. In T(osefta), for example, the story is told as an example of the way in which the mishnaic rule worked out in practice. According to the rule the exposition should not take place before any person who is not suitably qualified and then only before one person at a time. This is exactly what we find happening in the story.[7] Thus the

SYNOPSIS I

	MEKILTA	TOSEFTA	JERUSALEM TALMUD	BABYLONIAN TALMUD
1		A story of R. Johanan	A story of R. Johanan	Our rabbis said:
2		b. Zakkai	b. Zakkai	A story of R. Johanan
3		who was	who was going on a	b. Zakkai
4		riding upon	road riding upon	who was
5		an ass	an ass	riding upon
6				the ass
7				and was going on a road.
8		when R. Leazar b. Arak	And R. Eleazar b. Arak	And R. Eleazar b. Arak
9		who was driving the ass	who was going	who was driving the ass
10		behind him said to him	after him said to him	behind him said to him
11		Rabbi teach me	Rabbi teach me	Rabbi teach me
12		one section of the	one section of the	one section of the
13		story of the chariot	story of the chariot	story of the chariot
14		He said to him	He said to him	He said to him
15		Have I not	Have not	Have I not
16		said to you	the sages taught	taught you
17		from the beginning		
18		that they do not teach	Not	Not
19		the chariot with one	the chariot	the chariot with one
20		person, unless he is a	unless he is	person, unless he is a
21		sage able to understand	wise and able to	sage able to understand
22			understand	
23		from his own knowledge	from his own knowledge	from his own knowledge

	MEKILTA	TOSEFTA	JERUSALEM TALMUD	BABYLONIAN TALMUD
24		He said to him	He said to him	He said to him
25	If not, give me	Let me now discuss	Rabbi give me	Rabbi give me
26	permission to speak		permission to speak	permission to speak
27	before you	before you	something before you	something before you
28				which you have taught
29		He said to him	He said to him	me. He said to him
30		Speak on.	Speak on.	Speak on. Immediately
31				R. Johanan b. Zakkai
32				got down from his ass
33				and wrapped himself and
34				sat upon a stone under
35				an olive-tree. Eleazar
36				said to him, Rabbi,
37				why did you get down
38				from the ass? Johanan
39				answered, Is it right
40				that you expound the
41				story of the chariot
42				with the shekinah with
43				us, the ministering
44				angels accompanying us
45				with me riding upon an
46				ass?
47			So it happened that	Immediately
48	R. Eleazar b. Arak	R. Leazar b.Arak	R. Eleazar b. Arak	R. Eleazar b. Arak
49	was expounding	began and expounded	began	began
50		the story of the	the story of the	the story of the
51		chariot.	chariot.	chariot
52				and he expounded it.

Line	MEKILTA	TOSEFTA	JERUSALEM TALMUD	BABYLONIAN TALMUD
53		R. Johanan b. Zakkai	R. Johanan b. Zakkai	
54		got down from his ass	got down from his ass	
55		and wrapped himself		
56		in his *tallith*		
57			He said, It cannot be	
58			right that I should	
59			hear of the glory of my	
60			creator while I am	
61			riding upon an ass.	
62		The two of them	They went and	
63		sat down on a stone	sat down	
64		underneath the	underneath	
65		olive-tree	a tree	
66		and he discussed		
67		before him		
68	until fire was glowing		Fire came down from	Fire came down from
69	all round		heaven and surrounded	heaven
70			them and the minister-	
71			ing angels were	
72			dancing before them	
73			like wedding-guests	
74			in the presence of	
75			the bridegroom.	
76			An angel replied	
77			from the middle of	
78			the fire and said,	
79			According to your words	
80			Eleazar b. Arak is	
81			the story of the	
82			chariot.	
83				and encompassed all the
84				trees which were in the
85				field.

	MEKILTA	TOSEFTA	JERUSALEM TALMUD	BABYLONIAN TALMUD
86			Immediately all the	All of them
87			trees opened their	began
88			mouths and sang a song	and sang a song.
89				What was the song they
90				sang? Praise the LORD
91				from the earth, dragons
92				and deeps, fruitful
93				trees and all cedars,
94				praise the LORD.
95			Then all the trees of	
96			the forest began to	
97			rejoice.	
98				An angel answered from
99				the fire, This indeed
100				is the story of the
101				chariot.
102			Thus when R. Eleazar b.	
103			Arak finished the story	
104			of the chariot	
105	Then when R. Johanan	He	R. Johanan	R. Johanan
106	b. Zakkai saw that		b. Zakkai	b Zakkai
107	the fire was			
108	glowing all around,			
109	he descended from			
110	the ass			
111	and kissed him	stood up and kissed him	stood up and kissed him	stood up and kissed him
112		on the head	on the head	on the head
113	and said to him	and said	and said	and said
114	R. Eleazar b. Arak,			
115	Blessed is she who			
116	bore you			

	MEKILTA	TOSEFTA	JERUSALEM TALMUD	BABYLONIAN TALMUD
117		Blessed is the LORD	Blessed is the LORD God of	Blessed is the LORD
118		God of Israel who	Abraham, Isaac and Jacob who	God of Israel who
119		has given a son to	has given a wise son to	has given a son to
120		Abraham our father	Abraham our father	Abraham our father
121		who knows how	who knows how	who knows how
122		to understand		to understand
123				and to investigate
124		and to expound	to expound	and to expound
125		the glory of his	the glory of our	the story of the
126		father in heaven.	father in heaven.	chariot
127		Some expound well	some expound well	Some expound well
128		and do not perform well	and do not perform well	and do not perform well
129		perform well and	perform well and	perform well and
130		do not expound well	do not expound well	do not expound well
131		Eleazar b. Arak	Eleazar b. Arak	Eleazar b. Arak
132		expounds well	expounds well	expounds well
133		and performs well	and performs well	and performs well
134	Blessed are you	Blessed are you	Blessed are you	Blessed are you
135	Abraham our father	Abraham our father	Abraham our father	Abraham our father
136	that this man	that Eleazar b. Arak	that Eleazar b. Arak	that Eleazar b. Arak
137	has come forth	has come forth	has come forth	has come forth
138	from your loins	from your loins	from your loins	from your loins
139		who knows how to		
140		understand and expound		
141		the glory of his father		
142		in heaven.		
143	He was wont to say	R. Jose b. R. Judah		
144	If all the sages of	says, R. Joshua		
145	Israel were in one	discussed (the chariot)		
146	side of a scales	before R. Johanan b.		
147	and R. Eleazar b.	Zakkai. R. Akiba		
148	Arak in the other,	before R. Joshua and		
149	he would outweigh	Hananiah b. Kinai		
150	them all.	before R. Akiba.		

redactors of the different collections could offer this story as an example of the correct procedure to follow. The close link between the Mishnah and the story which we find in T is absent from B(abylonian Talmud) and J(erusalem Talmud) where the story occurs merely as part of a larger complex of material dealing with mystical matters.

When we examine the form of the story, we find that it falls into three basic parts:

a. An introduction in which the scene is set and a request is made by the pupil (Eleazar) that the teacher (Johanan) should recite part of the traditional exposition of the chariot-chapter, which leads to a quotation of the Mishnah (lines 1–24).

b. There then follow the account of the exposition by the pupil and the consequences of the exposition (fire etc.).

c. Finally there is the pronouncement of a series of blessings by the teacher on the pupil because of his successful exposition.

Consideration of these three parts of the story reveals that a major problem is the relationship between the first part and the other two. In the second and third parts we have a description of Eleazar expounding before Johanan, whereas the opening section presupposes that it is Johanan who will recite. The introduction clearly indicates that it is Eleazar who is seeking information on the chariot-chapter from his teacher (lines 11–13). Therefore, one would have expected Johanan to have been the one to expound the chariot-chapter. It would appear then that we have in this story a conflation of two separate incidents in the life of Eleazar, the first of which concerned Eleazar's request to his teacher to learn about the secrets of the chariot, and the second spoke of one occasion when Eleazar demonstrated his ability in the presence of his teacher. The two have probably been conflated in their present context to show how the mishnaic requirements were fulfilled.

This is done particularly in the opening section where the Mishnah is quoted in full and so provides the proper introduction to Eleazar's exposition. The fact that the first two parts of the final form of the story both take place in the context of a journey[8] could be an indication that originally the introduction to both stories was similar (lines 1–10). This would mean that the extent of the story dealing with Eleazar's request to learn something about the chariot of God was probably confined to lines 11–23. There is no reason why the story of Eleazar's exposition should not have included an introduction similar to the one we find in our present version, with the setting immediately followed by a request by Eleazar to expound the chariot-chapter (lines 1–10, 25ff.).

In the third section of the story the material hangs together rather loosely.[9] Several of the sayings have parallels in other parts of the rabbinic tradition. Lines 127–133 are found also in b. Yebamoth 63b. Here they serve as a redactional comment on Simeon b. Azzai's encouragement to propagate the race. In the eyes of the commentator on that passage Ben Azzai's remark sounded strange, as it was well known that Simeon remained celibate. He is thus congratulated for his exposition of the scriptures but criticized for not practising what he preached. Lines 134–138 are to be found in a similar form in Aboth 2.8 where they are spoken of Joshua b. Hananiah. The conclusion of the M(ekilta) account is also found in the same context once again linked with another disciple of Johanan, Eliezer b. Hyrcanus. Even though there is a consistent attestation that these last two mentioned sayings should be linked with Johanan, there is obviously uncertainty about which disciple they were originally spoken to. It is likely that in the case of both sayings it was considered appropriate to include them in this particular context, in which a privileged disciple is allowed to expound one of the most significant and profound parts of the scriptures. Such a privilege would only have been granted to the favourite disciple. As far as lines 134–138 are concerned, it is possible that we may be dealing with a proverbial saying which was used by Johanan but included here at a later time as a comment on the blessing of Johanan in lines 117–126. Here it will be noted that Johanan congratulates his pupil on two counts: his ability to expound (line 124) and his ability to understand (line 122).[10] As far as Johanan is concerned, there is more to the exposition of the story of the chariot than mere recitation of a particular set of words, for exposition has to be matched by understanding. This is surely the point which is being made by the additional passage in lines 134ff. It indicates that Eleazar's success is based on something more than mere exegetical ability, for this is matched by an insight into the real meaning of the text of Ezekiel 1. Thus it would appear that the nucleus of the story of

Eleazar's exposition of the chariot-chapter is to be found in lines 30–104 together with the first congratulation and blessing in lines 105–126.

Nevertheless within this original nucleus there is a considerable variety in the way in which the story is told. Our task now is to move behind these differences in an attempt to reconstruct the earliest version of the story. Recent discussion of the passage has been divided over which version offers us the earliest account of Eleazar's exposition. On the one hand we find Bowker, Neusner and Halperin[11] arguing that the brief account in M is the earliest with the rest as more complicated versions of M's simple story. On the other hand we find Goldberg completely repudiating the value of the account in M in favour of the versions in B and J.[12] But an examination of the four versions of the story would seem to indicate that it is the version in T which is most likely to be the earliest.[13] This is supported by an investigation of the differences which exist between the different versions. It is not possible here to examine all the variations between the four versions in detail. What will be attempted is an assessment of the more significant differences for the question of priority.

In lines 53–65 (B: 31–36) T has the fullest account of Johanan's descent from his ass, wrapping in the *tallith* (the Jewish prayer-shawl) and sitting under an olive-tree on a stone. Indeed, J omits all reference to the *tallith*. This omission probably indicates that the account in J represents a stage in the development of the story when interest in such details had diminished, and other elements had assumed a greater significance.[14] It is clear that in B and J the presence of the fire and the angels are much more important elements as compared with the precise details of the actions of Johanan as he prepares for the exposition. A similar change can be discerned in line 65 (B 36), where there ceases to be interest in the precise type of tree under which the two rabbis sat, and so the specific reference in T and B to the olive-tree becomes merely a tree.[15] It is understandable why J should omit the reference to the wrapping in the *tallith*, for in this version (and in B) part of the confirmation on Eleazar's ability to expound the mysteries of the chariot-chapter is the appearance of fire and angels (lines 68–101). The sight of these phenomena would have been the sign to Johanan that heaven had set its seal of approval on Eleazar's exposition. Wrapping in the *tallith* might be taken as a means of preventing Johanan from seeing these sights. Any doubt about Johanan's ability to see the supernatural occurrences which attended Eleazar's recitation could easily be removed by omitting all reference to the wrapping in the *tallith*.

The most striking difference between T and all the other versions of the story is the omission in T of all reference to the fire which attended Eleazar's exposition. T, like M, also omits all the references to the angelic attendance and the heavenly anthem (lines 70–100). The significance of the omission has been differently interpreted.[16] Nevertheless, it is no easy matter explaining why it should be that, if T is dependent on the talmudic versions, it should have omitted the references to the fire and the angels. The point is that these supernatural phenomena are the objective criteria by which Johanan is able to pronounce his satisfaction with Eleazar's recitation. It is difficult to see why T should have wanted to change a version of the story which included the supernatural elements. The same question arises in comparing the accounts in T and M. It is true that M does not contain any angelic voice pronouncing satisfaction with Eleazar's exposition, but the descent of the fire is surely a sign that Eleazar has successfully completed his task.[17] Although the longer accounts in B and J may seem to have the effect of giving greater significance to the exposition of the chariot-chapter,[18] it should be remembered that the presence of fire with a rabbi is not necessarily a sign that the chariot-chapter is being interpreted. It is also a feature of legends which tell of exposition of all parts of the Torah.[19] Indeed, the close similarity between the exposition of the chariot and other parts of the scriptures is well illustrated by a legend concerning Simeon b. Azzai (Shir ha-Shirim R. 1.10.2). On one particular occasion Simeon was sitting expounding while fire played around him. R. Akiba was told and concluded that Simeon was expounding the chariot-chapter. When asked, however, Simeon revealed that he was merely linking different parts of the scriptures together. A similar occurrence is said to have taken place at the house of Abuyah, father of the apostate Elisha, when he invited several famous rabbis to the party celebrating the circumcision of his son. While the majority of guests spent their time dancing and enjoying themselves, R. Eleazar and R. Joshua spent their time interpreting the scriptures by showing how the three parts of the Bible were linked. While they expounded fire came down from heaven (j. Hagigah 77b).[20] The similarity between the results of expounding the Torah and the chariot-chapter is in all likelihood because of the presence of fire in both the giving of the Torah (Exod. 19.16) and the vision of the chariot (Ezek. 1.4) in the Bible. What is more, there is evidence to suggest that the Jewish liturgy had made a close link between the two passages, as the first chapter of Ezekiel was prescribed as a reading from the prophets for *shabuoth*, the Feast of Weeks, which celebrated the giving of the Torah to Israel (b. Megillah 31a).[21]

But where does all this lead us in our account of the development of the traditions about Eleazar's exposition? It would appear that the motif of fire, far from being a means of extolling the significance of the exposition of the chariot-chapter, is best explained as an inclusion to show that the phenomena attending the interpretation of Ezekiel 1 were in fact exactly those which were to be found when the various parts of Scripture were expounded. The inclusion of an element like this would, of course, become imperative when the chariot-chapter was isolated from the rest of Scripture as a passage of special importance. The inclusion of the fire would show that in fact there was no difference between the phenomena attending exposition of Ezekiel 1 as compared with the rest of the scriptures. Although the addition of the reference to fire cannot itself be considered as a glorification of the exposition of the chariot-chapter, the same cannot be said of the other secondary features present in the talmudic versions, the presence of the angels and the angel's confirmation of the correctness of Eleazar's exposition.[22] The presence of the angels at the authentic exposition is only to be expected, as they too were not in a position to look upon God. Therefore, listening to Eleazar's exposition would reveal to them the secrets of God's throne and nature (cf. 1 Enoch 14.18; 1 Pet. 1.12).[23] So a good case can be made out for the priority of T, in so far as it preserves a version of the story which has not yet included the presence of fire during the recitation of Eleazar.

Finally, we should note that in Johanan's blessing of Eleazar the latter is congratulated for his ability 'to expound the glory of his heavenly father' (lines 121–126). Unlike T and J, however, B has here 'to expound the story of the chariot' (lines 124–126). The reason for this alteration is not too difficult to see. The phrase 'the story of the chariot' refers to the whole of Ezekiel's vision. The phrase in T and J, however, is much more specific. It indicates particular interest in the glory of God himself enthroned above the firmament (Ezek. 1.26f.)[24] and not the details of the chariot and its living creatures as a whole. The version in B once again reflects a time when an attempt was being made to play down the significance of the meditation on the first chapter of Ezekiel. This was done by turning attention away from the potentially explosive verses at the end of the chapter by suggesting that interest was in the chapter as a whole. The rest, while obviously important, included far less dangerous material than the conclusion of the chapter. Thus the version of the blessing of Eleazar in T and J suggests that the part of the chapter which really interested them (and probably the angels in J as well!) was the brief and veiled reference to God enthroned in glory.

So this brief survey of some of the important differences between the versions of our story indicates that the two longest versions in B and J are later developments of the shorter versions in T and M. The close literary relationship between T, B and J, as the synopsis indicates, does probably suggest that the talmudic versions were directly dependent on T, and it is conceivable that the version in M (or something very like it) with the motif of the fire also contributed to the talmudic accounts. Of the two versions in M and T we have had reason to suppose that M betrays later influence because of the inclusion of the reference to the fire. That is not to suggest that M is dependent on T, for there is little sign of any close relationship between the two accounts. Nevertheless the presence of certain elements in T, which are absent in other versions, and the fact that T does not appear to have known about the presence of fire during the exposition suggest that it is this version of the story which should form the basis of any reconstruction of the earliest form of the exposition of the chariot-chapter of Ezekiel.[25]

Although the story of Eleazar b. Arak's exposition is the most important evidence concerning R. Johanan b. Zakkai's involvement in matters of an esoteric kind, the two Talmuds offer us a story about a similar exposition by two of Johanan's pupils. This passage also must be considered in this context. As with the previous story the two elements of this exposition have enough similarities to produce it in synoptic form. Nevertheless there are once again significant differences between the two forms of the story, as the following synopsis indicates:

SYNOPSIS II

	JERUSALEM TALMUD (j. Hag. 77a)	BABYLONIAN TALMUD (b. Hag. 14b)
1	When R. Joseph the priest and R. Simeon	When these things were told R. Joshua, he
2	b. Nathanael heard these things	and R. Jose the priest were going along the
3		road. They said, Let us also expound the
4		story of the chariot
5	they also began [to expound] the story of	R. Joshua began and expounded.
6	the chariot	
7	They said it was in the first day of the	That day was in
8	month of Tammuz	the month of Tammuz. Nevertheless the
9		sky was thick with clouds
10	and yet the earth trembled	
11	and a bow appeared in the cloud	and a kind of bow appeared in the cloud
12		and the ministering angels gathered and came
13		to listen like people who gather to witness
14		the musical entertainment for a bridegroom
15		and a bride. R. Jose went and related
16		these happenings to R. Johanan b. Zakkai.
17		He said, Blessed are you and blessed is
18		the one who bore you. Blessed are my
19		eyes which have seen this. In my dream I
20		and you were reclining on Mount Sinai
21	and a bath qol came forth	and a bath qol was given on our behalf
22	and said to them	from heaven
23		
24	The place is made ready for you and the dining	Come up here, come up here.
25	couches are prepared for you. You and your	Great dining couches and handsome beds
26	disciples	are prepared for you. You and your
27	are destined for the third class.	disciples, and your disciples' disciples are destined for the third class.

The thing which strikes one immediately is that there is uncertainty over the precise identification of the rabbis concerned. Although J's Joseph is in all likelihood the same as B's Jose the priest, the difference over the second rabbi in the pair is difficult to reconcile. The prominence of Joshua as a disciple of Johanan makes it likely that B has replaced a reference to a little known teacher (Simeon b. Nathanael, cf. Aboth 2.8f.) by including a more prominent member of Johanan's school. An additional factor which suggests that this in fact is the kind of development which has taken place is the presence of R. Joshua in the chain of tradition dealing with the history of the exposition of the chariot-chapter in the rabbinic schools e.g. Tos. Hag. 2.2 (synopsis i, lines 143ff.). Thus the account in B is a later development than in J.[26]

Once again in our story we are confronted with supernatural phenomena similar to those in three versions of Eleazar's exposition. Here, however, there is one important difference. It is not fire which is present when the exposition is started but a bow in the cloud. In addition, B does mention the presence of angels (lines 11–15), as in Eleazar's exposition in B and J, but there is no mention of their presence in J. The significance of the bow in the clouds can be understood when we see the point of the reference in line 8. We are told that the exposition took place in the month of Tammuz, in other words in high summer when there would not have been a cloud in the sky. Thus the exposition of the chariot by the two rabbis has created a situation in which the sky clouds over and a bow appears in the cloud. What we have here is a clear allusion to the events mentioned in the first chapter of Ezekiel when a cloud appeared from the north (Ezek. 1.4) and the glory of God which was revealed to the prophet was compared to a rainbow (Ezek. 1.28: 'like the appearance of the bow that is in the cloud on the day of rain, so was the appearance of the brightness round about'). This reference is not meant to indicate a change in the meteorological situation at the time of the exposition, but to suggest that in the experience of the two rabbis the precise phenomena which Ezekiel himself experienced in his vision by the river Chebar were re-created all over again.

This is the main difference between the presence of fire in the account of Eleazar's exposition and the reference to the bow in the cloud in this story. The latter is positive evidence that at this time it was believed that the exposition of the chariot-chapter was more than merely an intellectual exercise in which traditions were remembered and discussed,[27] for the impression is given that the recitation itself brought about in the imaginations of the rabbis a re-enactment of that first experience of God's glory which came to the prophet Ezekiel by the river Chebar.

The story ends with a heavenly promise of the future blessedness of the disciples of the rabbis (in B the promise comes as part of a vision of Johanan, see lines 19ff.).[28] Despite the differences which are to be found between the two accounts, the significant thing, as far as we are concerned, is that these representatives of nascent rabbinic Judaism still consider that mystical or apocalyptic experiences like the *bath qol* had a part to play in their religious life.

So we have now examined the earliest traditions at our disposal concerning rabbinic involvement in the exposition of the first chapter of Ezekiel. But the question inevitably arises whether our critical examination has enabled us to get anything like far enough back to the circumstances of that early exposition. Can we be sure, for example, that the story of Johanan and Eleazar is not a late construction, even in the form we have it in T, to demonstrate the way in which the Mishnah should be put into practice? This last possibility has to be admitted, but there is one important fact about the story of Eleazar and Johanan at least, which indicates that we should take its authenticity seriously, namely that the main character in the story, apart from Johanan, is Eleazar b. Arak. It is not without significance that this teacher is not viewed very favourably in rabbinic sources. The main criticism of Eleazar was that he separated himself from the mainstream academy at Javneh (Koh. R. 7.7; ARN 14; b. Shabb. 147b). According to the later tradition this separation led to a lack of efficiency in the discussion of halakic issues and with it suspicions about his reliability as a representative of the traditional position. In addition, it was suspected that his separation also involved him in gaining more pleasures from the delights of life than from the study of the Torah. Consequently very few legal decisions are preserved in his name, not only because contacts between his disciples and the mainstream schools were broken, but also, because there was suspicion among later authorities about his worth.[29] Indeed doubts about Eleazar are in fact voiced in the Babylonian Talmud's version of the chain of tradition of exposition of the chariot:

> R. Joshua lectured before R. Johanan b. Zakkai, R. Akiba lectured
> before R. Joshua, Hananiah b. Hakinai lectured before R. Akiba. But
> R. Eleazar b. Arak does not count. One who himself lectured and
> others lectured before him, he counts; one who lectured himself, but
> others did not lecture before him, he does not count. But there is
> Hananiah b. Hakinai before whom others did not lecture, yet he is
> counted. He lectured before one who did lecture before others.

This negative evaluation of Eleazar, and the attempt to get round the embarrassing fact that the tradition clearly indicates that it was indeed Eleazar who was the favoured pupil of Johanan, add great weight to the value of our story. If such an event had been invented in the rabbinic schools to offer an example of the master's practice of the Mishnah, it would surely not have included a teacher about whom doubts had been expressed. This applies just as much to the second century as later, for the chain of tradition provided any would-be creator of such a story with a ready-made companion for Johanan in the person of Joshua. Indeed, it is probably no accident that the story of the two pupils of Johanan who expound the chariot-chapter in its form in B not only includes reference to Joshua but also incorporates Johanan himself (line 16). Thus there is good reason to suppose that a core of reliable historical information may well be extracted from the story of Johanan and Eleazar.

With this point in mind let us turn now to the question of the significance of the earliest version of this story for our investigation of the character of early rabbinic mysticism. Having decided that the supernatural phenomena in B and J are later additions and do not form part of the experience of the first exponents of the chariot-chapter,[30] we are faced with a version which tells us virtually nothing about the exposition itself, and, unlike the other versions, no clue is given why Johanan should have seen fit to pronounce the blessing upon Eleazar. As we have seen, the fire and the angelic pronouncement are both lacking in T, and so there is no external confirmation of the success of Eleazar's enterprise. What, we may ask is the basis for Johanan's praise of Eleazar?

It is possible that Eleazar had already received a body of traditional material in which selected verses from the rest of Scripture were used to explain the chariot-chapter. Now he shows his competence in repeating these passages before his teacher. In later times it seems likely that there may have been a relatively fixed interpretation of the chapter. In b. Hagigah 13a, for example, we find that the traditions about the chariot were divided into sections corresponding to the different subjects contained in the chapter:[31]

> Nor the story of the chariot in the presence of one. R. Hiyya taught: The headings of the sections may be transmitted to him. R. Zera said: The headings of sections may be transmitted only to the head of a court and to one whose heart is anxious within him, . . . how far does the story of the chariot extend? Rabbi said: As far as the second I saw. R. Isaac said: As far as *hashmal* . . .

But Johanan's congratulation of Eleazar suggests that his exposition was deserving of praise for more than his ability to recite ideas which had already been taught to him. He is praised not only because he can expound well but also because he can perform well or fulfil what he has set out to accomplish (lines 127ff.). Competence at exposition is not enough by itself. Indeed, according to Johanan, there are those who are perfectly competent at exposition, but their performance is inadequate. Thus it would appear that much more is required of the successful exponent than merely recitation of a fixed body of material. Can we say more about this additional requirement?

Although we have already had reason to question whether the saying about exposition and performance originated with Johanan, it would appear to be consistent with his congratulation of Eleazar. In lines 122 and 124 we note that there are two parts to Johanan's blessing. Eleazar is able both to expound and to understand, or make intelligible, the glory of his heavenly father. Thus the additional comment about exposition and performance is completely at one with what Johanan has himself said in his blessing of Eleazar. This extra requirement which Eleazar managed to fulfil can probably be illustrated by a passage in Tos. Megillah 4.28: 'They said to R. Judah: 'Many have expounded the chariot but have never seen it' and the parallel in b. Megillah 24b: 'It has been taught: they said to R. Judah: Many have gazed in order to expound (the mysteries of) the chariot, but they never saw it'.[32]

This is an ancient comment, linked with R. Judah who lived in the second half of the second century AD, and is found in its earlier form in T. It reflects what was thought about the exposition of the chariot-chapter at this period and indicates that more was often expected of the merkabah-exposition than mere interpretation, even if the majority had to be content merely to interpret the chapter. Indeed, it would appear that many embarked successfully on the task of expounding the chariot in the hope that they might also have a vision of it as well, but in this the majority were disappointed.[33] The two parts which made up the interest in the chariot correspond with what we find in the story of Johanan and Eleazar, although there it is exposition and understanding which are mentioned. In the light of the passage from Megillah one assumes that Johanan could congratulate Eleazar for his insight, because his exposition had been a means of him having a vision of Ezekiel's chariot. The form and content of Eleazar's exposition had been such that it had enabled his teacher to see again the glory of the chariot which had once appeared to Ezekiel. He was thus in a position to congratulate his pupil, not simply because of what he had heard but also because of his own experience.[34] Eleazar had thus not only expounded well but had also fulfilled what was expected, in the sense that he had enabled his teacher to see in his mind's eye the mysteries of the divine throne-chariot.[35]

Whether Eleazar also had a vision of the chariot we cannot say, but it would seem that the basis for Johanan's blessing of his pupil rests on his own experience, which arose directly out of Eleazar's interpretation. Are there any other indications that visions may have formed part of the earliest recorded interest in the chariot among rabbis? Four other points would seem to confirm the interpretation already given.

First of all, we have already noticed that there is another story about the exposition of the chariot-chapter involving members of Johanan's circle. This story does appear to give us evidence that the exposition could offer the participants the possibility of seeing again the vision which had appeared to Ezekiel. The presence of the cloud and the bow, on what should have been a day without rain, was intended as an indication that the situation which confronted the prophet could also be revealed to later visionaries.

Secondly, reference must also be made to a story, which we shall have to consider in some detail later, namely, the discussion between Simeon ben Zoma and R. Joshua. In this story we learn that Ben Zoma is engaged in the other main branch of Jewish mysticism, the exposition of the account of creation. He is particularly interested in the verses which speak of the firmament separating the upper and lower waters (Gen. 1.6–7). He is apparently so carried away with his speculation on this passage that he fails to notice that R. Joshua has greeted him. When pressed by R. Joshua about his activity, Ben Zoma tells him that he was having a vision (so Tos. Hagigah 2.6 *tsopheh*)[36] of the space between the upper and lower waters. This enabled him to gain some insight into the width of the firmament between the upper and lower waters. This story would seem to suggest that, in his reflection on the passage dealing with creation, Ben Zoma pictured the part of the cosmos which interested him in his mind's eye. Thus evidence from the other main branch of Jewish mystical lore indicates that speculation on the scriptures involved a vision of the contents of the passage for the interpreter of the text.

Thirdly, reference should be made to the passages in the apocalyptic literature which we have already examined where God's throne and his heavenly court are described. We noted that in these accounts there is a great variety of imagery used, indicating a considerable degree of speculation on the subject of the throne of God and its environs. We concluded that there was enough evidence to suggest that some of these visions now included in the Jewish and early Christian apocalypses offer some indication of the kind of visions which were experienced by those who interested themselves in the chariot-chapter of Ezekiel. Although the starting-point for these visions may well have been the first chapter of Ezekiel, other biblical passages have been utilized to fill out the detail and to explain obscurities in that chapter. It is worth recalling that in Revelation 4 we do possess John of Patmos's account of his vision of the celestial throne-chariot. This vision obviously owes much to Ezekiel 1, but it has also been influenced by Isaiah 6 and other passages from Scripture to offer a picture of the throne-chariot which differs substantially from the original. In all likelihood we have in that chapter the product of visionary imagination of John of Patmos, which took as its starting point the chariot-chapter of Ezekiel. Thus the evidence from apocalyptic literature also confirms that in the circles which produced this literature interest in Ezekiel 1 was not confined to explanation of the meaning of the text but included an exposition which resulted in a vision of the chariot as well.

We must ask whether we should attach any significance to one aspect of the story which receives particular attention in the account in T, namely Johanan wrapping himself in his *tallith* and sitting on a rock under the olive-tree. It may well be that we should simply follow B and interpret this as an act of reverence based on Johanan's conviction that when Eleazar began his exposition the *shekinah* was with the rabbis (lines 39f.).[37] Nevertheless such an explanation is missing in T, and, what is more, the act of reverence in B is more closely linked with Johanan's descent from the ass. Does the mention of the act of Johanan in T have a significance which was lost in the course of transmission? Perhaps a tentative suggestion could be made to indicate that the reference to the *tallith* may have more than a passing relevance for our subject.

The *tallith*, or prayer shawl, was (and is) a garment of some importance for Jewish piety. This is because it is the piece of Clothing to which are attached the tassels *(tsitsith)* mentioned in Numbers 15.37–39:

> The LORD said to Moses, Speak to the people of Israel, and bid them to make tassels on the corners of their garments throughout their generations, and to put upon the tassel of each corner a cord of blue [*tekeleth*]; and it shall be to you a tassel to look upon and remember all the commandments of the LORD to do them' . . .

As early as the mid-second century AD we find that a close link is made between the observance of the commandment about the tassels on the corners of the *tallith* and receiving the presence of the *shekinah*. Thus for example we read the following saying of R. Simeon b. Yohai: 'The one who is scrupulous in observing this precept is worthy to receive the presence of the *shekinah*. It is written here, That you may look upon him' (b. Menahoth 43b).

In a similar vein R. Meir, a younger contemporary of R. Akiba said as follows: 'It does not say, And you shall look upon it, but And you shall look upon him. Scripture thus demonstrates that it is reckoned to the man who fulfils the commandment concerning the tassels as though he welcomed the presence of the *shekinah*' (Sifre on Nu. par. 115).

In both these passages the masculine accusative pronoun in

Numbers 15.39 *(re'ithem 'otho)* is taken as a reference to God, not to the thread of blue or the tassels, both of which are feminine. But R. Meir's interpretation of the significance of the Numbers passage gives us even more indication that a close link was made between the tassels on the corners of the *tallith* and the throne of glory itself. This was because in the tassel there was a thread of blue:

> It was taught: R. Meir used to say: Why is blue specified above all other colours? Because blue is like the sea, the sea is like the firmament, the firmament is like the throne of glory, as it is said, Underneath his feet was the appearance of work of sapphire-stone and like the very heaven for clearness (Exod. 24.10). And it is written, Like the appearance of sapphire-stone was the likeness of the throne (Ezek 1.26).[38] (b. Men 43b.)

Here R. Meir is arguing that, by virtue of possession of the thread of blue in each tassel, the wearer of the *tallith* has a reflection of the colour of the throne of glory itself. Whether at this early stage we can argue that gazing at the thread of blue in the tassels on the *tallith* formed part of the visionary's preparation to see again the throne-chariot of Ezekiel we cannot be sure. Nevertheless it is apparent that in later *midrashim* the importance of the thread of blue for mystical study is made quite clear: 'That you may look upon it. It says him and not her (as we would expect as *tsitsith* and *tekeleth* are feminine). If you do this, it is as if you were seeing the throne of glory which is like the thread of blue.'[39]

What we can be sure of is that a connection between the thread of blue and the throne of glory had been made at a fairly early stage. The interpretation certainly goes back to R. Meir. Indeed, it probably antedates him as we find R. Simeon b. Yohai offering a similar interpretation of the passage, suggesting that such ideas were already a part of the stock of interpretations of the thread of blue by this time. In the light of this material it is not out of the question that the preservation of the wrapping in the *tallith* in T could reflect part of the earliest preparation for the vision of the chariot.[40] Looking at the thread of blue in the tassels on the *tallith* may have assisted the visionary in his vision of the throne-chariot and the glory of God himself.

The evidence is insufficient to be sure of exactly what the character of the meditation on the *merkabah* was in Johanan's day, but it is possible that some form of vision may have been part of the early rabbinic meditation on the chariot-chapter of Ezekiel. Although these texts have an important part to play in the evaluation of early rabbinic thought, what is most significant from the point of view of the history of apocalyptic is that these accounts give us a glimpse, however elusive, of the kind of situation in which such visions may have been received. We have in these stories a setting which may go some way to explain the origins of at least small parts of the apocalyptic literature. Exposition of certain key passages seemed to have paved the way for visions of heaven as well as further revelations about man's destiny as is apparent from Synopsis ii, lines 21ff. While it would be rash to assume immediately that rabbinic mysticism is the natural continuation of apocalyptic, there do seem to be signs that some sort of connection did exist.

It is very tempting to assume that the sudden appearance of interest in the first chapter of Ezekiel with R. Johanan b. Zakkai points to the effect of the fall of Jerusalem on Jewish spirituality. After this event views hitherto alien to Pharisaism gradually infiltrated nascent rabbinic Judaism. We should, however, be wary of assuming that lack of evidence about the existence of such interests before AD 70 is at all significant. As we saw earlier, our knowledge of the teachings of the pre-70 sages is very sketchy. This means that we cannot suppose that the silence of our sources necessarily implies rejection of such activities. Indeed, whenever we date the exposition of Eleazar before Johanan (and there is no reason why it should not have taken place before the Jewish War),[41] there is every indication that meditation upon the chariot-chapter had for a long time formed part of Johanan's religious life. We can hardly expect that such interests would have suddenly invaded the religious consciousness of one who was in 70 already an old man, even allowing for the devastating impact the destruction of the Temple would have had upon him. We may suppose then that the chariot-chapter and the experiences it offered had for a long time been of some significance to Johanan.

Despite having said this, however, one must point out the importance of this part of Johanan's religious heritage in the aftermath of AD 70, when the crisis facing his faith in his ancestral religion would have been profound. As Neusner points out, passages like Ezekiel 1, which are so closely linked with the consequences of the destruction of Jerusalem and its Temple by Nebuchadnezzar, would have been particularly apposite to Johanan as he sought to come to terms with the destruction of the city.[42] The experience of God's reality, which the exposition of the chariot-chapter offered, and allied experiences like the heavenly prediction of blessedness for the teacher and his disciples (lines 21–24), offered some security to the fathers of rabbinic Judaism amidst the perplexities of a bewildering period. It is not difficult to see in the chariot-mysticism the same kind of assurance as that vouchsafed by the earlier apocalypses. Just as John of Patmos offered his apocalypse as a means of giving confidence to those who may have been on the point of suffering for their faith, so Johanan found in his study of the chariot-chapter a means of supporting his religious convictions at a time when their credibility was being severely tested.

CHAPTER 12

The Problems posed by the Esoteric Tradition in the time of Rabbi Akiba

THE PRECISE RULES governing the exposition of the chariot-chapter, and particularly the dire warning to those who speculate on 'matters too difficult for them' (Sirach 3.21ff. quoted by R. Eleazar in j. Hagigah 77c), point to a period when interest in such issues had become a cause for concern. The terse formulation of the Mishnah by its admonitory tone deliberately excludes any encouragement to those who would interest themselves in speculation. No attempt at all is made here to promote the study of significant texts like the chariot-chapter and the story of creation, as is done, for example, in the Tosefta, where the account of Eleazar's exposition is pictured as a privilege, the goal of any diligent student of the Torah. Tradition has it that the mishnaic ruling goes back to R. Akiba, the great teacher who flourished in the opening decades of the second century and perished in the Second Revolt (j. Hagigah 77a). It is difficult to ascertain how much weight we ought to attach to this attribution, but at least it is symptomatic of the fact that it was during the last years of his life that Judaism had to weather the storm of heterodoxy, not least the conflict with gnosticism. It is the part which the rabbinic mystical tradition played in this difficult time which most concerns us in this section.

Despite the terse formulation of the Mishnah concerning the exposition of the chariot-chapter room is still left for the competent sage to speculate freely on the matter. Inevitably any situation which leaves room for a highly personal experience must be fertile ground for the growth of idiosyncratic and even heterodox beliefs. Even if the rabbis confined themselves to the scriptures to explain the meaning of Ezekiel 1, there was still obviously a vast range of possible texts which could be called into use to this end. While difference of opinion is something which is always allowed for in the rabbinic literature, there were occasions when, and issues about which, there had to be a minimum of divergence. One famous example is the disagreement between R. Eliezer b. Hyrcanus and his contemporaries over the *halakah*. Even if this story does not reflect the historical situation in Eliezer's life, it epitomizes the problem facing early rabbinic Judaism as it sought to make its views accepted by as many people as possible:[1]

> . . . R. Eliezer declared it clean, and the sages declared it unclean . . . On that day Eliezer brought forward all the arguments in the world, but they did not accept them . . . He said to them, If the Law agrees with me, let it be proved from heaven. A heavenly voice went forth and said, Why do you dispute with R. Eliezer, since in all matters the Law agrees with him? But R. Joshua exclaimed, It is not in heaven' (b. Baba Metsiah 59a–b cf. j. Moe'd Qatan 3.1).

As can clearly be seen in this story the position of Eliezer on all matters is guaranteed by the heavenly voice. Nevertheless, even though his position corresponds with the will of God, he is still in a minority in the rabbinic college and his ruling has to be rejected. We see here a definite suspicion of the direct revelation even in a case where the individual concerned was speaking according to the traditions of the sages; it is the opinion of the majority which should be heeded. This is a safeguard against the rise of idiosyncratic views, which may, according to the belief of a particular teacher, be inspired by God himself. An emphasis on the traditional view as agreed by a majority decision counteracts any tendency to individual divergence, especially on matters which are central to religion.

In b. Sanhedrin 97b–98a there is an account of a discussion between R. Joshua and R. Eliezer on whether the final redemption of Israel depended on repentance or not. Both teachers lived at the end of the first century, and it would appear that we have a record of an early debate on this issue:

> R. Eliezer said: If Israel repent, they will be redeemed, as it is written, Return ye backsliding children, and I will heal your backslidings. R. Joshua said to him, But is it not written, ye have sold yourselves for nought; and ye shall be redeemed without money. Ye have sold yourselves for nought, that is for idolatry; and ye shall be

redeemed without money, that is without repentance and good deeds? R. Eliezer retorted to R. Joshua, But is it not written, Return unto me, and I will return unto you? R. Joshua rejoined, But is it not written, For I am master over you; and I will take you one of a city and two of a family, and I will bring you to Zion? R. Eliezer replied, But it is written, In returning and rest shall ye be saved. R. Joshua replied, But is it not written, Thus saith the Lord, The redeemer of Israel, and his Holy One, to him whom man despiseth, to him whom the nations abhorreth, to a servant of rulers. Kings shall see and arise, princes also shall worship? R. Eliezer countered, But is it not written, If thou wilt return, O Israel, saith the Lord, return unto me? R. Joshua answered, But it is elsewhere written, And I heard the man clothed in fine linen, which was upon the waters of the river, when he held up his right hand and his left hand unto heaven and swore by him that liveth for ever that it shall be for a time, times and a half; and when he shall have accomplished to scatter the power of the holy people, all these things shall be finished. At this R. Eliezer remained silent.

This rather protracted alternation between different scriptural passages, which are used to support the two different points of view, is of interest to us because of the conclusion of the debate. With the quotation from Daniel 12.7 Eliezer falls silent and does not offer any further passage. Urbach has pointed out that, when Joshua sought support for his argument in the words of an apocalyptic vision, R. Eliezer saw no further possibility for continuing the argument, for it was precisely this view that he opposed.[2] What seems to have happened is that the altercation ground to a halt at the point where the apocalyptic vision was brought in. Up to that point the dispute had centred on the *interpretation* of the scriptures. With the quotation from Daniel 12.7, however, the debate moves away from the discussion about the meaning of the text to the divine pronouncement on the matter by the angel. The fact that an answer had been given in Daniel's vision to the matter, which the two rabbis were debating, made any further discussion completely superfluous. This passage then is further evidence of the way in which apocalyptic played its part in rabbinic debates by offering what appeared to be authoritative answers to disputed issues. As such it could cut right across the detailed exegesis of the scriptures practised in the rabbinic academies.

One way of guarding against heretical teaching in the early

church was by tracing the authority of church leaders in particular places back to the apostles. The chain of tradition served to legitimate the teaching of the church officials over against those who claimed new revelations on the nature of the faith. It is a device which is made much of by Irenaeus (*Adv. Haer.* ii. 2–3; iii. 3–4 cf. Tertullian *De Praescript. Haer.* 20–21) but already makes an appearance in a less sophisticated form in the Pastoral Epistles (e.g. 1 Tim. 6.20). Similarly in the sections dealing with the interpretation of Genesis 1 and Ezekiel 1 a chain of authoritative exposition is given, starting with R. Johanan b. Zakkai, and including R. Joshua and R. Akiba. This was obviously a means of directing those who were interested in matters of an esoteric kind to a recognized teacher in their own generation. It should be pointed out that the chain goes no further back than Johanan and stops with a pupil of Akiba, R. Hananiah b. Hakinai (c. AD 120).[3] The fact that it goes back only to Johanan is indicative of the importance the authors of the chain of tradition placed on Johanan's position within the esoteric movement. It would appear that the chain was formulated in the second century as it goes no further than Akiba's disciple. This suggests that it was only at this particular point in time that such a chain of tradition was required. Once again we see that there is evidence that in the opening decades of the second century problems were posed by the interest in the chariot-chapter.

But the difficulties of this period are epitomized for us in a very famous rabbinic story which speaks of the four who entered a garden (*pardes*). Before we embark on an investigation of the difficulties confronting an explanation of this story the four versions of the story are here given in synoptic form (ShSR. 1.4; Tos. Hag. 2.3f., j. Hag. 77b; Hag. 14b). Only in the case of the version in T(osefta) do we have the story told without any other material inserted. The versions in B(abylonian Talmud), J(erusalem Talmud) and S(hir) h(a) S(hirim Rabbah) contain explanatory material in the form of stories about the rabbis mentioned in the original account. Most interest is concentrated on Elisha b. Abuyah (*Aher*), whose career and apostasy was obviously a matter of major interest to the redactor of the J account. Because there is so much material concerning Elisha in B and J, it has not been reproduced in the synopsis. Where material has been added to the story general reference has been made to its character at the appropriate point in the story.

SYNOPSIS III

	BABYLONIAN TALMUD	JERUSALEM TALMUD	TOSEFTA	SONG OF SONGS R.
1	Our rabbis taught:			The king brought me
2				into his chambers. (ShS 1.4)
3	Four men entered	Four men entered	Four men entered	Four men entered
4	a garden. They were	a garden	a garden.	a garden.
5	Ben Azzai, Ben Zoma,		Ben Azzai, Ben Zoma	Ben Azzai, Ben Zoma
6	Aher		Aher	Elisha b. Abuyah
7	and R. Akiba		and R. Akiba	and R. Akiba
8	R. Akiba said to them,			
9	When you approach the			
10	stones of pure marble,			
11	do not say, Water,			
12	water, for it is			
13	written, He who speaks			
14	lies will not tarry			
15	in my presence			
16		One looked and died	One looked and died	
17		One looked and was	One looked and was	
18		struck.	struck.	
19		One looked and cut the	One looked and cut the	
20		plants.	plants.	
21		One entered in peace	One went up in peace	
22		and came out in peace	and came down in peace	
23	Ben Azzai looked	Ben Azzai looked	Ben Azzai looked	Ben Azzai looked
24	and died	and was struck	and died	and was struck
25	Concerning him	Concerning him	Concerning him	Concerning him
26	scripture says	scripture says	scripture says	it is said
27	Precious in the sight		Precious in the sight	
28	of the LORD is the		of the LORD is the	
29	death of his saints		death of his saints	

	BABYLONIAN TALMUD	JERUSALEM TALMUD	TOSEFTA	SONG OF SONGS R.
30		Have you found honey?		Have you found honey?
31		Eat what is sufficient		Eat what is sufficient
32		for you		for you
33	Ben Zoma looked	Ben Zoma looked	Ben Zoma looked	Ben Zoma looked
34	and was struck	and died	and was struck	and died
35	Concerning him	Concerning him	Concerning him	And concerning him
36	scripture says	scripture says	scripture says	it is said
37	Have you found honey?		Have you found honey?	
38	Eat what is sufficient		Eat what is sufficient	
39	for you,		for you,	
40	lest you be filled		etc.	
41	with it and vomit it.			
42		Precious in the sight		Precious in the sight
43		of the LORD is the		of the LORD is the
44		death of his saints		death of his saints
45	Aher	Aher looked	Elisha looked	Elisha b. Abuyah
46	cut the plants	and cut the plants	and cut the plants	cut the plants
	Additional material	*Additional material*		*Additional material*
	(i) Ben Zoma is asked for his opinion on two points of law.	Various stories about Elisha starting off with the way in which he interfered with children as they studied the Torah. All are intended as explanations of line 46.		The story of Elisha's interference with children studying Torah as explanation of line 46.
	(ii) Ben Zoma's meditation on the story of creation and his discussion with R. Joshua.			
47	Concerning him	Concerning him	Concerning him	Concerning him
48	scripture says	scripture says	scripture says	it is said
49	Do not allow your mouth	Do not allow your mouth	Do not allow your mouth	Do not allow your mouth
50	to bring your flesh	to bring your flesh	to bring your flesh	to bring your flesh
51	into sin	into sin	into sin	into sin
52		etc.	etc.	

	BABYLONIAN TALMUD	JERUSALEM TALMUD	TOSEFTA	SONG OF SONGS R.
	Additional material Various stories about Elisha and his pupil R. Meir, starting with the account of his vision of Metatron	*Additional material* Story of how Aher betrayed Jews.		R. Akiba entered in and came out in peace And he said, It is not that I am greater than my companions. But the sages taught as follows in the Mishnah: Your deeds will bring you near, and your deeds will keep you away. And concerning him it is said, The king brought me into his chambers
53	R. Akiba went up in	R. Akiba entered in	R. Akiba went up in	
54	peace and came down	peace and came out	peace and came down	
55	in peace	in peace	in peace	
56				
57				
58				
59				
60				
61				
62				
63				
64				
65	Concerning him	Concerning him	Concerning him	
66	scripture says	scripture says	scripture says	
67				
68				
69	Draw me; we shall	Draw me; we shall	Draw me; we shall	
70	run after you	run after you	run after you	
71	The ministering angels			
72	attempted to push			
73	R. Akiba away also.			
74	The Holy One, blessed			
75	be He said to them,			
76	Leave this elder alone,			
77	for he is worthy to			
78	avail himself of my			
79	glory.			

The similarity of this story to the account by Paul of the rapture of the man in Christ to the heavenly paradise (2 Cor. 12.3) has led many to assume that in the Jewish story we have the account of a similar experience to the one described by the apostle.[4] There is much evidence which superficially supports such a connection. After all, the context in which the story occurs in the Tosefta and the two Talmuds is dealing with interest in the heavenly world, unseen to normal human perception.[5] But it is the presence of the Hebrew word *pardes*, usually translated 'garden', which is taken to be a reference to the paradise of God in heaven. Those who are reluctant to find here evidence of a heavenly ascent made by the four rabbis named in the story consider that entry into the garden should be regarded as a metaphorical description of mystical or gnostic speculations.[6]

One of the main reasons why the story has been regarded as an ascent into heaven has been an excessive reliance on the version of the story in B. A glance at the other versions of the story, however, reveals that they omit the important passage in B (lines 8–15, 71–79) which has been regarded by Scholem, among others, as indicative of a mystical ascent. The omission in the other versions is noted by Scholem, but no comment is passed on the matter.[7] The addition records Akiba's advice when one is confronted during the ascent with stones of marble which resemble water.[8] Scholem argues convincingly that this reflects actual problems facing the mystics in their ascent to heaven.[9] There are other indications in B that the entry into the garden is here understood as a mystical ascent. Thus in lines 53–55 the verbs 'enter' and 'come out' have disappeared and are replaced by 'go up' and 'come down',[10] contrasting with the opening of the story where entry into the garden is presupposed. In b. Hagigah 15b (bottom – lines 71ff.) there is clear evidence that B has understood Akiba's entry as an ascent to the divine presence, for the ministering angels wish to prevent Akiba from reaching God. God has to intervene so that Akiba can come into his presence. It is probable that the beginnings of an understanding of the story as an ascent into heaven is also to be found in ShS R., for the story is attached to the text 'The king has brought me into his chambers'. Lines 56–68 seem to be intended to show that Akiba's deeds had enabled him to enter the divine presence without any mishap.

The question is whether such an interpretation is also applicable to the forms of the story which do not have the additions in B. We have had reason to suggest that this may already have been the case in ShS. But is it possible to argue that the understanding of the story as a heavenly ascent only belongs to later interpretations and was not the original intention of the story? If we look at the other versions, we note that the story merely records the fact that four rabbis entered a garden and describes the consequences of their entry on each one of them, without any suggestion that it was heaven that they entered. Comparison of the other three versions with B indicates that they offer us an earlier version of the story before its interpretation as a heavenly ascent had been made explicit. But it is possible to go back even further in the history of tradition than a story which told of the entry of four rabbis into a garden.

There is evidence from the version in J that originally there may have been a form of the story in which neither the names of those concerned nor the scriptural texts commenting upon their action in the garden were included. In J we find that the names of the four rabbis are not mentioned until the activities of the four individuals have been described (lines 23ff.). It is thus quite likely that at the beginning of the version in J (lines 3–4 and 16–22) we can isolate a simple story about four men who entered a garden. Originally this story need have had no contact at all with its present context, though of course it is not found in this simple form anywhere else. The version in T also preserves the form of the simple story, as, apart from the introduction of the names (lines 5–6) we have exactly the same form of the story as in J (lines 16–22). In both it is then repeated, in order that the names of the rabbis and the scriptural passages can be added to this simple story. So we can see that the second stage of development of the story of the four (and probably also its inclusion in its present context) involved identification of the four mentioned in the original story with actions of four famous teachers at the beginning of the second century[11] and the explanation of their activities through the use of appropriate passages from Scripture.[12] At a later stage still we have the insertion of further explanatory material in the form of relevant incidents from the lives of the rabbis concerned. We can see that the version in T has not integrated the story of the discussion between Joshua and Ben Zoma into the story, nor, as in B, J and ShS, does it include material from the life of Elisha (Aher) to

explain the enigmatic phrase 'cutting the plants' (line 46).[13]
Finally in the last stage of development we have the additions in
B and the change of the verbs (lines 53–55), reflected also in
some manuscripts of T, which definitely make the story into a
heavenly ascent. We cannot be certain whether the story of the
Four ever had an independent existence outside a context dealing with mystical matters.[14] Nevertheless, it seems that the
identification of different layers of tradition may reveal a variety
of interpretations of the story during the course of its development. Much has been written recently about the meaning of the
most developed form of the story, and there is no need to go
over this ground once more.[15] We can agree completely with
those who argue that the version of the story in B has become a
description of a heavenly ascent. What we must ask ourselves,
however, is whether the meaning of the story as we have it in
the other three versions is necessarily the same as the version
in B.

It is frequently assumed that mention of the word *pardes* in the
story points to an apocalyptic flavour to the story. But it is
wrong to assume that in this particular context the word is being
used in its technical sense as a reference to the Garden of Eden,
as the Greek *paradeisos* does in the Septuagint (Gen. 2.8–10;
Ezek. 28.13; 31.8; cf. Rev. 2.7).[16] Indeed, as Urbach has pointed
out, there is no evidence from early rabbinic literature that *pardes*
was used as the equivalent of *gan 'eden*.[17] What we would have
to suppose is that the usage in our story is unique in early
rabbinic literature if we see here a reference to the heavenly
paradise. There is also a lack of evidence for the use of entry into
the garden as a metaphor for involvement in gnostic speculations or mystical studies.[18] In the light of these facts we are
justified in looking for a meaning for the earlier form of the
story, which does not presuppose a heavenly ascent but merely
speaks of entry into a garden as a way of commenting on the
lives and activities of four famous rabbis.

That we are right in distinguishing between the meaning of
the story in B and other versions receives support from T. In
Codex Vienna of T the story of the four is illustrated by two
short parables (cf. Sifra on Lev. 26.12):[19]

'They tell a parable. What is this matter [the entry of the four into
pardes] like? It is like the garden of a king over which a balcony had

been constructed. What is a man to do in this situation? He should look but should not let his eyes feast[20] on what he sees.

Still another illustration has been offered. What is this matter like? It is like a street which passes between two other roads, one of fire and one of snow. If a man inclines one way, he is burnt with fire; if the other, he is frost-bitten. What is a man to do? To pursue the middle course, not deviating either one way or the other.'

In the first story about the garden of the king we have the use of *pardes*, exactly the same word as is used in the story of the four but here quite clearly used in its usual sense.[21] It is hard to believe that in the mind of the compiler of this passage the word *pardes* is being used in two different ways within the space of a few lines. It would appear then that the meaning of the word in both instances corresponds to the way in which it is usually used in rabbinic literature and means simply a garden. In other words, both stories in which *pardes* occurs are to be understood in a metaphorical sense and do not presuppose a heavenly ascent. Both these stories are appended to the story of the four in order to illustrate its meaning. The point made by the first story is that any person who has the opportunity to look into a king's garden should not take advantage of such opportunity by sitting and looking into it all the time, with the result that he cannot take his eyes off it. As an explanation of the story of the four it seems that it is a warning not to be so fascinated with what one finds in the garden that the object of infatuation becomes a distraction. The second parable urges caution when one is faced with snow and fire as one goes on a journey. The sensible man is going to be the one who avoids the perils of heat and cold and pursues a course between them. When applied to the story of the four this second parable would seem to indicate that entry into the garden offered perils similar to those suffered by the man who journeys along a path surrounded by snow and fire. Any distraction one way or the other can lead to disaster. In the garden disaster met three of those who entered. They had not practised moderation and had suffered for this. Only the fourth member of the quartet had taken the appropriate precautions and had avoided the distraction which prevented him from coming out again safely. Both additional parables in T suggest that the way in which the story of the four should be understood is as an encouragement to moderation, an avoidance of infatuation and extremes.[22]

So the story of the four was intended as a warning to readers, by pointing to the way in which entry into the garden affected three of the rabbis, and, in the person of R. Akiba, an example of correct behaviour.[23] It is only the fourth of the quartet who entered and came out of the garden without any harm either to himself or the garden. In all versions of our story it is stated that only the first three rabbis 'looked' *(hetsits)* after entering the garden; nowhere is this said of the fourth.[24] An understanding of the significance of the word may be gained by reference to the first of the illustrative parables in T quoted above. This says that, in a situation where he is able to look into a king's garden from a balcony, a man should look but not derive so much pleasure from it that he cannot stop himself gazing at it. The point is not that the looking is wrong, but that one should not fix one's gaze on one particular object and so run the risk of being distracted by it. When we turn to the story of the four, the fact that only Akiba is represented as coming out unharmed, without looking, suggests that it was what they saw in the garden which caused the other three their problems. Unlike R. Akiba nothing is said about them coming out of the garden again unharmed. They were thus distracted by what they had seen and detained in the garden to the detriment, in two cases, of themselves, and, in the third, of the garden. Clearly the story intends to teach that entry into the garden is no crime providing that the impact of the entry does not impair one's ability to come out unharmed.

Our investigation so far indicates that a story about four men who entered a garden and what happened to them after they had entered has been used to illustrate certain aspects of the lives of four rabbis who flourished in the early part of the second century. In this illustration only one survived the entry without harm, whereas the other three were affected by what they saw and prevented from coming out of the garden. We have also had reason to suspect that the purpose of the story was to encourage moderation and care and discourage infatuation with certain matters.

But what aspects of the lives of these teachers does the story set out to describe in this metaphorical way, and what were the particular issues which demanded moderation to avoid the risk of distraction? Are we to suppose that the version of the story, without the additions which make it into an account of an ascent to heaven, is merely a metaphor for mystical study? This obviously makes some sense, for, as we shall see later, there is evidence to link Ben Zoma and Elisha with such activities. Nevertheless there is very little early evidence to suggest that Akiba and Ben Azzai were deeply involved in such matters.[25] Also we have already noted that entry into a garden is not normally used as a metaphor for engagement in mystical or apocalyptic activity. The mystical connotations of the passage are given to it by its context in Hagigah. Indeed, there would probably be no good reason for supposing that entry into the garden was synonymous with mystical activity in the account in ShS if we did not possess the parallel versions in Hagigah. Although one does not want to minimize the importance of the context for the understanding of the story, the various factors already mentioned suggest that the specifically mystical elements within the story itself are not as obvious as is often assumed. Consideration should, therefore, be given to another interpretation which includes mystical involvement but is not confined to this narrow set of interests.

All we are allowed to conclude from the story itself is that the doings of four rabbis have been linked with a story about the entry of four men into a garden, whose aim was to enter and come out again without any harm. Unfortunately, only one of those who entered came out unharmed, for the rest were variously affected by what they saw in the garden. If we leave aside the mystical setting for the time being, the natural interpretation of such a story, in which rabbis are mentioned, would be to assume that entry into a garden was a metaphorical way of describing the involvement of these four teachers in what occupied them most, namely the exposition of the scriptures. To see the story in this sense obviously does not exclude mystical connotations, for the commitment of any rabbi to the exposition of the scriptures and the application of them to new situations led him sooner or later to consider the meaning of passages like Ezekiel 1 and Genesis 1. There was a great responsibility resting upon the student of the scriptures as he attempted to make sense of the revelation of God and to pass on unharmed what he himself had received to future generations. It was in fact a potentially dangerous exercise which could have dire consequences for the unwary. In the story of the four then we have a metaphorical description of the way in which involvement with the scriptures affected four teachers. For three of them the results were disastrous. Only the fourth succeeded in carrying on his activities unharmed. It was his example and teachings, therefore, which were the ones to follow, a point clearly illustrated by the citation from Scripture applied to him: 'Draw me after you; let us make haste' (ShS 1.4).

But what evidence is there that such an interpretation has any validity? There are two pieces of evidence which may suggest that our interpretation is on the right lines. First of all we must look at a parable from Shemoth R. 30.8, which compares the gift of the Torah to Israel by God to a king who allowed his sons to enter his garden:

> He spoke his word to Jacob. R. Abbahu said in the name of R. Jose b. Hanina [*c.* AD 250]: It is like a king who had a garden (*pardes*), and he planted all kinds of trees in it. No one entered it but the king himself, for he was its keeper. When his sons reached their maturity, the king said to them, My sons, I have been keeper of this garden and have not allowed anyone to enter it. Look after it yourselves as I have done. Thus did God speak to Israel: Before I created the world, I prepared the Torah . . . I did not give it to one of the nations but to Israel.

God's gift of the Torah to Israel is likened to the way in which a king gave his private garden to his sons to enter and look after it. In this parable entry into the garden is compared to the privilege granted to Israel of the keeping and study of the Torah.

The use of such a metaphor would be particularly applicable to four rabbis who were in particular responsible before God for the gift of the Torah. In the light of this parable from Shemoth R. the story of the four should be seen as a commentary on the results of the occupation of certain teachers with the scriptures. Even in a context dealing with mystical matters an account of the way in which four teachers treated the Torah would be particularly relevant, especially when such study would involve them in dealing with potentially dangerous material like the stories of creation and the chariot.

The second passage includes the parable about the ways of fire and snow in a different context in Hagigah 77a:

> 'There was once a young pupil of Rabbi who expounded one section of the chariot-chapter without the approval or knowledge of Rabbi and he became leprous. This Torah is like two paths, one of fire and one of snow. If one deviates to one side, one dies in the fire. If one

deviates the other way, one dies in the snow. What should a man
do? He should pursue a middle course.

Involvement in Jewish religion is compared to a situation where
a man is liable to perish in the extremes of temperature. The
only way in which he is going to save himself is by pursuit of a
middle course. The study of the Torah will present a man with
similar problems. Only by avoiding the dangers which the
Jewish religion presents and refusing to be attracted by passages
which may lead one astray will a man be able to keep himself
from danger. The pupil of Rabbi is cited as an example of a
person who was so interested in the chariot-chapter that he
could not resist the temptation to investigate it without his
teacher's permission. The consequences of his disobedience,
arising out of his infatuation with a dangerous part of the
scriptures, is offered as a salutary warning to all those who
occupy themselves in the study of the Torah.[26]
    It can be argued then that the earliest function of the story of
the four within its present context concerns the results of the
occupation of four rabbis with the study of the Torah, including
the passages which were of particular interest to the mystic. The
success or otherwise which they made of this venture would
obviously be influential on later assessment of them as examples
for future generations. But for a complete understanding of the
reason for the choice of these rabbis we must now turn to other
information, in order to elucidate what particular aspects of the
lives of the four are referred to in the cryptic references in the
story. Obviously the scriptural citations, which function as a
commentary on the results of the entry, are going to be of prime
importance, but other traditions, some of which are additions to
the story, about these teachers must also be utilized.
    There is some confusion in the tradition about the conse-
quences of Ben Azzai's entry into the garden. While B and T say
that he died as a result of his entry (lines 23–29), J and ShS
connect death with Ben Zoma (lines 33–36 and 42–46) and say
that Ben Azzai was struck in some way by his entry (lines 23–26
and 30–32). The versions in J and ShS correspond with later
stories about Ben Azzai which tell of him being struck 'by eleven
thousand iron bars'.[27] Confusion between the two is understandable if originally there were no names attached to the story.
It is quite likely that the two in the story who were not over-

whelmingly evil or righteous could have been confused. Clearly the composer of our secondary stage of the tradition had firmly fixed in his mind the link between Elisha and the mutilation of the plants in the garden, and Akiba and entry and exit without disaster. Nevertheless traditions about the other two teachers may have led to an alteration in the identification as the story was passed on. There are three reasons for accepting the priority of the version in B and T:

a. Although J's first reference to the four in lines 16–22 has the order 'one died' then 'one was struck'. It reverses this order when it comes to identify the four with the teachers. Thus J shows knowledge of the same order as B and T but for some reason has reversed it when the figures are identified.

b. There is good reason for linking Ben Zoma with the figure who died. In the account of his discussion with R. Joshua (see below) we find at the end a reference to Ben Zoma's departure. This is often taken as a way of referring to Ben Zoma's death.[28] It would be understandable, therefore, why the order in B and T should be reversed, as it fitted better with other material about Ben Zoma.[29]

c. The scriptural passage which is applied to Ben Zoma in B and T (lines 33–41) makes much better sense of what we know about his mystical activities than can be said about any tradition concerning Ben Azzai.

So it would seem that the order in B and T is to be preferred as representing the earlier identification of the four in the story.

It is the case of Ben Azzai which offers us the greatest problems in finding an appropriate event in his life to which the story can refer. The activities of the other three rabbis in the garden are all explicable as metaphors for their deeds. Are we to suppose that it is the same with Ben Azzai? Is the reference to Ben Azzai's death to be understood only figuratively? It is not easy, from what we know of Ben Azzai's life and utterances, to ascertain exactly what death, understood in a figurative sense, could possibly refer to. It seems best to conclude with Bacher that in the case of Ben Azzai we do not have metaphorical language used here but a reference to this teacher's death.[30] He suggests that Ben Azzai may have been a victim of the Hadrianic persecution. The only possible reason for the breakdown of the metaphorical description of the activities of the four teachers was the fact that an earlier story was being used in which death was one of the consequences facing those who entered the garden. When the time came to utilize his story in its present context, difficulties were obviously met in understanding the reference to death in the original story metaphorically. Hence it became necessary in the case of one of the four to abandon the quest for a figurative interpretation and to rest content with referring to an actual event in the rabbi's life.

The case of Ben Azzai calls for an interpretation of the story which is not related solely to the narrow area of exposition of subjects of mystical interest, for the traditions about him show little evidence of a connection with such activities. Of course, it is possible that such material has been suppressed, but the story of the four is not in itself enough indication that Ben Azzai was renowned for his involvement in such matters. The only possible exception is the story in ShS R. 1.10 which we have already examined. According to this story fire played around Ben Azzai as he expounded the scriptures. On hearing of this Akiba assumes that Ben Azzai must have been expounding the chariot-chapter. The question we must ask is whether Akiba's suspicions were aroused by the person who was doing the expounding or the supernatural phenomena which accompanied the exposition. In the light of the fact that in the more developed accounts of the exposition of the chariot-chapter by Eleazar b. Arak the fire plays a prominent part we may be justified in supposing that in this story it was the fire which was the indication to Akiba that the chariot-chapter was being expounded.

Apart from the fact that Ben Azzai remained celibate (something which has been taken as an indication of gnostic influence), the traditions about him hardly lead us to suspect his religious standing.[31] Indeed, it is not without significance that the passage of Scripture applied to Ben Azzai (Ps. 116.15) is far from critical and contrasts with the texts applied to Ben Zoma and Aher.[32] Death, far from being a punishment, was something glorious in God's eyes, an apt comment if Ben Azzai suffered a martyr's death. In the light of our attempt to see the entry into the garden as a metaphor for the study of the Torah it is quite appropriate to see martyrdom in the Hadrianic persecution as a direct result of his devotion to the Torah. Of course, in rabbinic legend R. Akiba was also supposed to have been a victim of this persecution (b. Berakoth 61b). The important difference between

Ben Azzai and R. Akiba is that the latter was probably an old man when he suffered a martyr's death whereas Ben Azzai was considerably younger than Akiba.[33] The former's involvement in his ancestral religion and his devotion to Torah did not bring worldly success, only a martyr's crown. The message to later students of the example of Ben Azzai is: despite the great mysteries about God and his universe which can be revealed by the study of the Torah, it is essential to count the cost of the rabbi's life-long commitment to the exposition of Torah. This means that we would have an assessment of Ben Azzai which was not as negative as those made of Ben Zoma and Aher. If this is the case (and the scriptural quotation applied to Ben Zoma would seem to reinforce the suggestion), the story has a chiastic structure in which only the middle pair are singled out for special censure.

When we turn to examine the reference to Ben Zoma, we find that the result of his entry into the garden was some kind of affliction. This is frequently understood to be a reference to madness which was the direct consequence of his involvement in mystical matters.[34] Apart from the later material such an interpretation depends for its validity on a story which we shall examine below in which one of Ben Zoma's contemporaries, R. Joshua, pronounces the former 'outside' *(mibahuts)*. But, as we shall see, such an interpretation of this phrase does not arise naturally from the context. The story of the four allows us to conclude that Ben Zoma was in some way afflicted by his entry, and the scriptural citation suggests that this was because he found in the garden something highly desirable and became so obsessed with it that it affected him (lines 37–41). As far as Ben Zoma's life and his study of Torah are concerned, the two passages which we shall consider now point to an excessive interest in the opening chapter of the book of Genesis, the story of creation. It would appear that a case can be made for Ben Zoma's affliction being the direct result of his great interest in this chapter which led him to become too interested in such speculative interests that it affected his religious life.

The account of Ben Zoma's conversation with Joshua, which leads to the former revealing that he was interested in the story of creation, is to be found in four different versions, Tos. Hagigah 2.6, j. Hagigah 77b, b. Hagigah 15a, and Bereshith R. 2.4. The story itself is found in slightly different contexts in the four versions. In Bereshith R. it obviously forms part of the exposition of the opening chapter of Genesis. In the other three versions, however, there is little uniformity on the position it is given within the tractate Hagigah. In B, for example, it is integrated into the story of the four. In T and J on the other hand it stands separately. In T it comes after the story of the four and the two explanatory parables, and in J follows the story of Eleazar and Johanan and Simeon and Joseph but is before the story of the four. The four versions are here produced in synoptic form (p.325ff.).

Whilst the account in B(ereshith) R(abbah) offers the most extended form of the initial questioning of Ben Zoma by Joshua (lines 10–26), it is J which spends most space on the discussion on the relationship between Genesis 1.6f., 1.2 and Deuteronomy 32.11 (lines 42–57). B and BR show most independence and agree in details against the other two accounts, e.g. the estimate of the distance between the waters (lines 32–33). B alone omits the close link between this incident and the supposed death of Ben Zoma (lines 67–68), and in its place suggests that the enigmatic reference to Ben Zoma being 'outside' is a reference to the incorrectness of Ben Zoma's interpretation of Genesis 1. Despite the differences which do exist the essential elements are the same in all the versions:

a. Joshua's greeting and Ben Zoma's refusal to reply (lines 10–12).

b. An enigmatic question by Joshua (lines 17–18).

c. Ben Zoma's confession that he was looking at the narrow space between the waters (lines 28–34).

d. The extent of the space interpreted by linking the hovering in Gen. 1.2 with another occurrence of the word in Deut. 32.11 (lines 37ff.), (though in B it is merely a comparison between the spirit of God and a dove).

e. Joshua's comment on Ben Zoma's activity (lines 64–65).

Three points in particular call for comment: Joshua's question, Ben Zoma's description of his activity and Joshua's comment upon it.

In B, T and J the form of Joshua's question is much the same (line 17).[35] In all versions the question is prompted by the silence of Ben Zoma. The form of the question thus seems to have

SYNOPSIS IV

	JERUSALEM TALMUD	TOSEFTA	BABYLONIAN TALMUD	BERESHITH R.
1			Our rabbis taught:	Once Simeon b. Zoma
2				was sitting gazing
3	A story concerning	A story concerning	A story concerning	
4	R. Joshua	R. Joshua	R. Joshua b. Hananiah	R. Joshua
5	who was going along	who was going along	who was sitting on top	passed by
6	the road	the street	of the Temple mount	
7	and Ben Zoma came	and Ben Zoma came	and Ben Zoma saw him	
8	alongside him	alongside him		
9		He drew near to him but	but	
10	Joshua greeted him	did not greet him	did not stand up before	and greeted him twice
11			him	
12	and he did not reply			and he did not reply
13				On the third occasion
14				he did not reply Joshua
15	Joshua said to him	Joshua said to him	Joshua said to him	said to him in some
16				agitation
17	Whence and whither,	Whence and whither,	Whence and whither,	Whence are the feet
18	Ben Zoma?	Ben Zoma?	Ben Zoma?	Ben Zoma?
19				He replied, not from
20				nothing, Rabbi. Joshua
21				said to him, I call
22				heaven and earth as
23				witness that I am not
24				departing from here
25				until you show me whence
26				are the feet

	Jerusalem Talmud	Tosefta	Babylonian Talmud	Bereshith R.
27	Ben Zoma replied	Ben Zoma replied	Ben Zoma said to him	Ben Zoma said to him
28	I was reflecting on	I was looking at the work	I was looking at	I was reflecting on
29	the work of creation	of creation	the space between the	the work of creation
30			upper and lower waters	
31	and there is only a	and there is only a	and there is only	and there is only
32	space a hand-	hand-	three fingers	two or three fingers
33	breadth wide between	breadth between	breadth between	breadth between
34	the upper and lower	the upper and lower	them	the upper and lower
35	waters	waters		waters
36			as it is said	Scripture does not say
37		as it is said	The Spirit of God was	The Spirit of God
38		The Spirit of God was	hovering on the face	breathes
39		hovering on the face	of the waters	
40		of the waters		
41				but hovers
42	'Hovering' is used			
43	here [Gen. 1.2]			
44	similar to the way it			
45	is used in the			
46	following passage			
47	(Deut. 32.11), Like an	and, Like an	like a	like a
48	eagle stirs up its nest	eagle stirs up its nest	dove which hovers over	bird which hovers and flutters
49	it hovers over its	etc.	its young	on its wings,
50	young. What does	As		
51	hovering mean? It	this eagle flies over		
52	means there, touching	its young,		
53	and yet not touching.			
54	It is exactly the same			
55	in the first passage,			
56	touching and yet not	touching and yet not	without any touching	
57	touching	touching,		
58		so there is only a		and its wings
59		hand-breadth between		touch and yet do
60		the upper and lower		not touch

JERUSALEM TALMUD

62 R. Joshua
63 said to his disciples
64 Ben Zoma is
65 outside
66 It was not many days
67 before Ben Zoma
68 departed.

TOSEFTA

R. Joshua
said to his disciples
Ben Zoma has long ago
been outside
It was not many days
before Ben Zoma
departed.

BABYLONIAN TALMUD

R. Joshua
said to his disciples
Ben Zoma is still
outside

BERESHITH R.

R. Joshua turned and
said to his disciples
Ben Zoma has gone

The days were few
for Ben Zoma
to be in the world.

arisen as a result of suspicions about Ben Zoma, and this leads us to wonder whether there is any deeper significance in the form the question takes. A comparison with the second part of the Mishnah indicates that Joshua may have been asking Ben Zoma whether he was indulging in inquiry into 'what is above, what is beneath, what was beforetime and what will be hereafter' (M. Hagigah 2.1). That the question indeed is about Ben Zoma's involvement in such matters would seem to be confirmation by another passage. Exactly the same words as are used in Joshua's question are to be found in a saying which talks about man's beginning and end in Aboth 3.1:[36]

> 'Akabya b. Mahalalel says: Consider three things and you will not fall into the hands of transgression. Know *whence* you have come and *whither* you are going, and before the face of whom you are about to give account and reckoning. Whence you have come – an offensive drop and whither you are going – to a place of dust.'

With his suspicions aroused by Ben Zoma's silence Joshua may have suspected that Ben Zoma was involved in meditation of a speculative kind on matters of importance for apocalypticist and gnostic alike. Consequently Joshua asked him, 'Whence and whither?'[37]. In other words he was asking him whether he was in fact thinking about the origin and destiny of man and the universe.

Ben Zoma eventually divulges the fact that he was looking at the space between the upper and lower waters and the width of the firmament which separates them (lines 28–36).[38] He ascertains the size of the distance by reference to Genesis 1.2 and Deuteronomy 32.11. The point of the comparison is to show how close the waters could be. They might appear to touch, but this in fact was not the case (lines 51–53). As has already been pointed out, there are certainly indications in Ben Zoma's reply that he was not merely involved in an intellectual exercise but was having a vision as well of certain parts of the created world. This point is made most clearly in the version in T and B (though not in J and BR) (lines 28–29), where Ben Zoma's response, literally translated, says 'I was having a vision (*tsopheh*) of the work of creation'.[39] Here exposition of Scripture and visionary activity are closely linked. We have an example here of the way in which passages like Genesis 1 and Ezekiel 1 were expounded, for the story would seem to confirm our impression that in the course of the exposition obscure details of the original passage were illustrated by recourse to other texts. In our story the problem confronting Ben Zoma was the width of the space between the waters, about which, of course, nothing is said in the original. According to J and T he solves this problem by linking another part of the creation story (v. 2), which speaks of the spirit of God hovering *(merahepheth)* on the face of the waters. One assumes that the justification for using this verse in connection with Genesis 1.6, which makes no mention of hovering, is because the waters are mentioned in both verses 2 and 6. This event is explained by the use of Deuteronomy 32.11, where the word 'hover' also occurs *(yeraheph)*. In that verse reference is made to a bird hovering over its nest. So Ben Zoma has some indication of the gap between the waters by comparing it with the gap which exists between a bird and its young as it hovers over the nest. The use of one part of Scripture to illustrate another part is exactly the same as is found in midrash generally. The main difference here is that this is not just an academic exercise. The new passages which were brought in to explain the original extended the visionary possibilities for the teacher concerned. So in this particular case Ben Zoma is able to see a space only a hand-breadth wide between the waters as a result of his application of Genesis 1.2 and Deuteronomy 32.11 to the interpretation of Genesis. 1.6–7.

Discussion of this section cannot be left, however, without bringing up the question of the relationship between the different versions. It will be seen from the synopsis that J and T make mention of the passage from Deuteronomy 32.11. BR contents itself with a rather general reference to a bird, whereas B alone makes mention of the dove. Thus although we may assume that Ben Zoma compared the narrow space with the hovering of a bird, it is necessary to ascertain whether this rested on a link with Deuteronomy 32.11 via Genesis 1.2 or merely arose directly out of the connection between Genesis 1.6 and 1.2 and the suggestive participle *merahepheth*. If the second alternative is correct, then the hovering of the spirit may have led Ben Zoma to compare it with a dove. While certainty here is out of the question, the likelihood would seem to be that the development from the general comparison of B and BR to one which specifically alludes to scriptural parallels is more likely than vice versa. Of the accounts in B and BR one may suppose that the tradition moved from specific to general or in the opposite direction. The former seems more likely. As the precise significance of Ben Zoma's comparison could not be justified by Scripture directly, the tendency would be to modify the reference to the dove either into a general comparison as in BR, or to relate it more specifically with another relevant scriptural passage as in J and T.[40]

Joshua, however, is unhappy with Ben Zoma's explanation of his meditation and tells his pupils that Ben Zoma is 'outside' (line 65). There are three ways of understanding the meaning of this word.[41] First it could indicate that Ben Zoma was out of his mind. There is nothing in the account to suggest in any way that this was the case. Second, it is not impossible that the word could refer to Ben Zoma's mental state at the time when he was talking to Joshua. He was not mad but in a state of ecstasy. The etymological similarity between the Hebrew *mibahuts* and the Greek *ekstasis*, used, for example, to describe Peter's state in Acts 10.10 is worthy of note. Joshua's comment would then be a means of telling his disciples that from his conversation with Ben Zoma he had ascertained that the latter was in a state of ecstasy.[42] This is an attractive suggestion but cannot be supported by parallel uses of the phrase *mibahuts*. So it is probably the third explanation which is to be accepted, namely that Ben Zoma was outside the bounds of permitted study on the subject of creation, because he had confused the different parts of the creation-story.[43] The account of the separation of the waters (Gen. 1.6f.) took place on the second day of creation, but Ben Zoma has linked this closely with the hovering of the spirit of God over the undivided waters on the first day. Joshua may have objected to this sort of confusion, because it was the first step along the road to the elaborate expansions of Genesis 1 which we find in the gnostic literature.[44] Thus R. Joshua is not objecting here to Ben Zoma's activity so much as the fact that he has transgressed the bounds of what is permitted in normal exposition of the text. The comment of Joshua in B and T shows that this incident only confirms supicions which Joshua had long held about Ben Zoma's orthodoxy on this issue. According to B (line 64) Ben Zoma is still outside (the bounds of permitted study). Linked with this particular interpretation of the word 'outside' is the final comment in lines 66–68 in J, T and BR. This has been interpreted as a reference to the death of Ben Zoma, but looks like a comment on the consequences of Ben Zoma's aberrant visionary meditation.

This interpretation of the story receives some confirmation from a brief statement about Ben Zoma's views in Bereshith R. 4.6 (on Gen. 1.7):

> This is one of the verses with which Ben Zoma shook the world – 'and God made': this is a strange thing. Is it not by a command *(ma'amar)* [of God]?

The passage suggests that this was not the only verse over which Ben Zoma's interpretation caused disquiet. The problem with the verse from Genesis 1 in question is that it is the first use of the verb *'asah* as opposed to *bar'a* in Genesis 1. This could indicate that Ben Zoma had qualms about the notion of God as maker, an indication of possible gnostic tendencies.[45] If we are to ascribe the comment, 'Is it not by a command of God?' to Ben Zoma,[46] it shows that he circumvented the problem of God actually making anything by resorting to explaining the verse as a reference to the mediatorial act of the divine fiat. In this respect he seems to go well beyond Philo in *De Opificio Mundi*, where, with the exception of man, the emphasis is on God himself as the creator (e.g. par. 171 where the word *demiourgos* is used).[47]

Here too we have indications that Ben Zoma was considered to be wayward in his views on cosmogony. It would appear, therefore, that in the context of the story of the four, Ben Zoma's fate (synopsis iii, lines 33–41) was closely bound up with his excessive interest in one part of the Torah, the story of creation. He refused to practise moderation in his study of the scriptures and insisted on concentrating on that part of them which was particularly attractive to him (lines 37–38). As a result he was afflicted by this infatuation and lost his spiritual equilibrium. The case of Ben Zoma was an example and a warning to readers of the dangers of narrow concentration on one part of Scripture, especially when it is such a difficult and dangerous passage as the story of creation.

Elisha b. Abuyah or *Aḥer* (i.e. another, this oblique way of referring to Elisha indicates his notoriety in rabbinic tradition) is in every respect the most intriguing character of the four mentioned in our story. A glance at the tractate Hagigah in the two Talmuds will reveal the vast number of stories which circulated about this figure who abandoned his ancestral faith. His apostasy is reflected in the story of the four, for he is the only one whose entrance into the garden resulted in the destruction of the garden itself (Synopsis iii, lines 45–46): he is said to have cut the plants.[48] If we are right in seeing entry into the garden as a metaphor for the study and the careful preservation of Jewish religion, Elisha's activity would seem to indicate a negative attitude towards Judaism, a point which is clearly illustrated by some of the legends which circulated about him.[49] More can be ascertained about what this 'cutting of the plants' could mean by examining the scriptural passage which is cited as an explanation of his activities in the garden viz., Ecclesiastes 5.6, 'do not allow your mouth to bring your flesh into sin' (lines 47–52). It would appear from this comment that it was something which Elisha said which was thought to have led him into a life of sin.

What was it that Elisha said which was the cause of his downfall? Very few of Elisha's utterances and activities give us convincing reasons why he should have turned his back on his religion. The bulk of the stories about him reflect the results of his decision to abandon his faith rather than explanations of the circumstances which led him to such a decision. Attempts to explain his apostasy as the result of the growing influence of Hellenism are hardly satisfactory, despite the fact that one story circulating about him suggested that he delighted in Greek songs (b. Hagigah 15b bottom).[50] One theme which does run through many of the stories about him is the fact that his apostasy was the result of an inward conviction that there was no place left for him in the Jewish faith.[51] There does not seem to be any question of harassment by the rabbinic authorities or even excommunication. Indeed, the accounts about R. Meir's devotion to his former teacher and his attempts to draw him back to his former beliefs show that the reason for apostasy was based on a firm personal conviction that there was no longer any possibility for him of a relationship with the God of Abraham, Isaac, and Jacob.

Several incidents in the life of Elisha are offered by the sources as reasons for his apostasy. In j. Hagigah 77b (bottom) and Koh. R. 7.8 it is his reflection on the apparent injustice of God which leads him to abandon his faith. On one occasion he saw a man transgress Deuteronomy 22.7 on the sabbath and escape punishment. On another occasion he saw a man who kept the Torah in every detail bitten by a snake. The inability to explain such events, it is said, led him to abandon his religion. An alternative explanation is that he saw the tongue of a fellow rabbi in the mouth of a dog (probably a victim of the Hadrianic persecution), which led him to believe that there was little point in studying the Torah. The juxtaposition of these stories in our sources shows that at the time of the composition of these tractates the precise reason for Elisha's apostasy was no longer known, hence the need to incorporate several explanations side by side.

There are two stories, however, which tell us of occasions when Elisha received a *bath qol*, a voice from heaven, which told him that there was no possibility of repentance for him. In other words we do have traditions, which offer some explanation of the *inner* conviction of Elisha that it was useless for him to continue in his ancestral religion any longer. The first of these tells of an occasion when Elisha was riding upon an ass by the synagogue on the Day of Atonement:

> That is enough, Meir, said Elisha, the sabbath-limit extends only as far as this. How do you know, said Meir? From the hoofs of my horse, replied Elisha. How is it that you possess so much wisdom and yet you do not repent? I cannot, said Elisha. Why not, said Meir? I was once riding along by the synagogue on the sabbath (which was also the Day of Atonement) and I heard a *bath qol*, proceeding from the Holy One saying: Return children, apart from Elisha b. Abuyah who knows my might but still opposes me.

Although this story is frequently attested in the traditions about Elisha,[52] it does not offer a completely convincing explanation of Elisha's apostasy. For one thing, Elisha is already at the time of the *bath qol* committing a culpable offence by riding on the Day of Atonement (so M. Betsah 5.2). The fact that Elisha was committing such an obvious offence makes it likely that the event described occurred after his abandonment of Judaism. Nevertheless Elisha's lack of concern for the observance of the Torah should not disguise the fact that Elisha is still concerned that his pupil should not transgress the Law. There is no suggestion in this story that Elisha is so disillusioned with Jewish religion that he encourages others to abandon it. His refusal to observe the *halakah* is based on his convictions about his destiny and is peculiar to himself and to no one else. This story still does not give us the reason why Elisha should have provoked the divine displeasure.

It is the other event which refers to a *bath qol* which demands our attention, however. This is the account of his confusion over the position of the angel Metatron in heaven, which B at least offers as an explanation of the phrase 'cutting the plants' (lines 45–52). In this story Elisha interprets Metatron sitting in heaven as a sign that there are *two* sources of divine power. The fact that this story is omitted in J and ShS and replaced by the story of Elisha discouraging young students in the *beth ha-midrash* from pursuing their studies[53] has been taken as an indication that the story about Metatron is late.[54] Nevertheless there is some evidence to suggest that J may in fact have known of the story of Metatron but decided to omit it to avoid encouraging speculation about this angel. Some indication that this was in fact the case is given by the hint of a reference to Ecclesiastes 5.6 in J which seems to point us not only to the first part of the verse but the rest of it as well (see line 52). The verse from Ecclesiastes is, therefore, worth quoting in full:

> Do not let your mouth bring your flesh into sin, and do not say before the angel[55] that it was a mistake; why should God be angry at your voice and destroy the work of your hands[56] (my translation).

The redactor of the version in J seems to want to take full account of the rest of the verse, and it is the second part of the verse which is particularly appropriate to the account of Elisha's reaction when he saw Metatron sitting in heaven. The use of this particular verse in all the accounts of the story of the Four suggests that a more important place than is the case usually should be given to the story of Elisha's confrontation with the angel Metatron, despite the late elements found in the story. We have two accounts of this story. One is to be found in B and the other as an addition to the late mystical text Hebrew Enoch.[57] Translations of both passages are given here (p.335f.).

The version in Hebrew Enoch is more elaborate and looks like a later development of the account in B. Not only is the angel Metatron portrayed sitting on a throne like God's throne, but he is also surrounded by angelic attendants very much like God himself. So glorious is he, in fact, that Elisha was filled with the sort of trepidation more appropriate to a theophany (lines 22–23 and 27–29). In Hebrew Enoch Metatron is a judge in the heavenly court (line 9f.), whereas in B he is merely the heavenly scribe who records the merits of Israel. The different pictures of

SYNOPSIS V

	3 ENOCH 16	b. HAGIGAH 15a
1		Aher cut the plants, concerning him it is
2		written, Do not let your mouth cause your
3		flesh to sin. What does this refer to?
4	R. Ishmael said, The angel Metatron the	
5	prince of the presence, the glory	
6	of the whole heaven said to me: At	
7	the beginning I was sitting on a great	
8	throne at the door of the seventh hall	
9	and I was judging the sons of heaven,	
10	the heavenly household, by the	
11	authority of the Holy One, blessed be He. I	
12	allotted greatness, dominion, dignity, rule,	
13	honour, praise, a diadem and a crown	
14	of glory to all the princes of the	
15	kingdoms, when I was sitting in the	
16	heavenly court with the princes	
17	of the kingdoms sitting before me on my	
18	right hand and on my left by the authority	
19	of the Holy One, blessed be He.	
20	When Aher came to gaze upon the	He saw Metatron, to whom was given
21	vision of the *merkabah*, he	permission to write down the merits
22	looked at me, and he was afraid	of Israel
23	and trembled before me.	
24		Tradition teaches that in heaven there
25		is no sitting, no rivalry, no division
26		and no weariness

336

3 ENOCH 16

27 His soul was so agitated even to
28 leaving him because of fear, horror
29 and dread of me, when he saw me sitting
30 on a throne like a king and ministering
31 angels sitting before me like servants
32 and all the princes of the kingdoms
33 around me adorned with crowns. At that
34 moment Aher opened his mouth and said
35 It is true; there are two powers in
36 heaven
37 Immediately a *bath qol* came from heaven
38 from the *shekinah* saying
39 Return, backsliding children apart
40 from Aher. At that time 'Aniyel, the
41 honoured, glorified, beloved, wonderful,
42 revered and fearful prince with a
43 commission from the Holy One, blessed be He
44 came and smote me with sixty lashes of fire
45 and made me stand on my feet.
46
47
48   See lines 37–39
49
50

b. HAGIGAH 15a

Perhaps (God forbid) there are two powers

See lines 48–50

Behold they led forth Metatron and they
smote him with sixty lashes of fire.
They said to him, When you saw him
why did you not rise before him?
Power was given to him to strike out the
merits of Aher. A *bath qol* came forth and
said, Return backsliding children apart from
Aher.

Metatron reflect the different versions of the Enoch-tradition. Enoch's position as a scribe and heavenly witness is the oldest part of the tradition (Jub. 4.23; Test. Abraham Rec. B 11; 1 Enoch 12; Targum Ps. Jonathan on Gen. 5.24). On the other hand, we have evidence of Enoch as a much more exalted figure, identified with the heavenly Son of Man who sits on God's right hand and judges mankind (cf. 1 Enoch 71.14f.). The account in Hebrew Enoch presupposes a cosmology in which there are seven heavens,[58] but no mention is made of a series of heavens in B. Metatron's throne stands outside the entrance to the seventh (and highest) heaven, within which is God's throne. We must presume that Elisha was able to see both Metatron and God within the seventh heaven, in order to understand how he could have made the comment that there were two powers in heaven. In B, however, it seems that Metatron sits close to God recording the merits of Israel.[59]

The character of the story in B does not place so much of the blame on Elisha. In fact the first thing to take place after Elisha's mistaken comment is the punishment of Metatron (lines 43ff.). The comment of Elisha was just as much a mistake on Metatron's part as Elisha's, for he failed to stand up when he saw the rabbi (lines 45–48). A difference can also be seen in the comment which Elisha makes (line 35). The version in Hebrew Enoch hints that Elisha's vision merely confirmed suspicions which he already entertained that in fact there were two powers in heaven.[60] In B, on the other hand, Elisha seems to be surprised by what he has seen. What he saw was apparently completely against his preconceived ideas about the heavenly world (lines 24–26). Elisha's fault is that he blurted out a view, which all his training and theology had taught him could not be true.[61] His sin was interpreting the power given by God to an angel to sit and write the merits of Israel as a sign that there were two divine powers in heaven. Elisha should have known better and not let his knowledge of heavenly things lead him to a conclusion which struck at the heart of his theological convictions.

The exclamation of Elisha and his vision of Metatron have been regarded as very late stories, much influenced by gnostic, or even later, ideas, created in order to denigrate Elisha.[62] But the similarities with gnostic ideas are only superficial. While it is true that two powers are mentioned, Metatron is far from being the demiurge of fully developed gnosticism, for his power and authority are very much derived from God himself. Indeed, if later Jewish writers had wanted to discredit Elisha by implicating him in gnostic ideas, we might have expected much closer links with gnostic teaching. Nevertheless the fact that our two accounts come from relatively late sources may make us reluctant to use them to interpret the reason for Elisha's apostasy. But apart from the use of the name Metatron, which is hardly found in earlier literature,[63] there is nothing in the version in B which differs in any respect from ideas current in the time of Elisha and familiar to us from the apocalyptic material.[64]

As we have seen, there is early evidence to suggest that a heavenly scribe who wrote down the merits of individuals was well established in Judaism and was closely linked with the legends which developed about Enoch. In addition, we have already seen that in Jewish apocalyptic literature there was the development of beliefs about an exalted angelic figure who shared the attributes and characteristics of God himself, e.g. Apocalypse of Abraham 10 and 17f. In this apocalypse the angel Jaoel, like the angel Metatron is said to have the name of God dwelling in him (b. Sanhedrin 37b and Heb. Enoch 12) and is described with terminology more usually reserved for God himself. Such examples suggest that Elisha's position was perhaps understandable, if not justifiable. If his interest in mystical and apocalyptic matters had led him to make such a judgement as the one we find in line 35, then clearly such speculations had driven him to strike at the roots of Jewish religion. That such tendencies were not necessarily confined to Elisha can be illustrated by a debate between R. Akiba and R. Jose about the significance of the plural 'thrones' in Daniel 7.9:[65]

One passage says: His throne was fiery flames and another, Till thrones were placed and the Ancient of Days sat. There is no contradiction, one throne for God and one for David. This is the view of R. Akiba. R. Jose the Galilean said to him, Akiba, how long will you go on profaning the shekinah. Rather it is one for justice and one for mercy. Did Akiba accept it from him or did he not accept it? Come and hear; one for justice and one for mercy – this is the view of R. Akiba. R. Eleazar b. Azariah said to him, Akiba what do you have to do with the haggadah? Stop your talk and turn to leprosy-signs and tent-covering. Rather one for a throne and one for a stool; the throne to sit upon and the stool for the feet, as it is said, Heaven is my throne and earth is my foot-stool' (b. Hagigah 14a).

Concerning a passage in which the thrones are closely linked with the chariot-chapter of Ezekiel (Dan. 7.9; 'its wheels were a flaming fire' cf. Ezek. 1.15) Akiba indicates that a human being sits alongside God and is thus on the same level as God.[66] We note that Akiba feels compelled to accept the interpretation of Jose which removes the difficulty by interpreting the passage metaphorically. The comment of Akiba so disturbed Eleazar that he suggested to Akiba that he deal with matters in which he had competence and leave haggadah to others. The point of importance as far as we are concerned is that implicit in Akiba's interpretation is a similarity with the mistaken view of Elisha in suggesting that another figure could sit alongside God, apparently with equal power.[67]

Our investigation has led us to the conclusion that Elisha's occupation with the Torah led him to speculations about the heavenly world which ultimately caused his mistaken views which struck at the roots of his religion (Aher cut the plants). Whilst Hebrew Enoch 16 clearly regards Elisha as one who did expound the chariot-chapter of Ezekiel (lines 20–21), all the story in B allows us to suppose is that he was in fact interested in God and the attendants of his throne, like his contemporary Akiba. What is certain is that there was a mystical side to Elisha's life, for the apocalyptic heavenly voice was the basic reason for his refusal to return to his religion. If he had placed the traditions of his fathers before his experience, he would not have allowed himself to be haunted by a conviction that repentance was an impossibility merely on the basis of what he thought was a divine revelation.

We have thus sought an explanation of the famous story of the Four, at least in its earliest form, not as an account of a heavenly ascent but as a metaphorical description of the consequences resulting from the occupation of four teachers of the early second century in the study of the scriptures. In two cases, namely Ben Zoma and Elisha, it seems likely that they may have been fairly deeply involved in apocalyptic matters. But this arose out of their study of the scriptures as a whole, of which Genesis 1 and Ezekiel 1 were but a small part. Nevertheless these passages obviously assumed an importance out of all proportion to their position within the whole gamut of God's revelation. It was therefore necessary to offer a warning to any student of the scriptures to avoid the pitfalls of study which so affected at least two of the four. If an interpretation of the story of the four who entered the garden on these lines seems to be a diminution of its significance, we should remember that the first half of the second century AD saw traditional interpretations of the scriptures being challenged for particular ends by Christians and gnostics alike. When study of the Torah led famous teachers into heterodoxy, it is not surprising that in the story of the four an attempt should be made to offer a timely reminder to all those involved in mystical matters as to the right path to follow. The inclusion of R. Akiba in the story and the scriptural passage which is added urges the students of Torah to follow his example: 'Draw me after you, we shall make haste'.

The Later Mystical Tradition

Our study of early Jewish mysticism has shown that a detailed study of the way in which tradition developed can reveal some of the contours of esoteric speculation concerning God and the heavenly world. Clearly, by the time of the final form of the story of the four who entered *pardes* we find that the belief in the heavenly ascent formed an important part of mystical experience. This notion, which has its part to play in the earlier apocalypses, clearly dominates the mystical literature which has come down to us. The interest in the heavenly world and its secrets continued to have a significant role within Jewish religious experience. Investigation of this ongoing mystical interest is a long and complicated story taking us into the medieval period and the speculations of the kabbalistic literature.[68] But the story of Jewish apocalyptic is incomplete without some indication of the way in which some of these ideas lived on in rabbinic circles even though only the briefest glimpse can be offered here.

No discussion of Jewish mysticism can fail to acknowledge the debt which is owed to Gershom Scholem whose major studies on the subject have pioneered study in this area and offer the student a reliable guide to the later developments. His interests have not been confined to the later manifestations of mystical interest, for he it was who demonstrated how much contact must have existed between the earliest rabbinic mystics and the apocalyptic speculations which we have examined earlier in this book. Thanks to him it is becoming clear that we are not dealing with an interest which had only marginal significance for Jewish religion but, as our previous investigations have shown, was linked with some of the most prominent teachers of the tannaitic period. Thus mysticism was not considered an alternative to the observance of the Torah and the ongoing interpretation of it, for within the mystical texts which are known to us interest in mystical matters was the direct consequence of years of basic study and based upon it.[69] However much the mystical lore of Judaism may have contributed to heretical tendencies of fringe groups there was a determined effort to limit the mystical expertise to those who, on the basis of their grounding in the *halakah*, would be less likely to misrepresent Jewish religious tradition.

The character of the later mysticism is well illustrated by the so-called *hekaloth* literature, which, among other things, describes the heavenly palaces through which the mystic must journey to reach God's presence. All these texts are pseudonymous in character with the names of prominent *tannaim* like R. Ishmael, R. Akiba and R. Nehuniah b. Hakanah cited as the mystagogues.[70] The texts themselves are on the whole rather uninspired collections of accounts of the different heavens, the angelic beings which guard the entrances to them, the preparations which are needed for the ascent, extensive angelology and many hymns of praise to God. The fact that much space is devoted in this literature to the problems confronting the mystic gives weight to the supposition that we are dealing here with the literary relics of actual directions for the mystical ascent. The same is probably true of the numerous hymns[71] which enable the one who recites them to understand the transcendence of God as he approaches the most holy part of heaven. Although obviously the climax of the ascent is the ascertaining of the secrets of God's throne-chariot and the mystery of the divine nature it is evident that this attracts much less attention in these texts than we might expect.

Nevertheless interest in the form of the divinity attracted particular attention and engendered a type of mystical speculation in its own right. This consisted of fantastic descriptions of the body of God with enormous measurements being given to the different limbs of the deity. It is given the title *shi'ur komah*, the measurement of the body.[72] This speculation derived its inspiration from the highly suggestive description of God in Ezekiel 1.26f., although the lack of inhibition in the way in which God is described contrasts with the restraint of the biblical passage. Such frank anthropomorphism may seem crude in the extreme until one realizes that the measurements given are so immense that the point of speculation ultimately stresses God's majesty and transcendence.[73] Nevertheless not all commentators have been impressed with such refined theological explanations, and the Karaite writer al-Qirqisani has some very disparaging comments to make about the influence of this kind of speculation among the Jews of his own day:

> They attribute to Him (human) likeness and corporeality, and describe him with most shameful descriptions; (they assert) that he is composed of limbs and has a (definite) measure. They measure each limb of His in parasangs. This is to be found in a book entitled 'Shi'ur Qomah,' meaning the measure of the stature, i.e. the stature of the creator.[74]

The late date of al-Qirqisani and the manuscripts which contain the bulk of this type of speculation should not prevent us from accepting that this form of speculation goes back to a very early date. While our study of the apocalypses indicated that there was a growing reluctance to speak of the figure on the throne, there are signs that the seeds of the later speculation on God's form are evident in 1 Enoch 14 and Daniel 7. What is more, Scholem has offered evidence of such ideas at the time of Origen (early third century AD), when he interprets a reference in Origen's *Prologus in Canticum* to Jewish reserve towards Shir ha-Shirim as the result of a link between the description of the figure of the lover and the body of God.[75]

What is crucially important to recognize about this is that the climax of the mystical ascent does not consist of a union between the mystic and the divine but the understanding of those secrets which normal human beings are prevented from perceiving. Knowledge of the dimensions of the divine nature brings the mystic to the very heart of his religion. The point is well made in the final verses of the apocalyptic section of Revelation. After the description of the new Jerusalem John affirms that the throne of God and the Lamb will be in it (Rev. 22.3) and God's servants 'shall see his face' (v. 4). The fascinating details of the heavenly courts and the frightening aspect of the celestial guards are all incidental to this main concern, to which all the minute preparation and the endurance of danger during the ascent are subordinated.

Relics of this esoteric tradition are numerous but not readily available to those who cannot read Hebrew, and even then few Hebrew texts are available in published versions. A study of early apocalyptic is not the place to go into the detail of this material, so attention will be confined in this section to two texts which are available in English as a means of offering an introduction to this aspect of Jewish religion. The first of these is in fact not an apocalypse at all, and in its present form cannot be dated much earlier than the eighth century AD. This is the Pirke de Rabbi Eliezer.[76] Despite the fact that the work as we have it is rather late there is little doubt that it contains much earlier material, much of it having parallels in earlier rabbinic collections. It is, therefore, a useful compendium of certain aspects of rabbinic teaching concerned with mystical subjects. The document has the framework of the biblical story from creation to Exodus, though a great deal of extraneous material is included under the different chapter headings. The most significant thing from our point of view is the prominent position given to four subjects which loom large in the earlier apocalypses, namely creation (ch. 3ff.), the divine throne (ch. 4), the secrets of the calendar (ch. 7f.) and eschatology (ch. 51). The essential continuity with earlier apocalyptic speculation is evident in the following passage which describes God and his throne:

> God is sitting on a throne high and exalted. His throne is high and suspended above in the air. The appearance of his glory is like the colour of amber. And the adornment of a crown is upon his head, and the ineffable name is on his forehead. One half is fire the other half is hail, at his right hand is life and at his left is death. He has a sceptre of fire in his hand and a veil is spread before him, and his eyes run to and fro throughout the whole earth, and the seven angels which were created first, minister before him within the veil, and this is called *pargod*. His footstool is like fire and hail. Fire is flashing continually round his throne, righteousness and judgement are the foundations of his throne. And the likeness of his throne is like a sapphire throne with four legs, and the four holy *hayyoth* are fixed to each leg, each one has four faces and each one has four wings . . .

The telling of the story of Adam and Eve gives the opportunity to indulge in a discussion of Adam's sin, a subject to which certain apocalypticists had given their attention. In this account it is the envy of the ministering angels which is the fundamental reason for Adam's fall (ch. 13) and their cunning way of leading him astray by tempting him through the woman rather than directly.

Much closer in form to the traditional apocalypses is the so-called Hebrew or 3 Enoch.[77] This purports to offer a report by R. Ishmael of his journey to the seventh heaven and of the secrets which the exalted angel Metatron revealed to him. The opening chapters tell of the ascension of Enoch and the way in which he was transformed into the angel Metatron, his coronation and position of authority among the hosts of heaven. The later chapters offer extravagant angelological speculation demonstrating the way in which the nascent speculation about the angels in the earlier apocalypses has reached extravagant proportions.[78] The process which had made its start much earlier (e.g. 1 Enoch 71.7), in which different parts of the divine throne-chariot are transformed into angels reaches its climax. In Hebrew Enoch 25 the wheels of the chariot (*ophannim*) have become an angelic band. Although the bulk of this material offers rather turgid descriptions of the various inhabitants of the world above, and especially the various angelic bands which accompany the throne-chariot, towards the end of the work there is a revelation of the secrets of the future which are written on the heavenly veil.[79] As far as its cosmology is concerned, it appears to conform to that which we find in b. Hagigah 12b, where there are seven heavens, in the highest of which God is located. The hierarchy is rather complicated with the angels in each heaven doing homage to those who are to be found in the heaven above (ch. 18). The picture which emerges in this work is of a God far removed, not only from the lowest orders of angels but also the inhabitants of the earth. But there is no question of any theological dualism here, as there is a clear grasp of the fact that God is ultimately in control. That is not to say, however, that there is no room for misunderstanding in this extravagant system. As we have already seen, the position granted to an exalted angel like Metatron could easily be interpreted in a dualistic way, a fact which God's remoteness only tended to emphasize.

On reading documents such as these one may be tempted to ask whether the vast lists of divine names and the vast number of angelic beings who are mentioned are really anything more than an attempt to satisfy the curiosity of the devout about the world above. A glance at the closing sections of Hebrew Enoch reveals that precisely the same kind of concerns are emerging here as are dominant among the apocalypticists at the beginning of the Christian era. The point can be most clearly made by quoting the following passage from Hebrew Enoch 44.7–10:

> And I saw the spirits of the Patriarchs Abraham Isaac and Jacob and the rest of the righteous whom they have brought up out of their graves and who have ascended to heaven. And they were praying before the Holy One, blessed be He, saying in their prayer: Lord of the Universe, how long wilt thou sit upon thy throne like a mourner in the days of his mourning with thy right hand behind thee and not deliver thy children and reveal thy kingdom in the world . . . Then the Holy One, blessed be He, answered every one of them saying: Since these wicked do sin so and so, and transgress with such and such transgressions against me, how could I deliver my great right hand in the downfall by their hands?

As in 4 Ezra and Syriac Baruch the position of Israel in the world is a theme which is near to the heart of the writer of Hebrew Enoch. A natural consequence of the sight of God's majesty is to ask when that glory would be revealed in the world of men. As the years went by it became an ever more pressing question for Israel. This section in Hebrew Enoch seeks to offer an explanation. First of all, it stresses how much the righteous in heaven share the concern of God's people on earth. Even the archangel Michael is compelled to ask God why he seems to be so far away from his people (Heb. Enoch 44.10). The answer is a fairly conventional one. God's glory has not been revealed because of the sins of Israel. What is more, the apocalypse shows that the reason for God's apparent inactivity is his choice to place his right arm, with which he will redeem his people, behind his back. Perhaps the lengthy description of the angels makes it less apparent that the author of this apocalypse is no less concerned with the attempt to explain history than works like Revelation or Daniel. These final chapters of Hebrew Enoch are evidence of a return to that theme which had occupied the attention of most apocalypticists: the contrast between the circumstances of history in the present and the divine promises to Israel. The answer given in Hebrew Enoch is essentially that of the other apocalypses. The course of history and the appropriate time God will intervene to deliver his people are mapped out on the celestial veil.

Similar concerns emerge within the angelology and hymns of the other *hekaloth* texts.[80] Within Hekeloth Rabbati, for example, the ascent to the heavenly world is closely related to the attempt to seek an explanation of the way in which the Roman power had mistreated Israel (3f.). Here we see yet again the way in which the opportunity to gain access into the divine presence is used to elicit an answer about some of the most pressing issues of the day. The stark contrast which existed between the real world in which Israel found itself and the world of the throne-chariot of God makes it completely comprehensible why many should have felt the need to retreat to this world of light in the face of gloom which surrounded them on every side. Throughout the whole of the early Christian era there were probably few periods when Jews did not feel acutely the tension between promise and fulfilment, or rather the lack of it. Consequently the opportunity of direct contact with the world of light reinforced those ties of allegiance with God when they were strained to breaking-point. It is surely no coincidence that the theme of many of the hymns in these works is God the creator, an affirmation that a chaotic world was ultimately under the control of the one who was enthroned above the cherubim.

While it is true that at first sight early rabbinic traditions seem to stand apart from the bulk of the apocalyptic literature, our investigation has suggested that first impressions may not necessarily be a true reflection of the relationship between the two branches of literature. It is true that most of our investigation has not been concerned with the extravagant imagery used to portray the last days, such as we find, for example, in the book of Revelation. Nevertheless we have found in our examination of a small part of rabbinic tradition an aspect of rabbinic thought which appears to offer us links with some of the products of the early apocalypticists. Interest in the first chapters of Ezekiel and Genesis, and the resulting speculation on the nature of God, man, and the universe, may not have been the dominant concerns of the rabbis of the late first and early second centuries AD. It would, however, be wrong to dismiss these elements as merely an aberration of a few eccentric teachers or an irrelevant extravagance on the periphery of the essentially legalistic rabbinic religion. The fact that one of the architects of early rabbinic Judaism, R. Johanan b. Zakkai, played such a prominent part in the meditation on Ezekiel 1 suggests that we are not dealing here with a subject which was only of peripheral importance. What is more, it is clear from our examination of developments in rabbinic interest in apocalyptic matters in the decades after Johanan's death that it had assumed a position within rabbinic Judaism out of all proportion to its importance within the whole gamut of Jewish faith. The dire warning in the second part of M. Hagigah 2.1 reflects a time when there was great unease about the potential dangers arising from the speculation which both chapters engendered. Thus we are probably not faced here with a few teachers indulging in speculative pursuits while the majority regarded them with suspicion, for it is likely that most rabbis were interested in the chariot-chapter and the account of creation, though only a few allowed such activities to lead them astray from the heart of Jewish piety.

The significance of these traditions about the exposition of the chariot-chapter and the story of creation is the different perspective we gain concerning interest in such matters as compared with the apocalyptic literature. In the rabbinic texts we are dealing with traditions which tell us about the activities of real historical personages. It is precisely when we want to ascertain the setting of the visions and speculations of apocalyptic literature that we are left in the dark. Their origin is shrouded in obscurity behind the façade of pseudonymity, and the fictitious setting in the life of some great hero of Israel's past can all too easily, and with some justification, lead to the conclusion that much of the material in the apocalypses was artificially composed and does not reflect actual experiences. Our examination of rabbinic exposition of Genesis 1 and Ezekiel 1 has left us with the impression that what started as an expository exercise soon turned into a vision, as the parts of the chariot and the cosmos appeared in the imagination of the visionary. All these were enriched and enlivened by the introduction and influence of other scriptural passages, not to mention influence from the imagination of the visionary himself. These early rabbinic texts give us a glimpse into the way in which such visions may have been constructed, and so, if any of the apocalypses do contain relics of such visionary activity, it is probably the rabbinic accounts which allow us to reconstruct something of their genesis.

But that, of course, is to beg the crucial question. How far, in fact, can we legitimately consider rabbinic mysticism to be a continuation of apocalyptic? There can be no denying that differences do exist both in form and content between the apocalypses and early rabbinic texts. Our study of some of the earliest rabbinic material dealing with mystical matters has suggested that there are basic interests common to both. The fictitious settings of most of the apocalypses and the halakic niceties of the bulk of rabbinic literature should not blind us to the fact that the interests of rabbinic mysticism are in fact shared in part by the apocalypticists. Interest in God's throne and its attendants has an important part to play in the apocalypses, and moreover, the idea of revelation of what is hidden, the heart of apocalyptic, is found in the rabbinic expositions of Genesis 1 and Ezekiel 1. Not only did visions form part of the experiences of certain exponents, but this experience itself was inspired by Scripture as a whole, enabling a man to gain new insights into the mysteries of God and his world. In a real sense there was the possibility of disclosure of new insights with every exposition of the chariot-chapter and the story of creation. On each occasion knowledge of the scriptures and the biblical images were utilized afresh, and new texts were brought into use, in order to reveal the meaning and expand the available knowledge about matters as obscure as these. A glance at the visionary experience of John of Patmos shows us the way in which a variety of scriptural images came to the assistance of the seer as he sought to describe what was above and what was to be hereafter (M. Hagigah 2.1, cf. Rev. 4.1). Thus the speculations of the apocalypticists on heaven, earth, and the future of man are essentially the concerns of the rabbinic mystic. 'Concern over the mysteries' (Sirach 3.23) and 'meddling with matters that are beyond you' (ibid.) are characteristic of both movements. There is not enough evidence to suggest that apocalyptic and rabbinic mysticism should be identified. It would seem, however, that in certain respects rabbinic mysticism inherited the mantle of apocalyptic, and its esoteric lore deserves to be included in any discussion of apocalyptic at the beginning of the Christian era.

Part Five

Apocalyptic in Early Christianity

ONE OF THE dangers in isolating apocalyptic for particular attention is the tendency to ignore elements within a religious tradition which are closely related to the phenomenon under investigation. We noticed in regard to Jewish experience that belief in
the immanence of God formed an equally significant part of the
understanding of God as that contained in the ongoing apocalyptic tradition of Judaism. Likewise in early Christianity the
apocalyptic belief concerning the knowledge of God and his
mysteries is just one facet of a direct awareness of God and his
will, though the means of communicating the revelation may
differ slightly from Jewish apocalyptic. The New Testament
apocalypse illustrates the point. The inclusion of this document
in the canon is itself testimony of the important role the visions
of the apocalypticists had for the early Church, but the book of
Revelation is regarded by its author as a *prophetic* writing (Rev.
22.7), despite the fact that its framework (Rev. 1.1) and contents
put it clearly within the category of apocalyptic literature. In this
respect the book reflects one of the deep-seated beliefs of early
Christianity, that the Spirit of God which had inspired the
prophets of old had returned and was at work in the world
among the followers of Jesus. The identification of a typical
apocalypse, both in form and content, with the prophetic word
by John of Patmos is an indication that we are dealing here with
two related types of religious experience.

The first Christians believed that they had received knowledge
of God in many different ways.[1] It is apparent from Acts and
1 Corinthians that prophecy and glossolalia were fairly widespread in the early Church. The divine message imparted by
these means is seen as just as much a disclosure of God's will as
any vision. Indeed, in 1 Corinthians 14.26ff. it would appear
that the revelation of hidden things is identified with the
prophetic word: 'Let two or three prophets speak, and let the
others weigh what is said. If a revelation [*apokalypsis*] is made to
another sitting by, let the first be silent' (1 Cor. 14.29–30). For
Paul then the apocalypse was not confined to visions but
included any means by which God communicated his ways to
his elect (cf. Rom. 1.17f.).[2] Indeed, it is probably true to say that
the understanding of direct revelation from God centred mainly

351

on the inspiration of the spirit. While there was some abuse of this *charisma* within the Church (e.g. Didache 11ff.), as well as early reluctance to trust it completely (1 Thess. 5.19 and 1 John 4.1), it continued to have a significant role well into the second century.[3] The psychological implications of prophetic inspiration in early Christianity remain unclear. If one is justified in reading into Paul's advice to the Corinthians (1 Cor. 12–14) some kind of polemical tone, there may be reason to suppose that prophecy at Corinth was marked by an ecstatic state which was unacceptable to the apostle (1 Cor. 14.32),[4] as later Montanist prophecy was to mainstream Christianity.[5] Whatever the psychological state of the Christian prophet, however, it is probable that we are dealing here with an understanding of God's dealings with man which is not far removed from that found in the apocalypses. The compulsion to place the oracles on the lips of some great figure of the previous prophetic era had disappeared, at least in the earliest period, but the conviction remained the same: God speaks to his people directly through those appointed to be agents of his word. As such apocalyptic in early Christianity must be seen as part of the much wider phenomenon of charismatic religion which characterized the Christian movement.

The same point can be made also about the way in which early Christians expressed their conviction about their relationship with God in Christ.[6] In Paul's view the new life in Christ was characterized by the indwelling spirit (Rom. 8.9). This was the mark of being 'in Christ' and led Paul to talk of the believer both as an individual and corporately as the locus of God's dwelling in the world (1 Cor. 3.16; 6.19).[7] The idea of the community as the temple of the Holy Spirit is just one aspect of the way in which early Christian writers emphasized the immanence of God with the community of believers. Thus not only does God manifest himself through words of rebuke and exhortation and acts of power, but by his indwelling in the individual through the Spirit living testimony is offered of his presence through lives which are beings transformed after the pattern of Christ's (2 Cor. 4.11; Gal. 5.24). In not dissimilar terms the author of the Fourth Gospel speaks of the individual who loves Christ and keeps his commandments as the one to whom the Father and the Son will come and with whom they will make their home (John 14.23). The mutual indwelling, which is such a distinctive feature of the Farewell Discourses, likewise stresses the presence of God in the world. Indeed, the ongoing life of the community represents a continuation of the mission of the Son (John 20.21), whose life was dedicated to the fulfilment of his Father's will (John 7.16).

These are just a few of the ways in which early Christian writers spoke about the relationship between God and his world. Detailed consideration of them would take us too far away from our immediate task: to trace the impact of one mode of revelation on early Christianity. Although it would be a mistake to think of apocalyptic as in any way separate from these ideas, it would appear that with apocalyptic we are dealing with a religious outlook whose contours are distinctive enough for us to differentiate it from related ways of experiencing the divine. Of course, it is easier to make the division in Judaism than in early Christianity. In the latter the idea of inspiration and God-given, direct revelation, independent of the normal channels of divine communication, such as the Torah, is a much more widespread phenomenon, whereas in Judaism the distinctive perspective of apocalyptic, while not unique,[8] was not merged within the total charismatic framework as it was in early Christianity. Providing that we remember that apocalyptic forms a part of a much larger complex of beliefs concerning the possibility of man's direct relationship with God, it is entirely appropriate to examine the contribution which Jewish apocalyptic made to early Christian thought.

Discussion of apocalyptic within early Christianity has been much influenced by preconceived ideas about the essence of Jewish apocalyptic. At the beginning of this study we saw how there was a tendency to assume that it was a relatively simple exercise to specify the theological characteristics of apocalyptic. The concentration on these characteristics of apocalyptic has tended to dominate the way in which the relationship between Jewish and Christian apocalyptic has been studied. In practice, apocalyptic in early Christianity usually refers to a certain body of eschatological beliefs, centring on the return of the heavenly Son of Man, the doctrine of the two ages, the cosmic disorders which precede the end and the hope for a new world beyond this one.[9] In his summary of apocalyptic which precedes his study of it in early Christianity, P. Vielhauer correctly enumerates the *literary* characteristics of the apocalypses, but it is clear that, as far as he is concerned, it is the *theological* characteristics

of Jewish apocalyptic which are more important for understanding its impact on early Christianity.[10] As we saw earlier,
many of these characteristics of apocalyptic are either too infre-
quent in the apocalypses to be considered in any way typical or
merely part of the eschatological beliefs of Judaism at this time,
and as such hardly deserving to be labelled apocalyptic. Consequently, the examination of apocalyptic in early Christianity
tends to concentrate on eschatological material of a particular
type rather than to investigate the way in which the spirit of
apocalyptic, as it has been outlined in this study, has made its
presence felt in New Testament theology. Thus the investigation
of apocalyptic in Christianity is usually the attempt to trace the
way in which early Christians imbibed a type of eschatology,
which, it is thought, corresponds to that which is contained in
the apocalyptic literature.

Typical of recent study of apocalyptic in early Christianity is
the survey of J. D. G. Dunn, which owes much to the discussion
of the subject by Vielhauer.[11] Dunn lists a number of essential
literary characteristics of Jewish apocalyptic (pseudonymity, the
survey of the whole history, its esoteric character, etc.) and then,
on the assumption that they too are characteristic of the whole,
adds a number of theological characteristics (two ages, pessimism and hope, the eschatological climax, imminence of the
end, supernatural and cosmic dimensions, and divine
sovereignty and control). On the basis of this characterization he
then turns to the New Testament.[12] He starts with John the
Baptist and argues that the element of judgement by fire is
influenced by apocalyptic. He rightly points to the links between
the Baptist and Jesus and detects the following examples of
apocalyptic theology in Jesus' teaching: a) Language of the two
ages (Mark 3.29 etc.) and particularly the kingdom of God, is to
be understood 'as a radically superworldly entity which stands
in diametric opposition to this world.' b) The dualism between
light and darkness, this age and the age to come, is to be found
in Jesus' conviction that the present age was one which was
dominated by spiritual powers opposed to God (Mark 1.23–27;
3.22ff.) c) In the eschatological teaching the trials preceding the
end (Mark 13.14ff.), the cosmic catastrophes and the belief in
resurrection are all said to indicate apocalyptic influence (Mark
12.25f.) d) The supernatural and cosmic events of the end-time
(Mark 8.38), e) The proclamation of the kingdom underlines

Jesus' 'belief not only in its transcendent character but also in the divine sovereignty which controls events leading to its full establishment.'

Similarly when he examines the teaching of the early Church, Dunn points to the resurrection of Jesus, the belief in his imminent return and the hope of a renewed community centred on Jerusalem as signs of apocalyptic influence. Elsewhere in early Christian literature passages like 1 Thessalonians 4.16 and the final form of Mark 13 are seen as testimonies to the abiding influence of this type of religion. So that he can conclude that 'Christianity began as an apocalyptic sect within Judaism . . . which in its apocalypticism was in substantial continuity with the message of the Baptist and Jesus.'[13]

Some of these ideas do have some parallels in the Jewish apocalypses, and, in the case of the notion of the divine control of history, we have a significant link with the eschatology of the apocalypticists, particularly in passages like Mark 13.20 and 2 Thessalonians 2.3ff. Likewise Jesus speaks of the trials and tribulations which must be endured before the elect are finally vindicated (Mark 13.7ff.). But to speak of these ideas as distinctively apocalyptic is unjustified. The messianic woes and the divine control of human history are both ideas which are to be found elsewhere in Jewish eschatology.[14] What Dunn has indicated is the way in which eschatology dominated early Christian theology. Most of the ideas he collects point to early Christianity as an eschatologically-orientated community, whose expectation about the future is distinguished, not so much by the so called 'apocalyptic' elements, but by the earnest conviction that the hopes of Judaism were already in the process of being realized. They believed that the final climax of history was imminent, not because they had utilized a particular brand of eschatology, but because their beliefs about Jesus and their experience of the Spirit had led them to understand their circumstances in this particular way. The early Christians coincided with those apocalypticists, who expected an imminent coming of the kingdom, only in respect of their common belief that history itself appeared to them to justify such an expectation. For some apocalypticists it was the political circumstances of their day, whether it be the desecration of the Temple by Antiochus or its destruction by Titus which fired eschatological expectation; for the early Christians it was their belief that God had raised Jesus from the dead, and as a result, he had become the first of those who would be raised from the dead in the near future (1 Cor. 15.20).

The question arises, however, whether we can speak of New Testament apocalyptic if we ignore those eschatological passages whose contents have earned them the label 'apocalyptic'. Revelation immediately springs to mind as an obvious example of apocalyptic in early Christianity. Here is a whole book which purports to contain disclosures in the form of visions about God's plans for his world. In this it is completely consistent with what we have ascertained about apocalyptic in Judaism. Its emphasis is on the disclosure of that which hitherto had been hidden but which God permitted the seer to ascertain by means of visions.

Into the same category as Revelation fall the various reports of visions which we have in early Christian literature. In these the recipients clearly believe that they see something normally hidden from them which has a profound impact on their outlook on life. Although not forming part of a longer apocalypse with a whole series of disclosures, the accounts of visions in early Christian literature evince exactly the same kind of outlook as is found in Jewish apocalyptic. Indeed, in the case of the visions which Paul alludes to in 2 Corinthians chapter 12, the example is so akin to what we may term the traditional heavenly journey in apocalyptic literature that we have further confirmation that we are dealing with the same kind of piety.

It will be seen from this that the emphasis in this study of early Christian literature is on the way in which the distinctive spirit of the Jewish apocalypses has manifested itself in the New Testament. It is not, therefore, a catalogue of all the possible links which exist between the New Testament writings and the Jewish documents. That there are other contacts must be freely admitted, particularly with regard to the topic of eschatology. Nevertheless this study does not set out to point to all these links, which, in most instances, were borrowings from the common stock of Jewish eschatology. Rather it is our concern to show how the quest for knowledge of the divine through revelation and the theological beliefs which attended such a quest have infiltrated the thought-world of early Christianity. It is, therefore, a question about the impact of a 'vertical' rather than a 'horizontal' way of thinking on early Christian doctrine.[15] Apocalyptic may have contained eschatological teaching, but the point cannot be denied that its hope for the future on a horizontal plane is always matched by the conviction that on a vertical plane these hopes already in some sense existed with God and could be ascertained by the visionary fortunate enough to enter God's presence and receive this information. It is this aspect of apocalyptic which particularly demands our attention here.

CHAPTER 13

Reports of Visions in Early Christian Literature to AD 200

The Gospels

SINCE THE TIME of J. Weiss and A. Schweitzer there has been much debate about Jesus' attachment to apocalyptic, which, of course, is usually taken to mean a particular brand of eschatological teaching.[1] In recent study of the teaching of Jesus there has been a tendency to admit that, while Jesus may well have been influenced by the eschatological teaching of Judaism, there is an absence of the distinctive features of apocalyptic from his message. The message of the kingdom stresses the fact that the age to come has already made its start in his own ministry (Luke 11.20).[2] There are signs that Jesus shared with the apocalypticists some of the eschatological beliefs of the first century, particularly the idea of the messianic woes and a degree of historical determinism (Mark 13.8ff.). But while it may be true that some of the characteristic features of the apocalypses are absent from the teaching of Jesus and are replaced by the parables, it would seem to be a mistake to suppose that Jesus remained unaffected by the thought-world of apocalyptic. Indeed, there is evidence to suggest that on certain occasions Jesus did receive visions which resemble the visions of apocalyptic.[3]

According to all our sources a decisive event took place in Jesus' life when he was baptized by John at the river Jordan.[4] Reconstruction of the nature of this experience and the significance which it had for Jesus is not easy. Doubt has frequently been cast on the historicity of the details of the account, even if it is conceded that Jesus did actually undergo some kind of dramatic spiritual experience at his baptism.[5] Despite the similarity which exists between the various versions in the four Gospels (and for that matter that contained in the Gospel of the Ebionites in Epiph. *Pan.* 30.13, 7) the slight differences which are to be found give some indication of the way in which the story developed and was understood by later writers.

Matthew's addition in chapter 3.13–15 indicates a certain embarrassment on the part of the evangelist over the fact that Jesus the messiah appears to have needed to have been baptized by a less important figure. In Matthew the experience of Jesus has been made a public proclamation of his messiahship, as is demonstrated by the way in which the verb 'he saw' is moved to a position after the reference to the open heaven (Mark 1.10, cf. Matt. 3.16; Luke 3.21). The process is continued in Matthew 3.17, for here the heavenly voice no longer addresses the remarks to Jesus alone but to anyone who happened to be listening. Mark's description of the incident suggests that it was a private experience.[6] Indeed, the language is remarkably similar to the introduction of Ezekiel's vision of God: 'the heavens were opened and I saw visions of God' (Ezek. 1.1) as well as other visionary reports in the New Testament and elsewhere in Jewish tradition (e.g. Acts 10.11; 7.56; Rev. 4.1; John 1.51).[7] The addition in Matthew 3.13ff. and Luke's attempt to objectify the incident by making the descending spirit into a dove (Luke 3.22 'the Holy Spirit descended upon him in bodily form as a dove', cf. Mark 1.10 'the Spirit descending upon him *like* a dove') indicate that it is the Marcan version which is the least pretentious and most likely to preserve the original version of the story subsequently modified by the other evangelists.[8]

Although it may be possible to point to the version in Mark as the earliest version of the story, we must ask whether we are justified in finding in this version any reminiscence of the experience of Jesus himself. Many commentators tend to answer this question in the negative.[9] Dibelius, for example, argues cogently that, if in fact we had a reflection of Jesus' own experience at Jordan in these words, the event would have been passed on as a saying of Jesus rather than a story recorded in the third person.[10] In the light of visionary reports in the Old Testament and elsewhere in the New Testament this objection appears to have considerable force. Indeed, another saying of Jesus, which we shall have reason to examine in more detail later, Luke 10.18, takes the form of a report by Jesus himself of the sight of Satan falling from heaven. The difference with the latter, however, is that it is incorporated in a context consisting mainly of sayings of Jesus. By contrast, the account of the baptism is in a narrative framework. We must ask, therefore, whether it is this narrative framework which has been the reason for the change from an autobiographical account to the narrative form in which we find the baptism story in canonical gospels. By way of comparison we may refer to the vision of Peter reported in Acts 10.11.[11] This is found in a narrative context, and the vision itself is described in the third person. It seems likely, therefore, that in the course of transmission, when such stories as these were given some kind of framework, experiences which may originally have been reported in the first person were altered when inserted into a narrative to fit that particular context. After all, it would have been most inappropriate at this point in the gospel for the evangelists to have preserved an account of Jesus' baptism in the first person, when the story gives no indication that this was the moment when Jesus reported what he had seen. Thus it seems likely that the lack of any direct report from Jesus is the result of the influence of the context in which the vision now finds itself. Indeed, we can see that the pronouncement by God in Mark 1.11 has been changed from the second person to the third person in Matthew 3.17. In other words, the Matthew version has a perfectly rounded narrative which does not include any hint of an original autobiographical account, whereas the Mark version possibly retains in the words of the voice from heaven some indication of the personal nature of the experience as originally recorded.[12]

Thus a greater measure of authenticity must be allowed for this account of the beginning of Jesus' ministry.[13] This does not, of course, exclude the possibility that the baptism may have been preceded by a much longer period of preparation, as well as a propensity on Jesus' part to expect revelations from God. The evidence does not allow us to speculate further on this, however, and we are left with the baptism as the decisive moment in Jesus' life when he became conscious of a vocation to act as the eschatological emissary of God.

When examining the story, it is by no means easy to explain why the early Church should have invented the form of visionary experience which is mentioned in our sources. Indeed, the history of research into the baptismal accounts shows how difficult it has proved to be to make sense of the reference to the descending dove. For that matter, the variety of opinion which exists concerning the origin of the words of the heavenly voice shows that, unlike the temptation narrative in Matthew and Luke, we are not dealing here with a mere repetition of Scripture.[14] In this respect the use of the Old Testament in Revelation may be important as an illustration of the way in which Scripture has been used in visionary material. There are numerous allusions to the Old Testament, yet, as W. G. Kümmel points out, 'there is not a single word for word quotation.'[15] This shows how a mind saturated in the scriptures can utilize the imagery to express the character of the vision. There is no conscious attempt to quote Scripture. It is just the case that the many facets of the Bible, especially those with a visionary content, tend to determine the way in which the visionary expresses his experience verbally. The elusive nature of the significance of Jesus' baptism is best explained in a similar way.

Interpretation of the significance of what Jesus saw and heard is no easy matter. Our interest centres here on the vision rather than the meaning of divine sonship, which is the divine proclamation to Jesus. Although the Spirit is closely linked with the inspiration of the prophets in the Old Testament (e.g. Ezek. 8.3; Isa. 61.1), the comparison of the Spirit with a dove is somewhat perplexing, to say the least.[16] It would appear, however, that the tendency which we have noted in Luke to *identify* the Spirit with the dove marks a move away from the original intention of the account, which regarded the reference to the dove as a way of describing the descent of the Spirit rather than the form of the Spirit itself.[17] Thus it was the way in which the dove came upon Jesus, rather than its outward form, which attracts such a comparison. If we take it in this way, one must ask whether the often-quoted rabbinic story concerning Simeon b. Zoma should be rehabilitated to explain the significance of the descent of the dove.[18]

In this story, which we have already discussed in another context,[19] the early second century teacher Simeon b. Zoma is reported to have meditated upon the first chapter of Genesis, and, as a result, to have gazed on the small gap which existed between the upper and lower waters. This vision led him to compare the small amount of room which there is when a bird

362 The Open Heaven

hovers over its nest. In the version of the story which we find in
the Babylonian Talmud the hovering of the spirit of God is
compared to a dove. It is this version, we suggested, which
probably reflects the earliest version of Ben Zoma's meditation
and indicates that within the cosmological speculations of rabbinic Judaism the hovering of the spirit over the waters could be
likened to the way in which a dove hovers over her young.

Now while there is nothing in the story of Jesus' baptism to
suggest that he was particularly interested in the celestial waters, it is by no means impossible that Jesus was interested in the
story of creation at his baptism, and it is this which may have
given to the baptismal vision its distinctive character. If Jesus
had thought at all about the Spirit of God it would only be
natural for his thoughts to have turned to the reference to it in
the first chapter of Genesis. If so, any consideration of Genesis
1.2 could easily have led to a comparison of the activity of the
Spirit with the bird hovering over its nest. Such a comparison is
likely, in view of the fact that of the two other occurrences of the
verb *riḥeph* in the Hebrew Bible one is used definitely of a bird
hovering over the nest (Deut. 32.11).[20] Consequently any
thought about the Spirit of God in Genesis 1.2 would have led
to a comparison of its movement with that of a bird. But two
questions present themselves: first, why should Jesus have been
thinking at that particular moment about the Spirit of God; and
secondly, why should his thoughts have turned to the first
chapter of Genesis?

It hardly needs to be pointed out that the message of John the
Baptist was thoroughly eschatological. This means that Jesus at
his baptism must have been very conscious of a fervent eschatological expectation which was engendered by John's preaching.
As C. K. Barrett has put it: 'Jesus' acceptance of John's baptism
meant that he was moving in the same circle of prophetic and
eschatological concepts as the Baptist.'[21]

Thus on the occasion of his baptism Jesus must have been
very much aware that a new act in salvation-history was to take
place in the near future. Indeed, in several sayings of Jesus the
decisive nature of John's preaching within the divine plan is
stressed (Luke 16.16), which shows that even after his call Jesus
acknowledged the immense importance of John for his own
understanding of the circumstances of his mission.

According to our sources part of John's eschatological preaching involved a reference to the Holy Spirit (Mark 1.8; Matt. 3.11; Luke 3.16).[22] Although there are differences between Matthew and Luke on the one hand and Mark on the other, there does not seem any good reason to deny the presence of a reference to the Spirit in John's preaching. Indeed, it fits well with what we know of Jewish expectation at the time of Jesus that the last days would be marked by a return of the Spirit (e.g. Tos. Sotah 13.2), though this is usually seen as the inspiration of prophecy rather than as a purifying force.[23] So Jesus would have been encouraged by John's own preaching to expect the coming of the Spirit.

It has become clear that the eschatological imagery of Judaism was very much influenced by the notion of the return of the universe to its pristine state at the creation.[24] So the Spirit of the end-time would be none other than that same Spirit which had hovered over the waters at creation. In some such way as this, it could be argued, Jesus had linked the Spirit spoken of by John with the Spirit mentioned in Genesis 1. But while Genesis 1 may have formed the framework for his vision, unlike Ben Zoma, he did not watch in a detached way a particular part of the cosmos but saw that Spirit which had been active in creation coming towards himself. It had ceased to be merely part of an earlier aeon but had now descended upon him and led him to conclude that he was the anointed agent of God (cf. Luke 4.16).

The important thing to note about the baptism of Jesus is that a vision marked the decisive moment in his life, which convinced him that he was to be the one who was to inaugurate God's kingdom.[25] Although the words of the heavenly voice speak of the personal relationship between God and Jesus, the vision is not merely a private experience assuring the individual of his own destiny but one which leads its recipient to the service of God. In this respect Jesus is at one with the prophets of old whose call-visions were always the preludes to the more important activity of acting as spokesmen of God (Isa. 6.8; and Ezek. 2.1). Thus visions, whatever their contents and however extensive the information which may be offered in them, are ultimately subordinate, and a prelude, to the task to which the visionary believes himself to be called. Interest in the contents of the vision and the experience for its own sake is something which is alien to the Old Testament accounts and, in the case of his baptismal experience, to Jesus as well.

If we find ourselves in some difficulty over the reconstruction of precisely what Jesus experienced at his baptism and have to resort to conjecture to explain the significance of the imagery used in the account, we are in a worse predicament when we turn to the story of Jesus' temptation in the wilderness. In comparing the accounts in the synoptic Gospels we find a considerable difference between Matthew and Luke on the one hand and Mark on the other. The bald statement in Mark that the temptation took place over a period of forty days (Mark 1.12f.) is expanded by both Matthew and Luke. Despite the difference in the order of the second and third temptations both produce substantially the same versions of the three temptations. There were probably several versions of the temptation story circulating in the early Church,[26] and it is not easy to consider the detail of the versions in Matthew and Luke as authentic reflections of the debate which was going on in Jesus' own mind about the nature of his ministry.[27] Indeed, the way in which the book of Deuteronomy has influenced the present form of the temptation story in these two Gospels points in the direction of later reflection.[28] But the witness to this event in various parts of the early Christian literature suggests that there is a historical nucleus to the story. Reference to fasting, for example, is reminiscent of the preparations mentioned in some apocalypses for visions (Matt. 4.3; Luke 4.2, cf. Dan. 10.2).[29] Whether the sight of the kingdoms of the world and the placing of Jesus on the pinnacle of the Temple have any basis in the experience of Jesus cannot now be decided.[30]

That Jesus did have a vision, in which he at least witnessed the fall of Satan, is confirmed by the isolated saying in Luke 10.18, which is uttered by Jesus in its present context after the disciples return from their mission and report to him the way in which the unclean spirits have been subject to them: 'And he said to them, "I saw Satan fall like lightning from heaven." '[31]

The context certainly suggests that Jesus saw the fulfilment of the fall of Satan in the glad tidings which his disciples brought to him about the subjugation of the powers of darkness, though it would not be correct to suppose that Jesus' words are to be understood merely as a picturesque comment on the disciples' activity.[32] The authenticity of the saying is not often doubted, though the meaning is obscure.[33] What we have here is not an account in the first person of a vision as it happens in the style, say, of Acts 7.56, but a reference by Jesus to an experience which happened some time previously, whose contents are recalled at a later time (cf. 2 Cor. 12.2ff.). Whether the present context (that is after the return of the seventy) is original is uncertain. It is more likely to reflect the concerns of the redactor of this section who found an appropriate saying which served as a comment on the success of the disciples. But whatever its original setting in the life of Jesus, the indications are that Jesus here recalls a visionary experience which had important consequences for his understanding of his ministry. That this is the case is confirmed by the way in which he speaks in similar terms to the vision in parables like Mark 3.22ff., cf. Matt. 12.24ff. and Luke 11.15ff. His exorcisms mark the practical outworking of the conviction which is expressed in this visionary report. Satan has fallen from heaven, and the dominance of the power of evil has been eradicated.

Two other New Testament passages may cast light on this saying. In language which is completely devoid of the apocalyptic traces which we find in Luke 10.18, John 12.31 expresses a similar conviction, when it speaks of the ruler of this world on the point of being cast out.[34] Judging from its present context it would appear that this saying also is an isolated logion with a history in the Johannine tradition before its inclusion here.[35] John chapter 12, verses 31 and 32 look like two separate sayings which have been put together here because of their relevance to the theme of judgement and its link with the cross of Jesus. Unlike its synoptic counterpart this saying refers to the ejection of the ruler of this world as an event which is still to take place. Despite the element of futurity, the adverb 'now', and the following saying about the lifting up of Jesus from the earth, indicate that the moment of judgment is to take place when Jesus is lifted up on the cross.

Much closer in every way to Luke 10.18 is the vision of John recorded in Revelation 12.7ff. In contrast to John 12.31 this vision of the war in heaven refers to a glimpse which the seer is permitted to have of an event which had already taken place.[36] The decisive victory by Michael over the powers of Satan had already been won, and as a result Satan could no longer stand in God's presence to act as accuser of the elect. Instead Michael, the representative of God's people before the celestial tribunal (Dan. 12.1, Slav. Enoch 22.6; 33.10), is able to put the case of the elect with impunity. The ejection of Satan from heaven is a cause of rejoicing for the elect (Rev. 12.10), as there is no one in heaven to prevent them achieving their eternal destiny. They now have to be aware of Satan, who has come down to earth to wreak havoc in the short time that is left to him (Rev. 12.12). Although the earthly consequences evident in John's vision are not explored in the report of Jesus' vision (though they may be hinted at in v. 19f.), the idea of the fall of Satan is a theme which is seen by both visionaries as having decisive consequences for salvation-history. In their different ways both visions stress the consequences of an event in heaven for the history of mankind. The fall of Satan is the prelude to a dramatic change in the relationship between God and man; in both it is an event of eschatological significance.[37] Within the framework of Jesus' teaching this account of a vision indicates that Jesus had witnessed such an event in his visionary state and was convinced that he was seeing the consequences of what he had glimpsed in his vision being realized through the establishment of God's kingdom in earth.

Despite the fact that reports about visions play a very small part within the framework of the gospel-tradition as a whole, the examples which are to be found focus on the very heart of Jesus' mission. To that extent we can suggest that visions may have played a central role in directing Jesus' understanding of his office, though, as we have argued, their importance did not lead to any excessive attachment to the experience itself at the expense of the mission for which they provided the impetus.

Before turning to reports of visions outside the Gospels consideration must be given to one passage in the synoptic Gospels which is to be regarded as an experience of the disciples rather than Jesus himself. The Transfiguration is mentioned in all three synoptic Gospels, and its position in the Gospel of Mark so soon after the confession of Peter suggests that it has a role to play in the revelation of divine sonship which goes on throughout the gospel, a point confirmed by the use of the isolated logion in chapter 9.1 as the prelude to the story.[38] Thus in our earliest gospel we have a story which plays a very important part within the structure of the Gospel as a whole. The character of the story has led commentators to ask whether it is an intrusion into the earthly life of Jesus of Nazareth, and the suggestion has been made that we have here a misplaced resurrection story.[39] Nevertheless there have been those who have interpreted the story as a vision experienced by the disciples, and the viability of this interpretation has been championed by Lindblom.[40] It is true that there are similarities with certain Old Testament theophanies, particularly in respect of the prostration of the disciples (in Matt.) (Ezek. 1.28), the heavenly voice (Gen. 22.11) and the glorious appearance of Jesus (cf. Dan. 10.5f.). But two passages in particular call for our attention.

The description of Abel in the Testament of Abraham (Rec. A) 12 and the Great Glory on the throne in 1 Enoch 14.20 are not dissimilar to the description of the transfigured Jesus.[41] In 1 Enoch 14.20f. two aspects of the divinity are mentioned, his clothing ('his raiment was like the sun, brighter and whiter than any snow') and his face. Precisely these two elements are mentioned in Matthew 17.2 and Luke 9.29, though no mention is made of Jesus' face in Mark.[42] The presence of a man with shining raiment is thus remarkably like the two passages just quoted, both of which are intimately linked with the vision of the throne-chariot. No less than five words are used in both the Greek of 1 Enoch 14.20f. and the synoptic accounts of the Transfiguration, namely, sun, face, white, snow (in some manuscripts)[43] and the clothing (which involves a different Greek word, *himatia* in the Gospels and *peribolaion* in 1 Enoch). What is more, the word translated 'dazzling' *(exastrapton)* in Luke 9.29 is reminiscent of the use of the word *astrape* (lightning) on two occasions in 1 Enoch 14 (vv. 11 and 17, cf. Ezek. 1.4). Indeed, in the description of the angel in Daniel 10.6, the appearance of that being is said to resemble lightning. Finally, as we have already noted, Matthew 17.6 has the disciples falling on their faces, a typical reaction to a theophany or angelophany (cf. Ezek. 2.1; Dan. 10.9). These similarities suggest that it is in the direction of the apocalyptic theophanies and angelophanies that we should look for an explanation of the material in this passage.

In addition, the similarity with the vision of the risen Christ in Revelation 1.13ff. suggests that such views of Jesus were not out of the ordinary in the early Church. The categories in which Jesus is described go beyond anything which we know about the messiah.[44] Whoever saw the vision and whatever the occasion, attributes more usually linked with God himself or his angelic envoy have here been given to Jesus.[45] Whether Peter and his companions could have seen Jesus in this light before the resurrection cannot now be ascertained. The fact that this story continued to be a part of the pre-Easter tradition about Jesus makes the objections to taking the story as a misplaced resurrection-appearance very weighty indeed.[46] It would, therefore, be a mistake to exclude the possibility that we have in this story a reflection of an experience when certain disciples, and particularly Peter,[47] may have believed that they had seen Jesus in the form of an angelic envoy. Whether such a vision ever formed part of Jesus' self-disclosure can no longer be decided,[48] though it would appear to be most unlikely.

The Acts of the Apostles

Equally difficult to evaluate is the account of the experience of the disciples on the day of Pentecost.[49] The reason is that this account is now closely bound up with Lucan redaction, not to mention his own understanding of the significance of glossolalia.[50] The question is whether we have any historical nucleus to this story at all. Our particular concern is not with the phenomenon of glossolalia but the vision which appeared to the Christian group as they assembled together. That the phenomenon of the flames of fire is to be interpreted as a vision is indicated by the use of the verb 'appear' (ophthesan), which is to be found elsewhere in Acts and the New Testament as an introduction to a description of what was seen in a vision (Luke 1.11; Acts 9.17; 26.16; 1 Cor. 15.6ff.; Rev. 11.19; 12.3).[51] Study of Jewish traditions about the Feast of Weeks has naturally gone on in order to assist in the interpretation of the passage as a whole,[52] and it is the close link between this festival and the giving of the Torah on Sinai which has attracted most attention. As we know from Exod. 19.16 fire was a prominent feature of the theophany in the description of the giving of the Torah. According to b. Megillah 31a the first chapter of Ezekiel was the reading from the prophets for this particular festival. Indeed, reference to tongues of fire is often found in rabbinic legends about the exposition of the Torah.[53] Such a Jewish background could well have provided the raw material for such a vision as the one described in Acts 2.3, but whether the presence of this feature is a reflection of Luke's sources or the contribution of the redactor himself is now impossible to tell. One can only echo E. Lohse's comment on the Pentecost account: 'The most one can say is that very probably Luke utilized a tradition concerning the first outbreak of mass-ecstasy in Jerusalem.'[54]

Any hesitation which we may have had with the last two stories is less necessary with two further accounts of visions in Acts, the vision of Stephen and that of Peter before the conversion of Cornelius. Stephen's vision in Acts 7.56 is typical of apocalyptic. As in the Mark version of the baptism of Jesus it is said that the heavens open, and the proto-martyr has a glimpse of God with the Son of Man standing at his right hand though, unlike the baptismal vision of Jesus, this does not serve as a means of authenticating the divine call. Visions in such a setting as this have parallels in other literature,[55] and it serves as a final assurance to the dying martyr that he has been accepted by God, and, at the same time, a sign of rejection of the opponents' point of view.[56] A superficial glance at the passage might suggest that it was the claim to visionary experience which led the mob to react so violently against him.[57] Nevertheless it is clear from Acts 7.54 that it was what he had said in his speech which had so inflamed his hearers. Their reaction to him was dictated by his indictment of Jewish disobedience to God. According to Luke, Stephen's words had already angered his hearers, and, when he started to claim a vision of the heavenly world, they did not want to hear any more (v. 57).

There can be little doubt about the authenticity of the vision. Despite the appropriateness of the vision for Luke who wanted to stress the absence of Jesus in heaven until the Parousia (Acts 1.11), Luke is using a source here. This is indicated by the way in which he relates the contents of the vision twice, and the occurrence of the phrase 'Son of Man', unique in Acts. On the first occasion (v. 55) he uses his own words to describe what Stephen saw, leaving the reader in no doubt that it was in fact Jesus who appeared to Stephen.[58] The verse is full of Lucan vocabulary, viz. the verb 'look' (*atenizo*) and the reference to the filling with the Spirit (cf. Acts 4.8). It is most unlikely that Luke created the contents of Stephen's vision and then wrote a slightly different introduction to explain the contents of the vision which he had invented. Thus there is every indication that we have here, at the very least, a summary of the contents of what Stephen saw on the occasion of his martyrdom.

The meaning of Stephen's vision is, with one exception, relatively straightforward. After all Stephen only claims to see

God seated in heaven with the Son of Man standing at his right hand. The exception, of course, is the reference to the Son of Man standing in heaven. Not only is this the only use of the phrase 'Son of Man', together with the article, outside the Gospels, a matter of interest in its own right, but also the fact that the Son of Man stands rather than sits has been the subject of considerable debate.[59] Three interpretations have been offered:[60] a) Jesus stands to welcome the pro-martyr, b) Jesus stands to take up his messianic office, and c) Jesus, like the angels, stands before God. It is not our intention here to discuss the rival interpretations, save to point out that two levels of meaning are more than likely. The first two could equally well represent the Lucan understanding of the vision (of these the first is to be preferred), whereas the third may indicate the significance of the reference to standing in Stephen's own mind. As we have pointed out above, there is nothing in the vision which would lead the hearers to stone Stephen on the grounds of heretical teaching, except perhaps for the presumptuous claim to have received a vision. In the light of the story of the confrontation between Metatron and Elisha which we looked at earlier, the scene in heaven which Stephen describes leaves the hearer in no doubt of the subordination of the Son of Man to God. Unlike Metatron who continued to sit when Elisha had his vision of the dwelling of God, the Son of Man stands at God's right hand. In this respect Stephen's statement could be regarded as less open to misunderstanding than a similar comment of Jesus recorded in parallel versions in Mark 14.62 and Luke 22.69, but parallel to 1 Enoch 49.2 the Elect One 'standeth before the Lord of Spirits' (cf. Rev. 5.6). In the light of the identification which we find in the Similitudes between the Elect One and the Son of Man, this verse offers an important parallel to the standing of the Son of Man in Acts 7.56.[61] Thus the Son of Man stands in Stephen's vision precisely because that was his subordinate position in the heavenly court.

The vision of Stephen is an indication that visions did have their part to play in at least one group within the early Church. The question is whether visions also formed part of the spirituality of other groups within the early Church. After all, Stephen does appear to have been a member of a splinter-group within the Church,[62] and his religious outlook need not have been the same as that of the central figures in the primitive community.

Nevertheless, the hints which we have already had from the Transfiguration and the Pentecost story that such experiences did form part of the religion of the main group, are supported by the evidence of Acts 10.11.

According to Acts 10, one of the main reasons for Peter's subsequent decision to preach to the Gentile centurion, Cornelius, was a vision which he had received, telling him that the barriers between clean and unclean had been broken down, and, by implication, the barriers which existed between the people of God and the Gentiles. When Peter comes to justify his decision to take the gospel to the Gentiles and to eat with them (Acts 11.3), part of his argument rests on the vision he had received (Acts 11.5f., cf. 10.28). In the context of Acts the vision was part of the divine initiative which gave the impulse for the spread of the gospel. Along with the outpouring of the Spirit (Acts 10.44f.; 11.17), it was a sign that God's hand was at work in this particular enterprise.

Can we assume that Luke's portrayal necessarily reflects the historical realities of the beginnings of the involvement of Peter in the Gentile mission? Many questions have been raised about the authenticity of Peter's speech,[63] but the rest of the chapter has not escaped critical attention.[64] As far as the vision itself is concerned, doubts have been expressed about the applicability of this particular vision to the issue of preaching the gospel to the Gentiles. Its major concern seems to be the eating of foods, a fact which is borne out by the introduction to the following chapter (Acts 11.3; cf. Gal. 2.11ff.). Accordingly, it has often been suggested that a vision dealing with an incident which arose as a result of a dispute over table-fellowship has been inserted in the context of the story of the conversion of Cornelius as an illuminating comment on this particular story.[65] That Peter should have had such a vision as this at the height of the dispute about table-fellowship with Gentiles is quite understandable. But according to the context given to the vision by Luke there is no suggestion that Peter has had any reason to meditate on the consequences of the admission of Gentiles to the Church. The vision comes as a 'bolt from the blue' to prepare Peter for the arrival of the envoys from Cornelius. Although one does not want to exclude the latter possibility, it seems preferable to suppose *either* the vision has been inserted in its present context by Luke, even though originally it was intimately bound up with an incident, now unknown to us, concerning the validity of table-fellowship with Gentiles and the eating of unclean food; or Luke has retold the story of Cornelius in such a way that he wanted to stress the divine initiative in the Gentile mission by omitting any suggestion that Peter was already considering the implications of that mission, which might in turn have led to the vision. The second alternative seems to me to be the more likely, not least because we are not left to speculate about another context for the vision. In view of the fact that some kind of mission to the Samaritans had already gone ahead, it is by no means impossible that the leaders of the Church were already wrestling with the issue of Gentile admission, and, what is more important for this passage, the implications of such a decision. It is the applicability of the vision to this second point which makes it possible to see how it could originally have formed part of the complex of events associated with the preaching to Gentiles.

The vision itself has a typical feature of the revelation of the heavenly secrets, the open heaven.[66] According to Luke, Peter experienced this vision in a state of ecstasy (Acts 10.10), a point which is repeated by Peter when he comes to report the vision to the church in Jerusalem (Acts 11.5). The vision takes place at an appointed time of divine service (v. 9).[67] The verb of seeing which is used of Peter's vision (theoro) is found elsewhere in contexts describing visions (Acts 7.56; Luke 10.18; cf. Luke 24.39). Unlike Stephen, Peter does not look into the heavens but merely sees an object descending, containing a vast number of creatures. The fact that the sheet, full of the different creatures, actually descends from heaven is an indication that all the creatures contained in it are acceptable to God (cf. Rev. 21.2). In his state of hunger[68] Peter is commanded to kill and eat what is in the sheet to satisfy his hunger. But the fact that it contains animals which a Jew was forbidden to eat prevents Peter from following the command. There is then a dialogue between Peter and the divine voice (v. 14f.) about the rectitude of such an act, with the affirmation by the latter that what has been cleansed by God should no longer be considered unworthy of Peter's attention. The vision ends without Peter actually carrying out the command in the vision, but it has sufficient impact on the apostle to cause him to wonder about the precise significance of what he has seen (v. 17, cf. Dan. 7.15).

Whatever our view of the original setting of the vision, one very important point emerges from it. We have a clear example here of a vision being used, together with other extraordinary manifestations (Acts 10.44ff.), as the basis for taking decisions of far-reaching consequences (cf. Acts 11.17).[69] Whether we see the context of the vision as merely Lucan redaction or not, one cannot deny the central position which it has been given in the development of Christian ideas. It is not difficult to see why the church in Jerusalem should need to question Peter closely on this matter. The consequences of the action of Peter were so far reaching, that it is easy to see why later rabbinic tradition registers a certain degree of caution when religious experience is claimed as the basis for decisions affecting the ethical stance of the community.[70]

The disquiet is also quite apparent in early Christianity. While it would be wrong to portray James as an opponent of the charismatic element in the early Christian movement, as 'patriarch' in Jerusalem it was his task to hold the balance between the developments which owed much to belief in divine inspiration and a more traditional way of coming to decisions (Acts 15, especially v. 28).[71] The fact that James was Jesus' brother makes the possibility that we have here a dynastic authority rather than a charismatic one.[72] James's attempts to extend his authority outside Jerusalem (Gal. 2.12), however necessary they may have appeared to him,[73] are a sign that the mother church in Jerusalem wanted to keep a close watch on the way in which the views of Christian communities were developing outside Palestine. Indeed, it is significant that the emissaries from James who come to Antioch rebuke Peter for indulging in precisely that activity which the vision in Acts 10 had allowed, namely, table-fellowship with Gentiles.

The affirmation of the validity of direct inspiration in deciding how early Christians behaved must have proved extremely difficult for those whose view of authority demanded guidance only from a recognized hierarchy. Although Luke's account of the early Church gives little evidence of a rift over this issue, the seeds of dissension are present in the importance which was attached to visions by certain members of the early Church (Acts 8.26; 9.10; 10.11; 11.13; 12.9; 16.9f.; 22.17; 27.23), not least because in certain instances these visions mark a turning point in the Church's development.[74] Steps which are taken as the result of religious experience inevitably lead to dissension, as those who distrust such methods question the validity of enterprises based merely on an individual's conviction. The importance which was attached to direct revelation cut across the more conventional ways of ascertaining God's will through the interpretation of Scripture. An appeal to experience conferred on the revealed opinion an authority which, because of its directness, appeared to be more in touch with the divine will than the more laborious exegetical process, where difference of opinion was a fact of life. Experience and exegesis need not have been mutually exclusive modes of revelation, providing that the former did not put forward a view which it was difficult to justify by means of the latter. When, however, an opinion is canvassed as the divine will which seems to go against the totality of current practice, conflict between the experiential and exegetical approaches is inevitable. Thus, when Peter or Paul claimed that they were justified in their actions with regard to the Gentile mission, either in whole or in part on the basis of revelation, it became well nigh impossible to resist the question of the validity of that claim, not least as far as Paul was concerned, whose claim to apostolic authority was far less secure than that of Peter. This, of course, is an issue which keeps appearing in several of Paul's letters, and occupies his attention in the first two chapters of Galatians. However passionate Paul's appeals may appear to be and however clear he himself was about the validity of what he had experienced, the stories which were circulating about him (Acts 21.21) led to a great deal of suspicion about his claim to be an emissary of Christ (1 Cor. 15.8, cf. Acts 9.1). This necessitated a visit to Jerusalem for those claims to be examined by the church there (Gal. 2.1ff.).[75]

The Pauline Letters

Mention of Paul brings us to a discussion of those passages in the New Testament where Paul speaks of the importance of visions for his own religious life. Central among these, of course, is the story of his conversion on the road to Damascus. The problem presented by Paul's conversion still leaves many unsolved questions. Attempts to explain the event as the result of Paul's growing dissatisfaction with the life under the Law as reflected in a passage like Romans chapter 7 would be accepted by few today.[76] Whatever thoughts he was engaged in on the way to Damascus,[77] he became convinced that the criminal, whose followers he was in the process of persecuting, was in fact the messiah.

Unfortunately our information about this important event is rather scanty. It is true that we have no less than three parallel accounts of Paul's conversion in Acts (Acts 9.3–8; 22.6–11; 26.12–18). Even if we were in a position to use these accounts to identify the nature of Paul's experience, they furnish us with very little information. The indications are that Luke wishes us to understand that it was a vision that Paul experienced. Indeed, according to Acts 26.19 Paul describes what he has seen as an *optasia* (vision), a term which is used in Daniel 10.16 (Theod.) of Daniel's vision of the angel (cf. Luke 1.22; 24.23).[78] But despite the fact that we possess three versions of the story in Acts, there is evidence that in their present form they owe a great deal to Luke;[79] they cannot be used in the first instance as evidence of the nature of Paul's experience.

When we turn to Paul's own letters, we find that the apostle is distinctly reluctant to say much about the experience. While there are only a few occasions when he has reason to speak of his inner life, he exhibits precisely that concern to preserve the visions from the readers of his letters which we would expect of a Jewish rabbi.[80] Only occasionally does he allow the veil to fall away, so that glimpses of his inner life can be seen. He tells the Corinthians about his use of glossolalia (1 Cor. 14.18), and at one point is driven to speak of a heavenly ascent which he made (2 Cor. 12.2ff.). But even here the experience is described in such a way that very little is divulged about it. As far as his conversion is concerned, Paul talks occasionally of 'seeing Jesus' (1 Cor. 9.1), the decisive resurrection appearance which qualified him to be an apostle (1 Cor. 15.8f.), and makes the briefest references to the conversion in Galatians 1.12 and 16.

There has been much discussion of the nature of the appearance of Jesus to Paul, spoken of in 1 Corinthians, chapters 9 and 15, particularly in relation to the resurrection stories in the Gospels.[81] It is not our concern to review this debate at this point, but to seek to ascertain from the information available to us the character of Paul's experience. The apostle leaves his readers in no doubt in 1 Corinthians that he considers that the appearance of Jesus to himself was of the same order of importance as that to the rest of the apostles. Indeed, in both places he uses the verb of seeing (*heōrakan* in 9.1 and *ōphthe* in 15.8) when speaking of how he perceived Jesus. As has often been pointed out, Paul uses precisely the same terminology of his own experience as that of the other apostles. He is, however, forced to admit that there is a difference between himself and the other apostles, for he describes himself as 'one untimely born' (*ektrōma*). This translation disguises the fact that *ektrōma* means an 'abortion' or 'miscarriage' rather than a child born *later* than expected, which is how the historical circumstances might lead us to interpret the RSV translation. It is best, therefore, to understand this as a reference to the fact that Paul comes on the scene as a fully-fledged apostle much earlier than he should have done. He was like a premature baby, in the sense that he differed from the rest of the twelve in that he did not have that lengthy period with Jesus which was the prerequisite for apostleship. His introduction into the circle of apostleship was far too early, without the qualifications which the rest possessed but with the claim to the same authority as them.[82] As far as the character of the experience is concerned, Paul tells in these passages that he saw Jesus. It is not clear whether that meant visionary experience,[83] apprehension of a truth hitherto unrealized[84] or physical perception.[85]

When talking of his conversion in Galatians (1.12 and 16), Paul talks of God 'being pleased to reveal his son to me'. The Greek phrase *en emoi*, which is here translated 'to me' should probably be treated as a simple dative rather than indicating anything internal in the character of the disclosure.[86] What is here revealed to Paul is not the significance of Jesus so much as a vision of Jesus. Like John of Patmos Paul receives a disclosure of Jesus, a figure temporarily hidden from human gaze, but revealed from heaven to the apostle.[87]

The use of the verb *apokalupto* in the Pauline corpus is normally linked with the unveiling of people and events at the end with the exception of Romans 1.17f. and Galatians 3.23. Thus we find the verb used of the unmasking of the sons of God, that is a revelation of their identity which may not be apparent at the present time (Rom. 8.19).[88] Similarly the identity of the man of lawlessness will be unmasked in the future (2 Thess. 2.6 and 8). This is no supernatural agent of the powers of evil, even if his inspiration may be from that quarter.[89] The future will also test the real quality of a man's work (1 Cor. 3.13), for the refining fire of judgement will be a characteristic of the dawn of the future age. Nevertheless this process of unmasking is not confined to the future. For the disclosure of the gospel based on faith is something which has already taken place (Gal. 3.23) as also has the righteousness of God (Rom. 1.17). Indeed, the wrath of God, which has its origin in heaven, is already being revealed against the wickedness of man (Rom. 1.18).

Paul does not use the verb in connection with the revelation of Christ in the future. Indeed, it is used in this way only once in the New Testament at Luke 17.30. In the two cases where he speaks of the revelation of Christ he prefers to use the cognate noun *apokalypsis* (1 Cor. 1.7; 2 Thess. 1.7, cf. 1 Pet. 1.7 and 13). It seems to me that these passages should in the first instance be used as the most relevant comparison with the use of the verb in Galatians 1.16, for both have as their object Christ. In the light of 1 Cor. 1.7 and 2 Thess. 1.7 it is difficult to see how one can interpret Gal. 1.16 in any other way than as a reference to the revelation to Paul of the hidden Christ who is now in heaven. Thus we can speak of a proleptic disclosure to the apostle of one who would only be revealed from heaven to the whole world in the future.[90] Similarly the revelation of Jesus Christ which Paul talks of is a disclosure of the Lord who is now in heaven removed from human sight, and who directly commissioned the apostle.[91]

Galatians 1.12b is intimately linked with the preceding sentence. There is a clear contrast here between the *para anthropou* (from man) and *dia apokalypseos Iesou Christou* (through a revelation of Jesus Christ), interrupted by the denial that any man had taught Paul.[92] Paul affirms that he did not receive his gospel from any man but, perhaps a little unexpectedly, he does not contrast this with the phrase 'but from Jesus Christ'. Instead, he feels the need to speak of a revelation of Jesus Christ. Two points should be made here. First of all, Paul is dealing with the origin of his gospel. As such, his main concern is to contrast the suggestion of his opponents that his gospel has a purely human origin, and is therefore only indirectly linked with Christ, with his belief that it comes directly from Christ himself. Thus the comparison is between *anthropou* and *Iesou Christou*. The gospel which he has received is just as much the result of a direct confrontation with Jesus as the gospel purveyed by the other apostles. Secondly, we must consider the significance of the insertion of the word *apokalypsis*. The question inevitably arises, in response to Paul's assertion that he received his commission personally from Jesus, how this could have happened. The answer is that it was because of a disclosure of Jesus, who was now in heaven seated at God's right hand. He was temporarily unveiled to Paul in his glory and commissioned the apostle and told him the content of the good news which he now proclaimed. In the light of what we have said already about the significance of the use of *apokalypsis* in a passage like 1 Cor. 1.7, the indication is that here too we have a reference to a disclosure of Jesus, but in this instance a special privilege granted to a particular individual to see beforehand the glorious lord who would be revealed to all the world in the future. Such an interpretation is then completely consistent with the use of the word *apokalypsis* in 2 Cor. 12, where the disclosure certainly appertains to heavenly realities.[93]

In conformity with the rest of Jewish apocalyptic Paul thinks of another dimension to reality, in heaven, which is hidden to all but the select few, but which he has been privileged to know. For Paul and the apocalypticists the distinction which modern scholars make between objective and subjective appearances and visionary and spiritual perception is totally artificial. The heavenly world above was a reality, whose existence was accepted by all Jews, even if few had direct knowledge of it. On occasion, however, 'the heavens opened' or 'a door opened in heaven' and that reality became apparent to the apocalyptic seer. What had hitherto been hidden was now visible to him. As far as the seer was concerned, it was part of the same totality of reality as his normal life, the only difference being that only in extraordinary circumstances was he allowed to be directly aware of it. Thus when Paul sees the risen Lord, we may describe it as a vision of a heavenly being, but within the thought-world of Paul's day that meant the drawing back of the veil to disclose that other dimension of reality which was normally hidden. The fact that it was the risen Lord in heaven, who appeared to Paul by means of revelation, was the dominant issue for Paul, not whether he had only seen him in a vision or as a physical form. Thus one must see the conversion of Paul as a vision of essentially the same type as others mentioned by Paul, and in particular those referred to in 2 Cor. 12.1. The difference for Paul was that the Damascus vision marked the decisive step in turning the persecutor into the apostle to the Gentiles. Using language which the prophets before him had used to describe their call by God (Gal. 1.15)[94] Paul speaks of the decisive event in his life as one which God had prepared long before, that he should be the chosen instrument of his will. Like the prophets, Paul sees in his confrontation with the heavenly Jesus not only the basis for the call but the character of the commission as well. In contrast to Stephen who had been permitted to look into heaven at the end of his life, Paul had been privileged to see the exalted Lord right at the outset of his life as a Christian, and this was the decisive step in his acceptance of the messiahship of Jesus.

A glance at Acts indicates that Paul had several visionary experiences in addition to that at his conversion (e.g. Acts 22.17; 27.23). Little reference is made to these, however, in the letters. There is one exception and that is to be found in 2 Cor. 12.2ff., which speaks of a heavenly ascent made by Paul some fourteen years before the writing of that letter. The intensity of this experience had made such an impact on the apostle that he felt able to use this as an indication of his spiritual endowment.[95] It is not absolutely clear if Paul refers to this because of the claims made by his opponents in Corinth, though it has often been suggested that this in fact was the case.[96] It is probably better to assume that Paul is merely resorting to similar tactics to his opponents rather than directly matching the experiences of the false teachers with his own.[97]

In a discussion of the claim to apostolic authority (cf. 2 Cor. 11.5) it probably seems a little strange that Paul did not mention his experience on the Damascus road as an example of his visionary prowess. Its absence may indicate that this may have been one of the points at issue with his opponents, who distrusted the claim which Paul made on the basis of it (cf. Gal. 1.12). But, what is more, the fact that he does not mention it is an indication that Paul was not simply trading his own experiences with the claims of the opponents. Instead he offers the Corinthians features of his own life which, he believes, qualify him to be an apostle.[98] Such an interpretation seems to be confirmed by the section which precedes the account of the visions and revelations. In 2 Cor. 11.23ff. Paul answers the question about his position in relation to the superlative apostles, not by direct comparison, but by relating the events of his own life which he considered were the real marks of the apostolic office. There is no reason to suppose that in chapter 12 he suddenly changed to compare himself directly with his opponents. Rather, he continues a presentation of his credentials, which extended, though it pained Paul to have to boast about it (2 Cor. 12.1), to his visionary experiences.

Paul speaks of 'visions and revelations of the Lord'. This introduction seems to confirm the impression given by Acts that Paul had a number of such experiences to speak of,[99] though in the event he mentions only one (or at most two). The words translated visions (*optasia*) and revelations (*apokalypsis*) are those which we find elsewhere in the New Testament of visions (e.g. Luke 1.22; Acts 26.19) and disclosures of things in heaven (Rev. 1.1; Gal. 1.12). The presence of both words here is best interpreted as the use of synonymous expressions (cf. 1 Thess. 5.1).[100] We argued earlier that the object of the revelation on the Damascus road was the risen Christ, and there is no reason to suppose that the situation is any different here. Paul here speaks of visions when he has seen the Lord in glory.[101] Although nothing is said in the subsequent report about what Paul had seen in heaven, a comparison with other apocalyptic visions suggests that there was usually something to be seen, even if it was not always God himself, in addition to the verbal communications which the seer received (2 Cor. 12.4).[102] The fact that reference to the content of the vision is omitted in the description of the vision(s) merely reflects the reserve which Paul shows in speaking of the experience[103] and does not indicate the absence of a vision of God or Jesus. When he speaks of the revelation of Christ in 1 Cor. 1.7 and 2 Thess. 1.7, there can be little doubt that in these instances Christ is the object, not the author, of the revelation. What Paul is saying in 2 Cor. 12.1 is that the Lord who would be revealed at the climax of history had been revealed to him before this event through the medium of visions.

Paul then describes the experience itself. An examination of verses 2–4 reveals that the passage falls into a clearly defined structure with two major sections:

a. I know a man in Christ fourteen years ago.
b. Whether in the body or out of the body I do not know, God knows

c.   Who was snatched up to the third heaven

 i.   I know such a man
 ii.   Whether in the body or out of the body I do not know, God
       knows
 iii.   That he was snatched up to Paradise
        He heard unspeakable words which it is not possible for man to
        utter[104]

It is clear from the above that Paul felt the need to speak about this experience in this rather stylized way, giving only the vaguest of hints concerning the precise nature of this overwhelming experience.[105] What is not clear is whether Paul is referring to two separate experiences in the two parts of this structure, one experience which had two definite parts, of speaking of the same event in parallel terminology.[106] Most reject the first opinion in the light of the absence of any date at the beginning of the second section, a feature which is to be found in many Jewish visionary accounts (Isa. 6.1; Ezek. 1.1; Jer. 1.1ff.; Dan. 10.1; Amos 1.1; and Zech. 1.1). What is more, the absence of any indication of progression from verse 2 to verse 3 has suggested to many commentators that the third option is the one which should be favoured.[107]. But the fact that Paradise is occasionally said to be located in the third heaven (e.g. Slav. Enoch 8; Apoc. Moses 37.5) should not disguise the fact that the parallelism between the two sections is not as complete as is often supposed. Thus it is only after the man in Christ has been lifted up into Paradise that he hears the unutterable words (v. 4).

It would appear, therefore, that there is reason to suppose that we are dealing with two parts of the same experience rather than parallel accounts of it.[108] The visionary often goes through various parts of the heavenly realm before reaching his destination, the presence of God himself. As he goes, he describes the various stages of his journey through the heavens (e.g. T. Levi 2ff.; Asc. Isaiah 7ff.). It is only at the highest point of the ascent that the seer is shown the divine secrets (1 Enoch 71.3f.; Slav. Enoch 22ff.). The fact that the audition is mentioned only after the ascent to Paradise probably indicates that the latter is the final stage in the journey to the presence of God himself. Unlike the Jewish parallels, which indicate that the climax of the heavenly ascent has been reached by reference to a vision of God (e.g. Apoc. Abr. 18) or describing the seventh heaven and its inhabitants (Slav. Enoch 22), Paul merely speaks of reaching Paradise. Another difference which emerges is the absence of any reference to other parts of the heavenly world which he passed through on the way, except, that is, for the third heaven. This is certainly unusual, and the closest parallel is the vision of John of Patmos in Revelation 4.1, where the seer starts his description of his ecstatic experience by describing the climax of the visionary's ascent, the throne of God itself.[109] Nothing whatever is said in 2 Corinthians about the lower parts of the heavenly world, and the absence of other cosmological references from Paul's account is an argument for the identification of the two ascents.

While one must admit this difficulty, the fact that the audition is mentioned only after the reference to Paradise is a reason for supposing that another dimension to Paul's experience is being spoken of here. The Greek word *paradeisos*, derived from a Persian word meaning an orchard, had an important part to play in the Greek Old Testament as a way of referring to the Garden of Eden (Gen. 2.8–10, 15; cf. Ezek. 28.13), though it is used in a Hebrew form *(pardes)* in a non-technical sense in the MT of Song of Solomon 4.13, Ecclesiastes 2.5 and Nehemiah 2.8,[110] the way in which it continued to be used in later Hebrew.[111] In Jewish literature in Greek the LXX usage continued, but in some texts Paradise took on an eschatological aspect as protological ideas tended to influence the formation of eschatological beliefs (T. Levi 18.10; Rev. 2.7, cf. 4 Ezra 8.52).[112] In the present age Paradise is said to be located in heaven, to be revealed only in the last days (1 Enoch 70.4; Syr. Baruch 4.3 and 6; 4 Ezra 4.7f.; Life of Adam and Eve 25.3). In the Testament of Abraham (Rec. A) 11 and 20 it signifies the place of blessedness for the righteous[113] though in earlier literature Paradise is still located on earth (Jub. 4.22; 1 Enoch 32.3).[114]

Of all the material which has been quoted two passages in particular concern us. First of all, Revelation 22.1ff. shows that Paradise is the place where God's own presence is to be found. It may be the abode of the righteous dead, but for John the centre of the celestial city is the garden where God and his throne are to be found (Rev. 22.3). The importance of this passage is that it sees Paradise as the place where the presence of God dwells. This emphasis is also to the fore in the Life of Adam and Eve 25, where Adam is caught up to the Paradise of righteousness and sees God surrounded by angels.[115] In the light of these two passages, what Paul seems to be describing here is an ascent through the heavens until he reaches Paradise, the dwelling of God himself. It is a glimpse, in other words, of the world above as it exists now with God but which is to be revealed in all its glory in the future.

At the climax of his heavenly ascent Paul reports that he heard 'things that cannot be told' (RSV). As with the apocalyptic seers Paul's audition only comes at the end of the ascent when the apostle reaches the presence of God. Unlike the apocalypticists, however, Paul does not feel that he is in a position to communicate what he has heard. This is either because the words were in a divine or angelic language (cf. 1 Cor. 13.1),[116] or the communication was of such momentous importance that, for the time being at least, Paul felt the need to keep the mystery to himself.[117] Of these alternatives the latter seems preferable, so one can only hazard a guess at what the content of these mysteries may have been. The fact that Paul seems to have had a reservoir of divine secrets, which he disclosed as occasion demanded, may lead one to suppose that it was secret teaching of the sort we find in passages like Romans 11.25 and 1 Corinthians 15.51. Whether Paul thought that what had been revealed to him on the occasion of his ascent to Paradise could never be communicated to others is unclear. But the fact that he divulges other mysteries to his churches as the need arises may have led him to do the same with 'the things that cannot be told'.[118]

Paul's repeated emphasis in verses 2 and 4 that he was unable to comment on the precise nature of his physical state has occasioned much discussion. Clearly parallels are available which illustrate the ascent of the soul as well as a corporeal ascent to heaven.[119] The dominant view of the apocalypses stressed the corporeal ascent to heaven, but there are hints that the writers reckoned with the possibility that there was a temporary separation of the visionary from his body during his ascent (e.g. 1 Enoch 71.1; Asc. Isa. 6.10; 7.5). Rather than attempting to explain this double reference as part of Paul's polemic against Judaizers and gnostics in Corinth, we should probably follow Lindblom's suggestion and see in this reference an indication of the overwhelming impact the experience had on the apostle, with the result that he was at a loss to explain adequately how he had experienced the ascent.[120] Providing that one acknowledges the temporary nature of such heavenly ascents, there is no reason why a Jewish apocalypticist should not have reckoned with the possibility of a temporary separation of the self from the earthly body while he went into God's presence. Indeed, if the Ascension of Isaiah is anything to go by, such a separation also involved transformation during the ascent into angelic form (Asc. Isa. 7.25, cf. Slav. Enoch 37.1f.; 2 Cor. 3.18). Such a temporary separation Paul himself seems to countenance in other contexts (Phil. 1.23; 2 Cor. 5.13),[121] and this would not be unusual in the circumstances of the heavenly ascent. In fact one is tempted to ask why Paul did not state unequivocally that the experience was of an ecstatic nature when it involved the ascent to heaven. The reason for his perplexity probably lies in the parallel material which we assembled earlier.[122] We found that in the Jewish apocalypses there are indications that the apocalypticist may have experienced physical sensations during the vision in addition to the consciousness of being outside the body when he made the ascent. It is probably such twofold effects which Paul is hinting at when he refers to his uncertainty about the precise nature of his experience.

The most striking thing about the way in which Paul speaks of his experience is the fact that he relates it, not, as we might have expected, in the first person, but in the third person. He talks about 'a man in Christ' whom he knows (2 Cor. 12.2). That there is identification between this man and Paul is not in doubt as verses 5 and 7 show. This unwillingness of Paul to speak directly of his visionary experiences has been variously explained,[123] the most popular explanation being Paul's modesty and his desire to boast only of his weakness (v. 5).[124] As a result he refuses to speak of his visionary activity directly and prefers instead to talk about the experience as if it were of another person. Such modesty arises quite naturally out of the context, where Paul is anxious to stress his weakness (2 Cor. 11.23ff.; 12.10). It is not unnatural to suppose, therefore, that Paul wanted to play down the honour, which his visions may have given to him, by speaking of them in this oblique fashion.

Nevertheless, one must go on to ask whether such self-effacement as is found here is the result of Paul's deliberate attempt to separate the suffering apostle from such experiences or whether he utilized an already existing literary form in the description of this experience which enabled him to play down his involvement in it.[125] The attempt of Bousset to explain the distinction by reference to Paul's dualistic anthropology has not met with much favour,[126] yet it has the merit of taking seriously the clear division which Paul wishes to make between himself as the suffering apostle and the man in Christ who is taken up to Paradise. There may not be two conflicting aspects of one personality, but there does appear to be an attempt by the apostle to distinguish between his normal self and his visionary self by using language which appears to suggest two separate individuals.[127] The evidence from contemporary sources suggests that a number of idioms were open to the apostle to express this separation, but which one is used here is not easy to decide.

The decisive factor in reaching a decision on the idiom which has influenced Paul must be the immediate context in which the distinctive phraseology is to be found. In fact, if we turn to Jewish apocalyptic literature for a parallel to this literary form, we are confronted immediately with the device of pseudonymity, where visions are ascribed to some other figure than the actual recipient.[128] Although there is no question of pseudonymity here,[129] the distancing of oneself from a visionary experience, by speaking about it in the name of another, is the literary style of Jewish apocalyptic. Thus the form of this section indicates that Paul throughout is utilizing an idiom familiar to him from Jewish apocalyptic in which the visionary speaks of his own experience in this impersonal way.[130] The use of this form has the advantage of enabling Paul to continue to emphasize his weakness without losing the opportunity to do that which is 'not expedient' (2 Cor. 12.1), namely boast about his own stupendous knowledge of the world above.

That Paul is using the traditional language and style of Jewish apocalyptic is apparent from the cosmological framework which he employs. But another indication that this is the background of the language here is his use of the Greek verb *harpazo* to describe his rapture to heaven (vv. 2 and 4). The use of this word could be seen as the result of Paul's attempt to stress that the experience was an involuntary rapture rather than a carefully planned and prepared for heavenly journey.[131] The same verb is used on other occasions in the New Testament to speak of the taking up of human beings to heaven (1 Thess. 4.17; Rev. 12.5).[132] It is also used of the dramatic removal of Philip to

Azotus in Acts 8.39. But the most significant use of all is to be found in Wisdom 4.11 in a passage which refers to the translation of Enoch. In the Greek versions of Enoch's removal by God in Genesis 5.24 and Sirach 44.16 the verb *metatithemi* is used and in Sirach 49.14 *analambano* (cf. 1 Enoch 12.1 Gk).[133] In the description of the righteous man who was lifted from the earth in Wisdom 4.11 (a story which is clearly dependent on Gen. 5.24, though Enoch's name is never mentioned), the verb *harpazo* is used.[134] This passage offers us clear evidence of the use of *harpazo* in connection with the heavenly ascent of a figure who plays a central role as the pseudonymous recipient of heavenly visions in Jewish apocalyptic literature. The presence of this verb in 2 Corinthians 12.2ff., therefore, suggests the ultilization of a term which was used on occasion as a way of describing the transportation of the visionary hero of the past to the world above.[135]

Thus in 2 Corinthians 12.2ff. Paul briefly allows the readers of his letters to glimpse one aspect of his inner religious life. The passage, despite its brevity and vagueness, still gives some indication of the debt which Paul owed to apocalyptic ways of thinking. This may not always be apparent in his letters, but the paucity of evidence cannot disguise the fact that at certain key points in his life such ways of thinking provided an important framework for his understanding of God and his purposes.

Extra-Canonical Writings

When we turn to extra-canonical writings, several passages demand our attention. First of all, consideration must be given to a work which we have had reason to mention on several occasions already, the Ascension of Isaiah.[136] There are good reasons for dating this at the end of the first or at the very beginning of the second century AD.[137] In its present form the work is clearly Christian (e.g. 3.13ff, 4.9; 9.5), though its cosmology is essentially Jewish.[138] The apocalypse falls quite clearly into two parts. The first (ch. 1—5) tells of the martyrdom of Isaiah, and the second describes a heavenly ascent made by the prophet and his vision of the descent of the Beloved to earth and his return back to heaven again (ch. 6—11).

The work as a whole is the earliest apocalypse from the beginning of the Christian era, which resembles the Jewish apocalypses in including a fictitious setting and attribution to a figure of Israel's past. The most important part of the work, as far as we are concerned, is the final section, which describes the ascent of the seer through the heavens. On his way to the seventh (and highest) heaven Isaiah describes the inhabitants of each heaven, culminating in his description of the glory in the seventh heaven, where, along with the invisible God, are situated the pre-existent Christ, the angel of the Spirit and the righteous dead. The description of the heavens is uniform until the seer reaches the sixth heaven. Up to that point he has described how in each heaven there is a throne surrounded by angels, but the sixth and seventh heavens contain no throne (8.7). When at last he reaches the highest heaven, Isaiah describes the descent of the Saviour (the Beloved) through the lower heavens. In order to complete his descent to earth, the Beloved has to change his form as he descends through each successive heaven, thus escaping the notice of the inhabitants of the lower heavens. After his death and resurrection he ascends back to the seventh heaven in triumph over the heavenly powers.[139] There is evidence of a traditional futurist eschatology in the opening chapters of the work (4.14), but this has almost completely disappeared in the final chapters. Like the ascent of Enoch in Slavonic Enoch we have an essentially non-eschatological apocalypse. Its concern with the secrets of heaven, and especially the mystery of the descent of the Beloved, makes it a work of considerable importance for the history of apocalyptic.

The strange sect of the Elchesaites must be mentioned briefly in any survey of visions in early Christian literature.[140] The movement had its origins at the very beginning of the second century (Hippolytus *Ref.* ix, 13.3f.) probably east of Palestine (Epiphanius *Pan.* xix, 2.10ff.; liii, 1.1ff.), a fact which seems to be confirmed by the presence of an Aramaic formula in one of the references to Elchesai's teaching (Epiph. *Pan.* xix, 4.3). A man named Alcibiades from Syria was responsible for bringing the book of Elchesai to Rome *c.* AD 220. This fact, together with a description of how the original book of Elchesai came to be received, is described in Hippolytus *Ref.* ix, 13.1ff.:

> . . . Alcibiades came to Rome and brought with him a book. Of it he said that Elchesai, a righteous man, had received it from Seres in Parthia and had transmitted it to a certain Sobiai. It had been

The Open Heaven

communicated by an angel, whose height was twenty-four *schoinoi*, which is ninety-six miles, his breadth four *schoinoi*, and from shoulder to shoulder six *schoinoi*, and the tracks of his feet in length three and a half *schoinoi*, which is fourteen miles, and in breadth one and a half *schoinoi*, and in height half a *schoinos*. And with him there was also a female figure, whose measurements, Alcibaides says, were commensurate with those mentioned; and the male figure was the Son of God, but the female was called the Holy Spirit.[141]

The origin of the book is said to be oriental. The reference to the Seres in Parthia is a way of referring to the Chinese.[142] Whatever the truth of this statement the vision which led to the receiving of the book has several clear links with the angelology of Jewish Christianity and ultimately is inspired by Jewish ideas. The enormous size of the two figures described here recalls the description of the resurrection in the Gospel of Peter (10.40) and certain of the angelophanies in the Shepherd of Hermas (e.g. Sim. ix. 12.8).[143] The identification of the Holy Spirit with a female figure is found in the fragment of the Jewish Christian Gospel of the Hebrews in Origen *Comm. in Joh.* 2.12.[144] The other fragments which we possess of the Elchesaite teaching cannot be said to be distinctively apocalyptic in their outlook. The main concern is with ethical problems facing the group, including post-baptismal sin (Hippol. *Ref.* ix. 15.3). The point which most interests us is the setting in which the original teaching was communicated. This fringe-Jewish Christian group emphasized the divine origin of the teaching. Like John of Patmos, who gave his own work an authority which is unparalleled in early Christian literature (Rev. 22.18f.), the book of Elchesai, by virtue of its angelic origin, is deemed to offer an important contribution to the understanding of the divine will for man. As Daniélou points out, what we have in this movement are some of the distinctive features of Jewish Christianity, albeit in a more primitive form than we find them, say, in Hermas.[145] Nevertheless the fragments which we do possess are testimony to the way in which the value of apocalyptic visions was kept alive within these circles.

Better known, but giving evidence of the same kind of religion, is the Shepherd of Hermas. This is the title given to a long, diffuse work containing visions, extensive exhortations and complicated allegories. It was probably written about the middle of the second century in Rome and shows the abiding influence of apocalyptic well into the second century.[146] Doubt has been cast on whether Hermas should be considered an example of apocalyptic at all.[147] The absence of eschatological material has led some to suppose that, while outwardly it has the appearance of an apocalypse, the lack of any teaching on the future should exclude it from inclusion among the apocalyptic writings.[148] We have already argued that eschatological teaching is not necessarily an essential feature of an apocalypse, and there are one or two texts where eschatology has little or no importance within the secrets revealed to the seer. Nevertheless, there is a sense in which Hermas does mark a change in the character of apocalyptic, a change which in some respects is already anticipated in Revelation itself.

In Revelation 11—13, it will be suggested, we have various visions whose imagery is used to communicate a message about the present situation and the present responsibilities of the Church. The various images are not to be seen, therefore, as a prediction of future personages and events but a picturesque way of talking about the true meaning of the present. This is the type of apocalyptic which we find in Hermas. Although Hermas retains many of the trappings of apocalyptic, like the open heaven (Vis. i, 1.4) and the spiritual rapture (Vis. i, 1.3), there is a complete absence of any vision of the heavenly world. It is true that Hermas frequently meets angelic beings,[149] but these are emissaries sent from the world above rather than angels who accompany the seer during the heavenly ascent. Hermas, like Jewish apocalyptic before it, contains several examples of visions followed by interpretation, e.g. Visions iii, 1.6ff. Indeed, in this work the various elements of the visions have been interpreted so completely, that it is impossible to resist the conclusion that a long process of reflection on any original visions has gone on.

A glance at the fourth vision, when Hermas sees the great sea-monster, will illustrate the point and may enable us to see whether there are traces of actual visions to be found in this collection:

> The fourth vision which I saw, brethren, twenty days after the former vision was a type of the persecution [*thlipsis*] which is to come. I was going into the country by the Via Campana. The place is about ten furlongs from the public road, and is easily reached. As I walked by myself I besought the Lord to complete the revelations and visions which he had shown to me by his holy church, to make me strong and give repentance to his servants who had been

offended, to glorify his great and glorious name because he had thought me worthy to show me his wonders. And while I was glorifying him and giving him thanks, an answer came to me as an echo to my voice, Do not be double-minded, Hermas. I began to reason in myself and to say, In what ways can I be doubled-minded after being given such a foundation by the Lord, and having seen his glorious deeds? And I approached a little further, brethren, and behold, I saw dust reaching, as it were to heaven, and I began to say to myself, Are cattle coming and raising dust? and it was about a furlong away from me. When the dust grew greater and greater, I supposed that it was some portent. The sun shone out a little and lo, I saw a great beast like some Leviathan, and fiery locusts were going out of his mouth. The beast was in size about a hundred feet and its head was like a piece of pottery. And I began to weep and to pray to the Lord to rescue me from it, and I remembered the word which I had heard, Do not be double-minded, Hermas. Thus brethren, being clothed in faith of the Lord and remembering the great things which he had taught me, I took courage and faced the beast. And as the beast came on with a rush it was as though it would destroy the city. I came near to it, and the Leviathan for all its size stretched itself out on the ground, and put forth nothing except its tongue, and did not move at all until I had passed by it. And the beast had on its head four colours, black, then the colour of flame and blood, then golden, then white.[150]

While Hermas is walking through the countryside , he is obviously in a receptive frame of mind for receiving visions (Vis. iv, 1.3). He hears a voice telling him not to doubt and there then follows the vision of the sea-monster. When Hermas prays for deliverance from the beast, he recalls the words telling him not to be double-minded. As a result of his faith he finds that he manages to pass by the terrible monster without any harm. Afterwards the ancient lady appears to Hermas and explains to him the significance of the beast. The main elements of the interpretation of the vision centre round Hermas' faith and the significance of the four colours which the beast has on its head (Vis. iv, 1.10). This last element is pressed into service as a means of speaking not only about this age but also about the glory which is to come. Clearly there is an attempt here to draw out every possible ounce of meaning from this aspect of the vision. The main point of the vision seems to have been to show Hermas that an unwavering faith would enable the Church to withstand the tribulation which was to come upon it (Vis. iv,

2.4ff.). In comparison with this, the long interpretation of the significance of the colours wanders away from the original intention. The fact that the colour of the beast was not originally important would seem to be confirmed by the vision itself. In Visions iv, 1.10 the reference to the colours on the head of the monster seems to be tacked on after the original sight of the beast, as if a need was felt to mention the colours in the vision, because of their importance for the later interpretation. Nothing whatever is said about them when Hermas first describes the monster in iv, 1.6. Doubtless the origin of this vision is to be found in the reservoir of contemporary mythology available to the apocalypticist.[151] But this vision is no literary construction to suit the details of the interpretation which the seer wishes to communicate to the Church. The lack of any reference in the interpretation to the fiery locusts coming out of the mouth of the beast hardly fits in with a vision which has been constructed merely to provide significant elements for an allegorical interpretation. The core of this vision, therefore, is no artificial construction, but later reflection has made it the basis of an elaborate allegory.

The dominant concern of the Shepherd of Hermas is as a means of teaching correct Christian attitudes rather than disclosing the mysteries of heaven by the medium of apocalyptic revelations. The apocalyptic framework assists in the imposition of a new type of teaching within the Church,[152] especially that concerning the discipline of repentance. The problem of post-baptismal sin was one that caused difficulties to the growing Church.[153] Hard-line teaching on the matter can be found hinted at in Hebrews 6.4; 10.28ff. and 12.6ff., but such a position was rather unrealistic. The matter was dealt with in a rather limited way by the author of 1 John, who divided sin into different grades of seriousness (1 John 5.16). By the middle of the second century the problem had become immense. In response to this the visions which are received by Hermas hold out the possibility of forgiveness after baptismal regeneration (e.g. Sim. ix, 23.2; Mand. iv, 3 and Vis. ii, 2.4f.). The apocalyptic form thus gives the teaching an authority which it would certainly not have if it had been merely the opinion of one of the members of the Roman church, however important he may have been.

There is another aspect to the function of apocalyptic within the Shepherd of Hermas which deserves comment. This resembles the function of apocalyptic as it is found in parts of Revelation. In the letters to the seven churches the readers of the letters in the different churches are let into the assessment of heaven of their spiritual progress (or lack of it). Churches which feel that they are on the point of giving up and feel utterly helpless are encouraged by being told how much their devotion is recognized by God (Rev. 2.9ff.), whereas those which feel self-confident are severely rebuked (Rev. 2.4; 3.15ff.). On a personal level in Visions i, 3 (cf. Vis. iii, 1.4f.) Hermas is shown that God's anger against himself arises from his indulgent attitude towards his sinful relatives. Thus this vision serves to enable the individual believer to know the precise reason for his estrangement from God. As far as the community as a whole is concerned, Visions ii, 2 contains a revelation whose purpose is to challenge the complacency of the Church by presenting them with God's view of their performance as Christians. Thus the preacher's call to repentance is reinforced in these instances by the affirmation that God has spoken directly to his representative through visions. No longer can the community escape its responsibility by asserting that the charge is merely from men, as the use of apocalyptic is a means of bringing them face to face with the demand of God himself.

The Evidence of Montanist Visions and the Passio Perpetuae

The writings of the second century hardly allow us to trace the influence of apocalyptic on nascent Christianity with any degree of certainty. There are occasional hints in Ignatius' letters that some of the communities which he was addressing were influenced in one way or another by such notions and that the spirituality of the Bishop of Antioch himself may have been open to such ideas (Trallians 5.2).[154] Unfortunately the other extant works from the early part of the second century do not allow us to ascertain whether apocalyptic continued to play a dominant role. Nevertheless, the presence of apocalyptic visions in the Roman church at the middle of the second century, and what is more important, the degree of authority which was attached to them, gives an air of plausibility to the suggestion of those, like Daniélou, who think that apocalyptic theology continued to have a pervasive influence well into the second century.[155]

The book of Revelation shows that Asia Minor was another area which was influenced by the apocalyptic spirit. Asia Minor continued to offer fertile soil for this type of religion,[156] and it is no surprise that towards the end of the second century Phrygia should have been the place where the enthusiastic movement called Montanism arose. The Montanist movement was characterized by the fervent belief in the imminence of a new age, a heightened moral earnestness and a revival of the prophetic charisma.[157] The movement must have been partly a reaction to the waning of religious enthusiasm in the second century churches as eschatological expectation diminished,[158] whatever the contribution from the indigenous religions of the area, whether pagan, Jewish, or Christian.[159] Its characteristic feature was its emphasis on prophecy, and it was called by the Montanists a 'new prophecy' (Eus. *EH* v, 16.3). The conviction which the Montanists held to that there was the possibility of further revelations from God makes this movement one which we should examine briefly in connection with the persistence of the apocalyptic spirit in the early Church.

As in the earliest Church revelation came to the Montanists through various means, though it is inspired utterance which tends to dominate the accounts of the Montanist charisma. The evidence would seem to suggest that the prophetic inspiration came by means of an ecstatic state.[160] We may suppose that such ecstatic states were true also of the earliest Christian prophets, though our lack of information on this point does not make the tracing of links with earlier Christian prophecy at all easy.[161] Our main concern, however, is not the Montanist prophecy as such, but with the question whether visions of an apocalyptic type also formed part of their spirituality. In other words, is it true to see a continuation of the apocalyptic religion in the particular form which we have it in Revelation in this later movement? That visions do seem to have played a part in their religious outlook is confirmed by Eusebius (*EH* v, 16.14). He reports the death of a certain Theodotus during an ascent to heaven.[162] Such states of ecstasy accompanied by visions seem to have been fairly common. Indeed, it is during one of these visions, experienced by one of the leading women in the Montanist movement, either Priscilla or Quintilla, that one of the most distinctive beliefs of Montanism, the descent of the heavenly Jerusalem at Pepuza in Phrygia, makes its appearance:

In Pepuza she [either Priscilla or Quintilla] was asleep and Christ
came to her and slept with her in the same way she in her deceived
way said. She said: Transformed in the likeness of a woman, in a
bright robe, Christ came to me and put wisdom into me, and
revealed to me that this place was holy, and that here Jerusalem
comes down from heaven (Epiph. *Pan.* xlix, cf. Euseb. *HE* v, 18.2).[163]

Epiphanius is very disparaging about the claim which the
woman makes, but it is significant that he does not deny that the
woman did in fact experience a vision of this kind, even though
he himself is convinced that it is utterly spurious.[164] If
Epiphanius is right about the location of the dream, the
woman's presence in Pepuza would explain the fact that this
place should be mentioned in her dream. What is even more
remarkable, however, is the vision of Christ as a woman. The
presence of a woman in visions is, of course, fairly common (4
Ezra 9.38ff.; Rev. 17.3ff.). How far this way of looking at Jesus
derived from the significant role which women played in the
early stages of the movement is difficult to assess.[165] What is
clear is that such an element as this is unlikely to have been a
deliberate invention and thus reflects the visionary experience of
the Montanist prophetess.

The important role, which women played in the form of
Montanism known to Tertullian, can be illustrated by reference
to the occasion when a woman, who was wont to experience
dreams and visions during the liturgy, saw a vision of a soul:

At the moment there is in our midst a sister favoured with gifts of
various revelations, which she experiences in the church through a
state of ecstasy in the spirit during the sacred rites of the Lord's day.
She talks with angels, and sometimes even with the Lord, and sees and
hears mysteries (*sacramenta*). She understands the hearts of some,
and distributes remedies to those who desire them. Whether during
the reading of Scripture, the singing of psalms, the preaching of
sermons, the offering up of prayers, matters from all these are
offered to her for her visions. It may be that we had discoursed
about the soul, when that sister was in the spirit. When the divine
service was completed and the people dismissed, it is usual for her
to recount to us what she has seen (for they are examined most
carefully, in order to test their validity). Among other things, she
said, a soul has been shown to me in bodily form, and a spirit was
wont to appear to me, but not of void and empty character, but such
as could be grasped, soft and transparent, and of an ethereal colour,

and in form resembling that of a human being in every respect. (Tertullian *De Anima* 9)[166]

Tertullian tells this story because of the importance he attached to it in his discussion of the nature of the soul. Obviously, as far as he is concerned, a vision of this type may be regarded as valid evidence of the nature of the existence of the individual in the world beyond. Although due emphasis is given to the fact that such experiences were carefully investigated after the divine service had been completed (a sign that the community was not completely credulous as far as the various claims to visionary experience were concerned), there is little doubt that, once the authenticity of what the visionary had said has been established, it is treated with due regard by Tertullian. As far as the experiences of the woman are concerned, one matter remains unresolved. We are left in the dark as to the character of her ecstasy. Whether she experienced an ascent into heaven to see God and the angels is unclear. Nevertheless Tertullian's account does offer us important insights into the origin of such experiences within his community. He tells us that the various parts of the liturgy offered the raw material for the woman's vision. Words and images from her everyday surroundings usually form the basis for the vision which follows, and, presumably, any instructions which are likely to come from the world beyond. Indeed, in this particular instance Tertullian seems prepared to hazard a guess that the reason for the woman's vision of the soul may well have been the fact that this matter was being broached at some point during the service.

The importance of this passage is that it offers direct testimony to the nature of visions, which can only be surmised from the biblical evidence. Scholars have for a long time pointed to the various contents of the Temple in Jerusalem as the raw material for the visions of Ezekiel and Isaiah. At a later time one can conjecture that a cloud of dust and the refraction of the sun's rays may have been responsible, together with a vivid imagination, for Hermas' vision of the great sea-monster discussed above. Earlier we argued that the imagery of Scripture had an important part to play in the visions of apocalyptic literature. This vision of the soul and Tertullian's analysis of the origin of the woman's visions, are an important testimony to the way in which such visions came into being.[167]

The Montanist movement was an important factor in the continuation of visionary experience in the third century. The defection of Tertullan to the Montanists shows that its influence was by no means confined to Asia Minor, nor was orthodox Christianity free from the impact of its spirituality. The zeal for martyrdom was always endemic within early Christian spirituality,[168] and when it became linked with Montanist rigour it is not difficult to see the way in which a yearning for martyrdom grew within the early Church. There are various collections of the acts of the martyrs, and it is one of these which demands our attention, the *Passio Perpetuae*.[169]

In about AD 202 in Carthage a young woman named Perpetua was martyred along with several other believers. There is evidence to suggest that she may have been influenced by Montanist Christianity, if not a Montanist herself.[170] In the *Passio* an account is given of her martyrdom, but in addition there is also what appears to be a kind of prison diary which includes three visions of Perpetua and one of her fellow-prisoners, Satyrus. In the view of several commentators the visions in particular contain the experiences of the martyrs themselves.[171] Despite some similarities with other apocalyptic literature, and in particular the Shepherd of Hermas, the visions are full enough of their own idiosyncrasies to demand that their contents be given due consideration.

The second and third visions of Perpetua contain less interesting material than the first. The second falls into two parts and deals with the fate of Perpetua's unregenerate brother. During prayer she is reminded of her brother who had died in infancy, and her intercessions for him lead to a vision of him in a gloomy place, still bearing the wound from which he had died. He is unable to drink from a pool of water which stands before him. Later she has a further vision in which her brother appears revivified and with the wound healed. On this occasion we are told that he is able to drink from the pool of water. Perpetua gleans from this that her brother is no longer undergoing the torments of the underworld.[172] In the third vision her imminent fate in the arena has made such an impact on Perpetua that she sees herself taken into the arena. She is surprised, however, to find that it is not the wild animals which are confronting her there but an Egyptian dressed for a gladiatorial contest. A very tall man appears who promises Perpetua a branch if she should triumph and slaughter with the sword if she should fail. Perpetua then gets ready for the fight and is transformed into a man. She eventually triumphs, takes the branch from the man and is kissed by him. The significance of the vision is then interpreted for her as her imminent triumph over the Devil in the arena. The character of this vision is essentially different from the first. It arises directly out of her imminent death which was on Perpetua's mind at the time, and its content is thus directly related to her own immediate concerns.

The first vision comes to Perpetua while in a perceptive frame of mind, and there are several features which demand our attention. It is full of images which are only indirectly concerned with the matters which were at the forefront of her conscious mind:

> I saw a golden ladder of marvellous height, reaching up even to heaven, and very narrow, so that persons could only ascend on it one by one; and on the sides of the ladder was fixed every kind of weapon. There were swords, lances, hooks, daggers; so that if any one went up carelessly, or not looking upwards, he would be torn to pieces, and his flesh would cleave to the iron weapons. And under the ladder itself was crouching a dragon of wonderful size, who lay in wait for those who ascended and frightened them from the ascent. And Satyrus [one of Perpetua's fellow-prisoners] went up first, who had subsequently delivered himself up freely on our account, not having been present at the time we were taken prisoners.[173] And he attained the top of the ladder, and turned towards me and said, Perpetua, I am waiting for you;[174] but he said, be careful that the dragon does not bite you. And I said, in the name of the Lord Jesus Christ he shall not hurt me. And from under the ladder itself, as if in fear of me, he slowly lifted up his head. And I went up, and I saw an immense extent of garden, and in the midst of the garden a white-haired man sitting in the dress of a shepherd, of a large stature, milking sheep; and standing round were many thousand white-robed ones. And he raised his head and looked upon me and said to me, Thou art welcome daughter. And he called me, and from the cheese as he was milking he gave me as it were a little cake, and I received it with folded hands; and I ate it, and all who stood around said, Amen. And at the sound of their voices I was awakened, still tasting a sweetness I cannot describe. (*Pass.* 1)

There are several elements here which are reminiscent of Jewish apocalyptic tradition. This is all the more remarkable as Perpetua

does not appear to have been a believer for very long (1.1).
Whether there was familiarity with texts like the Shepherd of
Hermas during the catechumenate is now impossible to say,
though some knowledge of this text seems certain. The ladder to
heaven recalls Jacob's vision in Genesis 28,[175] but it is not the
ladder which is the centre of interest but the difficulties which
attend the ascent of it. Threats to the mystic as he ascends to
heaven are well known from later Jewish mystical material. In
Hek. R. 17ff. for example, much space is devoted to a description of the threats posed by angelic beings, who examine the
worthiness of those who would enter the innermost sanctum of
heaven. From early Christian literature we have a similar notion
emerging in the Ascension of Isaiah 9.1. When Isaiah is on the
point of gaining access to the seventh heaven, a voice asks 'How
far shall he ascend who dwells among aliens?' Fortunately for
Isaiah Christ speaks up for him and permits him to ascend (Asc.
Isa. 9.2). It is the one who is set over the sixth heaven who
forbids the visionary to ascend further without permission (cf.
Heb. Enoch 1.3 and 7).[176] The threat posed by the dragon recalls
the similar beast in Revelation 12 and the Shepherd of Hermas
Visions iv, 1.6. In the passage in Revelation the male child who
is born to the woman and the woman herself are terrorized by
the dragon. Later in that chapter (v. 17) the dragon goes off to
terrorize the other offspring of the woman who are identified
with the followers of Jesus. The threat to the ascent to heaven
from the powers of darkness and the consequent possibility of
communion with God being forbidden is an issue which all
these apocalyptic texts reflect in their different ways.

Once in heaven Perpetua sees a garden. It is difficult to resist
the conclusion that we have a reference to Paradise here, where
the righteous dwell (cf. Luke 23.43; Test. Abraham Rec. A 10).[177]
As Daniélou rightly points out, the description of the shepherd
(cf. *Hermas Vis.* v, 1.1) with his enormous stature, is similar to
the description of the resurrected Christ in the Gospel of Peter
10.40 (cf. *Passio* 10.8 and *Hermas Vis.* v, 1.1).[178] In both this vision
and that of Satyrus reference is made to the white-haired
appearance of the exalted figure (*Pass.* 1.3; 4.2). The similarity
with Revelation 1.14 cannot be ignored, where, as we have seen,
the risen Christ is described with the appearance of the Ancient
of Days in Daniel 7.9.[179] There is a passage in j. Yoma 5.2, where
Simeon the Just, when in the Holy of Holies on the Day of

Atonement, was wont to see an old man dressed in white. This is either a reference to God himself or an angel decked out with divine attributes.[180] A passage like this makes it difficult to resist the conclusion that the vision of Perpetua does in fact owe much to the Jewish apocalyptic tradition.

While a heavenly ascent is presupposed in Perpetua's vision, there is a lack of the distinctive features of the world above familiar to us from a vision like that contained in Revelation 4. This deficiency may be due to lack of familiarity with the traditional imagery used in such visions but, more likely, is the fact that the description of the world above plays a subordinate role in the relevance of its content to the situation confronting the prisoners. The vision serves as a message to the prisoners about the obstacles on their way to glory. It steels Perpetua in her resolve to do all in her power to resist the beguiling pleas of those who would prevent her martyrdom. This becomes apparent in the story which follows when the second attempt by Perpetua's father to persuade her to recant is narrated. Thus the threat to Perpetua's ascent into heaven is interpreted as the attempts of those who would prevent her from reaching the realm above through martyrdom.

The first two visions of Perpetua are not totally unexpected. Indeed, the visions concerning her deceased brother clearly arise in a state of great anxiety about his eternal destiny. As far as the first vision is concerned, we are told that Perpetua's brother, who was also a catechumen, had suggested to his sister that she should ask God for a vision, so that she would be able to ascertain what her fate would be. A woman imprisoned for her faith was in a position to make such a request. In the light of this Perpetua asks for a vision.

The vision of Satyrus is related without any description of preparation. It falls into two clearly defined halves. The first deals with the ascent of the martyrs to heaven, whereas the second concerns a meeting with two church officials who are at enmity with each other. The state of affairs in the Church is rebuked, and it is implied that a failure to repent will mean exclusion from heaven. As in Revelation 2—3 and in Hermas (e.g. *Vis.* ii, 2) the second half of this vision is a way of offering what the visionary believes is the standpoint of heaven on a current dispute which is raging within the community. Our particular concern, however, is with the first part of the vision, which describes the ascent to heaven:

> We had suffered and were gone forth from the flesh, and were
> beginning to be borne by four angels into the east; and their hands
> touched us not. And we floated not supine looking upwards, but as
> if ascending a gentle slope. And being set free, we at length saw the
> first boundless light; and I said, Perpetua (for she was at my side),
> this is what the Lord promised us; we have received the promise.
> And while we are borne by these four angels, there appears to us a
> vast space which was like a pleasure-garden, having rose trees and
> every kind of flower. And the height of the trees was after the
> measure of a cypress, and their leaves were falling incessantly.[181]
> Moreover, in the pleasure garden four other angels appeared, brigh-
> ter than the previous ones, who, when they saw us, gave us honour
> and said to the rest of the angels, 'Here they are, here they are',
> with admiration. And those four angels who bore us, being greatly
> afraid, put us down; and we passed over on foot the space of a
> furlong in a broad path . . . And the angels said to us, 'Come first,
> enter and greet your lord.'
>
> And we came near to a place, the walls were such as if they were
> built of light; and before the gate of that place stood four angels,
> who clothed those who entered with white robes. And being
> clothed we entered and saw boundless light, and heard the united
> voice of some who said without ceasing, Holy, Holy, Holy. And in
> the midst of that place we saw as it were a hoary man, sitting,
> having snow white hair and with a youthful countenance; and his
> feet we saw not. And on his right hand and on his left were
> twenty-four elders and behind them a great many others were
> standing. We entered with great wonder, and stood before the
> throne; and the four angels raised us up and we kissed him, and he
> passed his hand over our face. And the rest of the elders said to us,
> 'Let us stand'; and we stood and made peace. And the elders said to
> us, 'Go and enjoy'. And I said, 'Perpetua, you have what you wish'.
> And she said to me. 'Thanks be to God, that joyous as I was in the
> flesh, I am more joyous here'. (*Passio* 4.1–3).

Here the contacts with earlier apocalyptic literature are more
prominent. The journey of the souls to the east and to the space
like an orchard (*viridarium*) reflects early Jewish beliefs about the
location of Paradise in the east (e.g. 1 Enoch 32). Indeed, so
close is the similarity of this section with 1 Enoch 32.3 that it is
difficult to resist the impression that there may be some direct
knowledge of this text: 'And I came to the garden of righteousness, and from afar off trees more numerous than these trees

and great . . . and the tree of knowledge . . . that tree is like the fir.'

Two stages of the ascent are presupposed in the vision. The first to the great space and the second to the walls of light. If the author of this vision had known 1 Enoch in its Greek form, one wonders if the walls of light also are derived from the heavenly journey in 1 Enoch 14, especially verse 10.[182] At the entrance to God's dwelling there stood four angels who clothe those who would enter with white robes. Although it is not stated explicitly, it would appear that these angels act as guardians of the celestial palace. Only those who are given white robes are allowed into the divine presence. The church officials, whom Satyrus meets in the second part of his vision, are left outside. Here we have another example of the threat which angels posed to humans in the heavenly world similar to that found in Perpetua's vision.

When they have entered the walls, we have a description of the divine presence which owes a great deal to Revelation 4, as is evident from the references to the twenty-four elders and the singing of the *trisagion*. The clothing of the martyrs in white robes derives from Revelation 6.11, cf. 7.9. Appropriate clothing for entry into the divine presence is an element which we meet occasionally in Jewish apocalyptic. In Slavonic Enoch 22.8ff., for example, God says to Michael: 'Go and take Enoch from out his earthly garments and anoint him with my sweet ointment and put him into the garments of my glory.'(cf. 1 Enoch 62.15; Hermas Sim. viii, 2; Asc. Isa. 9.9; 9.30).

In both visions of heaven in this short work the divine being is described in the same way. Reference is made in both cases to his aged appearance. This might lead us to suppose that we have a purely Jewish influence here, a sight of God rather than Christ (cf. Rev. 4.1). The youthful aspect of the figure, however, makes it more likely that it is a christophany. If this is the case, then the martyrs do not see God enthroned in glory surrounded by the twenty-four elders. It is Christ who appears with the characteristics of God himself. Justin in his Dialogue with Trypho had spoken of certain Old Testament theophanies as visions of the pre-existent Christ (ch. 75—80, 125ff.). Such an idea is at least as old as John 12.41. Here we find a reference to Isaiah seeing the glory of Christ. This must be a reference to Isaiah 6.1 which is here treated as a reference to a vision of

402 *The Open Heaven*

Christ himself.[183]

Both these visions are a remarkable testimony to the persistence of Jewish and Christian apocalyptic ideas in early Christianity. It is not surprising in the light of the Montanist movement that there was an interest in visions in African Christianity, but what causes most surprise is the fact that the form in which these visions are couched still has its roots in the apocalyptic of Judaism, whose literary remains, as we know, were preserved, thanks to the interest of early Christians. This fascinating document also testifies to the abiding impact of apocalyptic on early Christianity. The literary evidence of such influence may not in fact be very substantial, but its significance for understanding the origin and growth of the Christian movement should not be underestimated. Despite the possibility of abuse, the apocalyptic spirit pervaded early Christianity and continued to exercise a decisive influence on its outlook throughout the second century.[184]

CHAPTER 14

Revelation

Date and Setting

IN SOME RESPECTS the precise dating of Revelation does not radically affect the exegesis of the document, as the issues which appear to confront the writer can be understood in broadly similar terms whenever we date it. Nevertheless some idea of the general setting may assist us in understanding why particular subjects should be of greater concern to the visionary than others. This document ought to be one of the easiest to date in the whole of the New Testament. The references in Revelation 17.8ff. certainly appear to give some kind of clue as to the particular historical setting.[1] The interpretation of the vision of the harlot seated upon the beast with seven heads suggests that John meant his readers to understand that the beast represented the Roman principate and the woman the city itself. But while most interpreters would be in agreement thus far, differences emerge over the precise identification of the kings who are hinted at in 17.10, though most agree on the setting in which the vision was written.

Of all the critical issues relating to the New Testament which have been discussed in scholarly circles over the past hundred years[2] it is probably true that, until recently, a date for Revelation some time in the last decade of the first century, during, or just after, the reign of Domitian, has attracted the widest amount of support from both conservative and radical scholars.[3] Recently a view which was widely held in the nineteenth century has been rehabilitated, which suggests that a date in the late sixties for Revelation would be more appropriate.[4] There is much to be said for this suggestion, as it appears to make good sense of the historical allusions in chapter 17. If we leave aside the testimony of early Christian tradition which favours a date during Domitian's reign[5] and concentrate on these verses, a good case can be made out for acceptance of the view that John was writing round about AD 68. But let us first consider the reference in verses 9 to 11, which is the basis of the discussion of the date of Revelation:

> This calls for a mind with wisdom: the seven heads are seven mountains on which the woman is seated; they are also seven kings, five of whom have fallen, one is, the other has not yet come, and when he comes he must remain only a little while. As for the beast that was and is not, it is an eighth but it belongs to the seven, and it goes to perdition.

Assuming, as most commentators do, that we have here a reference to a number of Roman emperors, we have then to decide which John is referring to in this verse. Do we simply start with either Julius Caesar or Augustus and number the first five emperors consecutively? Is it right to include all the emperors in the list, including, for example, the three so-called soldier-emperors (Galba, Otho and Vitellius) who reigned for such a short time in the troubled years after Nero's death? In response to these questions one must say that, while a start with Julius Caesar cannot be ruled out (he is the first in a similar list in Sib. Oracles v. 12), it is probably correct to start with Augustus. The question is, however, whether one wants to end up with a Domitianic date. If one starts with this in mind, one's approach to the list will be affected, for a Domitianic date cannot be achieved without some juggling of the various emperors' names. Even if the three soldier emperors are omitted, we are still left with a date in Vespasian's reign (kings one to five, Augustus to Nero, six Vespasian, seven Titus), though it would enable us to identify the eighth with Domitian. Accordingly various schemes have been adopted for selecting the five who have fallen, principally one which starts the list with Caligula either on the basis of the fact that he was the first to reign after the Christian mission began[6] or on the basis of the fact that the emperors from Caligula onwards were all persecutors of the people of God.[7]

But, if we leave on one side for the moment the attempt to locate Revelation in the reign of Domitian and assume that the simplest solution ought to be given the prime consideration, we shall start with Augustus and, as is the case in both Suetonius'

Twelve Caesars and Sibylline Oracles v. 13ff., include the so-called soldier-emperors. This would mean that the five who have fallen start with Augustus and end with Nero, the one who is refers to Galba, and the next who remains for just a little while refers to the challenge to Galba from another pretender to the principate. Even if we are unwilling to tie the date so closely to Galba's brief period of office, the date could be said to be at some point during AD 68 when there was a political vacuum, with several claimants to the principate. No other explanation of these verses matches the simplicity of this interpretation, which, one may assume, would also have been the most obvious to the original readers of the document.

It would, however, be wrong to suppose that these verses are without exegetical difficulties on other grounds. A glance at them will reveal several peculiar features. First of all, the heads of the beast are given a double interpretation (v. 9). Not only do they symbolize the seven kings but also the seven hills (of Rome). The latter are not mentioned again. There is the possibility that we may have here a later gloss, or more likely, an attempt by the visionary to draw out every ounce of meaning from his vision.[8] Whoever inserted this sentence wanted his readers to be in no doubt whatsoever about the identity of the beast and the nature of the burden which it bore. Also, as the interpretation of the original vision progresses, there is a change of interest in verse 11 away from the heads of the beast, which are said to represent seven kings, to the beast itself. The eighth which is one of the seven is in fact 'the beast that was and is not'. We have a similar oscillation between the beast and its heads in 13 verses 12 and 14, where the characteristics predicated of the head are applied to the beast as a whole. It is probably right to assume, therefore, that each head in some sense represents the beast as a whole and its activities in its own period of dominance. But there is a sense in which the eighth king in particular, as the last in the process, is the embodiment of all that has gone before.[9] This king, who comes in the future, has all the marks of the final eschatological manifestation of evil. Like the beast, whose origin and inspiration are demonic (v. 8), the eighth king continues in this tradition, but he it is who goes back to perdition. In other words he is the last in the line of representatives of the beast, the final embodiment of the works of darkness. The reference in verse 11 to the fact that the eighth is one of the seven looks like a reference to a belief which existed at this time that the emperor Nero, one of the five who had already fallen, was likely to return at some point in the future from the past (Suet. Nero 57).[10] It is thus an earthly figure who is mentioned here, but because of the demonic inspiration and his final destruction this figure takes on the appearance of an eschatological 'antichrist' (cf. 2 Thess 2.3ff.).

There is some difficulty attaching to the explanation of the ten horns in verse 12. In the light of the demonic character of the eighth king some commentators have been reluctant to see here references to historical personages but merely demonic powers who appear at the end-time.[11] But while one does not want to deny that this prediction is firmly fixed within the eschatological predictions, it would seem to me to be unjustified to assume that the manifestations of the powers of evil in the future were necessarily to be supra-human beings. The evidence of Revelation 13 itself shows how John could see in historical persons and institutions the power of the demonic, without necessarily regarding the human beings who perpetrated the evils as in any sense demons themselves. Thus the reference in verse 12 seems to me best taken as a prediction of certain historical occurrences which will attend the rise of the last king. Probably the best explanation is to see them as the leaders of the Parthian hordes, who would come on the scene when the eighth king (*Nero Rediturus*) would arrive from the east to challenge the authority of the empire he once ruled.[12]

Thus this chapter is certainly open to an interpretation which sees its origin within the years following the death of Nero. There are good reasons from the content of Revelation itself for regarding this as the most likely date for its writing.[13] The upheavals which followed Nero's death could well have been indications to those who were looking out for the signs of a new age that things were now beginning to move in that direction. The early Christians themselves lived in the expectation of Christ's imminent return.[14] While it would be wrong to suppose that this belief completely dominated their thinking (but cf. 2 Thess 2.2ff.), the great uncertainty which was felt throughout the empire during AD 68 could hardly have failed to stir up the hopes of Jews and Christians that their deliverance was nigh.[15] Indeed, as we have already seen, Jewish eschatology gave an important role to the messianic woes as a necessary prelude to the End, when wars, dissension and the like would characterize human relationships. The outbreak of unrest during this period could not have failed to awaken the hopes of those who were looking for God's deliverance, however lukewarm that hope may have become.[16]

Two issues must be considered, however, before we can be completely happy with a date for Revelation in the last years of the sixth decade of the first century. First of all, some examination is necessary of the strength of the Domitianic date for Revelation. Second, the problem has to be faced that the political situation facing Christians in Revelation finds no real parallels during the Jewish war, or for that matter in the reign of Vespasian, the other likely date, assuming a straightforward interpretation of the reference to the kings in chapter 17. For this reason the Domitianic date has seemed so attractive. It offers us a situation when various sources do speak about persecution of various kinds, and in particular with reference to the imposition of the imperial cult.

One of the main reasons for continued support of a Domitianic date which was first supported by Irenaeus (*Adv. Haer.* v. 30.3) is the fact that Christians were persecuted by Domitian (Melito of Sardis in Eus. *EH* iv. 26.9), and it is this persecution which John is alluding to, particularly in chapter 13. In a remarkable reconstruction of the situation in Asia Minor, Stauffer argues for an extensive harassment of Christians during this period.[17] It is true that Domitian had a tendency towards megalomania which led him to claim for himself the title *dominus ac deus noster* (Suetonius Domitian 13). Nevertheless evidence from Roman historians gives us very little reason for supposing that Domitian moved in any systematic way against the Christians.

According to Suetonius (Domitian 12) Domitian did extend the range of levy of the Jewish tax (formerly the half-shekel tax paid by every Jew for the upkeep of the Temple but confiscated by Vespasian in AD 70), to include all those with any Jewish connections. This probably resulted in attacks being made on anyone with Jewish sympathies, who was thus liable to the tax, even if in fact he was not a proselyte.[18] According to Dio (*Hist.* lxviii, 1.2), in Domitian's reign some had been accused of *maiestas* or the Jewish life. Dio also tells us about the fate of Domitian's cousin, Flavius Clemens, who was executed in 95, and his niece, Flavia Domitilla, exiled on the grounds of 'atheism' (*atheotes*). This was a charge, Dio tells us, 'on which many others who were drifting into Jewish ways were condemned' (*Hist.* lxvii. 14.1–3). There is thus some evidence to suggest that Domitian had taken some action in Rome, apparently against people of noble birth with Jewish sympathies. Smallwood has argued that during the last years of Domitian's reign atheism counted as a form of treason, and the main evidence of this crime was the neglect of the state-cult.[19] This would, of course, have been a special problem to Jewish converts and to those who set out to observe the essence of the Jewish religion. Any form of idolatry was absolutely abhorrent, and worshipping the genius of the emperor or hailing him as a god would have appeared blasphemous to such people.

All this adds up to little more than evidence of harassment of those who were thought to have any Jewish connections,[20] (which at this time would almost certainly have included Christians), and a move against certain noble citizens in Rome for their Jewish beliefs. None of this amounts to a systematic attempt to move against the Christians throughout the empire.[21] What the seer has in mind in Revelation 13 is not an occasional incident when a few individuals took action against local Jews, but a more widespread outburst with some official recognition (13.11ff.) in an attempt to victimize those who did not acknowledge the emperor by worshipping before his statue (12 and 15). But, even if the evidence from outside the New Testament hardly justifies the kind of reconstruction which we find in Stauffer's essay, at least it does offer us *some* evidence that moves were taken against those with Jewish connections during Domitian's reign.[22] With the exception of Nero's outburst against the Christians after the fire in Rome (Tacitus *Annals* xv.44) there is no evidence to suggest that Christians or Jews were subject to any form of persecution, whether official or unofficial, during the last years of the sixties.[23] In view of the lack of any evidence for a persecution of Christians at this time it is necessary to see whether such an early date can fit in with the social and political situation in Asia Minor in these years.

It is obvious that of all the New Testament writings Revelation is the one which is the product of its Jewish background. Not only is the debt to Jewish apocalyptic great but the religious outlook in the document is still dominated by distinctively

Jewish practices (e.g. Rev. 2.14 and 20). Although there is considerable animosity towards 'the synagogue of Satan' (Rev. 2.9; 3.9), this is the product of sectarian animosity such as we find in the Dead Sea Scrolls (e.g. 1QpNah 3.1f.).[24] The Jewish nation still has its part to play in the future (Rev. 7.4ff.), and the impression given by the author is that the communities which he was addressing all thought of themselves as very much part of the ancient people of God, differing from non-Christian Jews only in their convictions about Jesus.[25] The letter to the Colossians also gives evidence of a considerable degree of Jewish influence on the beliefs and practices of Christian communities in Asia Minor (Col. 2.16ff.).[26] Christianity in many towns and cities in Asia Minor had its origins within the Jewish communities of those areas. Whatever the differences which existed between the beliefs and practices of the Christians and the non-Christian Jews, there was probably very little to distinguish Jews from Christians as far as outsiders were concerned until towards the end of the first century. Thus, whatever pressure was placed on Jewish inhabitants it was almost certainly bound to have repercussions on the Christians too. The type of Christianity presupposed in Revelation inevitably led pagans to see a close link between that religion and other forms of Judaism.

It would appear from archaeological work carried out in Asia Minor that Jews had an increasingly important role within the life of the cities of Asia Minor.[27] Far from being a frightened minority the Jewish community frequently had important privileges to practise its religion and exist as a recognized enclave within a city. Josephus in *Ant.* xiv.223ff. gives us a list of some of these rights which indicate that Jews were a religious community with a recognized position in many of the cities. What is more, the prosperity of some Jews meant that more and more they played their part within the civil life of the city. But inevitably the more Jews were recognized as a part of society, and the more they became involved within the life of a city, the greater the pressure upon them to conform to the *mores* of that city. The emergence from the ghetto meant greater integration and acceptance of the values of the area. In those cases where Jews had received Roman citizenship there was an added obligation to recognize the dominion of the emperor even if religious scruples prevented them from demonstrating this loyalty in the usual way.

For any prosperous Jewish member of the cities of Asia Minor the war of AD 66–70 presented him with conflicting loyalties. On the one hand there was his loyalty to the Roman state which had so often upheld the privileges granted to the Jews. These were of such a kind that Sevenster can comment that their position 'must have been very annoying to a great number of people.'[28] Such annoyance would have particularly marked at a time of unrest throughout the empire, in which the co-religionists of the Jews of Asia Minor were engaged in a long and costly rebellion against Rome. On the other hand, there were the bonds of kinship and religion which linked these Jews with their separated brethren in Palestine. Philo's Embassy to Gaius shows how sensitive Jews in the Diaspora were to events in their homeland and the challenge to the Jewish conscience presented by Caligula's proposal to erect a statue of himself in the Temple.[29] The fact was that, however fanatical the Jews in Palestine may have been in their zeal to be rid of the Roman yoke and however lukewarm the attitude of Diaspora Judaism towards the revolt may have been, the Palestinian Jews were fighting for an ideal which the Jews of the Diaspora would have kept alive year by year as they observed the Passover ritual.

Even if Jews in Asia Minor showed no sympathy for the revolt itself, it is difficult to see how they could have avoided the suspicion of the inhabitants of the city in which they dwelt, for the simple reason that they were linked by the ties of religion with the rebels in Palestine. What form is this hostility likely to have taken? Could it in fact have extended to putting pressure on Jews to show their allegiance to Rome by participating in the imperial cult, exactly as we find reflected in Revelation 13? An examination of the lists of privileges granted to Jews does not include explicit reference to freedom from participation in the worship of the local gods. Lack of reference to freedom from participating in the imperial cult is not surprising, as many of these rights were granted before the dominance of that cult in the religion of Asia Minor.[30] Sevenster summarizes the position in the following way: 'It cannot be said that not a single obliga-tion to worship the Emperor was imposed on the Jews, but it can be said that the privileges were so comprehensive that they imposed no ritual acts on the Jews that were incompatible with obedience to their laws.'[31] The fact is, however, that, as far as the evidence goes, any one who wished to insist that Jews show their allegiance to Rome in the conventional way may have been within his rights to do so. The lack of any *explicit* exemption from the imperial cult left open the possibility for those who were minded to do so to exploit this loophole to the full. In a situation where those with any kind of Jewish link would be under pressure to show their loyalty to Rome, no better way of doing this could be devised than insisting that Jews should express their allegiance by doing homage before a statue of the emperor.[32]

Now whether pressure of this kind was ever in fact put upon Jews in Asia Minor we do not know. Josephus has nothing to tell us about the situation of Jews in that part of the world during the revolt. Nevertheless consideration of some other evidence suggests that Jewish privileges, however long standing, may have come under threat at this time. This can be illustrated by reference to other passages in Josephus. Even in times of peace we find Jews in Asia Minor being the victims of the displeasure of their fellow-countrymen. In 16 BC the Ionians petitioned M. Agrippa that he should withdraw Jewish privileges, arguing that if the Jews were to be their fellows they should join in the worship of the Ionian gods (*Ant.* xii, 125 cf. *Ant.* xvi, 27ff.). Another incident is reported in *Ant.* xix, 300, where young men from Dora, near Caesarea, brought a statue of the emperor and set it up in a Jewish synagogue. Here there is clear evidence that there was dissatisfaction among the populace about Jewish unwillingness to participate in the homage due to the emperor. More important still are two incidents which took place during and just after the Jewish War.

First of all, according to *BJ* vii, 407ff., Josephus reports the case of a band of *sicarii* who fled from Palestine to Egypt but were handed over by the Jewish community to the Roman authorities. Every kind of torture was inflicted upon them in the hope that they would be compelled to acknowledge Caesar as lord. Nothing, however, persuaded the men to recant and they perished without defiling their consciences. Now it is true that this particular incident involves men who had been directly involved in the revolt in Palestine, but it does reveal that in certain circumstances the Romans were prepared to make allegiance to Caesar a test for those who were suspected of holding rebel views.

The second incident also took place during the war. In *BJ*

vii, 40ff. Josephus relates how at the beginning of the war feelings began to run very high against the Jewish population of Antioch (vii, 46). At this time a certain Antiochus, an apostate Jew, stirred up the people of Antioch. He furnished proof of his apostasy from Judaism by sacrificing after the manner of the Greeks (vii, 50 *epithuein hōsper nomos esti tois Hellēsin*). This led to the demand that a similar act should be performed by Jews of the city, and those who refused to sacrifice in the way specified were massacred.[33] This second incident reveals the extent of anti-Jewish feeling which was to be found in one city of the Diaspora. The fact that Josephus does not make mention of any further incidents should not lead us to suppose that this was an isolated outburst. The likelihood is that what happened in Antioch was also true of other cities. The temptation for Jews to follow the example of the Antiochus mentioned in this story must have been enormous, for it offered a way of demonstrating one's complete disassociation from an unpopular group whose reputation among the gentiles was probably never lower. While we may agree with Mary Smallwood when she says 'Rome made no attempt to force the cult in its direct form after AD 70',[34] we must bear in mind the fact, which is illustrated by the event in Antioch, that pressure probably came in the first instance from the local populace. That is not to deny the fact that this would in all likelihood coincide with official hostility, implied if unexpressed. Whenever the official attitude was rather negative, anti-Semitic feeling tended to increase. Philo makes this point in the *Embassy to Gaius* 135ff., where he argues that official hostility to Judaism was the direct cause of anti-Semitism in Alexandria.

All this leads one to suppose that the situation in the Jewish War would have been one where there was a likelihood that Jews and Jewish sympathizers would have been under great pressure in the Diaspora to dissociate themselves from the position of their co-religionists in Palestine. In this situation it would not be surprising to find many Jews apostatizing, and, on occasion, the imperial cult may have been used as a device whereby Jewish loyalty to Rome could be tested. The latter possibility is more likely to have been true of Asia Minor than any other part of the empire, for it was in that province particularly that the imperial cult was so firmly rooted and linked with the indigenous religious practices through the *commune Asiae*.[35]

Thus the evidence, such as it is, makes it likely that in Asia Minor during the Jewish War there may have been harassment of Jews and some semi-official compulsion to renounce their religion and their beliefs, which were the cause of the unrest in Judaea, by means of recourse to the imperial cult as a test of allegiance to Rome.

Whether this actually happened or not is in fact immaterial to the interpretation of Revelation. All we need to know is that such a fear may have been prevalent among Jews in the Diaspora. It has long been recognized that nowhere does John suppose that a persecution had already begun. The letters to the seven churches make no mention of the imperial cult and only occasionally do they presuppose that any kind of persecution had been suffered by the communities (Rev. 2.13). Lack of references to persecution should not be taken as a reason for ascribing the letters to a different date from the apocalypse proper (Rev. 4—22). Like the apocalypse proper the letters fear a coming time of tribulation (Rev. 2.10, cf. 13). John the visionary and prophet is not merely reacting to circumstances as they exist, but in his visions he is expressing the conviction about what is likely to happen in the immediate future. The circumstances suggest to the seer that a time of trial is going to come on the Church, when its members will be tempted to follow the masses in their adulation of the beast (Rev. 13.3). especially as it would mean freedom from economic sanctions (13.17) and even death (Rev. 13.15).[36] What John expresses in his visions, therefore, is not the actuality of persecution and death for the saints but the possibility of that in the near future. Thus in our attempt to locate the date and setting of Revelation we have to ask ourselves what circumstances best explain a situation where the seer of Patmos fears a time when those in authority would take the unusual step of insisting that all, irrespective of their religious sensibilities, would be compelled to worship before the statue of the emperor. The historical circumstances presented by the Jewish War and the apparent break-up of the empire seem to offer the most appropriate time of writing of the book of Revelation.

The Composition of the Book of Revelation

The history of the study of this document over the past hundred years has been characterized by a welter of opinion concerning its sources, redaction and structure. The variety of material within the book, and the difficulties in relating the various parts to each other, have suggested sources from different origins and settings as well as a series of editions of the book.[37] The problems, however, have frequently been exaggerated. Although there are one or two perplexing passages, the work has a unity of style and purpose which demands that we take seriously the possibility that its present form is in the main the responsibility of one author.[38] Although we would want to argue that a substantial number of authentic visions have been included, there is no doubt that redaction of that material took place to enable the book to have the considerable degree of order which it manifests. The attempts at source-criticism have hardly been successful,[39] and, in the light of this, it is incumbent upon the exegete to do all in his power to attempt an understanding of the text as it stands. If this task proves impossible, he may then have to resort to theories of multiple editions of the work. It is not too great an assumption to suppose that whoever edited the final form of the text had some method before him and was not guilty of adding material in a haphazard fashion. Indeed, when one compares Revelation with the Similitudes of Enoch, which is certainly a conglomeration of disparate material, it is quite apparent how different the New Testament document appears in its carefully constructed form.[40]

The three opening chapters go closely together and with the concluding verses of chapter 22 (8–21) stand apart from the apocalypse proper and form a framework into which it has been inserted.[41] After the introductory sentences John describes his original call-vision, which, as we have already seen, owes much to the vision in Daniel 10.5ff. While in a state of ecstasy inspired by the Spirit (Rev. 1.10), he sees the risen Christ, who tells him to write what he sees and to send it to seven churches in Asia Minor (1.19). The content of this vision includes not only the apocalypse proper, which is marked by a new stage in John's spiritual perception (4.2 'At once I was in the Spirit'), but also the communications of the risen Christ to the angelic representatives of the seven churches.[42] This material is just as much part of the heavenly disclosures as that which follows in chapter 4 to 22. These opening chapters have a significant role within the apocalypse as a whole. In a sense the revelations which come in chapters 4ff. are dependent on these letters. They not only confirm the correctness of the call to repentance but offer hope of imminent salvation or judgement depending on the response of the different churches. The fact is that John is not here interested in passing on his eschatological disclosures simply to satisfy the curiosity of his readers about the subject of eschatology. The revelation about that which is to come merely intensifies the words of warning and encouragement which are contained in the letters.[43] In this respect Revelation is at one with other eschtological passages in the New Testament. Rarely, if at all, do we find apocalyptic mysteries, whether eschatological or otherwise, being passed on as material which is of interest in its own right. They function within the framework of the spiritual needs of the community addressed. In 1 Thess. 4.15f. the eschatological passage is included to give comfort to those who were perplexed by the death of their loved ones before the parousia, whereas in 2 Thess. 2.2ff. it serves to dampen the zeal of those who believe that the end has already arrived. Eschatological teaching in the New Testament always serves to answer a particular pastoral problem. This is equally true of Revelation, where the faltering belief of some (2.9) and the complacency of others (3.2) demand the challenge which the promise of future bliss offers to those who remain obedient.

Although the first three chapters form an important part of the apocalypse, there can be no denying the new dimension to John's experience which is reached in 4.2.[44] Whereas John had previously seen the vision of Christ with him, now he speaks of an open door in heaven and transference through that door to the world above (cf. T. Levi 2.6).[45] This leads into a section which extends to the end of chapter 5 and deals with the heavenly world and the exaltation of the Lamb. This is preparatory to the material which forms the core of the book, the sequence of seven seals, trumpets, and bowls, all of which arise directly out of the exaltation of the Lamb and the right which he has as a result to open the sealed scroll. Many have noted the parallelism which exists between the three series of sevens, which has led some to suppose that we have parallel events mentioned in these chapters.[46] A comparison of the material in chapters 6; 8—9; 11.15–19 and 16 will reveal how much overlap there is between the series of seals, trumpets, and bowls:

SEALS	TRUMPETS	BOWLS
1 White horse comes forth to conquer	1 Hail and fire: third of earth burnt up	1 Evil sores
2 Red horse takes peace from earth	2 Mountain thrown into sea; third of sea turned to blood and third of creatures die	2 Sea becomes blood
3 Black horse: prediction of famine	3 Star falls from heaven; third of waters made bitter	3 Rivers become blood
4 Pale horse: quarter of the earth killed	4 Sun does not give its proper light	4 Men scorched
5 Souls of martyrs plead for vengeance	5 Air darkened with smoke WOE	5 Kingdom of beast in darkness
6 Earthquake and cosmic disorders	6 Angels kill a third of mankind WOE	6 Euphrates dried up
7 Silence for half an hour	7 Celestial worship and opening of ark in heaven	7 Noises and earth-quake which causes great damage

Now the subject matter here is all of a similar type and speaks of the terrible disasters which afflict the inhabitants of the earth once the eschatological process has started. But although there are the occasional overlaps, there does not seem to me to be enough evidence to suggest that we have here three parallel descriptions of the same events, even if one supposes that two are offered in a more summarized form than the third.[47] There can be little doubt that what the author has in mind here is a fixed number of messianic tribulations or woes.[48] There is nothing in the Jewish eschatological material,[49] which resembles the precise delineation of these woes as we find them in Revelation, though a fixed number does seem to be normal within eschatological beliefs of the period. Thus, for example, a quota of seven lots of tribulations precede the age to come in b. San. 97a[50] and twelve in Syriac Baruch 27. The question is whether John has offered parallel accounts of the same event or has extended an original series of seven to bring about the scheme which we now find in Revelation. The fact that there are not precise parallels between the three series leads one to suppose that the second alternative is to be preferred. Although it is difficult to see any intensification in the suffering and destruction caused by these events, there does appear to be the belief in the author's mind that the sequence of seals and trumpets has merely been a prelude to the final chapter of disasters listed in the seven bowls. Indeed, in chapter 15.1 it is explicitly stated that the seven plagues which are to come are the seven last plagues with which God's wrath is ended.[51] This is surely an indication that there is a definite progression through these chapters leading up to the climax of the eschatological process in chapter 19ff.

Thus the sequence of seals, trumpets, and bowls provides the basic framework of the eschatological material of Revelation. What follows the series of bowls marks the final stages before the new age. Chapters 17 and 18 are a digression which concentrates on the character and destruction of 'Babylon'. This amplifies a brief reference in 16.19, which makes mention of God's wrath against Babylon.[52] The opportunity is then taken in the next two chapters to take a closer look at the reason for her downfall and to indulge in rejoicing over her judgement. The sequence of events is then picked up again in 19.11 which was left off in 16.21. The messianic woes have now ended, and the final judgement comes, instigated by the rider on the white horse. This leads into the messianic age when those who had been slaughtered will reign with Christ for a thousand years, followed by the final judgement and the creation of a new universe (chs. 20—22). There is some difficulty in knowing why we should have apparent doublets in 19.11ff. and 20.11ff. (the judgement of the man on the white horse and the judgement before the great white throne) and 20.1f. and 21.1ff. (the messianic age and the new heaven and earth).[53] This sequence of events is best explained by what John's biblical sources dictated rather than any suggestion that some of the passages may be later insertions.[54] The variety which exists in eschatological expectation at this period makes it dangerous to suppose that John was working within a fixed framework of belief. While it is clear that he follows contemporary expectation in his inclusion of the messianic woes, the very variety of expectation made possible by the scriptural material at his disposal makes some kind of variation in the expression of eschatological belief inevitable.

There thus seems to be evidence in Revelation of a relatively straightforward eschatological scheme consisting of chapters 4—6; 8—9; 11.15–19; 16 and 19.11—22.5 with chapters 17—18 as an attempt to focus on that particular enemy of God and his

Church. The starting point for this eschatological progression is to be found in chapter 5 which in turn leads into a fixed number of tribulations which have to precede the coming of the new age.

Of course, this does not cover anything like all the contents of Revelation, and it is now necessary to explain the function of these other elements. These consist of what Kümmel calls 'interludes' in the sequences of seals, trumpets, and bowls.[55] The first of these passages, chapter 7, looks like a description of the last things and is parallel in its finality with chapter 20ff. as well as chapter 14. What we have here is certainly a vision connected with the final vindication of the election, but whose position here has been totally determined by its context. That is to say, we are not dealing with the climax of the eschatological tribulations, which, in the case of the seals is not reached until 8.1, but with a proleptic vision of the glory of the future which is included here because of its close link with what precedes it. The opening of the seals in heaven has unleashed a great wave of judgement and destruction on the earth, and this culminates in 6.17 with the words, 'for the great day of their wrath has come, and who can stand before it?' The answer to that question is then given in chapter 7,[56] particularly in verse 9: 'I looked, and behold, a great multitude which no man could number, from every nation, from all tribes and peoples and tongues, standing before the throne and before the lamb.' These are the ones who will be able to endure the wrath of God and the Lamb, for these are the ones who have been obedient to God (vv. 3 and 14).

Another link between chapters 6 and 7 is the word 'seal' (*sphragis/sphragizo*). The opening of the seals in heaven spells judgement for a world, which has rebelled against God, but for these who are faithful the coming of the new age is a time of promise. This is indicated by their being sealed (7.3). Although this will not protect from the tribulation which is to come (v. 14), it does guarantee their ultimate safety before God. In language which owes much to Ezekiel 9.4, the faithful are marked upon their foreheads, and they are thus designated as being the ones who would enjoy the bliss into which the thousands, whom John sees in his vision, are about to enter. The chapter thus reassures the faithful that the awful events of the eschatological tribulations are not a sign of eternal doom but of hope for those who are faithful to God. Thus the issues touched on in chapter 7 arise directly out of the first series of disasters which is directed towards mankind. The reason for the interruption of the sequence is intentional; the vision reassures the elect that the evils which are afflicting the earth are a temporary phenomenon which will not directly affect the joy which belongs to those who endure the great tribulation.[57]

The second, much longer, interruption in the sequence of seals, trumpets, and bowls, is to be found in chapters 10–15. Between the sixth trumpet (9.13–19) and the seventh trumpet (11.15–19) we have the vision of the angel and the command to prophesy before the world (10.11), followed by the vision of the two witnesses (11.1–13). There is clearly a deliberate interruption of the sequence here, as 9.20f. looks like a summary of the impact (or rather lack of it) on mankind of the preceding disasters. The reason for an interruption at this particular point is not easy to ascertain, and we may be in a better position to answer this question when we have looked at the contents.

The theme of 11.1–11,13 appears to be the character of prophecy. In 10.11 John is commanded to prophesy and immediately afterwards is shown a vision of the two witnesses whose activity is described in language derived from that used in the Old Testament of the prophets Moses and Elijah (11.6). Although in the different interpretations of this passage down the centuries it has been assured that we have a description of figures who would arise at the End,[58] the probability is that the intention of this vision is much more closely linked with the needs of the Church and is intended as a demonstration of the way in which the true prophet should live and the kind of sufferings which he should be prepared to undergo.[59] Thus the concern here is not with figures who would appear in the future but an illustration derived from biblical imagery of the obligations upon the Church in the present. It is the present which marks the dawn of the new age (5.5) and the return of the prophetic spirit (2.7). The task of prophecy, however, is not just an activity which is confined to the well-being of the Church, for, as in the prophetic ministries of old, it involves the prophet in speaking about and before the world.

If we are right to suppose that John is concerned in this vision with the task of the Church in the present, we may be able to see why this passage should have been included at this point. Thus far in the apocalypse John has seen part of the quota of messianic woes accomplished, the rest is still to come. It is at this particular point, however, that he turns his attention to the role of the Church in the present. In the accounts of history in the apocalypses it is often the case that the apocalypticist indicates the time of writing by changing from a fairly accurate presentation of past history to vague eschatological predictions. This can clearly be seen in the Animal-Apocalypse in 1 Enoch 85ff., where the precise historical writing is abandoned during the middle of the account of events during the second century BC, in favour of eschatological predictions (1 Enoch 90.13ff.).[60] While the pseudepigraphic framework and the total historical reviews are absent from the book of Revelation, there is reason to suppose that in the structure of the book the author does follow some kind of chronological time sequence. He indicates his interest in secular history in Revelation 17.9ff., and one must ask whether in chapters 10 and 11 the interruption in the sequence is here determined by chronological considerations. Up to this point John has spoken about the messianic woes only, with the exception of chapter 7 where the proleptic vision makes the general point about the eternal salvation of those who remain faithful. From chapter 10 onwards, however, John ceases to be a passive observer and is commanded directly to prophesy. This personal involvement indicates a change in perspective, from the description of that which had already taken place as the result of the triumph of the Lamb, to the present situation of the visionary.[61] John interrupts the sequence of trumpets at this point, because he believes that it is at precisely this point in the unfolding eschatological drama that he believes that he and the churches find themselves. It is, therefore, entirely appropriate for him to turn his attention at this particular point to issues which directly affect the life of the Church and its mission in the last days.

Further evidence of this is found in the fact that chapters 4 and 5 definitely refer to past historical events. Chapter 4 describes the situation in heaven before the advent of Christ, whereas chapter 5 speaks of the consequences of the triumph of the cross. John here glimpses past, not future events, and it may be supposed that from his own perspective some of the messianic woes had already passed. The apocalypticist in his vision sees the totality of past and future, and it is, of course, a history of which he himself is a part. Accordingly it is not surprising to find that at the point in history at which the apocalypticist stands there is a more direct concern with what may be expected in the future. John, however, is most interested in that part of history which started with the cross and ends with the new age, but, even within this short span, some of the events are going to have a more direct relevance for his readers than others, for the simple reason that they are the events which have still to come in the near future.

Whether we take the change of emphasis in chapter 10 as a sign that this marks the time of writing or not, there can be little doubt that the bulk of chapters 11—14 is concerned with issues which John believes will impinge directly on the communities for whom he writes. After the vision in chapter 11, which illustrates the character of the prophetic ministry, chapter 12 concentrates on two themes: the divine protection afforded to the Church from the marauding power of the Devil (12.1–6, 13–17) and the imminent threat which the Devil presents to the inhabitants of the earth as the direct result of his ejection from heaven (12.12). The second theme is then expanded in chapter 13. Chapter 12.17 has spoken of the way in which the dragon has made war on the offspring of the woman, who are identified as those 'who keep the commandments of God and bear testimony to Jesus'. One particular form of this threat to the elect is illustrated.[62] The Roman principate and the grandiose claims made for it are said to be inspired by the Devil (13.4). The major diabolical threat to the churches is a failure to recognize the true character of the imminent imposition of worship in the imperial cult in the region. Here then is a threat to the well-being of the community which arises directly out of the triumph of Michael and his angels (12.7ff.). The activities of the powers of darkness have been directed against the people of God, but it is the way in which that threat is about to manifest itself among the churches in Asia Minor which occupies the attention of the seer.

Chapter 14 stands in a similar relation to the preceding chapter as chapter 7 does to chapter 6. We saw that the message of the proleptic vision of the end arose directly out of the issues raised by the opening of the first six seals. The link between chapters 13 and 14 is to be found is the common use of 'name' (13.17, cf. 14.1). Freedom to buy or sell in the kingdom of the beast depends on being marked with the name of the beast (13.16f.). Without this mark economic sanctions, and even death (13.15), result for those who refuse to follow the beast. Those who are marked in this way are safe in the short term from the threats against their livelihood posed by the beast. In chapter 14 a completely different picture emerges. Here, as in chapter 7, we have a proleptic vision of of the final judgement. Those who stand with the Lamb on Mount Zion have his name and the name of God on their foreheads. These are the ones who have not compromised their religion by worship of the beast, whereas all those who have defiled themselves in this way can only expect eternal retribution (14.9f. cf. 13.8). The glimpse of the glory of the future shows that it is the ones who have been marked with the divine rather than the bestial name who will be the ones to triumph, whereas those who have preferred prosperity in the short term can only expect to be victims of the wrath of the Lamb in the future. The contrast is thus starkly drawn. Chapter 13 presents the immediate threat facing the church and the suffering which faithfulness to God will involve. On the other hand chapter 14 presents the other side of the coin, this time viewed *sub specie aeternitatis*. Those who endure the great tribulation are to be the ones who will stand with the Lamb on Mount Zion. Here then is a call to the elect to persevere and put up with temporary inconvenience and suffering (14.12).

Finally, chapter 15 acts as a transition to the resumption of description of the eschatological woes which had been left off in 11.15ff. This is most apparent in verses 1a and 6ff. where specific reference is made to the plagues which are to afflict the earth. Verses 2–4 stress the separation which exists between God and man. Reaching the other side of the sea of glass depends on the rejection of the claims of the beast (v. 2). These verses merely stress the point which has been made in the previous chapters, but this time in the light of the cosmology of Revelation 4. The heavenly sea which is before the throne is said to be full of fire. Like the Red Sea which separated the people of God from the Promised Land, this separates man from God. Those who would sing the song of deliverance on God's side of the sea have to be the ones who have overcome the lures of the beast (v. 2, cf. 13.4).

This survey of the contents of Revelation would appear to give us a scheme of the following kind:

1.1–8	Introductory material
1.9–20	Call-vision
2—3	The letters to the seven churches

4—5	The description of the heavenly court and the transformation of God's relationship with man as the result of the exaltation of the Lamb
6, 8—9 11.15–19 and 16	The sequence of seals, trumpets and bowls which describes the predestined quota of eschatological tribulations which must precede the new age. The whole process starts only as the result of the exaltation of the Lamb.
7	First interlude in the description of the tribulations: a vision which is intended to give hope and assurance to the Church amidst the disasters which surround it.
10.1—11.14 12.1—15.8	Second interlude in the description of the tribulations: a description of the effect of the eschatological events on the life of the Church

    (i)   10–11: the call to prophesy and the character of the prophetic office

    (ii) 12: the assurance of divine protection but also a message of an imminent threat from the Devil

    (iii) 13: the embodiment of evil in the threat of emperor-worship

    (iv) 14: the glory which will belong to those who refuse to worship the beast and the terrible consequences for those who give in

    (v) 15: Concluding vision which leads into the final outburst of the eschatological tribulations.

17.1—19.10	Particular attention devoted to 'Babylon' and her destruction
19.11—22.5	The climax to the eschatological process started in chapter 5
19.11ff.	The victory of Christ
20.1–6	The messianic kingdom
20.7–10	The release of Satan and the war against Gog and Magog
20.11–15	The resurrection and the last judgement
21.1—22.5	The new Jerusalem in a new creation
26.6–end	Concluding admonitions

The Message of Revelation

Recent scholarship has moved away from the belief that Revelation was written by John, the son of Zebedee[63] and acknowledges that all we can say about the author is what we can glean from the book itself: namely, he was a man called John who was imprisoned for his faith (1.9) and who had intimate knowledge of the situation of the churches which he addresses, information about which colours his vision.[64] The rejection of apostolic authority inevitably raises the question of the authority which John supposes himself to possess to address the churches in the way he does. If he had been an apostle or another church leader, his position in itself would have been enough to have guaranteed a hearing for his visions. John lays claim to none of these, however, and the source of his authority is stated clearly and simply in the opening chapter. Unlike contemporary Jewish apocalypticists John does not cloak his message in the garb of the historical events and persons of the past. Instead, he states that he is a companion in tribulation and a brother (1.9) but above all one who prophesies (1.3).[65] Because of this, his authority is not designated by any ecclesiastical office but by the conviction that the Spirit of God is speaking through him and the visions which he has received.[66] The basis for his right to speak to the churches is his conviction that the risen Lord has appeared to him and commanded him to reveal what he had seen and heard. Like the prophets of old he had been told directly, in his case by the exalted Christ, to speak to the people. It is because of this that he can give his book such authority (22.18f.), because they are the words and secrets of Christ himself.

It is this commission of 1.10ff. which undergirds all that follows. Like Micaiah ben Imlah, who saw into the heavenly world and as a result was able to report accurately what was about to take place (1 Kings 22.19), John unveils the mysteries of heaven (1.19). The impact of his message lies in the fact it is presented as the direct revelation from Christ. The view of the seven churches which is to be found in chapters 2 and 3 is presented not as John's assessment of their spiritual progress but as that of Christ. In these chapters the seer is let into the secret of the heavenly assessment of the lives of the Christians in the seven cities addressed. As a result of passing on this 'inside' information to the churches, their members could be challenged to recover their religious zeal (2.4f.), be encouraged in the face of tribulation (2.9ff.), told to reject heresy (2.6; 2.14; 2.20) and made to look beyond their own complacent view of the situation (3.17f.). Both the letters, which presuppose so much intimate knowledge of the individual members and the geography of the various cities,[67] and the apocalypse proper in chapters 4—22 arise from John's conviction that the visions vouchsafed to him would enable the Christians in these places to see historical circumstances in a completely new light.

The ascent to heaven (4.2) which enables John to view the heavenly court marks a new dimension in the rest of the apocalypse. Hitherto John had reported the words of the risen Christ who had appeared to him, but from chapter 4 onwards he speaks of what he has seen in heaven. As we have already noted, Revelation 4 offers an essentially Jewish picture of the heavenly dwelling of God,[68] in which John describes the situation in heaven before the advent of Christ. God sits on his throne surrounded by his celestial retinue, cut off from all but the gaze of the fortunate seer, who is privileged to have this glimpse of God in all his glory. His lordship and power over the whole of creation is hymned in typical Jewish fashion by his celestial court.[69] While it may be a reassuring picture of the fact of God's existence and a reaffirmation of the belief in his rule over the world, it cannot be denied that this is a rule which is only acknowledged in this vision by the heavenly court and the faithful few on earth. The contrast between the hymns of praise to the all-powerful God in heaven and the lack of evidence of the divine will on earth must have been most evident to the readers of the apocalypse. The antithesis between theological affirmation and historical reality could not have been more starkly put. The Christians were living in a world where the dominion of the creator was barely acknowledged, yet the seer was telling them about heavenly choirs which sang the praises of God as the king of the universe. The dualism, though implicit, is perhaps stronger in this chapter than anywhere else in the apocalypse. The world above, where God is acknowledged as lord, and the world below, where few acknowledge his dominion (cf. 11.1f.), exist side by side with little prospect of the dominion of the creator in his heaven being accepted by those who inhabit the world below.

The scene is completely transformed in chapter 5. John sees a scroll with seven seals which turns out to contain the divine will for the inauguration of the events leading up to the new age (6.1ff.).[70] Only when the seals of the scroll are broken can the whole process begin. Unfortunately, the stark contrast between the world above and the world below cannot be rectified until someone is found to open the seals and so inaugurate the process which will lead ultimately to God being put at the centre of the affairs of men. The fact that no one has been found worthy to open the seals is a matter for great regret to the seer (5.4), who, as a typical member of the people of God, longs for the demonstration of God's glory in the world below. John is told not to weep as the advent of the messiah will bring about the transformation (5.5). Dramatically, the messianic figure is then identified with a Lamb bearing the marks of slaughter, which stands in the midst of the court and then comes to take the scroll from God.[71] The picture here is similar to that in Daniel 7.13, where, in this case, a human figure comes to God and receives power and dominion. Until the Lamb comes to God, however, it is merely standing among the other members of the heavenly court.[72] It was the fact that he was a Lamb bearing the marks of slaughter which distinguished him from the rest,[73] however, and meant that he was to share the throne of God himself (7.17). At first he stands as a suppliant before the throne of God, but his death means that he has won vindication for himself and those who follow him (5.9) and worship from the angelic court. Like the Son of Man in 1 Enoch 71.16[74] the Lamb stands as a guarantee in heaven for the ultimate redemption of the redeemed, those who have washed their robes and made them white in the blood of the Lamb (7.14, cf. Heb. 6.19). But he is not merely a pledge of future glory for the elect, for his death and exaltation enable him to be the one to take the scroll with its plan for the inauguration of the last days, and to start that process by opening the seals. This process gradually unfolds throughout the sequence of seals, trumpets and bowls until the glorious future is finally established. The exaltation of the Lamb provides the impetus for all that follows in the unfolding story. Theologically, one can say that a start has been made in the attempt to bridge the gap between the divine intention for the world and the bleak reality of the situation. The sublime lordship of God, manifested in the vision in chapter 4, now has begun to make an impact on a world whose attitudes and outlook is so totally opposed to God. The change in the relationship between heaven and earth has happened because of the slaughtered Lamb.

The point of the sequence of seals, trumpets, and bowls is a way of stressing that the disasters which must afflict the earth are not a sign of divine absence from the world, but paradoxically God's involvement in human history. Such events are a necessary prelude to the new age in Jewish eschatology. All the action connected with the seals, trumpets, and bowls has its origin in heaven. In all cases, where certain events take place on earth immediately after the opening of a seal or the trumpet-blast, the point is being made that the new dispensation, inaugurated by the exaltation of the Lamb, has direct consequences for mankind. Thus the close bond which unites God with human history is emphasized throughout the vicissitudes of the events which are described on earth.

Obviously, the significance of these disasters looks very strange, even barbaric, to modern readers.[75] One has to face the fact that this was not something which John had to explain to his readers as they would, in all likelihood, have shared his beliefs about the way in which the new age would come about. The important thing is to attempt to understand them from John's own point of view before one indulges in attempts to explain the particular doctrine he espouses. What John does say about the various disasters is that they were intended to bring mankind to their senses (9.20f.). John does not regard the terrible happenings merely as the result of the vicious caprice of God. Nor should the point be missed that these events were in any way different in kind from other terrible catastrophes experienced by men. What John describes in his vision is a condensed form of all those terrible events which have afflicted men throughout their history, an intensive demonstration of the imperfections of the universe which mankind tolerates as acceptable and as part of the permanent fabric of things. In these events God, as it were, allows man to see for himself that, if only he is willing to recognize it, the whole universe is riddled with imperfections, which make the world an unsatisfactory place for human existence as it is. But the world as it is cannot be anything but imperfect and subject to these disasters when it refuses to acknowledge the lordship of the creator. Thus God allows the most obvious symptoms of the world's disorder to impinge directly on human existence, in the hope that mankind would recognize the cause of the imperfections and repent. The fact that the warning signs are not heeded means that only the direct overthrow of all that is opposed to God can ultimately free the universe of its imperfections. For John the conviction that God was ultimately sovereign carried with it the corollary that the inevitable coming of God's kingdom meant that all that continued to stand against God would be removed. The gradual coming of perfection demanded that it be fully reflected in the lives of men. Man's refusal to recognize his misuse of his powers could only perpetuate a system, where right suffers and injustice and disobedience continue to triumph. Any concession to the continuation of this process would be a rejection of the lordship of God and the final triumph of his will. Thus the inexorable tide of God's kingdom need not sweep all aside who are confronted by it, provided that they conformed to its norms and rejected the ideas and institutions which stood against it.

Within the process of the inauguration of the new age spoken of in the sequence of seals, trumpets, and bowls John includes other visionary material. The first insertion comes after the opening of the sixth seal when the process is halted so that the servants of God can be sealed (7.3f.). This is a note of reassurance to the faithful that the terrible disasters will not mean ultimate separation from God, providing that they follow in the footsteps of the Lamb (7.14). That does not mean that they will be spared all suffering, for the reaction of the unbelieving world will be frequently hostile (11.10 and 13.1ff.). What is certain is that obedience to God will finally receive its due reward. Likewise we have a concern for the role of the Church and the threat facing it in the much longer insertion in chapters 10—15. Once again a sequence of seven is broken (9.13) so that the material can be inserted. Its place within this sequence is a demonstration of the fact that the Church too lives in the last days, and its responsibilities must be outlined and its integrity safeguarded.[76]

In chapter 10, which acts as an introduction to the vision which follows, we have a twofold pronouncement. First of all, there is the promise that the climax to the whole eschatological process is nearing its end (10.6) with the imminent seventh trumpet-blast. This gives a clear sense of urgency to what follows, and in particular to the role of the churches in the present. The second part of the chapter describes how John ate a scroll (cf. Ezek. 3.1ff.), and is then commanded by an angel 'to prophesy about peoples, nations, tongues and kings' (10.11). It is this command which provides the setting for the vision which follows and must be used as the key to interpret the vision. It is better, therefore, to take the vision in 11.1–13 not as a prediction of eschatological events still to happen but as an illustration of the true nature of the prophetic office to which John is now called.[77]

But his call to prophesy cannot be isolated from the task of the church as a whole. John, therefore, intends his companions in tribulation to share with him the task of witness before the world. This link between the role of the individual prophet and the task of the Christian community at large is most clearly seen in 19.10, where the seer is placed on the same level as all who hold the testimony of Jesus. Thus, while the command at the end of chapter 10 is directed to John alone, it applies just as much to all those whose task it is to testify to the ways of God.[78] That is not to suppose that John thought that all Christians would necessarily pay the ultimate penalty for their witness as the two figures do in the vision (11.7). But the fact that only two lampstands are mentioned in 11.4, in comparison to the seven in 1.12, should not lead us to suppose that it was only a prophetic 'remnant' which was about to die for its actions.[79] As far as John is concerned, the possibility must remain that the role of ideal witness, as it is outlined in chapter 11, is one that is incumbent upon every Christian. This vision has as its major concern an issue which is of direct importance to the Church itself. The process of unveiling here switches from the account of the events leading up to the establishment of God's kingdom to focus on the Church itself and its role before the final stage of the messianic woes is completed.

Drawing on Old Testament imagery, particularly Ezekiel 40.3, John's vision starts with a command to measure the Temple of God as well as those who worship in it (11.1). This contrasts with the outer court which is left unmeasured and handed over to the nations of the world for a limited period. This is not a reference to the Temple in Jerusalem, though the idea obviously derives from the description of it. The point is that John is not here dealing with an actual building but the temple as a symbol of a greater reality. Just as the two witnesses are examples of the ideal witnesses to God and symbolize the Church as a whole, dedicated to the testimony to God, so also the place here is not to be identified with any particular location on earth.[80] The setting is any place where Christians find themselves having to stand up for the ways of God in the face of opposition from their opponents. The measurement of the Temple, therefore, is a sign of divine possession.[81] This small area which has been measured designates the paucity of evidence of God's dominion in a world which is *apparently* dominated by forces opposed to his ways. The present is thus depicted as a situation where forces opposed to God are rampant, and the evidence of God's presence in the world and adherents of his cause is, for a time, rather limited (v. 2). But in this situation God has decreed that he has not left himself without witness to his cause. In this context it becomes necessary for the Church, symbolized by the two witnesses,[82] to be free from destruction while they carry out their office.[83] That promise applies only long enough for them to carry out their task, and it does not mean that they are to be immune from all harm. The Church's Master died after his witness to God (19.10), and this is the fate of all those who follow in his path. Wherever their testimony is made and their words and persons rejected and destroyed, that place resembles the place which rejected Jesus and is at one with all those places which throughout history have refused to listen to the voice of God (11.8). But the physical destruction of those who witness to God is not the last word. Like their Master, the witnesses also will be given new life (11.11), and their vindication will in the end be a testimony to the folly of unbelieving mankind (cf. 1.7 and Wisd. 2.21—3.12). The conclusion of the whole episode is a great earthquake (11.13) which then leads into the seventh trumpet. This is a reminder that the prophetic activity of the community takes place in the very middle of the messianic woes. The promise of vindication of the martyrs is matched by the tribulations which now afflict an impenitent universe. Within the last times a world which now seems to have excluded God completely is not left without some indication of the demands of God which are exemplified in the lives of the righteous community.

When we turn to chapter 12, we are once again faced with a chapter whose message is directed to the Church. Two main features appear in this chapter: the persecution of the pregnant woman and her offspring by the dragon (12.1–6 and 13ff.) and the heavenly battle between the angelic forces of light, led by Michael, and the forces of darkness led by Satan (vv. 7–12). The first theme is best understood as a symbolic way of presenting the way in which the righteous community, from whom the messiah is born,[84] has been persecuted by the dragon. This rather general point which is made in this vision becomes more specific in chapter 13. The child who is born, though pursued by the dragon, is taken up to heaven. His presence in heaven is followed almost immediately by the vision of the war between Michael and Satan. It is tempting to suppose that the rapture of the messiah had a decisive effect on the position of Satan in heaven. Just as the exaltation of the lamb brought about the opening of the seals, so here the rapture of the male child brought about the decisive battle between the heavenly representative of the people of God and their accuser (12.10), so that the latter is thrown out of heaven never more able to bring complaints against the elect of God (cf. Rom. 8.33).[85] Those who follow the Lamb can be assured that there is no longer anyone to refuse them access to the presence of God (v. 11). Despite all the harassments of the evil one, to quote Paul in Romans, nothing will be able to separate the faithful from God (Rom. 8.39).

The promise of divine protection for the community from the destruction of the devil (v. 15f.) and the freedom from the challenge of the accuser in the heavenly tribunal does not alter the fact that the present is a time of great peril. The Devil has been thrown from heaven, knowing that he has been allowed only a very short period of freedom to do what he wishes on earth (v. 12). What is offered to the community is the vindication of faithfulness but also a warning that the wiles of the powers of evil are now at work in the world of men.

The form in which the wiles of the Devil manifest themselves is examined in detail in the following vision of the beasts from the sea and land, which are said to wield the authority of the dragon (13.4). Most commentators would agree that the specific issue which lies behind this vision is the threat of an imposition of emperor-worship in Asia Minor.[86] The beast which comes up from the sea is said to be the emperor's representative in the province of Asia Minor, the proconsul, who, as it were, came up from the sea annually when he landed at Ephesus. The head of the beast whose mortal wound had been healed is probably to be taken as a reference to the myth of the return of Nero which was current in the last years of the first century.[87] The fact that we have imagery derived from Daniel 7 here makes it likely that the issue at stake is the question of the relationship between the people of God and the secular power. The point is made most clearly that worship of the beast means worship of the Devil as well (v. 4). The vision sets out the great lure of following the beast, not least because so many people will be attracted in this way (v. 8). This, however, is no harmless act but an acknowledgement of another power instead of God, and, what is worse, tacit recognition that the power of darkness deserves as much, if not more, devotion than the creator himself.[88]

The second beast which comes out of the earth is the native group, known as the *commune Asiae*[89] which became responsible for promoting the imperial cult in Asia Minor. This activity is described in graphic detail in this vision, even to the extent of performing miracles similar to those of the prophets of old to impress the inhabitants of the earth (v. 13, cf. 1 Kings 18.38). Whether one should take this as a reference to some of the fraudulent devices, which were practised to persuade people of the supernatural character of the cult, cannot be said.[90] At any rate it is yet another warning to the Christians not to be taken in by the false claims made and the extravagant language which were nothing short of blasphemy (cf. v. 6). The consequences of not falling into line are manifold. Some clearly will be killed (v. 15), but others may have to suffer economic hardships (v. 16). Both are powerful incentives to the weak-willed to seek for peace from the harassment in the short term by giving into the demands to worship the beast.

In the vision in chapter 14 the opposite side of the picture is given. Whereas the threat of the beast and its propagandists means ostracism and death for those who refuse to bow down before it, chapter 14 shows that such an apparently futile protest guarantees future vindication. It is those who are free of the mark of the beast and are instead marked with the name of the Lamb and his father who will stand with the Lamb on Mount Zion in the future. Those who have given in and accepted the dominion of the beast will not be so fortunate. Their fate is painted in gruesome detail. The decision which faces the communities as the threat from the Devil intensifies is here portrayed in the starkest fashion. On the one hand there is the mighty Roman state characterized by its figurehead, the emperor, with power over the whole world and being spoken of in quasi-divine terms. It has so many marks of divine authority, that to many it seems impossible to deny that supernatural power must be behind such an institution. But, of course, the fact is that this power is demonic and not divine. Nevertheless, rejection of its claims means death or loss of status in the present. On the other hand there is the religion of the true people of God which makes a stand against the false claims of the state-religion even at the expense of personal fortune and well-being.

Nowhere in the apocalypse is the significance of apocalyptic more clearly seen than in its function in these two chapters. In them the seer removes the veil which hides the real character of the Roman state, so that his readers may see for themselves what the situation is really like. To those who are tempted to regard the Roman state and its emperors as an innocent institution ordained by God, John discloses their true character. Those who believe that swearing by the genius of the emperor is a quite harmless act are asked to think again. When the emperor is set up as a god and when demands are being made to worship him as such, there is a direct threat to true worship, which can only be inspired by the Devil. In the light of such claims any kind of religious compromise would be a denial of one's place within the people of God. Only those who have triumphed over the beast by refusing to worship it can pass into the presence of God (15.2). The use of apocalyptic here shows how short-term benefit in the form of freedom from persecution is not only a denial of one's integrity but also jeopardizes one's future destiny.

After the long interruption in the description of the sequence of the trumpets the final stage in the eschatological woes is started in 15.1 and 5 and described in detail in chapter 16. With the completion of the full quota of eschatological disasters John turns his readers' attention to the destruction of Babylon, whose rulers' claims had seemed to pose such an enormous threat to the life of the Church. He mentions her destruction in passing in 16.19, and then returns in chapters 17 and 18 to examine her character and her downfall. Whereas in chapter 13 the content of the vision had been the claims made for the Roman emperors and their power, interest in these chapters centres on the city which was the centre of their empire, referred to as Babylon.[91]

In chapter 17 John sees a vision of a woman in the wilderness sitting on a scarlet beast (v. 3). She is described as a harlot, who has participated in shedding the blood of the martyrs (v. 6). The picture of the woman supported by the beast contrasts with the vision of the perfect city, new Jerusalem in chapter 21, which is not supported from below but comes from above, from God himself.[92] The emphasis in John's vision of the harlot is on one whose continued existence depends on the support of the beast, which wielded the power of Satan (13.2). The grandeur is only of a transient kind, however, and depends entirely on the consent of the beast. This is clearly evident in 17.16ff. where the beast and its horns combine together to destroy the harlot. The imperfection of Rome, like the world at large, is the result of neglect of the divine will and has within itself the seeds of its own destruction. Although its power may appear to be all-pervasive, it is in fact very insecure, and the kings which appeared to guarantee its continued existence will in fact be the means of its overthrow (v. 16). Like the prostitutes with which she is compared Rome has grown rich illicitly (v. 4). Her gaudy splendour contrasts with the pristine purity of the virgin-bride, the symbol of the new Jerusalem in 21.2. The fall of Babylon is then greeted with a dirge reminiscent of oracles of doom in the prophetic writings (e.g. Isa. 13 and Jer. 51). Her position at the hub of the world's commercial activity and her arrogant self-confidence is shown to be completely ephemeral. Those who placed so much confidence in her have their illusions shown up for what they really are (18.11ff.).

After the digression which examines the character and downfall of Babylon the final stages of the eschatological process are reached. The beast which had brought about the overthrow of the harlot, together with all those who had promoted the worship of the beast and participated in its worship are destroyed (19.19f.). This is the fulfilment of that dominion over the world which had arisen as the result of the cross. The death of the Lamb had been acknowledged by God as the moment which marked the decisive change in the course of human history. This was still a victory which had to be acknowledged by men. The character of the rider on the white horse (19.13) is clearly seen in the fact that he comes in garments dripping with blood. This is not the result of the battle, because that has not yet taken place. He comes covered with his own blood, with the right to act as eschatological judge conferred upon him by his victory on the cross (cf. 5.5).[93] Early Christian writers looked back to Calvary and Easter as the moments when the decisive victory had been won (1 Cor. 15.20ff. and Col. 2.14f.).[94] The juxtaposition of the war in heaven with the rapture of the male child who has the characteristics of the messiah in 12.5ff. may reflect such a belief.[95] But by and large Revelation tends to see the cross as the moment which triggered off the sequence of events which would culminate in the final triumph of the messiah. The rider is acknowledged as king of kings and lord of lords (19.16), but this reflects the estimate of heaven already found in the hymns of 5.12. Although there seems to be a duplicate of this final battle in 20.7ff., the point of the two is completely different. The first in 19.11ff. deals with the destruction of the beast and its followers, whereas the second is concerned with the power behind the beast, the Devil himself.

With the final overthrow of the earthly power, which had been the cause of so much evil, the way is open for the kingdom of the messiah to be established in the world. The problem with the eschatology of Revelation is that we have few parallels from Jewish literature of, what one might term, a two-stage expectation for the future kingdom of God. A period of bliss within this world is the central feature of Jewish eschatology, however, and can be found in 4 Ezra 7.27ff. and Syriac Baruch 29f.[96] The tendency to concentrate on the description of the new Jerusalem in Revelation 21f. should not lead us to gloss over the importance of the messianic kingdom in 20.4–6. It is more than merely a prelude to the new age. The promises which John has made to the faithful in his visions have included vindication of the elect in the sight of the world (11.11). This vindication takes place when the martyrs reign with Christ.[97] In the millennium the apparent futility of the life of the martyrs is vindicated. Not only is it a question of a reward for their faithfulness, for these are the ones who are most qualified to exercise dominion with the messiah in his kingdom. Their lives in the previous order had shown that they had been able to live up to their calling as kings and priests (1.6f., cf. 5.10). Now they continue the role which had already been theirs but had hitherto remained hidden from the perception of the world at large (cf. Rom. 8.19). What shines through this brief reference to the millennium in Revelation is the inaugurated eschatology which is so familiar to us from the rest of the New Testament.[98] In the old aeon the Church is already anticipating its role in the new age; the glory of the age to come already has made its presence felt through the gift of the Spirit. Those who are obedient to God in the difficulties of the present are the ones who are best equipped to exercise dominion in God's kingdom on earth in the future (cf. Luke 22.29f. and 1 Cor. 6.2).

The inclusion of the messianic reign on earth in the eschatology of Revelation should warn us not to assume that apocalyptic eschatology had lost faith in history as the sphere of divine redemption and was concerned with events beyond history. Chapter 20.4ff. is at one with other examples of apocalyptic eschatology in stressing the viability of the creation as it is reflecting the will of God. There is nothing here to suggest that it is so corrupt that it is beyond hope. That is not to deny, however, that the picture of the messianic kingdom reckons with the need to make one important change as compared with the situation as it existed before. In this future kingdom the temptation to evil has been restrained by the binding of Satan (20.2). Thus the deception, which Satan had practised hitherto, and as a result led many astray (13.4), is now absent. This freedom from the pernicious influence of evil enables man to see more clearly than he otherwise would have done his obligations to God. The whole eschatological process in Revelation, therefore, is about God's activity in history. It starts with a historical event (the death of Jesus) and is introduced by the judgement of God working through events in history. It cannot be said that in this instance the future breaks into the present, as Rowley has suggested.[99] The whole of future history in Revelation is an evolution which arises directly out of past events, particularly the crucifixion of Jesus, and moves in and through the historical process to its conclusion. As John says little about history before the cross, we are not in a position to know what his attitude to God's activity in history had been in the period of Israel. If the Apocalypse is anything to go by, however, there can be little doubt that, like other apocalypticists, he never loses grasp of the fundamental truth of God's complete control. The only dualism which is to be found in heaven arises out of the contrast between promise and fulfilment. There is never any suggestion that God is not in control of what takes place. The disasters of the last days and the release of Satan for one final assault (20.7ff.) all speak of the utter control which God has over the forces of chaos.

After the destruction of Satan and the judgement of the whole of mankind on the basis of their works (20.12)[100] there comes the climax of the book, the vision of the new heaven and earth and the new Jerusalem coming down from heaven (21.1ff.). Inevitably, the process of purification must precede the description of what is to come, because the complete destruction of the forces opposed to God and his ways is the necessary prelude to that perfect state into which nothing profane can enter (21.27). It may seem rather strange that John should feel the need to have a second stage in his eschatological description, when he had already spoken of the bliss enjoyed by the martyrs. The point is that it is enjoyed by only a few (20.5). Whether pastoral problems have dictated the form of John's eschatology we cannot say, but there must have been some perplexity among Jews when passages like Syriac Baruch 29f. seemed to indicate that it was only those who were fortunate enough to be alive at the dawn of the new age who would be privileged to participate in it. This was a problem which Paul had to face in writing to the Thessalonians (1 Thess. 4.15f.). John offers all the faithful the promise of a hope for the future, whether they take part in the messianic kingdom or not. Of course, one cannot underestimate the significant contribution which the scriptural imagery would have made on the form of John's expectation.[101] Scripture told John that there was to be a new heaven and earth (Isa. 65.17), in addition to which it speaks elsewhere of a period of messianic bliss (Isa. 11.1ff.). In John's visions such elements have not been fused but juxtaposed to yield the type of two-stage eschatology which we find here.

The fact that Scripture provides the resources for John's visions should make us a little wary of reading too much into the significance of the reference to the new creation. This language may lead us to question whether what has just been said about an emphasis on history as the sphere of divine activity really explains what is to be found in Revelation 21f. The fact that John speaks of a new creation and the flight of the old creation from God's presence (20.11) may seem to indicate that type of dualism which one has come to associate with apocalyptic thought. Here after all is an example of the rigid break with the past, the need to destroy the old, the move away from that which is corrupt to the utterly new and God-given.[102] In the light of the presence of the millennium in Revelation which maintains the possibility of obedience to God in the old world under the right conditions, it would appear to be difficult to maintain that the reference to the new heaven and new earth is the product of the deep-seated eschatological dualism inherent in apocalyptic. That is not to deny that we have a reference to a new creation here. In the light of 21.1b it is impossible to justify the belief that it is simply a question of the renewal of the old aeon. But the significance of this vision derives from the presence of this promise in Scripture and not from any apocalyptic pessimism. There is no evidence to suggest that John wants to assert the complete discontinuity which exists between the old and the

new. While it is true that the descent from heaven of the new
Jerusalem speaks of the divine origin of the new city, man is not
denied any part in its building. Indeed, on the foundations of
the city are inscribed the names of the twelve apostles of the
Lamb (21.14). The point of this comment is that certain individuals did have their part to play in this divine edifice.[103] This is not
to deny the divine inspiration behind it, but asserts that men
and women, as they had during the messianic age, could indeed
act as the agents of God's eternal purposes. In a similar vein,
John speaks of the way in which the glory of the nations is
brought into the new Jerusalem (21.24). The influence of Scripture is once again all important (e.g. Isa. 60.11), but the presence
of this passage makes it difficult to speak here of a radical
dichotomy between the old and the new. As Caird says,
'nothing from the old order which has value in the sight of God
is debarred from entry into the new.'[104] The present age is not
without the indications of the divine will and the divine character manifested in human lives and achievements, but these are
seen in all their completeness in the future. In every age and,
perhaps one can also say, among all peoples there have been
signs of God's will being fulfilled, and it is, therefore, perfectly
appropriate that these products of the previous world-order
should find their place in the next. Without this, the significance
of inaugurated eschatology, which is such an important part of
early Christian thought, makes little sense. John's grasp of some
of the social implications of these beliefs may at times seem
rather tenuous, but he remains in no doubt that already it is
possible for those who believe in Jesus to act in the present the
roles of those who will play their part in the future order. To
admit this is to accept the possibility that, amidst the imperfections of the present, much of worth can be achieved which will
stand the test of entry into the new age (cf. 1 Cor. 3.13).

Much of John's description of the new creation is taken up
with a detailed plan of the new Jerusalem (21.10–21).[105] Apart
from this certain points are made about the character of life in
the new age. Every inhabitant of the new Jerusalem will be a
child of God (21.7). Here the promise to David and his descendants is extended to all the people of the new Jerusalem, just as
the idea of divine sonship is the property of all believers as well
as Jesus himself according to Galatians 4.6 and Romans 8.15.
Exactly this eschatological belief is to be found in Jubilees 1.24

(cf. 1.17) where God speaks in the following way about the future:

> . . . and I will create in them a holy spirit, and I will cleanse them so that they will not turn away from that day unto eternity. And their souls will cleave to me and to all my commandments, and they will fulfil my commandments, and I will be their father and they shall be my children. And they shall all be called children of the living God . . .[106]

The separation which exists between God and man, as the result of human sinfulness, is now removed, and God dwells with his people (21.3). Similarly, the disasters which afflicted the world and were symptomatic of rebellion against God are no more, and the travail which characterized human existence previously has now been abolished (v. 4). There is no need of a temple within the city, because the division between sacred and profane has been removed.[107] God's command to his people to be holy has now been fulfilled (Lev. 19.2; 26.11f; cf. 1 Peter 1.16; Rev. 1.6). Right at the heart of the new city is the throne of God and the Lamb, and the stream, which comes forth from this throne, revivifies the city. Chapter 22.2 describes the immediate environs of God in terms of Paradise, though this word is not used explicitly in this chapter (cf. Rev. 2.7). The leaves on the tree of life are 'for the healing of the nations', an indication that God had always offered the means of salvation to all who would repent.[108] The greatest glory of all, however, is the privilege, granted to all who are part of the new creation, to see God face to face (22.4). This was the greatest favour of all for any Jew (Exod. 33.20, cf. Isa. 6.5). They will also be stamped with the name of God. Thus the essential character of God, which had been part of man from the very beginning of creation (Gen. 1.26), will be apparent in the lives of those who are part of this new age.

This survey of the various parts of Revelation and the message which the visions set out to communicate to the reader indicates that we are dealing with a work which is not merely a conglomeration of various eschatological predictions. Even with the unfolding eschatological drama we have evidence of that pastoral concern of the opening letters in visions like 7; 11.1–13 and 12—13. But nowhere is the concern better manifested than in the conclusions to the seven letters (2.7f.; 2.17; 2.26ff.; 3.5f.; 3.12f.; 3.21). All the promises contained in these verses relate to participation in the new age, but the promise is intimately linked with the challenge to repent or stand firm. The significance of the apocalypse is that it attempts to make its readers aware of another dimension to human existence, which is not apparent as the result of observation of the world as it is. It is important for them to realize that the history of which they are a part is not a never-ending process, in which present structures and relationships are perpetuated. History is not without meaning, for the apparently haphazard string of events has to be set within the framework of the divine control. By appreciating the eschatological character of historical events John intends his readers to be equipped to make decisions, which are based on a full appreciation of the nature of the case and not on dangerous half-truths. It, therefore, is essential for followers of Jesus to see that the divine dimension in human existence is in fact ever present, though unseen, and that its effects will become apparent in due course. The belief that the present is all that matters, even if it means sacrificing one's integrity, is shown to be the ultimate disaster for man. The inherent evil of institutions, which are outwardly harmless, is stressed in no uncertain terms. The result is a document which sets out to offer its readers an apocalyptic dimension to life, in the sense that reality is explained within a framework, which shows the divine involvement in human existence and the inadequacy of an approach which does not take this seriously.

There is a tendency in Revelation, which is probably inevitable in a document whose eschatological belief is so dominant, for there to be a lack of concern for the role of the community in the present. The message is one of readiness to guard against the incursions of the powers of darkness, which will prevent the communities from reaching their goal. But Revelation does not urge its readers merely to hang on during the last stages of the present age so that they can receive their reward. Revelation 11 indicates that John is anxious that the Church should see that it has a role to play, however unsuccessful it may be, as part of the witness to God and his ways in this age (11.13, cf. 1 Pet. 2.12). The mission of the Church then is centred on its role as the standard-bearer of the ways of God and the living testimony to the inadequacy of a godless view of life. Revelation does not reject the need for change, but, like most eschatological treatises, it presupposes that real change can only occur if the results of the change coincide with the character of the new aeon. There can be no question of superficial reform which does not affect the underlying problem. Anything short of that is nothing but the attempt of man to tinker with a system which bears the marks of ultimate destruction and must, therefore, be rejected.

Conclusion

THE STUDY OF apocalyptic has witnessed the changing emphases and interests of the students of the Jewish and Christian religions. Attempts have been made to play down the importance of apocalyptic, with the result that its position has often been relegated to that of a bizarre eccentricity which was duly rejected by both religions. There is now a widespread recognition, however, that apocalyptic (as we have used the word throughout this study) and eschatological beliefs had a significant, perhaps central, role to play in early Christian belief. Few would deny the importance of eschatological concepts for the proclamation of Jesus, though whether an imminent expectation formed a central platform of his and the Church's message is still a debated issue. But the indications are that the apocalyptic outlook, which sought answers to ultimate questions through direct revelation, had its part to play in the foundation of the early Christian movement. Thus the hope for the future and the convictions about the contacts with another realm, such as we find them in the last book of the New Testament, are not merely deviations from mainstream Christianity, at least in its earliest period, but can with some justification be regarded as the essence of the Christian message.

Whereas the evidence which we possess seems to support such an assessment of the contribution of apocalyptic to earliest Christianity, the same cannot be said unequivocally for all aspects of Jewish religion. No doubt apocalyptic did have its part to play within first century Judaism, but the question is whether it is at the heart of the Jewish religion or merely a fringe phenomenon. As we have seen, there has been a tendency in recent study to suppose that apocalyptic, with its claims to direct experience of God, and Pharisaic Judaism, were not mutually exclusive in their approaches to theology. This position has been assumed throughout the foregoing discussion. Nevertheless one cannot but be aware of the uncertainties attaching to this view. Although the evidence from the apocalypses is sufficient to

443

enable us to sketch an outline of the apocalyptic movement, our task is nothing like as easy when we come to ask whether all groups within Judaism were infected by its spirit. This problem is particularly acute when we examine the earliest rabbinic evidence. Recent study has tended to suppose that the mystical ideas, current at a much later period, were also operative in the late first and early second centuries of the Christian era. Nevertheless a critical examination of the texts has indicated that the earliest versions of many of the most important stories will just not bear the weight of a thoroughgoing mystical and apocalyptic interpretation. What is more, it seems likely that they are susceptible of an interpretation which excludes any suggestion of mystical interest completely. But while fully accepting the problems presented by the rabbinic material and the dangers of building too much on an insecure foundation, it seems to me that there was probably an <u>essential continuity between the</u> <u>religious outlook of the apocalypticists and that of the earliest</u> <u>exponents of *merkabah*-mysticism among the rabbis</u>. Both seem to bear witness to the possibility that the study of Scripture could, in certain instances, lead to direct apprehension of the divine world.

The foregoing study has not placed very much weight on the eschatological material of the apocalypses. As has been pointed out, this should not be interpreted as a rejection of the significance of this element but the consequence of a recognition of the heterogeneous character of the apocalypses. The fact remains that the apocalypses offer the major witness to the character of early Jewish eschatology. Their importance in this respect, however, should not be taken as a basis for the definition of the religious outlook contained in them. This study would seem to indicate that an approach to apocalyptic which concentrates its attention on the hope for the future and the distinctive elements in that message of hope inevitably omits some of its most important characteristics. The future is important in the apocalypses but precisely because the destiny of the individual and his world is always one of those imponderables whose obscurities man longs to penetrate.

Although the trend of much recent study with its equation of apocalyptic and eschatology has been questioned, there is a sense in which aspects of recent study and the approach taken here coincide. Paul Hanson has argued that apocalyptic eschatology involved a retreat from the historical realm into a transcendent sphere, which alone would be appropriate for the fulfilment of the divine promises. In apocalyptic eschatology, he argues, the language of myth provided the terminology to speak of the world beyond where the divine purposes would be fulfilled. While there are grounds for questioning whether this explanation does justice to the eschatological material in the apocalypses, there is a sense in which the retreat from history does characterize the outlook of apocalyptic.

We have argued that the presupposition of apocalyptic is its interest in that which is secret. But the quest for contact with the hidden world of God and his angels is a potential threat to an interest in history. It must be said unequivocally that nowhere does apocalyptic deny the inevitability of the fulfilment of the divine purposes in history. Nevertheless its belief that contact can be made with the realm above undermines the concern for the historical fulfilment of the divine promises. When a man can receive assurance about existence by knowledge of the world above and a proleptic glance of eschatological bliss, the yearning for the realization of the promises inevitably diminishes. Knowledge of that which is already in existence can so easily become a matter of satisfaction in its own right, at the expense of the earthly realization in the future. Apocalyptic has within it the seeds of destruction of the historical eschatology. The vertical dimension of apocalyptic thought offered a retreat from reality, which could, and in gnosticism did, dispense with the need for historical fulfilment. To be part of the world of light can become an all-embracing salvation for the elect without any recourse to the vicissitudes of history. Knowledge of what is above and what is below, what is past and what is still to come, can become ends in themselves rather than means whereby the validity of the divine promises can be upheld.

The attempts to understand the past and to give new meaning to the religious inheritance have been features of all the great religions. Apocalyptic should be seen as part of this process. Although it sets out to make sense of what has been received, the means whereby it answered the questions thrown up by the religious traditions were in fact radical. The laborious task of interpreting the scriptures was at the heart of the Jewish attempt to understand the challenge of the present. Apocalyptic, however, looked to God for a direct answer. The proper understanding of difficult passages and the perplexing problems of the day were all susceptible, in the view of the apocalypticists, of an answer by means of vision, dream, or the intervention of a divine emissary. Herein lies the potential point of conflict with a religion which concentrates on exegesis as the key to its understanding of the divine will. The direct communion with the divine, claimed in the apocalypses, could bypass the minute study of the sacred text such as was practised in the rabbinic schools. That is not to say that experiential religion and exegesis were necessarily mutually exclusive within Judaism. We have argued that both formed an indispensable part of Jewish religion. Nevertheless there was always the possibility that the revelation would itself include innovations which could be regarded as at least as important as the Torah itself. This position is hinted at in 4 Ezra 14.47. Such a claim is not far removed from the gnostic apocalypses, which claim to have unique and authentic information about the cosmos and human existence. The apocalyptic literature by and large is not aberrant in its doctrine, but the means whereby it justified its beliefs was subversive of traditional methods of ascertaining the divine will and of the sacred scriptures themselves.

Although there is reason to suppose that the apocalyptic outlook was to be found in all streams of Judaism and throughout the nascent Christian movement, there was a reaction against certain aspects of its manifestation. The suspicion of the *bath qol* among certain rabbis may have been in part a reaction to claims to divine authority based on revelation alone. While this may have been partly because of the importance given to such claims within the Christian movement, it would be wrong to suppose that the whole of the early Christian Church accepted such revelations unquestioningly. Both Paul and the author of the Fourth Gospel centre the revelation of God in the person of Jesus and his death and resurrection. The hostile reactions to figures like Cerinthus, Elchesai and the Montanists all exhibit a growing suspicion of the claim to direct revelation, despite the fact that such claims were at the heart of the earliest Christian experience. Despite the fact that claims to revelation were the source of much heterodox teaching in early Christianity, not least among those gnostics who were least enthusiastic about history, the paradox is that it is the earliest example of revelatory literature, the New Testament apocalypse, which is the document which emphasizes most clearly the working out of the divine will on the historical plain.

This book has concerned itself entirely with the study of ancient Jewish and Christian texts. The fact is, however, that several of these texts are part of a canon of sacred Scripture, which is considered a source of enlightenment about God's activity in the world. I have deliberately refrained from engaging in the discussion of hermeneutical issues, not because these are unimportant, but because a superficial treatment would hardly do justice to the complex issues which such an investigation would present. There can be little doubt that the neglect of apocalyptic in recent decades is giving way to a more positive appreciation of its religious value, not only for the understanding of hope in a secular age but also because of its contribution to experiential theology. Such a change of heart does not make any easier the hermeneutical task, however. The bizarre nature of the symbolism and the outmoded cosmology and mythology present enormous problems to the interpreter. Nevertheless the more we appreciate that we have the relics of a living religion enshrined in these ancient texts, the greater our assessment of its value will be. Despite the culturally conditioned mythology, the concern of religious people to make sense of their past in the circumstances of the present, by resorting to attempted contacts with the world beyond, is a feature of religions in every generation and culture. But the fact that the apocalypses offer such important evidence of the dominance of eschatological beliefs within Jewish and early Christian religion is demanding a reappraisal of this element within contemporary Christianity. Continuity with the biblical revelation demands that one reckons with eschatology as the central pillar of Christian doctrine. The renewed interest in the idea of hope in the Chrisitian religion and the move away from an individualist piety to the cosmic dimension of divine activity have given renewed impetus to the need for sympathetic assessment of this element within early Christian belief. In that the apocalypses are our main witness to this aspect of belief, they will surely need to move to the centre of the stage in our attempts to probe the character of early Christian eschatology. If apocalyptic was the mother of Christian theology, then the outlook of the New Testament apocalypse should be seen as typical of early Christian belief and not an aberration. Eschatological enthusiasts in every generation have given its view of history a bad name. That should not prevent us from ascertaining the contribution which it has to offer to a Christian view of history and society. To be true to the religious outlook of the first Christians demands that we interact with the religious beliefs of apocalyptic in all its dimensions.

Notes

Introduction

1. A point well made in the little book by K. Koch *The Rediscovery of Apocalyptic*.
2. On apocalyptic and early Christianity mention must be made of E. Käsemann, whose essays have had such an important effect on the rehabilitation of the subject (see the collection on 'Apocalypticism' ed. R. W. Funk *JTC* 6). On the systematic front see e.g. W. Pannenberg *Jesus God and Man*, ed. Pannenberg *Revelation as History*, J. Moltmann *Theology of Hope*, and on the Pannenberg group W. R. Murdock 'History and Revelation in Jewish Apocalypticism', *Interpretation* 21 and H. D. Betz 'The Concept of Apocalyptic in the Theology of the Pannenberg Group', in *JTC* 6.
3. See the comments of J. J. Collins 'Apocalyptic Eschatology as the Transcendence of Death' *CBQ* 36.
4. C. K. Barrett, 'New Testament Eschatology', *SJT* 6 p.138f.
5. On the mystical quest in Philo see particularly E. R. Goodenough *By Light, Light. The Mystic Gospel of Hellenistic Judaism*.

Part One: **What is Apocalyptic?**

Chapter 1 *Knowledge of the Divine Mysteries through Revelation*

1. On this theme see W. Harnisch, *Verhängnis und Verheissung* pp.19ff. On the crisis facing religion in the Ancient World see the suggestive comments of J. W. Bowker, *The Religious Imagination and the Sense of God* and E. R. Dodds, *Pagan and Christian in an Age of Anxiety*.
2. Article '*Mysterion*', *TDNT* iv, p.815. Also D. Flusser article 'Apocalypse' *EJ* 3, col. 179: 'The major purpose of apocalyptic writings is to reveal mysteries beyond the bounds of human knowledge', J. B. Frey *DB* Supplement i, 327f., J. Schreiner *Apokalyptik* p.80, Hengel 'Pseudonymität' p.267 but cf. the change of emphasis in P. D. Hanson's (*RB* 78 p.35) 'Apocalyptic we define as the disclosure, usually esoteric in nature, of the prophetic vision of Yahweh's sovereignty (including his future dealings with his people, the inner secrets of the cosmos etc.), which the visions of visionaries have ceased to translate into the terms of plain history . . . because of a pessimistic view of reality.' See further now ed. J. Collins 'Apocalyptic' *Semeia* 14, M. Stone 'Lists of Revealed Things' and I. Gruenwald *Apocalyptic and Merkavah Mysticism*.

3. Cf. the parallels to apocalyptic which are to be found in M. Eliade, *Shamanism: Archaic Techniques of Ecstasy*, particularly pp.181ff. and id. *Myths, Dreams and Mysteries*, especially pp.57–122. See also W. James, *The Varieties of Religious Experience*, pp.366ff.

4. See e.g. G. Scholem *Major Trends in Jewish Mysticism* and id. article 'Kabbalah', in *Encyclopaedia Judaica* vol. X col. 489ff. and Scholem *Sabbatai Şevi*. On Christian mysticism mention may be made of E. Underhill, *Mysticism*, K. Kirk, *The Vision of God*, D. Knowles, *The English Mystical Tradition*, and F. von Hügel, *The Mystical Element of Religion*.

5. A good example of the sort of exegetical methods used at the beginning of the Christian era can be found in the seven *middoth* attributed to Hillel in ARN 37. Further discussion of this subject can be found in J. W. Doeve, *Jewish Hermeneutics in the Synoptic Gospels and Acts* especially pp.52ff.

6. The Greek word *apokalypsis* from which we derive the English words apocalypse and apocalyptic means a 'disclosure' or 'revelation'.

7. A major difficulty with the book of Daniel is the fact that it is bilingual, chapters 2.4—7.28 being written in Aramaic rather than Hebrew. This does not correspond to the division between legends and revelations, as the 'son of man' vision is in Aramaic. Various attempts have been made to solve this linguistic problem, on which see O. Eissfeldt, *Old Testament Introduction* pp.516ff. and H. H. Rowley, 'The Unity of the Book of Daniel' in *The Servant of the Lord*, pp.247ff.

8. Passages like Daniel 7.9f. had an important bearing on later eschatological ideas, not least the picture of the last judgement in Revelation 20.12f. In its present form, however, it must be doubted whether this heavenly assize in Daniel 7 is to be understood as an event which will take place at the end of history, but is rather a judgement passed in heaven, whose consequences will be ultimately felt by mankind.

9. Reference is made to an anointed one in 9.26, but this is probably an allusion to Onias III (cf. 2 Macc. 4.30ff.).

10. I.e. prophecies after the event. These are statements which have the appearance of predictions of the future, though in fact they are merely historical reports put on the lips of some great figure of the past to offer a pretence of being a prophetic pronouncement. On this subject see E. Osswald, 'Zum Problem der *Vaticinia ex eventu*', *ZAW* 75.

11. E.g. 1 Enoch 85ff., Syriac Baruch 53ff. This material is discussed by Rössler, *Gesetz und Geschichte* pp.55ff. and see below pp.136ff.

12. There is little doubt that the contents of Daniel 7 exercised a considerable influence on later Jewish apocalyptic. For example, in 4 Ezra 12.10f., the interpretation of the eagle-vision explicitly mentions the vision of Daniel as the basis for what the seer had just seen.

13. On the introductory stories in Daniel see G. Hölscher, 'Die Entstehung des Buches Daniel', *TSK* 92 and J. J. Collins, 'The Court-Tales in Daniel and the Development of Apocalyptic', *JBL* 94.

14. The differences between Revelation and Daniel should not be taken as an indication that the former is in fact not a typical apocalypse. On this see J. Kallas, 'The Apocalypse – an Apocalyptic Book', *JBL* 86 and B. W. Jones,

'More about the Apocalypse as Apocalyptic', *JBL* 87 and J. J. Collins 'Pseudonymity, Historical Reviews and the Genre of the Revelation of John' *CBQ* 39.

15. R. H. Charles's description of the work as 1 Enoch ought to be retained, since we have a considerable number of fragments which parallel the Ethiopic text in both Greek (see ed. M. Black *Apocalypsis Henochi Graece* and A. Lods *Le Livre de Hénoch*) and Aramaic (see now J. T. Milik *The Books of Enoch*). There is now a new edition of the Ethiopic text, ed. M. A. Knibb and E. Ullendorf, but the edition of the Ethiopic consulted was that by R. H. Charles *(The Ethiopic Version of the Book of Enoch)*. The translation in ed. R. H. Charles *Apocrypha and Pseudepigrapha* vol. ii, pp.163ff. and *The Book of Enoch*[2] will be presupposed wherever there is a translation of the texts offered here. Further literature to be found in A. M. Denis, *Introduction aux pseudépigraphes grecs d'Ancien Testament* pp.15ff. and J. H. Charlesworth, *The Pseudepigrapha and Modern Research* pp.98ff. No attempt has been made in these notes to give a complete summary of texts and studies relating to the Jewish apocalypses. Much relevant material can be found in the bibliographical books of Delling, *Bibliographie zur jüdisch-hellenistischen und intertestamentarischen Literatur 1900–70*, Eissfeldt, *Introduction* pp.603ff. and G. Nickelsburg, *Jewish Literature between the Bible and the Mishnah*.

16. The most recent edition with text, introduction and French translation is by A. Vaillant, *Le Livre des Secrets d'Hénoch*. There is an earlier English translation and commentary by R. H. Charles and W. R. Morfill, *The Book of the Secrets of Enoch*. See also Denis op. cit. p.28f.

17. For a discussion of the special case of Jubilees see pp.51ff.

18. English translation by R. H. Charles, *The Apocalypse of Baruch translated from the Syriac*. For other editions and literature see Denis op. cit. pp.182ff and bibliography *sub* Bogaert.

19. Text and introduction by J-C Picard, *Apocalypsis Baruchi Graece*. There is a new German translation by W. Hage in the series ed. by W. G. Kümmel *Jüdische Schriften aus hellenistisch-römischer Zeit*.

20. English translation and notes by G. H. Box, *Ezra–Apocalypse*. Further literature in Denis op. cit. p.92f. See now also M. Stone, *The Armenian Version of IV Ezra*.

21. An English translation with a short but valuable introduction can be found in the series *Translations of Early Documents* ed. G. H. Box. See also N. Bonwetsch, *Die Apokalypse Abrahams* and the literature cited in Denis p.37f.

22. The two recensions of the Greek version have been edited by M. R. James, *The Testament of Abraham*, on which see G. W. Nickelsburg ed. *Studies in the Testament of Abraham*,[2] *IOSCS Proceedings* ii. A translation of the Ethiopic version can be found in W. Leslau *A Falasha Anthology*; other literature in Denis pp.31ff. There is an English translation by G. H. Box *(The Testament of Abraham)* which includes translations of the Testament of Isaac and the Testament of Jacob. For a full discussion see M. Delcor *Le Testament d'Abraham*.

23. Greek version in R. H. Charles,*The Greek Versions of the Testaments of the Twelve Patriarchs* and M. de Jonge, *Testamenta XII Patriarchum*. Aramaic fragments of the Testament of Levi have been found in the Cairo Genizah, see R. H. Charles and A. Cowley 'An Early Source of the Testaments of

the Patriarchs', *JQR* 19, and at Qumran, see ed. J. T. Milik *Discoveries in the Judaean Desert* (Cave 1) pp.87ff. and id. 'Le Testament de Lévi en araméen, fragment de la grotte 4 de Qumran', in *RB* 62. Further secondary literature on the Testaments is to be found below at n.33 It is difficult to decide whether the Testament of Joseph should be classified as apocalyptic. It certainly includes a dream vision in chapter 19, but this is probably the result of influence of Genesis 37.5f and 40f. rather than the use of the apocalyptic framework. Its exclusion has few consequences for the present study. On this testament see the collection of papers in ed. G. W. E. Nickelsburg *Studies on the Testament of Joseph*.

24. This work is preserved as a whole only in Ethiopic. The early chapters under the title 'The Martyrdom of Isaiah' can be found in Charles, *Pseudepigrapha*. Translations of the whole can be found in Hennecke–Schneemelcher–Wilson, *New Testament Apocrypha* ii, pp.642ff. (by H. Duensing and J. Flemming) and by R. H. Charles (*The Ascension of Isaiah*).

25. A convenient text and translation is to be found in vol. ii of K. Lake, *The Apostolic Fathers* (Loeb edition).

26. Hebrew text with extensive introduction and English translation by H. Odeberg, *3 Enoch*, reissued, with a new introduction by J. Greenfield, in 1973. A new edition is promised in the Doubleday series ed. P. S. Alexander. Mention should also be made here of the various fragments which we possess of the lost pseudepigrapha, among which are several apocalypses. They are collected by A. M. Denis *Fragmenta Pseudepigraphorum quae supersunt Graece*. There is an English translation of certain texts by M. R. James *The Lost Apocrypha of the Old Testament*. Also of importance are the gnostic apocalypses, see ed. J. M. Robinson *The Nag Hammadi Library*.

27. On these apocalypses see M. Buttenwieser *An Outline of the Neo-Hebraic Apocalyptic Literature* and id. *Jewish Encyclopaedia* i, pp.675ff.

28. See A. Rubinstein 'Hebraisms in the Slavonic Apocalypse of Abraham', *JJS* 4.

29. So L. Rost *Judaism outside the Hebrew Canon* p.110 on the Slavonic Enoch and on the Testament of Abraham, F. Schmidt *Le Testament d'Abraham* Diss. Strassbourg, 1967, and G. H. McCurdy 'Platonic Orphism in the Testament of Abraham', *JBL* 61 and further Hengel 'Pseudonymität' p.268.

30. See J. T. Milik '4Q Visions de 'Amram et une citation d'Origène' *RB* 79, pp.77ff.

31. Text with translation and notes edited by J. Strugnell, 'The Angelic Liturgy at Qumran', *Supplements to Vetus Testamentum 7*.

32. Edition of the Latin text by G. Kisch *Pseudo-Philo's Liber Antiquitatum Biblicarum*. For literature on the work as well as a text and commentary see C. Perrot, P. M. Bogaert and D. J. Harrington *Pseudo Philon: Les Antiquités Bibliques*. There is an English translation by M. R. James *The Biblical Antiquities of Philo*. The vision of Cenez is quoted in full p.151.

33. See the survey of research in H. Dixon Slingerland, *The Testaments of the XII Patriarchs: a Critical History of Research*, M. de Jonge *Studies in the Testaments of the Twelve Patriarchs*.

34. See n.23 above for references to the Aramaic and Hebrew fragments of the Testament of Levi. A Hebrew fragment of the Testament of Naphtali has

been found in Cave 4 (J. T. Milik in *RB* 63). Further bibliographical information in Denis op. cit. p.52f.

35. On the development of the testament-form to include the apocalypse see A. B. Kolenkow 'The Genre Testament in the Hellenistic Jewish Milieu', *JSJ* 6, especially p.69: '. . . in the Hellenistic era, the literary genre of the patriarchal blessing would seem to have been enlarged by visions or trips to heaven which give the rationale for revelation of the future . . .' On the apocalyptic character of the Testament of Abraham see Hengel, 'Pseudonymität' p.265.

36. It is not clear whether J. G. Gammie would include the Testaments on the basis of his definition of apocalyptic ('The Classification, Stages of Growth and Changing Intentions of the Book of Daniel', *JBL* 95, p.193f.): 'A work may be classified as apocalyptic providing it contains (i) some form of revelation, whether of future events of heavenly contents, (ii) a cluster of sub-genres or component genres, (iii) a cluster of ideational elements common to works already agreed to belong to the apocalyptic literature.' In the light of what has been argued in this study, his first definition is to be welcomed without reserve, not least because it recognizes the possibility that apocalyptic can have interests which are not specifically eschatological. When, however, he argues that it can also be applied to a cluster of sub-genres or component genres, he runs the risk of allowing such a vague definition to include works which are not in the strict sense apocalyptic. We have noted that apocalyptic contains many features in common with other contemporary Jewish literature. In the light of this it is difficult to see how the presence of certain features in common with an apocalypse necessarily justifies a work, or part of a work, being called apocalyptic. A work like the Psalms of Solomon, for example, has several features in common with the apocalypses. Indeed, both H. H. Rowley, *The Relevance of Apocalyptic* p.71f., and D. S. Russell, *The Method and Message of Jewish Apocalyptic* p.57f. include it in their list of apocalyptic literature, but cf. the comments of Schreiner, *Apokalyptik* p.80. But we are dealing here with a work which takes its inspiration from the biblical liturgical texts, and there is no suggestion that a claim is being made to reveal divine secrets. Because it was written round about the same time as many of the apocalypses it could be expected to share some common theological themes with them.

37. On the Sibylline oracles see J. J. Collins, *The Sibylline Oracles of Egyptian Judaism*.

38. For a consideration of the importance of this type of religion in the ancient world see E. R. Dodds, *The Greeks and the Irrational* (on the Sibyl. p.71), A. D. Nock, *Conversion* and W. L. Knox, *St Paul and the Church of the Gentiles* pp.13ff.

39. Doubts are expressed about the apocalyptic characters of the Sibylline Oracles by J. J. Collins (op. cit. n.37) p.110, though for rather different reasons than those outlined here.

40. *Judaism and Hellenism*, i, p.210.

41. On the gnostic character of early rabbinic aphorisms see W. D. Davies 'Aboth Revisited', in *Christian History and Interpretation* pp.148ff.

42. J. J. Collins 'The Symbolism of Transcendence in Jewish Apocalyptic' *Biblical Research* 19 p.12 'the primary form of apocalyptic is not speculation on future events, but the living of life in the present', see also the same author's 'Apocalyptic Eschatology as the Transcendence of Death', *CBQ* 36.

43. See G. Scholem *Major Trends* pp.40ff. and now Gruenwald *Apocalyptic*.

Chapter 2 *Apocalyptic and Eschatology*

1. On 'apocalyptic' in modern literature see F. Kermode, *The Sense of an Ending,* especially pp.93ff. The view of H. Cox (*On Not Leaving It to the Snake* p.38) is typical of this modern understanding: 'Apocalypse creates a mood of world-negation, fatalism . . . and sometimes a virulent other-worldliness . . . Rational action is useless because powers outside history and beyond human control will quickly bring the whole thing to a blazing end', quoted and discussed in D. S. Russell, *Apocalyptic: Ancient and Modern* p.22f.

2. For example W. Schmithals, *The Apocalyptic Movement* pp.29ff; P. D. Hanson article 'Apocalypticism', in *IDB Supplement* pp.28ff; D. S. Russell, *The Method and Message of Jewish Apocalyptic* p.105f. There is a concise survey of the various attempts to define apocalyptic in F. Dexinger, *Henochs Zehn-wochenapokalypse* pp.6ff.

3. *The Rediscovery of Apocalyptic* pp.24ff. The formal characteristics are: (i) discourse cycles in which the seer is shown something important about the destiny of man, (ii) spiritual turmoil which leads to some kind of revelation, (iii) paraenetic discourses which offer a kind of 'eschatological ethic', (iv) pseudonymity, (v) symbolism drawing upon a vast reservoir of ancient mythology, and (vi) a long literary development and composite character. Of the eight leading ideas of apocalyptic which he lists the following may be mentioned: (i) imminent expectation of the end, (ii) the cosmic catastrophe which ushers in the end, (iii) the history of the world divided into fixed segments, and (iv) an extensive angelology and demonology. A similar definition is to be found in P. Volz, *Die Eschatologie der jüdischen Gemeinde* pp.4ff., W. Bousset, *Religion* pp.292ff., Vielhauer, 'Apocalyptic', *NT Apocrypha* ii, pp.587ff., and Schreiner *Apokalyptik* pp.70ff., though the latter points out how difficult it is to summarize its distinctive ideas (p.111), as also does P. D. Hanson *Dawn* p.8f.

4. W. Schmithals *The Apocalyptic Movement* p.14 (cf. p.17) 'For apocalyptic, revelation was in essence a revelation – *apokalypsis* – of an event in the future.'

5. Op. cit. p.30.

6. The confusion which has arisen in the use of the word has rightly been pointed out by P. D. Hanson in his article 'Apocalypticism' in *IDB Supplement* p.29: . . . 'the extension (of the term apocalyptic into biblical scholarship) invited confusion from the start by virtue of its arbitrariness, as connections were made first on the basis of various literary features, then on the basis of diverse doctrines or concepts . . . The significance of the use (of the word *apokalypsis* in Rev. 1.1) applies in the first instance to the definition of the literary genre 'apocalypse' rather than to the definition of

the phenomenon of apocalypticism'. Cf. the comments of M. E. Stone, 'Lists of Revealed Things' p.451.

7. E.g. E. Käsemann, 'On the Subject of Primitive Christian Apocalyptic', in *New Testament Questions of Today* p.109 n.1, 'I speak of primitive Christian apocalyptic to denote the expectation of an imminent Parousia', and E. Stauffer, 'Das theologische Weltbild der Apokalyptik', *ZST* 8 and in summary form in his *New Testament Theology* pp.19 and 258.

8. *The Relevance of Apocalyptic* p.38 and also P. D. Hanson, *The Dawn of Apocalyptic* pp.9ff. Further questioning of this distinction can be found in B. Vawter, 'Apocalyptic: its Relation to Prophecy', *CBQ* 22 and G. E. Ladd, 'Why not Prophetic-Apocalyptic?' *JBL* 76.

9. For a similar contrast between apocalyptic and scribal religion see D. Rössler *Gesetz und Geschichte* and below p.486 n.1 and the literature cited there.

10. *Jesus and his Coming* p.94f. So also T. W. Manson, 'Reflections on Apocalyptic', p.145; but cf. de Jonge, *Studies in the Testaments of the Twelve Patriarchs* pp.193ff.

11. See W. Bousset, *Die Religion des Judentums* pp.242ff. and P. Vielhauer, 'Apocalyptic' in *New Testament Apocrypha* vol. ii, p.587. D. S. Russell (op. cit. 264ff.) speaks of a new eschatology of a transcendent kind being an important element in apocalyptic.

12. This difference is noted and discussed briefly by R. Bauckham, 'The Rise of Apocalyptic', *Themelios* 3 p.10ff.

13. Critical problems concerned with both documents are discussed on pp.251 and 405.

14. See M. E. Stone, 'Lists of Revealed Things in Apocalyptic Literature'.

15. Indeed, it has been suggested by ·W. Harnisch, *Verhängnis* especially pp.240ff. that this particular doctrine arose within the late first century situation in which 4 Ezra was written, cf. Hengel, *Judaism and Hellenism* i, p.190 and Volz, op. cit. p.65f.

16. E.g. D. Rössler, op. cit., G. F. Moore, *Judaism* i, p.127f., R. T. Herford, *The Pharisees* especially p.188, T. W. Manson 'Some Reflections on Apocalyptic'.

17. Scholem, 'Towards an Understanding of the Messianic Idea in Judaism', pp.5ff., J. Bloch, *On the Apocalyptic in Judaism* particularly pp.31ff. and 57ff., J. Klausner, *The Messianic Idea in Israel* p.393, I. Levi, 'Apocalypses dans le Talmud' *REJ* 1 pp.108ff., W. D. Davies, 'Apocalyptic and Pharisaism', in *Christian Origins and Judaism*, A. Nissen, 'Tora und Geschichte', and J. B. Frey op. cit. p.345. On the absence of eschatological material in early rabbinic texts see A. J. Saldarini, 'Apocalyptic and Rabbinic Literature', *CBQ* 37 and for evidence of the continuing interest in such ideas, albeit in a less intense form, see id. 'The Uses of Apocalyptic in the Mishna and Tosefta', *CBQ* 39.

18. See E. P. Sanders, *Paul and Palestinian Judaism* especially pp.346ff.

19. See Nissen op. cit. p.260f. but cf. Schmithals op. cit. pp.46ff.

20. For further discussion of these traditions see J. Neusner, *The Rabbinic Traditions about the Pharisees before AD 70*. On the esoteric teaching of the scribal schools see the suggestive, though hypothetical, comments of J. Jeremias, *Jerusalem in the Time of Jesus* pp.237ff.

21. For further information see J. Klausner, *The Messianic Idea in Israel* pp.391ff. and E. E. Urbach, *The Sages* pp.666ff. and Schürer-Vermes-Millar, *History of the Jewish People* vol. 2 pp.488ff.

22. Op. cit. p.9f. On this see L. Ginsberg, 'Some Observations on the Attitude of the Synagogue towards the Apocalyptic–Eschatological Writings' *JBL* 41.

23. It is worth pointing out that works like 4 Ezra and Syriac Baruch are frequently linked with a Pharisiaic milieu, so Rost op. cit. pp.120ff., P. Bogaert, *L'apocalypse de Baruch* pp.370ff., F. Rosenthal, *Vier apokryphische Bücher aus der Zeit und Schule R. Akibas* especially pp.39ff., but cf. C. Thoma, 'Jüdische Apokalyptik am Ende des ersten nachchristlichen Jahrhunderts', *Kairos* 11 pp.134ff. and G. H. Box, *Ezra Apocalypse* pp.1viiiff.

24. Josephus' account of the events leading up to the war is to be found in *BJ* ii, 416ff. On Josephus' attitude towards the hopes of the Jewish people see M. de Jonge 'Josephus und die Zukunftserwartungen seines Volkes', in *Josephus-Studien* ed. O. Betz, K. Haacker and M. Hengel pp.205ff. On the complex political situation at the time of the outbreak of the Jewish war see now E. Schürer ed. G. Vermes and F. Millar, *The History of the Jewish People in the Age of Jesus*, vol. i especially pp.484ff. On the impact of the war on rabbinic Judaism see C. Thoma 'Auswirkungen des jüdischen Krieges gegen Rom (66–70/73) auf das rabbinische Judentum', *BZ* 12 and S. W. Baron, *Social and Religious History* ii, pp.89ff.

25. The most recent discussion of 1QM is that by P. R. Davies *(1QM: The War Scroll from Qumran)* with full bibliography.

26. From Aboth de R. Nathan Rec. B. ch.31. On this saying see Urbach op. cit. p.667.

27. b. Berakoth 28b and see W. D. Davies, *The Setting of the Sermon on the Mount* pp.256ff. and G. Forkman, *The Limits of the Religious Community* pp.90ff.

28. Translation from C. K. Barrett, *The New Testament Background: Selected Documents* p.163.

29. So e.g. Vielhauer op. cit. p.587. J. M. Schmidt, *Die jüdische Apokalyptik* p.174 has pointed out the interesting change which took place between the first and second editions of E. Schürer's *Geschichte des israelitisch – jüdischen Volkes im Zeitalter Jesu Christi*. In the first edition (1873) apocalyptic was given a separate section, but in the second edition (1886ff.) the eschatological teachings of the apocalypses were treated, along with similar doctrines, in a section on the messianic hope of Judaism. Schürer thus makes a clear distinction between the apocalypse as an appropriate designation of a literary form and the content of the apocalypses, which in many respects corresponds with similar ideas found in other Jewish literature, including the rabbinic sources.

30. See also Urbach op. cit p.676. A collection of similar material can be found in Strack–Billerbeck i, p.950. The messianic woes were known to R. Eliezer (c. A.D. 90) see Mekilta de R. Ishmael on Ex. 16.29 (*Wayyesa'* 5): R. Eliezer says: 'If you will succeed in keeping the sabbath, you will escape the three visitations: the day of Gog, the suffering preceding the advent of the messiah and the great judgement day.' (Lauterbach *Mekilta* ii, p.126).

31. See Russell op. cit. pp.217ff. and p.136.

32. Cf. the passage in b. Sanhedrin 99a which speaks of a fixed period for the messianic age: 'It has been taught: R. Eliezer said: The days of the Messiah will last forty years' etc.

33. See the material in Kuhn, article 'Gog' in *TDNT* i, p.790 and Strack–Billerbeck ii, pp.831ff.

34. Cf. Tosefta Berakoth 1.10 and b. Sanhedrin 94a and 95b.

35. Cf. J. Maier, *Vom Kultus zu Gnosis* p.12ff. The insistence on unity at this period makes openness to new ideas highly improbable (see Forkman op. cit. and Bokser, *Pharisaic Judaism in Transition* pp.28ff.).

36. Moore i, p.45ff. but cf. the interpretation of the saying in Urbach pp.255ff. and on the Manual of Discipline P. Wernberg-Møller, *The Manual of Discipline* particularly pp.69 and 85.

37. Moore, *Judaism* ii, p.378f. and Strack–Billerbeck i, p.829.

38. See also Urbach op. cit. p.667.

39. Cf. Urbach p.651: 'Some of the Sages not only knew compositions of this kind, but were actually close, in their spiritual leanings and turbulent imagination, to the circles from which they emanated, and were very susceptible to their ideas and visions'. Despite the fact that Urbach presupposes a distinction between the sages and the apocalypticists, he is in little doubt that close links did exist between the two. See also B. Reicke, 'Official and Pietistic Elements' *JBL* 79 pp.137ff.

40. Cf. the remarks of J. Barr in 'Jewish Apocalyptic in Recent Scholarly Study' in *BJRL* 58, particularly p.34f.

41. In this respect the work of P. D. Hanson *The Dawn of Apocalyptic* is very important.

42. Op. cit. p.42.

43. There is a brief but useful summary in M. Hengel, *Victory over Violence* p.55ff. but see also Schürer Vermes-Millar vol. i pp.484ff., S. W. Baron op. cit. i, pp.250ff., and Hengel, *Zeloten* pp.319ff.

44. A. Dupont-Sommer, *The Essene Writings from Qumran* speaks of the work as an 'immense and truly apocalyptic drama in which the destiny of the visible and invisible worlds was to be decided for ever'.

45. A. Dupont-Sommer op. cit. p.167 and Y. Yadin, *The Scroll of the War of the Sons of Light* p.14.

46. A. Dupont-Sommer op. cit. p.165.

47. Similar, though not exactly the same, ideas about the relationship between the community and the heavenly world are to be found in the Manual of Discipline and the Hymns (1QH) see H-W Kuhn, *Enderwartung und gegenwärtiges Heil* especially p.69f. and above pp.113ff.

48. So Dupont-Sommer op. cit. p.320.

49. Other passages are mentioned in Yadin op.cit. p.237.

50. Cf. Syriac Baruch 72.2 which seems to speak of a warrior messiah, though this emphasis is absent in the eschatological passage in 29.4. On this element in apocalyptic see Hengel, *Judaism and Hellenism* p.188.

51. So e.g. J. Jeremias, *New Testament Theology* vol. i, p.122.

52. History of research is given in G. R. Beasley-Murray, *Jesus and the Future* pp.1ff. and *A Commentary on Mark 13*. See also J. Lambrecht, *Die Redaktion der Markus-Apokalypse* and L. Gaston, *No Stone on Another*. There is a valuable comparison of the use of the Old Testament in Mark 13 and other eschatological discourses in apocalyptic literature in L. Hartmann, *Prophecy Interpreted*, especially pp.145ff.

53. Cf. the Apocryphon of John 1.30f. (*NHL* p.99) where the setting of the Temple-mount is the prelude to an apocalypse proper introduced by a reference to the open heaven, see W. C. van Unnik, 'Die geöffneten Himmel im der Offenbarungsvision des Apokryphons des Johannes', in *Apophoreta*.

54. It seems difficult to relegate the bulk of this chapter to later Christian prophets or redactors. N. Perrin's thesis (*The Kingdom of God in the Teaching of Jesus* p.131) that much of the language in this chapter has no parallels in the authentic Jesus-tradition does not necessarily indicate lack of authenticity. The facts can be equally well explained by arguing that such eschatological material is likely to have been confined to Jesus' private communication to his disciples on such matters cf. Mark 4.11.

55. So also W. G. Kümmel, *Promise and Fulfilment* p.99 ('these sayings do not constitute an apocalyptic revelation properly so-called') and Beasley-Murray p.223f. ('the similarities of form . . . are basic to any description of the end, but the parallels which would set Mark 13 in the class of genuinely apocalyptic writings are absent').

56. On the omission of typical eschatological themes see also Jeremias, *New Testament Theology*, vol. i, p.125. The importance of the theme of vindication of the suffering elect is singled out by M. D. Hooker, *The Son of Man in Mark* pp.148ff.

57. Cf. b. Sanhedrin 97a . . . 'pious men and saints will die, and the Torah will be forgotten by its students.'

58. Some indication of the variety of interpretations is offered by Beasley-Murray, *A Commentary on Mark 13* p.54.

59. On scriptural interpretation at Qumran see O. Betz, *Offenbarung und Schriftforschung in der Qumransekte* and F. F. Bruce, *Biblical Exegesis in the Qumran Texts*.

60. There is a concise survey of this aspect of the attitude to divine knowledge in the Qumran scrolls in Hengel, *Judaism and Hellenism* i, pp.221ff. On the link between the exegesis at Qumran and apocalyptic see I. Gruenwald 'Knowledge and Vision', *IOS* 3 p.74f.

61. Hennecke-Schneemelcher-Wilson *NT Apocrypha* ii, p.588.

62. Cf. H. Conzelmann 'Geschichte und Eschaton', *ZNW* 50 p.215ff. Though he has rightly pointed out that there is much in Mark 13 which still remains within the framework of existing history, there seems to be no reason to suppose that anything but v. 26 is to be regarded as an event of a supernatural kind.

63. Belief in a heavenly redeemer seems to be confirmed by 11Q Melch, though there does not seem to be sufficient evidence to see him as a messianic figure. On the relationship between this passage and the Son of Man issue see B. Lindars, 'Re-enter the Apocalyptic Son of Man', *NTS* 22

especially p.57f. It is significant that all the evidence which we possess of a heavenly redeemer in Jewish texts is of the same type as the New Testament beliefs about Jesus. All speak of an apotheosized man being the agent of deliverance in the future.

64. Cf. J. Pryke, 'Eschatology in the Dead Sea Scrolls', in ed. M. Black *The Scrolls and Christianity* p.46f.

Chapter 3 *Apocalypse and Apocalyptic*

1. On the significance of these chapters see J. J. Collins 'The Court-Tales in Daniel and the Development of Apocalyptic', *JBL 94*.

2. Also absent from the Apocalypse of Abraham, see Koch op. cit. p.25. On the ethical teaching which emerges in these sections see H. Maldwyn Hughes, *The Ethics of Jewish Apocryphal Literature*, and on the relationship between rabbinic and apocalyptic ethical teaching see e.g. A. Nissen op. cit. pp.260ff. (cf. Rössler pp.15ff. and 45ff.) and R. T. Herford, *Talmud and Apocrypha* pp.171ff.

3. Cf. Charles, *Pseudepigrapha* p.169 and *Book of Enoch* p.2f.

4. On the original form of the Book of Enoch without the Similitudes see the suggestion of J. T. Milik, *The Books of Enoch* especially p.58.

5. It is included in the category of apocalyptic by Nissen op. cit. p.246 n.6.

6. The ascent up the mountain became in later Jewish tradition an ascent into heaven; see W. A. Meeks, *The Prophet-King* especially pp.205ff.

7. G. I. Davies, 'Apocalyptic and Historiography', *JSOT* 5 p.22 and see the remarks of I. Gruenwald in 'Jewish Esoteric Literature in the Time of the Mishnah and Talmud', *Immanuel* 4 p.39f and id. *Apocalyptic* p.23f.

8. On the heavenly journey in the literature of antiquity see W. Bousset, *Die Himmelsreise der Seele*, C. Colpe, 'Die Himmelsreise der Seele innerhalb und ausserhalb der Gnosis', in ed. U. Bianchi, *Le Origini dello Gnosticismo* and G. Widengren, *Literary and Psychological Aspects of the Hebrew Prophets*, especially pp.94ff.

9. That an ascent to heaven is implied in Revelation 4.1ff. is suggested by E. Lohmeyer, *Die Offenbarung des Johannes* p.45 and Charles, *Revelation* i, p.110f, *contra* J. Lindblom, *Gesichte und Offenbarungen* p.221 n.18.

10. On the open heaven see W. C. van Unnik op. cit. above (p.458 n.53) and F. Lentzen-Deis *Die Taufe Jesu nach den Synoptikern* pp.99ff.

11. See below p.269. On IV Ezra see M. Stone, 'Paradise in IV Ezra', *JJS* 17.

12. On this passage see further p.97. On the connections with Ezekiel 1 see M. Black, 'The Throne-Theophany Prophetic Commission', in *Jews, Greeks and Christians*.

13. See pp.219ff and also T. F. Glasson 'The Son of Man Imagery', *NTS* 23.

14. Cf. Galatians 4.26; Hebrews 12.22; Revelation 21.2, and Strack–Billerbeck, ii, p.796.

15. There is some resemblance here to Philo's theological ideas, in which the total plan for human existence forms part of the mind of God, see Wolfson *Philo* i, pp.200ff.

16. Cf. the related idea of the seer glimpsing the decrees of God set down in the heavenly tablets e.g. 1 Enoch 81.1f.; 93.2; 103.2; 106.19 and G. Widengren, *The Apostle and the Heavenly Book* especially pp.22–39.

17. The exception to this rule is Daniel 7.1–14 which seems to speak of a vision of the heavenly world see below pp.85ff.

18. Noted by A. P. Hayman 'The Problem of Pseudonymity in the Ezra Apocalypse', *JSJ* 6, p.55f.

19. For further discussion of the throne-visions see below pp.85 and 219ff.

20. See Caird, *Revelation* p.63.

21. On Revelation see below pp.415ff.

22. See H. Gunkel, *Schöpfung und Chaos in Urzeit und Endzeit* pp.41–69. On Greek influence see T. F. Glasson, *Greek Influence in Jewish Eschatology* and J. J. Collins, *Sibylline Oracles* p.102ff.

23. So e.g. Koch op. cit. p.26 and Russell op.cit. pp.122ff.

24. The literature on this subject is extensive but particular reference should be made to the survey of the study of pseudonymity over the last century in ed. N. Brox, *Pseudepigraphie in der heidnischen und jüdisch-christlichen Antike*, J. A. Sint, *Pseudonymität im Altertum* (but see the review by M. Smith in *JBL* 78 p.188f.), F. Torm, *Die Psychologie der Pseudonymität im Hinblick auf die Literatur des Urchristentums* (only available to me in the form of the extract in Brox op. cit. pp.111ff.), K. von Fritz, ed. *Pseudepigrapha* 1 (particularly important are the essays by M. Smith, 'Pseudepigraphy in the Israelite Literary Tradition', and M. Hengel, 'Anonymität, Pseudepigraphie und "literarische Falschung"'), L. H. Brockington, 'The Problem of Pseudonymity', *JTS* n.s. 4, and B. M. Metzger, 'Literary Forgeries and Canonical Pseudepigrapha', *JBL* 91.

25. *The Relevance of Apocalyptic* pp.37ff.

26. See e.g. J. T. Milik, *The Books of Enoch* pp.22ff. and below p.255.

27. So Hengel, *Judaism and Hellenism* p.112f. and id. 'Anonymität, Pseudepigraphie und "literarische Falschung"', in ed. Fritz op. cit. (see n.24) cf. C. C. McCown, 'Hebrew and Egyptian Apocalyptic Literature', *HTR* 18.

28. There is complete absence of the legends of the supposed visionary, see above p.49.

29. There is a survey of examples of this legend in Bowker, *The Targums and Rabbinic Literature* p.187f.

30. Cf. Fragmentary Targum on Genesis 15.17; Tg. Jonathan on Isaiah 43.12; Syriac Baruch 4.4; 4 Ezra 3.13f; cf. Pseudo-Philo *LAB* 18.5.

31. On the figure of Enoch see H. L. Jansen, *Die Henochgestalt*, P. Grelot, 'La Legende d'Hénoch dans les apocryphes et dans la Bible', *RSR* 46, and H. Odeberg art. 'Enoch' in *TDNT* ii, pp.556ff.

32. The rabbis took rather different views about Enoch. On the one hand we find a very negative attitude in Ber. R. 25 (and the commentary in Theodor-Albeck ed. p.238), whereas in Hebrew Enoch (H. Odeberg *3 Enoch*) and the late legend *Hayye Henoch* (Jellinek *Beth ha-Midrasch* iv, pp.129ff.) a much more exalted picture of Enoch is to be found.

33. The link between priests and visions is illustrated by the material collected in Strack–Billerbeck ii, p.77f. and on the close relationship of cult to

heavenly world see J. Maier, *Vom Kultus zu Gnosis*, H. W. Kuhn, *Enderwartung und gegenwärtiges Heil* especially pp.66ff. and R. E. Clements, *God and Temple* especially pp.63ff.

34. 4 Ezra 10.21 seems to provide good evidence of this. See below p.253 and the works cited above p.456 n.23.

35. There is a useful discussion of this difficult issue in J. Bright, *History of Israel* pp.392ff.

36. See J. Neusner, *First Century Judaism in Crisis* and Schürer–Vermes–Millar op. cit. pp.523ff.

37. On the importance of the scribes see J. Jeremias, *Jerusalem in the Time of Jesus* pp.233ff.

38. So also J. Bloch, *On the Apocalyptic in Judaism* p.51, F. C. Burkitt, *Jewish and Christian Apocalypses* p.18, and Russell op. cit. p.135.

39. Russell op. cit. p.133, quoting H. Wheeler Robinson, 'The Hebrew Conception of Corporate Personality' in *Werden und Wesen des Alten Testaments* BZAW 66 pp.49ff.

40. Cf. Volz op. cit. p.5 who thinks that this concern with the past is an indication of the lack of originality of the apocalypticists and their dependence on the Old Testament.

41. Op. cit. p.136.

42. Russell op. cit. p.138 cf. Torm op. cit. p.21f. (quoted by J. M. Schmidt op. cit. p.278 n.134).

43. So, for example, J. W. Rogerson, 'The Hebrew Conception of Corporate Personality: A Re-Examination', *JTS* 21, and on T. Boman, *Hebrew Thought Compared with Greek*, see J. Barr, *The Semantics of Biblical Language* pp.8ff.

44. On the possibility of authentic visions in the apocalyptic literature see Kaufman art. 'Apokalyptik' in *Encyclopaedia Judaica* ii, col. 1145 and below pp.214ff.

45. There is a summary of the development of the Old Testament Canon by G. W. Anderson, 'Canonical and Non-Canonical' in ed. P. R. Ackroyd and C. F. Evans *The Cambridge History of the Bible* vol. i, pp.113ff.

46. The text is quoted in Bowker op. cit. p.41 n.3, where other material is also given. On the authority of antiquity see Brockington op. cit. p.20.

47. Further material in Strack–Billerbeck i, pp.125ff. and the discussion in P. Schäfer, *Die Vorstellung vom Heiligen Geist in der rabbinischen Literatur* p.112ff. and R. Leivestad, 'Das Dogma der prophetenlosen Zeit', *NTS* 19.

48. See e.g. P. R. Ackroyd, *Exile and Restoration* p.44.

49. For example, P. D. Hanson, *The Dawn of Apocalyptic*, O. Plöger, *Theocracy and Eschatology* and J. Schreiner, 'Die apokalyptische Bewegung' in *Literatur und Religion* p.217f.

50. See Schweizer article *Pneuma TDNT* vi, and Schäfer op. cit. pp.112ff.

51. Cf. Hengel, *Judaism and Hellenism* i, p.205f.

52. This is not to suggest that there are no pseudepigrapha among the early Christian documents. Rather it appears that its place was to be found in the earliest period among the epistles rather than the apocalypses, see M.

Rist, 'Pseudepigraphy and the Early Christians', in ed. D. E. Aune, *Studies in New Testament and Early Christian Literature* and cf. D. Guthrie, 'Epistolary Pseudepigraphy', in *New Testament Introduction* pp.671ff. In all probability it was with the waning of the primitive parousia-expectation that the eschatological character of the coming of the Spirit was gradually lost in favour of other doctrinal developments. On this question see M. Werner, *Die Entstehung des christlichen Dogmas* pp.185ff. and J. D. G. Dunn, *Unity and Diversity* pp.344ff.

53. See R. Meyer art. *Prophetes TDNT* vi, pp. 816ff. and Strack–Billerbeck i, pp.125ff. and Lieberman *Hellenism in Jewish Palestine* p.194.

54. So Hengel 'Pseudonymität p.267.

Part Two: **The Content of the Heavenly Mysteries**

1. Hebrew has 'he will reveal his secret to the humble'.

2. So Box and Oesterley in ed. Charles, *Apocrypha and Pseudepigrapha* i, p.326.

3. See G. A. Wewers, *Geheimnis und Geheimhaltung* p.46f. and H. F. Weiss, *Untersuchungen zur Kosmologie des hellenistischen und palästinischen Judentums* p.80.

4. But see now M. Hengel, *The Son of God* p.46f. and see below p.469 n.88.

5. Cf. the similar approaches to apocalyptic in Flusser op. cit. col. 179 and Frey op. cit. col. 328f.

Chapter 4 *What is Above:*
	the Mysteries of God, the Angels and Astronomy

1. On this expression see the collection of examples in F. Lentzen-Deis op. cit. (p.459 n.10 above) pp.99ff.

2. On Isaiah 6 see O. Kaiser, *Isaiah 1—12* p.78 and on Second Isaiah see F. M. Cross, 'The Council of Yahweh in Second Isaiah', *JNES* 12 and R. N. Whybray, *The Divine Counsellor in Second Isaiah*.

3. See further Cross, *Canaanite Myth and Hebrew Epic* p.186.

4. Cross op. cit. pp.36ff. and 147ff. On later developments see H. Ringgren, *Israelite Religion* pp.307ff.

5. On this passage see P. D. Hanson, *The Dawn of Apocalyptic* pp.113ff.

6. There is a useful survey of the different divine intermediaries in Moore, *Judaism* i, pp.357ff. and Urbach, *The Sages* i, pp.135ff. On concepts of the divine immanence see Urbach op. cit. pp.37ff.

7. On the heavenly journey in ancient religion see the works cited on p.459 n.8 above, and on the relationship between prophetic and apocalyptic inspiration see Widengren op. cit. pp.94ff. To these must be added C. Colpe, 'Die Himmelsreise der Seele als philosophie- und religionsgeschichtliche Problem', in *Festschrift für J. Klein* and A. Segal. 'Heavenly Ascent'.

8. We seem to be on the fringes of this in the visions of Zechariah. See now B. O. Long, 'Reports of Visions among the Prophets', *JBL* 95 and C. Jeremias, *Die Nachtgesichte des Sacharja*.

9. On Jewish cosmology see H. Bietenhard, *Die himmlische Welt* and N. Séd *La cosmologie juive* and on the origin and character of later Jewish cosmology see G. B. Sarfatti, 'Talmudic Cosmography', *Tarbiz* 35 (in Hebrew). There are important comments on the theological implications of such a cosmology in J. G. Gammie, 'Spatial and Ethical Dualism in Jewish Wisdom and Apocalyptic Literature', *JBL* 93, especially pp.360f and 366ff.

10. *Pseudepigrapha* p.304, and see also M. de Jonge in *Studies on the Testaments of the Twelve Patriarchs* pp.248ff.

11. On this passage see below pp.382ff.

12. On the cosmology of Revelation see P. Minear, 'The Cosmology of the Apocalypse' in *Current Issues in New Testament Interpretation*.

13. So Charles, *Pseudepigrapha* p.442.

14. Cf. J. Gray, *1 and 2 Kings* p.205.

15. A brief survey is to be found in Bietenhard op. cit. pp.11ff.

16. See further J. Maier op. cit., R. E. Clements, *God and Temple* and Bietenhard op. cit. pp.123ff.

17. Cf. 1 Chronicles 28.18f. On Exodus 25.40 see Childs, *Exodus* p.535.

18. Maier op. cit. p.127 and 'Das Gefährdungsmotiv bei der Himmelsreise in der jüdischen Apokalyptik und Gnosis', *Kairos* 5, pp.18ff. We may also note that the ceiling of the house is decorated with cherubim as was the case with Solomon's Temple, where both the inner and outer rooms were covered with the figures (1 Enoch 14.11 cf. 1 Kings 6.29).

19. This short reference provided the basis for the later speculation on the form of God known as the *shi'ur komah*, in which fantastic measurements are attributed to the limbs of the godhead. See Scholem, *Major Trends* pp.63ff. Maier, *Kultus* p.118 and Gruenwald, *Apocalyptic*. Among earlier scholars who discuss this speculation, mention must be made of the negative attitude taken towards the *shi'ur komah* by H. Graetz, *Gnosticismus und Judenthum* pp.102ff. and the interesting remarks on the ideas of the gnostic Marcus in M. Gaster, *Studies and Texts* ii, pp.133ff. (the passage discussed is Irenaeus *Adv. Haer.* i, 14.2 Foerster *Gnosis* i, p.204f.). See further below p.497 n.72.

20. Op. cit. p.39 (13.8).

21. *The Apocalypse of Abraham* p.62f.

22. See above pp.53ff.

23. On the various aspects of the throne-vision in Jewish apocalyptic see my article 'The Visions of God in Apocalyptic Literature', Bietenhard op. cit. pp.53ff., Gruenwald *Apocalyptic* pp.29ff.,J. Strugnell op. cit. (above p.452 n.31), and the examination of 1 Enoch 14 and Revelation 4 below pp.219ff.

24. On apocalyptic angelology see also Russell pp.257ff. According to Ber. R. 48.9 the names of the angels, Michael, Raphael, and Gabriel came from Babylon.

25. See further C. Jeremias op. cit. pp.81ff.

26. On the archangel Michael as the guardian angel of Israel see W. Lueken, *Michael* pp.13ff. and more recently J. P. Rohland, *Der Erzengel Michael* pp.10ff. On 1QM 17.5ff. see P. von der Osten Sacken, *Gott und Belial* pp.95ff. On the possibility of a Canaanite origin see J. Day, *The OT Utilisation of Language and Imagery Having Parallels in the Baal Mythology of the Ugaritic Texts* Diss. Cambridge pp.141ff.

27. See also 3 Enoch 17.8; 14.2; 26.12; 18.3. In Test. Naphtali (Heb.) we find the notion of angels connected with different nations and languages when God descends with seventy angels and commands them to teach seventy families descended from Noah seventy languages. On this type of angelology see Bousset p.324f., Russell pp.244ff., Hengel i, p.187, and Schäfer, *Rivilität* pp.27ff. and 60ff.

28. For a survey of the Jewish material see Russell op. cit. pp.254ff. Bousset, *Religion* pp.331ff., O. Böcher, *Der johanneische Dualismus* pp.23ff., and on Qumran dualism Osten-Sacken op. cit.

29. So Hengel i, p.190.

30. Cf. M. Rissi, *The Future of the World* p.34.

31. On heaven as a place of evil see Bietenhard p.205.

32. On this material see Hengel op. cit. p.231f., Russell op. cit. pp.249ff., Urbach op. cit. p.167f. The myth is found, in one form or another, in 1Q Gen. Apoc. 2, Jub. 4.15 and in the later rabbinic midrashim (see L. Ginzberg, *The Legends of the Jews* i.137 and v, 156f.).

33. But see now the discussion of these legends by Hanson and Nickelsburg in *JBL* 96 (below p.480 n.3).

34. But see further now M. Barker 'Some Reflections on the Enoch Myth', *JSOT* 15.

35. On the Old Testament material see W. Eichrodt, *Theology of the Old Testament* ii, pp.23–35 and F. Stier, *Gott und sein Engel im Alten Testament*. There is a brief discussion in A. R. Johnson, *The One and the Many in the Israelite Conception of God* pp.28ff.

36. Op. cit. p.24.

37. On this change see O. Procksch, 'Die Berufungsvision Hezekiels' *BZAW* 34 p.148f., id. 'Christus im AT', *NKZ* 44 p.79, H. Balz, *Methodische Probleme der NT Christologie* p.80, Maier, *Kultus* p.118. Colpe art., *ho huios tou anthropou* TDNT viii, p.421 n.151 and M. Black, 'The Throne-Theophany Prophetic Commission and the Son of Man', in *Jews, Greeks and Christians* p.39f., Zimmerli, *Ezechiel* i, p.210.

38. The MT reads *demuth kᵉmar'eh 'esh* in 8.2, but probably one should read *'ish* with LXX and the Old Latin. The *yodh* was probably omitted either because of the similarity with *kᵉmar'eh 'esh* in 1.27 or may have been changed to minimize anthropomorphism. See Zimmerli op. cit. i, p.191.

39. Eichrodt, *Ezekiel* p.58f., Procksch 'Die Berufungsvision' p.147, Zimmerli op. cit. p.210.

40. The reference to the glory of God in Ezek. 1.28 may well refer to the immediately preceding description of the human figure on the throne, so also Colpe op. cit. p.418 n.151. Confirmation of the identity of the figures

in Ezek. 1.26f. and 8.2 is to be found in the targum on Ezekiel. Although it remains fairly close to the MT it paraphrases 1.27 in the following way: 'And I saw like the appearance of bronze, like the appearance of fire in the midst of it, round about the appearance of glory, which no eye was able to behold, nor was it possible to look at it . . . and below I saw as it were the appearance of fire and its brightness . . .' At the second occurrence of the description of the human figure in 8.2 it paraphrases similarly: 'And I saw and behold an appearance like the appearance of fire, like the glory which no eye was able to behold, nor was it possible to look at it and below, the appearance of fire . . .' The veil of reverence which is drawn over the human figure in Ezek. 1.27, by emphasizing that it was not possible to look upon it, is also stressed in the targum on Ezek. 8.2. For the Aramaic text see A. Sperber, *The Bible in Aramaic* vol. iii.

41. See the works cited in n.37 above.

42. Op. cit. p.94.

43. Op. cit. p.82f.

44. Balz's theory is criticized by U. Müller, *Messias und Menschensohn* p.34f., particularly in relation to the interpretation of Dan. 7.13f.

45. Cf. Zimmerli op. cit. i, p.210.

46. See below pp.219ff.

47. A. Feuillet 'Le Fils de l'Homme de Daniel et la tradition biblique' *RB* 60 especially pp.183ff. is another who would trace the idea back to Ezek. 1 and also the works by Procksch above p.464 n.37.

48. On the Canaanite background to Dan. 7 see Colpe op. cit. pp.418ff., J. A. Emerton, 'The Origin of the Son of Man Imagery' *JTS* 9 and J. Day op. cit. pp.141ff. Criticisms of the Canaanite hypothesis are made by Müller op. cit. p.35.

49. On the clouds as a symbol of divinity in Dan. 7.13 see R. B. Y. Scott, 'Behold he cometh with clouds' *NTS* 5 pp.128ff. Colpe op. cit. p.420 and Emerton op. cit. p.231f. cf. Müller op. cit. p.27, who suggests that the clouds are merely a sign that the scene takes place in heaven.

50. O. Procksch in the articles cited above (e.g. 'Christus im AT', p.78) makes much of the fact that the prophet sees not God himself but his image cf. Eichrodt, *Theology of the Old Testament* ii, p.33. That the nouns which qualify the anthropomorphic statements can be said to signify such ideas seems unlikely.

51. On this reading see also Bousset *Religion* p.303, J. Montgomery, 'Anent Dr Rendel Harris's Testimonies', *The Expositor* 22 p.214 and H. R. Balz op. cit. p.69. The latter thinks that the reading is very ancient. See now J. Lust, 'Dan. 7.13 and the Septuagint'.

52. See below p.101.

53. T. Holtz, *Die Christologie der Apokalypse des Johannes* p.116 n.3 and O. Plöger, *Das Buch Daniel* p.148 note the connection with Ezek. 1. So e.g. Plöger: 'Die Zeichnung der Erscheinung ist eine Variation zur Theophaniezeichnung in Ezek. 1.26f. (8.2), das Leinengewand, das gleichwohl den Körper erkennen lässt, könnte an Ezek. 9.2 orientiert sein, um deutlich zu machen, dass es sich um eine mit den Zügen einer

Theophanie ausgestatte Botenerscheinung handeln soll'). Also J. Montgomery, *Daniel* p.420 and N. Porteous, *Daniel* p.151, Black op. cit. p.61.

54. It is not impossible that the similarity in colour which exists between *ḥashmal* used of the man in Ezek. 1.27 and *nᵉhosheth qalal* used of the creatures in Ezek. 1.7 may explain the reason for the absence of the word *ḥashmal* in Dan. 10.6. The yellow-coloured brightness of the heavenly man suggested to the seer not *ḥashmal* but *nᵉhosheth qalal* of Ezek. 1.7.

55. *A Critical and Exegetical Commentary on the Book of Daniel* p.256f.

56. On this development see the summary in W. Bousset, *Die Religion des Judentums* pp.342ff. and Hengel op. cit. i, pp.153ff. Among the more important studies are H. Ringgren, *Word and Wisdom*, B. L. Mack, *Logos und Sophia* and U. Wilckens, 'Sophia', *TDNT* vii. Some reserve is expressed about certain aspects of this material in G. F. Moore 'Intermediaries in Jewish Theology', *HTR* 15.

57. On this see Holtz op. cit. p.117.

58. See further Montgomery, *Daniel* p.407.

59. On these verses and their relationship with Dan. 10 and Jewish angelology see Holtz op. cit. pp.116ff. and G. Kretschmar, *Studien zur frühchristlichen Trinitätstheologie* p.222.

60. Of considerable similarity to the exalted heavenly being described in Rev. 1 and the Apocalypse of Abraham 10 is the description of the angel in Joseph and Asenath 14. He is said to be a man who is in all respects like Joseph, but his arrival is reminiscent of a theophany, with references to an open heaven (14.3) and prostration by Asenath. On this passage see now C. Burchard, *Der dreizehnte Zeuge* pp.59ff. The use of Dan. 7.9 in Jewish angelology is probably reflected in the strange story about the High Priest, Simon the Just, recorded in j. Yoma 5.2. When in the Holy of Holies on the Day of Atonement he was apparently accustomed to see an old man dressed in white (cf. the vision of Akatriel to R. Ishmael in b. Berakoth 7a and see Scholem *Jewish Gnosticism* p.51 and A. Marmorstein *The Old Rabbinic Doctrine of God* ii, p.49f.).

61. Cf. what is said of Metatron in b. San. 38b and Heb. Enoch 12. In the Samaritan Memar Marqah 1.2 and 9 (cf. 2.12 and 5.1) Moses is called God's vice-regent and is said to be crowned with the name of God (*Elohim* not the *tetragrammaton*). See further W. Meeks, *The Prophet King* pp.232ff.

62. In a *shi'ur komah* text (*merkabah shelemah* 37a) quoted in Scholem, *Major Trends* p.64 chrysolite is used to describe the body of God: 'The appearance of the face is like that of the cheek-bones, and both are like the figure of the spirit and the form of the soul, and no creature may recognise it. His body is like chrysolite etc.' see further Gruenwald, *Apocalyptic* p.214f.

63. In b. Hag. 12b the archangel Michael is said to have a priestly function. Holtz thinks that the christophany in Rev. 1.13ff. portrays Christ as High Priest, see p.118, cf. Hofius *Der Vorhang vor dem Thron Gottes* p.15.

64. On this see further below p.112.

65. Cf. Slav. Enoch 1.5; 1 Enoch 71.2 and see further below p.302f.

66. On this passage see the remarks of E. R. Goodenough, *Jewish Symbols* v, pp.103ff. and Meeks op. cit. pp.241ff.

67. Cf. Charles op. cit. i, p.259.

68. So now J. Theisohn, *Der auserwählte Richter* pp.31ff.

69. On the throne of God in the Similitudes and its background see Theisohn op. cit. pp.68ff.

70. Charles, *Enoch* p.69.

71. Charles loc. cit.

72. The only possible exception is 62.2 where the Ethiopic reads *wanabara*. A. Dillman, *Das Buch Henoch* was probably correct to emend the text to *wa'anbaro* (see Charles, *Ethiopic Versions* p.112). The Ethiopic as it stands is to be translated 'The Lord of the Spirits sat on the throne of glory', whereas the emendation turns the verb into a causative yielding the following translation: 'The Lord of Spirit caused him to sit on the throne of glory'. The emendation seems to be justified in the light of the lines which immediately precede and follow it, which demand that what is being spoken of be referred to the Elect One. The emendation is accepted by Charles loc. cit., Beer in Kautzsch, *Apokryphen und Pseudepigraphen* ii, p.271 and Theisohn op. cit. p.87.

73. It would be wrong to place too much emphasis on the way in which the throne is linked with the title Head of Days and not Lord of Spirits, but is it possible that there may have existed in the author's mind some distinction between God in his physical aspect, enthroned in glory, and God as a spiritual being? 48.2 may presuppose some kind of distinction; 'And at that hour the Son of Man was named before the Lord of Spirits and his name before the Head of Days', It is, of course, possible that this parallelism may be just a poetic way of referring to the same person (cf. Ps. 95.1; Isa. 44.6; Ps. 78.35). Indeed, there is some parallelism in the following verse (48.3), ('Before the sun and the signs were created, before the stars of heaven were made'), so great care is needed to avoid making too much of the parallelism in 48.2. Nevertheless in the light of the fact that the throne is not linked with the Lord of Spirits there may be something in the distinction which is to be found in this verse.

74. On the throne in the Similitudes see n.69 above.

75. It would appear that a new start is made in v.5, and the best explanation is that we have two versions of Enoch's ascent to heaven, cf. E. Sjöberg, *Der Menschensohn im äthiopischen Henochbuch* pp.147ff.

76. E.g. Jubilees 4.18ff. (though this passage places the Garden of Eden on earth) Test. Abraham (Rec. B) 11; Slav. En. 64.5; Tg. Ps. Jon. on Gen. 5.24 and see H. Odeberg in *TDNT* ii, pp.556f.

77. So also Denis, *Introduction* p.36f. On the question of the relationship between the different recensions see the essays by G. Nickelsburg and F. Schmidt in *Studies in the Testament of Abraham IOSCS Proceedings* ii, and the literature cited there.

78. Cf. the parallel expression from Hekaloth R. 19 'carriage of light' and Odes of Sol. 38.1.

79. On the figure of Abel see the view of F. Schmidt, quoted by Nickelsburg op. cit. p.36: 'In the Hebrew original of Rec. B. it was the Son of Man who was judge. The Greek translator understood *ben adam* to mean son of Adam and identified him with Abel'. (*Le Testament d'Abraham: introduction,*

édition de la recension courte, traduction et notes Diss. Strassbourg 1971 i,
p.64f.). Cf. the remarks of F. H. Borsch, *The Son of Man in Myth and History* p.170, id., *The Christian and Gnostic Son of Man* p.117.

80. There may be some borrowings from Egyptian and Greek mythology, see
    G. H. McCurdy, 'Platonic Orphism in the Testament of Abraham' *JBL* 61,
    but he has to admit the close links which also exist with the Jewish
    apocalyptic tradition (p.224). The description of heaven with two thrones,
    one outside the gate and one inside is similar to Heb. Enoch 10: 'R.
    Ishmael said: Metatron, the Prince of the Presence, said to me: All these
    things the Holy One, blessed be He, made for me: He made a throne
    similar to the throne of glory . . . and he placed it at the door of the
    seventh hall and seated me on it.' In Rec. A. Adam sits outside the gates
    on a golden throne and his appearance is said to be 'like that of his
    master', which in the present context can refer only to the glorious Abel.
    We have already had reason to link Abel's throne with the throne of
    glory, and thus it seems possible that the sort of pattern which we find in
    Heb. Enoch is repeated in the Testament of Abraham also. There is the
    possibility that the basic picture we have in Heb. Enoch has been
    reinterpreted. The scene with Metatron outside the door and God inside
    the heavenly palace has been identified with Adam and Abel respectively.
    There is some evidence to support this in the Arabic version, where the
    identification of the judge with Abel is not made, though we still have
    Adam sitting outside the door.

81. See A. S. van der Woude and M. de Jonge '11Q Melchizedek and the
    New Testament', *NTS* 12 and the articles by J. Carmignac ('Le document
    de Qumran sur Melchizedek', *RQ* 27), who challenges the identification
    with a heavenly being and M. Delcor 'Melchizedek from Genesis to the
    Qumran Texts and the Epistle to the Hebrews', *JSJ* 2 pp.115ff., who
    discusses Carmignac's interpretation.

82. Translation from G. Vermes, *The Dead Sea Scrolls in English*.

83. On the figure of Melchizedek in Jewish and Christian tradition see F.
    Horton, *The Melchizedek Tradition*.

84. Another text which must be mentioned and which speaks of the close
    relationship between an earthly figure and a heavenly being is a fragment
    of the Prayer of Joseph quoted in Origen's Commentary on John ii.31:
    'And I (Jacob), when I was coming from Mesopotamia of Syria, Uriel the
    angel of God came forth and said that I had come down to earth and
    tabernacled among men, and that I was called by name Jacob'. While
    nothing whatever is said here about this angel being the one to sit on the
    divine throne, it offers us further evidence of connections which were
    being made between exalted heavenly beings and heroes of Israel's past.
    The unique aspect of this fragment, however, is that, at least according to
    Origen, the earthly life of the father of the Jewish nation should be seen
    as the incarnation of a heavenly being. For a full discussion of this
    important text, together with an extensive bibliography, see J. Z. Smith,
    'The Prayer of Joseph', in *Religions in Antiquity* and A. F. Segal, *Two Powers in Heaven* pp.199ff.

85. On the dating of Hebrew Enoch see Odeberg p.23ff. and P. S. Alexander
    op. cit. below p.497 n.77.

86. See G. Macrae, *Elements of Judaism and Gnosticism* pp.104ff. and below p.496 n.62.

87. On this whole subject of the Jewish origin of the two power controversy see now A. F. Segal, *Two Powers in Heaven*, the comments in Bietenhard op. cit. pp.264ff. and H. F. Weiss op. cit. p.324ff.

88. There are signs that the value of Jewish angelology for Christology has been appreciated by recent commentators. See especially M. Hengel, *The Son of God* p.46f. A. F. Segal, *Two Powers in Heaven* pp.182–219. Among earlier studies mention must be made of W. Lueken, *Michael* pp.133ff., M. Werner, *Die Entstehung des christlichen Dogmas* with the response by W. Michaelis, *Zur Engelchristologie im Urchristentum*, also J. Bakker, 'Christ an Angel?' *ZNW* 32. On the contribution of angel-christology to doctrinal development see J. Barbel, *Christos Angelos*, G. Kretschmar op. cit. (p.466 n.59) and J. Daniélou, *The Theology of Jewish Christianity* pp.117ff.

89. O. Michel, *Der Brief an die Hebräer* especially pp.131ff.

90. On Phil. 2.6–11 see R. P. Martin, *Carmen Christi* especially pp.235ff. Most commentators interpret the name differently see e.g. Deichgräber op. cit. p.138, and O. Hofius, *Der Christushymnus Philipper 2.6–11* especially pp.86ff.

91. Cf. Bornkamm art. *mysterion TDNT* iv, p.816 n.2.

92. On knowledge in the Qumran hymns see M. Mansoor, *The Thanksgiving Hymns* and the material cited there. To this may be added B. Reicke, 'Da'ath in the Dead Sea Scrolls', in *Neotestamentica et Semitica* and H-W Kuhn, *Enderwartung und gegenwärtiges Heil* pp.139ff.

93. On this see O. Betz, *Offenbarung und Schriftforschung in der Qumransekte* particularly pp.73ff. and G. Vermes, *The Dead Sea Scrolls: Qumran in Perspective* pp.105ff, which offers an excellent summary of the sect's attitude to Scripture.

94. See Urbach p.304 and Moore i, p.254f.

95. Op. cit. See also B. Gärtner, *The Temple and the Community in Qumran and the New Testament* pp.92ff., D. E. Aune, *The Cultic Setting of Realised Eschatology in Early Christianity* pp.29ff., N. Kehl, 'Erniedrigung und Erhöhung in Qumran und Kolossä', *ZKT* 91 and R. Laurin, 'The Question of Immortality in the Qumran Hodayot', *JSS* 3.

96. Kuhn op. cit. p.91f.

97. P.56f. but cf. S. Holm-Nielsen, *Hodayoth* p.66f. who advises caution in the use of later rabbinic material.

98. On this phrase see Kuhn op. cit. pp.70ff.

99. On resurrection here see Kuhn p.78f., Holm-Nielsen p.187 and Laurin op. cit.

100. So P. Wernberg-Møller, *The Manual of Discipline* p.152.

101. On the notion of an actual heavenly ascent in these passages Kehl op. cit. p.34f. and Kuhn pp.52ff.

102. Kuhn pp.70ff. and 182ff. On the cultic background of Jewish mysticism see Maier, *Vom Kultus zu Gnosis*.

103. On the way in which the Qumran scrolls spiritualize cultic terminology see G. Klinzing, *Die Umdeutung des Kultus in der Qumrangemeinde und im Neuen Testament*, especially pp.50ff.

104. It is difficult to justify the sharp distinction between apocalyptic and priestly backgrounds found in Kuhn p.153f. and 183. He fails to note the aspects of realized eschatology already implicit in apocalyptic.

105. See R. G. Hamerton–Kelly, 'The Temple and the Origins of Apocalyptic' *VT* 20.

106. The present experience of heaven seems to be presupposed in the following passage from Philo's *De Vita Contemplativa* 11f., where Philo describes the life-style of the *Therapeutae*: 'But it is well that the *Therapeutae*, a people always taught from the first to use their sight, should desire the vision of the existent and soar above the sun of our senses and never leave their place in this company which carries them to perfect happiness. And those who set themselves to this service, not just following custom nor on the advice and admonition of others but carried away by a heaven-sent passion of love, remain rapt and possessed like bacchanals or corybants until they see the object of their yearning'. Despite the obvious Hellenistic garb of the description there do appear to be some similarities here with the experience of the Qumran group. Emphasis is laid on the happiness brought about by participation in the community and the yearning to see the vision of God in the present.

107. Some parallel, though not identical, material has been found among the Enoch fragments from Cave 4 at Qumran. These are discussed in detail and compared with the material in 1 Enoch in J. T. Milik, *The Books of Enoch* pp.274ff. See also Vermes op. cit. (p.469 n.93) pp.175ff and 191.

108. See Odeberg in *TDNT* ii, p.556f., and Milik, *Enoch* p.8.

109. On the calendar in Judaism see J. Goudoever, *Biblical Calandars* and especially A. Jaubert, *The Date of the Last Supper*, who examines the apocalyptic material.

110. S. Talmon ('The Calendar Reckoning of the Sect from the Judaean Desert', *Scripta Hierosolymitana* 4 p.167) has suggested that the reference in 1QpHab 11 to the pursuit of the Teacher of Righteousness by the Wicked Priest may have been the result of a discrepancy between the official calendar and that which was used at Qumran.

111. See below pp.306f and 375f.

Chapter 5 *What is Below: Man and his World*

1. On this see Weber op. cit. pp.341ff.

2. For the background see F. M. Cross *Canaanite Myth* p.36f.

3. *Enoch* p.16. E. Rau, *Kosmologie, Eschatologie und die Lehrautorität Henochs* pp.254ff., (especially p.258 on 77.4ff.) and see also P. Grelot, 'La géographie mythique d'Hénoch et ses sources orientales', *RB* 65.

4. On the affinities between Wisdom and apocalyptic see the literature cited

below p.478 n.24ff, M. A. Knibb, 'IV Ezra and Apocalyptic' (forthcoming), and Gruenwald, *Apocalyptic* pp.4ff.

5. On the theology of 4 Ezra see W. Harnisch, *Verhängnis und Verheissung der Geschichte*, E. Breech, 'These Fragments I have shored against my Ruins' *JBL* 92, A. L. Thompson, *Responsibility for Evil in the Theodicy of 4 Ezra* and A. P. Hayman, 'Pseudonymity in 4 Ezra', *JSJ* 6. There is a useful summary of recent research on the theology of 4 Ezra in E. P. Sanders, *Paul and Palestinian Judaism* pp.409ff. Our concern here is not with a detailed discussion of the composition and the development of the argument of the book itself but with a consideration merely of its contents as an illustration of the sort of issues with which some apocalypticists were dealing.

6. Cf. the use of a similar parable in Tos. Hagigah 2.5 and j. Hagigah 77a.

7. See particularly A. Marmorstein, *The Doctrine of Merits in Old Rabbinic Literature* and most recently E. P. Sanders op. cit.

8. So also Harnisch pp.248ff. and Breech op. cit. p.272.

9. Cf. Sanders op. cit. p.417f.

10. There is, therefore, no polemic against heretics of any kind whose position is represented by the question of the seer; so Breech op. cit. pp. 267ff.

11. See the remarks of G. Forkman, *The Limits of the Religious Community* pp.87ff.

12. Nevertheless commentators often describe this as a pharisaic apocalypse, see above p.456 n.23.

13. On this material see Harnisch op. cit. pp.72ff.

14. *The Mystery of the Kingdom of God* p.53.

Chapter 6 *What had Happened Previously: The Interest in Past History in Apocalyptic*

1. This is a matter which has received considerable attention in the study of the apocalyptic literature. Among the important literature on the subject must be mentioned M. Noth, 'The Understanding of History in Apocalyptic' in *The Laws of the Pentateuch and Other Essays*, D. Rössler, *Gesetz und Geschichte* especially pp.55ff., Russell op. cit. pp.217–34, Hengel, *Judaism and Hellenism* i, pp.181ff. for the relationship with hellenistic ideas, and most recently G. I. Davies, 'Apocalyptic and Historiography' *JSOT* 5, where other material is mentioned.

2. We see in the Deuteronomic history, the Priestly work and the books of Chronicles this concern with the totality of history, with the theological implication that there is a desire to see the divine plan manifesting itself through the whole of history.

3. So e.g. Schmithals op. cit. p.17: 'Of course, the apocalyptists' concern was not to relate past history with the help of *vaticinia ex eventu*, particularly since these were all taken from familiar writings, but to give credibility to the predictions which referred to the future.' But see the criticism of Davies op. cit. p.21.

4. On the historical background see H. H. Rowley, *Darius the Mede and the Four World Empires in the Book of Daniel*. On the non-Jewish background of the four kingdoms see the concise summary in W. G. Lambert, *The Background of Jewish Apocalyptic* and K. Müller, 'Die Ansätze der Apokalyptik'.

5. On this see G. Reese, *Die Geschichte Israels in der Auffassung des frühen Judentums*. Unfortunately this work was not available to me when this section was written.

6. On this see F. Dexinger, *Henochs Zehnwochenapokalypse und offene Probleme der Apokalyptikforschung*, especially pp.117ff. and on the historical difficulties of 93.8 especially p.131f., Rössler op. cit. p.57f. and Milik, *Enoch* p.48f., who dates the apocalypse *c.* 100 BC.

7. Charles, *Pseudepigrapha* p.420 sees a reference here to events in the Maccabaean period and offers for comparison the event mentioned in Josephus, *Ant.* xx, 9.7. The matter is also discussed by Rowley in *The Relevance of Apocalyptic* pp.134ff. On problems facing Jews in the reign of Hadrian see E. M. Smallwood, *The Jews under Roman Rule* pp.428ff.

8. On this vision see Harnisch op. cit. pp.250ff.

9. Harnisch op. cit. pp. 260ff. Although the eagle vision certainly concentrates on the history of the present and the immediate future, it is difficult to regard the vision of the clouds as so totally eschatologically orientated as Harnisch thinks (see Rössler op. cit. p.69 n.1). The interest in the whole of Israel's history hardly fits in with a concern merely for the last stage of the present age. History is here a matter of interest in its own right (cf. Davies op. cit. p.21).

10. *Contra* Harnisch p.264f.

11. See R. Le Déaut, *La Nuit Pascale* especially pp.214ff. and 279ff.

12. Cf. rabbinic ideas concerning the righteous man taking upon himself the yoke of the kingdom, see Strack–Billerbeck i, p.176ff. This is in a sense the realization in the present of God's future reign but on the individual level (N. Perrin, *The Kingdom of God in the Teaching of Jesus* pp.90ff.).

13. On this whole subject see particularly J. B. Schaller, *Genesis 1 und 2 im antiken Judentum* (though he seems to omit discussion of Slav. Enoch 25ff. and *LAB* 28) and H. F. Weiss, *Untersuchungen zur Kosmologie des hellenistischen und pälastinischen Judentums*, especially pp.75ff. On the discussion of the subject in early rabbinic Judaism see above pp.323ff. Evidence of speculation is already to be found in the LXX on Gen. 1 see A. Schmidt, 'Interpretation der Genesis aus hellenistischen Geist', *ZAW* 86.

14. The material in Jubilees 2 and 4 Ezra 6 has been investigated in detail by O. H. Steck, 'Die Aufnahme von Genesis 1 in Jubiläen 2 und 4 Esra 6', *JSJ* 8 and Weiss op. cit. p.127f.

15. Steck op. cit. p.176 and Conzelmann art. *phos* in *TDNT* ix.

16. On this see Box, *Ezra-Apocalypse* p.85. The Latin has *'creasti spiritum firmamenti'*. Steck. op. cit. p.174 attaches little significance to this phrase.

17. The Magariya believed that the world was created by an angel see N. Golb, 'Who were the Magariya?' *JAOS* 80, H. Wolfson, 'The Pre-Existent Angel of the Magharians and al-Nahawandi' *JQR* li, R. M. Grant, 'Les êtres intermédiaires dans le judaisme tardif' in *Le Origini dello Gnosticismo* p.149

and E. Bammel, 'Die Höhlenmenschen' *ZNW* 49. See also the reference to them in 'Al-Qirqisani's Account of the Jewish Sects' tr. A. Nemoy, (*HUCA* 7 p.326f.). According to the Tripartite Tractate from Nag Hammadi 112 (*NHL p.86*) Jews say that it was by angels that God created cf. *Contra Celsum* 5.6 and the teaching of Cerinthus (Irenaeus *Adv. Haer.* i, 26). See A. F. Segal op. cit. pp.121ff.

18. On this see Bietenhard op. cit. pp.95ff. and M. Philonenko, 'La cosmogonie du livre des Secrets d'Hénoch' in *Religions en Egypte hellénistique et romaine* and Weiss op. cit. p.126f.

19. Cf. Bietenhard op. cit. p.97. There is some evidence here of a link with gnostic ideas, see A. Altmann, 'Gnostic Ideas in Rabbinic Cosmology', in *Essays Presented to J. H. Hertz* especially pp.19ff.

20. See Weiss op. cit. pp.181ff.

21. Cf. the description of the creation of the throne of Sabaoth in the Untitled Work 153.1ff. (ed. Böhlig and Labib, *Die koptisch-gnostische Schrift ohne Titel aus Codex II von Nag Hammadi* p.53) and 105 (*NHL* p.166).

22. See further A. Schmidt op. cit. above n.13.

23. Translation follows mainly that by M. R. James, *The Biblical Antiquities of Philo* p.165f. For the Latin text see G. Kisch, *Pseudo-Philo's Liber Antiquitatum Biblicarum*. There is also a new translation in French in the series Sources Chrétiennes *Les Antiquités Bibliques* vol. 1. See further M. P. Wadsworth, *The 'Liber Antiquitatum Biblicarum' of Pseudo-Philo*.

24. For the various readings in the different MSS for this sentence see *Les Antiquités Bibliques* i, p.229 and Kisch op.cit. p.196.

25. So *Les Antiquités Bibliques* ii, p.162 and C. Dietzfelbinger in *Jüdische Schriften aus hellenistisch-römischer Zeit* 11.2 p.196.

26. On *LAB* 60 see *Les Antiquités Bibliques* ii, p.232f.

27. Translation G. Friedlander, *Pirke de Rabbi Eliezer* p.16

28. This order follows the order of creation espoused by the house of Shammai according to b. Hagigah 12a.

29. See Bousset, *Religion* p.402 n.1, and Weber op. cit. pp.217ff. An example from rabbinic Judaism is the passage in b. Hag. 12b. On Philo see Wolfson, *Philo* vol. i, p.366ff.

30. *Les Antiquités Bibliques* ii, p.163.

Chapter 7 *What is to Come*

1. See Volz op. cit. p.173ff. and Klausner, *The Messianic Idea in Israel* pp.49ff.

2. See Russell op. cit. pp.271ff.

3. For this theme in Jewish eschatology see the material dealing with Gog and Magog assembled in Strack–Billerbeck iii, pp.831ff.

4. This passage is discussed by Urbach op. cit. p.677f.

5. Davenport op. cit. p.41 sees a link here with the calm of the Maccabaean period.

6. Particularly in Volz op. cit. and earlier R. H. Charles, *Eschatology*.

7. A detailed study of this section of 1 Enoch can be found in E. Rau, *Kosmologie und die Lehrautorität Henochs* pp.42ff.

8. See also Russell op. cit. pp.287ff.

9. See also Milik, *Enoch* p.44.

10. Charles, *Pseudepigrapha* p.259 and Russell op.cit. pp.284 and 287 cf. Milik op. cit. who speaks of God's abode on the hill of the Temple.

11. On the universalist elements in Jewish eschatology see Volz pp.356ff. and Russell op. cit. p.299f.

12. So Milik op. cit. p.45.

13. The last three weeks appear in the Ethiopic at 91.12ff. Charles rightly conjectured that they should follow after 93.10, a fact supported by the Aramaic fragments see Milik op. cit. pp.265ff. On the interpretation of the Apocalypse of Weeks see Dexinger op. cit. pp. 117ff. and also J. P. Thorndike, 'The Apocalypse of Weeks and the Qumran Sect', *RQ* 3.

14. Further interpretations listed in Dexinger op. cit. p.130.

15. Cf. Dexinger op. cit. who rightly points out that the situation on earth had already been dealt with 91.14, so there is no need to deal with it further here. The Aramaic fragments make it unlikely that a destruction of the earth on the pattern of Isa. 65.17; Rev. 21.1 and 2 Pet. 3.10ff. is presupposed here, see Milik op. cit. pp. 265ff.

16. On concepts of immortality in Judaism see H. Cavallin, *Life after Death* and with particular regard to the origin of the resurrection-belief G. Nickelsburg, *Resurrection Immortality and Eternal Life in Judaism*.

17. J. Davenport, *The Eschatology of the Book of Jubilees* lists other passages which contain eschatological elements pp.47ff. See also M. Testuz, *Les idées religieuses du livre des Jubilées* pp.165ff.

18. Quoted above p.157.

19. It is denied by Davenport p.40 n.1, who thinks that these verses reflect the restlessness of the dead until they have been avenged, but cf. Cavallin op. cit. p.37.

20. On this theme see Harnisch op. cit. pp.19ff.

21. On the interpretation of the historical allusions see Box in *Pseudepigrapha* pp.608ff. and Harnisch op. cit. pp. 250ff.

22. Cf. the saying of Jesus quoted by Papias according to Irenaeus *Adv. Haer* v, 33.3f.: 'The days shall come wherein vines shall grow, each having ten thousand shoots and on one shoot ten thousand branches, and on one branch ten thousand tendrils, and on every tendril ten thousand clusters, and in every cluster ten thousand grapes, and every grape when it is pressed shall yield five and twenty measures of wine . . . and all animals shall use those foods which are got from the earth and shall be peaceable and in concord one with another, subject unto men with all obedience.' (Translation from J. Jeremias *Unknown Sayings of Jesus* p.33). On this see A. Resch, *Agrapha* p.166f., J. J. Jeremias, *Unknown Sayings of Jesus* pp.34ff. and F. F. Bruce, *Jesus and Christian Origins outside the New Testament* p.85.

23. So Russell op. cit. p.295, but see Bogaert op. cit. ii, p.94.

24. According to this version of the promise God is said to share in the inheritance with Azazel. This seems to arise from the conflict between good and evil arising from Adam's sin rather than a rejection of this world as totally under the domination of the power of evil. Box op. cit. p.65 n.11 is wrong to suppose that there is a completely dualistic notion here. It is apparent from the end of ch. 20 that Abraham also is perplexed by this yoking of God with the representative of evil. It is the people of God which is God's stake in the world, whereas the rest of mankind are the lot of Satan (ch. 23). They have been given to Azazel, so that he can be loved by them. Note the way in which the direction of affairs is still very much the result of God's initiative.

25. See Box op. cit. p.77.

26. Box op. cit. p.78.

27. See for example the discussions of the Jewish background of the title *christos* in O. Cullman, *The Christology of the New Testament* pp.111ff. and F. Hahn, *The Titles of Jesus in Christology* pp.136ff. On the messiah in the OT see H. Ringgren, *The Messiah in the Old Testament*. For a general survey of Jewish messianism see the article *'christos'* by Hesse, de Jonge, and van der Woude in *TDNT* ix and J. Klausner, *The Messianic Idea in Israel*. On the Qumran evidence A. S. van der Woude, *Die messianischen Vorstellung der Gemeinde von Qumran*.

28. So also Russell op. cit. p.309.

29. See Theisohn op. cit. especially pp.94ff.

30. So Charles, *Pseudepigrapha* p.260.

31. Art. *'christos'*, *TDNT* ix, p.515.

32. Jewish evidence in Strack–Billerbeck iii, p.489.

33. On this question see above p.187.

34. Bibliographical information can be found in C. Colpe art. *'ho huios tou anthropou'* in *TDNT* viii, p.400f.

35. J. Jeremias, *New Testament Theology* vol. i, p.270 n.2 suggests that Sib. Or. v, 256ff. may also be evidence of a Son of Man belief, but this whole passage is to be regarded as a Christian addition.

36. See e.g. S. Mowinckel, *He that Cometh* pp.346ff. and among others H. E. Tödt, *The Son of Man in the Synoptic Tradition* pp.22ff.

37. Among recent advocates of this view may be named R. Leivestad, 'Der apokalyptische Menschensohn als theologisches Phantom', *ASTI* 6, id. 'Exit the Apocalyptic Son of Man', *NTS* 18 and C. F. D. Moule 'Neglected Features of the Son of Man Problem', in *Neues Testament und Kirche*, and M. D. Hooker, *The Son of Man in Mark*. Most recently P. M. Casey, *The Son of Man*.

38. The identity of the saints of the Most High is uncertain. They could be angels or the righteous nation or both. See the most recent discussion in J. J. Collins, 'The Son of Man and the Saints of the Most High' *JBL* 93 and among the earlier discussions 'Les Saints du Très-Haut en Daniel VII' in J. Coppens and L. Dequeker, *Le fils de l'homme et les Saints du Très-Haut en Daniel VII*.

476 Notes to Pages 179–184

39. The detail about the fourth beast in vv. 21f. seems to be a return to the vision, which is suggested by the opening words of v. 21 ('And I looked') and the reference to the horn and the Ancient of Days which are part of the original vision. This could be a later interpolation, so e.g. O. Plöger, *Das Buch Daniel* p.115, M. Noth, 'Zur Komposition des Buches Daniel', in *Gesammelte Aufsätze zum AT* ii, pp.11ff. and Colpe op. cit. p.420. Whoever wrote these verses clearly did not presuppose an identification between the Son of Man and the saints. They show that the return to the vision speaks of the suffering, not of the Son of Man who is a triumphant figure, but of the saints themselves.

40. On the angels of the nations see above p.90.

41. *Contra* Plöger p.113 cf. Müller op. cit. p.24.

42. On this see above p.97.

43. Quoted also by Müller op. cit. p.29 n.36.

44. On heavenly ascents in the OT see A. Schmitt, *Entrückung-Aufnahme-Himmelfahrt.*

45. See above p.465 n.49.

46. On this verse see Montgomery, *Daniel* p.214f.

47. On the identification with Michael see Müller op. cit. p.27, Collins, *Apocalyptic Vision,* 'Saints of the Most High', and J. Day, *The Old Testament Utilisation of Language and Imagery Having Parallels in the Baal Mythology of the Ugaritic Texts* Diss. Cambridge 1977, pp.141ff. who argues for a Ugaritic background. On Michael see W. Lueken, *Michael* and J. P. Rohland, *Der Erzengel Michael.*

48. *Contra* A. Bentzen, *King and Messiah* p.74f.

49. On the history of interpretation of Dan. 7 see P. M. Casey, *The Interpretation of Daniel 7* Diss. Durham and now id. *The Son of Man.*

50. So also Theisohn pp.34ff.

51. See in particular, Milik *Enoch* pp.89ff. and in addition to the works cited on p.475 n.37 above see J. Y. Campbell, 'The Origin and Meaning of the Term Son of Man', *JTS* o.s.48.

52. Source critical studies of 1 Enoch are numerous. Among the more important are H. Appel, *Die Komposition des äthiopischen Henochbuchs* and more recently U. Müller op. cit. K. Müller, 'Menschensohn und Messias' *BZ* 15 pp.162f., and H. R. Balz, *Methodische Probleme* pp.97ff. For a review of earlier source-critical work see E. Sjöberg, *Der Menschensohn im äthiopischen Henochbuch* pp.1ff.

53. This emendation is decisively, and rightly, rejected by Sjöberg op. cit. pp.154ff.

54. E.g. P. Billerbeck, 'Hat die Synagoge einen präexistenten Messias gekannt? *Nathanael* 4 and J. Lagrange, *Le Judaïsme avant Jésus Christ* pp.244ff.

55. So also Theisohn op. cit. p.49. Examples of the overlap between the two titles are as follows: pre-existence, E(lect) O(ne) 39.6f. (doubted by K. Müller op. cit. p.169), S(on of) M(an) 48.3; sits on the throne EO 45.3, SM 69.27; characterized by righteousness 62.2, SM 46.3; judgement EO 45.3, SM 46.4.

56. So e.g. U. Müller op. cit. p.59, Colpe op. cit. p.426, Sjöberg pp.147ff. and K. Müller op. cit. p.172. See also M. Black, 'The Eschatology of the Similitudes of Enoch', *JTS* 3.
57. For parallel material from Jewish literature see Billerbeck op. cit. (above p.476 n.54) and Hammerton-Kelly, *Pre-existence* pp.15ff.
58. Cf. F. H. Borsch, *The Son of Man in Myth and History* for an attempt to set Jewish man-ideas in a broader religious setting, also C. H. Talbert, 'The Myth of a Descending – Ascending Redeemer'.
59. See Charles, *Book of Enoch* p.86 and Colpe op. cit. p.423.
60. On this see most recently the discussion by P. M. Casey, 'The Use of the Term "Son of Man" in the Similitudes of Enoch' *JSJ* 7, especially p.28.
61. Special mention should be made here of two articles by B. Lindars, 'Re-enter the Apocalyptic Son of Man'. *NTS* 22 and 'The Apocalyptic Myth and the Death of Christ', *BJRL* 57, especially p.377.
62. The Messiah in 4 Ezra 13 is said to be pre-existent also by M. E. Stone, 'The Messiah in 4 Ezra', in *Religions in Antiquity* p.303. See also de Jonge, *TDNT* ix, p.516, and Klausner op. cit. p.358f.
63. On this issue see above pp.248ff.

Part Three: **Towards an Understanding of the Origins of Apocalyptic and the Dates of the Apocalypses**

Chapter 8 *A Survey of Recent Study on the Origins of Apocalyptic*

1. See e.g. Russell op. cit. pp.73ff. and Bloch op. cit. pp.28ff. For a history of the study of this particular subject see J. M. Schmidt, *Die jüdische Apokalyptik.*
2. On this period see E. Bickermann, *From Ezra to the Last of the Maccabees.* There is a concise summary in P. R. Ackroyd, *Israel under Babylon and Persia.*
3. *The Relevance of Apocalyptic* pp.11ff.
4. See most recently J. J. Collins, 'The Court Tales in Daniel and the Development of Apocalyptic', *JBL* 94 cf. also the significant comments of G. Hölscher, 'Die Entstehung des Buches Daniel' *Theologische Studien und Kritiken* 92, who emphasizes the importance of the legends (especially p.136f.).
5. Russell op. cit. p.73 stresses the continuity between the two but like Rowley wants to see in apocalyptic an important development of prophecy, see above p.25.
6. See particularly *The Dawn of Apocalyptic,* his article in *IDB Supplement* 'Apocalypticism', 'Jewish Apocalyptic against its Near Eastern Environment' *RB* 78 and 'Old Testament Apocalyptic Re-examined' in *Interpretation* 25.
7. Op. cit. pp.113ff.

8. P. R. Ackroyd, *Exile and Restoration* p.118f.

9. It should be pointed out that Hanson himself recognizes that there must be some flexibility in the way in which one seeks to understand apocalyptic (*Dawn* p.8f.).

10. See particularly O. Plöger, *Theocracy and Eschatology* and S. B. Frost, *Old Testament Apocalyptic*. There is recent discussion of the relationship of the oracles of Isa. 24ff. to apocalyptic in W. R. Millar, *Isaiah 24—27 and the Origin of Apocalyptic*. He prefers the description proto-apocalyptic for this passage.

11. So also J. Lindblom, *Die Jesaja-Apokalypse* p.102, though one would not agree with all the elements which he considers to be typical of apocalyptic.

12. On this see Eissfeldt op. cit. p.394 and on the unity of the book see Fohrer, *Introduction* p.428.

13. On the final chapters of Ezekiel see now T. Levenson, *The Theology of the Program of Restoration* and on the relationship to apocalyptic B. Erling 'Ezekiel 38—39 and the Origins of Jewish Apocalyptic', in *Ex Orbe Religionum*. On the visions of Zechariah and their relationship to apocalyptic see C. Jeremias, *Die Nachtgesichte des Sacharja*, especially pp.228ff., R. North, 'Prophecy to Apocalyptic via Zechariah' *Supplements to VT* 22, briefly Russell op. cit. p.90f., and H. Gese, 'Anfang und Ende der Apokalyptik, dargestellt am Sacharjabuch', *ZTK* 70.

14. Zimmerli op. cit. ii, p.998 notes the link with Ezek. 8.2

15. Jeremias op. cit. especially pp.88ff.

16. See K. W. Carley, *Ezekiel Among the Prophets* pp.13ff.

17. Eissfeldt op. cit. p.439 suggests some time between 350 and 200 BC.

18. A similar point is made by R. Meyer in 'Prophetes' *TDNT* vi, p.813.

19. See J. Lindblom, *Prophecy in Ancient Israel* p.148.

20. LXX translates this word by the Greek *horasis*.

21. On this see above p.68.

22. Hanson, *IDB Supplement* p.29.

23. For the history of this particular background see Schmidt op. cit. especially pp.298ff.

24. *Old Testament Theology* ii, p.306f. See also his *Wisdom in Israel* p.280f. Von Rad made changes to this section in the fourth German edition which are not reflected in the English translation. It is important to note this as much of the ongoing discussion takes into account von Rad's own continuing contribution to the debate, which is reflected in this edition. See now Gruenwald, *Apocalyptic* pp.3ff.

25. See the comments of Koch op. cit. p.42f.

26. Particular mention should be made of P. von der Osten-Sacken, *Die Apokalyptik in ihrem Verhältnis zu Prophetie und Weisheit*, though the Wisdom influence is not discounted by von der Osten-Sacken (op. cit. p.63).

27. Cf. Koch's remark op. cit. p.45: 'the radical difference between this non-eschatological book (Ecclesiasticus) and the book of Daniel – written less than twenty years later – where eschatology is the dominating focus, surely becomes the glaring problem'.

28. Possible eschatological themes in Wisdom of Solomon can be found in ch. 18—19 in a passage dealing with the Exodus.

29. See particularly H-P Müller, 'Mantische Weisheit und Apokalyptik' in *Supp. to VT* 22 pp. 268ff. and Collins, 'Court Tales' pp.231ff. On the non-Israelite background see A. L. Oppenheim, *The Interpretation of Dreams in the Ancient Near East.*

30. See von Rad op. cit. p.306 and 309 and 'The Joseph Narrative and Ancient Wisdom' in *The Problem of the Hexateuch and Other Essays* and cf. the description of the Essenes given by Josephus in *BJ* ii, 159.

31. On the divine pronouncement in Job see R. Gordis, *The Book of God and Man* pp.117ff and now Gruenwald, *Apocalyptic* pp.4ff.

32. On Ezra see also A. P. Hayman, 'Pseudonymity in 4 Ezra', *JSJ* 6, especially p.55f and A. L. Thompson op. cit.

33. So e.g. Collins, 'Court Tales' pp.230ff.

34. For this discussion see particularly O. Plöger, *Theocracy and Eschatology* and H. Ringgren, *Israelite Religion* p.305f.

35. Plöger op. cit. pp.37ff., Rössler op. cit. pp.38ff., J. Schreiner, *Alttestamentlich-jüdische Apokalyptik: eine Einführung* pp.179ff., who argues for a playing down of eschatology by the Chronicler, and Hanson, *Dawn of Apocalyptic* p.276f.

36. Plöger op. cit. p.41f.

37. Plöger op. cit. pp.47ff.

38. See Schreiner op. cit. (n.35) p.165ff. and S. B. Frost, *Old Testament Apocalyptic.*

39. See now H. G. M. Williamson, *Israel in the Books of Chronicles* p.135 and the literature cited here.

40. On the *ḥasidim* see J. Morgenstern, 'The Hasidim-who were they?' *HUCA* 38 pp.59ff., who traces their origins back to the post-Exilic period, Plöger op. cit. pp.26ff. and 46ff., Hengel op. cit. pp.175ff. and A. Tcherikover, *Hellenistic Civilisation and the Jews* pp.196ff. cf. the critical remarks of P. R. Davies, 'Hasidim in the Maccabean Period', *JJS* 28.

41. Cf. Plöger op. cit. p.23f. On the link between apocalyptic and the *ḥasidim* see J. Schreiner in 'Die apokalyptische Bewegung' in Maier and Schreiner, *Literatur und Religion* pp.240ff.

42. Hengel op. cit. p.189, Charles, *Book of Enoch* and Milik op. cit. p.43.

43. On the significance of the find at Murabba'at see Hengel op. cit. p.175 and for the text *DJD* ii, p.163. This speaks of the fortress of the *ḥasidim*, which Hengel takes to be a reference to Qumran.

44. On this see Meyer *'Pharisaioi' TDNT* ix, p.14, W. Beilner 'Der Ursprung des Pharisäismus', *BZ3* especially pp.245ff., and Plöger op. cit. p.20 and 51f.

45. So Rost op. cit. pp.129ff. and K. Schubert, *The Dead Sea Community* pp.10ff.

46. *Jerusalem in the Time of Jesus* p.238.

47. On the halakah at Qumran see L. Schiffman, *The Halakhah at Qumran* and J. M. Baumgarten, *Studies in Qumran Law.*

48. On the possibility that some apocalypses are Pharisaic see above p.456 n.23.

Chapter 9 *An Attempt to Elucidate the Origins of Apocalyptic Visions*

1. Cf. Eissfeldt, *Introduction* p.528f.

2. So Russell op. cit. p.159 and see also the survey in Schmidt op. cit. pp.218f. and 279ff.

3. See e.g. P. Hanson, 'Rebellion in Heaven', *JBL* 96 pp.195ff. and G. W. Nickelsburg, 'Apocalyptic and Myth in 1 Enoch 6–11', *JBL* 96 pp.383ff.

4. Russell op. cit. pp.183ff. The sharp dichotomy between scriptural exegesis and experience as suggested e.g. in D. J. Halperin, *Merkabah and Ma'aseh Merkabah* p.327f. seems to drive an unjustified wedge between the exegetical and the experiential. See further on this Gruenwald, *Apocalyptic* pp.19ff.

5. See Montgomery, *Daniel* pp.377ff.

6. See above p.52 and cf. O. Betz op. cit. p.80f.

7. Steck op. cit. p.181 and Harnisch op. cit. p.25.

8. E.g. de Jonge in *TDNT* ix, p.516.

9. Cf. the way in which different parts of Ezek. 1 merge together in the angelophany in Dan. 10.5ff., see above pp.99f.

10. See also above p.85ff and my article 'The Visions of God in Apocalyptic Literature' *JSJ*. Also I. Gruenwald, *Apocalyptic* pp.32ff. and 62ff.

11. A matter which still interests the author of the Qumran *merkabah*-fragment, see J. Strugnell, 'The Angelic Liturgy at Qumran' *Supplements to Vetus Testamentum* 7 pp.318ff.

12. Charles emends the Greek *horos cheroubin* to *horasis cheroubin* as reflected in his translation 'visions of cherubim' (*The Book of Enoch* p.39). The Ethiopic *qala* is to be preferred, however, especially in the light of 4Q S1 which speaks of the 'still voice of the godly ones' cf. Ezek. 1.24. Milik, *Enoch* p.200 retains *oros* and says 'the term *oros* is without doubt . . . a boundary stone, *stele*; we are dealing here with two sides of the throne carved as sphinxes (=*cheroubin*)'.

13. Cf. Milik op. cit. p.194 where a fragment speaks of snow. The snow-like character of the exterior of Herod's temple is mentioned by Josephus *BJ* v, 233.

14. On this passage see E. W. Nicholson, 'The Interpretation of Exod. 24.9–11', *VT* 24.

15. See below p.313.

16. *Jewish Gnosticism* p.14 and *Major Trends* p.52f., also Gruenwald, *Apocalyptic* pp.87ff.

17. See p.83 and n.16.

18. Milik op. cit. supposes that a plural originally existed here, p.199f.

19. One Aramaic fragment which Milik thinks is part of 1 Enoch 14 uses the same Aramaic word (*sh^{e}bil*) of the fiery stream as is found in 4Q S1, *Enoch* p.199 and pl. XIII.

20. Bietenhard op. cit. p.75.

21. So K. Schubert, *Die Religion des nachbiblischen Judentums* p.89 and Scholem, *Major Trends* p.44.

22. On the living creatures in Revelation see J. Michl, *Die Engelvorstellungen in der Apokalypse des hl. Johannes* pp.5ff. and Gruenwald, *Apocalyptic* p.68.

23. So E. Lohmeyer, *Die Offenbarung des Johannes* p.45 and Gruenwald, *Apocalyptic* p.63f.

24. See the discussion in Charles, *Revelation* i, pp.128ff., Bietenhard op. cit. p.57f. Gruenwald, *Apocalyptic* p.64f. and cf. Michl, *Die 24 Ältesten in der Apokalypse des hl. Johannes*, who argues that they are the righteous of Israel's past.

25. Milik op. cit. p.199 points to a link with 1 Enoch 14.

26. See Scholem, *Major Trends* pp.57ff. and P. Prigent, *Apocalypse et Liturgie* pp.46ff.

27. Cf. Jörns, *Das hymnische Evangelium* pp.168ff.

28. Cf. the remarks of A. Vanhoye, 'L'utilisation du livre d'Ez dans l'Apocalypse' *Biblica* 43, especially p.462 and 472, where the originality in the use of Ezekiel is stressed.

29. Cf. Sjöberg op. cit. p.110: 'If one wants to know God in all his glory, one must know also these cosmological mysteries . . . the glory of God as creator is revealed through them.'

30. On this passage see further Odeberg, *3 Enoch* p.141.

31. On the different attempts to justify this possibility see the summary in Schmidt op. cit. pp.171f.; 218ff.; 277ff. and the suggestive comments in M. E. Stone, 'Apocalyptic: Vision or Hallucination'. For an attempt to take seriously the possibility of real experience in the book of Enoch see Widengren, *Literary and Psychological Aspects* pp.108ff.

32. See Russell op. cit. p.169f. and Oepke, 'existemi' *TDNT* ii, and O. Betz op. cit. p.137. See also the fasting necessary as a preparation for revelation of divine secrets in the text published in Scholem, *Jewish Gnosticism* p.111 19a (fol. 55b) cf. 14 (fol. 54a). On this see further Gruenwald, *Apocalyptic* pp.99ff.

33. Cf. Ezekiel 2.8ff. and Odes of Solomon 19.1. See further Box, *Ezra-Apocalypse* p.318, Russell op. cit. p.171.

34. For examples of the link between intoxication by drugs and visions from outside the Judaeo-Christian tradition see Eliade, *Shamanism* p.400.

35. Cf. the vision of Cenez Pseudo-Philo Biblical Antiquities 28: . . . 'the holy spirit that dwelt in Cenez leapt upon him and took away from him his sense . . . And it came to pass after Cenez had spoken these words and his sense returned unto him; but he knew not that which he had spoken neither that which he had seen . . .' and *The Life of St Teresa* 20.

36. Cf. Eliade p.36.

37. Cf. Eliade op. cit. p.140.

38. In Hekaloth R. 18 (Jellinek *Beth ha-Midrasch* iii, p.96) and Scholem, *Jewish Gnosticism* p.16f, Gruenwald, *Apocalyptic* pp.150ff.

39. Lindblom, *Gesichte* p.59 n.3, id. *Prophecy in Ancient Israel* pp.128ff. Mention also ought to be made of the physiological effects of Eliphaz's night vision in Job 4.13ff, which seems to contain elements of the impact which a visionary experience had on an individual.

40. A passage noted also by Scholem to which he attributes similar significance, *Major Trends* p.52.

41. On the sensation of heat see further Lindblom, *Prophecy* p.13, Eliade op. cit. p.437 and 474ff. and F. von Hügel, *The Mystical Element of Religion* ii, p.19.

42. See M. H. Weil and H. Shubin, *The Diagnosis and Treatment of Shock* pp.248ff. and von Hügel op. cit. ii, p.24.

43. There is more than a passing similarity to the ascent described in the liturgy of Mithras (A. Dieterich *Eine Mithrasliturgie* p.7). See also the material in Eliade op. cit. pp.407ff. and 477ff. and the summary in *Myths, Dreams and Mysteries* p.9.

44. But note Meeks' cautionary remarks on such an interpretation of traditions of Moses' ascent in 'Moses as God and King' in *Religions in Antiquity* p.369f.

45. See the survey in Lindblom, *Gesichte* pp.206ff. to which may be added H. E. Weber, 'Zum Verständnis der Offenbarung des Johannes' in *Aus Schrift und Geschichte*.

46. See e.g. W. G. Kümmel, *Introduction to the New Testament* pp.462ff. and above pp.415ff.

47. *Gesichte*, especially pp.218ff.

48. On the basis of the criteria which he enunciates it is difficult to see why he is so reluctant to limit the quantity of authentic visionary material to this relatively small amount. Although one does not want to deny the existence of a considerable degree of redaction in the book as we have it, there seems no reason to suppose that the bulk of the material in it did actually originate in a series of visions.

49. On this see Lindblom, *Prophecy* pp.137ff.

50. Cf. Charles, *Revelation* ii, p.102 and Beasley-Murray, *Book of Revelation* p.251.

51. See above pp.61ff.

52. On the unity of Daniel see Plöger, *Theocracy* p.10ff. and above p.450 n.7.

53. The idolatry of Terah, Abraham's father which is mentioned in ch. 4 is spoken of again in ch. 26.

54. Cf. H. Appel, *Die Komposition des äthiopischen Henochbuchs* p.20ff.

55. The Greek version speaks of Enoch being taken up (*elemphthe*) cf. Sir. 49.14 (*anelemphthe*). He already seems to have a divine position in heaven.

56. *Prophecy in Ancient Israel* pp.17 and 44 and *Gesichte* p.45 n.19. Not all Lindblom's examples are equally convincing. Thus the visions of Birgitta do not contain anything like a complete separation between the ordinary self and the visionary self. Contrary to what Lindblom says, the address in the visions is to Birgitta, the Bride of Christ, not to her *alter ego*. See e.g. W. P. Cumming, *The Revelations of St Birgitta* p.1 (Book 1).

57. *Prophecy* p.44.

58. *Prophecy* p.128. See also R. B. Y. Scott 'Isa. 21.1–10: the Inside of a Prophet's Mind' *VT* 2.

59. On this matter see the discussion in O. Kaiser *Isaiah 13—39* p.126.

60. On these verses see Lindblom *Gesichte* p.42f., Dunn, *Jesus and the Spirit* pp.214ff. and above pp.381ff. On the stylized form and its relationship to visionary experience Hengel 'Pseudonymität' p.277.

61. Cf. the very suggestive comments by Austin Farrer, *The Revelation of Saint John the Divine* pp.23ff. on the interaction between Scripture and the visionary mind. Although he is convinced that Revelation was the result of a literary process, many of his remarks apply equally well to our hypothesis that the visions arose as the result of the scriptural images forming the basis 'of fresh shapes expressive of a fuller truth' op. cit. p.28.

Chapter 10 *Dating the Apocalypses*

1. Of the books available in English on questions of introduction O. Eissfeldt, *The Old Testament: An Introduction* is probably the best. Unfortunately L. Rost, *Judaism outside the Hebrew Canon* is somewhat superficial, but it does offer a useful introduction to the literature. Special mention must also be made of A. M Denis, *Introduction aux pseudépigraphes grecs d'Ancien Testament*. Despite its title it contains very valuable comments on most of the apocalypses at one place or another. The bibliographical information is invaluable. Mention should also be made of the following works which offer a survey of secondary literature on the pseudepigrapha and related works: J. H. Charlesworth, *The Pseudepigrapha and Modern Study* and G. Delling, *Bibliographie zur jüdisch-hellenistischen und intertestamentarischen Literatur* 1900–1970, and on the history of the study of apocalyptic J. M. Schmidt, *Die jüdische Apokalyptik* and now Nickelsburg, *Jewish Literature*.

2. In 'On the History of Early Christianity' in *Marx and Engels on Religion* p.289 and *Marx and Engels: Basic Writings* (ed. L. Feuer) p.217.

3. A similar point can be made with regard to targumic literature. There are some who consider that the *targumim* are repositories of very early Jewish exegesis, e.g. G. Vermes, *Scripture and Tradition* and 'Bible and Midrash: Early OT Exegesis' in *The Cambridge History of the Bible* vol. 1 and M. McNamara, *The New Testament and the Palestinian Targums*, J. W. Bowker, *The Targums and Rabbinic Literature*. On the question of dating targumic material see A. D. York 'The Dating of Targumic Literature' *JSJ* 5. A rather negative attitude towards the *targumim* can be found in E. P. Sanders, *Paul and Palestinian Judaism* pp.25ff.

4. For cautious attitudes with regard to pre-Christian gnosticism and possible influence on the New Testament see R. McL. Wilson, *Gnosis and the New Testament* and E. Yamauchi, *Pre-Christian Gnosticism*. There is much important material relating to this issue in ed. U. Bianchi, *Le Origini dello Gnosticismo*.

5. The most controversial example of such a method in recent years has been W. Schmithals, *Gnosticism in Corinth*. On the relationship with early Christology see e.g. J. T. Sanders, *The New Testament Christological Hymns*.

6. *The Rediscovery of Apocalyptic* p.27.

7. We are now in a position to see the extent to which a later translation departed from the original Aramaic by comparing some of the more extensive Aramaic fragments from Cave 4 at Qumran with Greek and Ethiopic translations of 1 Enoch. It should be pointed out that some of the

reconstructions offered by Milik are hypothetical in the extreme. Nevertheless there are enough fragments of reasonable length to make a comparison possible.

8. This applies particularly to J. Hindley's attempt ('Towards a Date for the Similitudes of Enoch' *NTS* 14) to date the Sim. during the Parthian wars of AD 113–117. Even if one agrees with his interpretation of the historical allusion here (for a critical comment see J. Jeremias, *New Testament Theology* vol. i., p.269 n.5), it is clear that we are dealing with material which is itself probably of a completely different origin from that dealing with the Son of Man.

9. For an earlier date see the views expressed in R. H. Harrison *Introduction to the Old Testament* pp.1110ff.

10. So Milik, *Enoch* pp.41ff.

11. Milik, *Enoch* p.48f. cf. Dexinger op. cit. p.188f. who links it with circles of *ḥasidim*.

12. So also Daniélou, *The Theology of Jewish Christianity* p.13 and J. A. T. Robinson, *Redating the New Testament* p.239 n.98.

13. On the fall of Jerusalem as a factor in dating New Testament documents see now J. A. T. Robinson op. cit. pp.13ff.

14. How much weight can be attached to 4 Ezra 3.1 'in the thirtieth year after the downfall of the city', (i.e., AD 100, if this is a reference to the fall of Herod's temple), is uncertain (see further Box, *Ezra-Apocalypse* p.xxviii). Rost op. cit. p.124 thinks that this is only a round number and is not to be taken literally. Harnisch accepts a date towards the end of the first century and certainly before the Bar Kochba revolt for both apocalypses (p.11). On this question see Box op. cit. pp.xxiff, also W. O. E. Oesterley, *An Introduction to the Books of the Apocrypha* p.152.

15. See above p.156.

16. On Johanan see the summary of the problems facing late first century Judaism in Neusner, *First Century Judaism in Crisis*.

17. On this see Box op. cit. p.76 n.12.

18. J. T. Milik, *Ten Years of Discovery in the Wilderness of Judaea* pp.96ff, F. M. Cross, *The Ancient Library of Qumran* pp.37ff and Vermes, *The Dead Sea Scrolls* pp.29ff.

19. For a survey of the significance of the Qumran discoveries for study of the Pseudepigrapha see G. Vermes, *The Dead Sea Scrolls: Qumran in Perspective* pp.209ff.

20. *Enoch* p.48

21. See C. Bonner, *The Last Chapters of Enoch in Greek* p.76.

22. Milik op. cit. pp.22ff. would date some of the legends earlier than passages like Gen. 6.1, especially p.31. See further M. Stone, 'The Book of Enoch and Judaism in the Third Century B.C.E.', *CBQ* 40 (1978) pp.479ff.

23. See *Pseudepigrapha* p.170f. for a list of similarities. Box sees the two apocalypses as representatives of rival views in Judaism see his *Ezra-Apocalypse* pp.lxviii but note the links pointed out by Harnisch op. cit. p.240. See also B. Violet, *Die Apokalypsen des Esra und des Baruch* p.xlixf.

24. On the possibility of an earlier source in vv. 9f. and 13 see particularly Noth op. cit. p.11ff. (n.39 on p.476 above), Colpe *TDNT* viii, p.420 and Plöger, *Das Buch Daniel* pp.105ff.

25. *The Relevance of Apocalyptic* pp.78ff.

26. E.g. Charles, *The Book of Enoch* p.2.

27. He asserts that 1 Enoch 14 is dependent on Dan. 7 in *The Book of Enoch* p.34, but cf. p.liif.

28. Op. cit. p.83.

29. See above p.87.

30. See Emerton op. cit. p.229 and J. Day op. cit.

31. See e.g. M. H. Pope, *El in the Ugaritic Texts* p.34: 'I will make thy grey hair flow with blood', but cf. the remarks of Colpe op. cit. p.417.

32. C. Gordon, *Ugaritic Literature* p.15. See further Colpe op. cit. p.418 n.146 and J. Gray, *The Legacy of Canaan* p.118.

33. Cf. Emerton's ingenious suggestion about the way the ideas were preserved op. cit. p.240f.

34. So also now T. F. Glasson, 'The Son of Man Imagery: Enoch XIV and Daniel 7' *NTS* 23. He appears to have changed his position as compared with the third edition of his book *The Second Advent* p.6f.

35. E.g. Rowley op. cit. p.96 and Milik op. cit. p.107ff.

36. W. R. Morfill and R. H. Charles, *The Book of the Secrets of Enoch* p.xxv and Hengel 'Pseudonymität' p.275.

37. A. Vaillant op. cit. pp.viii–xiii and Daniélou op. cit. p.16 and see below p.261.

38. Cf. Denis op. cit. p.29 and see the comments in Charles op. cit. (n.36) on ch. 24ff.

39. On this text see M. Delcor, *Le Testament d'Abraham* especially pp.73ff.

40. Denis op. cit. p.36.

41. A particular problem arises with the story of Joseph and Asenath. See P. Battifol, *Le livre de la prière d'Asenath* and C. Burchard, *Untersuchungen zu Joseph und Aseneth* pp.99ff.

42. Other obvious Christian elements are listed in Charles ed. pp.lxiff and see now de Jonge in *Studies on the Testaments of the Twelve Patriarchs* pp.193ff.

43. See James ed. p.92.

44. Vaillant op. cit. p.x.

45. Op. cit. p.16.

46. LXX Gen 5.24; Sir. 44.16; 49.14; Heb. 11.5 and see P. Grelot, 'La légende d'Hénoch', *RSR* 46.

47. One is a little suspicious of the reference in 24.1, where Enoch is commanded to sit on God's *left* hand with Gabriel. Nothing is said about a person sitting at God's right hand, but early Christian texts may lead us to suspect that a reference to Christ may be implied here (Acts 2.33; Col. 3.1; Heb. 1.3) and further D. M. Hay, *Glory at the Right Hand*.

48. Even the Christian origin of this idea could be challenged. There is

probably enough evidence from Jewish sources and non-Christian gnosticism to suggest that ideas similar to this were already in existence, probably closely linked with Wisdom and angelic beings. See the survey of background material for Christology in M. Hengel in *The Son of God*, C. H. Talbert, 'The Myth of a Descending Redeemer in Mediterranean Antiquity', *NTS* 22 and W. Meeks, 'The Man from Heaven', *JBL* 92.

49. Against Daniélou op. cit. pp.174ff.

50. *The Testaments of the Twelve Patriarchs* pp.lxiff. For a history of research see H. D. Slingerland, *The Testaments of the XII Patriarchs: A Critical History of Research*, to which must be added M. de Jonge, *Studies in the Testaments of the Twelve Patriarchs*.

51. *The Testaments of the Twelve Patriarchs*.

52. See above p.81.

53. There is reference to the heavenly cult (3.5), an idea which can be paralleled in b. Hagigah 12b, see Bietenhard op. cit. p.123.

54. On this relationship see now Theisohn op. cit. pp.149ff.

55. See above p.475 n.37.

56. It is unlikely to have arisen as a polemic within mainstream Judaism, where there was considerable reserve towards Enoch as is illustrated by the interpretations of Gen. 5.24 found in Ber. R. 25, on which see the notes in the Theodor–Albeck ed. p.238, Bowker op. cit. pp.144ff., and Grelot op. cit. above n.46.

57. See B. Lindars, 'Re-Enter the Apocalyptic Son of Man' *NTS* 22. On the date of the Similitudes see now e.g. J. C. Greenfield and M. E. Stone, 'The Enochic Pentateuch and the Date of the Similitudes', *HTR* 69; M. A. Knibb, 'The Date of the Parables of Enoch', and C. Mearns, 'Dating the Similitudes of Enoch', both in *NTS* 24.

Part Four: **The Esoteric Tradition in Early Rabbinic Judaism**

1. So, for example, D. Rössler, *Gesetz und Geschichte*. From their different perspectives G. F. Moore, *Judaism* and W. Bousset, *Die Religion des Judentums* are both guilty of a similar differentiation between apocalyptic and rabbinic Judaism. A much more balanced assessment of the part played by apocalyptic in rabbinic Judaism is given by J. Bloch, *On the Apocalyptic in Judaism*, A. Nissen, 'Tora und Geschichte im Spätjudentum', *NT* 9, and most important of all, Gruenwald, *Apocalyptic*.

2. Bornkamm, *Mysterion TDNT* iv, p.817.

3. See the definition of Scholem, *Major Trends* pp.1ff. For a discussion of the wider influence of esoteric interests in early rabbinic Judaism see G. A. Wewers, *Geheimnis und Geheimhaltung in rabbinischen Judentum*.

4. On this passage see Wewers op. cit. p.64.

5. A. Goldberg, *Untersuchungen über die Vorstellung von der Schekhinah in der frühen rabbinischen Literatur* pp.385ff. On the immanence of God in rabbinic literature see J. Abelson, *The Immanence of God in Rabbinic Literature* and on the Holy Spirit in rabbinic literature see P. Schäfer, *Die Vorstellung vom heiligen Geist*.

6. Kadushin, *The Rabbinic Mind* p.211f.

7. So also J. Jeremias, *Jerusalem in the Time of Jesus* pp.239ff., G. Wewers, *Geheimnis und Geheimhaltung* and H. Bietenhard, *Himmlische Welt* pp.86ff.

8. Cf. Tos. Megillah 4.34: 'And the chariot-chapter? One should read this to many'.

9. The first chapter of Ezekiel was apparently the reading from the prophets, or *haftarah* for *shabu'oth*, the Feast of Weeks. See b. Megillah 31a and further Strack–Billerbeck ii, p.602f. and D. J. Halperin, *Merkabah and Ma'aseh Merkabah according to Rabbinic Sources* pp.87ff.

10. See Wewers op. cit. pp.6f., 10, and 119f. and Halperin op. cit. pp.33ff. On the date and authorship of the Mishnah see Halperin op. cit. pp.48ff.

11. On the influence of the *merkabah* chapter on gnostic ideas see below pp.496 n.62.

12. See Wewers op. cit. p.265 n.30 but see the alternative interpretation suggested by Halperin op. cit. pp.51ff. The fact that the prohibition with regard to the *merkabah*-chapter is quoted in isolation in the story of Johanan and Eleazar cannot be taken as an indication that this prohibition may have circulated separately (*contra* Halperin op. cit. p.55). One would not expect a quotation of the whole mishnah in this context.

13. Jastrow suggests as meanings for *bin* in the *hiphil* 'perceive, make intelligible, find analogies between cases'. He offers the following translation for our passage: 'a student able to speculate by himself' (also Halperin op. cit. p.46f.). Scholem, *EJ* article 'Kabbalah' col. 498 similarly offers a rather general translation; 'one who already has an independent understanding of the matter'. The fact that the word is used in b. Hagigah 13a (bottom) in the story about the child who was reading the book of Ezekiel and understood the meaning of *ḥashmal* (Ezek. 1.27) suggests that word as used in this context indicates insight into the real meaning of the text. Thus Soncino is probably right to translate 'he apprehended what *ḥashmal* was'. According to this story the consequence of the accuracy of his understanding was that fire came forth from the *ḥashmal* and consumed the child. The point is obviously that in some way the child had so accurately pictured the *ḥashmal* that the realism of his understanding destroyed him.

14. Cf. Tos. Hagigah 2.7 which provides additional material to show the dangers of speculation outside certain fixed boundaries and thus indicates that the second paragraph of the mishnaic warning is in part at least a reference to a speculative interest in aspects of creation, so Wewers op. cit. p.9, Weiss op. cit. p.81. On this see Halperin op. cit. pp.169ff.

15. See G. Scholem, *Major Trends in Jewish Mysticism* pp.46, 66, 110f. and 392 n.66 but cf. Wewers p.327f. n.45.

16. Maier, *Kultus* p.137 and I. Gruenwald, *Apocalyptic and Merkavah Mysticism*.

17. Nevertheless archaeological evidence now makes it difficult to speak with any certainty about popular theology. It would appear that there was much more speculation on the nature and form of God than was once recognized, see Goodenough, *Jewish Symbols* and M. Smith, 'The Shape of God' in *Religions in Antiquity*.

18. So e.g. Moore, *Judaism* i, p.384.

19. Doubts about the book of Ezekiel, because of the dangers inherent in the interpretation of the first chapter, are well illustrated by the story of the child recorded in b. Hagigah 13a (see also n.13 above): 'There was once a child who was reading Ezekiel at his teacher's house and he understood what *ḥashmal* was. As a result fire came forth from the *ḥashmal* and consumed him. As a result they sought to suppress the book of Ezekiel. Hananiah b. Hezekiah said to them: "If he was a sage, then all are sages."' Hananiah's comment suggests that such a disaster would not befall anyone who was qualified to embark on exposition of the chariot-chapter, i.e. a *ḥakam*. The whole story thus serves as a warning to those who would involve themselves in such matters of the real dangers of the subject-matter of the chapter.

Chapter 11 *The Meditation of Rabban Johanan Ben Zakkai and his Circle on the Chariot-Chapter*

1. So, for example, Maier, *Kultus* pp.11ff.

2. On this period see J. Neusner, *A Life of Rabban Johanan b. Zakkai* and G. F. Moore, *Judaism* i, pp.83ff.

3. On this particular story see also E. E. Urbach, 'The Traditions about the Religion of Esoteric Groups in the Tannaitic Period' (in Hebrew) in *Studies in Mysticism and Religion for G. Scholem*; J. Neusner, *The Development of a Legend* pp.240ff.; id. 'The Development of the *Merkavah* Tradition' in *JSJ* 2; A. Goldberg, 'Der Vortrag des Ma'asse Merkawa: eine Vermutung zur frühen Merkawamystik', *Judaica* 29 and J. W. Bowker, 'Merkabah-Visions and the Visions of Paul', in *JSS* 16. On the chain of tradition and the exposition before Johanan, N. Séd 'Les traditions secrètes et les disciples de Rabban Yohanan b. Zakkai', *RHR* 184, Wewers op. cit. pp.145ff., Halperin op. cit. pp.194ff., Gruenwald, *Apocalyptic* pp.75ff. and id. 'Yannai and the Hekhalot Literature', *Tarbiz* 36.

4. The texts used for the following translations are J. N. Epstein and E. Z. Melamed, *The Mekilta of R. Simeon b. Yohai* (Hebrew) p.158f., S. Lieberman, *The Tosefta (Seder Mo'ed)*, B. Behrend, *Talmud Yerushalmi* and L. Gold-schmidt, *Der babylonische Talmud*. There are some variations in the Erfurt MS of the Tosefta (Zuckermandel's ed.). For these differences see Bowker op. cit. p.164f. and Halperin p.195f.

5. A good example of the application of this method is to be found in J. Jeremias, *The Parables of Jesus*, especially part ii.

6. An example of the application of such techniques to rabbinic material is to be found in the works of Neusner cited above in n.3 and Halperin loc. cit.

7. See Séd op. cit. p.54ff., Wewers op. cit. pp.152ff. and Halperin op. cit. pp.43 and 211.

8. The setting of discussions during a journey is a device which is often used. It applies also to the account of the exposition of Jose and Joshua in b. Hagigah 14b, see below. A similar device is found also in Mekilta de R. Ishmael (*Shabbata 1*) where three rabbis are said to be walking along a road discussing sabbath-observance.

9. So also Urbach op. cit. p.3.

10. B also mentions a third reason for congratulating Eleazar (line 123): his ability to investigate the profundities of the chariot-chapter.

11. Bowker op. cit. p.169, Neusner op. cit. p.249 and Halperin op. cit. pp.215ff. The position of the dismounting of the ass in M *after* the appearance of the fire is regarded by Halperin as a decisive argument in favour of the priority of M (p.219f.). He has shown that there is a similarity between M and other contexts where a superior dismounts in the face of an inferior character's ability (p.218f.). But such a change is just as likely to have been introduced by the redactor of M. Halperin points to a parallel to the descent from an ass and wrapping in the cloak in Tos. Pesahim 2.15f. (p.217f.). In the latter instance we have the solemn rite before the cancellation of vows. The descent and the wrapping may have formed part of a deliberate and pre-determined action before such a solemn moment. Such an action may have formed part of the ritual of *merkabah* exposition and need not, therefore, have been artificially introduced into the story of Eleazar and Johanan in T and B (*contra* Halperin op. cit. p.218). The fact that T contains no explanation of the descent of the ass makes it just as likely that M changed the order of events to conform with the pattern of the recognition of an inferior by a superior as T altered M. Although certainty in this matter is out of the question, Halperin has not offered convincing arguments to shake the belief that the version without the supernatural detail is the earlier.

12. Op. cit. p.13. Goldberg speaks of M as 'completely unreliable textual evidence'. See also Gruenwald *Apocalyptic* p.84f.

13. Neusner's main objection to the priority of T is the addition of a second blessing in this version (lines 134ff.) and the omission of Johanan's word of praise of Eleazar (M: lines 143ff.). Two points should be made: (a) *All* accounts, including M (lines 115–116 and 134–138), have two blessings by Johanan and (b) we have already noted that the last part of the story is a collection of heterogeneous material (as Neusner himself admits) which has little to do with the main story. Even if we were able to show that part of this final section in T was later than M (and that is by no means certain), this would not affect our assessment of the main part of the story. See further Gruenwald 'Yannai' pp.260ff.

14. Some account of this sort of process is given by Goldberg op. cit. pp.10ff.

15. Due note should be taken of the fact that later versions of a story sometimes tend to increase irrelevant circumstantial detail. E. P. Sanders, *The Tendencies of the Gospel Tradition* p.272 warns against any simple theory of the development of a tradition based on the omission of circumstantial detail. As far as T is concerned, however, the inclusion of these details and the omission of the fire is hardly explicable if it forms the latest version of the story.

16. Bowker op. cit. p.169 and Goldberg op. cit. p.13 both assume that T knew of the presence of the fire. The former suggests that its omission is an indication of the process whereby the possibility was removed that the *merkabah*-versions could be seen by bystanders. But this would mean that T would have to be regarded as later than the versions in B and J which increase the amount of supernatural phenomena in the account. If T were

the midpoint in the process of development between M and B and J, we would have to suppose that the talmudic versions *reversed* the process whereby the vision became a private affair. In view of the close links which exist between T, B and J it is not easy to justify the opinion that T is a later rewriting of the earlier accounts.

17. *Contra* Wewers op. cit. p.151.

18. So also Maier, *Kultus* p.137.

19. This point is well demonstrated by Urbach op. cit. pp.4ff. and Wewers op. cit. p.151 and 156, and on the link between Sinai and the *merkabah* see Halperin op. cit. 221ff.

20. The verbal similarities which exist between the M account of the exposition and the passages just mentioned, when the scriptures as a whole are expounded, are worth quoting. They would seem to confirm that some kind of parallel was being drawn between exposition of the chariot-chapter and the rest of the scriptures:
Mekilta: '. . . until the fire was glowing all around him . . .'
Shir ha-Shirim R. '. . . and the fire was glowing around him . . .'
j. Hagigah '. . . and the fire was glowing around them . . .'

21. See Strack–Billerbeck iii, pp.598ff. and Urbach loc. cit.

22. On these elements see also Wewers op. cit. pp.150ff., Maier, *Kultus* p.137, id. 'Das Gefährdungsmotiv bei der Himmelsreise in der jüdischen Apokalyptik und Gnosis', *Kairos* 5 and Neusner, *Legend* p.98.

23. Also relevant to the addition about the angels in B and J is the version of Gen. 28.12 in the Palestinian *targumim* e.g. Targum Neofiti 1: 'And he dreamed and behold a ladder was set on the earth and the top of it stretches to the end of the heavens. And behold the angels who accompanied Jacob from the house of his father came to tell the good news to the angels on high, saying, Come, see a righteous man whose features are set on the throne of glory. And they were anxious to look upon him. And behold angels from before the LORD came and were descending and looking at him'. On this passage see F. Lentzen-Deis *Die Taufe Jesu* and my article 'John 1.51 and the Targumic Tradition', *NTS* forthcoming.

24. See above p.487 nn.15 and 16.

25. So also Séd op. cit. p.53f. and Urbach op. cit. p.11

26. Cf. Wewers op. cit. p.155 and p.331 n.70, *contra* Maier, *Kultus* p.138 n.159.

27. So also Moore op. cit. i, pp.411ff. See also Gruenwald, *Apocalyptic* p.76.

28. On Johanan's dream see Goldberg 'Rabban Yohanans Traum: Der Sinai in der frühen Merkawamystik' *Frankfurter judaistische Beiträge* 3. Urbach op. cit. p.6 has pointed to the contrast which exists with Johanan's hesitancy about his future destiny in b. Berakoth 28b.

29. W. Bacher, *Die Aggada der Tannaiten* i, p.71 n.3.

30. Cf. Goldberg p.19f. who interprets the supernatural phenomena as part of the ecstatic experience of the *merkabah*-mystics. He suggests, for example, that the rustling among the trees could be taken by the mystic in his ecstatic state as the singing of angels (lines 86ff.).

31. Goldberg op. cit. p.17 thinks that the *merkabah* tradition was composed of fixed combinations of scriptural verses. See Gruenwald, *Apocalyptic* p.76f.

32. On this passage see also Urbach op. cit. p.7, nn.25 and 26. Urbach rightly suggests that a vision of the *merkabah* is hinted at in this passage. Although Halperin op. cit. p.303f. is right to point out that in the tannaitic period there was exposition of the chariot-chapter without any vision of it, there is nothing in this passage to suggest that this was not the intention of the expositors. In that respect the slight alteration in B correctly understands the significance of the original. See further Gruenwald, *Apocalyptic* p.82.

33. The reply of R. Judah which is included in B is also of interest. He points to the importance of the inward perception of the individual and suggests that in some cases people did not have the qualities to enable them to go further than mere exposition of a particular passage.

34. So also Bowker op. cit. p.158 and Maier, *Kultus* p.17.

35. So also N. Séd op. cit. p.56.

36. This is the verb used in the passage which we have already considered in b. Megillah 24b and was a favourite word in later mystical literature used of the vision of the chariot, see Scholem *Major Trends* p.358 n.18 and Wewers op. cit. p.268.

37. So Goldberg, *Schekhinah* p.402f. and Wewers op. cit. p.152.

38. A close link between Exod. 24.10 and Ezek. 1.26 is made also in Targum Ps. Jonathan on Exod. 24.10. Note also the link between the blue of the high priest's mitre and the colour of heaven in Josephus *Ant*. iii, 183.

39. For a collection of later material linking the thread of blue with the divine throne-chariot see B. Z. Bokser, 'The Thread of Blue', in *PAAJR* 31 and R. Eisler, *Weltenmantel und Himmelszelt* pp.224–7.

40. Mystical significance was also attached to the wrapping in the *tallith* itself see R. Loewe, 'The Divine Garment and the Shi'ur Komah', *HTR* 58 and see further Halperin op. cit. p.248 n.111.

41. For a date before the war see Wewers op. cit. p.152 and Neusner, *Life* p.140.

42. See also Neusner *Life* p.140 n.5, *Development of a Legend* p.68 n.1, *First Century Judaism in Crisis* and Wewers op. cit. p.207 and see above pp.126ff on 4 Ezra and Syriac Baruch.

Chapter 12 *The Problems posed by the Esoteric Tradition in theTime of Rabbi Akiba*

1. On the value of these traditions see J. Neusner, *Eliezer b. Hyrcanus* especially vol. ii p.410ff., also A. Guttmann, 'The Significance of Miracles for Talmudic Judaism', *HUCA* 20 pp.373f. and Urbach op. cit. p.118f.

2. The passage is discussed by Urbach *Sages* p.669f.

3. On this chain see also Wewers op. cit. p.143, Sed. op. cit. pp.60ff. and Halperin op. cit. pp.149ff.

4. E.g. G. Scholem, *Jewish Gnosticism* p.14, id. *Major Trends* p.52f., L. Blau, *Das altjüdische Zauberwesen* p.115f., J. Maier, *Kultus* p.18, id. *Das Gefährdungsmotiv* p.27f., Bacher op. cit. i, p.333 and Gruenwald *Apocalyptic* pp.86ff. There is a survey of interpretations of the passage in Wewers

op. cit. pp.175ff., though he thinks that this is to be identified with visionary experience (p.186), so also A. Goldberg, 'Der verkannte Gott', *ZRGG* 26 p.19 n.11. Rashi's comment on the passage also presupposes a heavenly ascent: 'They went up to heaven by means of a name'. Likewise the *Tosafoth* confirms the fact that such an interpretation was widespread by saying 'It only *appeared* to them that they ascended'. For recent attempts to dissociate the story of the four from *merkabah*-mysticism see Halperin op. cit. pp.153ff. and Fischel *Rabbinic Literature and Greco-Roman Philosophy* (see below n.14).

5. In T the story of the Four follows the account of Eleazar's exposition before Johanan, being joined to the latter by the chain of tradition which serves to link Johanan and Akiba. The position is similar in the talmuds, though extra material is added after the account of Eleazar and Johanan in the form of the exposition of the chariot by two pupils of Johanan, and, in J, there is also the story of Ben Zoma's discussion with Joshua. On the structure of this section see Halperin op. cit. pp.125ff.

6. H. Graetz, *Gnosticismus und Judentum* pp.94ff., M. Joel, *Blicke in die Religionsgeschichte* i, p.163.

7. *Major Trends* p.361 n.44, but the point is noted by Urbach op. cit. pp.12ff.

8. This addition plays an important part in A. Neher's interpretation of the story in 'Le voyage mystique des quatre' *RHR* 140 and A. Goldberg 'Der verkannte Gott'.

9. *Major Trends* p.52, *Jewish Gnosticism* p.15f.

10. Present also as variants in some manuscripts of the Tosefta. See Lieberman op. cit. p.381 and Bacher op. cit. p.333 n.1.

11. These four teachers are frequently mentioned together in collections of teaching, e.g. ARN 23ff. where the order is Ben Zoma, Elisha, Ben Azzai and Akiba.

12. There is no good reason to suppose that the addition of the scriptural passages is a later stage in the development of the tradition. We may suppose that the citations from Scripture were added to the story at the same time as the identification of the four and, therefore, provide an invaluable clue to the meaning of the story in its present context.

13. Part of the additional material in B (Hagigah 14b bottom and 15a top) includes halakic questions put to Ben Zoma. In later times mystical experience was thought to lead to greater ability in solving disputed points of halakah, see Scholem, *Major Trends* pp.77ff.

14. An attempt has been made by H. Fischel, *Rabbinic Literature and Greco-Roman Philosophy* to explain the story of the four as an 'anti-Epicurean Stereotype', pp.5ff. Two points should be made: (a) Even if this was the original purpose of the story (and Fischel has made a strong case for such a function) it has no such meaning in its present context as Fischel admits (p.4f.); (b) Fischel assumes that the names of the four rabbis were linked to the story from the beginning. As we have seen, there are good reasons to suppose that this in fact was not the case.

15. For the interpretation which follows these lines see the works referred to above in notes 4 and 8.

16. It is unjustified to assume, as Billerbeck does, (iii, p.533) that *pardes* and *gan 'eden* are to be identifed in every case. It is true that in Slav. Enoch 8, The Life of Adam and Eve 25 and Testament of Abraham (Rec. B) 14 the paradise of righteousness is said to be located in heaven, and Scholem, *Jewish Gnosticism*, has pointed out that the phrase *pardes qushta* is to be found in the Aramaic fragments of 1 Enoch 32.2 and 77.3 from Qumran (J. T. Milik, *The Books of Enoch* pp.232 and 289). In both Aramaic fragments we do not have references to a heavenly paradise but to an earthly garden as in Jub. 4.22. In Bod. MS 1531 60a Elisha describes his ascent to heaven as 'going up to paradise', but apart from this there is scanty evidence for the use of *pardes* in its technical sense. See e.g. J. Jeremias *TDNT* v, p.766 'In the Hebrew and Aramaic sources the word keeps its profane sense. Only once does it have a transferred sense in the older rabbinic literature. In this instance it is used for metaphysical gnostic speculations, but the exception is due to Jewish–Greek influence. The consistent rabbinic term for the paradise of the first, the intervening, and the last time is *gan 'eden'*.

17. Urbach op. cit. p.13.

18. Graetz, *Gnosticismus und Judenthum* p.58, considers that involvement in gnostic or mystical matters is the meaning as also does Jastrow, *Dictionary* sub *pardes*.

19. The stories are not so closely linked with the story of the Four in the Erfurt MS where they follow the story of Ben Zoma and R. Joshua. In J the story of the two ways is found as a commentary on the illicit exposition of the chariot by a pupil of rabbi (j. Hag. 77a) and the garden of the king in j. Hag. 77c in a context dealing with creation (cf. ARN 28).

20. There is some textual variation here but see further Halperin op. cit. p.179 n.3.

21. *Contra* Wewers op. cit. p.58 and Maier, *Gefährdungsmotiv* p.26.

22. Urbach also places some weight on the value of the explanatory material in T, op. cit. p.13.

23. So also Wewers op. cit. p.183.

24. *Hetsits* is omitted in B and ShS in the reference to Elisha (line 45). Fischel op. cit. p.107 n.53 sees little significance in the omission of the word at this point in the story.

25. Apart from the story of the four the only early evidence to link Akiba with mystical matters is the chain of tradition and, as far as Ben Azzai is concerned, the story already mentioned in ShS R. 1.10. See further Bacher op. cit. i, 333ff. and Fischel op. cit. p.116 n.118.

26. See also the comments on this passage in Strack–Billerbeck i, 462f. and Wewers op. cit. p.164f. and p.58f.

27. See Scholem, *Jewish Gnosticism* p.15, and Goldberg, 'Verkannte Gott' p.21.

28. See the versions of Ben Zoma's discussion with R. Joshua lines 66–68 and Wewers op. cit. p.162f.

29. E.g. the series which includes the four in ARN 23ff. begins with Ben Zoma. It should be pointed out that Ps. 116.15, which is quoted here in connection with the one who died, is linked with Ben Azzai in Ber. R. 62.2, Shem. R. 52.3 and j. Abod. Zar. 3.1 (Goldberg 'Verkannte Gott' p.20).

30. Bacher i, p.408f. finds evidence for Ben Azzai's martyrdom in the list in

Ekah R. 2.2, though one must point out that doubt has been expressed about the historical value of this list. See *EJ* sub. 'Ten Martyrs' and Schürer/Vermes/Millar op. cit. p.552.

31. *Contra* Graetz op. cit. p.72f. He fails to note the positive view of marriage which Ben Azzai offers in b. Yebamoth 63b and the fact that his celibacy is the result of his devotion to the Torah ('my soul is in love with the Torah'). On this aspect of Ben Azzai's life see C. Rabin, *Qumran Studies* p.43f.

32. Cf. Ben Azzai's own discussion of this passage in Ber. R. 62.2 where he argues that God shows the righteous their future glory before death, a typical feature of the apocalyptic tradition as the Ascension of Isaiah reveals.

33. So *EJ* iv, col. 472 and b. Baba Bathra 158b. It would also appear that he was never ordained, on which see Rabin loc. cit., presumably because he never reached a mature enough age rather than any doubts about his capabilities, though M. Yebamoth 4.13 gives him the title 'rabbi'. There is one tradition in b. Berakoth 22a which is critical of Ben Azzai for his indiscretion (Strack–Billerbeck i, p.579), but there is little else which portrays him in an unsatisfactory light.

34. Jastrow op. cit. p.1135, Scholem, *Jewish Gnosticism* p.415, Bacher op. cit. i, p.421, Levy, *Wörterbuch* p.254.

35. Theodor–Albeck Bereshith Rabbah on Gen. 2.4, followed by the Soncino translation, considers that the passage has mystical significance. Jastrow op. cit. simply translates 'Whence art thou coming?' See further the works listed in nn.37 and 38.

36. On this saying see also W. D. Davies, 'Aboth Revisited' in ed. W. R. Farmer et al. *Christian History and Interpretation* p.150 and Lieberman, *How much Greek in Jewish Palestine?* p.138f.

37. Note the discussion in 4 Ezra 5.56 and the sketch of gnostic interest in the introduction to W. Foerster, *Gnosis* vol. i and also O. Betz, 'Was am Anfang geschah' in *Abraham Unser Vater* pp.24ff. See further S. Lieberman, *How much Greek in Jewish Palestine?* pp.135ff. and Urbach *Sages* p.189f. for a discussion of the relationship with gnostic ideas. It is not impossible that Ben Zoma's initial reply 'Not from where', indicating that he was not reflecting on the origin of the world, may have been construed by Joshua as a gnostic reply. After all *me'ayin* can mean 'from nothing' as well as 'from where'. The former could imply rejection of creation *ex nihilo*.

38. While there is certainly a close connection between Genesis 1 and the gnostic cosmogonies, e.g. in the Hypostasis of the Archons, there is little in the exposition of Ben Zoma to suggest the kind of pronounced gnostic influence suggested by Graetz op. cit. p.79, Weiss op. cit. p.102ff. cf. Urbach op. cit. p.13 and *Sages* p.189f. The questions of Jewish apocalypticists and mystics may have resembled those of the gnostics but their answers are completely different.

39. On *tsaphah* as a synonym for vision see Wewers op. cit. p.201.

40. I. Abrahams, *Studies in Pharisaism and the Gospels* First Series p.50 accepts the priority of B.

41. Rashi elsewhere suggests that Ben Zoma's knowledge departed from him.

42. So D. Daube in *Nir ha-Midrashia* pp.60–62, cf. Wewers op. cit. p.336 n.22.

43. So Bacher op. cit. i, p.424f., Strack-Billerbeck iii, p.362, Wewers op.cit. p.163, Weiss op. cit. p.103 n.4, and Graetz op. cit. p.80. If the chain of tradition in Tos. Hag. 2.2 is in any way accurate, it would suggest that Joshua was sympathetic to mystical ideas but had firmly fixed views on the matter, which allowed little room for divergence of interpretation.

44. So also Graetz op. cit. p.79. A good example of the way in which the opening chapters of Genesis were used by gnostics can be found in the Apocryphon of John 45.1ff. cf. C. H. Dodd, *The Bible and the Greeks* pp.99ff.

45. So also Graetz op. cit. p.78 and H. F. Weiss, *Untersuchungen zur Kosmologie des hellenistischen und palästinischen Judentums* p.106f. and on the connotations of the word *'asah* p.227f.

46. One problem with this passage is being certain about the source of the comment, 'Is it not by a command?' In the interpretation pursued here the comment has been taken as part of Ben Zoma's explanation of the use of the verb *'asah*. It is possible, however, that it could be a part of a later comment showing how the difficulty could be circumvented by relating the action to God's creative command. This may then mean that Ben Zoma was guilty of even more extreme dualistic views to remove God from any suggestion of involvement in 'making' the universe cf. the Magariya mentioned in Al-Qirqisani's *Account of the Jewish Sects* (*HUCA* 7 p.363f.).

47. The part of the Logos is mentioned in *Op. Mundi* 20 but cf. *De Spec. Leg.* i, 81.

48. For alternative explanations of the meaning of this phrase see Scholem, *Jewish Gnosticism* 2nd ed. p.16 and p.127, and Urbach op. cit. p.14.

49. E.g. those in b. Hag. 15a which speak of him consorting with a prostitute and murdering the students of the Torah. Even B is not too happy about accepting the authenticity of the latter (15a top)!

50. See S. Back *Elischa b Abuyah* pp.7–20. His analysis of a repetition of one saying of Elisha in ARN 24 with a view to establishing a growing Hellenistic influence is not convincing cf. also Graetz op. cit. p.62.

51. So also R. T. Herford, 'Elisha ben Abujah' in *Essays Presented to J. H. Hertz* p.218.

52. See Back op. cit. p.27.

53. E.g. in J 'Elisha came into the place of assembly and saw the children sitting before their teachers. He said to them: Why are they sitting here, they could be learning trades? This one could be a builder, that one a servant, that one a hunter and that one a tailor. When they heard this, they went away. Of him it is said, Do not let your mouth' etc.

54. So J. W. Bowker, *The Targums and Rabbinic Literature* p.149, A. Goldberg, 'Der verkannte Gott', p. 27, L. Ginzberg in *JE* v, 138f. and Back op. cit. p.26f. Halperin op. cit. pp.298ff. argues for a fourth century date. But see now the important discussion of this account and its background in A. F. Segal, *Two Powers in Heaven*, though he is reluctant to attach too much weight to the historicity of this particular story (p.63). So also Gruenwald *Apocalyptic* p.90.

55. Note that in the LXX we have *tou theou* as the translation of *ha-mal'ak*. Of course, the supposition that an angelic being was in fact a god as well is exactly Elisha's conclusion in the story of his confrontation with Metatron.

56. On this verse see C. D. Ginsburg, *The Song of Songs and Qoheleth* pp.340ff. Perhaps the Hebrew *ki* should in this context be translated 'for' (see Barton, *Ecclesiastes* p.122).

57. There is some discussion of the value of these stories in Milik op. cit. pp.130ff. He is unwilling to take seriously the possibility that there may be early elements in B's version. Even if 3 Enoch in its final form is later than was supposed by its editor (H. Odeberg *3 Enoch*), there seems every likelihood that B preserves earlier material, a point not considered by Milik. Although the story is given an important place in Graetz's consideration of the story of the four, he explains the story as the result of foreign (gnostic) influence on Elisha (p.45f.).

58. A succession of seven heavens with a series of thrones is already known to the early Jewish–Christian *Ascension of Isaiah* 7ff. (Hennecke–Schneemelcher–Wilson, *New Testament Apocrypha* ii, pp. 652ff.). See also the mystical 'Visions of Ezekiel' in S. Wertheimer *Batte Midrashoth* ii. On this facet of uranology see especially H. Bietenhard op. cit. pp.8ff.

59. Cf. Slav. Enoch 22—24 where Enoch sits at God's left hand.

60. Back op. cit. pp.29ff. sees a growing tendency to denigrate Elisha, e.g. the change from the surprised reaction in B to the comment in Heb. Enoch, with its implicit suggestion of previous consideration of dualistic ideas.

61. Segal op. cit. p.61. Bacher op. cit. i, p.415 n.3 suggests that a saying of Ben Azzai in Tos. Berakoth 3.4 (par. ARN 25) may be criticism of the attitude of Elisha who let his experience rule his judgement: 'If a man's knowledge is confused because of his wisdom it is a good sign. If, however, his wisdom is confused because of his knowledge, it is a bad sign'. The two qualities of wisdom and knowledge mentioned here turn up, it will be remembered, in M. Hagigah 2.1 in the discussion of the qualities required of a man who expounds the chariot-chapter. In this saying Ben Azzai says that priority should be given to wisdom. Elisha was an example of a man who did not allow his wisdom, derived from years of the study of the Torah, to prevail over his conviction that there was no possibility of repentance for him. Consequently his knowledge caused the end of his religious beliefs.

62. See Graetz op. cit. p.65 and G. Macrae, *Elements of Judaism and Gnosticism* Diss. Cambridge 1966 pp.104ff., who argues for direct influence on Elisha from ideas similar to those in Hypostasis of the Archons 143. On the links between gnosticism and early Jewish mysticism see Scholem, *Jewish Gnosticism*, G. Quispel, 'Gnosis and the New Testament' in ed. J. P. Hyatt *The Bible and Modern Scholarship*, J. Doresse, *The Secret Books of the Egyptian Gnostics* pp.285ff., A. Böhlig, 'Der jüdische Hintergrund in gnostischen Texten von Nag Hammadi', *Mysterion und Wahrheit* p.81f. R. A. Bullard, *The Hypostasis of the Archons* p.111, and F. T. Fallon, *The Enthronement of Sabbaoth*.

63. Scholem, *Jewish Gnosticism* pp. 43ff. See further now S. Lieberman in Gruenwald, *Apocalyptic* pp. 235ff.

64. See A. F. Segal op. cit. pp.182ff. and above pp.94ff.

65. On this passage see also A. Marmorstein, *The Old Rabbinic Doctrine of God* ii, pp.134ff. A. Goldberg, *Schekhinah* p.316, who thinks that it is anti-Christian polemic, Urbach, *The Sages* ii, p.998 n.76 and Segal op. cit. p.47.

66. As 1 Enoch 71 and Slav. Enoch 24.1 show, Akiba has good reason for linking the other throne with a human being cf. also 11Q Melch and Test. Abraham (Rec. A) 12. Perhaps an even more important passage as far as the interpretation of Akiba is concerned is 1 Chron. 29.23, 'And Solomon sat on the throne of the LORD to reign in place of his father David'. This verse proved to be the basis for much later speculation on the throne-chariot, see A. Jellinek, *Beth-ha-Midrasch* ii, pp.83ff. and v, pp.34ff. and E. R. Goodenough, *Jewish-Symbols in the Greco-Roman Period* ix, p.127, x, pp.99ff. and p.193.

67. On the problems which certain aspects of Jewish angelology posed for theology see H. Bietenhard op. cit. pp. 261ff.

68. In addition to Scholem's *Major Trends* see also his article 'Kabbalah' in *Encyclopaedia Judaica* (above p.450 n.4) and *Ursprung und Anfänge der Kabbala*. On the earliest period of *merkabah*-mysticism see now I. Gruenwald, *Apocalyptic and Merkavah Mysticism* and the summary in 'Jewish Esoteric Literature in the Time of the Mishnah and Talmud', *Immanuel* 4 pp.37ff.

69. *Jewish Gnosticism* pp.9ff.

70. There is a concise summary of the contents of this literature in *Major Trends* pp.43ff and Gruenwald, *Apocalyptic* pp.127ff.

71. See *Major Trends* p.57ff.

72. *Major Trends* pp.63ff. and *Von der mystischen Gestalt der Gottheit* pp.7ff.

73. Cf. Scholem *Major Trends* p.64 '. . . a feeling for the transmundane and the numinous still glimmers through these blasphemous-sounding figures . . .'

74. Translation from A. Nemoy 'Al-Qirqisani's Account of the Jewish Sects' *HUCA* 7 p.331.

75. On this see Scholem, *Jewish Gnosticism* pp.36ff. and S. Lieberman, 'Mishnath Shir ha-Shirim' ibid. pp.118ff., R. Loewe, 'The Divine Garment and the Shi'ur Qomah' *HTR* 58, N. de Lange, *Origen and the Jews* p.44f. and R. Loewe, 'Apologetic Motifs in the Targum to the Song of Songs' in ed. A. Altmann, *Biblical Motifs* pp.184ff.

76. Translation by G. Friedlander, from which the translation included here is taken. On the value of the traditions in PRE for earlier ideas see A. Goldberg 'Der verkannte Gott' p.25.

77. See above p.15 and also P. S. Alexander, 'The Historical Setting of the Hebrew Book of Enoch', *JJS* 28.

78. On this development see the comments of J. Strugnell op. cit. (above p.480 n.11) and Rowland op. cit. pp.143ff.

79. On the veil in Jewish mystical literature see O. Hofius, *Der Vorhang vor dem Thron Gottes* pp.5ff.

80. *Hekaloth Rabbati* can be found in A. Jellinek, *Beth ha-Midrasch* iii, pp.83ff. There is a useful summary of its contents and significance in M. Smith, 'Observations on Hekaloth Rabbati' in ed. A. Altmann *Biblical and Other Studies* pp.142ff. There is a *hekaloth* text published in Scholem, *Jewish Gnosticism* pp.101ff. There is a translation in German of a text from Jellinek op. cit. ii, pp.40ff. in *Aus Israels Lehrhallen* iii, pp.33ff. Further texts listed in Scholem, *Jewish Gnosticism* pp.5ff. and Gruenwald, *Apocalyptic* pp.127ff.

Part Five: **Apocalyptic in Early Christianity**

1. The point is well brought out in Lindblom, *Gesichte*, who gives due consideration to the various ways in which early Christians believed they experienced Christ cf. also, most recently, J. D. G. Dunn, *Jesus and the Spirit*, where a full bibliography can be found.

2. Cf. Dunn op. cit. p.212ff. and further D. Lührmann, *Das Offenbarungs-verständnis bei Paulus* p.32f., though one must reject the latter's exclusion of a visionary content to certain uses of *apokalypsis* (see e.g. p.40).

3. See von Campenhausen, *Ecclesiastical Authority and Spiritual Power*, especially pp.178ff.

4. So Conzelmann, *1 Corinthians* p.244.

5. Von Campenhausen op. cit. p.189. There is a tendency here to put a wedge between prophecy in the New Testament and the phenomenon which confronts us in Montanism for which there seems to be little justification, similarly R. A. Knox, *Enthusiasm* pp.39ff.

6. There is a summary in Lindblom, *Gesichte* pp.114ff.

7. The literature on the 'In Christ' formula in Paul is extensive. See the important study by F. Neugebauer, *In Christus*, and the useful summary in H. Conzelmann, *An Outline of New Testament Theology* pp.208ff. and further C. F. D. Moule, *The Origin of Christology* pp.54ff.

8. How much apocalyptic can be linked with the religious outlook of the charismatics discussed by A. Büchler, *Types of Jewish Palestinian Piety*, and G. Vermes, *Jesus the Jew* pp.58ff., is not easy to decide. There does seem to be evidence (Büchler p.98f.) that dreams were a part of Hanina's communication with the divine.

9. This is particularly evident in J. Baumgarten's study *Paulus und die Apokalyptik*, which devotes most of its attention to eschatological terminology in the Pauline corpus. This impetus has doubtless been the result of the contribution of E. Käsemann, see particularly the two essays 'The Beginnings of Christian Theology', and 'On the Subject of Early Christian Apocalyptic' found in *New Testament Questions of Today*, but see also the criticisms of Käsemann's approach to apocalyptic by W. G. Rollins, 'The New Testament and Apocalyptic' *NTS* 17, E. Fuchs, 'On the Task of Christian Theology' *JTC* 6 pp.69ff., and G. Ebeling, 'The Ground of Christian Theology', *JTC* 6 pp.47ff. A similar eschatological orientation is also evident in J. Becker, 'Erwägungen zur apok. Tradition in der paulinischen Theologie', *EvT* 30, and on Jesus A. Strobel, *Kerygma und Apokalyptik*, especially p.39f. For a survey of recent study on this theme see W. A. Beardslee, 'New Testament Apocalyptic in Recent Interpretation', in *Interpretation* 25.

10. *New Testament Apocrypha* ii, pp.581ff.

11. *Unity and Diversity in the New Testament* pp.309ff. The debt to Vielhauer is acknowledged on p.310. He does, however, note the variety of apocalyptic material (p.310), but this has had little influence on his presentation.

12. Op. cit. pp.316ff.

13. Op. cit. p.325.

14. See above pp.136ff.

15. For this type of language with regard to New Testament eschatology see O. Cullmann, *Salvation in History* pp.100ff. and on the vertical dimension of apocalyptic C. K. Barrett op. cit. (see above p.449 n.4), p.138f.

Chapter 13 *Reports of Visions in Early Christian Literature to AD 200*

1. J. Weiss, *Jesus' Proclamation of the Kingdom of God* and A. Schweitzer, *The Quest for the Historical Jesus*. Among earlier scholars who recognized the importance of the apocalypses particular mention should be made of W. Baldensperger's work.

2. On Jesus' proclamation of the kingdom of God see R. Hiers, *The Kingdom of God in the Synoptic Tradition* and N. Perrin, *The Kingdom of God in the Teaching of Jesus*. On the tendency to separate Jesus from apocalyptic see the summary in Koch op. cit. pp.57ff. and Rollins op. cit. 467ff.

3. So also Bultmann, *The History of the Synoptic Tradition* p.109f.

4. The most comprehensive study on this pericope is F. Lentzen-Deis, *Die Taufe Jesu nach den Synoptikern*, which contains a full bibliography to 1970.

5. So also Jeremias, *New Testament Theology* i, p.55, Bultmann op. cit. p.247. Interesting parallels are offered between the call of Jesus and Paul's conversion in H. Windisch, *Paulus und Christus* pp.134ff.

6. So also Lindblom, *Gesichte* p.64f., and Dodd, *Historical Tradition in the Fourth Gospel* p.259f.

7. A full account of this material is given in Lentzen-Deis op. cit. pp.99ff.

8. So also Lindblom, *Gesichte* p.65, Lentzen-Deis op. cit. p.56, and L. Keck, 'The Spirit and the Dove', *NTS* 17 p.67.

9. So Bultmann op. cit. p.247f. and C. K. Barrett, *The Holy Spirit and the Gospel Tradition* p.35.

10. *From Tradition to Gospel*, p.274.

11. See p.373.

12. Comparison with Acts 7.55 may give us some indication of how such personal reports become mere narratives. Luke prefaces Stephen's words with his own paraphrase of what he said. He has thus taken the step of writing a narrative-version of Stephen's vision, which could easily have replaced the original words of Stephen in an ongoing tradition.

13. So also L. E. Keck, 'The Spirit and the Dove' *NTS* 17 p.62 who says that it 'belongs to the oldest Palestinian Jewish Aramaic Christian traditions'.

14. For a background in Gen. 22 see G. Vermes, *Scripture and Tradition* pp.222f. The usual solution is to see here a link between Ps. 2.7 and Isa. 42.1, so Cullmann, *The Christology of the New Testament* p.66. Jeremias op. cit. p.54 prefers to concentrate only on Isa.42.1 and see Lentzen-Deis op. cit. pp.184ff. for a survey of interpretations.

15. *Introduction to the New Testament* p.464.

16. There is a full review of previous research in Lentzen-Deis op. cit. pp.3ff. and 170ff. Keck op. cit. pp.42ff., and S. Gero, 'The Spirit as a Dove at the Baptism of Jesus', *NT* 18. See also Odes of Solomon 24.1ff and 28.1ff.

17. So also Keck op. cit. p.63 and Jeremias p.52.

18. This was suggested by I. Abrahams, 'The Dove and the Voice' in *Studies in Pharisaism and the Gospels* pp.47ff. Although Lentzen-Deis op. cit. p.126 is quite prepared to find a background in Judaism for this imagery, he is less happy about the significance of the story of Simeon b. Zoma's meditation upon the first chapter of Genesis as a way into the understanding of the baptism of Jesus. As Billerbeck (op. cit. p.124) has pointed out (also Lentzen-Deis op. cit. pp.133f. and 176), the point of comparison in the Ben Zoma story is the movement of the Spirit, and there is no suggestion that the dove symbolizes the Spirit. But it is the movement of the Spirit which leads to the comparison with a dove in the gospels also (Keck op. cit. p.51ff). The difference between Ben Zoma and Jesus is that the latter is not merely a spectator of the action of the Spirit, for he is also touched by the brooding Spirit. Therefore, we find that the gospel accounts stress the descent of the Spirit as well as comparing its movements to that of a dove, in order to indicate the divine action in the events of Jesus' ministry. Keck loc. cit. rightly points to the fact that the Ben Zoma story emphasizes the comparison with the movement but fails to appreciate the possible eschatological implications of the study of the story of creation.

19. See above pp.323ff.

20. The other instance is Jer. 23.9 which is not relevant for our discussion as it is *Qal* rather than *Piel*.

21. Op. cit. p.35 cf. Dunn, *Jesus and the Spirit* p.67. On the life and ministry of John see e.g. C. H. H. Scobie, *John the Baptist*.

22. On the authenticity of this passage see Bultmann op. cit. pp.245ff. and Barrett p.125f.

23. On the link between spirit and prophecy see above p.461 n.47 and Schweizer, 'pneuma' *TDNT* vi, p.383f. On the spirit as a purifying force note the following passages from the Qumran scrolls 1QS 3.7–9, 4.21 and 1QH 16.12, 7.6, 17.26. See further O. Betz, *Offenbarung und Schriftforschung* pp.130ff.

24. See Bousset, *Religion* pp.283ff., Volz op. cit. especially p.417 and Jeremias op. cit. p.69f.

25. So also Dunn, *Jesus and the Spirit* pp.62ff. and also Hengel, *Nachfolge und Charisma* pp.41ff.

26. So Jeremias op. cit. p.73f., and Bultmann p.253. One obvious example is the quotation from the Gospel of the Hebrews in *Origen Comm. on Jn.* ii, 12.87: 'My mother the Holy Spirit, took me by one of my hairs and brought me to the great Mount Tabor'.

27. For parallel examples of the mental torment which holy men endured after such an overwhelming experience see Bultmann op. cit. p.253.

28. See e.g. B. Gerhardsson, *The Testing of God's Son*.

29. See above pp.228f. On the historical nucleus of the temptation-story see Jeremias op. cit. pp.70ff.

30. It is interesting to compare the Test. Abraham Rec. A 10, where the patriarch is said to see the whole world from the chariot in which he travels.

31. The verb *etheoroun* is a durative imperfect (see Moulton, *Prolegomenon* p.134 and *TDNT* vi, p.163 n.11), followed by a timeless aorist participle. It should be translated 'I watched him fall'. On this saying see also T. W. Manson, *Sayings of Jesus*, p.278.

32. So e.g. G. E. Ladd, *Theology of the New Testament* p.67.

33. Bultmann op. cit. p.161 and Jeremias op. cit. p.73.

34. Some versions of this verse seem to presuppose that the casting out of the ruler of this world is an ejection from heaven; it sy^S sa all read *kato* instead of *exo*, (so also Bultmann, *The Gospel of John* p.431 n.3).

35. Bultmann, *Gospel of John* p.431 cf. Brown, *The Gospel According to John* i, p.478.

36. See Caird op. cit. p.153. On the links between this verse and earlier tradition see P. von der Osten Sacken, *Gott und Belial* pp.210ff.

37. There is some late Jewish evidence which suggests that the casting out of Satan was regarded as part of the events of the end-time, see Lueken, *Michael* p.29.

38. So e.g. V. Taylor, *The Gospel According to St. Mark* p.386.

39. So Bultmann, *History* p.259f but see the recent criticisms of this view by R. H. Stein, 'Is the Transfiguration (Mark 9.2–8) a Misplaced Resurrection Account?', *JBL* 95, and earlier G. H. Boobyer, *St Mark and the Transfiguration* and H. Baltensweiler, *Die Verklärung Jesu*.

40. *Gesichte* pp.39ff. He points to the use of the phrase *ophthe autois* which is used elsewhere in descriptions of visions (Luke 1.11; Acts 2.3; 9.17; 26.16; 1 Cor. 15.3ff.; Rev. 11.19; 12.1 and 3). Also the conclusion of the vision with the reference to Jesus being left on his own (Mark 9.8 and par.) can be paralleled in certain OT visions (Gen. 35.13; Judg. 6.21; 13.20; cf. Luke 1.38; 2.15; Acts 10.7, 16; Rev. 22.8). In Matthew the event is explicitly described as *horama*, used elsewhere of a vision in Acts 7.31; 9.12 (in B and C); 10.3, 17, 19; 11.5. In 2 Pet. 1.16 the disciples are said to *epoptai* of the glory of Jesus. On the visionary aspects of the transfiguration story see also H. C. Kee, 'The Transfiguration in Mark: Epiphany or Apocalyptic Vision' in *Understanding the Sacred Text* and R. Hartstock 'Visionsberichte in den synoptischen Evangelien', pp.133ff.

41. Noted also by Albright/Mann, *The Gospel of Matthew* p.203 and by M. Lagrange, *L'Evangile selon Matthieu* p.335.

42. But cf. V. Taylor, *The Gospel of Mark* p.389.

43. *Chion* is a v. l. in Matt. 17.2 in D it vg sy^c and in Luke 9.29 in sy^c.

44. Cf. Lindblom, *Gesichte* p.63.

45. In the Slavonic Josephus Jesus is probably viewed as an angel. See the addition after *BJ* ii, 174 (in the Loeb ed. *BJ* vol. iii, p.648). Indeed, in the version of Peter's confession in the Gospel of Thomas logion 13 Peter confesses Jesus as a righteous angel. Does this also lie behind the confession of Jesus as 'the holy one of God' in John 6.69?

46. See Stein op. cit.

47. If there is any reason to suppose that some kind of visionary experience lies behind this account, Lindblom's suggestion that we have a vision in which the experience of Peter has played the dominant role may have something to be said for it (*Gesichte* p.62). One would then explain the presence of Moses and Elijah as the result of Peter's own religious background (on these figures see Baltensweiler op. cit. pp.39ff.). Peter's desire to build the booths (*skene*) may be understood in the light of Old Testament theophanies. On two occasions when Jacob experiences theophanies it is said that he erected a pillar where God had spoken to him (28.18 and 35.14 cf. 35.20: Ju. 6.24). Such an act as this may be reflected in the words of Peter who wanted to erect a memorial to this theophany. On the link between theophanies and holy places see Lindblom, 'Theophanies in Holy Places in Hebrew Religion', *HUCA* 32. Further explanations in Riesenfeld, *Jésus Transfiguré* pp.200ff. and 256ff. and Baltensweiler loc. cit.

48. Cf. M. Smith, *Clement of Alexandria and a Secret Gospel of Mark* pp.238f. and 243f. who thinks that the transfiguration is to be linked with a heavenly ascent.

49. With the exception of the conversion of Paul the treatment of the post-resurrection appearances has been omitted from this study. It must be admitted that some or all of these may have been visions, but the stories in the gospels do not allow us to suppose this with any certainty. For an examination of the post-resurrection appearances see Lindblom, *Gesichte* pp.78ff. and J. E. Alsup, *The Post-Resurrection Appearance Stories*, which includes an exhaustive bibliography.

50. See e.g. E. Haenchen, *The Acts of the Apostles* pp.173ff. and further on history and redaction in this chapter J. Kremer, *Pfingstbericht und Pfingstgeschehen*, and on the vision particularly pp.107ff.

51. Lindblom, *Gesichte* p.75 and Kremer op. cit. p.107. Luke did not think of the resurrection-appearances as visions. The use of *ophthe* in 24.34 represents the initial reaction of the disciples. At first they thought it was a vision. This view is then corrected in the following verses.

52. So e.g. Knox op. cit. p.195.

53. See above p.293, noted by Kremer p.113f. and 239ff. The phrase *glossai pyros* is actually found in the vision of God's throne and palace in the Greek of 1 Enoch 14.9 (Kremer op. cit. p.109 n.67).

54. Art. *pentekoste TDNT* vi, p.51 Lindblom, *Gesichte* p.109 n.44 speaks of mass-ecstasy cf. Dunn *Jesus* p.147f. but cf. Kremer op. cit. p.263.

55. See e.g. the visions in the *Passio Perpetuae* (above p.394), Martyrdom of Polycarp 5.2 and 9.1, Tg. Ps. Jon on Gen. 22.10 and see further E. Preuschen *Die Apostelgeschichte* p.45.

56. So Haenchen op. cit. p.295.

57. As suggested e.g. by Haenchen op. cit. p.292, but cf. Bruce, *The Acts of the Apostles* p.198.

58. J. O'Neill, *Theology of Acts* pp.88ff. questions whether in fact Stephen was a Christian.

59. See C. K. Barrett, 'Stephen and the Son of Man' in *Apophoreta*, M. H. Scharlemann, *Stephen: a Singular Saint* pp.15ff.

60. Following Haenchen op. cit. p.292.

61. For this particular interpretation see O. Bauernfeind, *Die Apostelgeschichte* p.120, cf. Bietenhard op. cit. pp.71 and 264.

62. On Stephen's position within early Christianity see O. Cullmann, *The Johannine Circle* pp.39ff., Scharlemann op. cit. pp.136ff. and J. Bihler, *Die Stephanusgeschichte im Zusammenhang der Apostelgeschichte* pp.187ff.

63. See e.g. U. Wilckens, *Die Missionsrede im Apostelgeschichte* pp.63ff, but cf. the discussion in G. N. Stanton, *Jesus of Nazareth in New Testament Preaching* pp.19ff.

64. Haenchen op. cit. p.355f.

65. So Dibelius, 'The Conversion of Cornelius', in *Studies in the Acts of the Apostles* p.112f., Bauernfeind op. cit. p.145.

66. On this feature see above p.499 n.7.

67. Cf. Lk. 1.11 and Strack–Billerbeck ii, p.77f.

68. Whether one should take this reference as a preparation for a vision is not clear from the text but see Lindblom, *Gesichte* p.54 and Haenchen op.cit. p.347.

69. One may compare the way in which a dream functions in Matt. 1.20 as Joseph debates the question of divorcing Mary when he finds her pregnant before he had had sexual intercourse with her. According to Matthew this vision was decisive in respect of his subsequent action (1.24). This is a point missed by Lindblom *Gesichte* p.27f.

70. See pp.306ff. and also Guttmann op. cit. above (p.49 n.1).

71. On the relationship of Acts 15 to rabbinic practice see the suggestions in B. Gerhardsson, *Memory and Manuscript* pp.245ff.

72. On this point see the valuable comments in E. Stauffer, 'Zum Kalifat des Jakobus' *ZRGG* 4. Parallels from Jewish practice would indicate that dynastic succession did form an important part within certain Jewish groups. The leadership of the Zealots was, according to Josephus, kept within one family (*BJ* ii, 433), see also S. G. F. Brandon, *Jesus and the Zealots* p.166f. The same is also true of the Hillelite school of Pharisaism, in which headship was passed on from father to son, see Urbach, *Sages* i, p.593f. As Jesus was unmarried, it is probably not surprising to find that the head of the Christian sect in Jerusalem should have been his brother, who, like Paul, only became a believer after the resurrection (1 Cor. 15.7 and Gospel of Hebrews in Jerome *De Viris Illustribus* 2). According to Eus. *EH* iii, 11.1 the see of Jerusalem was kept within Jesus' family after James' death.

73. On this passage see W. Schmithals, *Paul and James* pp.63ff.

74. So also Dunn, *Jesus and the Spirit* p.178.

75. On Paul's concept of authority see the summary in von Campenhausen, *Ecclesiastical Authority and Spiritual Power* pp.30ff. and most recently J. H. Schütz, *Paul and the Anatomy of Apostolic Authority* and Dunn, *Jesus and the Spirit* pp.271ff.

76. The point is made most succinctly by Dodd, *The Epistle to the Romans,* but see E. P. Sanders, *Paul and Palestinian Judaism* p.443 and the literature cited there.

77. It has been suggested by J. W. Bowker, 'Merkabah-Visions and the Visions of Paul' *JSS* 16, that Paul was engaged in the kind of meditation of the first chapter of Ezekiel, which occupied the attention of Johanan b. Zakkai and Eleazar b. Arak. His concentration on the accounts in Acts, however, must cast some doubt on this particular solution (see e.g. C. Burchard, *Der Dreizehnte Zeuge*), and the reliance on the account in the Mekilta de R. Simeon b. Johai must be seen in the light of the discussion above p.284. See now G. Quispel, 'Ezek. 1.26 in Jewish Mysticism and Gnosis', *VC* 34 and S. Kim, *An Exposition of Paul's Gospel*.

78. Lindblom, *Gesichte* p.47 but see the discussion of the Acts accounts in Burchard op. cit. above n.77.

79. Haenchen op. cit. p.327f. cf. Burchard op. cit. p.120f. Some indications of Lucan redaction can be seen from the following list: Acts 9.3 *exaiphnes,* of five occurrences in the New Testament, four are found in Luke/Acts; *lalethesetai* passive of *laleo* used at Acts 13.42, 45f.; 16.14; 22.10; 27.25; it is not found in Paul's letters; 22.5 *presbyterion* found only in New Testament at Luke 22.66 and 1 Tim. 4.14 (cf. C. F. D. Moule's opinion about Lucan authorship of the Pastorals in 'The Problem of the Pastoral Epistles', *BJRL* 47 and A. Strobel, 'Schreiben des Lukas? Zum sprachlichen Problem der Pastoralbriefe' *NTS* 15); *timoreo* in Acts 22.5 and 26.11; the word *Nazoraios* found seven times in Acts; 22.11 *cheiragogoumenos* only here and at 9.8; 26.13 *ouranothen* also at Acts 14.17; *dialekto* in 26.14 found only in Acts; *procheirizomai* in 26.16 only in Acts and *exaireo* in 26.17, five times in Acts but also at Matt. 5.29; Matt. 18.9 and Gal. 1.4. All this suggests that, whatever reminiscences Luke may have received concerning this event, it has been expressed in his own words.

80. So also J. Munck, *Paul and the Salvation of Mankind* p.34.

81. See e.g. W. Marxsen, *The Resurrection of Jesus of Nazareth* p.102 and also Alsup op. cit. pp.55ff. (p.502 n.49 above).

82. There is a discussion of the meaning of *ektroma* in Dunn *Jesus and the Spirit* p.101 with full bibliographical detail.

83. See Dunn *Jesus and the Spirit* p.100f. and Stuhlmacher *Das paulinische Evangelium* p.77 n.1. On this verse see K. Kertelge, 'Apokalypsis Iesou Christou (Gal. 1.12)', in *Neues Testament und Kirche* pp.266ff.

84. Marxsen op. cit. pp.101ff. cf. the discussion of Gal. 1.12 in D. Lührmann, *Das Offenbarungsverständnis bei Paulus* p.73f.

85. E.g. Rengstorf, *Die Auferstehung Jesu* p.58.

86. So also Blass–Debrunner para. 220 and Moule *An Idiom Book of New Testament Greek* p.76, but cf. Dunn *Jesus and the Spirit* p.105.

87. So Stuhlmacher op. cit. p.77f. (cont. of n.1 on p.77), but Baumgarten op. cit. p.153 thinks that there is a deliberate attempt by Paul to remove all visual aspects of such experiences. But in these cases it is a matter of what Paul chooses to tell his readers rather than any missing elements being indicative of the character of his experience. The fact that Paul concen-

trates on the words spoken to him does not in any way exclude the fact that he saw a vision, about which he chose to remain silent.

88. So also Cranfield, *Romans* p.409f.

89. *Contra* E. Best, *1 and 2 Thessalonians* p.283f. Rev. 13.2 shows how human persons and institutions can function as the embodiment of the demonic power in the last days without any suggestion that they are supernatural beings cf. 1 John 2.18ff.

90. See Stuhlmacher op. cit. p.77f.

91. So also Lindblom, *Gesichte* p.48. Acts 22.17 certainly refers to a vision of Jesus (on 2 Cor. 12.1 see below n.101). On Acts 22.17 see O. Betz, 'Die Vision des Paulus im Tempel', in *Verborum Veritas.* On the genitive in Gal. 1.12 see Kertelge op. cit. p.269 n.7.

92. The same double point is being made in 1.1 where the preposition *apo* denotes the origin of apostolic office and *dia* the means whereby that office has been initiated.

93. *Contra* Lührmann op. cit. p.41 and p.104f. especially 105 n.1. His views are subjected to criticism by Stuhlmacher op. cit. p.77 n.1.

94. See Munck op. cit. p.33f. It is interesting to note how Paul's language is taken up in the Mani text A. Henrichs and L. Koenen, 'Ein griechischer Mani-Codex', *Zeitschrift für Papyrologie und Epigraphik 5.*

95. It is thus not necessarily the case that Paul had to go back fourteen years for evidence of a suitable experience to relate to the Corinthians (*pace* Barrett op. cit. p.308), nor is it true that the experience had little significance for Paul (Baumgarten p.143). The importance of the visions for Paul is rightly stressed by H. Saake, 'Paulus als Ekstatiker', *NT* 15 pp.153ff. Attempts to link the experience with the conversion vision have not met with much success, see Windisch, *Der zweite Korintherbrief* p.373.

96. E.g. W. Schmithals, *Gnosticism in Corinth* p.211f. and R. Jewett, *Paul's Anthropological Terms* p.278. On Paul's opponents in 2 Cor. see D. Georgi, *Die Gegner des Paulus im 2 Korintherbrief* and the useful survey by C. K. Barrett, 'Paul's Opponents in 2 Corinthians', *NTS* 17.

97. So also H. Windisch op. cit. p.368.

98. Cf. E. Käsemann 'Die Legitimät des Apostels' *ZNW* 41 pp.63ff.

99. Windisch op. cit. p.369, E. Benz, *Paulus als Visionär* pp.88ff., and Lindblom, *Gesichte* pp.41ff. On 2 Cor. 12.2ff see now A. T. Lincoln, 'Paul the Visionary', *NTS* 25.

100. So also Windisch op. cit. p.368 and Lindblom *Gesichte* p.41f.

101. So also A. Schlatter, *Paulus der Bote Jesu* p.658, who points to the similarity with 1 Cor. 1.7. Cf. Bietenhard op. cit. p.165, Windisch p.368 and Baumgarten, *Paulus und die Apokalyptik* p.143, who prefer to take it as a subjective genitive.

102. Schmithals' attempt to make a distinction between the visions of apocalyptic and gnosticism on the grounds that the former are always concerned with the future is completely incorrect, op. cit. pp.379f. cf. Baumgarten op. cit. p.137f.

103. So also Munck op. cit. p.34f. cf. Baumgarten op. cit. p.153.

104. Cf. Bietenhard op. cit. p.164f., Windisch op. cit. p.371, Baumgarten p.140, and H. D. Betz, *Paulus und die sokratische Tradition* p.89.

105. On this stylized way of speaking see H. D. Betz op. cit. pp.84ff. The attempt to relate the formal expression in vv. 2ff. to Hellenistic material is hardly convincing, for the Jewish background looks more likely (op. cit. p.85 and above p.240).

106. See the discussion in Windisch op. cit. p.371 and Plummer, *Corinthians* p.344.

107. So e.g. Windisch p.171, Bietenhard p.164, Lührmann p.58 and Barrett p.310. See further now Lincoln op. cit. p.211.

108. See Betz p.91 n.336 and W. Bousset, *Die Himmelsreise der Seele* p.143 n.3, and cf. Clement of Alexandria *Stromateis* v, 11, 77.

109. Apoc. Abr. certainly presupposes a cosmology of seven heavens (19), but the patriarch says nothing about what he sees as he is taken up to the highest heaven where God's throne is located, though he does look into the heaven below after his vision of the throne-chariot.

110. The word *paradeisos* is found in the LXX at Neh. 2.8 and Eccles. 2.5.

111. See also Jeremais *'paradeisos'* TDNT v, p.766 and see Urbach op. cit. p.13.

112. Jeremias op. cit. p.767.

113. On this see Strack–Billerbeck iv, 1130f.

114. For the Aramaic *pardes qushta* in 1 Enoch 32.3 see Milik, *Enoch* p.232.

115. Noted in Strack–Billerbeck iv, p.1119.

116. Cf. Hermas Vis. i, 3.3 and see Strack–Billerbeck iii, p.449, Lindblom, *Gesichte* p.44. For the Hellenistic background see Windisch op. cit. p.377f.

117. On the secret teaching in apocalyptic see Slav. Enoch 23.1; T. Levi 8.19 and Asc. Is. 11.39. On the background to the concept of mystery in the New Testament see especially D. Lührmann, *Das Offenbarungverständnis bei Paulus* pp.113ff. G. Bornkamm, *'mysterion'* in TDNT iv, pp.802ff., R. E. Brown, *The Semitic Background to the Concept 'Mystery' in the New Testament*, Strack–Billerbeck i, p.659, and on this verse see Baumgarten op. cit. p.139 n.56.

118. It would be wrong to give the impression that Paul thought of the gospel as a series of mysteries to be disclosed to the Christians as they became more mature. Indeed, the gospel itself is the revelation of the supreme mystery (1 Cor. 2.7 cf. Col. 1.26f.), which, in different forms, is the possession of all believers. On this see Conzelmann *1 Corinthians* p.59f.

119. Windisch op. cit. p.374f., E. Grässer 'Kol 3.1–4 als Beispiel einer Interpretation *secundum homines recipientes'*, ZTK 64 p.151 n.34.

120. *Gesichte* p.44 and especially n.17 and Dunn *Jesus and the Spirit* p.214 and see above pp.231f.

121. Cf. Dunn *Jesus* p.215 and Lindblom *Gesichte* p.41.

122. See above pp.232.

123. There is a full range of parallel material in Windisch op. cit. p.369f.

124. E.g. Barrett op. cit. p.307f.

125. On the question whether Paul sought to isolate such experiences from the issue of apostolic authority see Lührmann op. cit. p.58 and Käsemann 'Die Legitimät des Apostels' *ZNW* 41 p.54

126. E.g. *Kyrios Christos* pp.172ff. cf. Deissner, *Paulus und die Mystik.*

127. So also Wendland, *Die Briefe an die Korinther* quoted by Barrett op. cit. p.307.

128. So also Stuhlmacher op. cit. p.77 n.1. and Baumgarten op. cit. p.142.

129. See the summary of views in Güttgemanns, *Der leidende Apostel* p.160f.

130. So also Lindblom, *Gesichte* p.45, Dunn, *Jesus and the Spirit* p.214f. and see also above p.240.

131. The distinction made between the ascents of the apocalypticists and the later rabbinic mystics by J. Maier (*Vom Kultus zu Gnosis* pp.17ff. 'Gefährdungsmotiv' pp.28ff. and M. Smith, 'Observations on Hekaloth Rabbati' cf. *Clement of Alexandria* p.155f.) is somewhat artificial.

132. See *TDNT* i, p.472.

133. In the Hebrew Sirach 44.16 reads 'Enoch walked with YHWH, a sign of knowledge for every generation', and 49.14, 'Few were created on earth like Enoch, and he also was taken up to the presence' *(nilqaḥ panim).*

134. Greek *euarestos to theo genomenos egapethe, kai zon metaxu hamartolon metetethe. Herpage me kakia allaxe sunesin autou.*

135. In b. Pesahim 50a the verb *ithnegid* is used to speak of the trance of R. Joseph (Strack–Billerbeck iii, p.531). Precisely the same word is used of Enoch's translation in Tg. Ps. Jonathan on Gen. 5.24 cf. S. Lieberman, *Hellenism in Jewish Palestine* pp.13ff.

136. Translations in Hennecke–Schneemelcher, Wilson *New Testament Apocrypha* vol. ii and R. H. Charles and G. H. Box, *The Apocalypse of Abraham and the Ascension of Isaiah.* Parts of the earlier chapters, but excluding the apocalypse, can be found under the title 'The Martyrdom of Isaiah' in Charles, *Pseudepigrapha* pp.155ff. On this work see N. K. Helmbold, 'Gnostic Elements in the Ascension of Isaiah', *NTS* 18 and Gruenwald, *Apocalyptic* pp.57ff.

137. See above p.252.

138. See above p.262.

139. There are probably relics of this type of understanding of the triumph of Christ in passages like Col. 2.14f., 1 Tim. 3.16 and 1 Pet. 3.22. See J. Daniélou, *Theology of Jewish Christianity* pp.233ff. and R. Longenecker, *The Christology of Early Jewish Christianity*, especially pp.58ff.

140. There is evidence of a close link between Elchesaites and Mani, see Henrichs and Koenen op. cit. (above p.505 n.94) pp.141ff. There are some similarities also with the apocalyptic origin of Cerinthus' message as it is reported in Eusebius *HE* iii, 28, 1f. Sources in Klijn and Reinink, *Patristic Evidence for Jewish Christian Sects.*

141. Translation from Hennecke op. cit. p.747f.

142. So Schoeps, *Theologie und Geschichte des Judenchristentums* p.326.

143. Cf. Daniélou op. cit. p.65. The possibility of a connection with the *shi'ur komah* speculation of the rabbinic mystics cannot be ruled out. Scholem, *Jewish Gnosticism* p.41 thinks that there was a link between Jewish-Christianity and this form of mystical doctrine.

144. Quoted above p.500, n.26.

145. Op. cit. p.66.

146. On critical matters see the short summary by Vielhauer in Hennecke op. cit. pp.629ff. and M. Dibelius, 'Der Hirt des Hermas' pp.421ff. The Muratorian Canon says that Hermas was brother of a bishop of Rome, Hennecke op. cit. i, p.45.

147. So Vielhauer op. cit. p.630.

148. On the eschatological teaching in Hermas see R. Bauckham, 'The Great Tribulation in the Shepherd of Hermas', *JTS* 25, and on the contact with earlier apocalyptic Daniélou op. cit. p.37.

149. On the angelology of Hermas see the discussion in L. Pernveden, *The Concept of the Church in the Shepherd of Hermas* pp.38ff.

150. Translation from K. Lake, *The Apostolic Fathers* ii, p.61f.

151. Cf. Dibelius op. cit. pp.482ff.

152. Dibelius op. cit. p.511.

153. See Vielhauer in *New Testament Apocrypha* ii, p.638f.

154. See C. K. Barrett, 'Jews and Judaisers in the Epistles of Ignatius', in *Jews Greeks and Christians*. That apocalyptic contributed to gnosticism seems to be demanded by some of the Nag Hammadi texts, see e.g. F. T. Fallon, *The Enthronement of Sabaoth*.

155. This is apparent throughout Daniélou's *Theology of Jewish Christianity* and *The Origins of Latin Christianity*.

156. See W. M. Calder, 'Philadelphia and Montanism' in *BJRL* 7, K. Aland, 'Der Montanismus und die kleinasiatische Theologie' *ZNW* 46, and W. Schepelern, *Der Montanismus und die phrygische Kulte* pp.159ff.

157. Texts relating to Montanism can be found in P. Labriolle, *Les sources de l'histoire du montanisme* and more detailed comment in id. *La crise montaniste*. See also N. Bonwetsch, *Die Geschichte des Montanismus*, and the concise summary in H. von Campenhausen, *Ecclesiastical Authority and Spiritual Power* pp.181ff.

158. Eusebius *EH* v. 16.7 tells us that Montanus' ecstatic state and his prophesying was 'not according to the Church's custom', a hint that the enthusiastic beginnings of Christianity had for long ceased to be regarded as anything out of the ordinary by the Church of a later time.

159. On the relationship of Montanism and Phrygian religion see Schepelern op. cit. pp.79ff. who considers that the later aspects of the movement owed something to Phrygian religion, even if its earliest manifestation does not come from that source. There may be a hint of considerable Jewish influence on Montanism, if we are follow the implication of the anti-Montanist polemic in *EH* v.16. This speaks of the lack of evidence which exists of persecution of the Montanists for their beliefs by members of the Jewish synagogues, see W. H. C. Frend, *Martyrdom and Persecution*

in the Early Church p.288, but cf. D. R. A. Hare, *Jewish Persecutions of Christians in the Gospel According to Saint Matthew* p.76 n.2. On the Jewish element in Montanism see also J. M. Ford, 'Was Montanism a Jewish-Christian Heresy?' *JEH* 17.

160. E.g. Tertullian *Adv. Marc.* iii, 24: 'For when a man is rapt in the spirit, especially when he beholds the glory of God, or when God speaks through him he necessarily loses his sense, because he is overshadowed with the power of God' cf. *De Anima* 45, *De Exhort. Cast.* x, 5 and Epiphanius *Pan.* xlviii, 4.

161. Cf. von Campenhausen op. cit. p.189, who places a little too much emphasis on the ecstatic element in Montanism. On prophecy in earliest Christianity see U. Müller, *Prophetie und Predigt im Neuen Testament*.

162. One wonders whether there is any connection between this story and the story of the four who entered *pardes* in its later versions, which speaks of the death of Ben Azzai during ecstasy, see Scholem, *Jewish Gnosticism* pp.15ff. and above p.322.

163. Labriolle, *Sources* p.139. This passage should be compared with the reference (Tertullian *Adv. Marc.* loc. cit.) to Jerusalem suspended in the sky for a period of forty days over Judaea.

164. So also von Campenhausen op. cit. p.187.

165. Schepelern op. cit. pp.7ff. Of course, the fact that early Christians identified Christ with the (female) figure of wisdom may account for the peculiarities of this vision.

166. Labriolle, *Sources* p.21.

167. Cf. *The Life of St Teresa* 29 'Once when I was holding the cross of a rosary in my hand, He took it from me into his own; and when He returned it to me, it consisted of four large stones much more precious than diamonds . . .' etc. See further Lindblom, *Prophecy* pp.41f. and 137ff.

168. See Frend op. cit. pp.178ff.

169. Latin and Greek Text ed. by C. I. M. I. van Beek, *Passio Sanctarum Perpetuae et Felicitatis* and J. A. Robinson, *The Passion of St. Perpetua*. On the significance of this material see Labriolle, *Crise* pp.338ff., E. R. Dodds, *Pagan and Christian in an Age of Anxiety* pp. 47ff., and Daniélou, *The Origins of Latin Christianity* pp.59ff. Translations from *Ante-Nicene Fathers*.

170. Montanist influence was particularly strong in N. Africa see Frend, *Martyrdom and Persecution*, pp.293ff. and 363ff.

171. So Daniélou loc. cit. Dodds op. cit. p.49 is less convinced about the authenticity of Satyrus' vision, but it is hardly the typical Christian vision which he supposes.

172. There is some similarity with the intercession of the righteous for the departed which we find in the Test. Abraham 14 (Rec. A), where the soul, whose righteous and wicked deeds are equally balanced, is saved as the result of the intercession of the patriarch and the archangel Michael.

173. The description of the vision shows clear signs here of subsequent reflection. The presence of Satyrus in the vision is explained, something which is unlikely to have formed part of the original memory of the experience by Perpetua.

174. Following the Greek *(perimeno)*; the Latin has *sustineo* (Robinson op. cit. p.66f.).

175. Jacob's ladder forms an important part of Philo's discussion of the mystical ascent in *De Somniis,* and it is also used by the rabbinic mystics as a way of comparing the ascent to heaven, see above p.22.

176. On the threat facing the mystic on his ascent to heaven see J. Maier, 'Das Gefährdungsmotiv bei der Himmelsreise in der jüdischen Apokalyptik und Gnosis' *Kairos* 5.

177. See Jeremias, *'paradeisos' TDNT* v, p.767f.

178. So Daniélou, *Origins* p.60 cf. *Theology of Jewish Christianity* p.120f.

179. Dodds op. cit. p.52f. says that it is pagan imagery.

180. See Hofius, *Vorhang* p.15 and also the Apocalypse of Paul 22 (*NHL* p.241): (Then we went) up to the seventh (heaven and I saw) an old man . . . (whose garment) was white. (His throne) which is in the seventh heaven (was) brighter than the son . . .' See Gruenwald, *Apocalyptic* pp.70ff.

181. J. A. Robinson op. cit. p.38 reads *canebant* for *cadebant.* If this is correct, we may note the parallel situation in the account of the exposition of the chariot-chapter by Eleazer b. Arak in the two talmuds (above p.287) where the trees of the field break out in song.

182. 1 Enoch 14.8ff. knows of two stages to the heavenly journey as also does 2 Cor. 12.2ff., assuming that our interpretation of that passage is correct.

183. So also Brown, *The Gospel According to John* i, p.487 and on the apocalyptic dimension of the theology of the Fourth Gospel see J. A. Bühner *Der Gesandte und sein Weg.*

184. This does not pretend to be an exhaustive survey. Much work remains to be done on the apocalyptic tradition in early Christianity. There are interesting ideas in *The Life of Pachomius* (W. Crum, *Theological Texts from Coptic Papyri* 1913 p.152, and see further K. Berger, *Die Auferstehung des Propheten* especially p.456f, 489, 567f).

Chapter 14 *Revelation*

1. But cf. P. S. Minear, *And I Saw a New Earth* pp.235ff.

2. For a discussion of this chapter and the question of date see A. Strobel, 'Abfassung und Geschichtstheologie der Apokalypse nach Kap. 17.9–12' *NTS* 10 and also the summary in W. G. Kümmel, *Introduction to the New Testament* p.466. There is a concise and lucid discussion of the date and setting in J. P. M. Sweet, *Revelation.*

3. E.g. D. Guthrie, *New Testament Introduction* pp.949ff. and N. Perrin, *The New Testament: an Introduction* p.80.

4. J. A. T. Robinson, *Redating the New Testament* pp.221ff. and now also A. A. Bell, 'The Date of John's Apocalypse', *NTS* 25.

5. Irenaeus *Adv. Haer.* v. 30.3 and see Guthrie op. cit. p.956f and Robinson loc. cit.

6. Strobel op. cit. p.437 thinks that the past history of Rome was of no concern to the apocalypticist, and the starting point for his view of history was the cross. There can be no doubt that the cross does play the decisive part in John's eschatology, but the fact that he includes a description of the throne-room in Rev. 4 which is 'unmodified' by the cross suggests that he does have a broader perspective than that suggested by Strobel.

7. On this see H. Kraft, *Die Offenbarung des Johannes* p.222 and Kümmel op. cit. p.468f. On the possibility of a later editing see the comment of M. Rissi, *The Future of the World* p.2.

8. Charles, *Revelation* ii, p.68 and Bousset, *Die Offenbarung Johannis* p.416 and Kraft op. cit. p.220f.

9. So Kraft op. cit. p.223.

10. 'In fact, twenty years later, when I was a young man, a person of obscure origin appeared, who gave out that he was Nero, and the name was still in such favour with the Parthians that they supported him vigorously and surrendered him with great reluctance.' The date suggested by Suetonius for the pretender, round about AD90, would fit better with a date for Rev. near the end of the first century. The significance of this material from Suetonius is that it confirms the existence of a *Nero Rediturus* myth. It is probably of little or no importance for the dating of Revelation. See further P. Prigent, 'Au temps de l'Apocalypse: II Le culte imperial au 1er siècle en Asie Mineure', *RHPR* 55, especially pp.227ff. and J. M. Ford, *Revelation* p.211f.

11. E.g. Kraft op. cit. p.223.

12. See note 10 and also Bousset op. cit. pp.408ff.

13. Two other pieces of evidence make Kümmel op. cit. p.469 favour the end of the first century. In 2.8–11 Smyrna has been persevering for a long time, though according to Polycarp (Phil. 11.3), the church did not exist in Paul's day. Secondly, 3.17 describes the community at Laodicaea as rich, though the city had been virtually destroyed by an earthquake in AD 60/61. There seems to be nothing in 2.8ff. which precludes a recent foundation for the church at Smyrna, however. Indeed, two points speak in favour of the community as a comparatively recent foundation. Not only are they said to be characterized by their poverty, hardly the sign of a flourishing and large religious group (cf. 2.4), but they are facing Jewish hostility. It is likely that Jewish hostility would have been particularly great soon after the defection of members of the synagogue to join the Christian movement (cf. Acts 17.5), see W. Ramsay, *The Letters to Seven Churches* p.272, and Charles op. cit. i, p.56. Evidence from Tacitus (*Annals* xiv, 27) indicates that Laodicaea recovered from the earthquake from its own resources without any help from the central authorities, an indication of the great wealth of the city. This is consistent with the picture of the city which we find in Rev. 3.17ff. and in no way precludes a date in the late 60s, so also Robinson op. cit. p.229f. See further on the letters J. M. Court, *Myth and History in Revelation* pp.20ff.

14. On this see A. L. Moore, *The Parousia in the New Testament*.

15. On the troubled history of this period see what remains of Tacitus' *Histories* and K. Wellesley, *The Long Year: A.D. 69*. For the eschatological

character of political upheavals see above p.156. Tacitus (*Histories* ii, 8) reports unrest in Asia Minor in 69 linked with the return of Nero (Prigent, *'Culte Impérial'*, p.227).

16. It has often been suggested that the vision in Rev. 11.1ff., which makes mention of the Temple, could well reflect the circumstances of the Jewish War, particularly when the outer court of the Temple was taken by the Romans and the Jewish patriots were besieged in the Temple, (see Robinson op. cit. p.238f. and Kraft op. cit. p.152 and further S. Giet *L'Apocalypse et l'Histoire*). If this vision reflects exactly the situation in the siege of Jerusalem, it could not have been written before AD 70, because we know that the situation when the outer court was taken by the Romans and the inner was besieged took place in that year (Josephus *BJ* vi, 70ff.). It seems unlikely, however, that a Jewish-Christian in Asia Minor would have known the precise details of the siege. What is possible, however, is that the military situation in Judaea after Vespasian had temporarily abandoned the campaign in AD 68 (Tacitus *Histories* v, 11), with the whole of the country subjugated apart from Jerusalem, might have been the inspiration for John's vision. The isolation of the holy city and its Temple in the midst of the hosts of the enemy may have formed the starting-point for John's vision. But, as many commentators have pointed out (e.g. G. B. Caird, *The Revelation of St. John the Divine* p.131), it is the symbolism rather than any historical interest which dominates John's thought. The city of Jerusalem is not a sacred place for John but a place of rebellion (11.8). Thus, while it may be possible that certain historical events were the starting-point for John's visions, these events became transformed as part of the vision and under the influence of the message which the symbols were intended to communicate. On this see now J. M. Court op. cit. pp.82ff.

17. *Christ and the Caesars* pp.147ff.

18. For further detail see E. M. Smallwood, 'Domitian's Attitude Towards the Jews and Judaism' *Classical Philology* li, pp.1ff. and Prigent, 'Au temps de l'Apocalypse I. Domitien', *RHPR* 54, pp.481ff.

19. Op. cit. pp.3ff. and also her *Jews under Roman Rule* pp.378ff.

20. Evidence from coins minted at the beginning of Nerva's reign suggests that he abolished an abuse where men and women were wrongly accused of living the Jewish life cf. Dio Cassius lxviii, 1.2; Smallwood, *Jews under Roman Rule* p.378; L. W. Barnard, 'Clement of Rome and the Persecution of Domitian' *NTS* 10 p.259; Prigent, 'Domitien' p.482.

21. It is hard to base a case for such an act on Pliny's reference to erstwhile Christians who had committed apostasy some twenty years before, i.e. at the end of Domitian's reign (*contra* Smallwood, *Jews under Roman Rule* p.381). Eusebius *EH* iii, 18 mentions moves against Christians in Rome only, and there is no evidence to suggest a link between them and the apostasy of certain Christians in Bithynia, which could have happened for a variety of reasons unconnected with state pressure cf. 2 Tim. 4.10.

22. On the religious beliefs of Flavia Domitilla see Smallwood in *Classical Philology* li pp.5ff., Barnard op. cit. p.259f. and P. Prigent. 'Au temps de l'Apocalypse: I. Domitien' *RHPR* 54 pp.470ff. Despite what Eusebius has

to say about her Christian faith (*EH* iii, 18) there seems to be no reason why it should not have been Jewish beliefs which occasioned her downfall as Dio indicates.

23. It is widely accepted that the statement of Sulpicius Severus in *Chronicle* ii, 29 that the Christian religion was officially proscribed must be viewed with considerable suspicion e.g. W. H. C. Frend op. cit., G. Ste Croix, 'Why were the Early Christians Persecuted' *Past and Present* 26 and on the difficulty of linking the Apocalypse with a Domitianic persecution B. Newman, 'The Fallacy of the Domitianic Hypothesis' *NTS* 10.

24. Kraft op. cit. p.61 thinks of a Christian dispute. In the light of later evidence it seems preferable to explain the reference as a dispute between Christian and non-Christian Jewish groups. Evidence from the Martyrdom of Polycarp 12 shows how Jews did ally themselves with the pagans against Christians. See further P. Richardson, *Israel in the Apostolic Church* pp.43ff. On Rev. 2.9 see Kraabel, *Judaism in Asia Minor* pp.27ff.

25. On Judaism in Asia Minor at this period see the survey of evidence both literary and archaeological in A. T. Kraabel, *Judaism in Asia Minor in the Imperial Period* and S. Johnson, 'Asia Minor and Early Christianity' in *Christianity, Judaism and other Greco-Roman Cults* vol. ii pp.98ff., S. Safrai and M. Stern, *The Jewish People in the First Century* i, pp.477ff., G. Kittel, 'Das kleinasiatische Judentum in der hellenistisch-römischen Zeit' *TLZ* 69 and F. Blanchetière, 'Juifs et non Juifs', *RHPR* 54.

26. The Jewish apocalyptic character of the Colossian false teaching makes it difficult to suppose that the Christianity of Asia Minor was merely an accretion from Palestinian Judaism introduced by Christians like John of Patmos. See further F. O. Francis 'Humility and Worship of Angels' in ed. Meeks and Francis, *Conflict at Colossae* and J. J. Gunther, *St. Paul's Opponents and their Background* pp.271ff.

27. Kraabel op. cit. pp.145ff., Johnson op. cit. p.98f.

28. J. N. Sevenster, *The Roots of Pagan Anti-Semitism* p.151. On attitudes to Jews see the concise collection of material from contemporary literature in J. Gill, *Notices of the Jews and their Country* and M. Stern, *Greek and Latin Authors on Jews and Judaism*.

29. E. M. Smallwood, *Legatio ad Gaium*.

30. On the imperial cult see L. R. Taylor, *The Divinity of the Roman Emperor* pp.181ff., S. Weinstock, *Divus Julius* pp.401ff., and K. Scott, *The Imperial Cult under the Flavians*, and on its impact in Asia Minor P. Prigent, 'Au temps de l'Apocalypse: II. Le culte impérial au 1er siècle en Asie Mineure' *RHPR* 55 pp.215ff.

31. Op. cit. p.151 cf. Smallwood, *Jews under Roman Rule* p.137, '(the right to opt out of the imperial cult) followed automatically on the grant of religious freedom and formed an integral part of it'.

32. Cf. Martyrdom of Polycarp 9.2: 'Therefore, when he was brought forward, the Proconsul asked him if he were Polycarp, and when he admitted it, he tried to persuade him to deny it, saying: Respect your age, and so forth as they are accustomed to say: Swear by the genius of Caesar, repent, say away with the atheists'.

33. Cf. *BJ* vii, 110f, where the citizens of Antioch petition Titus to expel the Jews from their city after the war, and failing that, to remove their privileges. Although Titus refuses, this is further indication that considerable animosity was felt towards the Jews of the Diaspora at this time.

34. *Jews under Roman Rule* p.348.

35. Ramsay op. cit. pp.114ff. and Prigent op. cit. (n.30) p.216f.

36. J. M. Ford, *Revelation* p.215 compares the situation in the reign of Decius (AD 249–251), where any one who did not have a certificate of having sacrificed to Caesar could not pursue ordinary trades.

37. On the history of interpretation see Bousset op. cit. pp.49ff., Lohmeyer, 'Die Offenbarung des Johannes 1920–1934' *TR* 6, and A. Feuillet, *The Apocalypse* pp.23ff.

38. So also Rissi op. cit. p.1f. On the unity of style see Charles op. cit. i, p.lxxxviii and p.1.

39. So also Kümmel op. cit. p.464.

40. .The attempt to look at the structure of the work as a whole is to be found also in G. Bornkamm, 'Die Komposition der apokalyptischen Visionen in der Offenbarung Johannis' *ZNW* 36 and E. Fiorenza, 'The Eschatology and Composition of the Apocalypse' *CBQ* 30, though with different conclusions from those reached here. See now the works by Sweet and Court.

41. This should not lead to the supposition that chs. 1–3 were written at a different time from the rest of the apocalypse, see e.g. Charles op. cit. i, pp.42 and 110 and most recently J. M. Ford op. cit. pp.55ff. and Kraft op. cit. p.50.

42. For the view that they were human representatives of the churches see the discussion in Kraft op. cit. pp.50ff and Strack–Billerbeck iii, p.790f. There is no reason why John should not have been privileged to act as a scribe to the angelic representatives of the churches (on the angelic representatives see Urbach, *The Sages* p.138f.). After all Enoch acts as the heavenly scribe (see Test. Abraham Rec. B 11), and men were frequently regarded as more privileged than the angels see P. Schäfer, *Rivalität zwischen Engeln und Menschen* especially pp.219ff. and Urbach op. cit. p.150f. Two explanations therefore must be considered: *either* (i) John acts as heavenly scribe to the angels of the churches and as a result becomes aware of heavenly secrets which he communicates to the churches; *or* (ii) John is shown heavenly letters, dictated by Christ, to the angels of the churches. The command to write in 2.1 would thus not be a command to John but to another being who writes letters to the angels (cf. 1 Enoch 89.61), which John in turn ascertains and in his letters communicates the divine knowledge to the churches. The difficulty with regarding John as the intermediary between Christ and the angels is not the function of man as an envoy of God to the angels (*contra* Kraft p.51), (1 Enoch 12—15 is evidence of this), but the fact that John's commission is to write to the churches themselves (1.10 and 1.19). Thus the second alternative is to be preferred. See further Sweet op. cit. p.73.

43. Cf. Fiorenza op. cit. especially p.561f.

44. See Charles op. cit. i. p.110.

45. So Lohmeyer, *Die Offenbarung des Johannes* p.45 but cf. Kraft op. cit. p.95.

46. E.g. Bornkamm op. cit. p.134f. and Kraft op. cit. p.12.

47. So e.g. Bornkamm op. cit. pp.135ff.

48. The term is actually used in 9.12 and 11.14, as a way of summarizing the series of disasters which have already taken place. According to 11.14 there should have been another 'woe', but no further mention is made of it, unless it refers to the last series of catastrophes described in ch. 16. One wonders whether the placing of the reference to the first woe after the fifth trumpet betrays knowledge of the series of twelve eschatological woes found in Syr. Baruch 27.

49. For parallel material see Strack–Billerbeck i, p.950.

50. This may give weight to Kraft's suggestion (op. cit. p.12) that one series of seven has been extended by John to include the three series as we have them now.

51. So also Feuillet op. cit. p.56.

52. So Kraft op. cit. p.211 and Charles op. cit. vol. ii, p.52.

53. See the discussion of the various difficulties in Charles op. cit. ii, pp.144ff.

54. A glance at Ezek. 37ff. will perhaps make the point. In Ezek. 37 we have the messianic era (cf. Rev. 20. 1–6), in ch.38f. the defeat of Gog and Magog (cf. Rev. 20. 7–10), then in 40ff. the coming of the new Jerusalem (cf. Rev. 21f.), a point made by Kraft op. cit. p.253 and Kuhn 'Gog' in *TDNT* i, p.790f.

55. Op. cit. p.457.

56. So also Kraft op. cit. p.123 and Charles i, p.183.

57. Whether ch. 7 is a vision which was experienced on another occasion and has been inserted at this point cannot be precisely determined. In view of the link which can be identified, however, between this chapter and what precedes, it is not impossible that the significance of the seals in ch. 6 provided the mental stimulus for the subject matter of this vision.

58. So Kraft op. cit. p.156f. For the symbolic approach see e.g. Caird op. cit. pp.131ff. and see further Court op. cit. pp.82ff. The history of the interpretation of this passage can be found in Bousset, *The Antichrist Legend* pp.203ff.

59. Cf. Fiorenza op. cit. p.566.

60. There is a comprehensive discussion of the relationship of Revelation to the apocalyptic view of history in Fiorenza op. cit. pp.541ff. See also J. J. Collins, 'Pseudonymity, Historical Reviews and the Genre of the Revelation of John' *CBQ* 39.

61. The only other places where John had actually intervened to ask about the sight which had confronted him are at 5.4 and 7.14. These two passages differ from 10.11 however, which is directed specifically at the seer.

62. Cf. Fiorenza op. cit. p.566.

63. E.g. Kümmel op. cit. p.470f. For the linguistic arguments against common authorship with the Fourth Gospel see G. Mussies, *The Morphology of Koine Greek*, especially p.351f. On the relationship with the Fourth Gospel see the recent discussion by E. Fiorenza, 'The Quest for the Johannine

School: the Apocalypse and the Fourth Gospel', *NTS* 23.

64. On the knowledge of local conditions see C. Hemer, *A Study of the Letters to the Seven Churches of Asia with Special Reference to their Local Background*.

65. On the role of prophets in Revelation see A. Satake, *Die Gemeindeordnung in der Johannesapokalypse* pp.47ff.; D. Hill, 'Prophets and Prophecy in the Revelation of St. John', *NTS* 18, and on prophecy in early Christianity, U. B. Müller op. cit.

66. On charismatic authority in the early Church see the summaries in von Campenhausen op. cit. pp.55ff. and 178ff. and Dunn, *Jesus and the Spirit* pp.176ff.

67. That is not to deny the universal significance of these letters (so e.g. Kraft op. cit. p.49), but the extensive local colouring evident in the letters (see Hemer op. cit.) makes a universal intention unlikely in the first instance.

68. On this chapter see the discussion on p.222.

69. Prigent, *Apocalypse et liturgie* pp.46ff. On the link with Christian worship see Deichgräber, *Gotteshymnus und Christushymnus in der frühen Christenheit* pp.44ff. and especially p.59, and O. A. Piper, 'The Apocalypse of John and the Liturgy of the Ancient Church' in *Church History* 20 pp.10–23, but on this theme note the cautionary comments of K.-P. Jörns op. cit. (above p.481 n.27).

70. Caird op. cit. p.71f.

71. The reference to the *arnion . . . hos esphagmenon* makes it impossible to see this chapter as one devoid of Christian influence (*contra* J. M. Ford pp.89ff.). There is nothing in contemporary Jewish apocalyptic symbolism which corresponds with the imagery of this chapter. Not only the reference to the slaughter of the lamb but also the fact that the Lamb is the central agent of the sending of the spirit into the world (cf. John 15.26 and Acts 2.33) is at one with early Christian belief, so rightly Caird op. cit. p.74f. On the title Lamb in Revelation see the surveys in Kraft op. cit. p.107f. and T. Holtz op. cit. pp.39ff. On the Christian character of Revelation see particularly M. Rissi, *Zeit und Geschichte in der Offenbarung des Johannes*.

72. So Charles op. cit. p.140 who says 'the text seems to teach that the Lamb, when first seen by the seer, appeared in the space between the circle of the living creatures and the twenty-four elders'. On the reference to the Lamb 'standing' cf. Acts 7.56 and 1 Enoch 49.2.

73. So Minear op. cit. p.77.

74. See the comments on the Lamb's exaltation in O. Hofius, *Der Christushymnus* p.35f. and Holtz op. cit. pp.27ff.

75. On the wrath of God in Revelation see A. T. Hanson, *The Wrath of the Lamb* pp.159ff.

76. So Caird op. cit. p.124.

77. This position is argued in detail by Satake op. cit. pp.123ff. and see Minear op. cit. pp.98ff., who calls it 'a picture of Christian prophecy'.

78. Cf. A. A. Trites *The Concept of Witness in the New Testament* p.163f.: 'To the seer's *sundouloi* is given the task of proclaiming the Christian message. The same task belongs to the *prophetai . . .* In fact all these words together

with *douloi* . . . are usually used as synonyms for the faithful Christian witnesses who are prepared to die for their faith'.

79. So Satake op. cit. p.129f. On the possibility of a smaller remnant see Beasley-Murray op. cit. pp.178ff.

80. So also Caird op. cit. p.131 cf. J. M. Ford p.180.

81. Beasley-Murray op. cit. p.181 and Sweet op. cit. p.183 say the measurement is a sign of preservation from destruction (so also Caird op. cit. p.130f.).

82. Two witnesses are needed in Jewish law. See Deut. 17.6 and 19.15 and further Trites op. cit. p.167f. The description of the witnesses depends on OT references to Moses and Elijah (2 Kings 1.10; 1 Kings 17.1; Exod. 7.17ff.), both of whom had to face rejection and suffering (Num. 14.2 and 1 Kings 19.10). In addition the witnesses are called 'olive-trees' (Zech. 4.14). In the latter passage it is used to refer to the king and the high priest. This is a fitting description of the Christians who are priests of God (Rev. 1.6) and will reign with the Messiah (20.6 cf. 5.10).

83. Satake pp.122ff. thinks that there is little concern with the witness before the world, especially in the light of the destruction spoken of in v. 13. It would, however, be wrong to deny the positive role which John seeks to give to the Church in this vision, as the reaction of the inhabitants on earth in v. 13 may indicate (so also Trites op. cit. p.169f.).

84. The myth of the birth of the male-child may draw on Near Eastern mythology. Evidence is collected in Bousset op. cit. pp.346ff. To this should be added 1 QH 3.7ff. and the Apocalypse of Adam 78ff. (*NHL* pp.260ff.). A history of the exegesis of the chapter is to be found in P. Prigent, *Apocalypse 12: Histoire de l'exégèse.* See also Court op. cit. pp.106ff.

85. So Caird op. cit. p.153f.

86. But see the interpretation of Minear op. cit. pp.249ff., who is unwilling to see a link with Nero. On the subject of the imperial cult see the discussion of Prigent op. cit. (p.511 n.10 above). Whatever the attitude of individual emperors may have been to this kind of devotion (and there is considerable evidence that many were suspicious of it), Asia Minor was an important centre for the promotion of imperial cult.

87. See above p.252. The number 666 is perhaps easiest explained by the total of the Hebrew letters of *NRWN QSR*. There is no difficulty with a sudden switch to Hebrew in the light of the Semitic background of the style and ideas of Revelation. Indeed, we may expect that a Jewish-Christian readership would have quickly worked out the allusion. This Hebrew form has now been found in Qumran see *DJD* ii, p.101 and plate 29. For alternative explanations of the number 666 see Caird op. cit. pp.174ff.

88. The description of the beast certainly appears to be a parody of the Lamb (so Kraft op. cit. p.176). For example, in 13.3 it is said that one of the heads of the beast 'seemed to have a mortal wound', an affliction which resembles that of the Lamb in 5.6. While John nowhere calls this figure an Antichrist, he clearly wants his readers to understand that there can be no compromise between the Lamb and Caesar. Their claims are mutually exclusive, for those made for Caesar are spurious, despite the appearance of grandeur and power.

89. See Ramsay op. cit. p.118f.

90. There is no evidence that the practitioners of the imperial cult performed miracles to entice would-be worshippers. In the light of this it is not surprising that some commentators have been more happy to interpret these verses of supernatural eschatological figures rather than human beings who were part of the normal fabric of society (see Kraft op. cit. p.179f.). But the evidence from early Christian eschatology suggests that the antichrist figures were usually thought of as men who were inspired by demonic forces. This is clearly the case with the 'antichrists' of 1 John 2.18, who are the schismatics who hold aberrant christological views. This is probably also true of 2 Thess. 2.3ff. see further above p.408. Obviously John in his vision sees the threat from the imperial cult as part of the last attempt of the Devil to lead men astray. It would, therefore, be inappropriate to suppose that all the events which he describes can be paralleled in the current activities of the province's institutions. His starting point may be the imperial cult familiar to him from the cities of Asia Minor, but this has become the focus of the threat of the Devil within that area, and as such one would expect it to include every kind of device to persuade the elect to be led astray from the paths of righteousness. The matter is discussed by Ramsay op. cit. pp.97ff., who thinks that it does refer to current practices in the imperial cult, though he admits that there is no other evidence for it.

91. On the link between Babylon and Rome see Caird op. cit. p.216.

92. On the relationship see Rissi op. cit. p.53.

93. So Rissi op. cit. p.24.

94. See further Cullmann, *Salvation in History* pp.166ff.

95. See Caird op. cit. p.153f.

96. See Strack–Billerbeck iii, pp.823ff. for further material.

97. It is unclear whether it is only those who have suffered death for their testimony to Jesus in the messianic kingdom or if all the faithful are included in this period. The former group is preferred by Beasley-Murray op. cit. p.293, Kraft op. cit. p.257, and Charles op. cit. ii, p.183.

98. Cf. Beasley-Murray op. cit. p.294f.

99. See above p.25.

100. For Rissi op. cit. p.36 there is no question of judgement on the basis of works. 'The decisive criterion in the universal judgement is that of belonging to Christ.' But in the light of 13.8 and 17.8 it is preferable to see this book as specifically containing the names of those who did not defile themselves by their involvement in the imperial cult.

101. See above p.419.

102. So e.g. Kraft op. cit. p.263 and Rissi op. cit. p.55f.

103. Cf. Caird op. cit. p.279.

104. Caird loc. cit.

105. On this section see particularly the comments of Rissi op. cit. pp.67ff.

106. The significance of this passage and its relationship with Revelation has been missed by Davenport op. cit.

107. Cf. Rissi op. cit. p.63 '. . . John places the whole city in a new relationship to the temple concept, in that he identifies it with the cubic, golden Holy of Holies, which is filled with God's glory.'

108. The rather optimistic interpretation of Rissi op. cit. p.80f. concerning the salvation of those who had been cast into the lake of fire really cannot be supported from Revelation.

Bibliography

Sources and Reference Works

Baillet, M., Milik, J. et al., Discoveries in the Judaean Desert. Oxford, 1955–1968.
Barrett, C. K., The New Testament Background: Selected Documents. London, 1961.
Battifol, P., Le livre de la prière d'Asenath. Paris, 1889.
Bauer. W., (tr. W. F. Arndt and F. W. Gingrich), A Greek English Lexicon of the New Testament. Cambridge, 1957.
Baynes, C., A Coptic Gnostic Treatise contained in the Codex Brucianus. Cambridge, 1933.
Beek, C. I. M. I. van, Passio Sanctarum Perpetuae et Felicitatis. Bonn, 1938.
Black, M. and Denis, A. M., Apocalypsis Henochi Graece et Fragmenta Pseudepigraphorum quae supersunt Graece. Leiden, 1970.
Blass, F. and Debrunner, A. (tr. R. W. Funk), A Greek Grammar of the New Testament and Other Early Christian Literature. Cambridge, 1961.
Böhlig, A., Nag Hammadi Codices III.2 and IV.2: The Gospel of the Egyptians. Leiden, 1975.
Böhlig, A. and Labib, P., Die koptisch-gnostische Schrift ohne Titel aus Codex II von Nag Hammadi. Berlin, 1962.
Bonner, C., The Last Chapters of Enoch in Greek. London, 1937.
Bonwetsch, N., Die Apokalypse Abrahams. Berlin, 1897.
Box, G. H., The Ezra-Apocalypse. London, 1912.
– The Apocalypse of Abraham. London, 1918.
– The Testament of Abraham. London, 1927.
Brock, S. P., Testamentum Iobi. Leiden, 1967.
Brooks, E. W., Joseph and Asenath. London, 1918.
Bullard, R. A., The Hypostasis of the Archons. Berlin, 1970.
Casey, R. P., Excerpta ex Theodoto. London, 1934.
Chadwick, H., Origen: Contra Celsum. Cambridge, 1953.
Charles, R. H., The Ethiopic Version of the Book of Enoch. Oxford, 1906.
– The Greek Versions of the Testaments of the Twelve Patriarchs. Oxford, 1908.
– The Book of Enoch. Oxford, 1912.
– The Apocalypse of Baruch translated from the Syriac. London, 1896.
– (ed.) The Apocrypha and Pseudepigrapha of the Old Testament. Oxford, 1913.
– The Book of Jubilees or the Little Genesis. London, 1902.
Charles, R. H. and Morfill, W. R., The Book of the Secrets of Enoch. Oxford, 1896.
Charles, R. H. and Cowley, A., 'An Early Source of the Testaments of the Twelve Patriarchs' JQR 19 (1907) pp.566ff.
Charlesworth, J., The Odes of Solomon. Oxford, 1973.
Cohen, A., The Minor Tractates of the Talmud. London, 1965.
Colson, F. H., Whitaker, G. and Marcus, R., Philo. (Loeb ed.) London, 1929–1962

Danby, H., *The Mishnah*. Oxford, 1933.

Delcor, M., *Le Testament d'Abraham*. Leiden, 1973.

Dieterich, A., *Eine Mithrasliturgie*. Leipzig, 1903.

Diez-Macho, A., *Neophyti I*. Madrid, 1968.

Dupont-Sommer, A., *The Essene Writings from Qumran*. Oxford, 1961.

– *Encyclopaedia Judaica*. Jerusalem, 1972.

Epstein, I. (ed.), *The Babylonian Talmud*. Soncino Translation. London, 1935–52.

Epstein, J. N. and Melamed, E. Z., *The Mekilta of R. Simeon b. Yohai*. Jerusalem, 1955.

Etheridge, J., *The Targum of Onkelos and Jonathan ben Uzziel on the Pentateuch with the Fragments of the Jerusalem Targum translated from the Chaldee*, repr. New York, 1968.

Freedman, H. and Simon, M., *Midrash Rabbah*. London, 1939.

Frey, J. B., *Corpus Inscriptionum Iudaicarum*. Rome, 1936 and 1952.

Fitzmyer, J. A., *The Genesis Apocryphon of Qumran Cave 1*. Rome, 1966.

Foerster, W., *Gnosis*. Oxford, 1972 and 1974 (Eng. Trs. of *Gnosis*. Zürich, 1969 and 1971).

Friedlander, G., *Pirke de Rabbi Eliezer*. London, 1916.

Gill, J., *Notices of the Jews and their Country by the Classical Writers of Antiquity*. London, 1872.

Ginsburger, M., *Thargum Jonathan ben Uzziel zum Pentateuch*. Berlin, 1903.

– *Das Fragmentthargum*. Berlin, 1899.

Ginzberg, L., *Legends of the Jews*. Philadelphia, 1911–1938.

Giversen, S., *Apocryphon Johannis*. Copenhagen, 1963.

Goldin, J., *The Fathers according to Rabbi Nathan*. New Haven, 1955.

Goldschmidt, L., *Der Babylonische Talmud*. Berlin–Leipzig, 1897–1912.

Gordon, C. H., *Ugaritic Literature*. Rome, 1949.

Halevy, A. A., *Midrash Rabbah*. Tel-Aviv, 1956.

Harrington, D. J., Perrot, C., Bogaert, P. M. and Cazeaux, J., *Pseudo-Philon — Les Antiquités Bibliques*. Paris, 1976.

Harris, R. and Mingana, A., *The Odes of Solomon*. Cambridge, 1911.

– *Hekaloth Zutarti* from a MS in the Bodleian Library Oxford (No. 1531 in Neubauer's catalogue fol. 38a–46a).

Harvey, W., *Irenaeus: Adversus Haereses*. Cambridge, 1857.

Hatch, E. and Redpath, H., *A Concordance to the Septuagint*. Oxford, 1897.

Hennecke, E. and Schneemelcher, W., *New Testament Apocrypha*. London, 1963. (Eng. Trs. of *Neutestamentliche Apokryphen*. Tübingen, 1959.)

James, M. R., *Anecdota Apocrypha*. London, 1892.

– *The Biblical Antiquities of Pseudo-Philo*. London, 1917.

– *The Lost Apocrypha of the Old Testament*. London, 1920.

– *The Testament of Abraham*. Cambridge, 1892.

Jastrow, M., *A Dictionary of the Targumim, the Talmud Babli and Yerushalmi and the Midrashic Literature*. New York, 1950.

Jellinek, A., *Bet ha-Midrasch*. Leipzig–Vienna, 1853.

– *Jerusalem Talmud*. Krotoschin, 1886.

Jonge, M. de, *The Testaments of the Twelve Patriarchs*. Leiden, 1978.

Kautzsch, E., *Die Apokryphen und Pseudepigraphen des Alten Testaments*. Tübingen, 1900.

Kittel, R. and Friedrich, G., (ed.), *Theological Dictionary of the New Testament*. Grand Rapids, 1964–76 (Eng. Trs. of *Theologisches Wörterbuch zum Neuen Testament*).

Kisch, G., *Pseudo-Philo's Liber Antiquitatum Biblicarum*. Notre Dame, 1949.
Klijn, A. F. J. and Reinink, G. J., *Patristic Evidence for Jewish Christian Sects*. Leiden, 1973.
Krauss, S., *Griechische und lateinische Lehnwörter in Talmud Midrasch und Targum*. Berlin, 1898.
Kümmel, W. G. (ed.), *Jüdische Schriften aus hellenistisch-römischer Zeit*. 1973–.
Lake, K., *The Apostolic Fathers*. London, 1912–13.
Lawlor, H. J. and Oulton, J. G. L., *Eusebius: the Ecclesiastical History*. London, 1927–28.
Levi, T., *The Hebrew Text of the Book of Ecclesiasticus*. Leiden, 1904.
Levy, J., *Chaldäisches Wörterbuch über die Targumim*. Leipzig, 1868.
Lieberman, S., *The Tosefta and Tosefta Kifshuta* (Seder Moed), New York, 1962.
Lods, A., *Le livre d'Hénoch*. Paris, 1892.
Lohse, E., *Die Texte aus Qumran*. Darmstadt, 1971.
Mansoor, M., *The Thanksgiving Hymns*. Leiden, 1961.
– *Midrash Rabbah*. Vilna, 1878.
Migne, J. P., *Patrologia Graeca*. Paris, 1857–66.
– *Patrologia Latina*. Paris, 1844–64.
Milik, J. T., '4Q Visions de 'Amram et une citation d'Origène', *RB* 79 (1972) pp.77ff.
– 'Le Testament de Lévi en araméen, fragment de la grotte 4 de Qumrân', *RB* 62 (1955) pp.398ff.
Moule, C. F. D., *An Idiom Book of New Testament Greek*. Cambridge, 1959.
Moulton, J. H. and Turner, N., *A Grammar of New Testament Greek*. Edinburgh, 1919–.
Nemoy, A., 'Al-Qirqisani's Account of the Jewish Sects' *HUCA* 7.
Odeberg, H., *3 Enoch*. Cambridge, 1928.
Peel, M. L., *The Epistle to Rheginos*. London, 1969.
Philonenko, M., *Joseph et Aséneth*. Leiden, 1968.
Picard, J. C., *Apocalypsis Baruchi Graece*. Leiden, 1967.
Preisendanz, K., *Papyri Graecae Magicae*. Berlin, 1928.
Riessler, P., *Altjüdisches Schriftum ausserhalb der Bibel*. Heidelberg, 1966.
Roberts, A. and Donaldson, J., *The Ante-Nicene Fathers: Translations of the Fathers down to AD 325*. Edinburgh, 1868–1872. (repr. Grand Rapids 1950–52).
Robinson, J. M. (ed.), *The Nag Hammadi Library*. Leiden, 1978.
Schechter, S., *Aboth de Rabbi Nathan*. Vienna, 1887.
Schenke, H-M., 'Das Ägypter–Evangelium', *NTS* 16.
Smallwood, E. M., *Documents Illustrating the Principates of Gaius, Claudius and Nero*. Cambridge, 1967.
Sperber, A., *The Bible in Aramaic*. Leiden, (1959–73).
Stern, M., *Greek and Latin Authors on Jews and Judaism Vol I: From Herodotus to Plutarch*. Jerusalem, 1974.
Stone, M. E., *The Armenian Version of IV Ezra*. Missoula, 1978.
Strack, H. and Billerbeck, P., *Kommentar zum Neuen Testament aus Talmud und Midrasch*. Munich, 1922–26.
Strugnell, J., 'The Angelic Liturgy at Qumran', *Supplements to Vetus Testamentum*. VII, Leiden 1960 pp.318ff.
Thackeray, H. St. J., Marcus, R., Wikgren, A. and Feldman, L. H., *Josephus*. (Loeb. ed.). London, 1926–65.
Theodor, J. and Albeck, H., *Midrash Bereshit Rabba*. Jerusalem, 1965.

Vaillant, A., *Le Livre des Secrets d'Hénoch*. Paris, 1952.
Vermes, G., *The Dead Sea Scrolls in English*. London, 1975.
Violet, B., *Die Apokalypsen des Esra und des Baruch*. Leipzig, 1924.
Wernberg-Møller, P., *The Manual of Discipline*. Leiden, 1957.
Wertheimer, S., *Batte Midrashoth*. Jerusalem, 1952–65.
Yadin, Y., *The Scroll of the War of the Sons of Light against the Sons of Darkness*. London, 1962.
– *The Ben Sira Scroll from Masada*. Jerusalem, 1965.
Zuckermandel, M. S., *Tosephta based on the Erfurt and Vienna Codices*. Jerusalem, 1937.

Secondary Literature

Abbott, E. A., *New Light on the Gospel from an Ancient Poet*, Cambridge, 1912.
Abelson, J., *The Immanence of God in Rabbinical Literature*. London, 1912.
Abrahams, I., 'The Dove and the Voice', in *Studies in Pharisaism and the Gospels*, First series. Cambridge, 1917 pp.47ff.
Ackroyd, P. R., *Exile and Restoration*. London, 1968.
Ackroyd, P. R. and Evans, C. F., *The Cambridge History of the Bible* vol. 1. Cambridge, 1970.
Aland, K., 'Der Montanismus und die kleinasiatische Theologie', *ZNW* 46 (1955) pp.109ff.
– 'The Problem of Anonymity and Pseudonymity in Christian Literature of the First Two Centuries', *JTS* n.s.12 (1961) pp.39ff., reprinted in ed. D. E. Nineham *Historicity and Chronology of the New Testament*. London, 1965.
Albright, W. F. and Mann, C. S., *Matthew*. New York, 1971.
Alexander, P. S., 'The Historical Setting of the Hebrew Book of Enoch', *JJS* 28. (1977) pp.156ff.
Alsup, J. E., *The Post-Resurrection Appearances of the Gospels*. London, 1975.
Altman, A., 'Gnostic Ideas in Rabbinic Cosmology' in *Essays Presented to J. H. Hertz*. London, 1942, pp.19ff.
Anderson, G. W., 'Canonical and Non-Canonical', in *The Cambridge History of the Bible* vol. 1. pp.113ff.
Appel, H., *Die Komposition des äthiopischen Henochbuchs*. Gütersloh, 1906.
Aune, D. E., *The Cultic Setting of Realised Eschatology in Early Christianity*. Leiden, 1972.
Bacher, W., *Die Agada der Tannaiten*. Strasbourg, 1903.
Back, S., *Elischa b. Abujah-Acher*. Frankfurt a. Main, 1891.
Baeck, L., *The Pharisees and Other Essays*. New York, 1947.
Bakker, J., 'Christ an Angel?', *ZNW* 32. (1933) pp.255ff.
Baldensperger, W., *Die messianisch-apokalyptischen Hoffnungen des Judenthums*. Strasbourg, 1903.
Baltensweiler, H., *Die Verklärung Jesu*. Zürich, 1959.
Balz, H. R., *Methodische Probleme der neutestamentlichen Christologie*. Neu-kirchen-Vluyn, 1967.
Bammel, E., 'Versuch zu Kol. 1.15–20', *ZNW* 52 (1961), pp.88ff.
Barbel, J., *Christos Angelos*. Bonn, 1964.
Barker, M., 'Slippery Words: Apocalyptic', *ET* 89 (1978), pp.324ff.
– 'Reflections on the Enoch Myth', *JSOT* 15 (1980), pp.7ff.

Barnard, L. W., 'Clement of Rome and the Persecution of Domitian' *NTS* 10 (1963–4). pp.251ff.

Baron, S. W., *A Social and Religious History of the Jews*. Philadelphia, 1952.

Barr, J., 'Jewish Apocalyptic in Recent Scholarly Study', *BJRL* 58 (1975–6), pp.9ff.

Barrett, C. K., 'The Eschatology of the Epistle to the Hebrews', in *The Background to the New Testament and its Eschatology*. pp.363ff.

– *The Gospel according to Saint John*. London, 1978.

– 'New Testament Eschatology', *SJT* 6 (1953), pp.136ff.

– *The Holy Spirit and the Gospel Tradition*. London, 1947.

– 'Stephen and the Son of Man', in *Apophoreta. Festschrift für Ernst Haenchen*. Berlin, 1964.

– 'Paul's Opponents in II Corinthians', *NTS* 17 (1970–71), pp.253ff.

– *A Commentary on the Second Epistle to the Corinthians*. London, 1973.

– 'Jews and Judaisers in the Epistles of Ignatius', in *Jews, Greeks and Christians*. Leiden, 1976, pp.220ff.

Bauckham, R. J., 'The Rise of Apocalyptic', *Themelios* 3 (1978), pp.10ff.

– 'The Great Tribulation in the Shepherd of Hermas', *JTS* 25 (1974), pp.27ff.

Bauer, W., *Orthodoxy and Heresy in Earliest Christianity*. London, 1972. (Eng. Trs. of *Rechtgläubigkeit und Ketzerei im ältesten Christentum* ed. G. Strecker. Tübingen, 1964.)

Baumgarten, J., *Paulus und die Apokalyptik*. Neukirchen-Vluyn, 1975.

Baumgarten, J. M., *Studies in Qumran Law*. Leiden, 1977.

Beardslee, W. A., 'New Testament Apocalyptic in Recent Interpretation', *Interpretation* 25 (1971), pp.419ff.

Beasley-Murray, G. R., *Jesus and the Future*. London, 1954.

– *A Commentary on Mark 13*. London, 1957.

– *The Book of Revelation*. London, 1974.

Becker, J., *Das Heil Gottes. Heils- und Sündenbegriffe in der Qumrantexten und im Neuen Testament*. Göttingen, 1964.

– 'Erwägungen zur apokalyptischen Tradition in der paulinischen Theologie', *EvT* 30 (1970), pp.593ff.

– *Untersuchungen zur Entstehungsgeschichte der Testamente der Zwölf Patriarchen*. Leiden, 1970.

Beckwith, I., *The Apocalypse of John*. New York, 1919.

Beilner, W., 'Der Ursprung des Pharisäismus', *BZ* 3 (1959), pp.235ff.

Bell, A. A., 'The Date of John's Apocalypse', *NTS* 25 (1978–9), pp.93ff.

Benz, E., *Paulus als Visionär. Eine vergleichende Untersuchung der Visionsberichte des Paulus in der Apostelgeschichte, und in paulinischen Briefen*, Abhandlungen der Geistes- und Sozialwissenschaftlichen Klasse. Mainz, 1952, pp.77ff.

– *Die Vision: Erfahrungsformen und Bilderwelten*. Stuttgart, 1969.

Berger, K., *Die griechische Daniel-Diegese*. Leiden, 1976.

– *Die Amen-Worte Jesu*. Berlin, 1970.

Berger, K., *Die Auferstehung des Propheten und die Erhöhung des Menschensohnes*. Göttingen, 1976.

Bernard, J. H., *A Critical and Exegetical Commentary on the Gospel according to Saint John*. Edinburgh, 1928.

Berry, G. R., 'The Apocalyptic Literature of the Old Testament', *JBL* 62 (1943), pp.9ff.

Best, E., *A Commentary on the First and Second Epistles to the Thessalonians*. London, 1972.

Betz, H. D., 'The Understanding of Apocalyptic in the Theology of the Pannenberg Group', *JTC* 6. (Eng. Trs. of 'Das Verständnis der Apokalyptik in der Theologie der Pannenberg-Gruppe'. *ZTK* 65 (1968), pp.257ff.)

- 'The Religio-Historical Understanding of Apocalyptic', *JTC* 6 (Eng. Trs. of 'Zum Problem des religionsgeschichtlichen Verständnisses der Apokalyptik'. *ZTK* 63 (1966), pp.391ff.)

- *Der Apostel Paulus und die sokratische Tradition.* Tübingen, 1972.

Betz, O., *Offenbarung und Schriftforschung in der Qumransekte.* Tübingen, 1960.

Betz, O., Haacker, K., and Hengel, M., *Josephus — Studien.* Göttingen, 1974.

Betz, O., (ed.) *Abraham unser Vater: Juden und Christen im Gespräch über die Bibel.* Leiden, 1963.

Betz, O., 'Die Vision des Paulus im Tempel von Jerusalem. Apg. 22. 17–21 als Beitrag zur Deutung des Damaskuserlebnisses', O. Böcher and K. Haacker ed. *Verborum Veritas.* Wuppertal, 1970, pp.113ff.

- 'Was am Anfang geschah: Das jüdische Erbe in den neugefundenen koptisch-gnostischen Schriften', in *Abraham Unser Vater*, pp.24ff.

Bianchi, U., (ed.) *Le Origini dello Gnosticismo, Supplements to Numen* 12. Leiden, 1967.

Bickerman, E., *From Ezra to the Last of Maccabees.* New York, 1962.

Bietenhard, H., *Die himmlische Welt im Urchristentum und Spätjudentum.* Tübingen, 1951.

- *Das tausendjährige Reich.* Zürich, 1955.

Billerbeck, H., 'Hat die Synagoge einen präexistenten Messias gekannt?' *Nathanael* 21 (1905), pp.89ff.

Black, M., 'The Eschatology of the Similitudes of Enoch', *JTS* n.s. 3 (1952), pp.1ff.

- 'The Throne-Theophany Prophetic Commission and the Son of Man', in *Jews, Greeks and Christians*, pp.57ff.

Blanchetière, F., 'Juifs et non Juifs. Essai sur la diaspora en Asie Mineure', *RHPR* 54 (1974), pp.367ff.

Blau, L., *Das altjüdische Zauberwesen.* Budapest, 1898.

Bloch, J., *On the Apocalyptic in Judaism.* Philadelphia, 1952.

Böcher, O., *Der johanneische Dualismus im Zusummenhang des nachibiblischen Judentums.* Gütersloh, 1965.

Bogaert, P., *L'Apocalypse syriaque de Baruch.* Paris, 1969.

Böhlig, A., *Mysterion und Wahrheit.* Leiden, 1968.

- 'Der jüdische Hintergrund in der gnostischen Texten von Nag Hammadi', in *Mysterion und Wahrheit.*

Bokser, B. Z. *Pharisaic Judaism in Transition.* New York, 1935.

- 'Thread of Blue'. *PAAJR* 31 (1963), pp.1ff.

Bonwetsch, N., *Die Geschichte des Montanismus.* Erlangen, 1881.

Boobyer, G., *St Mark and the Transfiguration.* Edinburgh, 1942.

Borgen, P., *Bread from Heaven.* Leiden, 1965.

- 'God's Agent in the Fourth Gospel', in *Religions in Antiquity*, pp.137ff.

Bornkamm, G., 'Die Komposition der apokalyptischen Visionen in der Offenbarung Johannis', *ZNW* 36 (1937) pp.132ff. reprinted in *Studien zu Antike und Urchristentum*, pp.204ff.

- 'Baptism and New Life in Paul'. in *Early Christian Experience.* London, 1969, pp.71ff.

- 'Die Hoffnung im Kolosserbrief – zugleich ein Beitrag zur Frage der Echtheit des Briefes', in *Studien zum Neuen Testament und zur Patristik.* Berlin, 1961.

– 'Die Häresie des Kolosserbriefes' in *Das Ende des Gesetzes*. Munich, 1952 pp.139ff. (Eng. Trs. in *Conflict at Colossae* pp.123ff.)
– *'mysterion'* TDNT iv, pp.802ff.
Borsch, F. H. *The Son of Man in Myth and History*. London, 1967.
– *The Christian and Gnostic Son of Man*. London, 1970.
Bousset, W., *Die Religion des Judentums*. (ed. H. Gressmann and E. Lohse). Tübingen, 1966.
– *Die Offenbarung Johannis*. Göttingen, 1906.
– *The Antichrist Legend*. London, 1896.
 Der Antichrist in der Überlieferung des Judentums, des Neuen Testaments und der alten Kirche. Göttingen, 1895.
– 'Die Himmelsreise der Seele', *ARW* 4 (1901), pp.136ff and 229ff (reprinted Darmstadt 1960).
– *Kyrios Christos*. Abingdon, 1970 (Eng. Trs. of *Kyrios Christos*. Göttingen, 1921).
Bowker, J. W., 'The Origin and Purpose of St. John's Gospel', *NTS* 11 (1964–65), pp.398ff.
– *The Targums and Rabbinic Literature*. Cambridge, 1969.
– *Jesus and the Pharisees*. Cambridge, 1973.
– 'Merkabah-Visions and the Visions of Paul' *JSS* 16 (1971), pp.157ff.
– *The Religious Imagination and the Sense of God*. Oxford, 1978.
Brandenburger, E., *Adam und Christus*. Neukirchen-Vluyn, 1962.
Brandon, S. G. F., *Jesus and the Zealots*. Manchester, 1967.
– *Religion in Ancient History*. London, 1969.
Breech, E., 'These Fragments I Have Shored Against My Ruins: the Form and Function of 4 Ezra', *JBL* 92 (1973), pp.267ff.
Bright, J., *The History of Israel*. London, 1972.
Brockington, L. H., 'The Problem of Pseudonymity', *JTS* 4 (1953), pp.15ff.
Brown, P., *The Making of Late Antiquity*. Cambridge Mass., 1978.
Brown, R. E., *The Gospel according to John*. London, 1971.
– *The Semitic Background of the Term 'Mystery' in the New Testament*. Philadelphia, 1968.
Brox, N., (ed.), *Pseudepigraphie in der heidnischen und jüdisch-christlichen Antike*. Darmstadt, 1977.
Bruce, F. F., *The Acts of the Apostles*. London, 1952.
– *Jesus and Christian Origins outside the New Testament*. London, 1974.
– *Biblical Exegesis in the Qumran Texts*. London, 1959.
Büchler, A., *Types of Jewish Palestinian Piety*. London, 1922.
Bühner, J. A., *Der Gesandte und sein Weg im 4. Evangelium*. Tübingen, 1977.
Bultmann, R., *The History of the Synoptic Tradition*. Oxford, 1963. (Eng. Trs. of *Geschichte der synoptischen Tradition*. Göttingen, 1931.)
– *The Gospel of John*. Oxford, 1971. (Eng. Trs. of *Das Evangelium des Johannes*. Göttingen, 1950.)
Burchard, C., *Untersuchungen zu Joseph und Aseneth*. Tübingen, 1965.
– *Der dreizehnte Zeuge*. Göttingen, 1970.
Burkitt, F. C., *Jewish and Christian Apocalypses*. London, 1913.
Burney, C., 'Christ as the *ARCHE* of Creation', *JTS* 27 (1926), pp.160ff.
Buttenwieser, M., *Outline of the Neo-Hebraic Apocalyptic Literature*. Cincinatti, 1901.
Cadman, W. H., *The Open Heaven*. Oxford, 1969.
Caird, G. B., *Principalities and Powers*. Oxford, 1956.

- *The Revelation of Saint John the Divine.* London, 1966.
Calder, W. M., 'Epigraphy of Anatolian Heresies', *Anatolian Studies in Honour of Sir William Ramsay.* London, 1923 pp.76ff.
- 'Philadelphia and Montanism', *BJRL* 7 (1923), pp.309ff.
Campbell, J. Y., 'The Origin and Meaning of the Term Son of Man', *JTS* 48 (1947), pp.145ff.
Campenhausen, H. von, *Ecclesiastical Authority and Spiritual Power in the Church of the First Three Centuries.* London, 1969 (Eng. Trs. of *Kirchliches Amt und geistliche Vollmacht.* Tübingen, 1953).
Carley, K. W., *Ezekiel among the Prophets.* London, 1975.
Carmignac, J., 'Un qumrânien converti au christianisme: L'auteur des Odes de Salomon', in *Qumran-Probleme* ed. H. Bardtke. Berlin, 1963, pp.75ff.
- 'Le document de Qumran sur Melchisédeq', *RQ* 7 (1970), pp.343ff.
Casey, P. M., *The Interpretation of Daniel vii in Jewish and Patristic Literature and in the New Testament.* Diss. Durham, 1976.
- 'The Use of the Term 'Son of Man' in the Similitudes of Enoch', *JSJ* 7 (1976), pp.11ff.
- *The Son of Man.* London, 1980.
Catchpole, D. R., 'Paul, Jesus and the Apostolic Decree', *NTS* 23 (1977), pp.428ff.
Cavallin, H., *Life after Death.* Lund, 1974.
Cerfaux, L., *Christ in the Theology of St. Paul.* Edinburgh, 1959. (Eng. Trs. of *Le Christ dans la théologie de Saint Paul.* Paris, 1951.)
Charles, R. H., *A Critical and Exegetical Commentary on the Book of Daniel.* Oxford, 1929.
- *A Critical and Exegetical Commentary on the Revelation of St. John.* Edinburgh, 1926.
- *Eschatology: The Doctrine of the Future Life in Israel, Judaism and Christianity.* (repr. with an introduction by G. W. Buchanan). New York, 1963.
Charlesworth, J. H., 'The Odes of Solomon – Not Gnostic', *CBQ* 31 (1969), pp.357ff.
- (ed.) *John and Qumran.* London, 1972.
- 'A Critical Comparison of the Dualism in 1QS 3.13—4.26 and the 'Dualism' Contained in the Gospel of John', in *John and Qumran*, pp.76ff.
- *The Pseudepigrapha and Modern Research.* Missoula, 1975.
- 'The History of Pseudepigrapha Research', in ed. W. Haase, *Aufstieg und Niedergang der römischen Welt* II.19.1. Berlin, 1979, pp.54ff.
Chilton, B. D., 'The Transfiguration: Dominical Assurance and Apocalyptic Vision', *NTS* 27 (1980), pp.115ff.
Clements, R. E., *God and Temple.* Oxford, 1965.
Collins, J. J., *The Sibylline Oracles of Egyptian Judaism.* Missoula, 1974.
- 'Jewish Apocalyptic against its Hellenistic Near Eastern Environment', *BASOR* 22 (1975), pp.27ff.
- 'The Symbolism of Transcendence in Apocalyptic', *Biblical Research* 19 (1974), pp.1ff.
- 'Apocalyptic Eschatology as the Transcendence of Death', *CBQ* 36 (1974), pp.21ff.
- 'The Court Tales in Daniel and the Development of Apocalyptic', *JBL* 94 (1975), pp.218ff.
- 'The Son of Man and the Saints of the Most High', *JBL* 93 (1974).
- *The Apocalyptic Vision of the Book of Daniel.* Missoula, 1977.

– (ed.), _Apocalypse: the Morphology of a Genre._ (_Semeia_ 14 1979) 1ff.

Collins, J., 'Pseudonymity, Historical Reviews and the Genre of the Revelation of John', _CBQ_ 39 (1977) pp.329ff.

Colpe, C., '_ho huios tou anthropou_' _TDNT_ viii, pp.400ff.

– 'Die Himmelsreise der Seele ausserhalb und innerhalb der Gnosis', in ed. U. Bianchi _Le Origini dello Gnosticismo._

– 'Die Himmelsreise der Seele als philosophie- und religionsgeschichtliche Problem', in _Festschrift für J. Klein_ (ed. E. Freis). Göttingen, 1967.

Conzelmann, H., 'Geschichte und Eschaton nach Mc 13', _ZNW_ 50 (1959) pp.210ff.

– _1 Corinthians._ Philadelphia, 1975. (Eng. Trs. of _Der erste Brief an die Korinther._ Göttingen, 1969).

Coppens, J., _L'Apocalyptique._ Louvain, 1977.

Coppens, J. and Dequeker, L., _Le Fils de l'Homme et les saints du Très-Haut en Daniel VII, dans les Apocryphes et dans le Nouveau Testament._ Louvain, 1961.

Court, J. M., _The Book of Revelation: its Historical Background and Use of Traditional Mythological Ideas._ Diss. Durham, 1973.

– _Myth and History in Revelation._ London, 1979.

Cranfield, C. E. B., _Romans 1—8._ Edinburgh, 1975.

Croix, G. Ste., 'Why were the Early Christians Persecuted?' _Past and Present_ 26 (1963), pp.6ff.

Cross, F. L. (ed.), _The Jung Codex._ London, 1955.

Cross, F. M., _The Ancient Library of Qumran._ London, 1958.

– _Canaanite Myth and Hebrew Epic._ Harvard, 1973.

– 'The Council of Yahweh in Second Isaiah', _JNES_ 12 (1953), pp.274ff.

Cross, F. M. (ed.), _Magnalia Dei._ New York, 1976.

Cullman, O., _The Christology of the New Testament._ London, 1959 (Eng. Trs. of _Die Christologie des Neuen Testaments._ Tübingen, 1957).

– _The Johannine Circle._ London, 1976 (Eng. Trs. of _Der johanneische Kreis._ Tübingen, 1975).

– _Salvation in History._ London, 1967 (Eng. Trs. of _Heil als Geschichte._ Tübingen, 1965).

Dahl, N. A., 'The Johannine Church and History', in _Current Issues in New Testament Interpretation,_ pp.124ff.

Dalton, W. J., _Christ's Proclamation to the Spirits._ Rome, 1965.

Daniélou, J., _The Theology of Jewish Christianity._ London, 1964.

– _The Origins of Latin Christianity._ London, 1977.

Daube, D., 'Ecstasy in a Statement by R. Joshua b. Hananiah', in _Nir ha-Midrashia._ Jerusalem, 1972.

Davenport, G. I., _The Eschatology of the Book of Jubilees._ Leiden, 1971.

Davies, G. I., 'Apocalyptic and Historiography', _JSOT_ 5 (1978), pp.15ff.

Davies, P. R., _1QM: The War Scroll from Qumran._ Rome, 1977.

– 'Hasidim in the Maccabaean Period', _JJS_ 28 (1977), pp.127ff.

– The Eschatology of Daniel', _JSOT_ 17 (1980), pp.33ff.

Davies, W. D., _Paul and Rabbinic Judaism._ London, 1953.

– 'Apocalyptic and Pharisaism', in _Christian Origins and Judaism._ London, 1962, pp.19ff.

– 'Aboth Revisited', in (ed.) W. R. Farmer, C. F. D. Moule and R. Niebuhr _Christian History and Interpretation._ Cambridge, 1967, pp.127ff.

– _The Gospel and the Land._ Berkeley, 1974.

– _The Setting of the Sermon on the Mount._ Cambridge, 1966.

Déaut, R. le, *La Nuit Pascale*. Rome, 1963.

Deichgräber, R., *Gotteshymnus und Christushymnus in der frühen Christenheit*. Göttingen, 1967.

Delcor, M., 'Le milieu d'origine et de développement de l'apocalyptique juive', in *La littérature juive entre Tenach et Mishna*. Leiden, 1974, pp.101ff.

– 'Melchizedek from Genesis to the Qumran Texts and the Epistle to the Hebrews', *JSJ* 2 (1971), pp.115ff.

Delling, G., 'stoicheion' *TDNT* vii, pp.666ff.

– *Bibliographie zur jüdisch–hellenistischen und intertestamentarischen Literatur 1900–1970*. Berlin, 1975.

Denis, A. M., *Introduction aux pseudépigraphes grecs d'Ancien Testament*. Leiden, 1970.

Dexinger, F., *Henochs Zehnwochenapokalypse und offene Probleme der Apokalyptikforschung*. Leiden, 1977.

Dibelius, M., *From Tradition to Gospel*. London, 1934.

– *Die Geisterwelt im Glauben des Paulus*. Göttingen, 1909.

– 'Die Isisweihe bei Apuleius und verwandte Initiationsriten', in *Botschaft und Geschichte* ii, pp.30ff. Tübingen, 1956.

Dibelius, M. and Greeven, H., *An die Kolosser, Epheser und Philemon*. Tübingen, 1953.

Dibelius, M., *Studies in the Acts of the Apostles*. London, 1956 (Eng. Trs. of *Aufsätze zur Apostelgeschichte* Göttingen, 1951).

– 'Der Hirt des Hermas' in *Die Apostolischen Väter*. Tübingen, 1923.

Dodd, C. H., *The Bible and the Greeks*. London, 1935.

– 'The Mind of Paul II', *New Testament Studies*. Manchester, 1953 pp.83ff.

– *The Fourth Gospel*. Cambridge, 1953.

– *Historical Tradition in the Fourth Gospel*. Cambridge, 1963.

– *The Epistle to the Romans*. London, 1932.

Dodds, E. R., *Pagan and Christian in an Age of Anxiety*. Cambridge, 1965.

– *The Greeks and the Irrational*. Berkeley, 1951.

Doeve, J. W., *Jewish Hermeneutics in the Synoptic Gospels and Acts*. Assen, 1954.

Doresse, J., *The Secret Books of the Egyptian Gnostics*. London, 1960 (Eng. Trs. of *Les livres secrets des Gnostiques d'Egypte* Paris 1958).

Dunn, J. D. G., *Jesus and the Spirit*. London, 1975.

– *Unity and Diversity in the New Testament*. London, 1977.

– *Christology in the Making*. London, 1980.

Ebeling, G., 'The Ground of Christian Theology', in *JTC* 6, pp.47ff. (Eng. Trs. of 'Der Grund der christlichen Theologie', *ZTK* 58 (1961) pp.227ff.).

Eichrodt, W., *Ezekiel*. London, 1970. (Eng. Trs. of *Der Prophet Hesekiel*. Göttingen 1965.)

– *The Theology of the Old Testament*. London, 1967. (Eng. Trs. of *Theologie des Alten Testaments*. Stuttgart, 1959.)

Eisler, R., *Weltenmantel und Himmelszelt*. Munich, 1910.

Eissfeldt, O., *The Old Testament: an Introduction*. Oxford, 1966. (Eng. Trs. of *Einleitung in das Alte Testament*. Tübingen, 1964.)

Eliade, M., *Shamanism: Archaic Techniques of Ecstasy*. London, 1964. (Eng. Trs. of *Le Chamanisme et les techniques archaiques de l'extase*. Paris, 1951.)

– *Myths, Dreams and Mysteries*. London, 1968. (Eng. Trs. of *Mythes, Rêves et Mystères*. Paris, 1951.)

Emerton, J. A., 'The Origin of the Son of Man Imagery', *JTS* 9 (1958), pp.225ff.

Erling, B., 'Ezek. 38—39 and the Origins of Jewish Apocalyptic', in *Ex Orbe*

Religionum. Leiden, 1972. i, pp.104ff.

Fallon, F. T., *The Enthronement of Sabaoth.* Leiden, 1978.

Farmer, W. R., *The Synoptic Problem.* New York, 1964.

Farrer, A., *The Revelation of St. John the Divine.* Oxford, 1964.

– *A Rebirth of Images.* Glasgow, 1949.

Feuer, L., (ed.) *Marx and Engels: Basic Writings on Politics and Philosophy.* London, 1969.

Feuillet, A., *The Apocalypse.* New York, 1965.

– 'Le fils de l'homme et la tradition biblique', *RB* 60 (1953), pp.170ff.

Fiorenza, E., 'The Eschatology and Composition of the Apocalypse', *CBQ* 30 (1968), pp.537ff.

– 'The Composition and Structure of the Revelation of John', *CBQ* 39 (1977), pp.344ff.

– 'The Quest for the Johannine School: the Apocalypse and the Fourth Gospel', *NTS* 23 (1976–7), pp.402ff.

Fischel, H., *Rabbinic Literature and Greco-Roman Philosophy.* Leiden, 1973.

Fischer, U., *Eschatologie und Jenseitserwartung im hellenistischen Diaspora Judentum.* Berlin, 1978.

Flusser, D., 'Apocalypse', *Encyclopaedia Judaica* iii, col. 179f.

Foerster, W., *Palestinian Judaism in New Testament Times.* Edinburgh, 1964. (Eng. Trs. of *Das Judentum Palästinas zur Zeit Jesu und der Apostel.* Hamburg, 1959.)

– 'Die Irrlehrer des Kolosserbriefes', in *Studia Biblica et Semitica.* Wageningen, 1966, pp.71ff.

Fohrer, G., *Ezechiel.* Tübingen, 1955.

Ford, J. M., 'Was Montanism a Jewish–Christian Heresy?', *JEH* 17 (1966) pp.145ff.

– *Revelation.* New York, 1975.

Forkman, G., *The Limits of the Religious Community.* Lund, 1972.

Francis, F. O., 'Humility and Angel-Worship in Col. 2.18', *ST* 16 (1962) pp.109ff.

Francis, F. O. and Meeks, W. A., *Conflict at Colossae.* Missoula, 1975.

Frend, W. H. C., *Martyrdom and Persecution in the Early Church.* Oxford, 1955.

Frey, J. B., 'Apocalyptique', in *Supplement to DB* i, (1928), pp.326ff.

Friedländer, M., *Der vorchristliche jüdische Gnosticismus.* Göttingen, 1898.

Fritz, K. von (ed.), *Pseudepigrapha I: Pythagorica, Lettres de Platon. Littérature pseudépigraphique juive.* Geneva, 1972.

Frost, S. B., *Old Testament Apocalyptic.* London, 1952.

Fuchs, E., 'On the Task of Christian Theology', *JTC* 6. (Eng. Trs. of *Über die Aufgabe einer christlichen Theologie*', *ZTK* 58 (1961) pp.245ff.)

Fuller, R. H., *The Mission and Achievement of Jesus.* London, 1967.

Gabathuler, H. J., *Jesus Christus.* Zürich, 1965.

Gammie, J. G., 'The Classification, Stages of Growth and Changing Intentions of the Book of Daniel', *JBL* 95 (1976), pp.191ff.

– 'Spatial and Ethical Dualism in Jewish Wisdom and Apocalyptic Literature', *JBL* 93 (1974), pp.356ff.

Gärtner, B., *The Temple and the Community in the Qumran Scrolls and the New Testament.* Cambridge, 1965.

Gaster, M., 'Das Schi'ur Komah', in *Studies and Texts.* London, 1928. ii, pp.1330ff.

Gaston, L., *No Stone on Another.* Leiden, 1970.

Georgi, D., *Die Gegner des Paulus im 2. Korintherbrief*. Neukirchen, 1964.
Gerhardsson, B., *Memory and Manuscript*. Lund, 1961.
– *Tradition and Transmission in Early Christianity*. Lund, 1964.
– *The Testing of God's Son*. Lund, 1966.
Gese, H., 'Anfang und Ende der Apokalyptik, dargestellt am Sacharjabuch', *ZTK* 70 (1973), pp.20ff.
Gibbs, J. G., *Creation and Redemption*. Leiden, 1971.
Giet, S., *L'Apocalypse et l'Histoire*. Paris, 1957.
Ginzberg, L., 'Some Observations on the Attitude of the Synagogue towards the Apocalyptic–Eschatological Writings', *JBL* 41 (1922), pp.115ff.
Glasson, T. F., *The Second Advent*. London, 1963.
– *Greek Influence in Jewish Eschatology*. London, 1961.
– 'The Son of Man Imagery: Enoch XIV and Daniel 7', *NTS* 23 (1977).
– 'What is Apocalyptic?', *NTS* 27 (1980), pp.98ff.
Gnilka, J., *Der Epheserbrief*. Freiburg, 1971.
Golb, N., 'Who were the Magariya?', *JAOS* 80 (1960), pp.347ff.
Goldberg, A., *Untersuchungen über die Vorstellung von der Schekhinah in der frühen rabbinischen Literatur*. Berlin, 1969.
– 'Der verkannte Gott. Prüfung und Scheitern der Adepten in der Merkawamystik', *ZRGG* 26 (1974), pp.17ff.
– 'Der Vortrag des Ma'asse Merkawa. Eine Vermutung zur frühen Merkawamystik', *Judaica* 29.
– 'Rabban Yohanans Traum: Der Sinai in der frühen Merkawamystik', *Frankfurter judaistische Beiträge* 3 (1975), pp.1ff.
Goodenough, E. R., *By Light, Light. The Mystic Gospel of Hellenistic Judaism*. New Haven, 1935.
– *An Introduction to Philo Judaeus*. Oxford, 1962.
– *Jewish Symbols in the Greco-Roman Period*. New York, 1953–65.
Goudoever, J., *Biblical Calendars*. Leiden, 1959.
Grässer, E., 'Kol. 3.1–14 als Beispiel einer Interpretation *secundum homines recipientes*', *ZTK* 64 (1967), pp.139ff.
Der Glaube im Hebräerbrief. Marburg, 1965.
Graetz, H., *Gnosticismus und Judenthum*. Krotoschin, 1846.
Grant, R. M., 'Les êtres intermédiaires dans le judaïsme tardif', in ed. Bianchi, *Le Origini dello Gnosticismo*, pp.141ff.
– *Gnosticism and Early Christianity*. London, 1959.
Gray, J., *1 and 2 Kings*. London, 1970.
– *The Legacy of Canaan*. Leiden, 1957.
Greenfield, J. C. and Stone, M. E., 'The Enochic Pentateuch and the Date of the Similitudes', *HTR* 69 (1976), pp.51ff.
– 'The Books of Enoch and the Traditions of Enoch', *Numen* 26 (1979), pp.81ff.
Grelot, P., 'La géographie mythique d'Hénoch et ses sources orientales', *RB* 65 (1958), pp.33ff.
– 'La légende d'Hénoch dans les apocryphes et dans la Bible', *RSR* 46 (1958), pp.4ff. and 181ff.
– 'Apocalyptique', in *Sacramentum Mundi*. 1967. i, pp.225ff.
Grillmeier, A., *Christ in Christian Tradition*. London, 1975.
Grözinger, K. E., 'Singen und ekstatische Sprache in der frühen jüdischen Mystik', *JSJ* 11 (1980), pp.66ff.
Gruenwald, I., 'Yannai and the Hekaloth Literature', *Tarbiz* 36 (1967), pp.257ff.

– 'Jewish Apocalyptic Literature', in ed. W. Haase *Aufstieg und Niedergang der römischen Welt* II, 19.1. Berlin, 1979, pp.89ff.
– 'The Jewish Esoteric Literature in the Time of the Mishnah and the Talmud', *Immanuel* 4 (1974), pp.37ff.
– *Apocalyptic and Merkavah Mysticism.* Leiden, 1979.
– 'Knowledge and Vision', *Israel Oriental Studies* 3 (1973), pp.63ff.
Gunkel, H., *Schöpfung und Chaos in Urzeit und Endzeit.* Göttingen, 1895.
Gunther, J. J., *St. Paul's Opponents and their Background.* Leiden, 1973.
Güttgemanns, E., *Der leidende Apostel und sein Herr.* Göttingen, 1966.
Guttmann, A., 'The Significance of Miracles for Talmudic Judaism', *HUCA* 20 (1947), pp.363ff.
Haenchen, E., *The Acts of the Apostles.* Oxford, 1971. (Eng. Trs. of *Die Apostelgeschichte.* Göttingen, 1965.)
Hahn, F., *The Titles of Jesus in Christology.* London, 1969. (Eng. Trs. of *Christologische Hoheitstitel. Ihre Geschichte im frühen Christentum.* Göttingen, 1963.)
Halperin, D. J., *Merkabah and Ma'aseh Merkabah, according to Rabbinic Sources.* Diss. Berkeley, 1977.
Hamerton-Kelly, R. G., *Pre-existence, Wisdom and the Son of Man.* Cambridge, 1973.
– 'The Temple and the Origins of Apocalyptic', *VT* 20 (1970), pp.1ff.
Hamerton-Kelly, R. G. and Scroggs, R., (ed.), *Jews Greeks and Christians.* Leiden, 1976.
Hanson, A. T., *The Wrath of the Lamb.* London, 1957.
– *Grace and Truth.* London, 1975.
– *Studies in Paul's Technique and Theology.* London, 1974.
Hanson, P. D., *The Dawn of Apocalyptic.* Philadelphia, 1975.
– 'Apocalypticism', in *IDB Supplement*, pp.28ff.
– 'Prolegomena to the Study of Jewish Apocalyptic', in *Magnalia Dei.*
– 'Rebellion in Heaven, Azazel and Euhemeristic Heroes in 1 Enoch 6—11', *JBL* 96 (1977). pp.195ff.
– 'Jewish Apocalyptic against its Near Eastern Environment', *RB* 78 (1971), pp.51ff.
– 'Old Testament Apocalyptic Re-Examined', *Interpretation* 25 (1971), pp.454ff.
Hare, D. R. A., *The Theme of Jewish Persecutions of Christians in the Gospel according to Saint Matthew.* Cambridge. 1967.
Harnisch, W., *Verhängnis und Verheissung der Geschichte.* Göttingen, 1969.
Harrison, R. K., *Introduction to the Old Testament.* London, 1970.
Hartingsveld, L. van, *Die Eschatologie des Johannesevangeliums.* Assen, 1962.
Hartmann, L., *Prophecy Interpreted.* Lund, 1966.
Hartstock, R., 'Visionsberichte in den synoptischen Evangelien', *Festgabe für Julius Kaftan.* Tübingen, 1920, pp.130ff.
Harvey, A. E., *Jesus on Trial.* London 1976.
Haufe, G., 'Entrückung und eschatologische Funktion im Spätjudentum', *ZRGG* 13 (1961), pp.105ff.
Hay, D. M., *Glory at the Right Hand.* Abingdon, 1973.
Hayman, A. P., 'Pseudonymity in 4 Ezra', *JSJ* 6 (1975), pp.47ff.
Helmbold, N. K., 'Gnostic Elements in the Ascension of Isaiah', *NTS* 18 (1971–2), pp.22ff.
Hemer, C. J., *A Study of the Letters to the Seven Churches of Asia with Special Reference to their Local Background.* Diss. Manchester, 1969.

Hengel, M., *Nachfolge und Charisma*. Berlin, 1968.
– *Judaism and Hellenism*. London, 1974. (Eng. Trs. of *Judentum und Hellenismus*. Tübingen, 1969.)
– *Die Zeloten*. Leiden, 1976.
– 'Anonymität, Pseudepigraphie und literarische Falschung in der jüdisch-hellenistischen Literatur', in ed. Fritz *Pseudepigrapha I*, pp.229ff.
– *Victory over Violence*. London, 1975 (Eng. Trs. of *Gewalt und Gewaltlosigkeit*. Stuttgart, 1971).
– *The Son of God*. London, 1976.
Herford, R.T., 'Elisha b. Abujah', in *Essays presented to J. H. Hertz*. London, 1942, pp.215ff.
– *Talmud and Apocrypha*. London, 1933.
Hesse, Jonge, de and Woude, van der, 'christos' *TDNT* ix, pp.493ff.
Hiers, R., *The Kingdom of God in the Synoptic Tradition*. Gainesville, 1970.
Hill, D., 'Prophets and Prophecy in the Revelation of St John', *NTS* 18 (1971–2), pp.401ff.
Hindley, J., 'Towards a Date for the Similitudes of Enoch' *NTS* 14 (1967–8), pp.551ff.
Hofius, O., *Katapausis. Die Vorstellung vom endzeitlichen Ruheort im Hebräerbrief*. Tübingen, 1970.
– *Der Vorhang vor dem Thron Gottes*. Tübingen, 1972.
– *Der Christushymnus Philipper 2.6–11*. Tübingen, 1976.
Hölscher, G., 'Die Entstehung des Buches Daniel', *TSK* 92 (1919), pp.113ff.
– 'Problèmes de littérature apocalyptique juive', *RHPR* 9 (1929), pp.101ff.
Holtz, T., *Die Christologie der Apokalypse des Johannes*. Berlin, 1962.
Hooker, M. D., *The Son of Man in Mark*. London, 1967.
– 'Were there false Teachers at Colossae?' in *Christ and the Spirit*, ed. Smalley and Lindars. Cambridge, 1973, pp.315ff.
Horton, F., *The Melchizedek Tradition*. Cambridge, 1976.
Hügel, F. von, *The Mystical Element of Religion as Studied in Saint Catherine of Genoa and her Friends*. London, 1923.
Hughes, H. M., *The Ethics of the Jewish Apocryphal Literature*. London, 1909.
Hurd, J. C., *The Origin of 1 Corinthians*. London, 1965.
James, W., *The Varieties of Religious Experience*. Reprinted London, 1960.
Jaubert, A., *The Date of the Last Supper*. New York. (Eng. Trs. of *La date de la cène*. Paris, 1957.)
– 'Le calendrier des Jubilés et de la secte de Qumrân', *VT* 3 (1955), pp.250ff.
Jellicoe, S., *The Septuagint and Modern Study*. Oxford, 1968.
Jeremias, C., *Die Nachtgesichte des Sacharja*. Göttingen, 1977.
Jeremias, J., *New Testament Theology vol. I* London, 1971. (Eng. Trs. of *Neutestamentliche Theologie*. Gütersloh, 1971.)
– *Unknown Sayings of Jesus*. London, 1964. (Eng. Trs. of *Unbekannte Jesusworte*. Gütersloh, 1963.)
– *Jerusalem in the Time of Jesus*. London, 1969. (Eng. Trs. of *Jerusalem zur Zeit Jesu*. Göttingen, 1962.)
– 'paradeisos' *TDNT* v, pp.765ff.
– 'War Paulus Witwer?', *ZNW* 25 (1926), pp.310ff.
– 'Die Berufung des Nathanael', *Angelos* 3 (1928), pp.2ff.
– 'Die älteste Schicht der Menschensohn-Logien', *ZNW* 58 (1967), pp.159ff.
– *The Prayers of Jesus*. London, 1967. (Eng. Trs. of essays from *Abba* Göttingen, 1966.)

Jervell, J., *Imago Dei*. Göttingen, 1960.

Joel, M., *Blicke in die Religionsgeschichte zu Anfang des zweiten Jahrhunderts*. Breslau, 1880–3.

Jörns, K. P., *Das hymnische Evangelium*. Gütersloh, 1971.

Johnson, A. R., *The One and the Many in the Israelite Conception of God*. Cardiff, 1961.

Johnson, S., 'Asia Minor and Early Christianity', in *Christianity, Judaism and Other Greco-Roman Cults*. Leiden, 1975, vol. ii, pp.74ff.

Jones, B. W., 'More about the Apocalypse as Apocalyptic', *JBL* 87 (1968), pp.325ff.

Jonge, M. de, *The Testaments of the Twelve Patriarchs*. Assen, 1953.

– 'Josephus und die Zukunftserwartungen seines Volkes', in *Josephus-Studien* ed. O. Betz, K. Haacker and M. Hengel. Göttingen, 1974 pp.205ff.

Jonge, M. de and Woude, A. S. van der, '11 Q Melchizedek and the New Testament', *NTS* 12 (1965–6), pp.301ff.

Jonge, M. de (ed.), *Studies in the Testaments of the Twelve Patriarchs*. Leiden, 1975.

Kadushin, M., *The Rabbinic Mind*. New York, 1965.

Kaiser, O., *Isaiah 1—12*. London, 1972. (Eng. Trs. of *Der Prophet Jesaja 1—12*. Göttingen, 1963.)

– *Isaiah 13—39*. London, 1974. (Eng. Trs. of *Der Prophet Jesaja 13—39*. Göttingen, 1973.)

Kallas, J., 'The Apocalypse – an Apocalyptic Book?', *JBL* 86 (1967), pp.69ff.

Käsemann, E., 'Die Legitimät des Apostels', *ZNW* 41 (1942), pp.33ff.

– *New Testament Questions of Today*. London, 1969.

– *Essays on New Testament Themes*. London, 1964.

– *Das wandernde Gottesvolk*. Göttingen, 1939.

– 'A Primitive Christian Baptismal Liturgy', in *Essays on New Testament Themes*, pp.149ff.

– 'The Beginnings of Christian Theology', in *New Testament Questions of Today*, pp.82ff.

– 'On the Subject of Primitive Christian Apocalyptic', in *New Testament Questions of Today*, pp.108ff.

Kaufmann, J., 'Apokalyptik', in *Encyclopaedia Judaica II* (1928), pp.1142ff.

Keck, L. E., 'The Spirit and the Dove', *NTS* 17 (1970–1), pp.41ff.

Kee, H. C., 'The Transfiguration in Mark: Epiphany or Apocalyptic Vision?', in ed. J. Reumann *Understanding the Sacred Text*. Valley Forge, 1972, pp.135ff.

Kehl, N., 'Erniedrigung und Erhöhung in Qumran und Kolossä', *ZKT* 91 (1969), pp.364ff.

– *Der Christushymnus im Kolosserbrief*. Stuttgart, 1967.

Kelly, J. N. D., *A Commentary on the Epistles of Peter and Jude*. London, 1969.

Kertelge, K., 'Apokalypsis Jesou Christou', in ed. J. Gnilka *Neues Testament und Kirche*. Freiburg, 1974, pp.266ff.

Kettler, F. H., 'Enderwartung und himmlischer Stufenbau im Kirchenbegriff des nachapostolischen Zeitalters', *TLZ* 79 (1954), col. 385ff.

Kim, S., *An Exposition of Paul's Gospel in the Light of the Damascus Christophany*. Diss. Manchester, 1977.

Kirby, J., *Ephesians: Baptism and Pentecost*. London, 1968.

Kirk, K., *The Vision of God*. London, 1931.

Kittel, G., 'Das kleinasiatische Judentum in der hellenistisch-römischen Zeit', *TLZ* 69 (1944), col. 9ff.

Klassen, W. and Snyder, G., (ed.), *Current Issues in New Testament Interpretation*. New York, 1962.

Klausner, J., *The Messianic Idea in Israel*. London, 1956.

– *Jesus of Nazareth*. London, 1925.

Klinzing, G., *Die Umdeutung des Kultus in der Qumrangemeinde und im Neuen Testament*. Göttingen, 1971.

Knibb, M. A., 'The Date of the Parables of Enoch', NTS 25 (1978–9). pp.345ff.

– *The Ethiopic Book of Enoch*. Oxford, 1978.

Knowles, D., *The English Mystical Tradition*. London, 1961.

Knox, R. A., *Enthusiasm: A Chapter in the History of Religion*. Oxford, 1950.

Knox, W. L., *Saint Paul and the Church of the Gentiles*. Cambridge, 1939.

Koch, K., *The Rediscovery of Apocalytic*. London, 1972. (Eng. Trs. of *Ratlos der Apokalyptik*. Gütersloh, 1970.)

Kolenkow, A. B., 'The Genre Testament in the Hellenistic Jewish Milieu', JSJ 6 (1975), pp.57ff.

Kraabel, A. T., *Judaism in Asia Minor in the Imperial Period*. Diss. Harvard, 1968.

Kraft, H., *Die Offenbarung des Johannes*. Tübingen, 1974.

Kremer, J., *Pfingstbericht und Pfingstgeschehen*. Stuttgart, 1973.

Kretschmar, G., *Studien zur frühchristlichen Trinitätstheologie*. Tübingen, 1956.

Kuhn, H. B., 'The Angelology of the Non-Canonical Jewish Apocalypses', JBL 67 (1947), pp.217ff.

Kuhn, H. W., *Enderwartung und gegenwärtiges Heil*. Göttingen, 1966.

Kuhn, K. G., 'The Epistle to the Ephesians in the Light of the Qumran Texts' in ed. J. Murphy-O'Connor *Paul and Qumran*. London, 1968, pp.115ff.

– 'Gog' TDNT i, pp.789ff.

Kümmel, W. G., *Introduction to the New Testament*. London, 1975. (Eng. Trs. of *Einleitung in das Neue Testament*. Heidelberg, 1973.)

– *Promise and Fulfilment*. London, 1961. (Eng. Trs. of *Verheissung und Erfüllung*. Zürich, 1956.)

Labriolle, P., *La crise montaniste*. Paris, 1913.

Ladd, G. E., 'Why not Prophetic-Apocalyptic?', JBL 76 (1957), pp.192ff.

– *The Theology of the New Testament*. Grand Rapids, 1974.

Lagrange, J., *Le judaïsme avant Jésus Christ*. Paris, 1931.

– *L'évangile selon Matthieu*. Paris, 1923.

Lähnemann, J., *Der Kolosserbrief*. Gütersloh, 1971.

Lambrecht, J., *Die Redaktion der Markus-Apokalypse*. Rome, 1967.

Lange, N. de, *Origen and the Jews*. Cambridge, 1976.

Laurin, R., 'The Question of Immortality in the Qumran Hodayot', JSS 3 (1958), pp.344ff.

Laws, S., 'Can Apocalyptic be Relevant?' in ed. M. Hooker and C. Hickling *What about the New Testament?* London, 1975, pp.89ff.

Leivestad, R., 'Das Dogma von der prophetenlosen Zeit', NTS 19 (1973), pp.288ff.

– 'Exit the Apocalyptic Son of Man', NTS 18 (1971–2), pp.243ff.

Lentzen-Deis, F., *Die Taufe Jesu nach den Synoptikern*. Frankfurt, 1970.

Levenson, T., *The Theology of the Program of Restoration of Ezek. 40—48*. Missoula, 1976.

Lieberman, S., *Hellenism in Jewish Palestine*. New York, 1950.

– *Greek in Jewish Palestine*. New York, 1942.

Lightfoot, J. B., *Saint Paul's Epistles to the Colossians and Philemon*. London, 1875.

Lincoln, A. T., *The Heavenly Dimension*. Diss. Cambridge, 1974.

- 'A Re-examination of "the Heavenlies" in Ephesians', NTS 19 (1972–3), pp.468ff.
- 'Paul the Visionary', NTS 25 (1978–9), pp.204ff.
Lindars, B., *The Gospel of John*. London, 1972.
- 'Re-enter the Apocalyptic Son of Man', NTS 22 (1975–6), pp.52ff.
- 'The Apocalyptic Myth and the Death of Christ', *BJRL* 57 (1974–5), pp.366ff.
Lindblom, J., *Prophecy in Ancient Israel*. Oxford, 1962.
- *Gesichte und Offenbarungen*. Lund, 1968.
- *Die Jesaja-Apokalypse*. Lund, 1938.
- 'Theophanies in Holy Places in Hebrew Religion', *HUCA* 32 (1961), pp.91ff.
Loewe, R., 'The Divine Garment and the Shi'ur Qomah', *HTR* 58 (1965), pp.153ff.
- 'Apologetic Motifs in the Targum to the Song of Songs', in ed. A. Altmann, *Biblical Motifs*. Harvard, 1966, pp.159ff.
Lohfink, G., *Die Himmelfahrt Jesu*. Munich, 1971.
Lohmeyer, E., 'Die Offenbarung des Johannes 1920–1934', *TR* 6 (1934), pp.269ff. and 7 (1935). pp.28ff.
- *Die Offenbarung des Johannes*. Tübingen, 1953.
Lohse, E., *'pentekoste'* TDNT vi, pp.44ff.
- *Colossians and Philemon*. Philadelphia, 1971. (Eng. Trs. of *Die Briefe an die Kolosser und an Philemon*. Göttingen, 1968.)
Long, B. O., 'Reports of Visions among the Prophets', *JBL* 95 (1976), pp.353ff.
Longenecker, R., *The Christology of Early Jewish Christianity*. London, 1970.
Lowe, J., 'An Examination of Attempts to Detect Developments in St. Paul's Theology', *JTS* 42 (1941), pp.129ff.
Lueken, W., *Michael*. Göttingen, 1898.
Lührmann, D., *Das Offenbarungsverständnis bei Paulus und in paulinischen Gemeinden*. Neukirchen, 1965.
Lust, J., 'Dan. 7.13 and the Septuagint', *Ephem. Theol. Lov.* 54 (1978), pp.62ff.
Lyonnet, S., 'St. Paul et le gnosticisme: la lettre aux Colossiens', in *Le Origini dello Gnosticismo*, pp.583ff.
- 'L'Epître aux Colossiens (Col. 2.18) et les mystères d'Apollon Clarien', *Biblica* 43 (1962), pp.417ff.
McCown, C. C., 'Hebrew and Egyptian Apocalyptic Literature', *HTR* 18 (1925), pp.357ff.
McCurdy, G. H., 'Platonic Orphism in the Testament of Abraham', *JBL* 61 (1942), pp.213ff.
Mack, B. L., *Logos und Sophia*. Göttingen, 1973.
McKelvey, R. J., *The New Temple*. Oxford, 1969.
McNamara, M., *The New Testament and the Palestinian Targum to the Pentateuch*. Rome, 1966.
- *Targum and Testament*. Shannon, 1972.
Macrae, G., 'The Jewish Background of the Gnostic Sophia Myth', *NT* 12 (1970), pp.86ff.
- *Some Elements of Jewish Apocalyptic and Mystical Tradition and their Relation to Gnostic Literature*. Diss. Cambridge, 1966.
Maier, J. and Schreiner, J., (ed.), *Literatur und Religion des Frühjudentums*. Würzburg, 1973.
Maier, J., *Vom Kultus zu Gnosis*. Salzburg, 1964.
- 'Das Gefährdungsmotiv bei der Himmelsreise in der jüdischen Apokalyptik und Gnosis', *Kairos* 5 (1963), pp.18ff.

Manson, T.W., 'Some Reflections on Apocalyptic', in *Aux sources de la tradition chrétienne. Melanges à M. Goguel*. Neuchâtel, 1950, pp.139ff.

Marmorstein, A., *The Doctrine of Merits in Old Rabbinic Literature*. London, 1920.

− *The Old Rabbinic Doctrine of God*. Oxford, 1927.

Marrow, S. B., 'Apocalyptic Genre and Eschatology', in *The Word in the World. Essays in Honour of F. L. Moriarty*. Cambridge, Mass., 1973, pp.71ff.

Martin, R. P., *Carmen Christi*. Cambridge, 1967.

− *Colossians. The Church's Lord and the Christian's Liberty*. Exeter, 1972.

Martyn, J. L., *History and Theology in the Fourth Gospel*. New York, 1968.

Mearns, C. C., 'Dating the Similitudes of Enoch', *NTS* 25 (1978–9), pp.360ff.

Meeks, W. A., *The Prophet King*. Leiden, 1967.

− 'Moses as God and King' in ed. J. Neusner *Religions in Antiquity*, pp.354ff.

− 'The Man from Heaven in Johannine Sectarianism', *JBL* 91 (1972), pp.44ff.

Metzger, B. M., 'Literary Forgeries and Canonical Pseudepigrapha', *JBL* 91 (1972), pp.3ff.

Michaelis, W., *Zur Engelchristologie im Urchristentum*. Basel, 1942.

− 'Joh. 1.51, Gen. 28.12 und das Menschensohn-Problem' *TLZ* 85 (1960), col. 561ff.

Michel, O., *Der Hebräerbrief*. Göttingen, 1966.

Michl, J., *Die Engelvorstellungen in der Apokalypse des hl. Johannes*. Munich, 1937.

Milik, J., *Ten Years of Discovery in the Wilderness of Judaea*. London, 1963. (Eng. Trs. of *Dix ans de découvertes dans le désert de Juda*. Paris, 1957.)

Milik, J. T., *The Books of Enoch*. Oxford, 1976.

Millar, F. G. B., *The Emperor in the Roman World*. London, 1977.

Millar, W. R., *Isaiah 24—27 and the Origin of Apocalyptic*. Missoula, 1976.

Minear, P. S., *And I Saw a New Earth*. Washington, 1968.

− 'The Cosmology of the Apocalypse', in ed. Klassen and Snyder *Current Issues in New Testament Interpretation*, pp.23ff:

Miranda, J., *Die Sendung Jesu im vierten Evangelium*. Stuttgart, 1977.

Miranda, J. P., *Marx and the Bible*. New York, 1974.

Moltmann, J., *Theology of Hope*. London, 1967. (Eng. Trs. of *Theologie der Hoffnung*. Munich, 1965.)

Monloubou, L. (ed.), *Apocalypses et Théologie de l'Espérance*. Paris, 1977.

Montefiore, H. W., *A Commentary on the Epistle to the Hebrews*. London, 1964.

Montgomery, J., *A Critical and Exegetical Commentary on the Book of Daniel*. Edinburgh, 1927.

Moore, A. L., *The Parousia in the New Testament*. Leiden, 1966.

Moore, G. F., *Judaism*. Cambridge, Mass., 1927–30.

− 'Christian Writers on Judaism', *HTR* 14 (1921), pp.197ff.

− 'Intermediaries in Jewish Theology', *HTR* 15 (1922), pp.41ff.

Morgenstern, J., 'The HASIDIM − Who were they?' *HUCA* 38 (1967), pp.59ff.

Morris, L., *Apocalyptic*. London, 1972.

Moule, C. F. D., *The Epistles of Paul the Apostle to the Colossians and to Philemon*. Cambridge, 1962.

− 'The Problem of the Pastorals: a Reappraisal', *BJRL* 47 (1964–5), pp.430ff.

− 'Neglected Features in the Problem of the Son of Man', in ed. J. Gnilka *Neues Testament und Kirche*. Freiburg, 1974.

− 'St. Paul and Dualism', *NTS* 12 (1965–6), pp.106ff.

− 'The Individualism of the Fourth Gospel', *NT* 5 (1962), pp.171ff.

− *The Birth of the New Testament*. London, 1962.

Mowinckel, S., *He that Cometh*. Oxford, 1956.

Müller, H. P., 'Mantische Weisheit und Apokalyptik', in *Supplements to VT* 22, pp.268ff.
Müller, K., 'Menschensohn und Messias', *BZ* 16 (1972), pp.161ff.
– 'Die Ansätze der Apokalyptik', in Maier and Schreiner *Literatur und Religion des Frühjudentums* pp.31ff.
Müller, U., *Prophetie und Predigt im Neuen Testament*. Gütersloh, 1975.
– *Messias und Menschensohn*. Gütersloh, 1972.
– *Zur frühchristlichen Theologiegeschichte*. Gütersloh, 1976.
Munck, J., *Paul and the Salvation of Mankind*. London, 1959 (Eng. Trs. of *Paulus und die Heilsgeschichte*. Copenhagen, 1954).
Murdock, W., 'History and Revelation in Jewish Apocalyptic', *Interpretation* 21 (1967), pp.165ff.
Mussies, G., *The Morphology of Koine Greek as used in the Apocalypse of St John*. Leiden, 1971.
Mussner, F., 'Contributions made by Qumran to the Understanding of the Epistle to the Ephesians', in ed. J. Murphy O'Connor, *Paul and Qumran*, pp.159ff.
Myers, J. M., *I and II Esdras*. New York, 1974.
Neher, A., 'Le voyage mystique des quatre', *RHR* 140 (1951), pp.59ff.
Neugebauer, F., *In Christus*. Göttingen, 1961.
Neusner, J., *The Development of a Legend*. Leiden, 1970.
– *The Rabbinic Traditions about the Pharisees before A.D. 70*. Leiden, 1971.
– *A Life of Rabban Yohanan b. Zakkai*. Leiden, 1970.
– *First Century Judaism in Crisis*. New York, 1975.
– *Eliezer ben Hyrcanus*. Leiden, 1973.
– ed. *Religions in Antiquity. Supplements to Numen 14*. Leiden, 1968.
Newman, B., 'The Fallacy of the Domitianic Hypothesis', *NTS* 10 (1963–4), pp.133ff.
Nicholson, E. W., 'The Interpretation of Exod. 24.9–11', *VT* 24 (1974), pp.77ff.
Nickelsburg, G. W., *Resurrection, Immortality and Eternal Life in Judaism*. Cambridge, Mass., 1972.
– 'Eschatology in the Testament of Abraham' *IOSCS Proceedings* ii 1972.
– *Studies on the Testament of Joseph*. Missoula, 1975.
– 'The Apocalyptic Message of 1 Enoch 92—105', *CBQ* 39 (1977), pp.309ff.
– 'Apocalyptic and Myth in 1 Enoch 6—11', *JBL* 96 (1977), pp.383ff.
Nissen, A., 'Tora und Geschichte im Spätjudentum', *NT* 9 (1967), pp.241ff.
Nock, A. D., *Conversion*. Oxford, 1933.
North, R., 'Prophecy to Apocalyptic via Zechariah', in *Supplements to Vetus Testamentum* 22.
Noth, M., 'Die Entstehung des Buches Daniel', *TSK* 92 (1919), pp.113ff.
– 'The Understanding of History in Apocalyptic', in *The Laws of the Pentateuch and Other Essays*. (Eng. Trs. of 'Das Geschichtsverständnis der alttestamentlichen Apokalyptik', in *Gesammelte Studien zum AT*, Munich, 1960.)
– 'Zur Komposition des Buches Daniel', in *Gesammelte Studien zum AT*. Munich, 1960, pp.11ff.
Odeberg, H., *The Fourth Gospel*. Uppsala, 1929.
– 'The View of the Universe in the Epistle to the Ephesians', in *Lund Universitets Årsskrift* 29 (1933).
Oepke, A., 'existemi' *TDNT* ii, pp.449ff.
– 'apokalypto' *TDNT* iii, pp.551ff.
Oesterley, W. O. E., *An Introduction to the Books of the Apocrypha*. London, 1935.

O'Neill, J. C., *The Theology of Acts*. London, 1970.
Oppenheim, A. L., *The Interpretation of Dreams in the Ancient Near East*. Philadelphia, 1956.
Osswald, E., 'Zum Problem der *Vaticinia ex Eventu*', ZAW 75 (1963), pp.27ff.
Osten-Sacken, P. von der, *Die Apokalyptik in ihrem Verhältnis zu Prophetie und Weisheit*. Munich, 1969.
– *Gott und Belial*. Göttingen, 1969.
Otto, R., *The Idea of the Holy*. Oxford, 1928.
Pancaro, S., *The Law in the Fourth Gospel*. Leiden, 1975.
Pannenberg, W., *Revelation in History*. London, 1969 (Eng. Trs. of *Offenbarung als Geschichte*. Göttingen, 1965).
Percy, E., *Die Probleme der Kolosser- und Epheserbriefe*. Lund, 1946.
Pernveden, L., *The Concept of the Church in the Shepherd of Hermas*. Lund, 1966.
Perrin, N., *The Kingdom of God in the Teaching of Jesus*. London, 1967.
– *The New Testament: an Introduction*. New York, 1974.
Philonenko, M., 'La cosmogonie du "Livre des secrets d'Hénoch",' in *Religions en Egypte hellénistique et romaine*. Paris, 1969, pp.109ff.
Piper, O. A., 'The Apocalypse of John and the Liturgy of the Ancient Church', *Church History 20*. (1950), pp.10ff.
Plöger, O., *Das Buch Daniel*. Gütersloh, 1965.
– *Theocracy and Eschatology*. Oxford, 1968 (Eng. Trs. of *Theokratie und Eschatologie*. Neukirchen, 1962).
Plummer, A., *A Critical and Exegetical Commentary on the Second Epistle of St. Paul to the Corinthians*. Edinburgh, 1915.
Pope, M. H., *El in the Ugaritic Texts*. Leiden, 1955.
Porteous, N., *Daniel*. London, 1965.
Preisker, O., *'embateuo'* TDNT ii, pp.535ff.
Prigent, P., *Apocalypse et liturgie*. Neuchâtel, 1964.
– *Apocalypse 12: histoire de l'exégèse*. Tübingen, 1959.
– 'Au temps de l'Apocalypse: I Domitien', RHPR 54 (1974), pp.455ff.
– 'Au temps de l'Apocalypse: II Le culte imperial au 1er siècle en Asie Mineure', RHPR 55 (1975), pp.215ff.
– 'Au temps de l'Apocalypse: III Pourquoi les persécutions?', RHPR 55 (1975).
Procksch, O., 'Christus im AT', NKZ 44 (1933), pp.57ff.
– 'Die Berufungsvision Hesekiels', in *Karl Budde zum siebzigsten Geburtstag* BZAW 34 (1920). pp.141ff.
– *Die Theologie des Alten Testaments*, Gütersloh, 1950.
Pryke, J., 'Eschatology in the Dead Sea Scrolls', in ed. M. Black *The Scrolls and Christianity*. London, 1969.
Quispel, G., 'Christliche Gnosis und jüdische Heterodoxie', EvT 14 (1954), pp.474ff.
– 'Gnosticism and the New Testament', in *The Bible and Modern Scholarship*, ed. J. P. Hyatt. New York, 1965, pp.252ff.
– 'The Origins of the Gnostic Demiurge', in *Kyriakon* ed. P. Grenfield and J. A. Jungmann. Münster, 1970, pp.271ff.
– 'Nathanael und der Menschensohn', ZNW 47 (1956), pp.281ff.
– 'Der gnostische Anthropos und die jüdische Tradition', *Eranos Jahrbuch* 22 (1953), pp.195ff.
– 'Ezek. 1.26 in Jewish Mysticism and Gnosis', VC 34 (1980), pp.1ff.
Rabin, C., *Qumran Studies*. New York, 1975.
Rad, G. von, *Old Testament Theology*. Edinburgh, 1962. (Eng. Trs. of *Theologie*

des Alten Testaments. Munich, 1957.)
– 'The Joseph Narrative and Ancient Wisdom', in *The Problem of the Hexateuch and Other Essays*. Edinburgh, 1966.
Ramsay, W., *The Letters to the Seven Churches*. London, 1904.
Rau, E., *Kosmologie, Eschatologie und die Lehrautorität Henochs*. Diss. Hamburg, 1974.
Reese, G., *Die Geschichte Israels in der Auffassung des frühen Judentums*. Diss. Heidelberg, 1967.
Reicke, B., 'Official and Pietistic Elements of Jewish Apocalypticism' *JBL* 79 (1968), pp.137ff.
– *The Disobedient Spirits and Christian Baptism*. Lund, 1946.
– 'Da'at and Gnosis in Intertestamental Literature', in ed. E. Ellis and M. Wilcox *Neotestamentica et Semitica*. Edinburgh, 1966, pp.245ff.
Reim, G., *Studien zum alttestamentlichen Hintergrund des Johannesevangeliums*. Cambridge, 1974.
Rengstorf, K., *Die Auferstehung Jesu*. Witten-Ruhr, 1960.
Resch, A., *Agrapha*. Leipzig, 1906.
Richardson, P., *Israel in the Apostolic Church*, Cambridge, 1969.
Riesenfeld, H., *Jésus Transfiguré*. Lund, 1947.
Ringgren, H., *The Messiah in the Old Testament*. London, 1956.
– *Israelite Religion*. London, 1966 (Eng. Trs. of *Israelitische Religion*. Stuttgart, 1963).
Rissi, M., *The Future of the World*. London, 1972.
– *Zeit und Geschichte in der Offenbarung des Johannes*. Zürich, 1952.
Rist, M., 'Pseudepigraphy and the Early Christians', in ed. D. Aune, *Studies in the New Testament and Early Christian Literature*. Leiden, 1972, pp.75ff.
– 'Apocalypticism', *IDB* i, pp.157ff.
Rivkin, E., 'Pharisaism and the Crisis of the Individual in the Greco-Roman World', *JQR* 61 (1970–1), pp.27ff.
Robinson, J. A. T., *Jesus and his Coming*. London, 1957.
– *The Body*. London, 1952.
– *Twelve New Testament Studies*. London, 1962.
– *Redating the New Testament*. London, 1975.
Robinson, J. M. and Koester, H., *Trajectories through Early Christianity*. Philadelphia, 1971.
Rogerson, J. W., 'The Hebrew Conception of Corporate Personality: A Re-examination', *JTS* 21 (1970), pp.1ff.
Rohland, J. P., *Der Erzengel Michael. Arzt und Feldherr*. Leiden, 1977.
Rollins, W. G., 'The New Testament and Apocalyptic', *NTS* 17 (1970–1), pp.454ff.
Roon, A. van, *The Authenticity of Ephesians*. Leiden, 1974.
Rosenthal, F., *Vier apokryphische Bücher aus der Zeit und Schule R. Akibas*. Leipzig, 1885.
Rössler, D., *Gesetz und Geschichte*. Neukirchen, 1960.
Rost, L., *Judaism outside the Hebrew Canon*. Abingdon, 1976 (Eng. Trs. of *Einleitung in die alttestamentlichen Apokryphen und Pseudepigraphen*. Heidelberg, 1971).
Rowland, C. C., 'The Visions of God in Apocalyptic Literature', *JSJ* 10 (1979) pp.138ff.
– *The Influence of the First Chapter of Ezekiel on Judaism and Early Christianity*. Diss. Cambridge, 1975.

– 'The Vision of the Risen Christ in Rev. 1.13ff', *JTS* 31 (1980), pp.1ff.
Rowley, H. H., 'The Unity of the Book of Daniel', in *The Servant of the Lord.* London, 1952.
– *The Relevance of Apocalyptic.* London, 1947.
– *Darius the Mede and the Four World Empires in the Book of Daniel.* Cardiff, 1935.
Rubinstein, A., 'Hebraisms in the Slavonic Apocalypse of Abraham', *JJS* 4 (1953), pp.108ff.
Rudolph, K., 'Randerscheinungen des Judentums und das Problem der Entstehung des Gnostizismus', *Kairos* 9 (1967), pp.105ff.
Russell, D. S., *The Method and Message of Jewish Apocalyptic.* London, 1964.
– *Apocalyptic: Ancient and Modern.* London, 1978.
Saake, H., 'Paulus als Ekstatiker', *NT* 15 (1973), pp.153ff.
Saldarini, A. J., 'The Uses of Apocalyptic in the Mishnah and Tosefta', *CBQ* 39 (1977), pp.396ff.
– 'Apocalyptic and Rabbinic Literature', *CBQ* 37 (1975), pp.348ff.
Sanders, E. P., *The Tendencies of the Synoptic Tradition.* Cambridge, 1969.
– *Paul and Palestinian Judaism.* London, 1977.
Sanders, J. T., *The New Testament Christological Hymns.* Cambridge, 1971.
Santer, M., 'The Text of Ephesians 1.1', *NTS* 15 (1968–9), pp.247ff.
Sarfatti, G. B., 'Talmudic Cosmography', (in Hebrew) *Tarbiz* 35 (1965), pp.137ff.
Satake, A., *Die Gemeindeordnung in der Johannesapokalypse.* Neukirchen, 1966.
Saunders, E. W., 'The Colossian Heresy and Qumran Theology', in *Studies in the History and Text of the New Testament.* Salt Lake City, 1967.
Schäfer, P., *Die Vorstellung vom heiligen Geist in der rabbinischen Literatur.* Munich, 1972.
– *Rivalität zwischen Engeln und Menschen.* Berlin, 1975.
Schaller, J. B., *Genesis 1 und 2 im antiken Judentum. Untersuchungen über Verwendung und Deutung der Schöpfungsaussagen von Gen 1 und 2 im antiken Judentum.* Diss. Göttingen, 1961.
Scharlemann, M. H., *Stephen: A Singular Saint.* Rome, 1968.
Schenke, H. M., *Der Gott-Mensch in der Gnosis.* Göttingen, 1962.
Schepelern, W., *Der Montanismus und die phrygischen Kulte.* Tübingen, 1929.
Schiffman, L., *The Halakhah at Qumran.* Leiden, 1975.
Schlatter, A., *Paulus der Bote Jesu.* Stuttgart, 1934.
Schlier, H., *Der Brief an die Epheser.* Düsseldorf, 1957.
Schmidt, J. M., *Die jüdische Apokalyptik.* Neukirchen, 1969.
Schmithals, W., *Paul and James.* London, 1963. (Eng. Trs. of *Paulus und Jakobus.* Göttingen, 1963.)
– *The Apocalyptic Movement.* Abingdon, 1975. (Eng. Trs. of *Die Apokalyptik: Einführung und Deutung.* Göttingen, 1973.)
– *Gnosticism in Corinth.* New York, 1971. (Eng. Trs. of *Die Gnosis in Korinth.* Göttingen, 1956.)
Schmitt, A., *Entrückung — Aufnahme — Himmelfahrt.* Stuttgart, 1973.
Schnackenburg, R., *The Gospel according to Saint John.* London, 1968. (Eng. Trs. of *Johannesevangelium I.* Freiburg, 1965.)
Schoeps, H. J., *Die Theologie und Geschichte des Judenchristentums.* Tübingen, 1949.
– *Paul.* London, 1961. (Eng. Trans. of *Paulus.* Tübingen, 1959).
Scholem, G., *Major Trends in Jewish Mysticism.* London, 1955.
– *Jewish Gnosticism, Merkabah Mysticism and Talmudic Tradition.* New York, 1965.

542   Bibliography

- *Von der mystischen Gestalt der Gottheit.* Zürich, 1962.
- *Sabbatai Sevi: The Mystical Messiah 1626–1676.* London, 1973.
- 'Kabbalah', in *Encyclopaedia Judaica* vol. x, col. 489ff.
- *The Messianic Idea in Judaism.* London, 1971.
- *Ursprung und Anfänge der Kabbala.* Berlin, 1962.
Schreiner, J., *Alttestamentlich-jüdische Apokalyptik: eine Einführung.* Munich, 1969.
- 'Die apokalyptische Bewegung', in *Literatur und Religion des Frühjudentums*, pp.214ff.
- 'Die Symbolsprache der jüdischen Apokalyptik', in ed. W. Heinen *Bildwort-Symbol in der Theologie.* Würzburg, 1969, pp.55ff.
Schubert, K., *Die Religion des nachbiblischen Judentums.* Freiburg, 1955.
- 'Der Sektenkanon von 'En Fescha und die Anfänge der jüdischen Gnosis', *TLZ* 78 (1953), col. 495ff.
- *The Dead Sea Community.* London, 1959.
Schürer, E., *Geschichte des israelitisch-jüdischen Volkes im Zeitalter Jesu Christi.* Leipzig, 1910–11.
Schürer, E., (rev. Vermes and Millar) *The History of the Jewish People in the Age of Jesus Christ,* (vol. i and ii) Edinburgh, 1971 and 1979.
Schütz, J. H., *Paul and the Anatomy of Apostolic Authority.* Cambridge, 1975.
Schweitzer, A., *The Quest for the Historical Jesus.* London, 1910. (Eng. Trs. of *Von Reimarus zu Wrede.* Tübingen, 1906.)
Schweizer, E., 'pneuma' *TDNT* vi, pp.332ff.
- 'soma' *TDNT* vii, pp.1024ff.
- *Church Order in the New Testament.* London, 1961. (Eng. Trs. of *Gemeinde und Gemeindeordnung im Neuen Testament.* Zürich, 1959.)
- *Der Brief an die Kolosser.* Neukirchen, 1976.
Scott, C. A., *Christianity according to Saint Paul.* Cambridge, 1927.
Scott, K., *The Imperial Cult under the Flavians.* Stuttgart, 1936.
Scott, R. B. Y., 'Behold He Cometh with Clouds', *NTS* 5 (1958–9), pp.127ff.
- 'Isaiah 21.1–10: The Inside of a Prophet's Mind', *VT* 2 (1952), pp.278ff.
Séd, N., 'Les traditions secrètes et les disciples de Rabban Yohanan ben Zakkai', *RHR* 184 (1973), pp.49ff.
- *La Cosmologie juive.* Paris, 1980.
Segal, A. F., 'Heavenly Ascent in Hellenistic Judaism, Early Christianity and their Environments', in ed. W. Haase *Aufstieg und Niedergang der römischen Welt* II, 23.2. Berlin, 1980.
- *Two Powers in Heaven.* Leiden, 1978.
Selwyn, E. G., *The First Epistle of Saint Peter.* London, 1946.
Sevenster, J. N., *The Roots of Pagan Anti-Semitism in the Ancient World.* Leiden, 1975.
Sint, J., *Pseudonymität im Altertum.* Innsbruck, 1960.
Sjöberg, E., *Der Menschensohn in dem äthiopischen Henochbuch.* Lund, 1946.
Slingerland, H. D., *The Testaments of the Twelve Patriarchs: A Critical History of Research.* Missoula, 1977.
Smallwood, E. M., *The Jews under Roman Rule.* Leiden, 1976.
- 'Domitian's Attitude towards the Jews and Judaism', *Classical Philology* 51 (1956), pp.1ff.
Smith, J. Z., 'The Prayer of Joseph', in ed. J. Neusner *Religions in Antiquity*, pp.253ff.
Smith, M., 'Observations on Hekaloth Rabbati', in *Biblical and Other Studies* ed.

A. Altmann. Cambridge, Mass., 1963, pp.142ff.
- 'Pseudepigraphy in the Israelite Literary Tradition', in *Pseudepigrapha I* ed. K. von Fritz, pp.189ff.
- 'The Shape of God and the Humanity of the Gentiles', in ed. J. Neusner *Religions in Antiquity*.
- *Clement of Alexandria and a Secret Gospel of Mark*. Cambridge, Mass., 1973.
Sneen, D., *Visions of Hope*. Minneapolis, 1978.
Stanton, G. N., *Jesus of Nazareth in New Testament Preaching*. Cambridge, 1974.
Stauffer, E., 'Das theologische Weltbild der Apokalyptik', *ZST* 8 (1931), pp.203ff.
- *New Testament Theology*. London, 1955. (Eng. Trs. of *Die Theologie des Neuen Testaments*. Stuttgart, 1948.)
- *Christ and the Caesars*. London, 1955. (Eng. Trs. of *Christus und die Caesaren*. Hamburg, 1952.)
- 'Zum Kalifat des Jakobus', *ZRGG* 4 (1952), pp.1ff.
Steck, O. H., 'Die Aufnahme von Genesis 1 in Jubiläen 2 und 4 Esra 6', *JSJ* 8 (1977), pp.154ff.
Stein, R. H., 'Is the Transfiguration a Misplaced Resurrection-Account?' *JBL* 95 (1976), pp.79ff.
Stier, F., *Gott und sein Engel im Alten Testament*. Münster, 1934.
Stone, M. E., 'The Messiah in 4 Ezra', in *Religions in Antiquity*. ed. J. Neusner pp.295ff.
- 'Paradise in IV Ezra', *JJS* 17 (1966), pp.85ff.
- 'Lists of Revealed Things in Apocalyptic Literature', in ed. F. M. Cross *Magnalia Dei*.
- 'Apocalyptic – Vision or Hallucination', in *Milla wa-Milla* 14 (1974), pp.47ff.
- 'The Book of Enoch and Judaism in the Third Century B.C.E.', *CBQ* 40 (1978), pp.479ff.
- *Scriptures, Sects and Visions*. London, 1980.
Strobel, A., *Kerygma und Apokalyptik*. Göttingen, 1967.
- 'Schreiben des Lukas? Zum sprachlichen Problem der Pastoralbriefe', *NTS* 15 (1968–9), pp.191ff.
- 'Abfassung und Geschichtstheologie der Apokalypse nach Kap. 17.9–12', *NTS* 10 (1963–4), pp.433ff.
Stuhlmacher, P., *Das paulinische Evangelium: I Vorgeschichte*. Göttingen, 1968.
Sweet, J. P. M., *Revelation*. London, 1979.
Swete, H. B., *The Apocalypse of St. John*. London, 1906.
Talbert, C. H., 'The Myth of a Descending–Ascending Redeemer in Mediterranean Antiquity', *NTS* 22 (1976), pp.418ff.
Talmon, S., 'The Calendar Reckoning of the Sect from the Judaean Desert', *Scripta Hierosolymitana (Aspects of the Dead Sea Scrolls* ed. C. Rabin and Y. Yadin) 4 (1958), pp.162ff.
Tannehill, R. C., *Dying and Rising with Christ*. Berlin, 1967.
Taylor, L. R., *The Divinity of the Roman Emperor*. Connecticut, 1931.
Taylor, V., *The Gospel according to Saint Mark*. London, 1966.
Tcherikover, A., *Hellenistic Civilisation and the Jews*. Philadelphia, 1961.
Testuz, M., *Les idées religieuses du livre des Jubilés*. Paris, 1960.
Thackeray, H. St. J., *The Relation of St. Paul to Contemporary Jewish Thought*. London, 1900.
Theisohn, J., *Der auserwählte Richter*. Göttingen, 1975.
Thoma, C., 'Auswirkungen des jüdischen Krieges gegen Rom (66–70/73) auf

das rabbinische Judentum', *BZ* 12 (1968), pp.30ff. and 186ff.
– 'Jüdische Apokalyptik am Ende des ersten nachchristlichen Jahrhunderts', *Kairos* 11 (1969), pp.134ff.
Thorndike, J. P., 'The Apocalypse of Weeks and the Qumran Sect', *RQ* 3 (1961), pp.163ff.
Tödt, H. E., *The Son of Man in the Synoptic Tradition*. London, 1965. (Eng. Trs. of *Der Menschensohn in der synoptischen Überlieferung*. Gütersloh, 1963.)
Trites, A. A., *The Concept of Witness in the New Testament*. Cambridge, 1977.
Tröger, K. W., 'Spekulativ-esoterische Ansätze (Frühjudentum und Gnosis)', in *Literatur und Religion des Frühjudentums*, pp.310ff.
Tupper, F., *The Theology of Wolfhart Pannenberg*. Philadelphia, 1973.
Turner, N., 'The Testament of Abraham: Problems in Biblical Greek', *NTS* 1 (1954–5), pp.219ff.
Unnik, W. C. van, 'Die geöffneten Himmel in der Offenbarungsvision des Apokryphons des Johannes', in *Apophoreta*, pp.269ff.
Unnik, W. C. van, (ed.) *La littérature juive entre Tenach et Mishna*. Leiden, 1974.
Urbach, E. E., *The Sages: their concepts and beliefs*. Jerusalem, 1975. (Eng. Trs. of *Hazal. Pirke 'Emunot we De'ot*. Jerusalem, 1969.)
– 'The Traditions about Esoteric Teaching in the Tannaitic Period' (in Hebrew) in *Studies in Mysticism and Religion*. Jerusalem, 1967, pp.1ff.
Vanhoye, A., 'L'utilisation du livre d'Ez. dans L'Apocalypse', *Biblica*, 43 (1962), pp.436ff.
Vawter, B., 'Apocalyptic: its Relation to Prophecy', *CBQ* 22 (1960), pp.33ff.
Vermes, G., *The Dead Sea Scrolls: Qumran in Perspective*. London, 1978.
– *Scripture and Tradition*. Leiden, 1973.
– 'Bible and Midrash', in ed. P. R. Ackroyd and C. F. Evans *The Cambridge History of the Bible*, vol. i, pp.199ff.
– *Jesus the Jew*. London, 1973.
Vielhauer, P., 'Apocalyptic' in Hennecke-Schneemelcher (tr. R. Wilson) *New Testament Apocrypha*. London, 1965, ii, pp.608ff.
Volz, P., *Jüdische Eschatologie von Daniel bis Akiba*. Tübingen, 1903.
Wadsworth, M .P., *The 'Liber Antiquitatum Biblicarum' of Pseudo-Philo*. Diss. Oxford, 1975.
Wainwright, G., *Eucharist and Eschatology*. London, 1971.
Weber, F., *Jüdische Theologie auf Grund des Talmud und verwandter Schriften*. Leipzig, 1897.
Weinstock, S., *Divus Julius*. Oxford, 1971.
Weiss, H. F., *Untersuchungen zur Kosmologie des hellenistischen und palästinischen Judentums*. Berlin, 1966.
Weiss, J., *Jesus' Proclamation of the Kingdom of God*. London, 1971. (Eng. Trs. of *Die Predigt Jesu vom Reiche Gottes*. Göttingen, 1892.)
Werner, M., *Die Entstehung des christlichen Dogmas*. Tübingen, 1954.
– *The Formation of Christian Dogma*, London, 1957 (an abridged Eng. Trs. of the previous work).
Wewers, G. A., *Geheimnis und Geheimhaltung im rabbinischen Judentum*. Berlin, 1975.
Whybray, R. N., *The Divine Counsellor in Second Isaiah*. Cambridge, 1971.
Widengren, G., *The Ascension of the Apostle and the Heavenly Book*. Uppsala, 1950.
– *Literary and Psychological Aspects of the Hebrew Prophets*. Uppsala, 1948.
Wilckens, U., 'sophia' *TDNT* vii, pp.465ff.

- *Die Missionsrede im Apostelgeschichte.* Neukirchen, 1961.
- 'Die Bekehrung des Paulus als religionsgeschichtliche Problem', *ZTK* 56 (1959), pp.273ff.
- 'The Understanding of Revelation within Primitive Christianity', in *Revelation as History.* London, 1969.
Williams, L., 'The Cult of Angels at Colossae', *JTS* 10 (1908–9), pp.413ff.
Williamson, H. G. M., *Israel in the Books of Chronicles.* Cambridge, 1977.
Williamson, R., *Philo and the Epistle to the Hebrews.* Leiden, 1970.
Wilson, R. Mcl., *Gnosis and the New Testament.* Oxford, 1968.
Windisch, H., 'Angelophanien um den Menschensohn auf Erde. Ein Kommentar zu Joh. 1.51', *ZNW* 30 (1931), pp.215ff.
- *Paulus und Christus. Ein biblisch-religionsgeschichtlicher Vergleich.* Leipzig, 1934.
- *Der zweite Korintherbrief.* Göttingen, 1924.
Wolfson, H. A., 'The Pre-existent Angel of the Magharians and al-Nahawandi', *JQR* 51 (1960), pp.89ff.
- *Philo.* Cambridge, Mass., 1948.
Woude, A. S., van der, *Die messianischen Vorstellungen der Gemeinde von Qumran.* Assen, 1957.
Yamauchi, E., *Pre-Christian Gnosticism.* London, 1973.
York, A. D., 'The Dating of Targumic Literature', *JSJ* 5 (1974), pp.49ff.
Zeitlin, S., 'Dreams and their Interpretations from the Biblical Period to the Tannaitic Time: a History Study', *JQR* 66 (1975), pp.1ff.
Zimmerli, W., *Ezechiel.* Neukirchen, 1969.

Indexes

INDEX OF ANCIENT SOURCES

OLD TESTAMENT

Genesis
1.— 146ff, 276, 494(38)
1.1 16, 147
1.2 147, 149, 324ff, 362
1.6 148, 301, 329f
1.7 220, 225, 331
1.26 79, 216, 439
2.8ff 315, 382
2.15 382
2.16 150
5.23 120
5.24 62, 109, 262, 386, 485(46), 486(56)
6.1 93, 154
9.12ff 59
14.17ff 109
15.12 62
15.17 53, 62
16.7ff 94
16.13 94
18.2 95
21.18 95
22.— 499(14)
22.11 95, 367
28.12 398, 510(175)
28.18 502(47)
31.11 95
35.13f 501(40), 502(47)
37.5f 452(23)
35.20 502(47)
40.— 452(23)
49.— 18

Exodus
7.17 517(82)
19.16 161, 222, 293, 368
24.10 153, 220, 303, 491(38)
24.12 51
25.4 102
25.9 83
25.40 83, 463(17)
26.35 224
28.4 102
33.20 84, 280, 439

Leviticus
16.2ff 83
19.12 439
26,11f 439

Numbers
14.2 517(82)
15.38f 102, 302f
16.22 104
24.17 32
27.16 104

Deuteronomy
4.2 20
10.14 83
17.6 517(82)
19.15 517(82)
22.7 332
32.8 89
32.11 324ff, 362
33.— 18
33.2 161

Joshua
5.14 41

Judges
1.13 16
3.9 16
3.11 16
6.21 501(40)
6.24 502(47)
9.7ff 61
13.3ff 94
13.20 501(40)

1 Samuel
15.27 201

1 Kings
6.14 83
6.19 83
6.21 221
6.29 219, 463(18)
7.23 225
8.27 83
8.38 432
17.1 517(82)
22.19 53, 78, 199, 424
22.20ff 199

2 Kings
1.8 202
1.10 517(82)
2.9 62
6.15f 41
18.9ff 143
23.10 125

1 Chronicles
24.7ff 224
28.18 463(17)
29.23 497(66)

2 Chronicles
4.7 224

Ezra
7.6 64
7.8 63
10.— 63

Nehemiah
2.8 382, 506(110)
8.— 63

Job
1.— 2.— 91
1.12 206
1.18 205
2.7 205
4.ff 205
4.12ff 481(39)
19.25ff 205
38.f 146, 205, 207
42.6 206

Psalms
2.7 499(14)
18.7ff 158, 161
45.6 102
46.2 125
49.16 63
68.33 83
73.24 63
78.35 467(73)
80.8f 61
82.1 79, 109
82.5 79
95.1 467(73)
97.5 161
99.1 96
116.15 322, 493(29)
148.4 83

Proverbs
8.22ff 184
8.27 149

Ecclesiastes
2.5 506(110)
2.14f 205
3.11 205
5.5f 334
9.9f 205

Song of Solomon
1.4   310
4.13   382

Isaiah
5.—   61
6.—   63, 279, 301, 394
6.1   79, 199, 219, 222, 381, 401
6.2   87, 223
6.3   223ff
6.5   439
6.8   365
6.9   199
10.5   195
11.1ff   437
13.ff   136, 434
13.10   158
13.13   158
20.24   202
21.1ff   231, 243
24.ff   197f
25.6   197
26.19ff   197
40.—   79
42.1   499(14)
44.6   467(73)
59.2ff   194
59.14ff   195
60.11   438
61.1   361
63.1ff   194
64.1   11, 80
65.17ff   195, 437, 474(17)

Jeremiah
1.1ff   381
1.11   236
2.21   61
4.19ff   231
14.1   202
14.12   158
16.6   202
21.7   158
23.9   500(20)
25.11f   215
45.1   64
51.—   434
51.13   238

Ezekiel
1.—   55, 199, 218ff, 276, 280, 301, 381, 394
1.1   54, 80, 359
1.4   97, 219, 293, 296, 367
1.5f   87, 97
1.7   99
1.10   223
1.12   103
1.13   99, 221, 224
1.14   219
1.16   99, 221
1.18   223
1.19f   219

1.22   153, 219, 220, 221, 225
1.23   99
1.24   99, 101, 480(12)
1.26f   85, 95f, 221f, 280, 294, 303, 341, 491(38)
1.27   86, 95f, 99, 280, 487(13)
1.28   59, 102, 224, 296, 367, 464(40)
2.—   58
2.1   100, 199, 365, 369
2.8ff   481(33)
3.1   428
3.2f   229
3.12   158, 201
3.25ff   201
4.—5.—   201
8.2   80, 95f, 201
8.3   97, 363
9.2   96, 99
9.4   418
10.—   87, 96, 219, 280
10.4   96, 280
13.12   158
14.21   158
15.—   61
17.7   61
19.10f   61
20.—   136
26.—32.—   136
28.13   99, 101, 224, 315, 382
37.ff   515(54)
38.—   515(54)
40.ff   194, 199, 515(54)
40.2   199
40.3   199f, 429
47.1   224

Daniel
1.—6.—   11
2.—   136f
2.ff   450(7)
2.28   14
2.29   26
2.31ff   12, 49, 137, 166, 204
2.35   137
2.36ff   137
2.44   166
3.25   182
4.13   49
4.19ff   204
5.13ff   204
5.14   204
5.16   204
5.24f   49
7.—12.—   11, 49, 204, 241
7.1ff   12, 14, 136f, 137, 166, 180, 255f, 431, 450(12), 460(17)
7.2   97, 170, 179, 186, 217

7.8   138, 179
7.9f   55, 78, 80, 85, 97, 100, 104, 179, 180, 186, 221, 255f, 276, 338, 398, 450(8), 466(60)
7.10   106, 108, 221, 224
7.11   166, 179
7.13   96, 100, 178ff, 183, 186f, 216, 257, 265, 426
7.14   179, 181
7.15   372
7.17ff   13, 137, 178, 179, 180, 181
7.21   476(39)
7.22   179, 181
7.25   167, 179
7.27   179, 181
8.—9.—   136f, 138, 166
8.3ff   12, 57
8.9ff   138, 251
8.15ff   12, 98, 154, 182, 200
8.16   88
8.19ff   57, 200
8.25   138
9.1ff   44, 215
9.3   228
9.24   215, 217
9.26   450(9)
9.27   44, 215
10.—12.—   136f, 138, 200
10.1   381
10.2ff   58, 228, 364
10.5ff   98f, 101, 182, 367, 414
10.9   100, 231, 367
10.10ff   88
10.12   228
10.13   89
10.16   375
10.20ff   56
10.21   58, 98
11.21   138
11.31   44, 251
11.34   211
11.45   138
12.1   88, 136f, 138, 156, 182, 365
12.2   12, 138, 167
12.7   308
12.11   12, 27, 44

Joel
2.10f   198
2.28ff   69
3.18ff   198

Amos
1.1   381
1.3ff   136
8.1ff   236

Micah
1.4   161

APOCRYPHA

1 Maccabees
1.54　251
2.42　211
4.36ff　251
4.44ff　69
7.13　211
9.27　69
14.41　69

2 Maccabees
3.24　104

De Vita Contemp.
11.f　470(106)
28　44

Op. Mundi
20　148, 495(47)
72　148
171　331

De Spec. Leg
i.81　148, 495(47)

Leg. Alleg
iii.96　148

Sacr. Abel et Cain
8　148

BJ
ii.159　479(30)
ii.174　501(45)
ii.433　503
v.233　480(13)
vi.70ff　512(16)

Apoc. Moses
— 37.5　383

Assumption of Moses
— 17
2.ff　136f, 140
3.— 4.—　140
6.2　140
6.8　140
9.1ff　140

Life of Adam and Eve
25.—　16, 136f, 382, 493(16)
25.3　382
33.1ff　16
48.4ff　89
49.1　17

4.30ff　450(9)

Sirach
3.21ff　75, 204, 205, 306
3.23　348
24.23ff　149
34.1ff　204
42.15ff　136
44.16　386, 485(46),
　　　507(133)
49.8f　219

PHILO

Quod Deus Immut
57　148

De Fuga
94　148

De Cher.
127.f　148

Legatio
135.ff　412

Haggai
1.— 2.—　194
2.7　158

Zechariah
1.— 14.—　194

JOSEPHUS

vii.40　412, 514(33)
vii.407ff　411

Ant.
iii.188　491(38)

JEWISH PSEUDEPIGRAPHA

Pseudo-Philo (Lab)
18.5　460(30)
28.—　16, 151ff, 481(35)
28.7　152
28.8　153, 154
28.9　152
60.2　152f

Prayer of Joseph
—　468(84)

Psalms of Solomon
17　42, 163, 172

Sibylline Oracles
—　20
iii.46　21

49.14　386, 482(55), 485(46),
　　　507(133)

Wisdom of Solomon
2.2　207
2.21ff　430
3.— 4.—　205
4.11　386
8.6　148
9.4　103
18.— 19.—　479(28)

1.— 6.—　89, 199, 201
1.1　383
1.2f　200
1.19　200
3.1ff　91, 200
4.1　200
4.2ff　200, 224
4.10　224
4.14　200, 517(82)
6.9ff　200
8.20　163
13.2ff　68, 201
13.4　202
13.6　202
14.4　158
14.8　224

viii.79　225
xii.125　411
xiv.223ff　409
xvi.27ff　411
xix.300　411
xx.9.7　472(7)

iii.767ff　21
iv.121　253
v.145　253
v.12　404
v.256ff　475(35)

Ezekiel the Tragedian
—　102

Joseph and Asenath
14.3　466(60)

Testaments of the Twelve Patriarchs
—　15, 18
Test. Joseph
19.1ff　163

JEWISH APOCALYPTIC LITERATURE

1 Enoch
—　50, 160
1.3ff　50, 161
1.8f　161
2.— 5.—　50

6.— 11.—　51, 92, 93, 160,
　　　250
6.1ff　154
7.1　93
8.3　93

9.1　88
9.6　93
10.13　92
10.17　161
11.2　161

1 Enoch (cont.)
12.— 16.— 93, 514(42)
12.1 64, 93, 337, 386
12.2 242
13.8ff 242
14.— 55, 84
14.— 36.— 93, 124f, 160,
    250
14.4ff 242
14.6 242
14.8ff 17, 63, 80, 84, 180,
    218f, 233, 241, 255f,
    276, 342, 510(182)
14.9 219, 220, 502(53)
14.10 83, 219, 401
14.11 219, 220, 367,
    463(18)
14.12 219
14.13 232, 242
14.14 219, 222, 231
14.15 78
14.17 219, 221, 367
14.18 83, 108, 219, 255,
    293
14.19 106, 219, 221, 255
14.20f 78, 85, 108, 222,
    255f, 367
14.22 219
14.25 242
15.1ff 199, 241
16.4 199, 242
17.ff 124
18.11 92
18.12 124
19.1f 124, 200
21.7 92
21.10 124
22.— 124
22.4 161
22.9 161
22.10f 161
24.— 125, 161
25.1f 124
25.3 125
25.5 162
26.— 124
27.— 124
32.2f 124, 170, 382, 400,
    493(16), 506(114)
37.— 71.— 104f, 165f,
    178ff, 250
39.6f 476(55)
40.2 88, 105
40.8 200
41.ff 120, 165
42.— 183
45.3 165, 184, 476(55)
45.4 166
46.1 104
46.2 104
46.3 476(55)
46.4 106, 165, 184, 476(55)
47.3 105

48.2 104, 185, 467(73)
48.3 467(73), 476(55)
49.2 372, 516(72)
51.1ff 166
54.6ff 88
55.1 104
56.5ff 166
58.1ff 166
60.2 104, 105
61.8 104, 165, 184
62.2 476(55)
62.7 185
62.9 165
62.10ff 106, 165
62.14 105
62.15 114, 166, 398
69.27 184, 476(55)
69.29 104
70.— 71.— 262
70.4 382
71.1ff 63, 105, 106, 184,
    383, 497(66)
71.2 87, 466(65)
71.3f 55, 227, 381
71.5ff 106, 467(75)
71.7 88, 344
71.8ff 88
71.10 85, 104
71.11 100, 231
71.13 104
71.14 104, 337
71.15f 166, 265
71.16 426
72.ff 51, 55, 120ff
76.f 125
77.3 493(16)
78.f 120ff
81.1f 460(16)
82.3f 121
83.ff 51, 252
85.ff 139, 140, 162, 420,
    450(11)
85.1f 58, 136f, 160
88.1 92
89.10ff 139
89.59ff 90, 143, 180
89.61 514(42)
90.1ff 139
90.6 162, 211, 252
90.8f 211, 252
90.11 252
90.13ff 139, 157, 158, 162,
    211, 252, 420
90.15 162
90.19 42, 162, 163, 164
90.20ff 158, 162
90.23ff 92, 162
90.26 162
90.30ff 163
90.33 163
90.35 163
90.37 163
91.ff 49, 252, 255

91.5ff 163
91.12ff 136f, 140, 156, 163,
    474(13)
91.14 474(15)
91.42 252
93.— 136f, 140, 156, 163
93.2 227, 460(16)
93.8 140, 164
93.10 474(13)
93.13 164
93.15 164
94.6ff 163
97.— 100.— 163
100.6 20
103.2 163, 460(16)
104.11 20
105.2 255
106.19 460(16)

Slavonic Enoch
1.5 466(65)
3.3 225
7.1 154
8.— 381, 493(16)
16.— 120
18.— 92, 154
20.1ff 82
21.5 82
22.1 82, 382, 496(59)
22.6 365
22.8ff 114, 398
22.11 89
23.1 227, 506(117)
24.— 33.— 148
24.1 94, 485(47), 497(66)
24.2 148
24.3 151
25.ff 17, 55, 148f
25.1 148, 149, 152
25.4 150
26.1 149
27.1 152
29.1ff 150
30.8ff 150
30.11 150
30.13ff 127
30.15 145, 150
33.6 50
33.10 365
36.2 262
37.1f 114, 384
39.2 28
40.1 19
42.— 92
53.2 145
64.5 467(76)
65.6f 28

Jubilees
1.1 51
1.23ff 167, 398
1.26ff 51, 167
2.2 88, 146f
2.7 147

Jubilees (cont.)
2.17   121
4.15   464(32)
4.17   64, 120
4.18   93, 467(76)
4.22   63, 93, 382, 493(16)
4.23   124, 170, 337
6.32ff   120
8.12ff   126
15.31f   90
23.9   167
23.13ff   156, 167
23.27   158
23.31   167

Syriac Baruch
1.— 2.—   50
1.1   63, 254
3.—   131
4.2ff   56, 133
4.3ff   382, 460(30)
5.7   228
6.—   63, 143, 254
9.2   228
12.5   228
14.—   131
14.7   132
15.5f   132
15.7   132, 170
17.1ff   132
19.6   216
19.14ff   132f
20.—   133
20.1f   133, 170, 254
22.1   53, 228
25.— 30.—   42, 157f, 171
27.1ff   33, 416, 435, 438,
          457(50)
29.3ff   171
30.4   171
31.ff   50
36.— 40.—   136f, 141, 172,
          239f
36.—   53, 60, 172, 180, 239
36.5   141
36.8   141
39.2f   239
39.5   239
40.1ff   239
43.1ff   50
44.12   173
47.2   228
48.—   50
48.40ff   132
49.ff   134, 172
53.— 74.—   53, 136f, 139,
          141, 173ff, 189,
          450(11)
54.15   132
54.19   132
55.1ff   133
56.6   132
67.6   141

68.4   141, 142
69.—   141
72.— 74.—   141
72.2   457(50)
76.f   50
78.ff   50
85.3   254
85.7   145
85.10   27, 171

Greek Baruch
—   81f
13.5ff   82

4 Ezra
1.— 2.—   250
3.1   50, 484(14)
3.4ff   50, 128, 216
3.7   54
3.13f   460(30)
3.20   216
3.21ff   128, 207
3.28   128
3.29ff   216
4.1   89
4.3ff   170, 207
4.7   382
4.8   53
4.11   128
4.21   128
4.26   128
4.50   27
5.1ff   157
5.23ff   128
5.34ff   128
5.56   494(37)
6.1ff   56
6.7   168
6.28   158
6.29   231
6.38ff   128, 147f, 216
6.40   148
6.55ff   216
7.—   128f
7.1ff   216
7.11   216
7.12   216
7.14   216
7.20f   168
7.26ff   129, 131, 168, 171,
          435
7.28f   187
7.31   25, 48
7.33ff   48, 158, 168
7.47   129
7.50   168
7.68   54
7.72   129
7.75ff   168
7.102ff   129
7.106ff   217
7.112ff   217
7.118   130
7.129   168

7.132   130
8.4ff   130
8.20   54
8.37   130
8.52f   130, 169, 382
9.ff   180
9.1   157
9.23ff   228
9.32ff   130
9.38ff   50, 53, 133, 169, 253,
          394
10.5ff   169
10.21   461(34)
10.25   169
10.45ff   131, 169
10.55   169
11.— 12.—   131, 136f, 140,
          170, 217, 234
11.12ff   217
12.10f   172, 186, 217, 450(12)
12.30ff   141, 170
13.—   170, 186f, 217, 477(62)
13.25ff   170, 186
13.29   157
13.35   187
13.37ff   42, 187
13.40   131, 170
14.—   19
14.9   187
14.10f   169
14.18ff   229
14.27ff   50
14.38f   64, 228
14.47   445
14.49   54
15.— 16.—   250

Apocalypse of Abraham
4   482(53)
9   228
10.f   338f
11   98
13   127
15.ff   17, 53, 80, 154, 233
17.f   84, 102, 114, 225, 227,
          231, 338f, 381
18.ff   55, 86, 88, 223, 276
19   82, 103, 506(109)
20   127, 199, 227, 474(24)
21   55, 144
22   57, 144
23   127, 474(24)
24   207
26   482(53)
27.ff   136f, 254
29   260

Testament of Abraham
(Greek Rec. A)
—   259, 264
10.ff   17, 53, 80, 398, 501(30)
11   107, 166, 382
12   367, 497(66)
13   260

Testament of Abraham (cont.)
14   493(16), 509(172)
20   382

Testament of Abraham
(Greek Rec. B)
8   225
11   64, 355, 467(76)
14   260

Apocalypse of Zedrach
—   87

Mishnah
Megillah
4.10   276

Hagigah
2.1   54, 75, 271, 277, 328,
        347, 348, 496(61)

Yebamoth
4.13   494(33)

Sanhedrin
10.1   34

Eduyoth
2.10   33

Aboth
1.1   67
2.8   290, 296
3.1   328
3.2   274
3.15   274
3.16   35
6.1   70, 272

Tosefta
Berakoth
1.10   457(34)
3.4   496(61)

Pesahim
2.15   489(11)

Megillah
4.28   299f
4.34   277, 487(8)

Hagigah
2.1   282ff
2.2   282, 296, 495(43)
2.3   309ff
2.5   471(6)
2.6   301, 323
2.7   487(14)

Sotah
13.2   68, 363

Sifre on Nu.
¶115   302

**Mekilta de R. Simeon B.
Yohai**
Mishpatim
20.1   283ff

Mekilta de R. Ishmael
on Ex. 16.29   456(30)

Testament of Levi
(Greek)
—   263
2.f   63, 381
2.6   78, 415
2.7   225
3.1ff   81, 264
3.2   92
3.4   83
3.5   486(53)
8.19   506(117)

RABBINIC LITERATURE

Babylonian Talmud
Berakoth
7a   466(60)
22a   494(33)
28b   32, 456(27), 490(28)
61b   322

Shabbath
147b   297

Pesahim
50a   507(135)
54a   41, 147, 149, 185

Megillah
3a   100, 272
24a   370
24b   299f, 491(36)
31a   293, 487(9)

Hagigah
12a   152, 473(28)
12b   81, 82, 153, 344,
        466(63), 473(29),
        486(53)
13a   299, 487(13), 488(19)
14a   338f
14b   220, 282ff, 309ff,
        488(8), 492(13)
15a   323f, 495(49)
15b   313, 332

Yebamoth
63b   290, 494(31)

Baba Metsiah
59a   307

Baba Batra
158b   494(33)

Sanhedrin
37b   338
94a   33ff, 457(34)
95b   457(34)
97a   33, 416, 458(57)
97b   307
99a   457(32)

Menahoth
43b   102, 303

Hullin
91b   100

Jerusalem Talmud
Berakoth
5a   36

9.3   19
10.1   19
18.5ff   259
18.10   381

Testament of Naphtali
—   16, 263, 404(27)

Testament of Amram
—   15

Yoma
5.2   398, 466(60)
Ta'anith
68d   32
Mo'ed Qatan
3.1 (81d)   307
Hagigah
77a   282ff, 306, 319, 471(6),
        493(19)
77b   292, 303ff, 323f, 332
77c   306, 493(19)
Abodah Zarahh
3.1   493(29)

Ber. R.
1.1   149
1.4   149
2.4   323f
4.6   331
25.—   460(32), 486(56)
48.9   463(24)
62.2   493(29), 494(32)

Shem. R.
28.—   100
30.8   319
47.7   67
52.3   493(29)

Shir Ha-Shirim R.
1.4   309ff
1.10   292, 322, 493(25)

Ekah R.
2.2   494(30)

Koh. R.
7.7   297
7.8   332

Hebrew Enoch
—   344
1.3   398
1.7   398
10   110, 468(80)
12   110, 338
14.2   464(27)
15   100
16   100, 335
17.8   464(27)
18   344
18.3   464(27)

Hebrew Enoch (cont.)
25 344
26.12 464(27)
35.2 100
44 345
45 227
48 91, 100, 111
48.9f 91

Shemoneh Esreh
— 32, 36

Visions of Ezekiel
— 496(58)

Pseudo-Jonathan
Genesis
5.24 64, 337, 467(76),
        507(135)
22.10 502(55)
28.12 490(23)

Exodus
24.10 491(38)

1QS
3.7ff 500(23)
3.15 35
4.15ff 35
4.21 500(23)
8.5 119
8.18 45
9.11 263
9.17 45
11.7f 116f

1QH
3.7ff 517(84)
3.20 116f
7.6 500(23)

Midrash Conen
— 149

Pirke de R. Eliezer
— 153, 343

Derek Erets Zuta
11 31

Aboth de R. Nathan
14 297
23.ff 492(11), 493(29)

TARGUMIM

Fragment Targum
Genesis
15.17 460(30)
28.13 490(23)

Neophyti I
Genesis
28.12 490(23)

DEAD SEA SCROLLS

11.10ff 116f
16.12 500(23)
17.26 500(23)

1QpHAB
7.1ff 45, 115
11 470(110)

1QM
1.11 40
10.8ff 104, 116
12.4ff 40, 117
15.14 40
17.5ff 89, 181, 464(26)
17.6 40

OTHER WORKS

Suetonius
— 405
Nero
57 406
Domitian
12 407
13 407

24 495(50)
25 32, 496(61)
28 493(19)
31 456(26)
37 450(5)

Hekaloth R.
3 346
13 22
17.ff 398
18 230, 481(38)
19 467(78)
20 274

Onkelos
Genesis
28.12 490(23)

Targum Jonathan to the Prophets
Isaiah
43.12 460(30)

1QpNah
3.1f 409

1Q Gen Apoc
— 18, 464(32)

1QSa
— 263

4Q S1
— 16, 86, 103, 106, 221,
    480(12)

11Q Melchizedek
— 109, 185, 264, 458(63),
    497(66)

Tacitus
Annals
xiv.27 511(13)
xv.44 408
Histories
ii.8 512(15)
v.11 512(16)

Dio Cassius
Histories
1xvii. 14.1f 408
1xviii.1.2 407, 512(20)

Mithras Liturgy
— 482(43)

NEW TESTAMENT

Matthew
1.18f 253
1.20 503(69)
1.24 503(69)
3.11 363
3.13ff 359
3.16 359
3.17 359
4.3 364
5.29 504(79)
12.24ff 365

17 396f
17.2 367, 501(43)
17.6 100, 367
18.9 504(79)
25.31ff 43, 264, 266
Mark
1.8 363
1.10f 16, 359
1.11 360
1.12ff 364
3.22ff 365

4.11 458(54)
9.2ff 366f
9.8 501(40)
12.18ff 34
12.35 114
13.— 43ff
13.2 43
13.4ff 43
13.9ff 43, 358
13.13 158
13.14ff 43, 44

Mark (cont.)
13.20 158
13.24f 46
13.26 43, 46, 182, 458(62)
14.62 183, 370

Luke
1.11 368, 501(40), 503(67)
1.22 63, 375, 380
1.27 253
1.38 501(40)
2.15 501(40)
3.16 363
3.21 359
3.22 359
4.2 364
4.16 363
9.— 366f
9.29 367, 501(43)
10.18 359, 364f, 372
10.19f 366
11.15ff 365
11.20 358
11.52 64
16.16 362
17.30 377
22.29 435
22.66 504(79)
22.69 370
23.43 398
24.23 375
24.40 372

John
1.51 359
5.27 266
6.69 501(45)
12.31 365
12.41 401
15.26 516(71)
Acts
1.11 369
2.1ff 368ff
2.3 368, 501(40)
2.17 47, 69
2.33 485(47), 516(71)
3.19ff 47
4.8 369
7.31 501(40)
7.54 369
7.55 369, 499(12)
7.56 16, 78, 359, 364, 369f, 372, 516(72)
8.26 373
8.39 385
9.1 374
9.3ff 375, 504(79)
9.10 373
9.12 501(40)
9.17 368, 501(40)
10.— 372
10.3 501(40)
10.7 501(40)
10.9 372

10.10 330, 372
10.11 16, 359f, 371f
10.14 372
10.16 501(40)
10.17 372, 501(40)
10.19 501(40)
10.28 371
10.44 371, 373
11.3 371
11.5 371, 372, 501(40)
11.13 373
11.17 371, 373
12.9 373
13.42 504(79)
13.45f 504(79)
14.17 504(79)
15.28 373
16.9f 373
16.14 504(79)
17.5 511(13)
21.21 374
22.5 504(79)
22.6ff 375
22.10 504(79)
22.11 504(79)
22.17 373, 379, 505(91)
23.6f 34
26.11 504(79)
26.12ff 375, 504(79)
26.14 504(79)
26.16 368, 501(40), 504(79)
26.17 504 (79)
26.19 375, 380
27.23 373, 379
27.25 504(79)

Romans
1.17f 376
7.— 374
8.15 438
8.19 376, 435
8.33 431
8.39 431
11.25 383

1 Corinthians
1.7 377, 378, 380, 505(101)
2.6ff 506(118)
3.13 377, 438
6.2 435
7.25 20
9.1 375
13.1 383
14.18 375
14.26f 70
15.— 172
15.3ff 501(40)
15.6ff 368
15.7 503(72)
15.8 374, 375
15.20 434
15.51 383
2 Corinthians
3.18 384

5.1f 114
5.10 259
5.13 384
11.5 379
11.23ff 379, 384
11.30 244
12.1 378
12.2ff 81, 244, 313, 365, 375, 378, 510(182)
12.4 380, 381, 385
12.5 384
12.7 244, 384
12.10 384
Galatians
1.— 2.— 374
1.1 505(92)
1.4· 504(79)
1.12 375f, 379, 380
1.15 378
1.16 375f
2.1 374
2.11f 371
2.12 373
3.23 376
4.6 438
4.26 459(14)

Philippians
1.23 384
2.11 113

Colossians
1.26f 506(118)
2.14 434, 507(139)
2.16 409
2.18 229
3.1ff 485(47)

1 Thessalonians
4.15ff 47, 385, 415, 437
5.1 380

2 Thessalonians
1.7 377, 380
2.3ff 406, 415, 518(90)
2.6ff 376

1 Timothy
3.16 507(139)
4.14 504(79)
6.20 309

2 Timothy
4.10 512(21)

Hebrews
1.1 113
1.3 113, 485(47)
1.4 113
6.4 391
6.19 426
7.2 109
9.11 113
10.28ff 391
11.4 109
11.5 485(46)

Hebrews (cont.)
12.6ff 391
12.9 104
12.22 459(14)

1 Peter
1.7 377
1.12 45, 293
1.13 47, 377
1.16 439
2.12 440
3.22 507(139)

2 Peter
1.16 501(40)
3.10ff 474(15)

1 John
2.18f 505(89), 518(90)
5.16 391

Revelation
1.1 11, 103, 380
1.3 424
1.6 435, 439, 517(82)
1.7 430
1.9 13, 235, 423
1.10 414, 424, 514(42)
1.12 429
1.13ff 98, 100f, 367, 398,
     466(63)
1.16 102, 108
1.18 230
1.19 20, 414, 424, 514(42)
2.— 3.— 50, 145, 392, 399,
     424
2.1 514(42)
2.4 392, 424, 511(13)
2.7 315, 381, 419, 439, 440
2.8ff 392, 511(13)
2.9 409, 415, 424
2.10 413
2.13 413
2.14 409, 424
2.17 442
2.20 409, 424
2.26 440
3.2 415
3.5 440
3.12 440
3.15 392
3.17 424, 511(13)
3.21 440
4.ff 413, 414, 420, 424
4.— 12, 55, 58f, 81, 114,
     180, 218, 235, 276,
     301, 399, 401, 421, 425
4.1 78, 348, 359, 382, 401,
     459(9)
4.2 80, 86, 414, 415, 424
4.3 59, 99, 102, 224
4.4 224
4.5 222, 224

4.6ff 220, 223, 224f
4.8 223
4.10 225
5.— 425
5.4 515(61)
5.5 419, 425, 434
5.6 370, 517(88)
5.9 426
5.10 435
5.12 434
6.ff 12, 156, 227, 415, 418,
     425
6.9 224
6.11 401
6.17 418
7.— 420, 514(57)
7.3 418, 428
7.4ff 409, 429
7.9 401, 419
7.14 418, 426, 428, 515(61)
7.17 100, 426
8.— 235
8.1 418
9.12 515(48)
9.13ff 419, 422, 428
9.20 158, 419, 427
10.— 15.— 419, 420, 428f
10.1 102
10.6 428
10.11 419, 428, 515(61)
11.— 14.— 60, 239, 421
11.1ff 419, 425, 428f, 441,
     442, 512(16)
11.4 429
11.6 419
11.7 429
11.8 430, 512(16)
11.11 430, 435
11.13 430, 440, 517(83)
11.14 515(48)
11.15f 419
11.19 235, 368, 501(40)
12.1ff 398, 421, 430, 439,
     501(40)
12.3 368, 501(40)
12.5 385
12.7 89, 92, 364f, 421, 430
12.10 366, 431
12.11 431
12.12 366, 421, 431
12.13ff 235, 421, 431
12.17 398, 421
13.f 13f, 407f, 410, 413,
     421f, 430
13.1f 92, 428
13.2 433, 505(89)
13.3 252, 413, 517(88)
13.4 421f, 431, 436
13.6 432
13.7 421
13.8 422, 431, 518(100)
13.9 50
13.11f 408

13.12ff 405, 432
13.15 413, 421, 432
13.16 432
13.17 413
13.18 44
14.— 418, 421, 432
14.9f 422
14.12 50, 422
15.1 417, 422, 433
15.2ff 224, 235, 422, 433
15.5ff 235
16.— 433, 515(48)
16.8 159
16.19 419, 435
16.21 417
17.18 417, 433
17.— 13, 58, 237f
17.1 200, 2238
17.3ff 237, 394, 433
17.4 434
17.6 433
17.8 403ff, 518(100)
17.9 238, 404f, 420
17.11 252, 404f
17.15 238
17.16ff 433
18.11ff 434
19.ff 417
19.9f 235
19.10 429, 430
19.11ff 46, 196, 235, 417,
     434
19.14 432
19.17ff 235, 434
20.1ff 515(54)
20.2 167, 417, 436
20.4 435f
20.5 437
20.6 435
20.7 33, 92, 434, 436,
     515(54)
21.3 224, 439
21.7 438
21.10ff 169, 438
21.14 438
21.24 440
21.27 436
22.1 224, 382
22.2 439
22.3 342, 382
22.4 439
22.5 12
22.6ff 50, 70
22.8 235, 414, 501(40)
22.10 27
22.16 103
22.18 20, 388, 424

EARLY CHRISTIAN LITERATURE

Shepherd of Hermas
Vis.
i.1.4   54, 391
i.3.3   392, 506(116)
ii.2   392, 399
ii.2.4   391
iii.1.6ff   389
iii.10.3   228
iv.1.1ff   389f
iv.1.6   391, 398
iv.1.10   390
v.1.1   398
Sim.
viii.2   401
ix.12.8   388
ix.23.2   391
Mand.
iv.3   391

Polycarp Philippians
11.3   511(13)

Gospel of Peter
10.40   388, 398

Ascension of Isaiah
—   82
2.4   92
3.13f   386
4.2   92, 252
4.9   386
4.14   387
6.10   230, 383
7.1ff   17, 230, 381, 496(58)
7.5   114, 230, 383
7.9   92
7.25   384
8.7   387
8.11   230
9.1   398
9.2   114, 398

9.5   386
9.9   224, 461
9.30   114, 401
11.2f   253, 262
11.34f   114
11.39   506(117)

Odes of Solomon
19.1   481(33)
24.1ff   500(16)
28.1f   500(16)
38.1   467(78)

Ignatius
Trall.
5.2   392

Justin
Dialogue with Trypho
75   401
125f   401

Irenaeus
Adv. Haer.
i.14.2   463(19)
i.26   473(17)
ii.2–3   309
v.30.3   407, 510(5)
v.33.3   474(22)

Hippolytus
Ref.
ix.13.3f   387

Origen
Contra Celsum
5.6   473(17)

Comm. Joh.
ii.12.8   388
ii.12.87   500(26)

Tertullian
De Anima
9   394f
45   509(160)
Adv. Marc.
iii.24   509(160)
De Exhort. Cast.
x.5   509(160)

Passio Perpetuae
—   396f
1.1   398
3.2   244, 397
4.—   233, 397, 398, 400
10.8   398
11.—   398f

Martyrdom of Polycarp
5.2   502(55)
9.1f   502(55), 513(32)
12   512(24)

Epiphanius
Pan.
xix.2.10ff   387
xix.4.3   387
xxx.13.7   359
xlviii.4   509(160)
xlix   393
liii.1.1ff   387

Eusebius
EH
iii.11.1   503(72)
iii.18   512(21)
iii.28.1f   507(140)
iv.26.9   407
v.16.3   393
v.16.7   508(158)
v.16.14   393
v.18.2   394

GNOSTIC TEXTS

Apocalypse of Adam
78ff   517(84)

Apocalypse of Paul
22   510(180)

Apocryphon of John
—   458(53)

45.1ff   495(44)

Gospel of Thomas
Logion
9   501(45)

Hypostasis of the Archons
—   494(38)

143.20ff   496(62)

Triparthe Tractate
—   473(17)

Untitled Work from Codex II
—   473(21)

INDEX OF SUBJECTS

Abel   107f, 467(79)
Abomination of Desolation   44

Abraham   53, 62, 127f, 451(21), 451(22)
Adam   107, 127, 130, 132,

134, 163, 169, 343
Admonitions   50
Akatriel   466(60)

Akiba 32, 220, 292, 306ff, 322, 338
Al-Qirqisani 342, 473(17), 495(46)
Alter Ego 243, 384f
Amram, Testament of 15
Ancient of Days 97f
Angel-Christology 100ff, 387f, 398, 401
Angelology: archangels 88; of Churches in Asia Minor 514(42); Exalted Angel 94ff, 338f, 466(60); interpretative 200; *mal'ak YHWH* 94, 495(55); of nations 89f, 162, 464(27); rebellious angels 93, 164
Animal Apocalypse 42, 139, 251f
Anthropomorphism 105ff, 342
Antiochus Epiphanes 13, 44, 138, 140, 166, 179, 210, 215, 251
Apocalypses: Christian influence 183, 253, 259ff; dates 248ff; eschatology in 156ff; legends in 49, 93; list of 15; structure and form 49ff
Apocalypse of Weeks 163
Apocalyptic: attempted definition 14, 70f, 453(36), 454(3); characteristics of 9ff, 70f, 453(36), 454(3); christianity and 360ff; circumstances leading to 22, 214f; encyclopaedic interests 28, 203ff; eschatology and 23ff; ethical teaching in 459(2); foreign influence 203, 209; gnosticism and 3, 444f; heavenly secrets in 76ff; influence on modern thought 23; origin of 193ff, 214ff, 245ff; pessimism in 195; prophecy and 194f; relationship to rabbinic mysticism 75, 212; setting 208ff, 214ff; types of visions 52ff; vertical dimension 119; wisdom and 203ff
Apotheosis 104ff, 458(63)
Ascension of Isaiah 386f
Asia Minor 393f, 407ff, 424, 431, 513(25)
Assize, Last 158, 167
Astronomical teaching 120ff
Ascents to heaven 17, 53,
80, 87, 199, 220, 223, 230, 313f, 397f, 425
Authority 373f, 391, 423f, 444
Azazel 93, 127, 261,474(24)

Babylon 433ff
Banquet 165, 171
Baptism of Jesus 358ff
Bar Kochba 32
Baruch 63ff, 451(18), 451(19)
Bath Qol 272f, 275, 295, 297, 307, 333, 339, 360, 372, 445
Behemoth 171
Ben Azzai 290, 292, 303ff, 320ff, 509(162)
Ben Zoma 300, 303ff, 321, 323ff, 361f
Biblical Antiquities of Pseudo-Philo 16

Cairo Geniza 263
Calendar 120f
Canaanite influence 79, 97, 257f
Canon, O. T. 31, 66f
Celibacy 322
Cenez, vision of 16, 151ff, 481(35)
Cerinthus 445, 473(17), 507(140)
Cherubim 88, 96
Christology 100ff, 178ff
Chronicles 209
Church in Rev. 419
Colossians 409, 513(26)
Commune Asiae 412, 431
Communion with heaven 113ff
Contemporaneity 64f
Corporate personality 64f
Cosmology 79ff, 263, 301
Covenant 30
Creation 146ff, 272, 276, 301, 323ff, 361f
Crisis 26
Cross 425, 430, 434
Cult: heavenly 83; influence of apocalyptic 63, 83, 118f, 220f, 225

Damascus experience of Paul 374ff
Daniel 11f, 26f, 49, 193, 204; and apocalyptic 11ff; Court tales 49, 204; date 251; relation to 1 Enoch 14 255f
Date of apocalypses 248ff; table 266
Descent–Ascent

Theme 485(48)
Determinism 12, 33, 35, 41, 57, 144
Dialogue form 53, 58, 61
Divine control of history 91
Divine Council 79
Divine intermediaries *see* hypostasis speculation
Domitian, and Rev. 403ff
Door in heaven 78, 359, 458(53)
Dove 324ff
Dragon 397
Dualism 92, 195, 425, 436f, 474(24)

Ecstasy 201f, 229f, 330, 393, 394
Elchesai 387f, 445
Eleazar b. Arak 279, 282ff, 322, 510(181)
Elect one, in Similitudes 476(55)
Eliezer b. Hyrcanus 290
Elijah 60, 181, 262, 419, 502(47)
Elisha b. Abuyah 303ff, 331ff, 493(16)
Emperors, Roman 403f, 431
Enoch 181, 262, 344, 460(31), 485(47), 514(42); apocalyptic seer 53, 80, 93, 241; journeys 93; literature ascribed to 344, 451(15), 451(16), 452(26), 483(7); Similitudes of 47, 104f, 165f, 178, 183f, 264f
Ephesus 431
Eschatology 160ff; apocalyptic 23ff; discontinuity between two ages 27f; function of 415; imminent expectation 35; rabbinic 29ff; realized in Rev. 435; transcendent 37ff, 173, 195
Essenes 113ff
Ethics 25, 459(2)
Evil 91ff
Exile 194f
Experience and Exegesis in apocalyptic 215f, 298, 328, 347, 374, 394f
Ezekiel 54, 359
Ezra 54, 127ff, 167f, 451(20); relationship to Syr. Baruch 255

Fasting 228ff
Fire 87, 290f, 368
Flavia Domitilla 512(22)

Flavius Clemens 407
Four who entered
  pardes 306ff

Gabriel 88, 94, 98, 182
Garden *see* paradise
Garments, heavenly 165,
  222
Gehenna 124f
Gematria 44
Gentiles 162, 163, 164,
  166, 174, 211, 260f, 371,
  428f
Geography 124ff
Glory, divine 95f, 280
Gnosticism 21, 249, 322,
  328, 330f, 337f, 444
God 104, 165;
  Theophanies 59f, 85, 95ff,
  180, 199, 218ff, 467(73)
Gog and Magog 33, 473(3)

Hades 92
Halakah 213
Hashmal 466(54), 487(13),
  488(19)
Hasidim 139, 162, 210f,
  252
Hayyoth 87f
Heavenly tablets 121,
  460(16)
Heavenly world 54f, 78ff,
  313f, 425
Hebrews 112f
Hekaloth literature 22,
  341f
Hell 124
Hellenistic Judaism 259
Hermas, Shepherd of 58,
  388f, 452(25)
Hillel 30, 450(5)
History: despair of 126ff,
  145, 444f; interest
  in 136ff, 471(2)
Historical reviews 13,
  136ff
Hodayoth 113ff
Holy of Holies 83f
Holy Spirit 353f
Human destiny 126ff, 328
Human existence, problem
  of 126ff, 345
Hymns, heavenly 341,
  346, 425
Hypostasis
  speculation 466(56)

Ignatius 508(154)
Imagery 58ff
Imperial cult 406ff, 432,
  513(30)
Intercession 29f
Isaiah 79

James, brother of

Jesus 375ff
Jamnia 64, 131, 254, 282
Jaoel 89, 94, 101f
Jerusalem 133, 162, 168,
  169, 188, 438; church in
  375ff; fall of 27, 31, 63,
  126, 169, 170, 253, 258,
  282, 304f, 484(13)
Jesus: baptism 360f; visions
  of 358ff
Jewish privileges in Asia
  Minor 513(25)
Jewish War against
  Rome 403ff
Jews in Asia Minor 409f
Job, book of 58, 205ff
Johanen b. Zakkai 31f, 64,
  254, 274, 279, 282ff, 346
John of Patmos 13, 403ff
John the Baptist 354, 362
Joseph and
  Asenoth 466(60)
Joseph 204, 451(23);
  Prayer of 468(84)
Josephus 456(24)
Jubilees 51, 167f
Judgement 167, 168, 260
Judgement scenes 106f

Kabbalah 340f
Kabod *see* glory

Ladder 397, 490(23)
Lamb 222, 415ff, 425f,
  516(71)
Legends 13, 62, 93, 241,
  450(13)
Letters to churches in
  Rev. 424
Leviathan 171, 390
Logos 148
Lord of Spirits *see* God

Ma'aseh Bereshith *see*
  Creation
Ma'aseh merkabah *see*
  Merkabah
Magariya 472(17), 495(46)
Mal'ak YHWH see
  angelology
Mani 505(94), 507(140)
Manna 171
Mantic Wisdom 204
Meir 302, 332f
Melchizedek 109
Merits 129f
Merkabah 16, 59, 80f, 95f,
  104f, 149, 180, 218ff, 273,
  276, 279, 282ff, 335f, 338,
  425, 467(72), 497(66)
Messiah 141, 163, 168,
  170, 176f, 182, 184, 263,
  430, 477(62)
Messianic Age 160ff, 168,

171, 202, 417, 435, 436f,
  474(22)
Messianic belief 29, 42,
  176ff, 263
Messianic woes 28, 43,
  156ff, 164, 261, 406, 416f,
  426f
Metatron 110, 312, 334ff,
  344, 370, 466(61)
Michael 82, 88f, 181f, 365,
  421, 430, 464(26), 466(63)
Millennium *see* Messianic
  Age
Monism 92
Montanism 393ff
Moses 60, 67, 419, 502(47)
Mystery 14, 44f, 506(117f)
Mysticism 272ff
Mythology 195, 389f

Name, divine 101ff
Nations *see* Gentiles
Nehuniah b. Hakanah 230
Nero Rediturus 406, 431
New Age 27
New Heaven and Earth in
  Rev. 437

Ophannim 88, 344
Open Heaven 53, 78, 359,
  369, 372, 378, 389, 415

Pachomios 510(184)
Paradise 53, 56, 127, 130,
  147, 168f, 170, 220, 309ff,
  381f, 398, 400, 493(16)
Pardes *see* Paradise
Parousia 47, 377f
Paul: conversion 374ff;
  rapture to third heaven
  and paradise 244, 313,
  379ff
Pentecost 368, 487(9)
Perpetua 236, 244, 396
Persecution 403ff
Peter 330, 371f
Philo 44, 148, 331, 459(19),
  501(45), 502(47), 509(175)
Phrygia 393
Post-exilic religion 193ff
Pre-existence 185, 187,
  387, 401
Preparation for
  Visions 228f
Prophecy: and apocalyptic
  68f, 194f, 201f; after Exile
  68f, 196ff; in Rev. 419
Proto-Apocalyptic 194ff
Pseudepigraphy 13, 61ff,
  198, 214, 240ff, 347, 385
Psychology of visions 243f

Qumran 251, 254;
  communion with heaven

Qumran *(cont.)*
    113ff; Melchizedek
    fragment 109f; merkabah
    fragment 86; War Scroll
    31, 38ff

Rabbinic literature: and
    eschatology 29ff; and
    gnosticism 306, 322, 328,
    330, 337f; and mysticism
    225, 230, 271ff
Rainbow 59, 102, 223, 295f
Resurrection 12, 28, 34,
    134, 166, 167, 168, 172,
    210, 502(49)
Revelation 11f, 26f, 28, 53,
    235ff; authorship 423;
    composition 413ff; date
    and setting 248, 403ff;
    Domitian and 403ff;
    message 423ff; survey of
    contents 422f; visions in
    235ff
Rivers of Fire 221
Rolle Richard 240
Rome 9, 141, 170, 172,
    403ff, 431f

Sabbath,
    eschatological 168
Saints of Most
    High 473(38)
Satan 91, 360, 364f, 430
Satyrus, vision of 233,
    396ff
Scribes 212
Scriptural interpretation *see*
    Experience and Exegesis
Secrets 78ff
Seraphim 88
Shekinah 80, 274, 302
Shemoneh Esreh 32, 36
Shi'ur Komah 85, 341,
    463(19), 466(62), 508(143)
Sibylline Oracles 20
Sicarii 411
Similitudes of Enoch *see*
    Enoch
Sin 128, 130, 132, 150

Sirach 204
Slavonic Enoch 28, 50, 82f
Son of Man 14, 97f, 104f,
    165, 178ff, 264f, 369,
    467(79)
Spirit, Holy 202, 229,
    324ff, 361, 388, 424, 435,
    439
Splitting up of divine
    functions 96, 334ff
Stephen 369f
Streams of fire 221
Suffering, problem
    of 126ff
Symbolism 12
Synopses: Eleazar and
    Johnanan 284ff; Elisha
    and Metatron 335f; Four
    who entered *pardes* 310f;
    Joshua and Ben Zoma
    325ff; Joshua and Jose 295
Synoptic
    'Apocalypse' 38ff

Tallith 302
Teacher of
    Righteousness 45
Temple 44, 166, 429 *see
    also* Cult
Temporary Eschatological
    Kingdom *see* Messianic
    Age
Temptation 366
Teresa of Avila 232f,
    481(35), 509(167)
Tertullian 394
Testament-form 17, 43
Testaments of Twelve
    Patriarchs 17, 451(23)
Theodicy 126ff
Theophany *see* God
Therapeutae 44, 470(106)
Third Isaiah 194ff
Thread of blue 102, 302f
Threat-motif 397, 401
Throne of God *see*
    Merkabah
Torah 29, 130f, 271f, 278,
    292

Traditio-Historical
    Criticism 283
Transcendent eschatology
    see Eschatology
Transfiguration 366f
Trisagion 401
Two ages 27f, 35, 168,
    170, 455(15)
Two power
    controversy 111, 334f

Universalism 209
Urim and Thummim 10
Vaticinia ex eventu 12,
    450(10)
Veil, celestial 221, 227,
    343, 345
Vertical dimension to
    apocalyptic 3, 357
Vision of Black and Bright
    Waters 173
Vision of Forest and
    Vine 172, 180
Visions: call 199, 363;
    criteria for deciding
    authenticity 235ff;
    fragments in
    non-apocalyptic works
    16; in early Christianity
    360ff; and martyrdom
    371, 399; of God 59, 84f,
    295f; possibility of
    authentic visions 66,
    214ff, 230ff, 240ff, 482;
    problems presented by
    122f; type and character
    52ff, 200
War Scroll *see* Qumran
Warrior Messiah 41f, 176f
Watchers 93
Waters, heavenly 220f,
    301, 362
Wisdom: and
    apocalyptic 203ff
Wisdom *see* Hypostasis
    speculations
Witness in Rev. 429f
Wrath 427f
Zealots 41, 411

INDEX OF AUTHORS

Abelson 486(5)
Abrahams 494(40), 500(18)
Ackroyd 461(48), 477(2),
    478(8)
Aland 508(156)
Albright 501(41)

Alexander 452(26),
    468(85), 497(77)
Alsup 502(49), 504(81)
Altmann 473(19)
Anderson 461(45)
Appel 476(52), 482(54)

Aune 469(95)

Bacher 321, 490(29),
    491(4), 493(25), 494(34f),
    495(43f), 496(61)
Back 495(50f), 496(60f)

Bakker 469(88)
Baldensperger 499(1)
Baltensweiler 501(39),
  502(47)
Balz 96, 464(37), 476(52)
Bammel 473(17)
Barbel 469(88)
Barker 464(33)
Barnard 512(20)
Baron 456(24), 457(43)
Barr 457(40), 461(43)
Barrett 2, 362, 449(4),
  456(28), 499(15f), 500(22f),
  503(59), 505(95), 506(124),
  508(154)
Battifol 485(41)
Bauckham 455(12),
  508(148)
Bauernfeind 503(61)
Baumgarten J. 498(9),
  504(87), 505(95f),
  506(104f), 507(128)
Baumgarten J. M. 479(47)
Beardslee 498(9)
Beasley-Murray 458(52),
  458(55), 482(50), 517(79f),
  518(97f)
Becker 498(9)
Beckwith 524
von Beek 509(169)
Beilner 479(44)
Bell 510(4)
Bentzen 476(48)
Benz 505(99)
Berger 510(184)
Best 505(89)
Betz H. D. 449(2),
  506(104f)
Betz O. 456(24), 458(59),
  469(93), 480(6), 481(32),
  494(37), 500(23), 505(91)
Bianchi 483(4)
Bickermann 477(2)
Bietenhard 463(9), 463(15),
  463(23), 464(31), 473(18),
  480(20), 481(24), 487(7),
  496(58), 497(67), 503(61),
  506(104)
Bihler 503(62)
Billerbeck 248, 476(54),
  500(18)
Black 451(15), 459(12),
  464(37), 477(56)
Blanchetièrre 513(25)
Blass-Debrunner 504(86)
Blau 491(4)
Bloch 455(17), 461(38),
  477(1), 486(1)
Böcher 464(28)
Bogaert 451(18), 452(32),
  456(23), 474(23)
Böhlig 496(62)
Bokser 457(35), 491(39)

Boman 461(43)
Bonner 484(21)
Bonwetsch 451(21),
  508(157)
Boobyer 501(39)
Borgen 525
Bornkamm 9, 469(91),
  486(2), 506(117), 514(40f),
  515(46f)
Borseh 468(79), 477(58)
Bousset 454(3), 455(11),
  459(8), 464(27), 465(51),
  466(56), 473(29), 486(1),
  500(24), 506(108),
  507(126), 511(8), 514(37),
  515(58), 517(84)
Bowker 291, 449(1),
  460(29), 461(46), 483(3),
  486(56), 488(3f), 489(11f),
  491(34), 495(54), 504(77)
Box 87, 148, 451(20),
  451(22), 456(23), 472(16),
  474(21), 475(25), 481(33),
  484(14), 484(17), 507(136)
Brandon 503(72)
Breech 471(5)
Bright 461(35)
Brockington 460(24),
  461(46)
Brown 501(35), 506(117),
  510(183)
Brox 460(24)
Bruce 458(59), 474(22),
  502(57)
Büchler 498(8)
Bühner 510(183)
Bullard 496(62)
Bultmann 499(3f),
  500(22f), 501(33f)
Burchard 466(60), 485(41),
  504(77f)
Burkitt 461(38)
Buttenwieser 452(27)

Caird 438, 460(20),
  501(36), 512(16), 515(58),
  516(70f), 516(76f),
  517(87f), 518(103f)
Calder 508(156)
Campbell 476(51)
von Campenhausen
  498(3f), 503(75), 508(157),
  509(161f), 516(66)
Carley 478(16)
Carmignac 468(81)
Casey P. M. 475(37),
  476(49), 477(60)
Cavallin 474(16)
Charles 100, 162, 184, 256,
  258, 451(15), 451(18),
  451(23), 452(24), 459(3),
  459(9), 463(13), 464(55),
  467(67), 472(7), 474(6),

475(30), 477(59), 479(42),
  480(12), 481(24), 482(50),
  484(20), 485(26), 485(36),
  485(42), 507(136), 511(8f),
  514(38), 514(44f), 516(72),
  518(97)
Charlesworth 451(15),
  483(1)
Childs 463(17)
Chilton 527
Clements 461(33)
Collins J. 449(3), 449(2),
  450(13), 451(14), 453(37),
  454(42), 459(1), 460(22),
  475(38), 476(47), 477(4),
  479(29), 515(60)
Colpe 459(8), 462(7),
  464(37), 465(40), 465(48),
  475(34), 477(59), 485(24)
Conzelmann 458(62),
  472(15), 498(4), 506(118)
Coppens 475(38)
Court 511(13f), 515(58),
  517(84)
Cox 454(1)
Cranfield 505(88)
Croix Ste. 513(23)
Cross F. M. 462(2), 470(2),
  484(18)
Cullmann 475(27),
  499(15), 499(14), 503(62),
  518(94)

Dahl 528
Daniélou 388, 392, 398,
  469(88), 484(12), 485(37),
  486(49), 507(139),
  508(143), 509(169),
  510(178)
Daube 494(42)
Davenport 473(5),
  518(106)
Davies G. I. 459(7), 471(1)
Davies P. R. 456(25),
  479(40)
Davies W. D. 453(41),
  455(17), 456(27), 494(36)
Day 464(26), 476(47),
  485(30)
le Déaut 472(11)
Deichgräber 469(90),
  516(69)
Deissner 507(126)
Delcor 468(81), 485(39)
Delling 451(15), 483(1)
Denis 451(15), 452(26),
  467(77), 483(1), 485(38)
Dexinger 454(2), 472(6),
  474(13), 484(11)
Dibelius 359, 499(10),
  503(65), 508(146f)
Dieterich 482(43)
Dietzfelbinger 473(25)

Dodd 499(6), 504(76)
Dodds 449(1), 453(38), 509(169), 510(179)
Doeve 450(5)
Doresse 496(62)
Dunn 462(52), 483(60), 498(1f), 500(21), 502(54), 503(74f), 504(82f), 506(120f), 507(130), 516(66)
Dupont-Sommer 457(44)

Ebeling 498(9)
Eichrodt 94, 464(35), 465(50)
Eisler 491(39)
Eissfeldt 450(7), 451(15), 478(12), 478(17), 480(1), 483(1)
Eliade 450(3), 481(34), 482(41)
Emerton 465(48), 485(30)
Engels 483(2)
Epstein 488(4)
Erling 478(13)

Fallon 496(62), 508(154)
Farrer 483(61)
Feuillet 465(47), 514(37), 515(51)
Fiorenza 514(40f), 515(59f), 515(62)
Fischel 492(4f), 493(24f)
Flusser 449(2), 462(5)
Foerster 494(37)
Fohrer 478(12)
Ford 509(159), 511(10), 514(36f), 516(71), 517(80)
Forkman 456(27), 457(35), 471(11)
Francis 513(26)
Frend 508(159), 509(168f), 513(23)
Frey 449(2), 455(17), 462(5)
Friedlander 473(27), 497(76)
Friedländer 530
von Fritz 460(24)
Frost 479(38)
Fuchs 498(9)
Gärtner 469(95)
Gammie 453(36), 463(9)
Gaster 463(19)
Gaston 458(52)
Georgi 505(96)
Gerhardsson 500(28), 503(71)
Gero 500(16)
Gese 478(13)
Giet 512(16)
Gill 513(28)
Ginsberg 456(22)
Ginsburg 496(56)
Ginzberg 464(32), 495(54)
Glasson 459(13), 460(22),

485(34)
Golb 472(17)
Goldberg 291, 486(5), 488(3f), 489(12f), 490(28f), 491(37f), 492(4f), 493(27), 495(54), 496(65)
Goldschmidt 488(4)
Goodenough 449(5), 466(66), 487(17), 497(66)
Gordis 479(31)
Gordon 485(32)
Goudoever 470(109)
Grässer 506(119)
Graetz 463(19), 492(6), 493(18), 494(31f), 495(43f), 496(57f)
Grant 472(17)
Gray 463(14), 485(32)
Greenfield 452(26), 486(57)
Grelot 460(31), 470(3), 485(46)
Grözinger 531
Gruenwald 449(2), 454(43), 458(60), 459(7), 463(19), 463(23), 466(62), 471(4), 479(31), 480(4), 480(10), 480(16), 481(22), 481(32), 486(1), 487(16), 488(3f), 490(27), 491(32f), 495(54f), 497(68f), 507(136), 510(180)
Gunkel 460(22)
Gunther 513(26)
Guthrie 462(52), 510(3)
Güttgemanns 507(129)
Guttmann 491(1), 503(70)
Haenchen 502(50f), 503(60f), 504(79)
Hage 451(19)
Hahn 475(27)
Halperin 291, 480(4), 487(9f), 488(3f), 489(11f), 491(32f), 491(5f), 493(20f), 495(54)
Hamerton-Kelly 470(105), 477(57)
Hanson A. T. 516(75)
Hanson P. D. 194f, 443, 449(2), 454(2), 454(3), 454(6), 455(8), 457(41), 461(49), 462(5), 464(33), 477(6), 478(22), 479(35), 480(3)
Hare 509(159)
Harnisch 449(1), 455(15), 471(5), 472(8), 474(20), 480(7), 484(23)
Harrison 484(9)
Hartmann 458(52)
Hartstock 501(90)
Hay 485(47)
Hayman 460(18), 471(5), 479(32)

Helmbold 507(136)
Hemer 516(64)
Hengel 21, 452(29), 453(35), 453(40), 455(15), 457(43), 457(50), 458(60), 460(24), 460(27), 461(51), 462(54), 464(27 & 32), 466(56), 469(88), 471(1), 479(40), 483(60), 485(36), 485(48), 500(25)
Hennecke 452(24), 458(61), 507(136)
Herford 455(16), 459(2), 495(51)
Hesse 475(27)
Hiers 499(2)
Hill 516(65)
Hindley 484(8)
Hofius 466(63), 469(90), 497(79), 510(180), 516(74)
Holm-Nielsen 469(97)
Hölscher 450(13), 477(4)
Holtz 465(53), 466(63), 516(71)
Hooker 458(56), 475(37)
Horton 468(83)
von Hügel 450(4), 482(41)
Hughes 459(2)
James M. R. 451(22), 452(26), 452(32), 473(23), 485(43)
James W. 450(3)
Jansen 460(31)
Jastrow 487(13), 493(18), 494(34)
Jaubert 470(109)
Jeremias C. 463(8), 464(25), 478(13)
Jeremias J. 455(20), 457(51), 458(56), 461(37), 474(22), 475(35), 484(8), 487(7), 488(5), 493(16), 499(5), 500(17f), 501(33f), 506(111), 510(177)
Jewett 505(96)
Joel 492(6)
Jörns 481(27), 516(69)
Johnson A. R. 464(35)
Johnson S. 513(25)
Jones 450(14)
de Jonge 263, 451(23), 452(33), 455(10), 456(24), 463(10), 477(62), 480(8), 485(42), 486(60)

Kadushin 487(6)
Käsemann 449(2), 454(7), 498(9), 505(98), 507(125)
Kaiser 462(2), 482(59)
Kallas 450(14)
Kaufmann 461(44)
Keck 499(8), 500(16f)
Kee 501(40)
Kehl 469(95)

Kermode 454(1)
Kertelge 504(83)
Kim 504(77)
Kirk 450(4)
Kisch 452(32), 473(23)
Kittel 513(25)
Klausner 455(17), 456(21), 473(1), 475(27), 477(62)
Klijn 507(140)
Klinzing 470(103)
Knibb 451(15), 471(4), 486(57)
Knowles 450(4)
Knox R. A. 498(5)
Knox W. L. 453(38), 502(52)
Koch 24, 449(1), 454(3), 459(2), 460(22), 478(25), 483(5), 499(2)
Kolenkow 453(35)
Kraabel 513(24f)
Kraft 511(7f), 512(16), 513(24f), 514(41f), 515(46f), 516(67f), 517(88f)
Kremer 502(50f)
Kretschmar 466(59), 469(88)
Kuhn H. W. 116f, 457(47), 461(33), 469(92)
Kuhn K. G. 457(33), 515(54)
Kümmel 458(55), 482(46), 499(15), 510(2), 511(7), 514(39), 515(63)
Labriolle 508(157f), 509(163)
Ladd 455(8), 501(32)
Lagrange 476(54), 501(41)
Lambert 472(4)
Lambrecht 458(52)
de Lange 497(75)
Laurin 469(95)
Leivestad 461(47), 475(37)
Lentzen-Deis 459(10), 462(1), 490(23), 499(4f), 500(16f)
Leslau 451(22)
Levenson 478(13)
Levi 455(17)
Lieberman 462(53), 488(4f), 492(10), 494(36), 496(63), 497(75), 507(135)
Lincoln 505(99f)
Lindars 458(63), 477(61), 486(57)
Lindblom 235, 243, 383, 459(9), 478(11), 478(19), 481(39), 482(41), 482(56), 483(60), 498(1), 501(40f), 502(47f), 503(68f), 504(78), 505(91f), 506(116f), 507(130f), 509(167)
Lods 451(15)
Loewe 491(39), 497(75)

Lohmeyer 459(9), 481(23), 514(37), 515(45)
Lohse 502(54)
Long 463(8)
Longenecker 507(139)
Lührmann 498(2), 504(84), 505(93), 506(107f), 507(125)
Lueken 464(26), 469(88), 476(47), 501(37)
Lust 465(51)
Mack 466(56)
Macrae 469(86), 496(62)
Maier 457(35), 461(33), 463(16), 463(19), 464(37), 469(102), 487(16), 488(1), 490(18f), 491(34), 507(131), 510(176)
Manson 455(10), 455(16), 501(31)
Mansoor 469(92)
Marmorstein 466(60), 471(7), 496(65)
Martin 469(90)
Marxsen 504(81)
McCown 460(27)
McCurdy 452(29), 468(80)
McNamara 483(3)
Mearns 486(57)
Meeks 459(6), 466(61), 482(44), 485(48)
Melamed 488(4)
Metzger 460(24)
Meyer 462(53), 478(18), 479(44)
Michaelis 469(88)
Michel 469(89)
Michl 481(22)
Milik 451(15), 452(23), 452(30), 452(34), 459(4), 460(26), 470(107), 472(6), 474(8), 476(51), 479(42), 480(12), 481(25), 484(10), 484(18), 485(35), 493(16), 496(57)
Millar 478(10)
Minear 463(12), 510(1), 516(73), 516(77f)
Moltmann 449(2)
Monloubou 538
Montgomery 465(51), 466(53), 476(46), 480(5)
Moore A. L. 511(14)
Moore G. F. 455(16), 457(36), 462(6), 466(56), 469(94), 486(1), 487(18), 488(2), 490(27)
Morgenstern 479(40)
Moule 475(37), 498(7), 504(79), 504(86)
Mowinckel 475(36)
Müller H. P. 479(29)
Müller K. 472(4), 476(52)
Müller U. 465(44), 476(41)

476(52), 509(161), 516(65)
Munck 504(80), 505(94)
Murdock 449(2)
Mussies 515(63)
Neher 492(7)
Nemoy 495(46), 497(74)
Neugebauer 498(7)
Neusner 291, 304, 455(20), 461(36), 484(16), 488(2f), 488(3f), 489(11f), 490(22f), 491(41f)
Newman 513(23)
Nicholson 480(14)
Nickelsburg 451(15), 451(22), 451(23), 464(33), 467(77), 474(16), 480(3), 483(1)
Nissen 455(17), 455(19), 459(2), 459(5), 486(1)
Nock 453(38)
North 478(13)
Noth 471(1), 475(39), 485(24)
Odeberg 452(26), 460(31), 467(76), 468(85), 470(108), 481(30), 496(57)
Oepke 481(32)
Oesterley 484(14)
O'Neill 502(88)
Oppenheim 479(29)
Osswald 450(10)
Osten-Sacken 464(26), 464(28), 478(26), 501(36)
Pannenberg 1, 449(2)
Pernveden 508(149)
Perrin 458(54), 472(12), 499(2), 510(3)
Philonenko 473(18)
Picard 451(19)
Piper 516(69)
Plöger 209f, 461(49), 465(53), 476(39), 478(10), 479(34), 482(52), 485(24)
Plummer 506(106)
Pope 485(31)
Preuschen 502(55)
Prigent 481(26), 511(10), 512(15f), 513(30), 514(35f), 516(69), 517(84)
Procksch 464(37)
Pryke 459(64)
Quispel 496(62), 504(77)
Rabin 494(31)
von Rad 203, 478(24)
Ramsay 511(13), 514(35), 518(89f)
Rau 470(3), 474(7)
Reese 472(5)
Reicke 457(39), 469(92)
Rengstorf 504(85)
Resch 474(22)
Richardson 512(24)
Riesenfeld 502(47)

Ringgren 462(4), 466(56), 475(27), 479(34)
Rissi 464(30), 511(7), 514(38), 516(71), 518(92f), 518(100f)
Rist 462(52)
Robinson J. A. 509(169)
Robinson J. A. T. 25, 455(10), 489(12), 510(4), 511(13), 512(16)
Robinson J. M. 452(26)
Rössler 450(11), 455(9), 455(16), 459(2), 471(1), 479(35), 486(1)
Rogerson 461(43)
Rohland 464(26), 476(47)
Rollins 498(9), 499(2)
Rosenthal 456(23)
Rost 452(29), 456(23), 479(45), 483(1), 484(14)
Rowland 463(23), 480(10), 490(23), 497(78)
Rowley 25, 193, 256, 450(7), 453(36), 455(8), 460(25), 472(4), 472(7), 477(3), 485(25)
Rubinstein 452(28)
Rudolph 541
Russell 65, 162, 453(36), 454(1), 454(2), 455(11), 456(31), 460(23), 461(39), 461(42), 463(24), 464(27), 473(2), 474(8), 474(23), 475(28), 477(1), 478(13), 480(2), 481(32)
Saake 505(95)
Safrai 513(25)
Saldarini 455(17)
Sanders E. P. 455(18), 471(5), 483(3), 488(15), 504(76)
Sanders J. T. 483(5)
Sarfatti 463(9)
Satake 516(65), 517(79f)
Schäfer 461(47), 464(27), 486(5), 514(42)
Schaller 472(13)
Scharlemann 503(59)
Schepelern 508(156f), 509(165)
Schiffmann 479(47)
Schlatter 55(101)
Schmidt A. 472(13)
Schmidt F. 452(29)
Schmidt J. M. 456(29), 477(1), 478(23), 480(2), 481(31), 483(1)
Schmithals 24, 37, 454(2), 455(19), 471(3), 483(5), 503(73), 505(96)
Schmitt 476(44)
Schoeps 507(142)
Scholem 220, 313, 340, 450(4), 454(43), 455(17),

463(19), 466(60), 466(62), 480(16), 481(26), 481(32), 482(40), 486(3), 487(13f), 491(36f), 492(7f), 493(16f), 494(35f), 495(48f), 496(63), 497(68f), 508(143), 509(162)
Schreiner 449(2), 453(36), 454(3), 461(49), 479(35)
Schubert 479(45), 480(21)
Schürer 456(21), 456(24), 457(43), 494(30)
Schütz 503(75)
Schweitzer 471(14), 499(1)
Schweizer 461(50), 500(23)
Scobie 500(21)
Scott K. 513(30)
Scott R. B. Y. 465(49), 482(58)
Sed 463(9), 488(3f), 490(24f), 491(3)
Segal 462(7), 468(84), 469(87), 473(17), 495(54), 496(61f)
Sevenster 513(28)
Sint 460(24)
Sjöberg 467(75), 476(52), 481(29)
Slingerland 452(33), 486(50)
Smallwood 472(7), 512(18f), 513(29f), 514(34)
Smith J. Z. 468(84)
Smith M. 460(24), 487(17), 497(80), 502(48), 507(131)
Sneen 543
Stanton 503(63)
Stauffer 407, 455(7), 503(72), 512(17)
Steck 472(16), 480(7)
Stein 501(39), 502(46)
Stern 513(28)
Stier 464(35)
Stone 449(2), 451(20), 454(6), 455(14), 459(11), 477(62), 481(31), 484(22)
Strobel 498(9), 504(79), 510(2), 511(6)
Strugnell 452(31), 463(23), 480(11), 497(78)
Stuhlmacher 504(83f), 505(90f), 507(128)
Sweet 510(2)

Talbert 477(58), 485(48)
Talmon 470(109)
Taylor L. R. 513(30)
Taylor V. 501(42)
Tcherikover 479(40)
Testuz 474(17)
Theisohn 467(68), 475(29), 476(50), 486(54)
Theodor 486(56), 494(35)
Thoma 456(23), 456(24)

Thompson 471(5), 479(32)
Thorndike 474(13)
Tödt 475(36)
Torm 460(24), 461(42)
Trites 516(78f)

Underhill 450(4)
van Unnik 458(53), 459(10)
Urbach 308, 315, 456(21), 456(26), 456(30), 457(36), 462(6), 469(94), 473(4), 488(3f), 489(9), 490(18f), 491(32f), 492(7f), 493(17f), 494(37), 496(65), 503(72), 514(42)

Vaillant 451(16), 485(37), 485(44)
Vanhoye 481(28)
Vawter 455(8)
Vermes 40, 469(93), 470(107), 483(3), 484(18), 498(8), 499(14)
Vielhauer 454(3), 455(11), 456(29), 508(146f)
Violet 484(23)
Volz 30, 454(3), 461(40), 473(1), 500(24)

Wadsworth 473(23)
Weber 470(1), 473(29)
Weber H. E. 482(45)
Weinstock 513(30)
Weiss H. F. 462(3), 469(87), 472(13), 487(14), 494(38f), 495(43f)
Weiss J. 499(1)
Wellesley 511(15)
Wernberg-Møller 457(36), 469(100)
Werner 462(52), 469(88)
Wertheimer 496(58)
Wewers 462(3), 486(3), 487(7f), 488(3f), 490(17f), 491(36f), 492(4f), 493(21f), 494(38f), 495(43f)
Whybray 462(2)
Widengren 459(8), 460(16), 462(7), 481(31)
Wilckens 466(56), 503(63)
Williamson H. G. M. 479(39)
Wilson 483(4)
Windisch 499(5), 505(95), 506(104f)
Wolfson 459(15), 472(17), 473(29)
van der Woude 468(81), 475(27)
Yadin 457(45)
Yamauchi 483(4)
York 483(3)

Zimmerli 464(37), 465(45), 478(14)
Zuckermandel 488(4f)